BUSINESS LAW AND PRACTICE

BUSINESS LAW AND PRACTICE

Alexis Mavrikakis

Stephen Allinson

Jacqueline Kempton

Nick Hancock

CLP

Published by

The University of Law,
2 Bunhill Row, London EC1Y 8HQ

British Library Cataloguing-in-Publication Data

A catalogue record for this book is available from the British Library.

ISBN 978 1 80502 166 7

Typeset by Style Photosetting Ltd, Mayfield, East Sussex

Tables and index by Moira Greenhalgh, Arnside, Cumbria

Preface

In writing this book, we have set out to describe the forms of business most commonly encountered in practice, the issues they face internally, their relations with outsiders and their possible tax liabilities. In doing so we follow the lifespan of these businesses from their birth through to their death.

The style we have adopted has been chosen in the hope that the contents will be readily understood and appreciated by someone who is totally unacquainted with the subject, as well as by someone with some prior knowledge. We hope that the inclusion of statutory references in the text will encourage the reader to consult the original source materials whenever further research into a topic is required. To this end, we have prepared a companion volume, *Business and Company Legislation*, which contains the up-to-date text of the key legislation referred to in the book.

This book is a collaborative effort. With thanks to:

Stephen Allinson for writing the chapters on insolvency

Jacqueline Kempton for writing the chapters on taxation

Nick Hancock for writing the chapters on sale of goods and competition

Lesley King for Appendix 4 on the interpretation of company accounts.

I'm also very grateful to David Stott for his advice and patience in the face of deadlines stretched, and to Claire Lawrence, Nick Hancock, Giles Hutchinson, Marie Calleja and Edward Jones for their many suggestions for improvement.

This book should not be relied upon for the provision of or as a substitute for legal advice.

The law is stated as at 1 May 2025.

This book is dedicated to the memory of our former colleague, Neil Duckworth, a great teacher and a lovely man.

Alexis Mavrikakis
George Town, Grand Cayman

Contents

Table of Cases

Table of Statutes

Locations in italics refer to proposed changes to the Companies Act 2006 by the Economic Crime and Corporate Transparency Act 2023

Table of Secondary Legislation

Table of Abbreviations

AIA	annual investment allowance
AIM	Alternative Investment Market
BPR	business property relief
BRO	bankruptcy restriction order
BRU	bankruptcy restriction undertaking
CA 1985	Companies Act 1985
CA 2006	Companies Act 2006
CAA 2001	Capital Allowances Act 2001
CDDA 1986	Company Directors Disqualification Act 1986
CGT	capital gains tax
CL	compulsory liquidation
CMCHA 2007	Corporate Manslaughter and Corporate Homicide Act 2007
CRA 2015	Consumer Rights Act 2015
CTA 2009	Corporation Tax Act 2009
CTA 2010	Corporation Tax Act 2010
CVA	company voluntary arrangement
CVL	creditors' voluntary liquidation
DBT	Department for Business and Trade
DRO	debt relief order
ECCTA	Economic Crime and Corporate Transparency Act 2023
EEA	European Economic Area
EEIG	European economic interest groupings
ERA 1996	Employment Rights Act 1996
FA	Finance Act (various years)
FCA	Financial Conduct Authority
HMRC	HM Revenue and Customs
GAAR	general anti-abuse rule
IA 1986	Insolvency Act 1986
ICTA	Income and Corporation Taxes Act 1988
IHT	inheritance tax
IHTA 1984	Inheritance Tax Act 1984
ITA 2007	Income Tax Act 2007
ITEPA 2003	Income Tax (Earnings and Pensions) Act 2003
ITTOIA 2005	Income Tax (Trading and Other Income) Act 2005
IVA	individual voluntary arrangement
LCT	lifetime chargeable transfer
LLP	limited liability partnership
LLPA 2000	Limited Liability Partnership Act 2000
LP	limited partnership
LPA	Law of Property Act
MVL	members' voluntary liquidation
NCA	non-cash asset

NED	non-executive director
PA 1890	Partnership Act 1890
PAYE	pay as you earn
PET	potentially exempt transfer
PSC	persons with significant control
QFC	qualifying floating charge
QFCH	qualifying floating charge holder
RLE	relevant legal entity
SE	*Societas Europaea* (European public company)
SGA 1979	Sale of Goods Act 1979
SGSA 1982	Supply of Goods and Services Act 1982
SIP	statement of insolvency practice
SPT	substantial property transaction
TCGA 1992	Taxation of Chargeable Gains Act 1992
TEU	Treaty on European Union
TFEU	Treaty on the Functioning of the European Union
TMA 1970	Taxes Management Act 1970
UCTA 1977	Unfair Contract Terms Act 1977
VAT	value added tax

PART I

STARTING A BUSINESS

Part I

- introduces the different types of business a new business owner might choose
- considers the advantages and disadvantages of the different types of business
- highlights some of the practical issues involved in setting up a business
- introduces some of the key principles of company law
- gives an overview of the key sources of company law

CHAPTER 1

The Different Types of Business

LEARNING OUTCOMES

After reading this chapter you will be able to:

- identify and compare the different types of unincorporated business operating in England and Wales
- identify and compare the different types of company operating in England and Wales
- weigh up the factors an entrepreneur will use in determining the most suitable type of business
- understand the practical matters that must be addressed when setting up a business.

1.1 INTRODUCTION

Businesses dominate our way of life. They feed us, clothe us, build our homes, transport us, entertain us, inform us, medicate us and employ us. They are the backbone of our capitalist society and the means by which the UK creates the economic wealth to remain (for now) the sixth largest economy in the world. Unsurprisingly, then, few lawyers can avoid them in practice.

Future corporate lawyers reading this book, who will of course specialise in advising on the activities of businesses, will doubtless be champing at the bit, full of eagerness to learn more, aware that a comprehensive understanding of the law governing businesses is a prerequisite to earning their daily bread.

Non-corporate lawyers of the future may well be decidedly less enthusiastic, perhaps already bemoaning the prospect of having to devote time to a subject which might at first seem irrelevant. However, it is worth noting at the outset that if, for example, you were working on a personal injury case for a client whose 3-year-old daughter had been knocked down by a van, understanding the significance of the type of business that owned the van would be essential in deciding against whom to make the claim and what financial resources might be available to pay damages. Or if you were acting for one party to a divorce and some of the matrimonial assets were tied up in a business, an understanding of how that business operates under the law would be essential if your client wished to get their share out of that business. Perhaps you might be acting for a client who was sacked for making drunken advances to colleagues at the office Christmas party. Once again, even in this situation, the type of business may affect your approach to the case. An understanding of the law of businesses, at least in outline, is therefore important for virtually all lawyers.

It is estimated by the Department for Business and Trade (DBT), the UK government body which oversees businesses, that at the start of 2024 (the latest time for which official figures are available) there were approximately 5.5 million active businesses in existence in the UK, which employed 27.75 million people and had an estimated total turnover of £4.9 billion. These businesses exist in a wide variety of different forms. We shall first consider what these different types are and then explore why an entrepreneur might choose to run their business using one form rather than another.

1.2 INCORPORATED AND UNINCORPORATED BUSINESSES

Businesses may be run either in unincorporated or incorporated form. Unincorporated businesses require few – or even no – administrative steps to be taken to be formed under the law. By contrast, incorporated businesses must undergo a formal registration process before they can legally exist. In addition, incorporated businesses are legal entities which have an existence separate from that of their owners. An unincorporated business is usually treated as being the same as its owners, with no separate legal status.

The most common forms of unincorporated business in the UK are the sole trader and partnership. The most common forms of incorporated business in the UK are the private limited company, the public limited company and the limited liability partnership. We shall now look at each of these in turn, together with some less common forms of business which you may come across in practice.

1.3 SOLE TRADER

A sole trader is, as the name suggests, someone who runs a business on their own as a self-employed person. This could be, for example, an electrician, or a dog-walker, or a hairdresser or a lawyer – a sole trader can operate in any trade or profession. No formal steps need be taken to set up as a sole trader, but the sole trader must register with HM Revenue and Customs (HMRC) for tax purposes. Sole traders are the largest group of businesses in the UK. According to DBT figures, there are approximately 3.1 million sole traders.

It is worth noting that a professional, such as a lawyer, who runs their business on their own is more usually known as a 'sole practitioner'. Sometimes sole traders of whatever type are instead referred to as 'sole proprietors'. Throughout the remainder of this book, 'sole trader' is the only term used.

The vast majority of sole traders (over 90%) work entirely alone, but some may have employees working for them. The business will still be a sole trader where there are employees, if the sole trader owns the business alone.

A sole trader earns their income from the money received from their customers or clients, and keeps all the profit themselves. The sole trader pays income tax as a self-employed person. See **Chapter 24** for further information on the taxation of sole traders.

In law a sole trader is personally liable for all the debts of the business. The business has no legal status of its own. This means that the sole trader's business assets and personal assets are treated as one and the same. If the business (eg, a florists) fails, it is not just the sole trader's business assets (such as the shop, flowers and delivery van) but also the sole trader's personal possessions, including any savings, house and car, which may be taken or sold to repay outstanding debts. Ultimately, if the sole trader is unable to pay off all the debts using their business and personal assets, the sole trader may be made bankrupt. This is known as 'unlimited liability'.

When the sole trader retires or dies, the business ceases, although the business or individual assets may be sold if a buyer or buyers can be found.

Therefore, a sole trader is a person who alone:

(a) has the right to make all decisions affecting the business;
(b) owns all the assets of the business;
(c) is responsible for paying income tax on all the profits of the business; and
(d) has unlimited liability for the debts of the business.

There is no single piece of legislation governing a business run by a sole trader. The law governing the sole trader's activities is to be found in various pieces of legislation, which can equally apply to individuals or businesses generally. For example, a sole trader must register for value added tax (VAT) if their business turnover exceeds a certain threshold; this applies equally to other types of business. Sole traders are also subject to the common law, just as are all other forms of business.

1.4 PARTNERSHIP

A partnership occurs where two or more persons run and own a business together, as opposed to when one person runs and owns the business themselves (sole trader – **1.3** above). The business may carry on any trade, for example running an organic dairy farm or plumbing, or any profession, including dentistry or architecture. There are currently approximately 356,000 partnerships in the UK according to DBT figures. One of the largest is Slaughter & May, the City law firm, with about 110 partners and in excess of 1,300 further employees. Most are much smaller, though, and approximately 75% consist just of the partners themselves and no employees.

Partnerships are governed principally by the Partnership Act 1890 (PA 1890). Under s 1 of this Act, a partnership is legally formed when two or more persons carry on a business with a view to making a profit. The partnership will be run on the basis of a contract, which may be written or oral. There are no formalities which need to be satisfied, such as registration with a public body, in order to form a partnership. This means that if you and a friend start baking macaroons with the intention of selling them to your fellow students to make some money for yourselves (rather than, say, for charity) and share the proceeds, you have formed a partnership under the PA 1890 even if you did not realise that this would happen. However, each partner must register with HMRC for tax purposes.

The partners will divide the profits or losses of the business between them. In a partnership made up solely of individuals, the partners are taxed separately as self-employed individuals, paying income tax on their share of the profits of the partnership. See **Chapter 25** for further information on the taxation of partners.

A partnership has no separate legal status. The partners therefore have unlimited liability for the debts of the partnership. This means that, as with a sole trader, if the partnership fails, creditors can pursue not just the assets used by the business but the personal assets of the partners themselves. This liability is also said to be joint and several among the partners, allowing a creditor the choice of seeking the full amount of a debt from any one individual partner or from all the partners together.

When a partner dies or retires, the partner will usually be bought out by the remaining partners so that the partnership continues. If this is not agreed then the partnership will come to an end.

In summary, a partnership consists of two or more persons who, on the basis of a contract (whether written or not) between them:

(a) share the right to take part in making decisions which affect the business or the business assets (although they may have agreed that one or more of their number will not be involved in day-to-day matters but only in fundamental decisions);
(b) share the ownership of the assets of the business (although they may have agreed that the firm will use an asset which is owned by one of the partners individually);
(c) share the profits of the business (although the partners may have agreed not to share these equally); and
(d) share unlimited liability for the debts of the business (although if one does not pay then the others must pay that person's share).

Chapters 13 to **18** cover the law on partnerships in much greater detail.

1.5 LIMITED PARTNERSHIP

This form of unincorporated business is established under the Limited Partnerships Act 1907 (LPA 1907). A limited partnership (LP) is similar to a partnership in that there must be at least one general partner who has unlimited liability (for general partners see **1.4** above) for all the debts of the partnership. However, unlike a normal partnership, an LP is permitted to have a limited partner whose liability is limited to the amount they initially invested in the business. The limited liability of the limited partner is, though, conditional on the limited partner:

(a) not controlling or managing the LP;
(b) not having the power to take binding decisions on behalf of the LP; and
(c) not removing their contribution to the LP for as long as it is in business.

If the limited partner breaches any of these rules then they will lose the protection of limited liability and, in the case of (a) and (b) above, be treated as a general partner with unlimited liability.

Limited partnerships were originally created over 100 years ago to encourage entrepreneurs to set up businesses by lessening some of the effects of unlimited liability which may arise from an ordinary partnership. However, over time the LP was outshone by another form of business, the limited company, which became the business format of choice, as it offered even greater protection from unlimited liability (see **1.9** below).

More recently there has been an increase in the use of LPs as they have come back into fashion for certain specialist financial businesses, such as investment funds and venture capital funds, which invest their clients' money in companies or property. There are potentially certain tax benefits for these businesses in using an LP, and they are generally very flexible and lightly regulated (the LPA 1907 is a blissfully short 17 sections). Crucially, there *may* be no need to make financial information on the business's operations available to the public. The structure is sometimes also used for joint ventures, where two separate businesses decide to collaborate in a business under one roof. Currently, there are over 57,500 LPs in existence.

Unlike ordinary partnerships, LPs must be registered with the Registrar of Companies (who also acts as the Registrar of LPs) in accordance with s 8 of the LPA 1907 before they can start trading. An application form containing the details set out in s 8A of the 1907 Act (such as the full names of the partners and the nature of the business) must be completed, signed by all of the partners and sent to the Registrar together with the applicable fee. This fee is £71. A standardised application form, known as Form LP5 and available on the Companies House website <www.gov.uk/government/organisations/companies-house>, must be used. There is no same-day registration service available, nor is it possible to register overseas LPs via a digital application. Once successfully registered, a certificate of registration will be issued and sent to the general partner or partners. The LP comes into existence on the date of registration on the certificate.

Limited partnerships are recognisable by the use of 'limited partnership' or 'LP' (or their Welsh equivalents 'partneriaeth cyfyngedig' or 'PC' for LPs set up in Wales) at the end of their names.

You can obtain further information on LPs from the Companies House website mentioned above.

Note that an LP should not be confused with a 'limited liability partnership' (LLP) under the Limited Liability Partnerships Act 2000, which is a different way to run a business (see **1.11** below.)

Since April 2017 it has been possible to set up a special form of LP, the Private Fund LP (PFLP). This is only available to private investment funds which do not deal with members of the public. There are financial and administrative benefits to the PFLP compared to a normal LP. This new form of LP has been created in order to win business from countries such as Luxembourg.

The rules governing LPs are set to be tightened up (when the relevant provisions of the Economic Crime and Corporate Transparency Act 2023 are brought into force) in an effort to combat the abuse of the LP for money laundering purposes. The LP was found to have had a key role in the €200 billion Danske Bank scandal, which came to a head in 2018. Limited partnerships were used to launder dirty money from Russia and other former Soviet Union countries. However, it was only following the illegal invasion of Ukraine by Russia in February 2022, with a spotlight once again being shone on the lax attitude by the UK Government, the financial services industry and law firms to the presence of criminally obtained ('dirty') money in the UK (including that belonging to members and supporters of the Russian Government), that the reform to LPs has risen to the top of the political agenda.

The reforms will include a tightening of the rules for registration of LPs, a requirement for an LP to have a connection to the UK and an obligation for LPs to submit annual confirmation statements of the information held on them. The Registrar will be given powers to strike off LPs that are dissolved or which the Registrar concludes are not in operation.

1.6 CONTRACTUAL CO-OPERATION

It is possible for two or more parties to run a business together on the basis of a co-operation agreement. This is a form of association which is less formal than a partnership and other forms of business. It might be as simple as an agreement to share costs and resources between the parties. The parties would enter into this type of agreement, for example:

(a) to explore and develop oil and gas fields;
(b) in property development; or
(c) to conduct research and development with a view to developing new products.

Such agreements are sometimes called joint ventures. You can find out more about joint ventures at **Appendix 3**.

In addition to the lack of formality of running the business in this way, there is the further advantage that the terms of the agreement can be kept confidential. The disadvantages include a lack of identity, a lack of organisational structure and the danger of the business becoming a partnership by fulfilling the criteria under s 1 of the PA 1890 (see **1.4** above).

The law governing this arrangement flows from the co-operation agreement itself, as well as from the common law.

1.7 COMPANY

A company is often what we think of when we imagine a business. A company in the UK is formed by registering certain documents with a public official, the Registrar of Companies, in accordance with the requirements of the Companies Act 2006 (CA 2006). So, whereas the partners in a partnership or a sole trader can start trading immediately, steps need to be taken to set up a company before it can start trading. As at the end of December 2024, there were approximately 5.4 million companies registered in the UK, with a total estimated annual turnover in excess of £5 trillion. The largest company by value in the UK (and also the 44th largest company in the world) at the time of writing is the biopharmaceutical company, AstraZeneca, worth a staggering £155 billion. It employs over 90,000 people in the UK and worldwide. Of course many companies are much smaller, and most in fact have only between one and four employees.

Businesses run as companies perform a wide range of economic activities, from manufacturing cars to providing online dating services, from the provision of banking and insurance services to selling cheeseburgers, from developing apps for smart phones to running retirement homes for the elderly. Formerly, solicitors could not operate their business as a company, but under provisions of the Legal Services Act 2007 (known colloquially as the 'Tesco Law'), which came into force in October 2011, law firms were for the first time allowed to become companies. The first two such companies were licensed by the Solicitors Regulation Authority (SRA) on 28 March 2012, and subsequently Gateley became the first UK law firm to join the stock market in 2015.

Perhaps the single most important effect of running a business through a company is that the company has a separate legal personality. This means that, unlike sole traders and partnerships, which in effect are the same as the people who own and run them, a company is a legal entity separate from both its owners and the people who run it on a day-to-day basis. The company is recognised by the law as a person – a special type of person known as a 'legal person', but nonetheless one which has its own rights and obligations. This concept will be examined in further detail in **Chapter 2**.

Although a legal person in its own right, a company still, of course, needs humans to take decisions on its behalf and to interact with the outside world. The decisions affecting the company's business or the company itself are made either by the company's directors or by its shareholders, or sometimes by both jointly. The directors of a company run the company on a daily basis, whereas the members (also known as shareholders) are the owners of the company who usually tend to get involved only in the more important decisions affecting the company. This division of responsibility, and the fact that decisions of the directors and members are taken at different meetings, imposes on a company a degree of formality which is absent from the running of a business by a sole trader or a partnership.

A company is usually formed under the CA 2006 by filing a series of documents with the Registrar of Companies at Companies House and paying the applicable fee. This fee is £50 for a digital application or using Companies House software, or £71 if the documents are submitted in paper form. Companies House aims to process paper applications within five days and electronic ones within 24 hours. In practice, 99% of applications are processed within 24 hours. Alternatively, it is possible to pay £78 for a guaranteed same-day registration service but this is only available using Companies House software. The registration process is usually done electronically. Once the company is successfully registered, the Registrar will issue a certificate of incorporation. The company legally comes into existence on the date of incorporation on the certificate.

Companies are not subject to income tax, as are sole traders and partners, but to a different tax specific to companies – corporation tax. It is ultimately the owners of the company, the members, who get to share in the profits made by the company. Companies must register with HMRC for corporation tax purposes once they have been formed, and usually also as an employer for PAYE and National Insurance purposes. See **Chapters 21** to **29** for further information on the taxation of companies.

A number of different types of company may be formed, and we consider them in turn below.

1.8 UNLIMITED COMPANY

A company may be either a limited company or an unlimited company. An unlimited company is defined in s 3(4) of the CA 2006 as a company which does not have any limit on the liability of its members. The members of a company are its owners. If the owners wish to run their business through an unlimited company then they will be required to use not only the company's assets but also, if necessary, their own personal assets to pay off the company's debts. This is the same principle as seen at **1.3** and **1.4** above in relation to sole traders and partnerships.

Unlimited companies are very rare in practice. There are only approximately 4,500 in existence. One example was Land Rover, the car manufacturer, which was a private unlimited company for a period until 2013, owned by the massive Indian conglomerate, Tata. The office of the former Prime Minister, from 2010–2016, David Cameron, is run as a private unlimited company. One key advantage to this type of company is that the company's finances do not normally have to be made public. More usually, entrepreneurs who wish to run their businesses with unlimited liability for the business's debts do so as a sole trader or partnership, and therefore we do not specifically consider unlimited companies any further in this book. It is worth noting, though, that much of what applies to limited companies applies equally to unlimited ones.

Further information on unlimited companies may be obtained from the Companies House website <www.gov.uk/government/organisations/companies-house>.

1.9 LIMITED COMPANY

A limited company is one in which the liability of its members is limited by its constitution (CA 2006, s 3(1)). We saw in **1.7** above that the members of the company are its owners. The constitution of the company sets out the rules which govern how the company should be run. If the owners of a business wish to run it using this type of company, it will allow them to limit their liability for the debts of the company. This is an extremely important point, and potentially a very big advantage in running your business. Why?

Let us compare two toy businesses which manufacture fluffy bunnies. The first, FLB Toys (FLB), is run as a partnership and the second, Fluffy Limited (Fluffy), as a limited company. Imagine that both businesses stop trading because not enough people want to buy fluffy bunnies. Both businesses owe their suppliers a significant amount of money. The owners of FLB, as partners in a partnership, face unlimited liability for these debts. If selling the assets used by FLB does not pay off all the debts then the partners must use their personal assets, for example their savings, or even sell their possessions, to settle the outstanding amounts owed. The owners of Fluffy, as members of a limited company, have only limited liability. This will be set out in the company's constitution (ie its rules of operation). The amount the members have to pay will be limited to the amount they have agreed to pay for their shares in the company and no more than this. So, if the assets of Fluffy are sold off and do not raise sufficient money to settle the company's debts then the members will not have to pay any more than they agreed to in buying shares, ie ownership of the company. This shortfall means that the suppliers will lose money.

As you have now seen, this concept of the owners of the business being able to limit their liability for debts of the business by using a limited company is potentially a very significant advantage to them. It explains much of the popularity of the limited company in the business world. Virtually all companies are run as limited companies. It should be noted, however, that in practice the question of liability for limited companies is more sophisticated than the outline given above, and we return to examine this concept in greater detail in **Chapter 2**.

1.9.1 Limited by shares or by guarantee?

A limited company may limit the liability of its members (ie owners) in one of two ways:

(a) by shares; or

(b) by guarantee (CA 2006, s 3(1)).

A company which is limited by guarantee is a much less common type of limited company. There are only approximately 186,000 in existence. It is usually used for organisations that are not seeking to make a profit, such as charities, members' clubs (eg sports clubs), professional societies and property management companies. Examples of companies limited by guarantee include Bupa, the healthcare company, Network Rail, which owns and operates the UK's railway infrastructure, and Oxfam, the charity. The members (ie owners) of the company guarantee, in the event that their company is wound up (ie brought to an end), that they will pay a specified sum to the creditors under s 3(3) of the CA 2006. The owners' liability is limited to that sum, regardless of the amount of the debts of the company. It is usually £1. A company limited by guarantee is therefore useful for non-profit organisations (examples of which are given above) which wish to limit their members' liability but have no need for the members to contribute large amounts of money to run the company. Another advantage to this type of company is that it is easier to make changes in ownership than in a company limited by shares.

A company which is limited by shares is by the far the most usual form of limited company, and with the exception of this chapter this book will deal only with such companies. They take two forms: a private company limited by shares, or a public company limited by shares.

1.9.2 Private limited company

Almost all of the companies in existence are private limited companies. This is therefore the most important type of company for our purposes and we shall be concentrating on it in this book (although reference will be occasionally made to other types of company where necessary).

One of the biggest private companies in the UK is Iceland Foods Ltd, which owns the British supermarket chain, Iceland. It has an annual turnover of £4.2 billion and employs over 25,000 staff. Nevertheless, private limited companies are just as likely to run much smaller-scale family-owned or High Street businesses.

The CA 2006 defines a private company in s 4(1) as 'any company that is not a public company'. We therefore need to identify what constitutes a public company in order to find out precisely what a private company is (see **1.9.3** below). In summary, though, a private limited company can raise money for its purposes only from a restricted circle of owner-investors. This is because, under s 755 of the CA 2006, it is prohibited for a private company to raise money from members of the public at large by issuing securities such as shares. A private limited company is easily identifiable by the use of 'limited' or the abbreviation 'ltd' (or the Welsh language equivalents 'cyfyngedig' or 'cyf') at the end of the company's name.

Chapters 2 to **11** address the law on private limited companies in much greater detail.

1.9.3 Public limited company

A public company is defined by s 4(2) of the CA 2006. It is a company limited by shares or by guarantee (see **1.9.1** above) and having a share capital which has complied with the requirements of the CA 2006 (or former Companies Acts) to enable it to be registered or re-registered as such (see **12.4.1** to **12.4.3** below). There are approximately 5,000 public companies currently in existence in the UK, including the biggest companies in the UK. Household-name companies such as BP (the oil and gas company) and HSBC (the financial services company) are public limited companies.

How a company achieves public company status is explained in detail at **12.4** below. Broadly, for a company to be a public company:

(a) the constitution (the set of rules which establish the company and govern it once it has been formed) must state that it is a public company;

(b) the words 'public limited company' or the abbreviation 'plc' (or the Welsh language equivalents 'cwmni cyfyngedig cyhoeddus' or 'ccc' for Welsh companies) must be included at the end of the company's name; and

(c) the owners of the company must invest a specified minimum amount of money for use by the company.

In essence, the big advantage to being a public company is that, unlike a private company, it can raise money from members of the public.

1.9.3.1 Publicly-traded company

If it wishes, a public company, but not a private one, may apply to join a stock market in the UK. Of the approximately 5.4 million companies registered in the UK and of the approximately 5,000 public companies, only about 1,230 have joined a stock market. The two main stock markets in the UK are the London Stock Exchange's Main Market and the Alternative Investment Market (known more usually as 'AIM') (see **1.9.3.2** and **1.9.3.3** below). These stock markets allow companies to raise large amounts of money by enabling investors to buy their shares quickly and easily. Publicly-traded companies are therefore the largest companies in the UK. Consequently, an entrepreneur will not set up a business from scratch as a publicly-traded company; this will be an option only if the business reaches a certain size, reputation or level of growth.

It is important to note that there is no obligation on a public company to join a stock market. Public companies which choose not to do so are usually referred to as 'unlisted'. One example is the retail chain John Lewis. Although this business describes itself as a partnership, and it certainly has a unique business model, it is in fact legally established as an unlisted public limited company, with its formal name being 'John Lewis plc'.

A publicly-traded company is subject to a significant amount of additional regulation which does not apply to an unlisted company.

1.9.3.2 Main Market

The Main Market is the principal stock market for publicly-traded companies. Vodafone Group Plc (the mobile phone operator) and Tesco PLC (the supermarket chain) are two examples of the approximately 700 UK public companies that have joined the London Stock Exchange's Main Market. Such companies must successfully complete a time-consuming and complicated procedure known as a 'flotation' or 'IPO' (Initial Public Offering) in order to join the Main Market. In doing so, each company must satisfy an array of conditions and publicly disclose a vast amount of information about the company and the business it runs. In general, only a large public company can apply to join the Main Market. One condition for joining is that the company must also be admitted to the Financial Conduct Authority's (FCA) Official List. Thus such companies are often known as 'listed companies'.

There is no way of telling from the company name whether a company is listed. Instead, this may be discovered by searching the London Stock Exchange's website, or be identified when the company's share price is publicly quoted, such as in the finance or business section of newspapers, or on financial websites or television.

Once it has completed the IPO, the listed company must comply with a series of onerous on-going requirements regarding its operations, with the aim of protecting members of the public who have invested in the company. These additional obligations, for example in the UK Listing Rules, are mostly found in the FCA's *Handbook*. They do not apply to public companies which have not joined the Main Market.

More information on listed companies may be found in **Public Companies and Equity Finance** and on the London Stock Exchange's website <http://www.londonstockexchange.com>.

1.9.3.3 AIM

AIM is the London Stock Exchange's alternative investment market. This stock market is targeted at smaller, ambitious public companies looking to grow in size. It also appeals to overseas companies. AIM is a separate market from the Main Market, and while some companies may choose to move from AIM onto the Main Market at some point (such as ASOS plc in February 2022), there is no obligation to do so. It was originally regulated much less stringently than the Main Market, but recent reforms to the Main Market have resulted in increased competition between the two stock markets. Currently, around 530 UK companies are quoted on AIM, such as Naked Wines (formerly Majestic Wine) and Boohoo (rebranding as Debenham Group). AIM companies are subject to additional regulations in the form of the AIM Rules drafted by the London Stock Exchange.

More information on AIM may be found in **Public Companies and Equity Finance**, and on the London Stock Exchange's website <http://www.londonstockexchange.com>.

The FCA also oversees the regulation of companies quoted on AIM.

1.9.4 Differences between private companies and public companies

There are significant differences between public companies and private companies, both under the law and in how they operate in practice. Similarly there are big differences between unlisted public companies and publicly-traded public companies. A brief overview of these differences is given below. Many of the differences require a detailed understanding of the various company law concepts involved, so we shall return to this topic in **Chapter 12.** You will understand the importance of the differences more easily then, after you have first fully considered the position of the private company alone.

1.9.4.1 Legal differences

The CA 2006 applies to both public and private companies, but there are many differences of detail. For example, we have already seen (**1.9.2** above) that as a result of s 755 of the CA 2006, a private company cannot offer its shares to the public at large whereas a public company can. Another difference is that a public company must have at least two directors (ie managers), but a private company need have only one (CA 2006, s 154). Generally, private companies are less regulated than public companies because they do not seek to raise money from the public at large but either from people who know the company already, or from specialist investors who understand the risks involved.

In addition, the CA 2006 has provisions which apply only to publicly-traded companies (see **1.9.3.1** above) rather than to unlisted public companies, and also provisions which apply to public companies which are listed on the London Stock Exchange's Main Market rather than quoted on AIM. Unlisted public companies are less regulated than publicly-traded companies because they have not joined a stock market. It is very easy for the public to invest in a company which has joined a stock market, and so in order to protect the public these companies are more heavily regulated. Also, public companies that have joined the Main Market are more tightly regulated than those which have joined AIM, as members of the public more usually invest in Main Market companies so the need to protect the public is greater there.

1.9.4.2 Practical differences

One example will suffice for now. It is possible for a private company to be owned by a single shareholder and managed by a single director. The shareholder and the director may even be the same person. Although it is possible for a public company to be owned by a single shareholder and to be managed by two directors, there will often be more shareholders and (possibly) directors. In the case of a publicly-traded public company there may well be many more. One example is BT plc, the telecoms company, which is listed on the London Stock Exchange's Main Market. It has around 640,000 individual shareholders (and additional shareholders in the form of professional institutional investors) and 11 directors. This goes to explain why the rules in the CA 2006 sometimes differ for public and private companies.

1.10 OTHER TYPES OF COMPANY

There are a number of other, less common forms of company which may be set up or operate in the UK. These usually have special characteristics regarding their area of operation or their geographical location, or certain historical connections. We shall now consider these briefly.

1.10.1 Community interest company

The community interest company (CIC) is a form of limited liability company (either limited by shares or by guarantee, either private or public) intended for businesses that wish to use their profits and assets for the public good and not for private profit. It is worth remembering that the overwhelming majority of people who set up a business do so to make money for themselves, and as much as they can. The CIC is very different. In the words of one director of a CIC, 'I love the idea of having a duty to the community rather than shareholders.' A CIC has altruistic, charitable aims and uses a business to improve communities rather than just to make money.

There are approximately 32,500 CICs in existence at the time of writing, including the Dizzy (retail) CIC (a charity shop which aims to promote a better understanding of diabetes), Madlug CIC (which seeks to give dignity to children in care by donating travel bags to them so they don't need to carry their possessions in bin liners) and the Gaydio CIC (the UK's first full-time FM radio station for the LGBT community).

Such companies are governed by the Companies (Audit, Investigations and Community Enterprise) Act 2004, and set up under the formalities of the CA 2006. A CIC must have the specific aim of providing a benefit to a community, and it must use its assets and profits to benefit that community. Throughout its lifetime it must meet this community interest test. Community interest companies may not be formed to run political parties or be involved in political campaigning, and they must also not be legal registered charities.

More information on CICs is available from the CIC Regulator's website, <www.gov.uk/government/organisations/office-of-the-regulator-of-community-interest-companies>.

1.10.2 Charitable incorporated organisations

The Charities Act 2006 introduced the broad legal framework for a new legal form of corporate structure which is designed specifically for charities, the charitable incorporated organisation (CIO). The Charitable Incorporated Organisations (General) Regulations 2012 (SI 2012/3012) set out the detail on how they will be established and operated.

Prior to January 2013, charities could be set up with a corporate structure, but such entities normally fall within the requirements of company law as well as charity law. In particular, they have to register both with the Charity Commission (responsible for overseeing charities) and the Registrar of Companies (responsible for setting up and storing information on companies), and provide accounts and other information to both. As the framework of a company was designed primarily for commercial organisations, this may mean that it is not always suitable for charities.

The CIO is intended to provide the advantages of a corporate structure, such as reduced risk of personal liability, without this burden of dual regulation. It is not subject to company law and is regulated only by the Charities Commission. The first new CIOs were registered on 3

January 2013, and rules allow existing charities to convert to CIOs. There are now approximately 31,500 CIOs in existence at the time of writing.

You can find out more about CIOs from the Charity Commission's website, <www.gov.uk/government/organisations/charity-commission>.

1.10.3 UK Societas

The UK Societas is a product of Brexit. Whilst the UK was a member of the EU, it was possible for a UK registered company to form a European public company in accordance with EU Regulation 2157/2001 on the Statute for a European Company. These companies are known as *Societas Europaea* (SE). They are a single company, or a group of companies, operating in different EU Member States which can operate as a single corporate entity subject to one set of rules valid in all Member States.

The European Public Limited-Liability Company (Amendment etc) (EU Exit) Regulations 2018 amended the Regulation and the European Public Limited Liability Company Regulations 2004 (SI 2004/2326) which supplemented it in the UK. As a result, the UK-registered SEs were converted into a new corporate form, the UK Societas. The UK Societas is only intended to be a temporary corporate form whilst it decides on which other UK corporate structure to adopt. There is, however, no deadline for this transformation to take place and there are currently only approximately 19 left in existence. It is not possible to set up a UK Societas from scratch. Further information on UK Societates is available from the GOV.UK website, www.gov.uk.

1.10.4 UK establishment by overseas company

This method of running a business applies only to a pre-existing foreign company (known as an 'overseas company') that wishes to operate in the UK and set up a regular physical presence here. The law is set out in the Overseas Companies Regulations 2009 (SI 2009/1801) which were made under authority granted in the CA 2006. All overseas companies that set up a branch (as defined in the 11th EU Company Law Directive 89/666/EEC) or any other place of business in the UK must register selected details of the establishment within one month of its opening.

The rules apply not just to companies from EU and EEA countries, but also to companies registered in any country outside of the UK. Registration is not required if the overseas company does not have a physical presence in the UK, for example if it operates solely over the internet or it appoints an agent in the UK to act on the company's behalf. Similarly, if the presence is only occasional, such as periodic visits by a representative of the company, there is no need to register the place where meetings take place or the representative's place of accommodation.

There are currently approximately 14,500 overseas companies with a UK establishment from jurisdictions as varied as the Cayman Islands, Liberia, Lebanon, the USA and China. One example is the overseas company, Deutsche Bank Aktiengesellschaft, the German financial services company. It has registered Deutsche Bank AG London as its UK establishment.

In order to register, the overseas company must submit a registration application form, OS IN01 (available on the Companies House website at <www.gov.uk/government/organisations/companies-house>), which includes information on both the overseas company and the UK establishment (such as the name), together with certain documents from the overseas company and the applicable fee. This fee is £71 for a paper application. There is no same-day registration service available, nor is it possible to register overseas companies via a digital application.

Further information on UK establishments is available from the 'overseas companies' section of the Companies House website noted above.

1.10.5 Company formed by special Act of Parliament

Historically, trading companies were sometimes established by a special Act of Parliament. This process was often used to establish railways and the public utilities (electricity, gas and water) in the UK. Such companies are now very rare (there are just 44 still in existence) and they will not be considered any further in this book.

1.10.6 Company formed by royal charter

Such a company is formed under the prerogative powers of the monarch by letters patent without using the powers of Parliament. In an era of parliamentary democracy in the UK, and as registration of a company under the CA 2006 (see **1.7** above) is much cheaper, quicker and more certain, this method of establishing companies is more of historic interest, but the right to form a company in this way does remain and is explicitly referred to in s 1040 of the CA 2006.

Many companies established by this method – including the British East India Company, originally granted a charter by Queen Elizabeth I in 1600 (and which eventually ruled large parts of India) – no longer exist. However, there are currently about 890 companies in the UK which have been established by royal charter. For example, the Royal Bank of Scotland, one of the UK's leading banking companies, was established by royal charter granted by King George I in 1727. In more recent times the powers have been used to establish non-profit corporations such as The Law Society, which represents solicitors in England and Wales.

1.11 LIMITED LIABILITY PARTNERSHIP

This is yet another way in which a business may be run. A limited liability partnership (LLP) is formed under the Limited Liability Partnerships Act 2000. It is basically a hybrid between a partnership and a limited company. It has a separate legal personality distinct from its owners like a company (see **1.7** above), and it offers its owners the protection from liability of a limited company (see **1.9** above). However, the LLP is run with the informality and flexibility afforded by a partnership, and the partners are taxed as if the business were a partnership rather than a company.

There are approximately 52,500 LLPs in existence in the UK at the time of writing. Many of the larger LLPs are professional firms (such as firms of solicitors or accountants) which converted to this format from partnership to protect themselves from the risk of personal liability. Two of the largest LLPs are DLA Piper International LLP and Allen & Overy LLP, the City law firms, having a turnover of approximately £3 billion and £2.1 billion respectively in the last financial year for which information was available.

Limited liability partnerships can be formed only by two or more members carrying on a lawful business with a view of profit. They therefore cannot be set up by an individual or by non-profit organisations. They are formed by filing a series of documents with the Registrar of Companies at Companies House and paying the applicable fee. This fee is £50 if the documents are submitted in digital form, or £71 for documents submitted in paper form. Alternatively, it is possible to pay £78 for a same-day digital registration service. The registration process is usually done electronically. Once the LLP is successfully registered, the Registrar will issue a certificate of incorporation. The LLP legally comes into existence on the date of incorporation on the certificate.

Individual members of the LLP must register with HMRC as self-employed.

Chapter 18 contains further information on this type of business, and see **25.6** for details of how LLPs are taxed.

Note that an LLP should not be confused with a 'limited partnership' (or LP) under the Limited Partnerships Act 1907 which is a different way to run a business (see **1.5** above).

1.12 UKEIG

The UKEIG is a product of Brexit. Whilst the UK was a member of the EU, it was possible for UK-based businesses to form a European economic interest grouping (EEIG). These are designed to enable businesses (or other entities such as universities) to form and maintain links with businesses from other EU Member States. In effect they are alliances between businesses in different Member States that wish to operate together across national borders. The aim of an EEIG is to facilitate the economic activities of its members. It is therefore intended to be an alternative to other types of pan-European co-operation such as a joint venture, or a merger or takeover (where one company buys another). It is important to note that EEIGs may be used only where the purpose is not to make profits. Pre-Brexit there were about 280 EEIGs with their main base in the UK. Pursuant to the European Economic Interest Grouping (Amendment) (EU Exit) Regulations 2018, EEIGs with their main base in the UK were converted into a new corporate form, the UKEIG. These are only intended to be a temporary corporate form whilst the UKEIG decides on which other structure to adopt. There is, however, no deadline for this transformation to take place and there are currently approximately 260 still in existence. It is not possible to set up a UKEIG from scratch.

Further information on UKEIGs is available from the GOV.UK website, www.gov.uk

1.13 WHAT TYPE OF BUSINESS IS BEST?

Faced with this array of different business formats, which one should the entrepreneur choose to run their business? If they have set up a business before then they may already know how they wish to do it; but if, like most people, they have no previous experience, they may well have only a rough idea of how to structure their business. In this case it is, of course, best for them to seek professional advice, although by no means do all people do this before starting up, particularly as money is usually scarce. In addition, as we have seen, a sole trader or partnership may be started without any formalities having to be fulfilled. Usually, though, an entrepreneur will initially approach their bank, an accountant or a small business adviser. It is often these people who would refer the entrepreneur to a lawyer.

The most common, and therefore the most important, types of business are the sole trader, partnership, limited company (both private and public) and the LLP. We shall therefore limit the following discussion to these types of business. There are various factors which most future business owners will want to consider before deciding which type to choose.

1.13.1 Can the entrepreneur set up this type of business?

A partnership and an LLP require at least two owners for these forms to exist, so only the sole trader or limited company is suitable for the sole business owner. A public company requires at least two directors.

There are certain restrictions on who may be involved with a company. Under s 157 of the CA 2006, a person aged under 16 cannot usually be a director of a company; neither can an undischarged bankrupt or (under s 159A of the CA 2006) a person who has been disqualified as a director under the Company Directors Disqualification Act 1986 (CDDA 1986). If any of these restrictions applies then of course the limited company is not an option, but the presence of such individuals would make it very difficult to establish a business of any type, not least because they are unlikely to appeal to possible co-owners of a business and due to the difficulties that such individuals would face persuading investors or banks to provide finance.

1.13.2 How much tax will the entrepreneur pay?

This is often a crucial factor in the decision as to how to run a business. Almost all businesses are set up to make money for their owners, and the less tax the business pays, the more profit will be available to expand the business and to reward the owners. The role of taxation in determining the most suitable type of business for an owner is explored in **Chapter 29**. Where tax differences are not critical, a number of other factors are significant, as discussed below.

1.13.3 What is the entrepreneur's attitude to risk?

As we have already seen (**1.3** and **1.4** above), the owners of unincorporated forms of business, such as a sole trader and a partnership, have unlimited liability for the debts of the business. If the business fails, and the UK Government's figures show that about 50% of businesses fail in their first three years, all of the owners' personal assets may be at risk and they may be made bankrupt. Sole traders and partners therefore live with the threat of bankruptcy on a daily basis, either because of financial misfortune or because of litigation. In the case of a partnership, this could be due to the misdeeds of one partner and not through the other partners' fault.

A limited company and the LLP have separate legal personality and are responsible for their own debts. The liability of the company's and LLP's owners is limited to an amount agreed at the time of the establishment of the business (see **1.9** and **1.11** above).

In principle, therefore, the limited company and the LLP have a significant advantage for the entrepreneur over the sole trader and partnership; but in practice people dealing with these forms of business, for example a bank lending money to them, will usually seek personal guarantees from the owners themselves to ensure that if the business fails to repay the loan, the lender can seek the money directly from the owners. A guarantee is simply a contractual promise to pay another's debt (here the company's or LLP's) if that person cannot or does not do so. In other words, by entering the personal guarantee the owners in effect potentially lose the benefit of limited liability, as they could be asked to pay the company's or LLP's debts out of their personal assets. Why would they do this? The commercial reality is that new businesses generally need banks (for their money) more than banks need their business. Banks are of course not charities but hard-nosed commercial organisations, and so they will usually take every form of protection or security to ensure that they are repaid their loans.

However, over time, if the business flourishes, the advantage of limited liability can be very beneficial in reducing the risks of personal liability for the owners, and it is for this reason that many law firms which were run as partnerships have now become LLPs.

There are further risks involved in running a company due to the high level of regulation imposed by the CA 2006 and other legislation. As we have seen, a private company requires at least one director to be appointed to manage the company, and a public company requires at least two. In new businesses run as companies, these directors are usually also the individuals who own the company. As directors they are subject to personal liability for fines and even to imprisonment under the CA 2006 if they fail to carry out their statutory duties. For example, fines may be imposed for a failure to file the necessary returns and documents with the Registrar of Companies on time, or for failure to maintain the company's own records (eg, under s 853L of the CA 2006, for failure to submit a confirmation statement). Directors may also be made personally liable under other legislation. Examples include ss 213 and 214 of the Insolvency Act 1986 (for fraudulent or wrongful trading respectively in the run up to the insolvency of a company), s 37 of the Health and Safety at Work, etc Act 1974 (for failure to ensure the health, safety and welfare of employees at work) and ss 1 and 2 of the Bribery Act 2010 (for offering or receiving bribes in the conduct of business). Liability may also arise for a breach of the director's general duties under ss 171–177 of the CA 2006 (see further **Chapter 6**).

1.13.4 What formalities are required?

The unincorporated businesses (sole trader and partnership) need meet no formalities to be established, whereas the incorporated businesses (company and LLP) must first undergo a registration process involving the submission of an application form, the payment of a fee and the preparation of legal documents. There is a cost and time delay in establishing an incorporated business.

This difference in formality between incorporated businesses and partnerships may have less substance than at first appears. The reason is that in practice a partnership may record the agreement of the partners as to how to run the business in writing in a partnership agreement. The preparation of this agreement will incur solicitors' fees. This step is recommended even though it is not legally necessary, as it helps to avoid uncertainty in the future in dealing with matters which arise from the running of the partnership.

Perhaps the bigger issue is compliance with formalities *after* the business has been set up. A significant advantage for an unincorporated business is that there are no formal requirements (except tax requirements with HMRC) once it has been established; no legal documents have to be prepared. A company, however, must comply with a series of legal requirements depending on its size, and must complete minutes of meetings, maintain certain statutory registers, and regularly file certain documents and even audited accounts with Companies House. These obligations represent both an administrative inconvenience and an additional expense, as these documents may need to be prepared by professionals who will charge a fee, as might Companies House for documents filed there. Limited liability partnerships must also file certain documents and accounts, but generally there are not as many requirements for LLPs as for a company.

Furthermore, a company must be run in accordance with strict rules laid down in the CA 2006. As we shall see when we look at company law, these rules govern how the decision-making process should be undertaken, who should take certain decisions and whether certain decisions can be taken at all. A sole trader and a partnership have freedom regarding how they wish to structure decision-making in their businesses, although in a large partnership this could lead to slow decision-making if, for example, all of the partners' agreement is required to run the business. An LLP has a similar freedom to organise its decision-making as a partnership.

1.13.5 Does the entrepreneur want to reveal information publicly?

The sole trader and partnership are generally not obligated to reveal any information about their operations to the public at large, except the identity of all partners and an address for service of documents, whereas both a company and an LLP must by law reveal a certain amount of information, including, crucially, certain financial information. A company in particular must make public a range of information about its affairs, its directors and its shareholders by filing returns and documents with the Registrar of Companies. The information on companies and LLPs is stored at Companies House and is available for public inspection, even online via the Companies House website, usually for a small fee.

Some entrepreneurs may not wish to reveal certain information about their business. For example, they may not want the state of the finances of their business to be known beyond their accountants, their bank and HMRC, in which case an unincorporated business (sole trader and partnership) would be the more attractive option. It is said that some law firms have remained partnerships rather than converting to LLPs precisely for this reason.

1.13.6 How much will it cost the entrepreneur to set up and run the business?

A sole trader or partnership may be set up without any costs as these types of business can trade straight away, although we have seen that often a partnership agreement will be drawn up. There are fees which must be incurred to form either a company or an LLP. However, these are usually quite low.

In terms of running the business there are, of course, certain costs (premises, wages, supplies, etc) which are the same regardless of the type of business chosen. Incorporated businesses (LLPs and companies) will usually cost more to run from an administrative point of view due to the compulsory regulations imposed on them. For the company in particular there can be significant extra burdens imposed under the CA 2006. The sole trader and partnership escape these obligations and therefore do not incur the cost of compliance.

1.13.7 Does status matter?

There may be a feeling on the part of persons trading with the business that a company is a more substantial business medium than a partnership or a sole trader. They may feel more reassured dealing with a company which has to undergo a registration process, make information public and is generally subject to greater regulation.

Also, in terms of raising money to fund the business's activities, both a company and an LLP can offer an additional form of security for loans (a floating charge) which is not available to a partnership or sole trader, which may be desirable for lenders such as banks. Companies also offer the advantage of generally having a wider pool of potential investors, which means that it may be easier to raise money to expand in the future.

Because of these reasons, third parties and lenders may therefore be more willing to deal with a company (and perhaps an LLP), and this may influence the decision of the entrepreneur as to what type of business to select.

1.13.8 Summary

A simplified summary of the pros and cons of the different business formats is set out below.

Sole trader

Advantages

(a) very easy to form;

(b) freedom to run as owner sees fit;

(c) sole decision-maker;

(d) all profits belong to owner.

Disadvantages

(a) unlimited liability for business debts;

(b) lacks status of incorporated forms;

(c) no day-to-day support for owner.

Partnership

Advantages

(a) very easy to form;

(b) freedom to run as owners sees fit;

(c) support of joint decision-making;

(d) all profits belong to owners (the partners).

Disadvantages

(a) unlimited liability for business debts;

(b) decision-making can be cumbersome;

(c) lack of written agreement can lead to uncertainty;

(d) lacks status of incorporated forms of business.

Limited company

Advantages

(a) limited liability for business debts;

(b) greater status than other forms;

(c) potentially larger pool of investors.

Disadvantages

(a) must register to set up;
(b) extra formality and costs to run;
(c) extra legal duties and potential liability for directors;
(d) information (including finances) made public;
(e) profits earned by company, not owners directly.

LLP

Advantages

(a) limited liability for business debts;
(b) freedom to run as owners sees fit;
(c) support of joint decision-making.

Disadvantages

(a) must register to set up;
(b) information (including finances) made public;
(c) some extra formality and costs to run.

1.13.9 Conclusion

It is important to note that although a lawyer can advise an entrepreneur on the legal and taxation implications of the different types of business, compare them, and highlight the advantages and disadvantages of each type, the lawyer will not decide what type of business the entrepreneur should set up. What is important for one entrepreneur may be less so for another. Ultimately it is the entrepreneur themselves who best understands their position, the risks they are prepared to take, and the costs and restrictions they are prepared to bear. So, after being advised, it is they who must take this decision themselves and live with its consequences, good or bad.

1.14 CHANGING THE TYPE OF BUSINESS

Having, it is hoped, weighed up the pros and cons of the different types of business and then decided upon the right type of business, the reality is that over time, particularly if the business does well, the owner or owners may decide to change to the form in which their business is run. Marks & Spencer, the retailer, is a good example of this. Michael Marks set up business as a sole trader in 1884. In 1894 he formed a partnership with Tom Spencer. In 1914 they transformed the business into a private limited company, and in 1926 it became a public limited company. The company has since joined the Main Market of the London Stock Exchange to become a publicly-traded company.

It is important to note then that the decision as to how to run a new business does not necessarily determine the status of that business forever. As a new business grows, the advantages and disadvantages of each type of business may produce different results from when it was first established. The business owners and advisers may therefore revisit the factors in **1.13** afresh. How a business can be changed from one type to another is covered in **Chapter 30**.

1.15 PRACTICAL CONSIDERATIONS

This book concentrates on the legal issues arising out of running a business, of which the choice of the type of business is the first. However, for the budding entrepreneur there are many other non-legal considerations which, at least in theory, ought to be weighed up before they reach the stage of choosing the type of business.

There are personal considerations, such as the physical and emotional pressures on the entrepreneur and their family in the start-up phase, caused by the inevitably long hours of work, the likely financial unpredictability, and the loss of existing employee benefits such as paid holiday, pension and paid sick leave if resigning from a current job.

Furthermore, has the entrepreneur considered whether they possess the necessary skills to succeed? Setting up a business will require self-confidence, the entrepreneur's belief in their product or service, the motivation to work very hard, including in the evenings and at weekends, and the strength of character to cope with setbacks and the possible risk of losing their home. Does the entrepreneur have the ability to undertake the financial planning for the business, to manage employees, to market and sell the product, to negotiate and nurture relationships with suppliers?

There is an abundance of practical considerations for the entrepreneur to bear in mind as well. How will they manage financially before the business generates sufficient income? Have they arranged finance to cover the start up of the business? Have they got a business plan? Do they have premises from which to operate the business? Do they meet health and safety standards? Do employees need to be hired? What are their plans for advertising and marketing? Do they need to protect a new invention? Are authorisations required to run that particular business?

Many of these issues require a consideration of the law. The entrepreneur and the new business may therefore have to deal with contract law, tax and accounting law, health and safety law, property law, employment law, data protection law, banking law, intellectual property law and environmental law. This can be overwhelming to the uninitiated, but help exists in the form of mentors and professional advisers (including lawyers), and, copiously, online. A particularly good online resource for the first-time entrepreneur is the UK Government's website at <www.gov.uk/set-up-business>.

In the next chapter we consider the private limited company and begin our detailed examination of company law.

CHAPTER 2

INTRODUCTION TO THE COMPANY

LEARNING OUTCOMES

After reading this chapter you will be able to:

- understand the principle of the separate legal personality of a company under English law
- identify occasions when the principle is not enforced
- explain additional key English company law concepts
- locate the main sources of English and EU company law

2.1 INTRODUCTION

If an entrepreneur chooses to run their business as a company then that company will be formed under s 7 of the CA 2006 by a process of registration. Registration involves the submission of certain documents and payment of a fee to the Registrar of Companies at Companies House. This process is explained fully in **Chapter 3**. In this chapter we concentrate on some of the key consequences which arise under company law when a company is formed, and we develop some of these in later chapters. We also consider the most important sources of company law.

2.2 THE KEY CONCEPTS

We have already seen (**1.7** and **1.9** above) that the formation of a company results in two fundamental consequences. They are that:

(a) a company has separate legal personality; and

(b) the members of a limited company have limited liability.

They are two of the most significant legal principles in English law and represent two of the biggest advantages for the entrepreneur in choosing to run their business as a company. An understanding of these and related principles, and their effects, is essential to a clear understanding of how and why a company operates as it does. We shall now look at them in more detail.

2.3 SEPARATE LEGAL PERSONALITY

The single most important effect of running a business through a company is that the company has a separate legal personality. This is the crux of what a company is. Although forming a company by registration without the need for royal charter or Act of Parliament had been permitted since the Joint Stock Companies Registration Act of 1844, it was only following the decision of the House of Lords in *Salomon v A Salomon and Co Ltd* [1897] AC 22 that the full extent of this principle was realised. The House of Lords held in its judgment that the company's acts were its own acts, not those of Mr Salomon personally. This was the case even though Mr Salomon was in effect the only person involved in running the company and owned the largest share of the company.

This principle means that unlike sole traders and partnerships, which in effect are the same as the people who own and run them, a company is a legal entity separate from both its owners (the members) and those people who run it on a day-to-day basis (the directors). The company is recognised by the law as a person – a special type of person known as a 'legal person', but nonetheless one which has its own rights and obligations separate from the 'natural persons' (ie the individuals) who own and run it.

This can be a strange concept to grasp immediately, so we shall examine some of the principle's effects in practice to shed light on what it means.

2.3.1 Ownership of property

One of the effects of separate legal personality is that a company owns its own property and it does not belong to the members (ie owners) of the company. Imagine that Mr Batman and Mr Robin set up a company, Gotham Limited, and become its members. The company manufactures capes. The capes which are made belong to the company, Gotham Limited, in its own right and not to Messrs Batman and Robin. The members certainly own the company, Gotham Limited, but they do not own Gotham Limited's property directly, the company itself does.

Another example of this is that if the company wishes to insure its property, it must do so in its own name and not in the name of, say, one of its members, for it is the company which owns the property and not the member. If the member were to insure the company's property, the insurance would not be valid and the insurer would not have to pay up if a claim was made, even if that member owned the whole company (*Macaura v Northern Assurance Co Ltd* [1925] AC 619).

2.3.2 Contracts

The principle of separate legal personality also means that it is the company in its own name which will enter into contracts with third parties and incur contractual rights and obligations. For example, Gotham Limited may enter into a contract to supply a customer, Kat Woman, with 100 black capes for £2,000. The contract will not be between Messrs Batman and Robin and Ms Woman.

Another example involves the employees of a company. Employees of a company will enter into an employment contract with the company rather than with any of the individuals involved in running the company. The company will therefore be the employer, even though others involved with the company, such as the directors, will decide upon the pay, responsibilities, and terms and conditions of employment.

2.3.3 Borrowing

As with individuals, a company is able to borrow money and give security over its assets. For example, Gotham Limited might mortgage the factory which it owns to a bank in order to borrow money from the bank to expand the company's business. This is really nothing more than another example of a company's freedom to contract. After all, the mortgage and the loan agreement (or the bank overdraft) are simply contracts between the borrowing company and the lending bank. However, borrowing money is such an important part of a company's existence that it bears highlighting separately.

It is also worth noting that there is nothing to stop a company from borrowing money from its members, or indeed its directors, assuming, of course, that they are willing to lend. The company is a separate legal person distinct from its members and directors, and is free to enter into such contracts.

2.3.4 Liability for debts

A company, being a separate legal person, can incur debts in its own name. What happens if a company does not or cannot repay its debts? The creditors who are owed money must take action against the company and not against the members or directors of the company. The members and directors have no direct liability for the debts of the separate entity, the company, which incurred them. Creditors cannot sue the members or the directors to pay off these debts, or seize their personal assets. They can sue only the company; and if successful, they will be allowed to seize the assets which the company itself owns. If these assets are insufficient to pay off the creditors' debts then the creditors will lose money. Such is the risk of doing business with a company. This was what happened in the *Salomon v Salomon* decision (see **2.3** above).

This brings us to the related matter of limited liability and the other main consequence which arises when a company is formed. The explanation given in the previous paragraph would seem to indicate that members have no liability for the debts of their company. Why, then, are members referred to as having 'limited' liability? This is because (as we saw at **1.9** above) the term 'limited liability' refers to the *members'* own liability rather than to the *company's* liability.

When a new company limited by shares is formed, a person becomes a member by buying shares in that company. In doing so that member becomes an owner of the company. The member will agree to hand over money to the company in return for the company issuing them with shares (which represent ownership of the company and which import certain other rights). These shares will have a fixed legal monetary value, known as the 'nominal' or 'par' value.

For example, let us assume that Gotham Limited issued 100 shares to Mr Batman and 100 shares to Mr Robin. The shares each have a nominal value of £1. Each member is liable to pay to the company the nominal value for the shares he has bought in the company. So Mr Batman, buying 100 shares of £1 each in Gotham Limited, would have to pay £100 for those shares. If he paid £100 at the time of purchase, as is usual, Mr Batman has satisfied his liability to the company. His liability as a member is described as 'limited' because it is limited to his paying the £100. As in our example, he has done so; he has satisfied this liability in full and he cannot be asked to contribute any further money to settle the company's debts.

Usually most members pay for their shares in full when they buy them (like Mr Batman) and so settle their liability to the company immediately. Sometimes, however, the member will agree with the company to pay only part of the value of the shares when he buys them. For example, assume that when Mr Robin bought his 100 shares of £1 each in Gotham Limited and became an owner, he agreed with the company that he would pay only £50 at the time of purchase and £50 at a later date. If the company is wound up and comes to an end (eg, because it can no longer pay its debts), under s 74(2)(d) of the Insolvency Act 1986 (IA 1986) any unpaid amount of the nominal value of the shares may be claimed from the members. Any unpaid amount therefore represents the extent of the members' liability. If the member has not paid the full amount of the nominal value then he is liable to pay the outstanding amount, and this represents his liability to the company. So, using our example, Mr Robin would be asked to pay the outstanding £50 to Gotham Limited if it was being wound up. That unpaid amount, and only that amount, is the extent of his liability to the company. A creditor cannot sue a member directly and claim his personal assets to settle the debts of the company. Mr Robin's liability is therefore described as 'limited' because it is limited to the amount that is unpaid on his shares in the company. It is a fixed, identifiable amount at the time he bought the shares. No further money can be demanded from Mr Robin, even if the company's debts exceed this amount. If Gotham Limited was wound up owing £10,000, Mr Robin would have to pay £50 and, as we saw in the preceding paragraph, Mr Batman nothing.

It is worth reminding ourselves of the contrasting position of a business owner, such as a sole trader or partner in a partnership, who has unlimited liability. Unlimited liability covers the situation where the business owner has to pay off *all* the businesses debts whenever they arise and for whatever purpose (see **1.3** and **1.4**), and even use their personal assets to do so. This explains why many business owners choose to run their businesses as companies. It also explains why companies promote business, as business owners are more likely to take on speculative business ventures if they know that their personal assets are protected if the company goes insolvent.

The required use of the term 'limited' or 'ltd' at the end of a private company's name, and the required use of 'public limited company' or 'plc' at the end of public company's name (see **1.9.2** and **1.9.3** above), therefore refers to the fact that the owners of that company have only limited liability to the company (to pay for their shares) and will not themselves be responsible for the company's debts. It alerts anyone dealing with the company that the company itself must pay its own debts.

2.3.5 Legal action

A company may sue and be sued in its own name. It is not for the members to sue on the company's behalf. If Ms Woman fails to pay the agreed £2,000 for the capes by the agreed deadline, Gotham Limited must bring a claim for breach of contract in the courts in its own name. Mr Batman and Mr Robin cannot sue on the company's behalf. Similarly, if Ms Woman discovers that the capes are the wrong colour (ginger rather than black), she may sue Gotham Limited in its own name for breach of contract. She cannot sue Mr Batman or Mr Robin as members, since they are not parties to the contract which was made between Gotham Limited and Ms Woman.

A company may also be made subject to criminal prosecution in its own right. For example, Asda Stores Ltd, the company running the Asda supermarket chain, was fined £22,000 in 2005 as a separate legal person under the Health and Safety at Work, etc Act 1974 and other legislation, when a worker was injured when trying to demonstrate to a supervisor that her overloaded trolley carrying frozen chickens was unstable. She was pinned under 145 kilos of chickens impaled on skewers. The trolley was defective and had not been repaired. Another worker at the same store received an electric shock when she cleaned a refrigerated cabinet with a damp cloth. She had not received training or been told to switch off the electricity before cleaning the cabinet.

A company may even be prosecuted for manslaughter in its own right under the Corporate Manslaughter and Corporate Homicide Act 2007. The first prosecution for corporate manslaughter under the Act resulted in Cotswold Geotechnical Limited being found guilty at Winchester Crown Court in February 2011. The company had committed a gross breach of duty by failing to protect one of its employees from working in dangerous conditions. The employee, a geologist, died when a trench he was working in caved in on him. The company (rather than any individual connected with the company) was fined £385,000. There have since been further convictions of companies, and numerous additional cases are being prosecuted or under investigation.

2.3.6 Continuity

A company as a separate legal person has its own lifespan independent of those who own or run it. It is 'born' on incorporation when it is registered (this now takes place under the CA 2006, but there are previous versions of the Companies Act) and 'lives' until it is wound up or liquidated. Therefore, unlike the company's members and directors, the company, being an artificial person, can 'live' forever. If members or directors retire or die, procedures exist under the law to ensure that their shoes may be filled by new individuals. Immortality beckons for the company. The Whitechapel Bell Foundry Limited in London was the UK's oldest manufacturing company. It made bells (Big Ben, etc) as a company continuously from 1570 to May 2017 when it closed its business due to falling demand. At the other end of the spectrum, the company that runs the bank, Monzo, and the company which trades as Castore, the sportswear manufacturer, were incorporated only in 2015.

2.3.7 Taxation

A company, being a separate legal person, is taxed separately from the members and directors of the company, and the liability to pay tax for the company's activities is the company's alone. Companies even pay their own type of tax, corporation tax, rather than the income tax and capital gains tax which individuals such as members and directors will pay. See **Chapters 21** to **29** for further information on the taxation of companies.

2.3.8 'Human' rights

As a separate legal person a company is also entitled to certain protections under the Human Rights Act 1998 which enacts the European Convention on Human Rights into UK law. Whilst a company is not, of course, a human being, and cannot be tortured (Article 3) or marry (Article 12), and does not have the right to life (Article 2), it is a legal person and does, for example, have the right to protection of property (Article 1 of the First Protocol), the right to a fair trial to determine civil and criminal matters (Article 6), and the right to freedom of expression (Article 10). This is the case even though such rights are usually referred to as 'human' rights.

2.3.9 Division of responsibility in a company

All of the above examples make clear that a company is a separate legal person with its own legal identity. However, being a person which is artificial rather than natural has one obvious disadvantage – a company cannot think or take decisions for itself. It is one thing to say, for example, that a company can own property, but how should the company decide whether it needs to buy property, which property to buy, how much to pay for it and how will it sign the legal documentation necessary to transfer ownership? A company of course must still rely on natural persons – humans – to take decisions and act on its behalf.

There are three main categories of individuals whom a company will need in order to function: workers, members and directors.

2.3.9.1 Workers

Workers, particularly employees, are beyond the scope of this textbook as they are generally much less important from a company law point of view than members and directors, even though they are of course invariably extremely valuable in keeping the business going. The relationship between businesses (including companies) and their workers is predominantly governed by employment law, which is a specialist legal subject in itself and a distinct area of practice. It will be touched upon in this book only when necessary to explain requirements of company law.

2.3.9.2 Members

The members of a company are the owners of that company. The company belongs to them. In a company limited by shares the members are more usually known as 'shareholders', for in order to become the owner of a company limited by shares it is necessary to own shares in that company. The term 'member' is used throughout the CA 2006 rather than 'shareholder'. This is because, as we saw in **Chapter 1,** there are different types of company, and the umbrella term 'member' covers the owners of these other types of company. For example, 'member' in the CA 2006 covers the owner of a company limited by guarantee as well as of a company limited by shares. As we shall be concentrating in **Part II** on companies limited by shares (overwhelmingly the most numerous type of company), we use the term 'shareholder' rather than 'member' of a company. The term 'shareholder' is simply a more precise definition of 'member' for the owner of a company limited by shares. We examine the role of the shareholder in greater detail in **Chapter 5**.

2.3.9.3 Directors

The directors run the company on a day-to-day basis. They owe numerous duties to their company to ensure that they always act in its best interests rather than for their own personal benefit. The directors also have an agency relationship with their company, having the power to take certain decisions and enter into contracts on its behalf. A director may also have an employment relationship with their company. We consider the role of the director in greater detail in **Chapter 6**.

2.3.9.4 Decision-making

The decisions affecting the company, or its business, are in practice made either by the company's directors or by its shareholders, or sometimes by both jointly. The directors will take the daily decisions affecting the business run by the company, such as entering into contracts (eg sales contracts, loans, employment contracts). The shareholders, being owners, usually get involved only in the more important decisions affecting the company, including changes to the company's constitution, eg changing the company's name. These decisions are usually taken at meetings of directors and shareholders respectively. The need for a decision-making procedure involving the directors and shareholders is therefore a necessary consequence of the company being a separate legal person. It enables the company to take decisions and run the business for which it was set up. Much of the company lawyer's work involves ensuring that the rules governing decision-making are complied with. We consider company decision-making further in **Chapter 8**.

2.3.10 Groups of companies

We have seen that a company, being a separate legal person, can own property in its own name (**2.3.1** above). This property includes shares in another company. In other words, one company may own some or all of another company, just as an individual may own shares in a company. By way of example, Tesco PLC, the supermarket chain, owns shares in well over 100 companies. In such a situation Tesco PLC is known as the 'parent' company and the companies it owns are known as its 'subsidiaries'. Many of these subsidiaries run separate parts of the business: Tesco Stores Limited runs the supermarkets, Tesco Personal Finance Group Limited runs Tesco Bank and its banking, insurance and credit card services, Tesco Fuel Limited runs the petrol stations, Tesco Home Shopping Limited runs the home delivery service, and Tesco Mobile Limited runs the mobile phone business. There are many other Tesco subsidiary companies which own property, run the employees' pension fund, own the overseas Tesco stores and invest money for Tesco.

Tesco PLC structures its business in this way to take advantage of separate legal personality. By splitting its operations into different companies, Tesco PLC is lessening the risk of financial problems in one part of the business affecting other parts. Say that Tesco Bank operated by Tesco Personal Finance PLC (TPFP) went insolvent. The debts of TPFP belong to that company alone and would not have to be paid off by Tesco PLC; Tesco PLC is only a shareholder of TPFP and therefore has limited liability. Also, the money and assets of the other Tesco companies, such as Tesco Stores Limited, running the supermarkets, will be unaffected as they too are separate legal persons. If, however, Tesco PLC itself directly owned all of the business, including Tesco Bank and the supermarkets, rather than through companies which it owned, the debts of Tesco Bank would have to be settled by money and assets generated from elsewhere in the business, such as from the supermarkets. If these debts were very large, this could threaten the existence of the whole company, even the profitable parts.

Despite some contradictory jurisprudence, this principle is generally upheld by the courts in their decisions. In *Adams v Cape Industries plc* [1990] Ch 433, the claimants for asbestos-related illnesses were unable to bring proceedings against a parent company as they worked for one of the parent's subsidiary companies. This was the case even though the subsidiary company had gone insolvent. However, in what may be a shift of emphasis, in *Chandler v Cape plc* [2012] EWCA Civ 525, a parent company was held liable for the asbestos-induced illness of an employee of its subsidiary company. The Court of Appeal established a number of principles for deciding the circumstances in which a parent company will be liable for the subsidiary's actions in health and safety matters. It seems as if such liability could extend to other areas, for example environmental liability.

An entrepreneur will therefore frequently use more than one company to run her business if it starts growing considerably, or if the business branches out into different areas.

2.4 SIDE-STEPPING SEPARATE LEGAL PERSONALITY

The principle that a company is a legal entity distinct from its shareholders is applied strictly by the courts. For example, if a creditor attempts to make the shareholders liable for the debts of the company then the claim will be dismissed. As we have seen from *Salomon v Salomon* (see **2.3** above), these debts are the company's alone. Nonetheless, the consequences that flow from the principle of separate legal personality as explained above may, in certain circumstances, be problematic in practice. The fact that the company is separate from its owners and managers can lead to unfairness, or have unintended or undesirable outcomes. Practice and the law have therefore developed to accommodate certain methods of bypassing the principle. Some of the more important examples are given below.

2.4.1 Giving a guarantee

Imagine that a farmer has grown a new fruit, the strawnana, a cross between a strawberry and a banana. The farmer wants to increase production and sell the fruit in supermarkets, but does not have enough money to buy the new heated greenhouses required to expand sales of the fruit. The farmer has just set up a company, Deviant Fruit Ltd, to run the business. The farmer has bought all 100 shares of £1 in the company and paid £100 to the company, and is the sole director. The farmer now approaches a bank, the Bank of Shires, to borrow £10,000 to buy the greenhouses. Deviant Fruit Ltd has virtually no assets (other than the £100 from the sale of its shares) as the business has not yet started trading. If the Bank of Shires were to lend the £10,000 to Deviant Fruit Ltd then it would risk losing all of its money if the new fruit did not sell and the company went bust. The farmer as a shareholder would be protected by the principle of separate legal personality and would lose only the £100 he invested by way of shares.

The Bank of Shires will be fully aware of the principle of separate legal personality and the potential disadvantage for it, as outlined above, if it were to lend the money to Deviant Fruit Ltd. As a result, it will not want to run the risk of lending the money to the company. Nevertheless, the Bank of Shires could get some assurance that if Deviant Fruit Ltd fails, the bank will still get its money back. One of the ways for it to do so is for the Bank to ask for a personal guarantee from the farmer as shareholder of the company. The farmer would agree contractually with the Bank of Shires that if the company which borrows the £10,000, Deviant Fruit Ltd, is unable to repay the loan to the bank, the farmer will pay the money to the bank. This would usually give the bank the comfort it requires. Although this arrangement upholds the principle of separate legal personality in law (Deviant Fruit Ltd is still in law responsible for its debts and not the shareholder), in practice it is being sidestepped by the use of contract law. The shareholder of the company, the farmer, is agreeing to pay back the debts of the company if the company cannot pay, which the farmer does not have to do.

Why, then, would the farmer agree to take on liability for debts which belong to the company? The practical reality is that the Bank of Shires will not lend any money without having in place some form of security that ensures its loan will be repaid. If the company cannot ensure that it will repay the loan or offer security, the bank will need security from someone else. The farmer, as the shareholder of the company, is the most obvious candidate, as he owns the company and wants the business to be successful. Unless the farmer can find other investors who will put money into the company, he will have to accept the requirement for a guarantee from the bank.

Other parties that deal with a company may also require personal guarantees from the company's shareholders, for example a landlord who enters into a lease with a company, to ensure that the landlord receives the rent if the company cannot pay.

2.4.2 The corporate veil

The consequences that arise from the principle of separate legal personality are sometimes described as the 'corporate veil'. Incorporating a company is said to establish a veil, or barrier, between the owners of the company, the shareholders, on the one hand and the company on the other. This flows from the principle of separate legal personality: that the company as a separate artificial person is responsible for its debts, property and actions rather than the company's shareholders.

There are, however, exceptional circumstances in which statute or case law 'pierces', or 'lifts' or 'looks behind' this corporate veil. Put simply, when this occurs the separate legal personality of the company is ignored. The result is that account can be taken of the shareholders in deciding the company's rights and obligations, or the shareholders themselves may be made liable for the company's acts. As the separate legal personality of companies is one of their greatest advantages, the corporate veil is lifted only in exceptional and limited circumstances, when all other, more conventional, remedies have proved to be of no assistance (*Prest v Petrodel Resources Ltd* [2013] UKSC 34).

Examples arise, for instance, in tax law. The Supreme Court in *Prest v Petrodel Resources Ltd* (above) reviewed the existing case law and provided much-needed clarification of the decisions of judges where the corporate veil has been lifted, noting that some judgments which purported to involve piercing the veil in fact did not involve it at all. The courts will usually look behind the veil only in cases of fraud or deliberate breach of trust, eg where companies are used to carry out fraud (*Re Darby, ex p Brougham* [1911] 1 KB 95) or to avoid existing obligations (*Gilford Motor Co Ltd v Horne* [1933] Ch 935). The courts seem to ignore the principle of separate legal personality in these cases in order to ensure that an appropriate remedy is available against individuals who have committed a wrong using a company that they control. The Supreme Court has held, however, that even where fraud may exist, it will not pierce the veil in order to hold a person controlling a company liable as a joint contracting party for a contract which the company, and not the controller, has entered into (*VTB Capital plc v Nutritek International Corp* [2013] UKSC 5).

2.4.3 Single economic unit

We saw in **2.3.10** that a group of companies may be used to lessen the risks of a business failure by taking advantage of separate legal personality. However, the practical reality in these groups of companies is that they are ultimately all owned by the same shareholders. The shareholders who own the parent company also indirectly own the subsidiary companies. If a shareholder, Mr Big, owns all of the shares in X Ltd, and X Ltd owns all of the shares in Y Ltd, the fact is that Mr Big controls not just X Ltd but Y Ltd too. The law recognises this reality, and in doing so sometimes treats these companies as if they were not independent legal persons.

Court decisions reaching this conclusion are now rare, and previous decisions ignoring separate legal personality among groups are quite controversial and currently thought to be specific to their facts.

Nevertheless, there are statutory rules which apply to groups of companies and treat them as if they are a single economic unit rather than entirely separate legal persons. For example, s 399 of the CA 2006 requires certain parent companies to prepare accounts for their groups of companies as if they were single companies, one aim being to ensure that shareholders of the parent company get to see the true financial state of their company. There is also special tax treatment of groups of companies to reflect the fact that, although comprising separate legal entities, they are usually run together. There are other examples in employment law, and in UK and EU competition law.

2.4.4 Liability of directors

There are various examples of statute imposing liability on directors for their involvement in running a company. For example, under s 214 of the IA 1986, a director of a company can be made personally liable to contribute money to the company's assets where the company has gone into insolvent liquidation (ie gone bust) and before that happened the director knew, or ought to have concluded, that there was no reasonable prospect of avoiding insolvent liquidation (see **7.13.10.1** below). Strictly this is not side-stepping separate legal personality at all. In fact the remedy upholds the principle by requiring the director to pay money to the separate person, the company. However, these provisions demonstrate that the company as a separate legal person is not always exclusively responsible for its acts. The individuals that run the company, the directors, may also have liability imposed on them in recognition of their critical role in acting on behalf of the company.

We explore the liability of directors further in **Chapter 7**.

2.5 OTHER MAJOR PRINCIPLES OF COMPANY LAW

The principle of separate legal personality and the effects which flow from it are at the core of company law. In addition, there are other important principles which underpin company law and which pervade the subject. These principles will be developed and explained further at appropriate points later in this book.

2.5.1 Transparency

As the owners of a company have only limited liability for the company's debts (see **2.3.4** above), companies are required to make a large amount of information available to the public.

The information which is made available includes:

(a) the identity of the company's shareholders, and the number and type of shares that they own;
(b) the identity and certain personal information about the company's directors;
(c) the identity of the company secretary (if any);
(d) the company's constitution (the internal rules which govern how the company should be run).
(e) the company's accounts; and
(f) certain decisions taken by the shareholders.

Provision of this information is intended to assist third parties (such as banks, or suppliers or new investors) in deciding whether they wish to deal with the company. They will be able to assess the company's financial strength and find out about the people involved with the company. In other words, it is a trade-off for the owners of a company having limited liability that the company must make available a significant amount of information about it. This obligation to make information public does not apply to sole traders and partners, as they are owners of businesses, with unlimited liability for those businesses' debts.

All of the information set out above is required by various provisions of the CA 2006. Failure to submit the information by the necessary deadline, or provision of incorrect information, may result in criminal sanctions being imposed on the company and individuals connected with the company, including the directors and company secretary (if any). Specific penalties will be highlighted throughout the book.

The CA 2006 requires that this information must be sent, usually using a prescribed form, to the Registrar of Companies at Companies House. Companies House is an agency of the Department for Business and Trade (DBT) whose functions include storing information which must be filed in accordance with the CA 2006 (and other legislation) and making it available to the public. The information is stored on a register kept at Companies House in accordance with s 1080 of the CA 2006. (It is not for nothing that Companies House's slogan is the unimpeachably accurate phrase 'for the record'.) The Registrar of Companies is designated under s 1061 of the CA 2006 as having responsibility for keeping this register. There are separate registrars for companies registered in England and Wales (based in Cardiff), Scotland (based in Edinburgh) and Northern Ireland (based in Belfast), as required by s 1060 of the CA 2006.

Most of the information on the register is publicly available. The register may be inspected by anyone (CA 2006, s 1085). It may be searched in person at one of Companies House offices (there is also an office in London), or more usually online at <www.gov.uk/government/organisations/companies-house>. Companies House offers free access to the vast majority of its digital information. The impact of the availability of such information can, for example, be seen in the article below on the former Prime Minister, Tony Blair.

More information on the filing process may be found at **3.15**.

Tony Blair and the £8million tax 'mystery'

Robert Mendick

Official accounts show a company set up by Mr Blair to manage his business affairs paid just £315,000 in tax last year on an income of more than £12 million. In that time, he employed 26 staff and paid them total wages of almost £2.3 million.

The accounts provide the strongest evidence yet of the huge sums generated by Mr Blair through his various activities since quitting Downing Street in June 2007.

He runs a business consultancy – Tony Blair Associates – which has deals with the governments of Kuwait and Kazakhstan among others and is a paid adviser to JP Morgan, an American investment bank, and to Zurich International, a global insurance company based in Switzerland. Mr Blair makes a further £100,000 a time from speeches and lectures while also presiding over a number of charities including a faith foundation.

Mr Blair has previously been criticised for cashing in on contacts made in Downing Street and these accounts will likely add to those concerns.

The documents also reveal that in the two years until March 31 last year, Mr Blair's management company had a total turnover of more than £20 million and paid tax of about £470,000.

The scale of Mr Blair's finances are shown in accounts lodged by Windrush Ventures Limited, just one of a myriad of companies and partnerships set up by the former prime minister. Windrush Ventures Ltd's "principal activity" is the "provision of management services" to Mr Blair's various other interests.

The accounts for the 12 months to March 31 were lodged with Companies House in the week between Christmas and New Year and made publicly available for the first time last week. Previously the accounts have contained almost no information because Windrush was classified as a small company. This time auditors appear to have been obliged to divulge more information because of the amount of money being handled.

The accounts show a turnover of £12.005 million and administrative expenses of £10.919 million, leaving Windrush Ventures with a profit of just over £1 million, on which Mr Blair paid tax of £315,000. The tax was paid at the corporate tax rate of 28 per cent.

Of those expenses, £2.285 million went on paying 26 employees at an average salary of almost £88,000. Windrush Ventures also pays £550,000 a year to rent Mr Blair's offices in Grosvenor Square, a stone's throw from the US embassy in Mayfair in central London and a further sum of about £300,000 on office equipment and furniture. But those costs amount to a little more than £3 million, meaning almost £8 million of "administrative expenditure" is unexplained in the accounts.

It is not known from the accounts what happened to that huge sum.

Tax specialists who have studied the accounts have told The Sunday Telegraph that the tax paid in 2010 of £154,000 and £315,000 in 2011 appears low because costs have been offset against the administrative costs, which remain largely unexplained.

One City accountant, who did not wish to be named, said: "It is very difficult to see what these administrative costs could be. It is a very large amount for a business like this. I am sure it is legitimate but it is certainly surprising.

"The tax bill of £315,000 is explained by the large administrative costs that are being treated as tax allowable."

Richard Murphy, a charted accountant who runs Tax Research LLP and has studied Mr Blair's company accounts, said: "There is about £8 million which we don't know where it goes. That money is unexplained. There is no indication at all why the administration costs are so high. What has happened to about £8 million which is being offset against tax?"

There is no suggestion that Mr Blair's tax affairs are anything other than legitimate. His accounts are audited by KPMG, one of the world's biggest accountancy firms. Mr Blair presides over 12 different legal entities, handling the millions of pounds he has received since leaving office. Another set of companies, which are run in parallel to Windrush Ventures, are called Firerush Ventures and appear to operate in exactly the same, oblique way.

The money paid into Windrush Ventures Ltd largely comes from Windrush Ventures No. 3 Limited Partnership, which appears to be where money is deposited before being spread around other companies, ultimately in Mr Blair's ownership. The limited partnership does not have to disclose publicly any accounts allowing its activities to remain secret.

Mr Murphy said last night: "It is in the limited partnership where things really happen. But that is the one Mr Blair keeps secret. We don't know how much money is in the LP. It is completely hidden. The question is why is Tony Blair running such as a completely secretive organisation?"

A spokesman for Mr Blair said last night: "The Windrush accounts are prepared in accordance with the relevant legal, accounting and regulatory guidance. Tony Blair continues to be a UK taxpayer on all of his income and all of his companies are UK registered for tax purposes."

The spokesman added that the accounts did not relate to any of Mr Blair's charitable activities, which raised money separately as independently registered charities.

The spokesman chose not to explain what happened to about £8 million of administrative expenses.

Source: *Daily Telegraph* 7 January 2012

2.5.2 Maintenance of capital principle

When a company is formed, the owners will invest money in the company by buying shares. The money invested by these shareholders in a company is known as share capital. In return for this investment the shareholders receive shares in the company which represent ownership of the company, and also usually have rights to a portion of any profits made by the company.

It is a fundamental rule of company law that the share capital belongs to the company and not to the shareholders. The share capital is treated as a special fund within the company and given extra protection by the law. This is so that it is available to repay the company's creditors should the company be unable to pay its debts. This is the maintenance of capital principle – that a reserve of money, the share capital, is maintained within the company, to be available for creditors as a last resort. Its effects are most clearly demonstrated in s 830 of the CA 2006. This provision allows a company to make distributions to its shareholders only out of distributable profits. Put simply, a company can pay money to its shareholders only from available profits which do not touch the share capital.

The reality, however, is that most private limited companies have a share capital of £100 or less. This means that £100 or less has been invested by the company's shareholders when buying shares in the company. In practice this amount of money will offer little comfort to creditors. It is simply too small an amount. Consequently, the aim behind the principle, namely, to ensure a protected fund for creditors, is not achieved. In recognition of the fact that the principle is simply not relevant in practice for many companies and their creditors, the CA 2006 permits private limited companies to avoid many of the rules which seek to maintain the company's share capital. Sometimes, in order to do so a company must follow a complex statutory procedure. The principle does have greater importance for public limited companies, though. We examine these rules in more detail in **Chapter 9**.

2.6 SOURCES OF COMPANY LAW

Company law governs the formation of a company and regulates it throughout its life. There is a large volume of company law. This is because the company is an artificial person with many rights and duties. There are both commercial and practical advantages if the law lays down how this legal person should behave, and also the rights and responsibilities of those who act on its behalf, own it and deal with it.

Company law is mostly contained in legislation passed by the UK Parliament. This may be in the form of primary legislation (an Act of Parliament) or secondary legislation (statutory instruments). Judge-made case law is another important source of company law. We look in greater detail at each of these sources below.

2.6.1 Legislation

The CA 2006 is the primary source of company law throughout the UK. There are some provisions particular to Scottish companies to take account of the differences between Scots and English law (eg, property law), and Welsh companies have rights regarding the Welsh language, but otherwise the rules apply equally across the three jurisdictions of the UK: England and Wales, Scotland and Northern Ireland.

Different systems of company law apply in the UK's Crown Dependencies. The Isle of Man Parliament, the Tynwald, has passed its own (much briefer!) Companies Act 2006, available at <http://legislation.gov.im/cms>. Guernsey companies are subject to the Companies (Guernsey) Law 2008, passed by the States of Deliberation and accessible at <http://www.guernseylegalresources.gg>. Jersey companies must comply with the Companies (Jersey) Law 1991 passed by the States of Jersey, which may be accessed at <http://www.jerseylaw.je>. These laws are much more important than they may at first appear, because these jurisdictions are very attractive to business owners in the UK due to the low or zero taxation rates for companies. All of these jurisdictions are, however, subject to Part 28 of the CA 2006 (see **2.6.2** below).

This book concentrates on the law applying to companies in England and Wales, although reference may occasionally be made to other jurisdictions.

2.6.2 Companies Act 2006

The CA 2006 is the longest statute passed to date by the UK Parliament, in its original form running to an epic 1,300 sections in 47 Parts with 16 Schedules. You will doubtless be pleased to read that as a result of periodic amendments it is now even longer! The CA 2006 came into force fully on 1 October 2009, with certain provisions being introduced over the previous two and half years in eight different stages. It replaced the former Companies Act, the CA 1985, after an extensive and fundamental review of company law. The CA 2006 is so long because it attempts to codify much (but by no means all) of company law in one place.

Although the law to which all companies in the UK are now subject is the CA 2006 and most companies currently in existence were formed under the CA 2006, a sizeable minority of companies in existence were formed under the CA 1985. This means that in practice lawyers cannot entirely ignore the CA 1985, even though it has now been repealed. Why? In particular, the constitutions of companies established under the CA 1985 are still broadly valid. As there have been some fundamental changes to company law brought in by the CA 2006, the corporate lawyer must therefore have an understanding of some of the principles under the old CA 1985 to advise these older companies how they should now operate under the CA 2006. These points will be raised where relevant throughout this book, in addition to the law of the CA 2006.

It is important to be clear at the outset that both categories of companies (and those formed under even earlier Companies Acts) are now subject to the law set out in the CA 2006.

Before we go any further, it is worth noting the coverage of the CA 2006 to get an overview of the material dealt with in the Act and the scope of company law in practice. We cover all of these topics in this book (to a greater or lesser extent), except where noted:

Part 1: General introductory provisions [covering some key definitions and the different types of company]
Part 2: Company formation
Part 3: A company's constitution
Part 4: A company's capacity and related matters
Part 5: A company's name
Part 6: A company's registered office
Part 7: Re-registration as a means of altering a company's status
Part 8: A company's members
Part 9: Exercise of a member's rights
Part 10: A company's directors
Part 11: Derivative claims and proceedings by members
Part 12: Company secretaries
Part 13: Resolutions and meetings
Part 14: Control of political donations and expenditure [we do not cover this specialist topic in this book]
Part 15: Accounts and reports [we consider this topic in outline only in **Chapter 6**]
Part 16: Audit [we consider this topic in outline only in **Chapter 6**]
Part 17: A company's share capital
Part 18: Acquisition by a limited company of its own shares
Part 19: Debentures
Part 20: Private and public companies
Part 21: Certification and transfer of securities
Part 21A: Information about people with significant control
Part 22: Information about interests in a company's shares [we do not cover this topic as it relates only to public companies]
Part 23: Distributions
Part 24: Annual confirmation of accuracy of information on register
Part 25: Company charges
Part 26: Arrangements and reconstructions
Part 26A: Arrangements and reconstructions: companies in financial difficulty
Part 27: Mergers and divisions of public companies [we do not cover this topic as it relates only to public companies]
Part 28: Takeovers [we not cover this topic as it relates only to public companies]
Part 29: Fraudulent trading
Part 30: Protection of members against unfair prejudice

Part 31: Dissolution and restoration to the register

Part 32: Company investigations: amendments [we do not consider this topic]

Part 33: UK companies not formed under companies legislation [we considered this briefly in **Chapter 1**]

Part 34: Overseas companies [we do not consider this topic in this book as we are concentrating on UK companies]

Part 35: The Registrar of Companies

Part 36: Offences under the Companies Act

Part 37: Companies: supplementary provisions

Part 38: Companies: interpretation

Part 39: Companies: minor amendments

Part 40: Company directors: foreign disqualification etc

Part 41: Business names

Part 42: Statutory auditors

Part 43: Transparency obligations and related matters [we do not cover this topic as it relates only to public companies]

Part 44: Miscellaneous provisions

Part 45: Northern Ireland

Part 46: General supplementary provisions

Part 47: Final provisions

The longer Parts are divided into Chapters. Part 13 on a company's share capital has 11 separate Chapters. There are also 20 Schedules at the end of the CA 2006, some of which we examine as we cover the related topic.

In order to ensure that you are consulting the most up-to-date version of the CA 2006, it is recommended that you access a version through an online legal research database, such as LexisLibrary or Westlaw. Alternatively, the Act may be found online at the UK Government's website <http://www.legislation.gov.uk> run by the National Archives. In light of its scope, amendments are made regularly to the CA 2006. The legal research databases will tend to incorporate these changes into the text of the Act more quickly than the National Archives website. That said, the National Archives' version contains some explanatory notes and commentary on the sections of the CA 2006, which can be very useful in helping to understand the purpose behind the section.

When reading the text of the CA 2006, it is important to remember that many defined terms are used throughout. These terms are often included either at the start of the relevant Part or Chapter, or separately as a section or part of a section of the Act. There is also an (incomplete) list of defined terms used in the Act in Sch 8. It is imperative, therefore, when reading a particular provision for the first time, to examine it very carefully and look for any definitions which will assist in determining the extent of the application of the rule you are considering. Also, be careful to determine the extent of the definition within the Act; it may be expressed to apply only to the particular section, Chapter, Part or Schedule, or to the whole Act.

The Economic Crime and Corporate Transparency Act 2023 has already made and will continue to make significant changes to parts of the Companies Act 2006 throughout 2025 and beyond. You should ensure that you consult an up-to-date consolidated version of the Companies Act 2006 at all times.

2.6.3 Statutory instruments

As is customary with an Act of Parliament, the CA 2006 being primary legislation does not itself contain the entirety of the rules governing companies. There are powers granted to the Secretary of State for DBT to make various regulations and orders under the Act. This secondary legislation takes the form of statutory instruments. There are over 200 provisions of the CA 2006 which allow for statutory instruments to be made, not all of which have been exercised yet.

For example, s 57 of the CA 2006 authorises the Secretary of State for DBT to make regulations setting out which letters, characters, signs, symbols and punctuation may be used in a company's name, and those which may not. The Secretary of State has exercised this power through the Company, Limited Liability Partnership and Business (Names and Trading Disclosures) Regulations 2015 (SI 2015/17). These Regulations state, amongst other things, that it is possible to use numbers and other symbols, such as @, £, ?, !, anywhere in the company's name. However, the symbols %, #, +, *, and = are permitted only if not used as one of the first three characters of the company's name. Seriously!

The online resources mentioned at **2.6.1** above provide links to the statutory instruments passed under the relevant sections of the CA 2006. Again, care should be taken that the most up-to-date version is referred to, as the statutory instruments themselves are sometimes amended or replaced.

2.6.4 Other legislation

The CA 2006 and supplementary statutory instruments by no means represent all of the legislation on company law – far from it in fact. Other pieces of legislation that include important provisions of company law are as follows:

(a) The Financial Services and Markets Act 2000, which, together with EU law retained in UK law post-Brexit via the European Union (Withdrawal) Act 2018, sets out the framework for the regulation of publicly-traded companies (see **1.9.3.1** above) and certain restrictions on their behaviour.

There are fundamental changes to this retained EU law regulating publicly-traded companies coming into force in 2026.

(b) The IA 1986, which regulates companies in financial difficulty and companies which come to an end.

(c) The CDDA 1986, which sets out the procedure for disqualifying unsuitable individuals from being company directors.

(d) The Criminal Justice Act 1993, which contains the criminal offence of insider dealing relevant to publicly-traded companies and dealings in their shares.

(e) The Corporate Manslaughter and Corporate Homicide Act 2007, which imposes liability on a company where it commits the unintentional but unlawful killing of a person, ie manslaughter.

(f) The Bribery Act 2010, which imposes liability on a company (and others) for bribery and failing to operate satisfactory internal anti-bribery systems.

(g) The Stock Transfer Act 1963, which includes law relevant to the transfer of ownership of securities (such as shares) in a company.

(h) The CA 1985 and the CA 1989. Although these have almost been completely repealed by the CA 2006, a few provisions have been retained, such as the powers to conduct investigations into companies under the CA 1985, and provisions under the CA 1989 about financial markets and insolvency, as these extend beyond companies and company law.

(i) From 1 September 2025, s 199 of the Economic Crime and Corporate Transparency Act 2023 will introduce a new criminal offence of failure to prevent fraud. This offence will apply to larger companies only, eg with annual turnover of over £54 million.

There are also many other statutes which, although not limited to them, apply to companies. For example, companies are subject to the Sale of Goods Act 1979, which governs contracts for the sale of goods, the Law of Property Act 1925, the Land Charges Act 1972 and the Landlord and Tenant Act 1954 (governing property ownership and rights), the Employment

Rights Act 1996 (governing employees' rights) and the self-explanatory Health and Safety at Work, etc Act 1974.

2.6.5 Case law

There is a huge volume of case law in existence. Some of it has been codified into, amended or repealed by company legislation. Some of it has filled in gaps in statutory law and will shape the advice given by lawyers, and possibly affect how companies operate.

2.6.5.1 Interpretation

Judges' interpretation of statute (be it the CA 2006 or other legislation), or of common law and equitable principles, is an important source of company law. For example, the UK Supreme Court handed down a decision in *Holland v The Commissioners for HMRC and another* [2010] UKSC 51 in February 2011, providing clarification on what it meant to be a 'de facto' director (see **6.3**), which is a term that is not defined in company legislation.

2.6.5.2 Supervision

As well as interpreting the law, the courts are given a range of supervisory powers over companies by company legislation. For example, under ss 994 to 999 of the CA 2006, a shareholder may petition the court to make an order if the company's affairs are being conducted in a manner which is unfairly prejudicial to all or some of the company's shareholders (see **5.6.3.14** below). The court may make such order as it thinks fit, including regulating the future behaviour of the company.

A court may also disqualify a director from being a director for up to 15 years under the CDDA 1986 for behaviour which falls short of the expected standard (see **6.10.6** below).

Certain county courts and the High Court have jurisdiction to hear company law matters in England and Wales (eg, as stated by s 1156 of the CA 2006 for matters arising under that Act). There is a special division of the Chancery Division of the High Court in London, known as the Companies Court, which has specialist judges to hear company law cases.

2.6.5.3 Criminal cases

Company legislation provides for an array of criminal penalties for failure to comply with company law. To determine the particular punishment, you must of course read the relevant section of the legislation, as there is tremendous variety in the offences. However, in summary, minor offences, particularly for failure to provide the required information under the CA 2006, are usually triable summarily, that is in a magistrates' court. If the defendant is found guilty, the penalty imposed will normally be a fine ranging from level 1 (£200) up to level 5 (unlimited amount) on the standard scale of fines. Other offences which may be more serious are triable either way, that is either summarily in a magistrates' court or on indictment in a Crown Court. A defendant, if found guilty of one of these offences, will usually be fined and/or sentenced to imprisonment. Fines in the Crown Court are unlimited. The maximum term of imprisonment will not ordinarily exceed two years, but there are some more serious offences (such as fraudulent trading under s 993 of the CA 2006) which may result in imprisonment for up to 10 years.

2.6.5.4 Law reports

There are both hard-copy company law reports and online legal research databases, such as Lexis+ and Westlaw, recording the decisions of the courts. The electronic versions have the merit of convenience and speed, but at times they may provide only a summary of the case that you require. You may in such circumstance therefore need to revert to the full hard-copy version. Company law reports may be found in one or other of the Chancery section of the Law Reports (Ch), All England Law Reports Commercial Cases (All ER (Comm)), BCC (British Company Cases) or BCLC (Butterworths Company Law Cases).

2.6.6 EU company law

Although the UK has now left the EU, some EU company law will continue to form part of UK law, at least in the short term, although under the Retained EU Law (Revocation and Reform) Act 2023, the UK courts have greater powers to depart from it if they wish.

European Union Regulations did not require further steps to be taken in order to become law in the UK. Thus, Council Regulation (EC) 2157/2001, which established the European public company, the SE (see **1.10.3** above), came into force in the UK on the date stated in the Regulation, 8 October 2004. Post-Brexit this Regulation has been maintained in English law with amendments to enable SEs registered in the UK to continue to exist (at least for now). However, they have been turned into 'UK Societates' subject to UK law.

2.6.7 Other sources

Although outside the scope of this book, it is important to note that there are many other sources of rules which apply to public companies and publicly-traded companies (see **1.9** above). Many of these rules do not exist in the form of legislation but as codes or guidelines. Some do not even have legal force, but are followed nonetheless in practice by these companies in order to keep their shareholders happy.

2.6.8 Relevance

The volume of company law may seem overwhelming to the new company lawyer. The thought of reading over 1,300 sections of the CA 2006 is enough to make even the most enthusiastic lawyer whimper, even before turning to the statutory instruments and the huge amount of case law. The good news is that most company behaviour is neither controversial nor novel. A decision or an action taken by a company will usually have been done many times before by other companies, and therefore the law on how the company should operate in such a situation and the consequences of its actions will be clear and unproblematic.

It means that overwhelmingly in practice, a company lawyer will already have set procedures to be followed to ensure that the company acts correctly and legally. The law contained in legislation or interpreted in cases will often already have been translated into practical guidance notes specific to that law firm. These notes often incorporate a summary of the relevant law, a detailed step-by-step guide as to how the company should make the decision and draft documents which can be tailored to the specific company. These notes therefore build on the experience of that particular law firm. This obviously aids the new corporate lawyer tremendously, but there are still plenty of occasions when a new situation crops up, a dispute arises or an uncommon event occurs, and then the corporate lawyer in practice, usually starting with the trainee, will have to turn to the legislation and case law, and to their research skills in order to advise on the matter.

PART II

RUNNING A BUSINESS AS A COMPANY LIMITED BY SHARES

Part II

- describes how a company limited by shares is formed
- explains how a company limited by shares is run in compliance with the CA 2006
- sets out how to join and leave a company limited by shares
- demonstrates how to finance a company limited by shares
- explains what liability may be incurred by a company limited by shares and its directors in running the business

CHAPTER 3

HOW TO SET UP A COMPANY

LEARNING OUTCOMES

After reading this chapter you will be able to:

- understand the process for registering a new company using paper or electronically
- apply the rules governing the choice and use of a company name
- identify the required documentation for setting up a company limited by shares
- complete a Form IN01 – application for registration for a new company
- consider what needs to be done after the company has been incorporated
- understand the role of shelf companies.

3.1 INTRODUCTION

Having made the decision to run their business as a company limited by shares, the entrepreneur will be keen to get the company up and running as soon as possible. In this chapter we shall see how a company is brought into existence in order to operate the entrepreneur's business. We examine the requirements of the CA 2006, consider the role of the Registrar of Companies, law firms and company formation agents, and see how the process unfolds in practice.

An entrepreneur can start their business as a company in one of two ways:

(a) either they set up a new company from scratch; or

(b) they can buy an existing shelf company.

We consider both of these methods below.

3.2 FORMING A NEW COMPANY FROM SCRATCH

A company does not exist until it has been formed. According to Companies House, over 890,000 new private limited companies were formed in 2024. The birth of a new company – its incorporation – takes place in accordance with s 7 of the CA 2006 by a process known as registration. We shall be concentrating on the registration of a *private* company limited by shares in England and Wales, although reference may be made to other types of company and jurisdictions where necessary.

3.2.1 What does registration involve?

Registration (also known as incorporation) generally involves preparing a number of documents and delivering them to the Registrar of Companies at Companies House, together with a fee.

The documents which must be prepared and delivered to the Registrar for a private company limited by shares are:

(a) an application for registration as a company;

(b) a memorandum of association for the company; and

(c) possibly articles of association for the company.

The documents may be prepared and delivered to Companies House either in electronic form, or in paper form by post.

Once the correct documentation has been submitted and the correct fee paid, the Registrar will check the documents to see that everything has been prepared properly and is in order. If they are satisfied that the requirements of the CA 2006 have been met, they will register the documents delivered to them and will then issue a certificate of incorporation for the company. The company comes into existence on the date stated on its certificate of incorporation.

In what follows we examine each of these stages and the legal and practical implications which arise, after first highlighting the differences between the electronic and paper systems of registration.

3.2.2 Electronic registration

The vast majority of new companies are registered electronically. There are two ways in which this can be done, using:

(a) the Companies House software filing service; or

(b) the Companies House Web Incorporation Service.

3.2.2.1 Software filing service

The software filing service uses special software which enables communication with Companies House, thus permitting the electronic filing of the registration documents for a new company.

The most common way of using the software service is via a company formation agent. A company formation agent specialises in registering new companies. Companies House maintains a list on its website – <www.gov.uk/government/organisations/companies-house> – of over 70 companies (together with links to their websites) that have the software to enable them to submit electronic incorporations. A person who wishes to register a new company may, in return for paying the service, simply enter the required information for the new company on one of these agents' websites (eg, for £14.99, through Tide), and the registration documents are then generated and sent electronically to Companies House by the agent on the individual's behalf.

Alternatively, Companies House maintains a list of software suppliers on its website from whom it is possible to purchase the necessary software. This would enable individuals to register a new company electronically themselves, rather than using the company formation agent's web-based service explained above. The cost of this software is such, however, that it does not make financial sense to buy it unless you incorporate new companies on a regular basis.

3.2.2.2 Web Incorporation Service

Companies House has an online Web Incorporation Service using its WebFiling system. This allows anyone to register a new company by using the Companies House website rather than by using the software filing service discussed in **3.2.2.1** above. An individual wishing to set up the new company simply enters the required information on the website and pays the fee, and Companies House will generate the necessary documents electronically.

You can access the service on the Companies House website at <www.gov.uk/government/organisations/companies-house>. On the homepage, click on the link for 'set up a company', then 'register your company'.

3.2.3 Paper registration

As an alternative to electronic registration, it is possible to register a new company using paper documents. Hard copies of the necessary documents and the fee must be sent to the Registrar of Companies at Companies House's main office in Cardiff.

3.3 DOCUMENTATION

Although anyone, including the entrepreneur themselves, is allowed to prepare and submit the documentation to register a new company, because of the need for legal documents, the volume of rules, the potentially complex concepts involved and the specialist technical language used, it will often be prepared either by a solicitor acting for the entrepreneur, or an accountant or by a company formation agent. As a trainee solicitor you may therefore be called upon to draft the necessary documentation, or to submit it electronically for a client of your law firm who wants to set up a company.

In order to submit the information electronically or to draft the documentation in paper form, you will first need instructions from your client on the key elements of the proposed new company. The new company will be owned partly or wholly by the entrepreneur, so it is they who will determine its key elements. What is the preferred name? How many directors will there be? Who will they be? How many shareholders will there be? Who will they be? And so on. You would request all the necessary information from your client (most law firms will have checklists ready), in the process possibly advising them on the alternatives or the impact of their choices. Once that information has been provided, you can start on preparing the documentation.

3.3.1 Application for registration

The application for registration of the company is required by s 9(1) of the CA 2006. The application must contain the following information:

(a) a statement that the subscribers wish to form the company for lawful purposes (as required by s 9(2)(e));

(b) the type of company being registered (as required by s 9(2)(c) and (d));

(c) the new company's proposed name (as required by s 9(2)(a));

(d) the address (including the country) of the new company's registered office which must be an appropriate address (as required by ss 9(2)(b) and 9(5)(a));

(e) a statement of capital and initial shareholdings (as required by s 9(4)(a));

(f) a statement of the new company's proposed officers (as required by s 9(4)(c));

(g) a statement of initial significant control (as required by s 9(4)(d));

(h) a statement of the intended registered email address of the company (as required by s 9(5)(aa));

(i) possibly a copy of the new company's articles of association (if required by s 9(5)(b)); and

(j) a statement of compliance (as required by s 9(1)).

The Economic Crime and Corporate Transparency Act 2023 will require additional statements in the application for registration once the relevant provisions have been brought into force:

(i) of each of the subscribers to the memorandum of association's forename, surname and address for service of documents (as required by new ss 9(3A) and 9A); and

(ii) that none of the subscribers to the memorandum of association is disqualified under the directors disqualification legislation (as required by a new s 9(4)(e)).

These amendments are expected to come into force by 2027.

3.3.1.1 Electronic registration

The electronic version of the application for registration consists of a number of requests for information on the website of the company formation agent or Companies House Web Incorporation Service. It is recommended that you look at the latter's website (see **3.2.2.2** above) to see what is involved.

Further information on how to use the electronic registration service is set out at **3.15.1** below.

3.3.1.2 Paper registration

The hard-copy application for registration is known as Form IN01. A copy may be found on the Companies House website at <www.gov.uk/government/organisations/companies-house>. A copy is also included in **Appendix 1**. It is highly recommended, though, that at some stage you search for the form on the Companies House website, as familiarity with the content of the website is very beneficial.

Detailed guidance on how to complete Form IN01, in case you are required to do this in practice, is set out at **3.15.2.1** to **3.15.2.7** below.

Both the electronic and paper versions of the application for registration of a new company must comply with the law and practice set out in **3.4** to **3.15** below.

3.4 TYPE OF COMPANY

We saw in **Chapter 1** that various different types of company may be formed. The application for registration must state whether the company is private or public, limited or unlimited, and limited by shares or by guarantee (CA 2006, s 9(2)(c) and (d)). It is the private company limited by shares on which we are concentrating in this book.

3.5 COMPANY'S NAME

Choosing the name of a company is not as simple as the client telling you what they want it to be called. Of course you must get this information from the client, but there are a number of detailed statutory rules which govern which name can, or cannot, be used for a company, and these must be complied with. As a consequence, when asking the client what they would like to call the new company, you should always ask for a couple of alternatives in case their first, or second, choice cannot be used.

3.5.1 Index of company names

Once you have obtained the preferred names from the client, the first step is to search the index of company names at Companies House. This is a free, 24/7 online service. The search is done via the website <https://find-and-update.company-information.service.gov.uk/company-name-availability>, which brings up the 'Company name availability checker'. This search is necessary because, under s 66(1) of the CA 2006, a company must not be registered with the same name as one already appearing in the index. This to avoid the confusion of people dealing with one company when they thought it was another.

Under the Company, Limited Liability Partnership and Business (Names and Trading Disclosures) Regulations 2015 (SI 2015/17), the 'same' name includes not just an identical name but also names which would be essentially the same if simple elements were disregarded. The Regulations set out which elements are to be disregarded. They include the status of the company, certain words, punctuation marks, symbols and plurals. In other words, if the new company name your client wishes to use differs from an existing name on the index only by these prescribed elements, it is treated as being the same name and so cannot be used. (There are certain very limited exceptions to this for a new company which will form part of the same group of companies.)

For example, the name 'Bands Limited' will be the 'same' as:

Bands Ltd
Bands Public Limited Company (or PLC)
Band-S Limited (or Ltd)
B and s Limited (or Ltd)
B & s Limited (or Ltd)
B & s International Limited (or Ltd)
www.Bands Limited (or Ltd)
Bands.co.uk Limited (or Ltd)
@B & s Limited (or Ltd)

And that is not the complete list! The extent of 'same names' is therefore neither particularly easy nor always obvious to identify. The good news is that using the online search service simplifies matters tremendously. If you type in the proposed name, the service will list the 'same' names. If one appears then a new name must be chosen and checked itself. If the name is not the same as any currently on the index then the client may use it, subject to what follows.

It is important to note that if the chosen name is not already in use by another company, there is no procedure for reserving that name. Consequently, there is no means of preventing the formation of a new company which bears the name the client has chosen between the date of the search and the date on which the application for incorporation is received by the Registrar. This is another reason for ensuring you obtain more than one proposed company name from the client at the outset.

3.5.2 End of company's name

Section 59 of the CA 2006 states that a private limited company must use either 'limited' or the abbreviation 'ltd' (or the Welsh language equivalents 'cyfyngedig' or 'cyf') at the end of the company's name. This makes it clear to people dealing with the company that it is a private company whose shareholders have limited liability, and that they can look only to the company and its money for payment of the company's debts. There are certain exemptions to this rule in the Company, Limited Liability Partnership and Business (Names and Trading Disclosures) Regulations 2015.

3.5.3 Prohibited names

A company may not use a name which, in the opinion of the Secretary of State for DBT, would amount to a criminal offence or is offensive (CA 2006, s 53). For example, it would not be possible to use swear words, or the name of one of the UK's 80 or so proscribed terrorist groups (including Al Qa'ida, ISIS/ISIL/DAISh, Boko Haram, the Irish Republican Army (IRA), the Ulster Defence Association (UDA), the Kurdish organisation PKK and the Sri Lankan Tamil Tigers (LTTE)).

The use of 'Red Cross' and 'Red Crescent' (the humanitarian organisations) is controlled by the Geneva Conventions Act 1957 and will not be allowed in a company name.

Under s 53A of the CA 2006, a company may not use a name which, in the opinion of the Secretary of State for DBT, would facilitate an offence involving dishonesty or deception, or under s 56A of the CA 2006, give the false impression of a connection to a foreign government or an international organisation.

3.5.4 Permitted characters and computer code

Under the Company, Limited Liability Partnership and Business (Names and Trading Disclosures) Regulations 2015, certain letters, characters, signs, symbols and punctuation may be used in a company's name, and certain may not. For example, it is not possible for the symbols %, #, +, *, or = to be used as one of the first three characters of the company's name (2015 Regulations, Sch 1, Table 3). Punctuation marks listed in Sch 1, Table 2 to the Regulations, for example brackets and an exclamation mark, may be used only in the format set out in Sch 1, Table 2. Symbols not included in the Regulations cannot be used anywhere in the company's name – for example, the symbols ®, ©, ™ or ÷ would not be permitted.

The name of the company also cannot exceed 160 characters including spaces. To put this in context, if a company was named Llanfairpwllgwyngyllgogerychwyrndrobwllllantysilio-gogogoch Limited (after the village on Anglesey), it would use up only 66 characters.

Section 57A of the CA 2006 prevents the use of a name which in the Secretary of State for DBT's opinion consists of or includes computer code. This is because computer code embedded in an IT database (eg at Companies House) can maliciously infect the systems of those who access it or download data to their own systems. The Registrar of Companies may choose a new name for a company whose name includes computer code (s 76C).

3.5.5 Names requiring approval

Certain 'sensitive' words or expressions that the client may wish to include in their new company's name will need prior approval. Some words will require the approval of the Secretary of State for DBT, while others will require the approval of both the Secretary of State and a regulatory body. The approval process is carried out by Companies House on behalf of the Secretary of State when the application is submitted. Companies House is happy to provide advice over the phone on the use of specific names (useful before the application is submitted), but it is always wise to check its conclusion against the various rules.

3.5.5.1 Connection with government or public authority

Names that suggest a connection between the company and HM Government, the Welsh Assembly Government, the Scottish administration, HM Government in Northern Ireland, local authorities (eg local and county councils) and 28 public authorities listed in the Company, Limited Liability Partnership and Business (Names and Trading Disclosures) Regulations 2015 require the approval of the Secretary of State for DBT under s 54 of the CA 2006.

For names suggesting a connection with the 28 public authorities (including the Scottish Parliament, the Law Commission and the House of Commons), the views of the body listed in the Regulations next to the authority must be sought first before seeking approval from the Secretary of State.

For example, a client who wishes to call their company 'Government Services Ltd' would need prior approval from the Secretary of State for DBT. Under s 56 of the CA 2006, a request must be made in writing, asking whether the Secretary of State or the body objects to the use of the name and, if so, why.

Association with the Government or public bodies can enhance a company's reputation. The aim of these rules is therefore to ensure that the public will not by misled by the use of the name. Approval will not be granted if the use of the name is not justified. If the client who wishes to call their company 'Government Services Ltd' is going to run a home-cleaning business in Dartford, approval will not be given and a new name must be chosen.

3.5.5.2 Other sensitive words

The Company, Limited Liability Partnership and Business Names (Sensitive Words and Expressions) Regulations 2014 (SI 2014/3140), made under s 55 of the CA 2006, set out further words and expressions which, if intended to be used in the new company's name, require prior approval by the Secretary of State for DBT alone, or after having requested the views of a designated body.

What words are sensitive? There are too many to commit to memory, so recourse must be had to the Regulations themselves. Schedule 1 to the Regulations sets out the sensitive words. It is worth noting that the list includes some very common words, as well as some seemingly innocuous ones. Examples include those which refer to geographical or physical extent such as 'Britain', 'British', 'England', 'Sheffield' and 'United Kingdom'. The aim of these rules is once again to protect the public. Someone dealing with a company called 'England Enterprises Group Ltd' will naturally assume it operates in England. If in fact the company operates only in Rhyl in Wales, the use of 'England' may be misleading. The company would probably not be granted approval to use England in its name.

Other examples cover names which indicate a certain standard and position in society, such as 'council', 'institute', 'society', 'trade union' and 'trust'. Others denote regulated professions such as 'banking', 'dental', 'fund', 'nurse', 'insurance' and 'university'. Others are self-explanatory: 'duke', 'prince', 'king', 'royalty' and 'windsor'.

Schedule 2 sets out the relevant body to be approached. If, for example, the client wishes to include the word 'dental' in the company name, a request must first be made to the General Dental Council, seeking its views on the use before seeking approval from the Secretary of State for DBT. Not all of the bodies are administrative in nature. If the client wishes to use the name 'Sheffield', approval must first be sought from the Company of Cutlers in Hallamshire (which seeks to promote the name of Sheffield and maintain the standards of cutlery and steel in Sheffield). If no body is mentioned then approval must be sought solely from the Secretary of State for DBT.

Section 56 of the CA 2006 again applies here, so a request must be made in writing to the body or Secretary of State, asking whether they object to the use of the name and, if so, why. The trainee lawyer would draft this letter on behalf of the client.

3.5.5.3 Approval beyond the CA 2006

There are further words or expressions, use of which in a company name requires prior approval. These are set out in different pieces of legislation, though, and not in the CA 2006. They predominantly consist of medical professions, but extend beyond this to control some words which may be surprising. For example, 'higher, stronger, faster' requires approval by the British Olympic Committee in order to protect the use of one of the main slogans of the Olympic Games.

A list of these additional words may be found in guidance issued by Companies House, 'Incorporation and names', available on its website at <www.gov.uk/government/organisations/companies-house>.

3.5.6 Challenging a company name

Approval of the company name as part of the registration process of the company may not be the end of the consideration of a company's name. After the company has been formed, the use of the name may still be challenged by third parties. It is worth noting that this is a relatively rare occurrence but one of which you need to be aware as a corporate lawyer.

3.5.6.1 Secretary of State for DBT's additional powers

The Secretary of State may direct a company to change its name after the company has been registered if it is the same as or too like a name already on the index of company names under s 67 of the CA 2006. This power might be used, for example, if a company name already being used was mistakenly accepted by the Registrar on the registration of a new company. The Registrar of Companies may choose a new name for a company if the company fails to change it having been directed to do so (s 76D).

Other powers are granted to the Secretary of State under the CA 2006 to change the company name if misleading information was given for use of a particular name (s 75), or if the name gives a misleading impression of the nature of the company's activities, posing a risk of harm to the public in the UK or elsewhere (s 76), or has been wrongly registered in breach of the CA 2006 rules on company names (s 76B).

The Secretary of State also has the power under s 76E to permit a name to be used which would otherwise breach the CA 2006 where it is necessary for national security or to prevent or detect serious crime.

3.5.6.2 Company Names Tribunal

Under s 69 of the CA 2006, any person may make an application to the Company Names Tribunal (CNT) to change a company's existing name if that company's name is the same as one in which the applicant has goodwill (defined as reputation of any description), or is sufficiently similar that it would be likely to mislead by suggesting a connection. The procedure is particularly intended for use where the company name has been registered to extract money or prevent someone (such as the applicant) from using the name, a so-called 'opportunistic' registration.

For example, in January 2011 a company names adjudicator at the CNT ordered an English company which had been registered in the name Botox Limited to change its name, as an American company, Allergan Inc, wished to set up an English company with that name. Allergan Inc is the maker of Botox, and Botox Limited had not traded. More recently, in April 2024 Jamie Oliver Enterprises Limited (one of the famous restauranteur's companies) was successful in an application against Jamie Oliver Catherine Limited which was ordered to change its name.

Although the vast majority of applications to the CNT succeed, where good faith can be shown in adopting the company name already registered, or where the applicant's interests are not adversely affected by the use of the name, the application will fail. In February 2011, Tektronix Inc, an American company, failed to have the name of Tektronix Limited, an unrelated English company, changed. This was because the parties registering the English company adopted the name in good faith, and the American company was unable to show that it had goodwill (ie a reputation to protect) in the UK.

You can find more information on the CNT and its decisions from its website at <www.gov.uk/government/organisations/company-names-tribunal>.

3.5.6.3 Passing off

A company may be liable for the tort of passing off if it uses a name which suggests that the company is carrying on someone else's business. If a claimant is successful, a court can order an injunction and damages or an account of profits. In order to avoid this risk, it is prudent to check for similar names in the phone book, via online searches and in trade publications, in addition to the search of the index of company names (see **3.5.1** above), before settling on a name.

3.5.6.4 Trade mark infringement

If a company name includes the name protected by a trade mark then the holder of a trade mark may bring a claim against the company for infringement of that trade mark. In order to avoid this risk, it is prudent to carry out a search of the Trade Marks Register. This may be done online on the Intellectual Property Office's website at <www.gov.uk/search-for-trademark>, or there is an online company name and trade mark checker available at <www.start.biz/business_names/search>.

3.5.7 Business name

A company, once it has been registered, may choose to operate with a trading or business name which is different from its registered name. 'PwC' is a trading name for the global accountancy firm, Pricewaterhousecoopers International Limited. PwC was introduced as a trading name as part of a rebranding of the company 'in order to strengthen, and modernise how it represents its worldwide network to its clients, its people and the communities in which it operates. The new branding includes visual elements, as well as an expression of what PwC really stands for', in the company's own words.

There are similar restrictions on the use of business names as apply to the company name proper, although there is no need to register a business name. The restrictions may be found in ss 1192 to 1199A of the CA 2006, and in the Company, Limited Liability Partnership and Business (Names and Trading Disclosures) Regulations 2015. Just as with the company name proper, possible claims may lie for passing off and trade mark infringement (see **3.5.6** above). In order to avoid breaching these rules, it is necessary to conduct the same searches as outlined above if the client decides to trade under a business name.

3.5.8 Conclusion

At first sight it may seem that the simple process of choosing a name is governed by an awfully bureaucratic and at times pedantic set of rules. However, the extent of the rules is a reflection of the influence of a company name in the real world. The use of a particular name can have a dramatic impact on people's perception of a company and their decision whether to trade with it. The use of names commanding authority and respect may induce individuals to part with money when they otherwise might not. The power of company names is illustrated by the worldwide recognition and influence of examples such as Apple, Coca Cola, Nike, BP, Gucci, Tesla and Google.

3.6 REGISTERED OFFICE

A company must have a registered office in accordance with s 86 of the CA 2006. This is an address to which communications and notices relating to the company may be sent, including legal documents and correspondence from the Registrar of Companies. The company can also keep many of its company records at the registered office, for example internal registers and minutes of meetings. It is for the client to choose this address.

The registered office must be at an 'appropriate address'. This is defined in s 86(2) as an address where in the ordinary course of events:

(a) a document addressed to the company, and delivered there by hand or by post, would be expected to come to the attention of a person acting on behalf of the company; and

(b) the delivery of documents there can be acknowledged as delivered.

It is usually either a place where the company carries on its business (eg offices or factory), or the address of its solicitors or accountants (especially if they are to deal with the administration of the company in the future) to ensure that legal and other important documents relating to the company are received straight away by the company's advisers.

The address must be provided on the application (CA 2006, s 9(5)(a)), and must include the country in which the registered office is situated (CA 2006, s 9(2)(b)). The country must correspond to the jurisdiction in which the company is being registered – England and Wales, Scotland or Northern Ireland. So a company to be registered in England and Wales cannot, for instance, have a registered office address in Inverness in Scotland.

If the address is in Wales, you will need to check with your client whether they wish to designate the company a Welsh company in accordance with s 88 of the CA 2006, or if they would prefer an England and Wales company, as there is a separate category for Welsh companies. There is no real legal significance at stake but potentially plenty of pride, and the ability to submit forms to the companies registrar in Welsh.

The Registrar of Companies may change a company's registered office address where they are satisfied the company is not authorised to use the address given (s 1097A).

3.7 REGISTERED EMAIL ADDRESS

A company must maintain an 'appropriate' registered email address under s 88A of the CA 2006. This is an email address where, in the ordinary course of events, emails sent to it by the Registrar would be expected to come to the attention of a person acting on behalf of the company.

3.8 STATEMENT OF CAPITAL

As we have seen already, ownership of a company limited by shares is demonstrated by ownership of shares. The shareholders are therefore owners of the company. The very first shareholders of the company are known as the 'subscribers to the memorandum of association'. We discuss the significance of this phrase further in **3.14** below.

The application for registration must include a statement of capital and initial shareholdings (CA 2006, s 9(4)(a)). This statement must comply with the requirements set out in s 10 of the 2006 Act.

Section 10(2)(a) and (b) of the CA 2006 require that the statement must include the total number of shares to be taken by the subscribers to the memorandum, the total nominal value (see **2.3.4** above) of those shares and the rights attaching to the shares. In addition, s 10(2)(ba) requires the total unpaid amount on the shares (if any) to be included. Remember that shares do not have to be paid in full when they are issued by the company (see **2.3.4**). The total received by the company is known as its capital (or money), hence the name of this statement.

A company will often be formed with just one type of share, but sometimes it may be formed with different types or 'classes' of shares. A company registered with just one class of shares is said to have 'ordinary' shares which will give the shareholder (the owner) the right to vote at shareholder meetings. Another company may be set up with two classes of shares which will usually be known as 'ordinary' and 'preference' shares. The rights attaching to the different classes of shares will usually be different. Normally the shareholder (the owner) of the ordinary shares will have the right to vote at shareholder meetings of the company, and the shareholder (the owner) of the preference shares will usually have no right to vote at shareholder meetings.

Why a company might want to have more than one class of shares (and an explanation of the different types) will be explored at **9.6** below, but for now it is sufficient to note that if the new company is being registered with more than one class, s 10(2)(c) of the CA 2006 requires that the application form must include an explanation of the rights of each class, and specify the total number of shares of each class and the total nominal value of each class.

Section 10(4) of the CA 2006 requires the statement to identify each subscriber to the memorandum, as well as how many shares each person will be taking, the nominal value, the class of share and the amount to be paid up (and any amount to be unpaid).

This information is very important, as it reveals the finance being put into the company when it is set up through the owners buying shares, and the identity of the owners of the company and how much of the company they own. It is also important to note that the client will decide how many shares they (and maybe others) will be buying when the company is set up, of what type and at what price. The only requirement is that each subscriber to the memorandum must take at least one share in the company (CA 2006, s 8(1)(b)). As a company may be formed with one or more shareholders (CA 2006, s 7), as a bare minimum the company may be formed with one share and one shareholder. However, often the company will be set up with 100 ordinary shares of £1 each.

3.9 STATEMENT OF INITIAL SIGNIFICANT CONTROL

A statement of initial significant control is required by s 9(4)(d) of the CA 2006, with further requirements imposed by s 12A. A 'person with significant control' (PSC) is defined in s 790C of and Sch 1A to the CA 2006. Broadly, it means any individual who owns more than 25% of the shares or voting rights in the company or has the right to exercise significant influence or control over the company. See **5.5** below for more details. It would include the very common situation in practice of a company being set up with just one shareholder (with 100% ownership) or two shareholders each owning an equal number of shares (with 50% ownership each). If there is no PSC on incorporation then a statement to this effect must be made instead.

Key information on the PSCs must be included on the statement contained in Form IN01 (CA 2006, s 12A(1)). For individuals this includes the PSC's name, home address (unless exempt), an address for service of documents, country of residence, nationality and date of birth and the reason why they are a PSC (CA 2006, s 790K).

The Economic Crime and Corporate Transparency Act 2023 (ECCTA) will amend s 12A by requiring an additional statement on incorporation that the PSCs have not been disqualified as directors of a company. This is expected to come into force by 2027.

ECCTA will require the identify of PSCs to be verified. See ***3.11*** *below for details of what verification involves. Section 12B of the CA 2006 will provide an option for those seeking to incorporate a company to state in the application (Form IN01) that any PSC has had their identity verified. (If a PSC arises after incorporation, the company has the option to state the PSC has been verified when notifying Companies House of the existence of the PSC.) In both cases, not making the statement will result in Companies House sending out a notice requiring identity verification of the PSC to take place within 14 days (s 790LM).*

This verification system is not yet fully in force. From 8 April 2025, individual PSCs can voluntarily have their identified verified. Compulsory verification is expected to start in autumn 2025 for new PSCs. Existing PSCs will have a year from this date to seek verification of their identity. The system is therefore expected to be completely operational by the end of 2026.

3.10 STATEMENT OF PROPOSED OFFICERS

A statement of proposed officers of the company is required by s 9(4)(c) of the CA 2006, with further requirements imposed by s 12. The company's officers here are its directors and (possibly) a company secretary.

3.10.1 Directors

We already know that a director is the person who manages the company on a day-to-day basis. The statement of proposed officers will include details of the very first director or directors of the company. In private companies there must be at least one director (CA 2006, s 154(1)). The client will therefore need to decide who is to be a director of their company. Small companies may well have just one director, who will often be the client themselves. Sometimes further directors are appointed if the tasks of running the company are to be shared. Certain individuals may not become a director, eg anyone aged under 16 (see **6.3.2.1** below).

Key information on the directors to be appointed must be included on the statement contained in Form IN01 (CA 2006, s 12(1)). For individuals this includes the director's name, home address (unless exempt), an address for service of documents, country of residence, nationality, business occupation and date of birth (CA 2006, s 163).

It is also possible for an existing company to act as a director. This may sound strange, but remember that a company is a person in law too, and one of the things that a person, human or artificial, can do is act as a director of a company. Obviously if a company is a director (known as a corporate director) then a human must act on the corporate director's behalf when performing its role as director of the other company. If a corporate director is to be appointed to the new company then a human director must also be appointed to the new company (CA 2006, s 155(1)). Also, different information must be provided on the application form for a corporate director (CA 2006, s 164). Note that the law regarding corporate directors is in the process of changing as a result of the Small Business, Enterprise and Employment Act 2015. See **6.3.1.7** below for further information.

In contrast to a private company, a public company must always have at least two directors (CA 2006, s 154(2)).

In all cases the company must make a statement that the proposed director has consented to act as a director of the new company on Form IN01 (CA 2006, s 12(3)). A procedure has been included in the CA 2006, s 1095(4A)–(4D), to allow for someone wrongly included on the register as a director to have their name removed.

The Economic Crime and Corporate Transparency Act 2023 (ECCTA) will amend s 12 by requiring proposed directors to confirm that their identity has been verified. Under a new s 167M of the CA 2006, an individual must not act as a director unless their identity has been verified or they come within an exemption. See ***3.11*** *below for details of what verification involves.*

This verification system is not yet fully in force. From 8 April 2025, individual directors can voluntarily have their identified verified. Compulsory verification is expected to start in autumn 2025 for new directors. Existing directors will have a year from this date to seek verification of their identity. The system is therefore expected to be completely operational by the end of 2026.

ECCTA will further amend s 12 by requiring a statement to be included by the subscribers to the memorandum that none of the proposed directors have been disqualified as directors or are otherwise ineligible to hold that office.

ECCTA will repeal s 163 requiring information on directors and replace it with a new s 167J of the CA 2006 requiring almost identical information.

These amendments are expected to come into force by 2027.

3.10.2 Director's address

The director must provide an address for service of legal documents in the application (CA 2006, ss 12(2)(a) and 163(1)(b)). This may be any address, including the director's home address or the company's registered office. If an address other than the director's home address is chosen then the director's home address must still be disclosed on the application (CA 2006, s 12(2)(a)), but it is not a part of the application which may be viewed by the public (CA 2006, s 242(1)).

The reason for giving the director a choice about revealing their home address on a document accessible by the public (via Companies House) is that, unfortunately, the information may be used for criminal purposes.

Perhaps the most high-profile example in recent years involved Huntingdon Life Sciences Limited. Seven animal rights activists, members of Stop Huntingdon Animal Cruelty (SHAC), were jailed for between four and 11 years in 2009 for trying to close down Huntingdon Life Sciences, an animal testing laboratory, by targeting suppliers to the company. Groups of extremists wearing masks would turn up at night with sirens, fireworks and klaxons.

They would daub slogans with paint on the victims' homes and cars. In some cases, families received hoax bombs, and many employees were targeted by campaigns falsely alleging they were paedophiles. The intimidation included the sending through the post of used sanitary towels said to be contaminated with HIV.

The details of companies, including names and addresses of employees, were uncovered in part through publicly available information on Companies House.

The people targeted also included lawyers. Six further members of SHAC were imprisoned for up to six years in December 2010 for criminal acts against companies and individuals who had dealings with the company.

A director who originally provides their home address when incorporating the company can subsequently make an application to the Registrar under s 1088 of the CA 2006 and the Companies (Disclosure of Address) Regulations 2009 (SI 2009/214) to remove it from the public register where there is a serious risk of violence or intimidation as a result of the activities of the company.

A proposed director of a company may apply to the Registrar for further privacy by having their home address removed from credit reference agencies' records under s 243 of the CA 2006 and the Companies (Disclosure of Address) Regulations 2009 (SI 2009/214) where there is a serious risk of violence or intimidation as a result of the activities of their company. A completed application form (Form SR04) and an additional fee of £100 must accompany the application for registration. Companies House provides further guidance on this subject its website in its somewhat unsettlingly-titled booklet, *Restricting disclosure of your address if you are at serious risk*. Victoria Beckham, formerly known as 'Posh Spice', was granted a confidentiality order under the CA 1985 following the arrest for threatening behaviour of an obsessed fan at her home.

The Economic Crime and Corporate Transparency Act 2023 will repeal s 163(1)(b) requiring information on a director's service address and replace it with a new s 167J(1)(c) of the CA 2006 requiring a service address for the director which can be the company's registered office. This amendment is expected to come into force by 2027.

3.10.3 Company secretary

The company secretary is an officer of the company who performs administrative tasks imposed by the CA 2006, such as filing documents with Companies House. However, under s 270(1) of the Act, a private limited company is not required to appoint a company secretary. In this situation the duties will be performed by a director or other authorised person. In most private companies formed under the CA 2006, no secretary is appointed initially.

If the client does decide to appoint a company secretary for the new company then, for an individual, the name and an address for service must be included in the statement of proposed officers on the application for registration (CA 2006, ss 12(1) and 277). Again, a company rather than a human may act as company secretary (known as a corporate secretary), with an authorised human carrying out the corporate secretary's tasks. In this case the information required for the application for registration is different, being set out at s 278 of the CA 2006.

Unlike a private company, a public company must always have a company secretary (CA 2006, s 271).

The company must make a statement that a proposed company secretary has consented to act for the new company on the application for registration (CA 2006, s 12(3)). There is no need for a company secretary to have their identity verified (see **3.11** below).

The Economic Crime and Corporate Transparency Act 2023 will repeal s 277 and s 278 and replace them with a new s 279G of the CA 2006 requiring a company to notify Companies House of the date of the appointment or departure of a company secretary within 14 days. For an appointment of a new secretary, s 279G requires a statement by the company:

- *setting out the required information on the secretary (contained in new s 279J (individual secretary) and s 279K (corporate secretary));*
- *confirming the secretary has consented to act as a secretary.*

A notification must also be sent within 14 days if the secretary's details change (new s 279H).

These amendments are expected to come into force by 2027.

3.11 IDENTITY VERIFICATION

Certain individuals involved with the company such as directors, PSCs and people who deliver required documents to the Registrar on behalf of the company must have their identified verified. Previously the company registration system broadly operated on trust, but there were examples of abuse and false information being registered. The verification system therefore seeks to ensure that information on the register is as accurate as possible and to reduce the risk of people deliberately filing incorrect information.

The identity of the persons concerned may be verified in one of two ways, either directly with Companies House or by an 'authorised corporate service provider' (ACSP) making a verification statement about the person concerned. This provider will be approved by the Registrar and perform the necessary identity checks on behalf of the individual.

3.11.1 Individual verification by Companies House

The Registrar's (Identity Verification and Authorised Corporate Service Providers) Rules 2025 and the Registrar's (Identity Verification by the Registrar) Rules 2025 (made under s 117 of the CA 2006) set out the detailed procedure to be followed in order to verify an individual director, PSC or person seeking to submit documents for a company directly with Companies House.

The individual must provide some personal information (their name, date of birth and residential address) together with an email address when applying to Companies House to be verified. The supporting evidence that must be provided by the individual (eg current passport) depends on which one of three possible ways of making the application is used. All three are made through the GOV.UK One Login service:

(1) the GOV.UK One Login ID Check app (using a smartphone);
(2) the GOV.UK One Login web channel (using a web browser);
(3) the GOV.UK One Login face to face service (via an in-person interview at a Post Office which must be booked online).

This method of verification is not yet fully in force. From 8 April 2025, individuals can voluntarily have their identified verified. Compulsory verification is expected to start in autumn 2025 for new directors, PSCs and people submitting documents for the company. Existing directors, PSCs and people submitting documents will have a year from this date to seek verification of their identity. The system is therefore expected to be completely operational by the end of 2026.

3.11.2 Individual verification by an ACSP

Please note that this method of verification is not yet in force. It is expected to start in spring 2026.

Under s 1110A of the CA 2006, an ACSP can make a 'verification statement' that an individual is verified. So, under this method, the ACSP verifies the individual instead of Companies House. Who may become an ACSP is set out in the Registrar's (Requirements Applicable to Applications to Become an Authorised Corporate Service Provider) Rules 2025 (made under s 117 of the CA 2006). One key requirement is that they must already be regulated by an anti-money laundering supervisory body. In practice, therefore, this method will be used by lawyers, accountants and others who already carry out checks on their clients, for example to comply with anti-money laundering legislation.

The Registrar's (Identity Verification and Authorised Corporate Service Providers) Rules 2025 and the Registrar's (Identity Verification by Authorised Corporate Service Providers) Rules 2025 (made under s 117 of the CA 2006) set out the detailed procedure to be followed for verification of the individual by an ACSP.

To start the verification process, the individual must first ask the ACSP to conduct an identity check and then provide supporting evidence as set out in the relevant rules (eg current passport). The ACSP will then check the suitability of the evidence and information provided.

3.11.3 Completion of verification

For verification of an individual by Companies House, if the process is successfully completed, the individual will be allocated an 11-digit unique identifier number (their 'Companies House personal code') which can then be used by Companies House to ensure that the person is who they say they are, and it will enable the individual to submit documentation to Companies House.

If verification is successfully completed by an ACSP, it will submit a verification statement to Companies House. Companies House will notify the individual that this has occurred and notify them of their unique Companies House personal code. This will permit the ACSP to submit documents at Companies House on their behalf.

3.12 STATEMENT OF COMPLIANCE

Sections 9(1) and 13 of the CA 2006 require a statement of compliance to be included on the application for registration. It states: 'I confirm that the requirements as to registration under the Companies Act 2006 have been complied with.' Each subscriber to the memorandum (original shareholder) of the company must make the statement, or an agent (such as a solicitor) may make it on the subscriber's behalf. It is included in Part 10 of Form IN01.

The Registrar of Companies may accept this statement as sufficient evidence of compliance with the CA 2006 registration procedure (CA 2006, s 13(2)). In practice this means that the Registrar will not have to check all the information on the application form before registering the new company.

3.13 ARTICLES OF ASSOCIATION

The articles of association (usually just referred to as the 'articles') are the second key document to be prepared for registration of the new company. The articles are the internal rules governing how the new company is to be run. For example, they set out how directors of a company should take decisions and exercise their powers. Consequently, the articles form an extremely important document, and we shall consider them further in **Chapter 4**.

However, in order to complete the application for registration, it is necessary to cover some initial points now.

At this stage it is necessary to note that every company must have a set of articles (CA 2006, s 18). Section 9(5)(b) may require a copy of the articles to be included with the application for registration of the new company being formed. It is for those setting up the company to decide which articles to choose. There are three options for the new company's articles of association. They might be:

(a) unamended model articles of association; or
(b) model articles of association with amendments; or
(c) bespoke articles of association.

3.13.1 Model articles

Model articles are a precedent set of rules for a limited company which will apply if a company does not choose its own rules. There are three different sets of model articles:

(a) for a private company limited by shares;
(b) for a private company limited by guarantee; and
(c) for a public company.

They are found in the Companies (Model Articles) Regulations 2008 (SI 2008/3229).

If a company opts to use unamended model articles of association, it means that its articles will be identical to the precedent set of articles. This ensures that the company will have internal rules in place to take decisions if the owners do not choose their own version.

In this case there is no need to attach a copy of the model articles to the application for registration. These articles are already publicly available (eg, on the Companies House website <www.gov.uk/government/organisations/companies-house>), and ss 18(2) and 20(1)(a) of the CA 2006 allow for this.

3.13.2 Amended model articles

The unamended model articles are not necessarily suitable for all companies. Companies come in many shapes and sizes, and these default rules on how the company is to be run may not reflect the practical reality of how a particular company is to be run. As a result, it is possible to amend the model articles and substitute different rules. This is option (b) in **3.13** above. In such a case only a copy of the changes to the model articles need be submitted with the application for registration (in accordance with s 20(1)(b) of the CA 2006).

3.13.3 Bespoke articles

A third option (option (c) in **3.13** above) is to replace the model articles in their entirety with a bespoke or tailor-made set of articles. In other words, the new company will have its own unique rules governing how it should be run. If this option is chosen then the complete set of new articles must be submitted with the application form (CA 2006, s 18(2)).

3.13.4 Which articles to use?

Only one of the three options discussed above may be chosen. There is no right or wrong answer here. It is a decision that will be taken by the client after consulting with her lawyers, taking into account the need for speed in setting up the company and the purpose for which the company is being used. The decision is not absolutely critical at this stage, because a company is able to change its articles at any time after it has been formed. Many law firms will have their own in-house precedents for options (b) and (c).

3.13.4.1 Electronic registration

Note that it may not currently possible to register new companies electronically with all of the three options for articles mentioned above. At the time of writing the Companies House Web Incorporation Service (see **3.2.2.2** above) allows only for option (a), where a new company is using unamended model articles (see **3.13.1**). The service cannot therefore be used at the moment if the company is to have option (b) or (c) articles (see **3.13.2** and **3.13.3**).

Registering a company electronically via a company formation agent (see **3.2.2.1** above) is possible, however, if the new company is to have any of option (a), (b) or (c) articles. Depending on the company formation agent, it may offer model articles unamended, various versions with amendments to the model articles or articles totally replacing the model articles.

3.13.4.2 Paper registration

This method may also be used to register a new company using any of the three different options for its articles.

3.13.5 Entrenchment

It is possible to include provisions in the company's articles which are entrenched (CA 2006, s 22). If included, these rules are more difficult to change in the future than the other, non-entrenched rules in the articles (see **4.4.3** below). The inclusion of such entrenched provisions must be notified to the Registrar on the application (CA 2006, s 23).

3.14 MEMORANDUM OF ASSOCIATION

This is the final document that must be prepared before a company can be registered. Under s 9(1) of the CA 2006, it must be submitted together with the application for registration and the articles (if required). A new company is formed under s 7(1) of the CA 2006 by one or more persons subscribing their names to a memorandum of association and complying with the other requirements of registration (as outlined above).

The memorandum must state that the subscribers wish to form a company and that they agree to become be members of the company taking at least one share each (CA 2006, s 8). It must be in the form set out in the Companies (Registration) Regulations 2008 (SI 2008/3014), which is also available on the Companies House website <www.gov.uk/government/organisations/companies-house>.

The subscribers are therefore the very first shareholders of the company. Remember, it is possible for a company to be formed with just one shareholder (known as a single-member company), and in this case there will of course be only one subscriber to the memorandum.

The memorandum is a very simple document requiring just the name of each subscriber, their authentication (eg a signature) and the date of authentication. An example of a memorandum for a single subscriber for the electronic registration of a new company may be seen in **Appendix 2**.

3.15 DELIVERY OF THE DOCUMENTS

The application for registration, the memorandum of association and the articles of association (if required) must be delivered to the Registrar of Companies at Companies House (CA 2006, s 9(1)) together with the applicable fee. As explained at **3.2.2** above, this is almost always done electronically, but it is still possible to deliver hard-copy documents by post (see **3.2.3** above). How does delivery take place in each case?

3.15.1 Electronic registration

As explained at **3.2.2** above, this may be done online through a company formation agent or the Web Incorporation Service of Companies House. Be aware that practice will vary depending on the formation agent used.

You must complete the application for registration online by providing the required information for the new company, such as the company name, in response to prompts on the screen. Provision of this information is relatively straightforward – it is simply a case of entering the instructions you have received from your client regarding the make up of their company.

No physical signatures are required on the application; instead a system of electronic authentication is used. This may involve ticking a box to agree with a statement, for instance consent to act as a director on the Web Incorporation Service, and/or the provision of three out of seven possible personal details (such as your father's first name, or the colour of your eyes).

Remember (**3.13.4.1** above) that at the moment the Web Incorporation Service can be used only by companies having unamended model articles, and in such a case no articles are actually submitted to Companies House. Company formation agents usually offer a selection of different amendments to the model articles, or sometimes totally new articles. If one of these pre-prepared versions meets the client's requirements then it is just a case of selecting which version to use; the amendments or the totally new set of articles will automatically be sent electronically to Companies House with the application.

The memorandum of association will be automatically and immediately generated online and sent to Companies House electronically together with the application. The memorandum will state that is has been 'authenticated electronically' by the subscribers.

Once payment of the fee has been made by credit card, the documents are submitted to Companies House electronically for consideration by the Registrar.

3.15.2 Paper registration

If hard copies of the documents are prepared instead of electronic versions then, after being drafted, they must be sent to the Registrar of Companies at Companies House's main office in Cardiff together with the correct fee, currently £71, payable by cheque. The address is included on Form IN01.

On all of the documents physical signatures are used instead of electronic authentication.

Companies House aims to process paper applications within 8–10 days.

*The Economic Crime and Corporate Transparency Act 2023 will significantly amend the rules for the delivery of documents to Companies House. Generally speaking, individuals will only be able to deliver documents on their own behalf (such as a director) if they have had their identity verified (see **3.11** above) or are exempt from verification under regulations which the Secretary of State for DBT will make in due course. Alternatively, if the document is to be delivered on someone else's behalf (such as the company) then this may only be done by people falling within the table set out in s 1067A(2) of the CA 2006, either having passed the relevant identity verification checks or because they are working for an 'authorised corporate service provider' (see **3.11** above).*

Section 1067A is expected to come into force in spring 2026.

3.15.2.1 How to complete Form IN01

The application for registration of a new company is known as Form IN01. Instructions on how to complete the form follow. Locate a copy of the form online (see **3.3.1** above), or use the version at **Appendix 1** and refer to it as we cover this material.

If you look at the top of the form on the first page, you will see that some basic but useful guidance has been included. As well as setting out what the form is (application for registration of a company), it states the provision in the CA 2006 requiring the form to be completed (s 9), that a fee has to be paid when the form is submitted, the type of entity for which the form may be used (private and public company) and that the form cannot be used to register an LLP (see **1.11** above). There is further assistance on how to complete the form in notes (usually numbered) on the right-hand side. For example, the first note states that the form must be typed, or completed in black block capitals if done by hand. This guidance is given on most pages. There is additional help on the last page. This is all very useful – particularly for the trainee solicitor in practice completing Form IN01 for the very first time.

Form IN01 contains 10 parts. In what follows, we complete the form for a private company limited by shares with one type of share to be registered under English law.

Note that the Economic Crime and Corporate Transparency Act 2023 will result in changes to the content of this form as described below. Check the Companies House website for the most up-to-date version.

3.15.2.2 Part 1 – Company details

Part 1 requires the following company details to be completed:

A1: Company name
Having performed the searches and complied with the law outlined at **3.5** above, this is where the full intended company name needs to be entered.

A2: Company name restrictions
This is relevant only if the proposed company name needs approval by a specified body (as explained at **3.5.5** above). A copy of the body's response must be attached to the application.

A3: Exemption from name ending with 'Limited'
This applies only to companies limited by guarantee, so it must not be completed when forming a company limited by shares, which is the most common form of company and the type on which we are concentrating.

A4: Company type
Form IN01 may be used to set up five different types of company, as explained at **3.4** above. The one of interest to us is the private company limited by shares. The second box should therefore be ticked.

A5: Principal business activity
A trade classification number should be inserted here. This number identifies a particular type of business activity. These numbers, also known as SIC codes, can be found in a list on the Companies House website. For example if the company being incorporated is running a business breeding camels, the number is 01440.

A6: Situation of registered office
One of four boxes must be completed, designating the country of the new company's registered office (as explained at **3.6** above). As we are looking at forming a company under English law, you would tick either of the first two boxes.

If the address is in England, you must tick the 'England and Wales' box.

If the address is in Wales and your client wishes to designate the company as a Welsh company (see **3.6** above), tick that box; or if your client would prefer England and Wales, tick that box.

A7: Registered office address
As well as the country of the registered office, the full intended address (including postcode) of the registered office must be stated on the application. This must be an 'appropriate' address as explained at **3.6** above (and conveniently set out in the guidance to this section of the form as well).

A8: Articles of association
One of the three options discussed at **3.13** above must be indicated here. Only one option should be selected.

If the first option is chosen for unamended model articles, the first box for a private company limited by shares should be ticked, and options 2 and 3 left blank. Remember that in this case there is no need to attach a copy of the model articles to the application form.

If it is decided instead to amend the model articles, the first box of option 2 for a private company limited by shares should be ticked, and options 1 and 3 left blank. In addition, a copy of the changes only to the model articles must be attached to Form IN01.

If the third option is selected and the model articles are replaced in their entirety with a bespoke or tailor-made set of articles, the first box for a private company limited by shares in option 3 should be ticked, and options 1 and 2 left blank. In this case the complete set of new articles must be attached to the application form.

A9: Restricted company articles
This box should be ticked only if the articles contain entrenched articles. This is discussed at **3.12** above.

A10: Restricted email address

An 'appropriate' email address should be entered here. What amounts to 'appropriate' is described at **3.7** above and in the guidance note on the form.

3.15.2.3 Part 2 – Proposed officers

Part 2 requires the details of the proposed company directors and, if one is to be appointed, the company secretary.

Sections B1 and B2 below should be completed only if a company secretary is being appointed and that secretary is an individual. If the company secretary to be appointed is itself a company, C1 to C4 should be completed instead (see below).

If the company will not have a company secretary then sections B and C should be left blank.

B1: Secretary appointment
Insert a title (such as 'Lady Muck') if desired, but this is not compulsory. Then include the full first names and surname (although if the individual is known by a title, there is no need to include the full name). Former names should also be included, but only if used for business purposes in the last 20 years. For example, if the secretary is a married woman who ran a sole tradership under her maiden name, that maiden name must be added.

B2: Secretary's service address
This can be the secretary's home address, but as this information will be available on the public register it is more usual to insert 'The Company's Registered Office'.

C1: Corporate secretary appointments
If a corporate secretary is to be appointed, insert the name and full address of the company acting as a corporate secretary.

C2: Location of the registry of the corporate body or firm
If the corporate secretary is registered in the UK, complete C3 only. If it is registered outside the UK, complete only C4.

C3: UK-registered limited companies

This will be the usual option. For example, for a corporate secretary registered as a company in England and Wales you must insert the company's registered number.

C4: Other corporate bodies or firms

Additional information is required here, including the type of entity (eg LLP) and the governing law (eg the State of Delaware, USA).

D1: Director appointments
Sections D1 to D4 should be completed for directors who are individuals. If the director to be appointed is itself a company then sections E1 to E5 should be completed instead.

Insert a title if desired, but this is not compulsory. Then include the full first names and surname (although if the individual is known by a title, such as 'Lord Fauntleroy', there is no need to include the full name). Former names should also be included, but only if used for business purposes in the last 20 years. For example, if the director is a married woman who was a director of another company under her maiden name, that maiden name must be added.

The remaining information is self-explanatory, save that for 'business occupation' often you will insert 'company director'.

D2: Director's service address
This may be any address, including the director's home address; but as it is used for the service of legal documents, and is publicly available, it is common to insert 'The Company's Registered Office'.

D3: New director's date of birth
The new director's full date of birth should be inserted.

D4: Director's usual residential address
This should be completed in full unless it has already been entered for D2, in which case state 'Same as service address'.

If the director has or is applying for a s 243 exemption (see **3.10.2** above), tick the box and submit a completed application Form SR04 and £100 fee (if exemption not already granted).

You will see on the form that there is space for two individual directors. If more are to be appointed then you will need to use a continuation sheet, available online at the Companies House website with Form IN01 (see **3.3.1** above).

E1: Corporate director appointments
If a corporate director is to be appointed, complete sections E1 to E4 as for C1 to C4.

3.15.2.4 Part 3 – Statement of capital

Part 3 requires the statement of capital. As we are dealing with a company limited by shares, this part must be completed. As explained at **3.8** above, the client will decide this information. Often the company will initially be set up with 100 ordinary shares of £1 each, but it there is no reason why it cannot be different.

F1: Statement of capital
Most companies will be set up with their shares in pounds sterling (£), so this will usually be the currency inserted in Currency table A. For a company with one type of share, insert 'Ordinary' in the second column.

In the third column include the total number of shares to be issued, eg '100'.

In the fourth column, take the total number of shares and multiply by the nominal value of the shares. The nominal value is the fixed legal value of the shares. So a £1 share has a nominal value of £1. If the company was to have 100 shares of £1 each, you would insert the figure '£100' here. Be careful though. Sometimes shares are issued at a premium. In other words, the company receives more than the nominal value. For example, a £1 share is issued in return for the shareholder paying £2. The extra £1 over and above the nominal value is the premium.

The figure to be included in this box in this case is still '£100' as that the total nominal value is still 100 x £1.

Final column: If the company is to receive only some of the money for the shares when the shares are issued (ie they are partly paid), insert the total unpaid amount. Say the 100 shares were £1 shares and it was agreed that they were to be paid up as to 50 pence when the company was formed and 50 pence at a later date. You would include '£50'.

If there is more than one class of share then each class must be listed separately, and the total figures for the last two boxes must be included where indicated.

At the bottom you must insert the totals of all different classes of shares, the total nominal value and the total amount unpaid, if any. For our company with 100 fully paid £1 shares, the three entries would be 100, £100 and a dash (' – ') or '£0' (as there is no unpaid amount) respectively.

If the company's share capital will include shares in a currency other than sterling, for example, if a company were to be set up with shares in euros (€), US dollars ($) or yen (¥), the entries to be made are the same as in F1 above, save that the currency will be described differently.

F2: Statement of capital
In this section you must set out the rights which attach to the shares. These will be laid down in the company's articles of association. They will cover matters such as voting rights and the right to a dividend (share in the company's profits). If the company has more than one class of share then the rights for each class must be set out. The easiest way to do this is to 'cut and paste' the rights from the articles. You may run out of space on the form, in which case you need to use continuation sheets for the statement of capital, available from the Companies House website with the Form IN01.

F3: Initial shareholdings
First, the name and address of the original shareholders of the company must be entered on the left-hand side in alphabetical order. There is no need to include the home address of the shareholders on this public document, the company's registered office address will suffice. The next six boxes have been explained previously, so for a shareholder who is to own all of the 100 shares of £1 fully-paid shares, the boxes would read, from left to right, 'ordinary', '100', '£/GBP', '£1', '–/0 ', '£1'.

If needed, continuation pages are available from the Companies House website with the Form IN01.

3.15.2.5 Part 4 – Statement of guarantee

Part 4 does not need to be completed for a company limited by shares, as in our case, as it is only relevant for a company limited by guarantee.

3.15.2.6 Part 5 – People with significant control

Either section H1 or section H2 needs to be ticked.

H1: Statement of initial significant control
If on incorporation there will be someone who will count as a person with significant control (PSC) in relation to the company, this box must be ticked.

H2: Statement of no PSC
This box should be ticked if there will be no PSCs on incorporation of the new company.

See **5.5** below for a full explanation of who is a PSC and why this is required. One test for a PSC is that there is a shareholder who owns over 25% of the company's shares. So, if there is one shareholder who will own all of the 100 shares, or two shareholders owning 50% each, they will be PSCs.

I1: Individual's details

Sections I1 to I7 should be completed for PSCs who are individuals.

Insert a title if desired, but this is not compulsory. Then include the full first names and surname, country of residence, nationality and month and year of birth of the PSC.

I2: Individual's service address

This may be any address, including the individual's home address, which is used for the service of legal documents. Note this address is made public.

I3: Individual's date of birth

The PSC's full date of birth should be inserted.

I4: Individual's usual residential address

This should be completed in full unless it has already been entered for I2, in which case state 'Same as service address'.

If the individual has or is applying for a s 790ZF exemption (similar to the exemption for a director – see **3.10.2** above), tick the box and submit a completed application Form SR07 and £100 fee (if exemption not already granted).

I5: Nature of control for an individual

This requires the individual PSC to identify how they are a PSC. There are different categories which reflect the tests under the law, eg tests based on ownership of shares and voting rights. If there is just one shareholder owning all 100% of the voting shares in the company, you would tick the last box '75% or more' for both ownership of shares and voting rights. If there were two shareholders each owning 50% of the shares, you would tick the first box 'more than 25% but not more than 50%' for both ownership of shares and voting rights.

I6 or I7 may need to be completed as alternatives to I5. These cover less common circumstances beyond the scope of this book, eg trust arrangements. Similarly, sections J and K of Form IN01 which deal with more complex scenarios involving companies and other bodies amounting to PSCs will not be covered in this book.

You will see on the form that there is space for two individual PSCs. If more exist then you will need to use a continuation sheet, available online at the Companies House website with Form IN01 (see **3.3.1** above).

3.15.2.7 Part 6 – Election to keep information on the public register (if applicable)

A private company can elect to keep certain information on the public register at Companies House rather than keeping individual registers at the company. Sections L1 to L5 cover the five different sets of information to which this applies, eg L1 allows for an election to keep the information on the company secretaries' register on the public register rather than on a register held at the company. A box under each of the five categories can be ticked if such an election is desired.

The Economic Crime and Corporate Transparency Act 2023 will remove the requirement on companies to keep their own individual company registers save for the register of members. The register of members will have to be kept by the company rather than relying on Companies House maintaining it centrally.

These amendments are expected to come into force by 2027.

3.15.2.8 Part 7 – Consent to act

This box must be ticked once consent has been obtained from each new director and the company secretary, if appointed.

3.15.2.9 Part 8 – Statement about individual PSC particulars

This box must be ticked where there is an individual PSC or PSCs. It confirms that the subscribers to the company have told the PSCs that their information is being included on Form IN01.

3.15.2.10 Part 9 – Lawful purpose statement

This box must be ticked, confirming that the subscribers setting up the company wish to form the company for lawful purposes.

3.15.2.11 Part 10 – Statement of compliance

Either section P1 or section P2 needs to be completed.

P1: Statement of compliance delivered by the subscribers
Under this option, all the subscribers to the memorandum sign their names.

P2: Statement of compliance delivered by an agent
Under this option, no subscribers sign but an agent signs on the subscribers' behalf. This might be the client's solicitor. In addition, the agent's name and full address must be provided.

There is no particular reason to favour either option, but some clients will wish to sign the document themselves so P1 will be used. Section P2 is useful when the client is unable to sign (eg, is out of the country), or if there are a large number of subscribers and use of the agent is more convenient.

3.15.2.12 Last page

On the last page you will see space to include presenter information. This is not compulsory, but you would complete this as a trainee in order that Companies House has a point of contact should there be a mistake or query regarding the form.

There is also the opportunity to choose the address to which the certificate of incorporation will be sent once the company is registered, and a useful checklist of steps to take before submitting the form.

3.15.3 Fee

The fee payable to Companies House for registering a new company depends on whether the documents are filed electronically or in hard copy form; and if electronically, depending on which type of service is used and whether the client wishes to use Companies House same-day incorporation service or the normal service. Note that company formation agents will sometimes charge more than the software prices quoted below to cover the cost of providing the registration service via their website.

Electronic (software)
Same-day: £78
Normal: £50

Electronic (Web Incorporation Service)
Normal: £50

Paper
Normal: £71

These fees are subject to periodic change. You should therefore always check the Companies House website for the current fees.

3.15.4 *Economic Crime and Corporate Transparency Act 2023*

The Economic Crime and Corporate Transparency Act 2023 (ECCTA) will significantly amend the rules for the delivery of documents to Companies House. Generally speaking, individuals will only be able to deliver documents on their own behalf (such as a director) if they have had their identity verified (see ***3.11*** *above) or are exempt from verification under regulations which the Secretary of State for DBT will make in due course. Alternatively, if the document is to be delivered on someone else's behalf (such as the company) then this may only be done by people falling within the table set out in s 1067A(2) of the CA 2006, either having passed the relevant identity verification checks or because they are working for an 'authorised corporate service provider' (see* ***3.11*** *above).*

Section 1067A is expected to come into force in spring 2026.

ECCTA further grants powers to the Registrar of Companies enabling documents to be submitted in electronic form only. This may result in future changes to the ability to submit documentation to Companies House in hard copy form. ECCTA also grants a new power under a new s 1068A of the CA 2006 to enable the Registrar to require two or more documents that need to be delivered to Companies House to be delivered together and not separately.

3.16 ROLE OF THE REGISTRAR

Once the application and supporting documents have been delivered to the Registrar of Companies at Companies House, either electronically or by post, the documentation will be checked. Under s 1081A of the CA 2006, the Registrar must ensure that the information on the register is accurate. Obviously this is not done by the Registrar personally (remember that hundreds of thousands of new companies are registered annually) but by one of the many Companies House employees.

Companies House will, for example, check that the necessary parties have had their identity verified (see **3.11** above), that the intended company name does not exist already, or is not the same as one in existence or does not need prior approval. It will also check that none of the proposed directors is disqualified from acting as a director of a company. Companies House can rely on the statement of compliance made in the application for registration (see **3.12** above), but its statutory objectives under s 1081A of the CA 2006 also require it to take a proactive role to maintain the integrity of the registers kept by Companies House.

Under s 14 of the CA 2006, if the Registrar is satisfied that the requirements of the Act as to registration (as outlined in this chapter) have been complied with, ie everything is in order, they will register the documents delivered to them. The Registrar will then issue a certificate of incorporation for the new company in accordance with s 15(1) of the CA 2006.

If the same-day registration service has been used, the documentation will be processed and the certificate will be issued on the same day. In fact, provided the documentation is sent before 3pm, and in order, the company will be formed on that same day. If the normal electronic registration service is used, this will usually be done within 24 hours; and postal applications of paper documentation will be completed within eight to 10 days.

The Registrar has a wide array of powers under the CA 2006 to reject documents for inconsistencies, to require additional information and to strike off a company registered on the basis of false information (ss 1073A, 1092A and 1002A respectively).

3.17 CERTIFICATE OF INCORPORATION

The certificate of incorporation will state (CA 2006, s 15(2)):

- the name and registered number of the company;
- the date of its incorporation;
- whether it is a company with limited or unlimited liability; and if limited, whether by shares or guarantee (usually it will be a company limited by shares);
- whether it is a private or public company; and
- whether the registered office is located in England and Wales, Wales, Scotland or Northern Ireland.

Under s 1066 of the Act, the company is given a registered number. This is a unique number which will identify the company throughout its life.

The certificate of incorporation is conclusive evidence that the new company has been properly formed and has been duly registered (CA 2006, s 15(2)). It is in effect the company's birth certificate.

Companies House will send a hard copy of the certificate of incorporation to the address submitted during electronic registration or included on the paper application, Form IN01. It will also email an electronic version for electronic registrations only. An example of a certificate of incorporation may be seen in **Appendix 2**.

If a new *public* limited company has been registered, it must also be issued with a trading certificate by the Registrar of Companies before it can do business or use its borrowing powers. This certificate confirms that the new company has met additional requirements relating to share capital under s 761 of the CA 2006, applicable only to public companies.

3.18 EFFECT OF REGISTRATION

On registration of the new company, of which the certificate of incorporation is conclusive evidence, a number of consequences follow, including:

(a) the company is formed with the name stated in the certificate (s 16(2));

(b) the company is capable of exercising all the functions of a company (s 16(3));

(c) the protection of limited liability begins (s 16(4) and see **2.3.4** above);

(d) the subscribers to the memorandum become shareholders of the company, owning the number of shares specified in the statement of capital (in the application for registration) (s 16(5)); and

(e) the proposed director(s) and company secretary (if any) of the company mentioned in the application take up their positions (s 16(6)).

In other words, once the certificate of incorporation has been issued, the company exists as a separate legal person (see **2.3** above).

Section 7(2) of the CA 2006 makes it clear that a company must not be formed for an unlawful purpose. If by mistake the Registrar registers a company which breaches this rule then the company may be stuck off the register by the court and it will be wound up. Such an action may be brought by the Attorney-General. A rare example arose in the case of *R v Registrar of Companies, ex p Attorney-General* [1991] BCLC 476, when the Registrar registered a company, Lindi St Claire (Personal Services) Ltd, which had been set up expressly for the purposes of running a prostitution business. The Registrar had previously rejected the business owner's preferred company name of 'Hookers Ltd'. Although prostitution itself is not illegal in the UK, the court found that it was not a lawful purpose for a company to be formed to carry on the business of prostitution.

Section 1002A of the Companies Act 2006 gives the Registrar the power to strike off a company (thereby ending its existence) if the Registrar has reasonable cause to believe that any information in the application for registration (Form IN01) or accompanying document or statement is materially misleading, false or deceptive.

3.19 POST-INCORPORATION STEPS

Although the entrepreneur now has formed the company they want to run their business, there are still some additional legal and practical matters which must be attended to before the company can begin to operate effectively.

3.19.1 The first board meeting

The new director or directors will need to hold the first meeting of the board of directors of the new company soon after incorporation because they will need to take decisions on a variety of matters. We examine the law and practice surrounding directors and their board meetings in **Chapters 6** to **8**. For now it is sufficient to be aware that directors take some key decisions on behalf of the company, and the board meeting is the forum at which they do so.

An indication of some of the steps which might be taken at the first board meeting of a company is given below. Note that it is not absolutely essential for the directors to deal with all these items at the first meeting. If more time, information or advice is needed, these decisions may be taken at a later meeting. Also, it is important to note that other matters may be dealt with that are not included here, such as a discussion of the company's future business plans.

3.19.1.1 Chairperson

A chairperson of the board of directors of the new company will usually be elected at the board meeting, and that person will then take charge of the meeting.

3.19.1.2 Incorporation

It is good practice for a report to be made on the incorporation of the company, and for a note to be made of the identities of the first director or directors and company secretary (if any).

As the company does not exist before its registration, the cost of forming the company cannot be incurred on behalf of the company, and those instructing, for example, a solicitor or company formation agent to form it are personally liable for any costs. However, once the company is in existence, it is common for the directors to decide that the expense of incorporating the company should properly come out of company funds.

3.19.1.3 Bank account

The directors will decide to open a bank account for the company. Although not legally necessary, a bank account is of course essential for the company to trade. The account will be in the company's name.

The bank will usually require a specified form of wording to be used by the directors in taking their decision. It will also require the directors to sign a mandate form, giving specimen signatures and specifying who is allowed to sign cheques on the company's behalf, and whether there is any limit on the amount for which cheques may be written. For example, in a company with more than one director, the directors might decide that any one director's signature is sufficient to sign cheques up to, say, £500, but that for any amount in excess of that sum two directors must sign the cheque.

3.19.1.4 Company seal

The directors may decide to adopt a company seal for the new company (CA 2006, s 45(1)). A company seal is one of the ways in which the company may execute (ie 'sign') documents. The seal will have the company's name engraved on it in legible characters (CA 2006, s 45(2)), and when applied it embosses the name of the company on the document. Examples of company seals may be seen at <www.bolsons.co.uk>. In addition to affixing the seal to a document, additional signatures will be required (eg, from a director and a witness) in accordance with the company's articles.

If the new company is to have a seal then it will be formally adopted by a decision of the board of directors.

However, a company does not have to have a company seal (CA 2006, s 45(1)). It may rely instead on s 44 of the Act, which allows for the signatures either of two authorised signatories (a director or the secretary (if any)), or of one authorised signatory and a witness. In practice many companies do not bother to adopt a seal.

3.19.1.5 Business name

As explained at **3.5.7** above, a company may choose to use a business name for trading rather than its company name. This is a decision for the directors, so if they want the company to do this they should take a decision to that effect at the first board meeting.

3.19.1.6 Accounting reference date

All companies must prepare accounts showing the company's finances for each financial year. The accounting reference date (ARD) is the last day in the company's financial year. It is therefore the date to which the company must make up its accounts each year.

When a new company is registered, its ARD initially will be the anniversary of the last day of the month in which the company was incorporated (CA 2006, s 391(4)). For example, if the date on the certificate of incorporation of a new company, Patriot Limited, is 11 September 2025, the company's ARD will be 30 September. The first set of accounts for Patriot Limited would therefore be prepared from 11 September 2025 to 30 September 2026. In subsequent years the accounts would be prepared for each year ending 30 September.

However, the directors of the new company may wish to change the date of the ARD. For example, some companies will wish to align the ARD with the end of the tax year, 5 April. If the directors agree to do this, they will take a decision specifying the new date at the board meeting. They must then file a Form AA01 (change of accounting reference date) with the Registrar of Companies at Companies House (CA 2006, s 392).

3.19.1.7 Auditor

All companies must prepare accounts (CA 2006, s 394). Many companies will have to have the accounts audited, ie checked by an auditor (a specialist accountant), to show that they have been prepared in accordance with applicable company law and accounting standards. Companies which do not need to have their accounts audited are 'dormant' companies (CA 2006, s 480), ie companies which are not currently trading, 'small' companies (CA 2006, s 477) and 'micro-entities' (CA 2006, s 384A) on which the burden would be disproportionate. See **6.7.1** (below) for definitions of small companies and micro-entities.

If the new company does need to have its accounts audited, an auditor will have to be appointed by the company. The board of directors will take this decision on behalf of the company at the first board meeting.

If no auditor is required, as may be the case with many newly-formed companies (because they are defined as 'small'), the directors may still take a decision to appoint accountants to prepare the accounts.

3.19.1.8 Directors' service contracts

The directors will often enter into service (ie employment) contracts with the new company, including terms as to remuneration, working hours, holidays and duration. The board of directors usually will take the decision to enter into such contracts on behalf of the company at the first board meeting, unless a particular director is to be appointed for a guaranteed term of more than two years. If this is the case then the fixed-term part of the contract must be approved in advance by the company's shareholders (see **6.8.2** below).

This rule seeks to prevent directors from abusing their position by entering into a long fixed-term contracts on behalf of the company which may cost it a lot of money if it subsequently wants to get rid of any director(s). There are further procedural protections at the board meeting regarding directors voting on company contracts with themselves (see **8.4.4** below).

3.19.1.9 Company records

An important part of running a company is keeping records about it, as required by the CA 2006. Section 1134 defines what these records are. They include, for example, registers containing information on the directors and shareholders of the company. These records must be written up on incorporation and amended from time to time to reflect any changes so that they are always up to date. If this requirement is not satisfied, any director or other officer of the company in default may be liable to a fine. The records will usually be produced at the first board meeting and approved by the directors (which is just a formality).

Further information on the keeping of company records may be found at **8.11.1** below.

The Economic Crime and Corporate Transparency Act 2023 will remove the requirement on companies to keep their own individual company registers save for the register of members. Instead, information will have to be notified to the Registrar to inform them of changes to the company. The register of members, however, will have to be kept by the company and can no longer be kept centrally at Companies House. This is expected to come into force by 2027.

3.19.1.10 Tax registrations

Companies House will automatically notify HMRC of the registration of the new company; and HMRC will then send to the company's registered office address an introductory pack concerning the tax affairs of the company.

Corporation tax

The pack will include a Form CT41G (new company details), which must be completed and returned to HMRC. This will initiate the company's registration for corporation tax purposes.

PAYE and National Insurance

The company will normally have employees working for it (eg, the directors themselves will usually be treated as employees of the company). The directors should register the company with HMRC to arrange for the deduction of income tax from salaries under the PAYE scheme, and for the payment of National Insurance contributions by the employees. It is possible to do this online via the UK Government's website at <https://www.gov.uk/new-business-register-for-tax>.

Value added tax

Most businesses, except those with a very small turnover, must register for VAT with HMRC. Again, this can be done in most cases online via the UK Government's website set out above. The company will then be allocated a VAT number.

The directors will approve the applications for tax registration at the first board meeting, and they will then be submitted.

A Streamlined Company Registration Service allows new companies to be registered and at the same time to register for tax with HMRC.

3.19.1.11 Insurance

The directors will approve arrangements for taking out insurance in the company's name, for example for any buildings or motor vehicles, for injury to employees or for occupier's liability.

3.19.2 Disclosure of company details

Under powers contained in s 82 of the CA 2006, the Secretary of State for DBT has made the Company, Limited Liability Partnership and Business (Names and Trading Disclosures) Regulations 2015 (SI 2015/17). The aim behind these Regulations is to ensure that anyone dealing with the company, or wishing to deal with it, knows its name, its legal status and where further information about the company may be found. A summary of the Regulations follows, but this is of course no substitute for reading the Regulations themselves (as you might have to do in practice).

The company must include its company name in characters legible to the naked eye at its registered office, the location where the company keeps its company records and all places of business, on all websites, all business letters and notices, all cheques, order forms, invoices, demands for payment and other business correspondence (whether paper or electronic). If any such office, location or place is shared by six or more companies, each such company must ensure either that its registered name is displayed for at least 15 continuous seconds at least once every three minutes (eg on an electronic display), or that its registered name is available for inspection on a register by any visitor to that place.

In addition, all websites, business letters and order forms must state the company's country of registration, its registered number and the address of the registered office. Further, all business letters must contain the names of either all or none of the directors.

If the company trades under a business name (see **3.5.7** above), the above requirements must still be met.

Stationery, websites and signs for the company must therefore be prepared in accordance with these rules.

3.19.3 Shareholders' agreement

It is common, but not compulsory, where there is more than one shareholder of a new company, for the shareholders to enter into an agreement as to how they will run the company. This agreement is a matter for the shareholders themselves as owners of the company, and it does not usually involve the company itself. Such agreements may be entered into at any time in the life of a company, but they are usually entered into on registration of the new company. Shareholders' agreements are discussed further at **5.6.2.2** below.

3.20 SHELF COMPANY

So far in this chapter we have considered one of two options available to an entrepreneur who wants to run their business as a company, namely, setting up a company from scratch which, when registered, will meet their requirements.

There is another option, however, and that is for the entrepreneur to buy a pre-existing company – a so-called 'shelf' or 'ready-made' company – and then make changes to it so that it is ready to run the entrepreneur's business.

The essential difference between the two methods is that whereas in setting up the company from scratch there is of course no company in existence at the start of the process, if the entrepreneur uses a shelf company it means they are buying a company that has already been registered and therefore already exists. Someone (a company formation agent or a law firm) will have registered the company already in anticipation of a client wanting to buy it and use it to run a business. This shelf company will not have traded but simply have been waiting, dormant, for someone to buy it, activate it and use it for their business.

Why use a shelf company? In certain circumstances it may be a quicker way of getting the client's business up and running in the form of a company than creating a company from scratch, because there is no need to go through the registration process. Registration of the shelf company has already been done. The company already exists. There will be the certificate of incorporation to prove this. Even though registration of a company from scratch is possible on the same day (see **3.16** above), if the entrepreneur wishes to form a company with various amendments to the model articles it can take time to draft those amendments. This must, of course, be done before the application for registration of a new company can be submitted, and so an existing shelf company with these amendments already in place will be up and running more quickly.

Shelf companies are generally available from two sources: company formation agents (or law stationers such as Oyez at <www.oyez.co.uk>), and law firms. Anyone can buy a shelf company from a company formation agent simply by going onto its website and paying for it. The agent will then send the buyer the certificate of incorporation, the memorandum and articles (and possibly other documentation, depending on the service paid for). At the time of writing it was possible to buy a shelf private limited company from 1st Formations at <http://<www.1stformations.co.uk> for £52.99 (including the £50 Companies House registration fee). It is possible to purchase shelf companies with unamended model articles and various different amended model articles.

Law firms often incorporate their own shelf companies so that they have one available for instant use when a client requires a new company. A law firm will have drafted the articles of its own shelf companies, and it will therefore not have to waste time reviewing the articles of a shelf company bought from a company formation agent. Typically, an entrepreneur who decides to run their business as a company, having being advised by a law firm, will purchase a shelf company from that law firm.

Shelf companies from law firms are therefore commonly used in practice where the law firm gives legal advice in connection with the formation of the business, where the articles involve amendments to the model articles or bespoke articles, if the company is to be involved early on in a complex transaction, such as the purchase of another business, or if time is of the essence.

It is called a shelf company because traditionally, once the company had been registered by the company formation agent or the law firm, the physical documents proving the company existed – the certificate incorporation, the memorandum and articles of association for example – would sit on a shelf in an office (of the law firm or agent), waiting until the company was bought and then activated.

3.20.1 Changes to the shelf company

If a shelf company is used then changes will need to be made to the company to ensure that it meets the client's requirements for her business. Although the company already exists, it will not yet be owned by the entrepreneur, neither will it be in the shape they need.

The changes described at **3.20.2** and **3.20.3** below will be made by the existing directors and shareholders of the company. Remember that these will be employees of the agent or law firm. Once these changes have been made, the remaining changes may be made by the new directors and shareholders. This process is usually referred to as converting, or adapting or transferring the shelf company.

Ensuring that these changes are implemented correctly is usually the job of the trainee solicitor. In order to do this it is necessary to have an understanding of how meetings of directors and shareholders work. We cover this in detail in **Chapter 8**. For now it is sufficient to understand what changes need to be made to the shelf company, and why.

As with setting up a company from scratch, decisions need to be taken as to what the company should look like after the changes are made by the client, sometimes after taking legal advice. Information on the matters discussed below would be obtained from the client before proceeding to carry out the changes, usually using a precedent checklist produced by the law firm.

3.20.2 Ownership

As the shelf company has already been registered, it will of course already have at least one subscriber to the memorandum who is now the first shareholder of the company. This shareholder will be an employee either of the company formation agent or of the law firm as it set up the shelf company. The share or shares which the agent or law firm owns must be transferred into the names of the entrepreneur, because ownership of shares represents ownership of the company. Until the shares are transferred into the name of the entrepreneur, it will not be their company.

Some shelf companies are set up with one shareholder, others with two. If there are two shareholders then both shareholdings must be transferred to ensure that the company is fully owned by the entrepreneur.

How shares are transferred is explained at **9.9** below.

3.20.3 Officers

As the shelf company has already been registered, it will of course already have at least one director (maybe two) and possibly a company secretary (although this is not necessary). The existing officers of the company will be employees of the agent or law firm. They will all have to resign their positions; in their place will be appointed the number of directors the entrepreneur decides they want, and a perhaps a company secretary. Clearly the entrepreneur will want their company to be one in which they (or someone they know) take the decisions as director and act as company secretary.

How directors and company secretaries are appointed and resign is explained in **Chapter 6**.

3.20.4 Name

The shelf company will have been formed with a name given to it by the company formation agent or law firm. The entrepreneur will usually want to change this name to one of their choosing as soon as possible, for as soon as the company starts to trade it will begin to build a reputation under that name.

The name of a company is changed by the shareholders passing a special resolution under s 78 of the CA 2006, or if an alternative procedure exists in the articles then by that procedure under s 79 of the CA 2006. This alternative procedure might, for example, be a decision of the directors (a board resolution).

3.20.5 Articles

The shelf company will have been formed with articles chosen by the company formation agent or law firm. The entrepreneur may wish to make amendments to these articles to reflect the way in which they wish the company to be run.

How the articles of association are amended is explained at **4.4.1** below.

3.20.6 Registered office

The shelf company will have been formed with a registered office, usually being the address of the company formation agent or law firm. The entrepreneur may want to change this to an appropriate address associated with their or the company's business, such as offices.

The registered office is changed by a decision of the directors (a board resolution).

3.20.7 Accounting reference date

See **3.19.1.6** above for an explanation of when the shelf company's first accounting reference date will be. The entrepreneur may wish to change this to something more suitable.

The accounting reference date is changed by a decision of the directors (a board resolution) and must comply with the additional requirements of s 392 of the CA 2006.

3.20.8 Other changes

The entrepreneur may wish to take advantage of the shelf company conversion to make further changes. For example, to raise money by increasing the company's issued share capital, as the shelf company may well have been formed with just one share of £1. This also allows for new shareholders to be brought on board by selling the new shares to them.

How a company issues new shares is explained at **9.3** below.

The matters set out in **3.19** above (chairperson, bank account, company seal, business name, auditor, service contracts, company records, tax registration, insurance, disclosure requirements and shareholders' agreement) may be dealt with at the same time.

3.21 CONCLUSION

We have now seen that a company may either be set up from scratch, or acquired as a shelf company and adapted to meet a client's needs. A summary checklist for each follows. In the remaining chapters of **Part II** we shall consider how the company operates on a day-to-day basis.

3.21.1 Matters to consider when registering a company from scratch

1. Type of company
   - Limited or unlimited?
   - Limited by shares or by guarantee?
   - Private or public?

Assuming a private company limited by shares, matters which arise in documentation to be submitted

2. How many shareholders? (Minimum 1)
3. How many shares?
   - What nominal value? Currency?
   - What price?
   - Fully paid on issue or partly paid?
   - More than one class?
4. Which articles?
   - Model?
   - Amended model?
   - Bespoke?
5. Company name
   - Allowed?
   - Already in use?
   - Approval needed?
6. How many directors? (Minimum 1)
   - Who?
   - Disqualified?
   - Personal information?
7. Company secretary
   - Optional
   - If yes, who?
8. Registered office
   - Country?
   - Full address – must be 'appropriate'?
9. Registered email
   - which address?
   - must be 'appropriate'?
10. Method of registration
    - Electronic?
    - Paper?

- Same-day?
- Normal?

Matters to be addressed post-incorporation

11. Chairperson of board meeting
    - Who?
12. Cost of incorporation
13. Bank account
    - Which bank?
    - Signatories?
    - Limit?
14. Company seal
    - Optional
15. Business name
    - Optional
    - If yes, permitted?
    - Already in use?
    - Approval needed?
16. Accounting Reference Date
    - When?
17. Auditor
    - Needed?
    - If so, who?
18. Directors' service contracts
    - Terms?
    - Approval needed?
19. Company records
    - Complete
20. Tax registration
    - Corporation tax
    - PAYE and NI
    - VAT?
21. Insurance
    - For what?
22. Disclosure of company details
    - Documents
    - Websites
    - Registered office
    - Places of business
23. Shareholders' agreement
    - Needed?
    - Parties?
    - Terms?

3.21.2 Matters to consider when converting a shelf company

1. Type of company
   - Limited or unlimited?
   - Limited by shares or by guarantee?

– Private or public?

Assuming a private company limited by shares

2. Existing shareholders transfer shares
   – To whom?
3. Director/s must resign
   – Who replaces?
   – Disqualified?
   – Personal information
4. Company secretary
   – Is there one?
   – If yes, must resign
   – Who replaces?

Shelf company now owned and run by client. Other matters to be dealt with

5. Change company name?
   – If yes, allowed?
   – Already in use?
   – Approval needed?
6. Change articles?
   – If yes, what amendments?
7. Change registered office?
   – If yes, what address?
8. Change registered email address
9. Change Accounting Reference Date?
   – If yes, to what?
10. Issue more shares?
   – If yes, how many?
   – Who will buy them?
11. Chairperson of board meeting
   – Who?
12. Bank account
   – Which bank?
   – Signatories?
   – Limit?
13. Company seal
   – Optional
14. Business name
   – Optional
   – If yes, permitted?
   – Already in use?
   – Approval needed?
15. Auditor
   – Needed?
   – If so, who?
16. Directors' service contracts
   – Terms?
   – Approval needed?

17. Company records
    - Update with new details
18. Tax registration
    - Corporation tax
    - PAYE and NI
    - VAT?
19. Insurance
    - For what?
20. Disclosure of company details
    - Documents
    - Websites
    - Registered office
    - Places of business
21. Shareholders' agreement
    - Needed?
    - Parties?
    - Terms?

CHAPTER 4

THE COMPANY'S CONSTITUTION

LEARNING OUTCOMES

After reading this chapter you will be able to:

- understand the role of the company's constitution
- identify the legal rules governing the existence and content of the company's constitution
- explain how and why a company can change its constitution.

4.1 INTRODUCTION

Every company has a constitution. This comprises certain key documents which evidence the existence of the company, state its current share capital (the amount of money shareholders have invested in the company by buying its shares) and, most significantly, set out the rules which govern how the company should be run. The constitution is important not just for its content but because it represents a special type of contract between the company, as a separate legal person, on the one hand, and the shareholders, the owners of the company, on the other. It also represents a special type of contract between the shareholders themselves. We shall explore these issues further in this chapter.

4.2 DEFINITION

The company's constitution is defined in ss 17, 29 and 32 of the CA 2006. It includes:

(a) the company's articles of association;

(b) its certificate of incorporation (see **3.17** above);

(c) its current statement of capital (see **9.3.1** below);

(d) copies of any court orders and enactments (ie legislation) altering the company's constitution;

(e) resolutions (shareholders' decisions) affecting the constitution;

(f) agreements involving shareholders which affect the constitution (see **5.6.2.2** below).

4.3 THE ARTICLES OF ASSOCIATION

The articles of association are the most important part of the company's constitution. As we saw at **3.13**, every company must have a set of articles of association which lays out the rules on how the company is to be run (CA 2006, s 18(1)). The articles form the company's internal rulebook.

There are many legal rules governing how a company should be run, all of which must be complied with, principally in the CA 2006 but also in decisions of judges under the common law. Nevertheless, company law in the UK seeks to allow a certain amount of flexibility to companies regarding how they run themselves, in recognition of the fact that companies are set up for different purposes and can vary tremendously in size. Certain provisions of the CA 2006 will therefore apply only if they are expressly included by the company's articles. The 2006 Act also allows certain, but by no means all, of its provisions to be excluded by the company's articles. In other words, the owners of each company may decide for themselves, up to a point, how it should be run by what they put in its articles. The articles of a particular company are therefore essential to help clarify what the powers of the directors, as managers of that company, and those of the shareholders, as owners of that company, are. The articles will also shed light on how decisions should be taken in that particular company. It is possible to include restrictions on what a company can do in the articles too.

The company's articles will always be available for inspection by the public because they are available for inspection at Companies House. This allows those thinking of dealing with the company to see how that company should be run and, if they are included, any restrictions on its operations. The articles must be contained in a single document and be divided into consecutively numbered paragraphs (CA 2006, s 18(3)). This makes it easier for everyone involved in the company or dealing with it to obtain a complete and clearly laid-out copy of the company's own rules.

We saw at **3.13** that there are three options for a company's articles, which will initially be chosen by those setting up the company. The articles will be:

(a) unamended model articles of association; or
(b) model articles of association with amendments; or
(c) bespoke articles of association.

The impact on a company of each of these options is examined below.

4.3.1 Unamended model articles

A company registered with no other articles will by default have unamended model articles as its articles (CA 2006, s 20(1)) (see **3.13.1** above). For companies considered in this book, this will be the set of model articles for private companies limited by shares. They are set out in the Companies (Model Articles) Regulations 2008 (SI 2008/3229). They were drafted under powers given to the Secretary of State for DBT by s 19 of the CA 2006. They apply to all private companies limited by shares formed on or after 1 October 2009 where no other articles are registered.

4.3.1.1 Use of model articles

The model articles comprise a set of minimum basic rules on running the company. They have been specifically drafted with small business owners in mind and to keep regulation to a minimum. They will therefore be used, rather than amended model articles or bespoke articles, if those forming the company are currently running a small business or do not wish to use anything more comprehensive, or if time is of the essence and a private company must be formed from scratch very quickly. However, remember that the entrepreneurs setting up a company have a choice and are not compelled to use the model articles.

4.3.1.2 Content of model articles

Table 4.1 shows which articles cover which matters in the model articles for a private company limited by shares.

Table 4.1 Content of the model articles for a private company limited by shares

Article numbers	*Subject*
1–2	Defined terms and liability of members
3–6	Directors' powers and responsibilities
7–16	Decision-making by directors
17–20	Appointment of directors
21–29	Shares
30–35	Dividends and other distributions
36	Capitalisation of profits
37–41	Organisation of general meetings
42–47	Voting at general meetings
48–51	Administrative arrangements
52–53	Directors' indemnity and insurance

Such is the importance of the articles of a company that we shall be considering them throughout the remainder of this part of the book. The provisions of the model articles will be explained as and when they become relevant, as we examine how a company operates and how those involved with the company take decisions on its behalf. These model articles are likely to remain the same or predominantly the same for many years to come, so they will still have relevance well into your career in practice.

One example of the content of the model articles will suffice for now. Article 21 states:

> (1) No share is to be issued for less than the aggregate of the nominal value and any premium to be paid to the company in consideration for its issue.
>
> (2) This does not apply to shares taken on the formation of the company by the subscribers to the company's memorandum.

This means that a company which adopts unamended model articles may issue only fully-paid shares after its formation (see **2.3.4** above). Issuing shares is a means by which a company may raise money for its purposes. Only those shares referred to in the company's memorandum, namely the very first shares of the company, may be issued partly paid (see **2.3.4** above). In other words, although it is perfectly possible for a company to issue partly-paid shares under English law (ie shares for which the company does not receive all the money at the time they are issued), by adopting unamended model articles the owners have decided that under its rules (art 21) it should not be allowed to do so. The advantage of including this rule, even though it is not necessary, is that it ensures that the company will receive and be able to use all the money for the shares at the time they are sold. If it sells £10,000 worth of shares it will get all the money immediately, and not (say) £5,000 at the time of the sale and £5,000 at some point in the future.

When considering the model articles it is important to ensure that you always check the definitions in art 1, as they will provide further clarification of the wording of the model articles. For example, the words 'shares' and 'paid' in art 21 are defined.

4.3.2 Amended model articles

When a company adopts unamended model articles it must abide by all of the 53 articles (see **Table 4.1** above). It will often be the case that some of these rules are not suitable for a particular company. For example, the company may wish to issue partly-paid shares, which would not be possible under art 21 of the model articles (see **4.3.1** above). Further, as the model articles represent a bare minimum set of rules, some entrepreneurs will want to set up their companies with additional articles to provide greater clarity on how the company should be run. In order to accommodate these changes, it is possible to adopt amended model articles (or adopt a different set of articles altogether, as explained at **4.3.3** below).

When setting up a new company with amended model articles, only a copy of the changes to the model articles need be submitted with the application for registration (in accordance with s 20(1)(b) of the CA 2006). The amendments or any new articles included are known as 'special articles' to distinguish them from the model articles themselves.

The first article of the amended model articles will include wording which expressly states that the model articles shall be the articles of the company except where they are modified or excluded by or are inconsistent with the special articles. This means that only the amendments to the model articles and entirely new articles need to be written down. In practice this means that when considering the articles of such a company, you will need to get a copy of the unamended model articles, and then read the special articles to see which of the 53 model articles this company has retained unamended, which of the model articles it has amended (and how) and which special articles are entirely new (and what they mean).

4.3.2.1 Special articles

Some examples of special articles which are used by companies amending model articles for a private company limited by shares are set out in **4.3.2.2** to **4.3.2.8** below. They represent some of the simpler amendments which are made to the model articles.

4.3.2.2 Directors' meetings

The provisions for holding directors' meetings and the way in which directors can take decisions under the model articles are very flexible. It may be appropriate in some companies to amend the model articles to make decision-making by the directors more formal, for example by requiring a minimum period of notice be given before a directors' meeting may be held (there is currently no such provision), or to limit the ability to take decisions by some electronic means, such as text messaging, by amending model art 10.

4.3.2.3 Directors' interests in transactions

In certain cases, art 14 of the model articles prevents a director who has a personal interest in a transaction with the company from voting at or participating in a board meeting dealing with the transaction. A special article may be included to allow directors to vote on and participate in any matter at board meetings, even where they have a personal interest in the transaction in question. Where the company has only one or two directors, such an article may prove useful, as it is common for directors in a small company to have such a personal interest (eg when discussing a proposed contract with another company in which one of the directors is a shareholder, or when deciding their own salaries). A personal interest might otherwise prevent a director from voting at a board meeting, and if an insufficient number of directors is present at the meeting who are entitled to vote, no decision can be taken on the transaction at the board meeting. (See further **8.4.3 below**.)

4.3.2.4 Directors' conflict of interests

In situations other than those suggested in **4.3.2.3** above, a director may still be in a potential position of conflict with their company which may breach their duties as a director under s 175 of the CA 2006. For example, if a director takes a decision on a contract between two different companies when the director is a director of both companies. Section 175 of the CA 2006 expressly allows a private company to permit the directors to authorise a situation which would otherwise breach s 175 (see **7.11.1** below) provided the articles do not prevent this. The model articles contain no such provision and will need to be amended if they are to include one.

4.3.2.5 Number of directors

The minimum number of directors for a private company is one, by virtue of s 154 of the CA 2006. The model articles do not state a minimum or maximum number of directors for a company, so any number may be appointed. However, some companies may wish to state expressly that the minimum number of directors shall be two, or even more. This is because, under the model articles, a single director can act alone, with all the powers given by the articles and company law. The shareholders may decide that their company's best interests are best served by there being at least two decision-makers on the board.

4.3.2.6 Absence of directors

There is no power in the model articles for a director to appoint a temporary replacement if the director should be out of contact for a period of time. Although the model articles do allow great flexibility as to the means by which directors may take decisions, some companies may nevertheless wish to include a formal arrangement to appoint an 'alternate' director, who will act during the director's absence with the powers set out in the special article.

4.3.2.7 Company secretary

A private company does not need to have a company secretary (CA 2006, s 270(1)), and this is reflected in the model articles. If the company does decide it needs one, it *may* choose to amend the model articles to include the powers of the secretary and the terms of such an appointment. However, this is not necessary and the appointment can be made under the directors' general powers under model article (MA) 3.

4.3.2.8 Issuing shares to new shareholders

This is a special article which gives the directors the freedom to sell new shares to new shareholders by removing the statutory pre-emption rights of existing shareholders. These rights, under s 561 of the CA 2006, allow the existing shareholders to be offered the chance to buy any new shares before they are offered to outsiders (see **9.3.3** below). This special article therefore enables the directors to get on with the business of issuing the new shares and raising the necessary capital for the company without having to call a shareholders' general meeting to ask the existing shareholders to waive these pre-emption rights.

4.3.3 Bespoke articles

A company may be set up with its own tailor-made set of articles without reference to the model articles. In this case the articles must be submitted when the company is set up (CA 2006, s 18(2)). A lawyer will be required to draft these bespoke articles, to ensure that the provisions of the CA 2006 and company law are complied with. The advantage of bespoke articles is that they can be drafted to the exact requirements of the private company's owners.

The bespoke articles will usually as a minimum cover the same topics as the model articles (sometimes using the exact wording of an article in the model articles), and may in addition include some or all of the special articles referred to at **4.3.2** above and other special articles dealing with additional matters affecting the company's operations.

4.3.4 Effect of the articles

Under s 33(1) of the CA 2006, the constitution of a company (of which the articles are the most important part) forms a contract between the company and each of its members. In addition, the constitution forms a contract between all the company's shareholders.

The effect of s 33 is to create contracts in circumstances when they would not otherwise exist under contract law. In particular, it ensures that parties have special contractual rights relating to the articles, which set out the rules of the company. For example, where a company, X Limited, issues shares to two different shareholders, there would ordinarily be no contractual relationship between the shareholders. Each shareholder has a separate contract with the company to buy shares. Section 33 creates an additional contract between the two shareholders on the basis of the articles. This helps to ensure that both shareholders abide by the articles, as a remedy may be available for breach of contract if the articles are not observed. (See **Figure 4.1**.)

Figure 4.1 Contract between the company and its shareholders under CA 2006, s 33

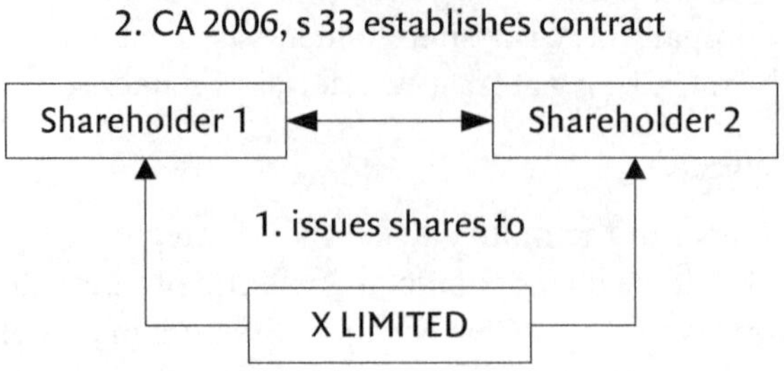

Section 33 also ensures that there is a contract where a shareholder in the company sells their shares to another shareholder. In **Figure 4.2** below, s 33 creates a contract between the new shareholder and Y Limited, and they must both abide by the articles.

Figure 4.2 Contract between the company and new shareholder under CA 2006, s 33

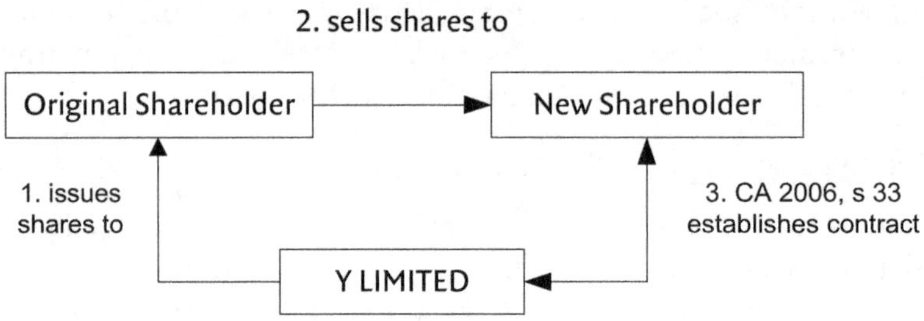

Section 33 in effect provides a means for a shareholder to take action against the company or against another shareholder for breach of their contractual rights as set out in the articles and in the rest of the constitution. However, it is important to note that the s 33 contract is a very different type of contract from a trading contract to buy and sell goods or services. The contract allows for action to be taken only in so far as it deals with membership rights (*Beattie v E and F Beattie* [1938] Ch 708). These include such entitlements as the right to vote, the right to attend general meetings and the right to a dividend if one is declared (see **9.8** below).

By contrast, anything which purports to bind the company and its members but which deals with rights other than those of a member in their capacity as member (such as the right to be a director (*Read v Astoria Garage (Streatham) Ltd* [1952] Ch 637), or the right to be appointed the company's solicitor (*Eley v Positive Government Security Life Assurance Co Ltd* (1876) 1 ExD 88) or how a shareholder will vote) will be unenforceable if included in the articles of the company. Such matters must therefore be dealt with in a separate contract, such as a shareholders' agreement (see **5.6.2.2** below).

It should be noted that the courts are much less keen to give effect to membership rights between shareholders of a company (ie as opposed to between a shareholder and the company) by a s 33 contractual claim. The only case in which an action between shareholders was successful was *Rayfield v Hands* [1960] Ch 1. There are, though, other possible remedies for an aggrieved shareholder, for example a petition to the court for unfair prejudice under s 994 of the CA 2006 (see **5.6.3.14** below).

As the articles amount to a contract, it is possible for additional terms to be implied if necessary to give effect to the contract, for example as a result of court proceedings about a dispute over the meaning of the articles (*Cream Holdings Ltd v Stuart Davenport* [2011] EWCA Civ 1287).

4.4 AMENDING THE CONSTITUTION

As a company evolves over time, the directors and shareholders may find that elements of the constitution which were, or were thought to be, suitable are no longer so. Circumstances change, and sometimes the company's constitution must be amended to reflect this. For example, if a shelf company has been used to start up a new business (see **3.19** above) then changes may be necessary immediately in order to structure the company in the way the entrepreneurs wish (eg, amendments to the model articles, as explained at **4.3.2** above). Alternatively, a company which has been owned by family members may bring in investors from outside the family, and changes may therefore be needed to the constitution.

The key constitutional document for a company is its articles. We therefore now consider how a company's articles may be amended. Note that it is possible to make more than one change to the articles at the same time (indeed to replace them entirely) and for the company to make amendments to its articles at any time throughout its existence.

There are two separate procedures for amending the articles. The first is for the amendment of ordinary articles. This will be relevant for the overwhelming majority of amendments to the articles. The second is for amending any so-called 'entrenched' articles. This is rarely used.

4.4.1 Amending the articles

The shareholders of the company must usually pass a special resolution to change the articles of a company (CA 2006, s 21(1)). We consider shareholders' resolutions in greater detail at **8.7.7.3** below. For now it is sufficient to be aware that a shareholders' resolution is simply a decision of the shareholders, and that being 'special' it must be passed by a majority of not less than 75% (CA 2006, s 283(1)). This again demonstrates why the contract which arises under s 33 is different from an ordinary trading contract. The fact that the articles, part of the company's constitution, can be changed without the complete agreement of all parties runs counter to the usual principles of contract law which ordinarily require unanimous agreement. The decision is made by the shareholders as owners of the company rather than by the directors managing the company, in recognition of the importance of the articles to the company's existence.

If the shareholders have sufficient votes to pass the special resolution, the articles of the company will be amended. The Registrar of Companies must be sent a copy of the articles as amended not later than 15 days after the amendment takes effect (CA 2006, s 26(1)). Usually the change takes effect immediately. In addition, a copy of the special resolution itself must also be sent to the Registrar of Companies within 15 days after it has been passed (CA 2006, s 30(1)). These two documents will be put on the company's file at Companies House and thus will be publicly accessible.

It should be noted that in a couple of exceptional cases the CA 2006 permits changes to the articles of a private company by an ordinary resolution of the company's shareholders. An ordinary resolution may be passed by a simple majority (ie over 50%) (CA 2006, s 282(1)) and is therefore potentially easier to achieve than a special resolution.

If the directors have authority under the articles to allot new shares in the company, an ordinary resolution of the shareholders may revoke, vary or renew this authority (CA 2006, s 551(8)). The reason why a special resolution is not required for such an amendment is that this directors' authority is often not included in the articles, and in such a case a decision to change it is usually taken by an ordinary resolution under the CA 2006. The directors' authority to allot is explained fully at **9.3.2** below.

Another example of a change to the articles by ordinary resolution is found in s 685(2) of the CA 2006, which relates to a special type of shares, known as 'redeemable' shares, sometimes issued by a company.

If necessary the court can rectify the articles, as seen in *Folkes Group plc v Alexander* [2002] 2 BCLC 254. In this case there was an amendment to the company's articles which was disputed. The court said that the literal interpretation of the amendment led to an absurd result. In order to give proper commercial effect to the articles, new words would be inserted in the articles by the court. Of course, this situation would arise only exceptionally.

4.4.2 Restrictions on amending the articles

The shareholders are nevertheless restricted in a number of ways as to the changes they can make to their company's articles.

4.4.2.1 Restrictions under the CA 2006

The shareholders cannot amend the articles so as to conflict with a mandatory provision of the CA 2006 (*Allen v Gold Reefs of West Africa* [1900] 1 Ch 656).

The CA 2006 contains provisions which are both voluntary and mandatory. Voluntary provisions are either those that will apply unless they are excluded by the company's articles, or those that will not apply unless the shareholders choose to include them in the company's articles. An example is s 31(1) of the CA 2006. This provides that 'unless a company's articles specifically restrict the objects of a company, its objects are unrestricted'. The objects of a company are the powers of the company. In other words, the basic rule in s 31 is that a company has unrestricted powers unless the shareholders specifically choose to place a restriction in the articles, such as that the company shall not borrow more than £50,000.

Mandatory provisions of the CA 2006 are those which cannot be excluded by the company's articles. For example, s 355(2) of the CA 2006 requires a company to keep a record of the proceedings of shareholders' meetings for 10 years. An attempt by the shareholders to include a provision in the company's articles reducing this period to one year would be void, and would in fact be a criminal offence under s 355.

How do you tell the difference between mandatory and voluntary provisions? Usually the voluntary provisions will explicitly state that they are subject to the articles. We saw that s 31 includes the wording 'unless a company's articles ...'. This qualifier is expressed in the CA 2006 in a number of different ways, including by phrases such as 'subject to the company's articles' or 'this section applies where provision is made in the company's articles to ...'. Mandatory provisions often state that an offence will be committed for non-compliance.

In addition, s 25 of the CA 2006 specifically provides that a shareholder is not bound by any change in the company's articles which forces that shareholder to buy more shares in the company, unless they expressly agree in writing to be so bound.

4.4.2.2 Common law restrictions

Generally, the shareholders can make a change to the articles only if it is 'bona fide for the benefit of the company as a whole' (*Allen v Gold Reefs of West Africa* [1900] 1 Ch 656). This is a complex test which has generated a large amount of case law and commentary. In very simple terms, whether or not the change is 'bona fide for the benefit of the company as a whole' is a subjective matter for the company's shareholders to decide (*Citco Banking Corporation NV v Pussers* [2007] UKPC 13). It is therefore not for the court to decide what is in the company's interests.

However, objectively, there may be amendments to the articles which cannot be said to benefit the company as a whole. Usually such cases involve the situation where the intention behind amending the articles was to discriminate against minority shareholders rather than to benefit the company as a whole. This may be seen especially in cases involving a change to the articles to allow the company to buy out certain shareholders. *Brown v British Abrasive Wheel Co Ltd* [1919] 1 Ch 290 is an example of such an amendment which was held to be invalid; whereas the amendment to the articles in *Shuttleworth v Cox Brothers and Co (Maidenhead) Ltd* [1927] 2 KB 9 was held to be valid.

4.4.3 Entrenched articles

Section 22 of the CA 2006 permits a company to include 'provisions for entrenchment' in its articles. We saw at **4.4.1** above that a special resolution under s 21 of the CA 2006 is the usual way to change a company's articles. An entrenched article contains extra procedures or conditions, which makes it harder to change than other articles.

An entrenched article may, for example, include a condition that on a shareholders' vote to amend it, a particular shareholder alone will always have a greater number of votes than the rest of the shareholders put together. In other words, that one shareholder will decide the fate of the article if a change to it is proposed. Such a provision might be included in an article appointing a specified person as a director where the director is also a shareholder. In effect such an article means that the other shareholders cannot remove that person as a director of the company without their consent. Note that s 22(3) of the CA 2006 permits an entrenched article to be amended by agreement of all the company's shareholders, or by order of the court, even if the conditions in that article are not met.

The CA 2006 seeks to make it difficult for a company to include such provisions in its articles because they can significantly restrict the freedom of the shareholders to take decisions. Under s 22(2) of the CA 2006, the entrepreneurs forming a company will only be able to include entrenched rights in the articles either when the company is first set up, or with the agreement of all the shareholders once the company has been registered. This latter change would therefore require a higher threshold than applies when changing other articles, since these require only a 75% shareholder vote in favour. However, at the time of writing, s 22(2) of the CA 2006 had not yet entered into force. This is because of concerns that the subsection as currently worded traps commonly-used articles which were not intended to be caught. Therefore, until such time as this problem is resolved by the DBT, an entrenched article may still be included simply by passing a s 21 special resolution. The rest of s 22 is already in force.

If the company's articles are amended to *include* an entrenched article then, in addition to the special resolution and copy of the new articles (see **4.4.1** above), the company must also send Form CC01 (notice of restriction on the company's articles, available on the Companies House website <www.gov.uk/government/organisations/companies-house>) to the Registrar of Companies.

If the company's articles are amended to *remove* an entrenched article then, in addition to the special resolution and copy of the new articles (see **4.4.1** above), the company must also send Form CC02 (notice of removal of restriction on the company's articles, available on the Companies House website noted above) to the Registrar of Companies.

Where a company's articles *already* include an entrenched article and any of the company's articles are altered (whether the entrenched article or not) then, in addition to the special resolution and copy of the new articles (see **4.4.1** above), the company must also send Form CC03 (statement of compliance where amendment of articles restricted, available on the Companies House website noted above) to the Registrar of Companies.

4.5 THE MEMORANDUM OF ASSOCIATION

This document was described in detail in **3.14** above and a copy may be found in **Appendix 2**. As the memorandum is a very simple document, and represents just a snapshot of the company and its owners at the time the company is formed, it does not form part of the company's constitution.

4.6 COMPANIES FORMED UNDER THE COMPANIES ACT 1985

What has been described in this chapter up to this point explains the law affecting a company formed under the CA 2006, which came fully into force on 1 October 2009. From that point in time, all new companies had to be set up under the 2006 Act. However, at the start of 2024 approximately 15% of private companies currently in existence were not formed under the CA 2006 but under its predecessors, including the CA 1985. Although the CA 1985 has been repealed, and the CA 2006 applies to *all* private companies whenever they were set up, the constitution of a company set up under the 1985 Act differs fundamentally from what has been explained above. The reality is that you will deal in practice with companies which were set up under the CA 1985 for many years to come. You will also therefore see the CA 1985 constitutional documents of such companies. They differ substantially from the documents for companies formed under the 2006 Act. It is therefore important to understand what these documents are and how they are now treated under the CA 2006.

4.6.1 Memorandum of association under the CA 1985

Before the CA 2006 came into force, the memorandum of association had a much more important role to play. Unlike the current memorandum, the CA 1985 memorandum was relevant throughout the life of the company. The old-style memorandum comprised five main clauses: the name, registered office, objects, shareholders' liability and authorised share capital. A draft copy of an old memorandum is included in **Appendix 2**.

On 1 October 2009, when the CA 2006 came into force, the memorandum became much less significant (see **3.14** above), the five main clauses of the memorandums of companies already in existence automatically becoming provisions of their articles (CA 2006, s 28(1)). This meant that the clauses could be changed by the company following the procedure described in **4.4.1** above, with the shareholders passing a special resolution under s 21 of the CA 2006.

4.6.1.1 Liability clause

The shareholders' liability clause of the old-style memorandum simply stated: 'The liability of the members is limited.' This is now automatically a provision in the articles due to s 28(1) of the CA 2006, and of course it will not need to be changed unless the company wishes to convert to being an unlimited company. This would be extremely rare in practice.

As all limited companies formed under the CA 2006 must state in their constitution that the liability of their shareholders is limited (CA 2006, s 3(1) – see, eg, art 2 of the model articles), both a company formed under the CA 1985 and a company formed under the CA 2006 are treated in exactly the same manner.

4.6.1.2 Objects clause

All companies in existence before 1 October 2009 had an objects clause in their memorandum. This clause set out the purposes for which the company was formed and included a statement of what it was empowered to do. Historically, if a company acted outside of its objects set out in the objects clause then it was said to have acted 'ultra vires' (beyond its powers). At common law, a transaction which was 'ultra vires' would be void as it was beyond what the company could legally do (*Ashbury Railway Carriage and Iron Co Ltd v Riche* (1875) LR 7 HL 673).

If business people like one thing above all else (other than making money of course), it is certainty in their business dealings. The doctrine of 'ultra vires' introduced an unwanted element of uncertainty, as there was always the possibility that a company's action would be found to be void for breaching its objects clause. Consequently, various devices were developed over time in order to minimise the risk of a company's act being found to be 'ultra vires'. One of these was the introduction by the CA 1989 of the 'general commercial company' objects clause, set out in the memorandum of association in **Appendix 2**. This wording allowed the company to carry on any business it wished and to do anything incidental or conducive to its business. However, this was introduced only in 1989, and companies set up before this date often have objects clauses running to many pages, comprehensively listing the business which the company was to carry on (so-called 'long-form' objects clauses) in order to avoid the company acting 'ultra vires'.

Even companies formed after 1989 would usually still use these 'long-form' objects clauses, because it was unclear whether a 'general commercial company' objects clause permitted the company to do everything it might want to do, eg selling off its whole business or donating money to charity.

The CA 2006 finally clarified the situation once and for all. It specifically removed the need for an objects clause altogether through s 31 of the Act, which provides that a company's objects are completely unrestricted unless the constitution provides otherwise. Section 31 therefore allows a company to carry on whatever activity it wants (within the law, of course).

Further, s 39 of the CA 2006 effectively abolishes the 'ultra vires' doctrine with regard to third parties dealing with the company. In other words, s 39 provides that an act undertaken by the company with an outsider (such as entering a contract) cannot be challenged if it is beyond the powers granted in the company's constitution. Both the company and the other party to the transaction are bound by the act. This is backed up by s 40(1), which states that the powers of the directors to bind a company (eg by entering a contact) are deemed to be free of any limitation under the company's constitution in favour of a person dealing with the company in good faith.

Although we have seen that ss 39 and 40(1) of the CA 2006 thus prevent a challenge to an act of the company due to a breach of its constitution externally (ie with third parties), there are still some possible consequences internally (ie within the company) if the company's objects are exceeded. If the company intends to act in breach of its objects (eg, by the directors deciding to enter a contract), there is a right for a shareholder to go to court to seek an injunction under s 40(4) to restrain the company from taking this action. However, this injunction must be sought *before* the act is undertaken (ie a legal obligation has been incurred). If the act has already been done (say, the contract has been signed), the shareholder can only take action against the directors (CA 2006, s 40(5)) for breach of their duty to the company. Directors are obliged under the CA 2006 to act within their powers, which includes observing any restrictions in the constitution (CA 2006, s 171).

Section 31 does preserve the right of a company to limit its objects if it chooses to do so, but in the vast majority of cases companies will now be formed under the CA 2006 without this limitation, to avoid the possible problems that still may arise if its objects are exceeded.

As mentioned at **4.6.1** above, the objects clauses of companies registered before 1 October 2009, being part of their memorandum of association, became part of the articles under s 28(1) of the CA 2006. In effect, such an objects clause will operate as an article which restricts the directors rather than the company (because of ss 39 and 40(1)). There is therefore still a risk of directors being held to be in breach of their duties to the company if they act outside the objects. The restrictions on these companies' objects, now being contained in the articles, may be removed by the shareholders passing a special resolution under s 21 of the CA 2006 to amend the articles (see **4.4.1** above). There is therefore a big incentive for most companies incorporated with an old-style memorandum to change their articles and remove their objects clause to avoid any potential problems.

If a company amends its articles so as to add, change or remove any part of (specifically) an objects clause, it must complete and send Form CC04 to the Registrar of Companies at Companies House (CA 2006, s 31(2)), together with the special resolution and a copy of the new articles.

To summarise the position with regard to the objects clause:

Company formed under CA 2006

(a) There is no need for an objects clause, as under s 31(1) the company's objects are unrestricted. This will be the usual scenario.

(b) The company may choose to place restrictions on its objects (s 31(1)) by passing a special resolution to amend its articles (s 21). This will be rare in practice.

(c) If it does so and the company acts in breach of its objects, it will have no impact on outsiders dealing with the company (s 39) but shareholders may either seek an injunction (s 40(4)) or sue the directors for breach of duty (s 40(5)).

Company formed under CA 1985

(a) The existing objects clause in the company's memorandum became part of its articles on 1 October 2009 (s 28(1)).

(b) If the company acts in breach of its objects clause, it will have no impact on outsiders dealing with the company (s 39) but shareholders may either seek an injunction (s 40(4)) or sue the directors for breach of duty (s 40(5)).

(c) The company may choose to amend its articles by passing a special resolution (s 21) to remove (or amend) the objects clause. If it removes its objects clause, its objects are unrestricted under s 31(1).

4.6.1.3 Authorised share capital

A company in existence before 1 October 2009 had to have a clause in its memorandum stating its authorised share capital. This was a cap on the amount of money which a company could raise by issuing shares to its shareholders. For example, in the memorandum set out in **Appendix 2** the company has an authorised share capital of £100 made up of 100 shares of £1 each. The company could not raise more than £100 from shareholders without following a complex statutory procedure to raise this amount. Under the CA 2006 the concept of an authorised share capital has been abolished. Instead, a statement of capital is made on incorporation of the company (see **3.7** above) and each time it decides to issue more shares after incorporation.

A company formed before 1 October 2009 will have had its former authorised share capital clause moved from the memorandum to the articles by s 28(1) of the CA 2006. It then operates as a restriction under the articles, and would need to be removed by amending the articles if the directors wished to issue more shares that would exceed the cap. So if a company had the clause mentioned above and it wanted to raise more than £100, it would need to amend its articles. How this is done is explained at **9.3.1** below.

4.6.1.4 Other clauses

A company formed under the CA 1985 may alter its name and registered office in the same way as a company formed under the CA 2006 (see **3.20.4** and **3.20.6** above).

4.6.2 Articles of association under the CA 1985

As has already been noted, a minority of private companies currently in existence were incorporated before the CA 2006 came into force. When these companies were set up, mainly under the CA 1985, a different set of model articles for a private company limited by shares could be chosen by the company's owners, or would automatically apply on incorporation if no other articles were registered. They are known as Table A articles (or more usually just 'Table A'). Table A could be adopted unamended or with amendments, as with the model articles (see **4.3** above).

Table A is still important today, because although new companies can no longer be formed with them, existing companies using Table A were not required to change their articles when the law changed on 1 October 2009. Existing companies were allowed to keep Table A. It is therefore essential for a corporate lawyer to be familiar with both versions of the articles. We shall refer to provisions of both the model articles and Table A where relevant throughout this part of the book.

4.6.2.1 Use of unamended Table A

Table A was intended to be a more comprehensive set of articles than were the model articles that replaced them. In particular, they were not specifically drafted for smaller companies but for all sizes of company. It follows, therefore, that Table A is considerably longer than the CA 2006 model articles, and covers more aspects of a company's operations.

Although companies with Table A articles may continue to operate under these rules (CA 2006, s 19(4)), as a number of major changes have been made to company law by the 2006 Act, certain Table A articles will be redundant, impose unnecessary extra administrative burdens or operate in a different manner under that Act. As a consequence, there are advantages for many existing private companies in amending their existing Table A articles to conform to the changes in the law. While some private companies have already done so, the reality is that many have not, particularly where legal advisers are not employed on a regular basis to advise a company.

4.6.2.2 Content of Table A

Table A's 118 articles were set out in the Companies (Tables A to F) Regulations 1985 (SI 1985/805) (amended in 2000 to allow for electronic communications in a company).

The main areas covered in Table A are as shown in **Table 4.2** below.

Table 4.2 Content of Table A articles of association

Article numbers	*Subject*
1	Definitions
2–35	Share capital and shares
36–63	Shareholders' general meetings
64–98	Directors and board meetings
99–101	Company administration
102–110	Company profits
111–116	Notices
117–118	Winding up and indemnity

The clauses of the old-style memorandum of association also became provisions of the company's articles with effect from 1 October 2009 (see **4.6.1** above).

4.6.2.3 Differences between the model articles and Table A

Some of the differences are listed here for ease of reference, but note that the practical significance of any difference will be explained where relevant throughout this part of the book when discussing the company's activities.

The key differences (there are others) between the new model articles for a private company limited by shares and Table A are that the new model articles:

- include a reference to the limitation of the members' liability (art 2) which was not in Table A (see **4.6.1.1** above);
- refer only to shareholders' 'general' meetings (art 37), whereas Table A refers to two different types of shareholder meeting: annual general meetings (AGMs) and extraordinary general meetings (EGMs);
- do not require the holding of an AGM, unlike Table A;
- do not include notice provisions for shareholders' meetings, unlike Table A;
- do not allow the use of a chairperson's casting vote in a shareholders' meeting, unlike Table A;
- do not deal with written resolutions, unlike Table A;

- allow proxies to vote on a show of hands, unlike Table A;
- do not make provision for the use of alternate directors, unlike Table A;
- do not require the directors to retire by rotation, unlike Table A;
- specify that directors' decisions are reached by majority decision or by unanimity, unlike Table A;
- specify that a unanimous decision of the directors may be made in any manner, whether or not there has been a formal board meeting, unlike Table A; and
- permit board meetings to be held by any method so long as each director can communicate to all of the others, and regardless of where each director is located, which is a much more relaxed regime than under Table A.

Some of these differences reflect the fact that rules which were in Table A are now contained in the CA 2006, but others reflect the deregulatory aspect of current company law in the UK for private companies, and the idea that private companies should be subject to the lightest regulation possible whilst still protecting investors and the public.

4.6.2.4 Amended Table A

As with the model articles, a company which adopted unamended Table A had to abide by all of its articles. In order to achieve rules more suitable for their purposes, many companies adopted special articles amending provisions of Table A.

The first article of a company which adopted amended Table A articles will include wording which expressly states that the Table A articles shall be the articles of the company except where they are modified or excluded by or are inconsistent with the special articles. When considering the articles of a company with amended Table A articles, you will need to get a copy of the unamended Table A and then read the special articles to see which of the 118 articles this company has retained unamended, which of the model articles it has amended (and how), and which special articles are entirely new (and what they mean).

Although companies with amended Table A articles may continue to operate under these rules (CA 2006, s 19(4)), as a number of major changes have been made to company law by the CA 2006, certain Table A articles will be redundant, impose unnecessary extra administrative burdens or operate in a different manner under that Act. As a consequence, as with unamended Table A articles, there are advantages for many existing private companies in amending their current amended Table A articles to conform to the changes in the law. As explained at **4.6.2.1** above, many private companies will not yet have done this.

4.6.3 Table A 2007

The provisions of the CA 2006 affecting private companies came into force in stages from 2007 until 1 October 2009. In order to deal with new companies which were set up in this period, when parts of the CA 2006 had already been implemented and before the new model articles came into effect on 1 October 2009, an interim set of Table A articles ('Table A 2007') was produced which companies could choose to use. They are based on the original Table A articles, but with amendments to reflect the changes made by provisions of the CA 2006 which came into force on 1 October 2007. Table A 2007 was ultimately replaced by the model articles. This means that only private companies formed between 1 October 2007 and 1 October 2009 could have these articles (assuming that they did not decide to adopt bespoke articles).

As the number of companies which adopted Table A 2007 represents a very small percentage of the total number of companies in existence, and as this percentage is shrinking every year, we do not consider Table A 2007 separately in this book, particularly as many of the issues which arise are covered in our analysis of Table A or the model articles. If you wish to consult

Table A 2007, you can find a copy on the Companies House website <www.gov.uk/government/organisations/companies-house>.

4.7 SUMMARY OF OPTIONS REGARDING ARTICLES

In light of the number of options which the law permits, and which you may come across in practice, there follows a summary of the different options for articles which may apply to private companies currently in existence, whether they were set up under the CA 2006 or before then. Only one of these options can apply. Remember that a company may change its articles at any time by following the statutory procedures in the CA 2006. You can check which articles apply to a company by searching the company's file at Companies House, as the latest version must always be submitted there.

Company formed under CA 2006

A private company formed *on or after* 1 October 2009 may have as its articles:

(a) unamended model articles; or
(b) amended model articles (with special articles); or
(c) bespoke articles.

Company formed under CA 1985

A private company formed *before* 1 October 2009 may have as its articles:

(a) Table A unamended with clauses from an old-style memorandum (usually where the articles have not been changed since 1 October 2009); or
(b) amended Table A (with special articles) and clauses from an old-style memorandum (usually where the articles have not been changed since 1 October 2009); or
(c) bespoke articles and clauses from an old-style memorandum (usually where the articles have not been changed since 1 October 2009); or
(d) Table A 2007 unamended with clauses from an old-style memorandum (usually where the company was formed between 1 October 2007 and 1 October 2009, and the articles have not been changed since 1 October 2009); or
(e) amended Table A 2007 and clauses from an old-style memorandum (usually where the company was formed between 1 October 2007 and 1 October 2009, and the articles have not been changed since 1 October 2009); or
(f) unamended model articles (if expressly adopted by special resolution since 1 October 2009); or
(g) amended model articles (if expressly adopted by special resolution since 1 October 2009); or
(h) bespoke articles taking account of changes in the CA 2006 (if expressly adopted since special resolution after 1 October 2009).

4.8 PROVISION OF CONSTITUTIONAL DOCUMENTS

A company must send a shareholder at their request a copy of certain of the company's constitutional documents, as set out in s 32 of the CA 2006. These include an up-to-date copy of the company's articles, its certificate of incorporation and its latest statement of capital. If the company does not do so, the officers of the company (eg the directors and any company secretary) may be liable to a fine. This provision ensures that the owners of a company have access to the key documents governing its existence and operation.

CHAPTER 5

The Company's Shareholders

LEARNING OUTCOMES

After reading this chapter you will be able to:

- explain the role of promoters and the different types of shareholder in a company
- understand how to become a shareholder of the company
- identify the rights granted to shareholders by law
- explain the significance of owning different numbers of shares in a company.

5.1 INTRODUCTION

The shareholders of a company are the owners of that company. In return for buying shares in the company (and therefore investing their money in it) the shareholders acquire certain rights. We saw at **2.3.4** above that an entrepreneur may use a private limited company to run her business and that she may become a shareholder in order to take advantage of limited liability. In other words, as owner of and investor in the company, she is liable to pay only for her shares in full and not the debts of the company. As owners and investors the shareholders play a very important role in the life of a company, and so we shall now look at their role in greater detail.

As explained at **2.3.9.2** above, although the term 'member' is used throughout the CA 2006, we are going to use the term 'shareholder' as we are considering only companies limited by shares in this part of the book, and a member of such a company is a shareholder.

5.2 PROMOTERS

We saw in **Chapter 3** that a new company is formed by a process of registration, and that on registration the entrepreneur becomes a shareholder of the company. The reality is that the affairs of the business that will be run by the company may require action to be taken before the company is formed. For example, there may be a contract into which an entrepreneur wants to enter straight away, before a company can be set up. At this time, as there is no company there are no shareholders. Individuals who decide to set up the company are known as 'promoters' before their company has been established.

5.2.1 Definition

A promoter is not defined in the CA 2006 but in guidelines set out in case law, such as in *Twycross v Grant* (1877) 2 CPD 469:

> [A] promoter ... is one who undertakes to form a company with reference to a given project and to set it going, and who takes the necessary steps to accomplish that purpose.

A promoter therefore includes both those who take the steps to register a company under the CA 2006 and those who start or operate the business that the company will run. It does not, however, include solicitors or accountants, or other professionals who act for the promoter in the setting up a company.

5.2.2 Responsibilities

The promoter is in a special position with regard to the as yet unformed company, as she will direct and oversee the initial stages of the formation of the company. This power gives rise to the possibility of abuse. Such abuse may arise, for example, where more than one entrepreneur or investor is involved, and one of them alone takes on responsibility for setting up the company or entering into contracts before the company has been formed. To mitigate this possibility of abuse, a promoter is placed in a fiduciary relationship with the company once it has been formed.

The primary fiduciary duty of the promoter is not to make a 'secret profit' when forming the company. This might arise if, for example, the promoter bought property for the new company in her own name (or purportedly in the new company's name) before it was formed and then sold it at a profit to the company once it was formed, without disclosing the fact that she has made a profit. In such a case the new company could rescind the contract, or make the promoter account to the company for the profit (ie make her hand over the money). It is possible for the promoter to keep such a profit, but only where she has properly disclosed her interest in the profit to the new company.

5.2.3 Pre-incorporation contracts

Another potential problem which arises for the promoter is incurring expenses and liabilities on behalf of the company before it has been set up. For example, someone must pay the costs of registration, or the investors might wish to enter into a contract straight away before the company is formed. Prior to incorporation, of course, the company does not exist. Any attempt to act on behalf of the company before the date stated on the certificate of incorporation has no legal effect as the company may ultimately never be formed. A person (the promoter) cannot act as agent of a company which does not yet exist. The company, when it is incorporated, has no obligation under any contract purportedly made on its behalf before its registration. These contracts, if made, are known as 'pre-incorporation contracts'.

The fact is, though, that in practice an entrepreneur (the promoter) may try to act on behalf of the company before incorporation. If this happens, the promoter does so at her own risk, as she is personally liable on any contract made (CA 2006, s 51); the company when formed does not have take over the contract.

So, say that the promoter enters into a contract to buy a piece of land (for a factory) on behalf of the company before it is formed. At this point in time, under s 51 of the CA 2006 the liability for the contract, for example paying the purchase price, is the promoter's alone and not the company's (as it does not exist). If, once the company is formed, the directors wish the company to be party to this pre-incorporation contract, they must enter into a contract of novation (an entirely new contract) with the seller of the land, replacing the pre-incorporation contract. If the directors refuse to do this then the promoter will have to pay the purchase price and become owner of the property herself. The seller of the land can enforce the contract against her as the contract was made with her. Such a situation is not usually a problem in practice, as the promoter very often goes on to be a shareholder and director of the new company.

If the promoter is unwilling to take on the risk of personal liability which arises on pre-incorporation contracts, it is possible for her to negotiate a draft agreement on the behalf of the yet to be formed company which the company will then execute once formed. Clearly, one of the big potential disadvantages to this approach is that no contract is made initially, which means that the other contracting party is not compelled to sign the contract once the company is formed.

Another possible solution is for the pre-incorporation contract to be signed by the promoter and become binding, but for it to include a contractual provision ending her personal liability for the contract if the newly-formed company takes over the contract on the same terms. Section 51 of the CA 2006 allows this by making the promoter personally liable, 'subject to any agreement to the contrary'.

5.3 JOINING THE COMPANY

There are two requirements as regards becoming a shareholder of a private company limited by shares and sharing in the potential risks and rewards of being its owner. Under s 112 of the CA 2006:

(a) the person must agree to become a shareholder of the company; and
(b) their name must be entered in the register of members (see **5.4** below).

The different circumstances in which a person may become a shareholder are set out below.

5.3.1 The subscribers to the memorandum

Those persons who signed the memorandum of association as 'subscribers' (see **3.14** above) automatically become the first shareholders of the company when the Registrar of Companies issues the certificate of incorporation (CA 2006, ss 112(1) and 16(5)). Their agreement to become shareholders is deemed given, and their name or names must be entered in the register of members (CA 2006, s 112(1)).

In a small new company, the subscribers will be the entrepreneurs who have registered their private company limited by shares in accordance with the procedures set out in **Chapter 3** in order to run their business. On registration they become the owners of the company.

5.3.2 Buying shares from the company

A company will often seek to raise money by issuing new shares to shareholders in return for money or money's worth (such as property). The company might decide to issue these new shares to the existing shareholders, or it might wish to bring in outsider investors and therefore new shareholders. The procedure for buying new shares from the company is called the allotment of shares. The allottee (the purchaser) agrees to become a shareholder by formally applying to the company to buy the new shares, and becomes a shareholder when their name is entered in the register of members (CA 2006, s 112(2)). The procedure for allotting new shares is discussed further at **9.3** below.

5.3.3 Buying shares from existing shareholders

Shares in a company are a form of property, and as such may be bought or sold. If an existing shareholder wishes to reduce or remove their financial investment in the company, they may try to sell some or all of their shares to another person. That other person who buys the shares will themselves become a shareholder of the company. When this happens, no new money is generated for the company. It is just a question of a change in the ownership of shares and thereby in the company itself.

The procedure for buying existing shares in a company is called the transfer of shares. The transferee (the purchaser) agrees to become a shareholder by submitting the share transfer (the contract for sale of the shares) to the company, and becomes a shareholder when their name is entered in the register of members (CA 2006, s 112(2)). The directors must enter the name of a person who has received shares by transfer in the register of members, unless the articles of the company give them discretion not to do so, in which case the transferee will not become a shareholder of the company and the shares will remain legally owned by the seller, ie the transferor. Most private companies give such discretion to their directors in their articles, in which case it is the directors who will decide whether the transferee can become a shareholder.

The procedure for registering a transfer of shares, including the right of the directors to refuse registration and its effects, is discussed further at **9.5** below.

5.3.4 Receiving a gift of shares

Shares, being property, may be given away instead of being sold. In such a case, the existing shareholder may choose to gift some or all of their shares. In either case, the recipient or recipients of the shares will become a new shareholder or shareholders in the company. Again, no new money is created for the company here, but ownership has changed. The process of becoming a shareholder by receiving a gift of shares is also known as the transfer of shares (as in **5.3.3** above). The recipient of the gift (the transferee) agrees to become a shareholder by submitting the share transfer (the document transferring ownership) to the company, and becomes a shareholder when their name is entered in the register of members (CA 2006, s 112(2)), subject to the directors not exercising any discretion to refuse to register the transfer of ownership. The procedure for gifting shares in the company, including the right of the directors to refuse registration, is discussed further at **9.5** below.

5.3.5 Inheriting shares

Shares may be bequeathed under a will (or, if none exists, will become subject to the rules of intestacy). The shares will, on the death of the shareholder, automatically vest in the personal representatives of the deceased. This is known as a transmission of shares (where the change occurs by operation of law). If this happens, the personal representatives may or may not be the same people as the ultimate beneficiaries of the shares (depending on the terms of the will or the intestacy rules). Therefore the transmittees (here the personal representatives) will either become the shareholders if they are the ultimate beneficiaries of the shares, or transfer the shares on to the ultimate beneficiary who will become the shareholder. In other words, a transmittee might be just a temporary holder of the shares, or may become a full shareholder. In the case of a transmittee who is just a temporary shareholder, the articles of the company will usually provide for limited rights of ownership until the shares are transferred to the ultimate owner. The beneficiary agrees to become a shareholder by applying to be registered as a new shareholder, and becomes a shareholder when their name is entered in the register of members (CA 2006, s 112(2)).

The procedure for dealing with an inheritance of shares in the company is discussed further at **9.10** below.

5.3.6 Insolvency of the shareholder

If the shareholder is an individual and goes bankrupt then the bankrupt's property, including their shares, will automatically vest in a trustee in bankruptcy. This too is known as a transmission of shares (because the change occurs by operation of law). The trustee in bankruptcy will try to sell the shares to raise money to pay off the bankrupt's debts. As in **5.3.5** above, the ultimate owner will become the new shareholder in the company. The trustee will usually hold only limited rights of ownership under the company's articles, as their involvement is only temporary. The purchaser agrees to become a shareholder by applying to be registered as a new shareholder, and becomes a shareholder when their name is entered in the register of members (CA 2006, s 112(2)).

A similar procedure exists if the shareholder is itself a company and goes insolvent.

The procedure for dealing with a transmission of shares in the company on insolvency is discussed further at **9.10** below.

5.4 THE REGISTER OF MEMBERS

We have seen that, irrespective of the method by which a person acquires shares, and having agreed to become a shareholder, it is only on entry of a person's name in the register of members that they become a shareholder of the company. Every company must therefore keep a register of those persons who own shares in it (CA 2006, s 113(1)).

Note that what is described below applies only to private companies and public companies which are not publicly traded (see **1.9.3** above). The system is very different for publicly-traded companies (which must be public companies), because they may have many thousands of shareholders and shares which will usually be held in electronic form, which is not currently possible for private companies.

Section 128B of the CA 2006 allows private companies to elect not to keep their own register of members (CA 2006, s 128D(2)), and alternatively they can ensure that the necessary information is filed and kept up-to-date on the central register for the company held at Companies House. All shareholders must agree for this election to be valid (CA 2006, s 128B(2)(a)), and the Registrar of Companies must be notified (CA 2006, ss 128B(3) and 128C(1)). During the time that this election not to have a register of members is in force, the company must notify the Registrar of Companies as soon as is reasonably practicable of any information that otherwise would have gone into the register of members (CA 2006, s 128E(2)). This election can be withdrawn and the register of members reactivated following the procedure in CA 2006, s 128J.

The Economic Crime and Corporate Transparency Act 2023 (ECCTA) will remove the right of a company to elect to keep its register of members centrally at Companies House. ECCTA will repeal ss 128B–128E and 128I. The effect of this change will be to ensure that all companies maintain their own register of members rather than relying on Companies House maintaining it. This amendment is expected to come into force by 2027.

5.4.1 Content and form

The register may be kept in hard-copy or in electronic form (CA 2006, s 1135). It must show:

(a) each shareholder's name and address (s 113(2)(a));

(b) the date of entry into the register of each shareholder (s 113(2)(b));

(c) the number of shares owned by each shareholder (s 113(3));

(d) the class of share (if there is more than one) (s 113(3)(a)(ii)); and

(e) the amount paid up on each share (s 113(3)(b)).

The register must be updated whenever necessary to reflect any changes in the membership of the company, for example when a new shareholder joins the company or when an existing one leaves. If a shareholder leaves the company then the date the shareholder left the company must also be included on the register (s 113(2)(c)).

The register of members is a very important document, as it records the past and current ownership of the company. It is therefore a criminal offence by the company and any officer of the company in default, punishable by a fine, if the register of members does not contain the correct information (CA 2006, s 113(7) and (8))

If the company is set up originally with just one shareholder, or becomes a company with only one shareholder due to the departure of an existing shareholder or shareholders, the register of members must, in addition to the information above, contain a statement that the company has only one member and the date upon which this happened (CA 2006, s 123(1) and (2)).

Similarly, if a company's membership increases from one to more than one, the register of members must in addition to the information mentioned above contain a statement that the company has ceased to have just one member, together with the date on which the number of members was increased (CA 2006, s 123(3)).

A failure to comply with these additional requirements will mean that the company and every officer in default is liable to a fine under s 123(4) and (5) of the CA 2006.

The Economic Crime and Corporate Transparency Act 2023 (ECCTA) will amend s 113 by requiring an individual name in the register of members to include the forename and surname, unless they are commonly know by a title (such as 'Dame'/'Lord') in which case that title may be used instead. It will also require the individual's address for service of documents.

ECCTA also states that where an individual's name is not entered in the register of members correctly, that does not affect their right to be a shareholder.

ECCTA will also create a new rule (s 113D) requiring a shareholder to notify their company of any changes to the information required to be included in the register of members within two months of the change (s 113E). The company will also acquire a new power to require a shareholder to provide the necessary information for the register of members within one month (s 113F).

These amendments are expected to come into force by 2027.

5.4.2 Entering information

Assuming that any rights available to the directors under the company's articles to refuse to register a new shareholder are not exercised, the directors should ensure that the new shareholder's name and other details are entered on the register as soon as possible to allow the shareholder to take up their rights as an owner of the company. Section 771(1) of the CA 2006 states that a company must register a transfer as soon as is practical, and in any event within two months after the date the transfer is submitted to the company.

The prospective new shareholder's status between the date on which they acquire the shares and the date on which their name is entered on the register of members, is that they are beneficially entitled to the shares but are not the registered legal owner of them. This means that the *original* shareholder will still be treated as the owner of the shares by the company and therefore will continue to receive notice of shareholder meetings and be entitled to attend them, and will also receive dividends (payments of profit from the company) if these are paid. However, they must vote at a meeting in accordance with the instructions of the prospective shareholder, and must account to the prospective shareholder for any dividend.

The court has the power under s 125 of the CA 2006 to rectify the register of members for an unwanted omission or entry, or for default or unnecessary delay in removing a shareholder's name when leaving the company. It may at the same time order the company to pay damages to a wronged person and settle any disputes regarding ownership. This power may therefore be used not just to rectify genuine mistakes in recording information in the register, but also where there is a dispute between the directors and the new shareholder, for example where the directors refuse to register a transfer of shares to the new shareholder after a reasonable time period has elapsed, even where they have no power to do so under the articles. For an example of rectification under s 125 following a dispute over ownership, see *Avenue Road Developments Ltd v Reggies Co Ltd* [2012] EWHC 1625 (Ch).

The Economic Crime and Corporate Transparency Act 2023 will amend s 771 by introducing a new rule that a company may not register the transfer of its shares unless it has all the information necessary to complete the register of members (see above). This is expected to come into force by 2027.

5.4.3 Inspection

Under s 114(1) of the CA 2006, where the company does not keep this information on the public register at Companies House, the register of members must be kept either at the company's registered office (see **3.6** above), or at its 'single alternative inspection location' (SAIL) if specified under s 1136 of the CA 2006 (see **8.11.4** below).

The register must be available for inspection to any shareholder free of charge and to any other person on payment of a fee (CA 2006, s 116(1)), and any person may make a copy in return for payment of a fee (s 116(2)). A request must be made to the company for inspection or copying in accordance with the requirements of s 116(4), including giving the person's name, address and the purpose for which the information is to be used. The company has five working days under s 117(1) of the CA 2006, either to comply with the request or to apply to the court to disallow the request (if it thinks the request is not for a 'proper purpose') and thus prevent inspection or copying of the register. The reason for these restrictions on access to the register is to protect the privacy of shareholders of a company if that company is involved in controversial work, such as that likely to provoke the ire of animal rights campaigners or anti-abortion campaigners (see **3.10.2** above). If the company allows the request, it must make clear the latest date on which amendments were made to the register (if any) and that there were no further amendments to be made (CA 2006, s 120(1)).

The Court of Appeal held that a request to inspect the register was not for a 'proper purpose' in *Burberry Group plc v Richard Charles Fox-Davies* [2014] EWCA Civ 604. In doing so it stated that the onus was on the company to show that the request was made for an improper purpose, and that the courts could take account of a guidance note from the Institute of Chartered Secretaries and Administrators (ICSA) (now known as The Chartered Governance Institute), which gives examples of proper and improper purposes, although this does not bind the court. The Court of Appeal also held the request to be invalid because the request (by a company seeking to trace missing shareholders for a fee) did not include all the required details, such as the shareholder's name.

The company and every officer in default (under s 118(1)) will commit an offence for failure, without a s 117 court order, to allow inspection or copying of the register; and the person making the request will commit an offence (under s 119(1)) if they knowingly or recklessly make a statement which is materially misleading, false or deceptive.

Under s 120A, the Secretary of State for DBT has the power to make regulations requiring a company to refrain from using or disclosing 'individual membership information' except in specified circumstances, where an application to the Registrar is made to request this. These regulations will enable shareholders to apply to the Registrar to prevent both the fact that they are, or were, a shareholder of the company and the personal information required to be included on the register of members from being divulged.

The relevant regulations are expected to be introduced in summer 2025. Please check the Companies House website for the latest information.

5.5 PSC REGISTER

Section 790M of the CA 2006 requires companies to keep a 'PSC register'. This is a register setting out details of persons with significant control (PSC) in the company. The idea behind the register is to increase transparency about who actually owns the company, with the aim of increasing trust for third parties dealing with it and to deter illicit activity through the use of companies. The register must be made available for public inspection. Note that this requirement applies only to private companies and public companies that are not publicly traded (see **1.9.3** above).

A 'person with significant control' is defined in s 790C of and Sch 1A to the CA 2006. Broadly, it means any individual who:

(a) owns more than 25% of the shares in the company (this would include non-voting shares, such as preference shares); or

(b) owns or controls more than 25% of the voting rights in the company (this would usually be ordinary shares); or

(c) has the right to appoint or remove a majority of the board of directors of the company; or

(d) has the right to exercise, or who actually exercises, significant influence or control over the company.

This definition extends to a 'relevant legal entity' (RLE) (CA 2006, s 790C(6)), which is not a real individual. The entity is deemed to be an individual for these purposes. In other words, not only must a human individual who owns, say, 30% of the shares in company Y be entered in company Y's PSC register, but so must company X, which owns a further 35% of company Y's shares.

Under ss 790D and 790E of the CA 2006, the company is placed under an obligation to investigate, obtain and update information relevant for the register. Additional obligations are placed on the individual or individuals concerned by ss 790G and 790H, to notify the company of their significant control.

The information to be included in the PSC register for individuals is set out in s 790K and includes the individual's name, date of birth, nationality, country of usual residence, residential address and address for service of documents. For a relevant legal entity this information comprises its corporate or firm name, registered or principal office, the legal form of the entity and the law by which it is governed, the register of companies in which it is entered and its registration number (if relevant).

Under the Register of People with Significant Control Regulations 2016 (SI 2016/339), there are three different levels of significant control which need to be notified and which need to be included in the PSC register:

(1) where the person holds more than 25% but not more than 50% of the shares in the company; or

(2) where the person holds more than 50% but less than 75% of the shares in the company; or

(3) where the person holds 75% or more of the shares in the company.

Under s 790E(5) the company must include this information on the PSC register within 14 days from the day after it becomes aware of a change or has reasonable cause to believe there has been a change.

Sanctions for breach of Part 21A are set out in Sch 1B to the CA 2006.

Pursuant to s 790X of the CA 2006, private companies can elect not to keep their own PSC register, and alternatively they can ensure that the necessary information is filed and kept up-to-date on the central register for the company held at Companies House.

In addition the company must notify Companies House when someone becomes a PSC or is no longer a PSC by using forms PSC01 to PSC09. For example:

- PSC01 is used when an individual becomes a PSC
- PSC02 is used when an RLE becomes a PSC

- PSC04 is used for a change in details (including when the percentage of shares crosses one of the 25%, 50% or 75% thresholds set out above)
- PSC07 is used when either an individual or an RLE ceases to be a PSC.

The deadline for filing is 14 days after the deadline of 14 days for completing the register mentioned above.

The Economic Crime and Corporate Transparency Act 2023 will remove the requirement for a company to maintain a PSC register. Furthermore, it will also remove the right of a company to elect to keep its PSC register centrally at Companies House. Under a new s 790LA of the CA 2006, a company will be required to notify Companies House of a person who becomes or ceases to be a PSC within 14 days. These changes are expected to come into force by 2027. For a new PSC, the information to be provided on the PSC will be the same as currently required by s 790K.

In addition, the notification may include confirmation that the person's identity has been verified in accordance with the new procedure under s 1110A (see ***3.11*** *above). This verification system is not yet fully in force. From 8 April 2025, individual PSCs can voluntarily have their identity verified. Compulsory verification is expected to start in autumn 2025 for new PSCs. Existing PSCs will have a year from this date to seek verification of their identity. The system is therefore expected to be completely operational by the end of 2026.*

A new s 790LC of the CA 2006 will require notification of any changes to the details of a PSC within 14 days. Also, under a new s 790LD, a company must notify Companies House of any changes to the information in an initial statement of PSC between submitting the application for registration of a new company and its incorporation within 14 days of becoming aware of the change. These changes are expected to come into force by 2027.

5.6 SHAREHOLDERS' RIGHTS

The shareholders of a company are the owners of the company. They own the company in proportion to the number of shares they hold. But what does it mean to be an owner of the company? The shareholder has an array of legal rights and some obligations in relation to the company which flow principally from both contract law and statute.

5.6.1 Limited liability

As we saw at **1.9** above, one of the greatest advantages of being a shareholder of a limited company is that the shareholder's liability is generally limited to paying the agreed price for their shares. Generally shareholders have no personal liability for the company's debts, however great those debts may be. This is because the company is a legal person in its own right. Any debts owed by the company are the responsibility of that company and not of any individuals involved in it (see **2.3.4** above).

5.6.2 Shareholders' contractual rights

The shareholders of a company have contractual rights which flow from two main sources. The first is the statutory contract created under s 33 of the CA 2006. The second are rights arising under a shareholders' agreement made between the shareholders.

5.6.2.1 Section 33 contract

We considered this contract at **4.3.4** above. Section 33 of the CA 2006 creates a special contract between the shareholder on the one hand and the company on the other, and also between the shareholders themselves on the basis of the company's constitution. We noted that 'membership rights' only, such as the right to vote or to a dividend (share of profit), were enforceable by a shareholder. The contract also imposes the obligation on the shareholder to observe the terms of the constitution, particularly the company's articles.

The articles may set out partially or fully the rights which attach to shares in a company. These rights are then exercisable by the shareholder. To the extent that there is nothing in the articles, recourse may be had to the CA 2006 and to the common law to identify the shareholder's rights regarding the shares. The rights will as a minimum cover sharing in the profits of the company, sharing in any surplus on a profitable winding up of the company and any voting rights at shareholder meetings.

5.6.2.2 Shareholders' agreement

It is also common for shareholders of a company to enter into a private contract with one another as to how they will behave in relation to their company (a shareholders' agreement). It is important to note that normally this does not involve the company itself. The company will not therefore usually be a party to this contract. In addition, it is not compulsory for the shareholders to enter a shareholders' agreement. It is for each shareholder to enter freely into the contract if the shareholder decides it is in their interests to do so. Ideally, all shareholders would enter the agreement so that they are all bound by its terms, but they cannot be compelled to do so.

Shareholder agreements may take many forms, and the need for them can arise in very different circumstances. Here, we consider the type of agreement which may commonly be entered into when a new, small private company is established to run the entrepreneurs' business.

The benefits of a shareholders' agreement

The importance of entering into the agreement is that it will bind all the parties to the terms, and the usual remedies for breach of contract will be available if any of the parties breaches the terms. A shareholders' agreement might typically include provisions as to what business the company can do, what matters require the shareholders' (rather than just the directors') consent, the transfer of shares, the issue of new shares and holding a directorship of the company.

Some of these matters will also (or alternatively) be dealt with in the company's articles, and in that case any requirements would apply to all shareholders (including future ones). This may be advantageous, but there may be greater benefits from including them in a shareholders' agreement, depending on the circumstances of the particular company and shareholders involved, for the following reasons:

(a) *A shareholders' agreement can deal with matters which are personal to the shareholders.* Including such personal rights in a shareholders' agreement means that they become contractually enforceable, whereas this would not be the case if they were included in the company's articles and reliance placed on the contract under s 33 of the CA 2006 (see **5.6.2.1** above). For example, the right for a specified individual to be appointed a director is a personal right and is not enforceable if included in the company's articles. By including the right to be appointed in the agreement, the shareholder would be able to seek damages or an injunction for breach of contract if other shareholders breached the agreement and did not appoint them as a director.

(b) *A shareholders' agreement can help protect a minority shareholder.* Under the usual contractual principles, all contracting parties must agree to amend the agreement. Each shareholder therefore has an equal say. By contrast, under the CA 2006, shareholder power is determined by the proportion of voting rights in the company, eg the articles of the company may be changed by special resolution under s 21 of the CA 2006 (see **4.4** above), which requires a 75% majority vote. The shareholders' agreement, however, might include a provision that all shareholders must vote to change the articles. In other words, the shareholders have agreed amongst themselves to raise the threshold from 75% to 100%. The consent of every shareholder is required not only to change the articles but also to amend the shareholders' agreement and the requirement for 100% support for changing the articles. If shareholders with 75% of the votes did vote to amend the articles against the wishes of the remaining 25%, the 25% shareholders could seek damages or an injunction for breach of contract against those shareholders voting for the change, whereas without the agreement there would be no such remedy.

(c) *The shareholders' agreement being a private contract does not need to be made publicly available.* Contrast this with the articles of association of all companies, which must be filed at Companies House and can be read by anyone (see **4.3**). The shareholders' agreement therefore allows for confidentiality.

There are, however, limitations as to what may be included in a shareholders' agreement. Nothing may be included that fetters the company's powers to exercise its statutory duties. For example, the company itself cannot include in its articles a provision that increases the threshold under s 21 of the CA 2006 to more than 75% before a resolution can be passed to amend the articles; only the shareholders can agree to do this privately. Also, the shareholders cannot agree to anything that would bind them as to how they might vote as directors, if they also held this position, as otherwise they might possibly breach their duties as directors (see **6.6**).

Typical clauses in a shareholders' agreement

Examples of what a typical shareholders' agreement might contain include the following:

(a) An undertaking that the company will not amend its articles without the consent of all parties.

(b) Similar undertakings regarding changes in capital or share capital structure.

(c) Requirements on unanimity among shareholders for major decisions (eg the sale of the business).

(d) Restrictions on borrowing and offering security over the company's assets.

(e) Agreements regarding further financing for the company.

(f) Agreement on dividend policy (ie sharing profit).

(g) Any disputes between shareholders to be referred to arbitration.

(h) The right for each party, or specific parties, to be a director and/or be employed or take part in management, or the right to nominate a specified number of directors.

(i) Agreement not to compete with the company's business.

(j) Agreement on treatment of intellectual property rights (if relevant).

(k) Provisions dealing with the departure of a shareholder.

(l) Provisions for the resolution of deadlock in decision-making.

Note that there is no reason why a shareholders' agreement cannot include a non-shareholder as a party, for example a director of the company who is not a shareholder in it.

5.6.3 Shareholders' statutory rights

A shareholder also gains a significant number of rights from statute, particularly from the CA 2006. Some of the more important rights are set out below.

5.6.3.1 Share certificate

A shareholder must receive from the company a share certificate within two months either of allotment (if new shares are being issued) under s 769(1) of the CA 2006, or of lodging the transfer with the company (if existing shares are being transferred from an existing shareholder) under s 776(1) of the Act. Under s 768(1), this document, which states how many shares the shareholder owns, is prima facie evidence of title to the shares (ie ownership). As such, it is crucial that the shareholder be given a copy of it by the company.

This does not apply to publicly-traded companies whose shares are in electronic form, which are subject to a different system.

5.6.3.2 Register of members

Assuming that any right to refuse to register a transfer of shares under the company's articles (if it exists) is not exercised by the directors, the new shareholder has a right to be entered in the register of members within two months of the transfer (see **5.4.2** above). We have seen that this step is essential for a shareholder to become a full shareholder of the company.

5.6.3.3 Key company documentation

A company must send copies of certain important documents about the constitution and finances of the company to its shareholders. For example, it must send to its shareholders, if these are requested, copies of the company's constitutional documents (CA 2006, s 32). These include up-to-date articles and the certificate of incorporation. This ensures that the shareholder has access to the key rules governing the running of the company.

Section 32 also allows the shareholder to request the company's current statement of capital. Further, under s 423, a copy of the company's annual accounts and accompanying reports must be sent to all shareholders each year. No request is required. This enables the shareholder to gain full access to information on the company's share capital and its financial situation.

A shareholder may also demand a copy of a director's service contract (CA 2006, s 229(1)).

5.6.3.4 Inspection of company information

Minutes of all general meetings must be kept at the company's registered office or at its SAIL (if specified under s 1136 of the CA 2006 – see **8.11.4** below). The company's shareholders must be permitted to read those minutes if they so wish (CA 2006, s 358(1)).

The various company registers (eg the register of members, directors, secretaries (if applicable) and charges (see **8.11.2** below)) must be made available for inspection by the shareholders at the company's registered office or SAIL.

In addition, other key information regarding the company must be made available for inspection by the shareholders, including the directors' service contracts, instruments creating charges and contracts relating to the buy-back of shares (see eg **9.5.3.2** below).

This transparency aims to empower the shareholders with knowledge of the most important individuals involved with the company, the key decisions it has taken and significant contracts it has entered.

The Economic Crime and Corporate Transparency Act 2023 will remove the requirement of a company to keep a register of directors, directors' addresses, secretaries and the PSC register. The register of members will be retained. These amendments are expected to come into force by 2027.

5.6.3.5 Voting rights

The right to vote at shareholders' general meetings is an extremely important right for shareholders of a company, as this is the way in which they exercise their powers and take decisions affecting the company. Whilst a company has some flexibility to regulate their meetings in its articles, the CA 2006 provides a number of protections for the shareholders. For example, instead of attending general meetings and voting in person, a shareholder has the right, under s 324(1) of the CA 2006, to send a proxy (a stand-in) to attend, speak and vote (both on a show of hands and a poll) in their place.

Shareholders may vote at general meetings in one of two ways:

(a) on a show of hands; or

(b) on a poll vote.

All shareholders with at least 10% of the company's shares have the right to demand a poll vote (CA 2006, s 321(1)). If a vote is taken on a show of hands, every shareholder has one vote; if a poll vote is taken, each shareholder has one vote for every share they own. This right will be exercised if a vote is first passed by a show of hands and produces an unfair result. For example, if there are three shareholders and two vote for the resolution but one votes against, the resolution is passed on a show of hands. But imagine that the one shareholder who voted against the resolution owns 80% of the company's shares. Clearly the vote on the show of hands would be unfair, as the two shareholders who passed the resolution own only 20% of the shares and they have overturned the wishes of the majority owner. A poll vote would result in the resolution being defeated by 80% to 20%, and fairness is restored.

5.6.3.6 Notice of general meetings

Under ss 307 to 311 of the CA 2006, all shareholders must be given proper notice of a shareholders' general meeting; and if this is not done, any business transacted at the general meeting is invalid. Notice is simply advance warning of and information about the meeting. Shareholders must be given sufficient information in the notice of the general meeting to enable them to know what is to be proposed. The exact wording of special resolutions must be set out, and enough information must given on any ordinary resolutions for members to decide whether they should attend in order to vote.

5.6.3.7 Written resolution

Shareholders of the company holding at least 5% of the total voting shares in the company (or less if the articles so specify) have the right to circulate a written resolution and an accompanying statement of up to 1,000 words under s 292(1) of the CA 2006. A written resolution is an alternative mechanism for shareholders to take decisions without having to hold a general meeting (see **8.9** below).

Any request from shareholders must be made in hard-copy or electronic form, be authenticated by the people making it, and identify the resolution and accompanying statement (CA 2006, s 292(6)). The company must then circulate the resolution and statement to all shareholders in hard-copy or electronic form, or by posting it on a website so far as reasonably practical, at the same time as and within 21 days after its submission (CA 2006, s 293).

This is a very important right for the shareholders to shape decision-making in the company. However, it should be noted that private company shareholders may be made to pay the company's expenses for circulating this statement (CA 2006, s 294(1)).

5.6.3.8 Written statement

Shareholders of the company have the right under s 314(1) of the CA 2006 to circulate a written statement of up to 1,000 words about a proposed resolution or other business of a shareholders' meeting. In contrast to the written resolution in **5.6.3.7** above, this is not an attempt by the shareholders to have a decision taken but to have their views circulated among all shareholders. This right is available:

(a) to shareholders holding at least 5% of the total voting shares in the company; or

(b) to at least 100 shareholders who hold at least an average of £100 of paid-up share capital (CA 2006, s 314(2)).

The second option will in practice be relevant only to much larger public companies, particularly those which are publicly traded, where 100 shareholders may not jointly own the required 5% of the company's shares.

Any request from shareholders must be made in hard-copy or electronic form, be authenticated by the people making it, and be deposited at the company's registered office at least one week before the relevant general meeting (CA 2006, s 314(4)). The company must then circulate the statement to all shareholders under s 315(1), either with the notice of the general meeting or, if that has already been sent out, as soon as possible thereafter.

Although an important right for the shareholders as owners of the company, because it counterbalances the directors' power (in managing the company) by enabling their views to be circulated in advance of the meeting, generally this provision will used by larger private companies and public companies where there are a larger number of shareholders who are not in regular contact with one another. It should be noted that private company shareholders may have to pay the company's expenses in circulating this statement (CA 2006, s 316(2)).

5.6.3.9 Removal of director and auditor

Section 168(1) of the CA 2006 permits the company's shareholders to remove a director of their company by passing an ordinary resolution (over 50% votes in favour) at a shareholders' general meeting, regardless of any agreement to the contrary (see further **6.10.3** below). This right reflects the reality that it is the shareholders who are the owners of the company and it is the directors who are managing the company on the shareholders' behalf. A majority vote of the company's owners should therefore have the right to determine who will manage their investment in the company.

Section 510(1) of the CA 2006 sets out a parallel provision allowing the company's shareholders to remove the auditor of their company by passing an ordinary resolution at a shareholders' general meeting, regardless of any agreement to the contrary. The auditor, if required, has a crucial role regarding approval of the company's accounts (see **6.11**). It is therefore important that the owners of the company have confidence in the auditor and that they can take action if they do not.

5.6.3.10 Court proceedings

Shareholders of the company have the right to go to court under the CA 2006 in relation to certain of the most important transactions which affect its share capital. For example, under s 721(1), any shareholder may apply to court to cancel a resolution approving the buy-back of shares out of capital (see **9.5.3.2** below).

The aim is to ensure that any valid objections are heard in full in relation to decisions which in practice return the company's protected pool of money, the share capital, to its shareholders rather than keeping it in the company.

5.6.3.11 Calling a general meeting

The usual way for general meetings to be called is by the directors (see **8.2** below). However, shareholders of the company holding at least 5% of the company's shares have the right to require the directors to call a general meeting of the shareholders (CA 2006, s 303(1)) by depositing a written request at the company's registered office. This so-called 'requisition' must comply with the requirements of the Act (see **8.7.3.2** below). If the directors do not take the required action then the requisitioning shareholders themselves may call a general meeting; or if this is not practical, they may go to court under s 306 of the CA 2006 (see **5.6.3.12** below) and ask the court to order a meeting to be held.

This right protects minority shareholders in a company, particularly where the directors and majority shareholders hold opposing views to the minority. It allows the minority to force a shareholders' meeting to be held which the directors would otherwise not call and, if desired, to have a resolution (decision) of their choosing voted upon.

5.6.3.12 Court-ordered general meeting

Any shareholder (and also a director) may apply to the court under s 306 of the CA 2006 for an order that a general meeting be held, if for some reason it is impracticable for one to be held otherwise (eg, where other shareholders are refusing to attend general meetings and it is therefore impossible to hold one which is quorate, ie with the minimum required for valid decisions to be taken). The court has the power to order the meeting to be called, held or conducted in any manner it sees fit. It can also make such ancillary directions as it might think appropriate. In the situation above, where a quorate meeting is impossible, the court might order that the quorum for a particular general meeting should be reduced to one, as happened in *Smith v Butler* [2011] EWHC 2301 (Ch), applying CA 2006, s 306(4), as a result of dispute between director-shareholders where two directors refused to attend board meetings leaving the remaining director unable to take decisions.

5.6.3.13 Breach of constitution

We saw at **4.6.1.2** above that shareholders may seek to restrain a breach of directors' duties before the event, or take action afterwards under s 40 of the CA 2006 if the directors exceed their powers under the company's constitution.

5.6.3.14 Unfair prejudice

If any shareholder feels that the company's affairs are being conducted in a manner which is 'unfairly prejudicial' to them, they have a right under s 994(1) of the CA 2006 to petition the court for a remedy. The complaint may be based on past, present or even anticipated future events, and the conduct may be unfairly prejudicial to all of the members or to only some or one of them (*Re a Company (No 004175 of 1986)* [1987] BCLC 574). Whether what has happened, is happening or will happen amounts to 'unfair prejudice' is judged on an objective basis, from the perspective of an impartial outsider. The conduct must be both unfair and prejudicial. The essential element of 'unfairness' is breach of the agreement between shareholders as to how the company is to be run (*O'Neill v Phillips* [1999] 1 WLR 1092). For the petition to be successful, the shareholder must also prove that they have been affected in their capacity as a shareholder, although this has been given a very wide interpretation (*Gamlestaden Fastigheter v Baltic Partners Limited* [2008] 1 BCLC 468).

In order to establish unfair prejudice, it is not necessary to prove that the value of the shareholder's shares has been adversely affected, although frequently this will have happened. Examples of potential unfair prejudice are:

(a) non-payment of dividends;

(b) directors awarding themselves excessive remuneration;

(c) directors exercising their powers for an improper purpose (eg to 'freeze out' a minority shareholder); and

(d) exclusion from management in a small company (eg one formed on the understanding that all those involved will share the running of the business and the profits).

In *VB Football Assets v Blackpool Football Club Ltd and Others* [2017] EWHC 2767 (Ch) the court found that on the facts improper payments out of the company, a failure to pay dividends and deliberate exclusion from company decisions were unfairly prejudicial to a minority shareholder whereas changes to the articles of association were not.

In *Re CF Booth Ltd (sub nom Booth v Booth)* [2017] EWHC 457 (Ch) it was held that there had been unfairly prejudicial conduct by a company's majority shareholders and directors maintaining a policy of paying no dividends while the directors were excessively remunerated.

In *Sharafi v Woven Rugs Ltd (in administration)* [2010] EWHC 230 (Ch), the conduct of a director in making payments to his personal company at the expense of the original company and its minority shareholders was held to be unfairly prejudicial under s 994.

If the court finds that a shareholder has suffered unfair prejudice, it may make any order it thinks appropriate under s 996(1) of the CA 2006. Examples of the types of order the court may grant are given in s 996(2) and include the most common remedy, namely, an order that the other shareholders or the company itself should purchase the shares of the petitioner at a fair value (CA 2006, s 996(2)(e)).

The Court of Appeal has held that the normal way of dealing with internal company disputes in small private companies where unfairly prejudicial conduct had been proved is an order for a share purchase under s 996 (*Grace v Biagioli* [2005] EWCA Civ 1022). In *Nagi v Nagi* [2006] Lawtel AC0111971, it was held that one director removing another director without notifying him amounted to unfair prejudicial conduct. A buy-out under s 996 was therefore ordered by the court. A more recent example may be seen in the decision in *In the matter of Home & Office Fire Extinguishers Ltd* [2012] EWHC 917 (Ch) after one of two director/shareholders attacked the other with a hammer after he was refused an advance on his salary and there was no prospect of the two working together again.

If a company is a 'quasi-partnership', ie a small group of participants who are both directors and shareholders, equitable considerations come into play. This makes it more likely that a court would grant an order under s 996 to buy out the disaffected party (*Strahan v Wilcock* [2006] EWCA Civ 13).

However, in *O'Neill v Phillips* [1999] 1 WLR 1092, the House of Lords made it clear that although the court's powers under s 996 of the CA 2006 were wide, that provision did not give an automatic right to withdrawal from a company where trust and confidence had broken down. For example, in *Re Phoenix Office Supplies Limited* [2003] 1 BCLC 76, the Court of Appeal held that the petitioner, who had voluntarily severed his links with the company, could not use a s 994 petition as a way of trying to obtain the highest price possible for the sale of his shares.

The Court of Appeal held, in *Fulham Football Club (1987) Ltd v Richards* [2011] EWCA Civ 855, that where the parties had agreed to binding arbitration to settle a matter of unfair prejudice, proceedings would not be allowed under s 994 of the CA 2006. This means that s 994 does not give a shareholder an inalienable right to bring a claim under the CA 2006.

5.6.3.15 Winding up the company

Any shareholder may make an application under s 122(1)(g) of the IA 1986 to have the company wound up on the ground that it is 'just and equitable' to do so, provided they can prove that they have a 'tangible interest', ie that the company is solvent and they will therefore get back some or all of the money originally invested. The court has granted such applications in a wide variety of situations, for example where the management is in deadlock, where the shareholders have no confidence in the management, where the company can no longer carry on the business for which it was formed and, in a quasi-partnership situation (eg a company owned 50:50 by two shareholders who are also the only two directors) where one of those involved is being excluded from management.

A petition for winding up is clearly the 'nuclear' option – a remedy of last resort – because if it is successful, the company will cease to exist and the shareholders will no longer have an investment, and the directors will no longer have a job even though the company is solvent. Therefore, a shareholder will usually petition the court for unfair prejudice under s 994 instead (see **5.6.3.14** above). See also **Chapter 19** on corporate insolvency.

5.7 THE SHAREHOLDER'S ROLE

Shareholders provide some or all of the financial backing for the company. The money produced by the sale of the shares from the company to its shareholders enables the company to commence and continue in business. In exchange for leaving their money with the company (having bought the shares), a shareholder may receive an income payment from the company (a dividend) and may benefit from the capital appreciation of the value of their shares. Equally, a shareholder's shares may decrease in value if the company is not successful.

The rights set out at **5.6** above give examples of the sorts of things that the shareholders of the company can do. However, many of those rights will in practice be exercised only if there is disagreement or a dispute between the directors and the shareholders (if different people), or between different shareholders (particularly between majority shareholders (owning over 50% of the voting shares) and minority shareholders (owning less than 50%)).

Normally it is the directors who make the day-to-day decisions affecting the company (eg, art 3 of the model articles for a private company), and they will involve the shareholders and call them to a meeting only when the need arises under the CA 2006, for example because it is required under s 21 of the Act in order to change the company's articles or under s 188 to authorise a service contract for a director which gives them job security for more than two years. Shareholders who are happy with the direction their company is taking and their dividend will usually let the directors get on and do their job. Their involvement will principally be through voting at general meetings. Shareholders of a company with model articles do have the right to direct their directors to do or refrain from taking action by special resolution (art 4), but this power will be exercised rarely in practice.

The effect of the directors having day-to-day control is that if the shareholders do not like the way in which the board is running the company, they cannot simply overturn the board's decisions. Instead they have the right to remove directors from office (see **5.6.3.9** above), and usually the right to appoint new directors, in the company's articles (eg, art 17 of the model articles for private companies), both by ordinary resolution. Thus, a majority of shareholders' votes could remove all the existing directors and replace them. It is not a decision which can be taken lightly, though, as it involves considerations of company law and employment law.

It is worth remembering that, particularly in smaller private companies, a shareholder may also be a director of the company (although is not required to be). In this case the law still requires that the roles are kept totally distinct, but in practice life will be easier, because a director who takes a decision as director will undoubtedly support it as a shareholder.

The degree of involvement by shareholders in their chosen company ultimately will vary considerably, depending on the size of their shareholding, the size of the company, the financial success of the company, and the wishes of the shareholders and the directors.

5.8 PROTECTION OF MINORITY SHAREHOLDERS

Having seen what the rights and role of a company shareholder are, it is important to note there are some key restrictions on what majority shareholders can do as owners of the company in order to protect the rights of the minority shareholders in that company. Shareholders acting together (or an individual) owning over 50% of the voting rights in a company are known as majority shareholders as they have a majority of the votes. Those shareholders holding less than 50% of the company's shares are known as minority shareholders.

5.8.1 Majority rule

Power amongst the shareholders of a company is determined by voting rights, which in turn depends on the type of shares owned (see **5.9** below). Put simply, usually, the more shares owned, the more power a shareholder has. Shareholder power is exercised in a company on the basis of what is known as 'majority rule'. If there is a disagreement among the shareholders then the owner or owners of a majority of the voting shares will decide the outcome.

The reality, however, is that most decisions affecting a company are taken by the directors who manage it on a day-to-day basis. The directors are subject to a raft of legal duties owed to the company (see **Chapter 6**). The question arises as to what should happen if the directors breach their duties to the company. The rule in *Foss v Harbottle* (1843) 2 Hare 461 answers this question. The rule has two elements to it. First, it is for the company itself, rather than an individual shareholder, to bring a claim for a wrong done to the company (the 'proper claimant rule'). Secondly, the courts will not interfere with the internal management of the company acting within its powers, so where a wrong is alleged against the company, it is for a majority of the shareholders to decide whether to make a claim on behalf of the company or to ratify that wrong by passing an ordinary resolution (the 'internal management rule').

The rule in *Foss v Harbottle* extends the principle of majority rule. If there is some irregularity in internal management, it is for the directors, rather than the shareholders, to decide whether to take action in the company name. If the directors cannot or will not take action, the majority shareholders may do so in the name of the company; a minority shareholder may not. Clearly, there is little point in allowing minority shareholders the right to commence legal action in the company name when the wrong can be ratified by an ordinary resolution passed by the majority. This rule has been applied in many circumstances, even where the minority shareholder alleged that the directors were acting in breach of EU competition law with the intention of damaging the company (*O'Neill v Ryanair Ltd* [1990] 2 IR 200). Thus, in many cases, the rule preventing minority shareholders from taking legal action is justifiable, as it means that the court's time is not wasted.

Although the principle of majority rule and the rule in *Foss v Harbottle* bring advantages to the running of a company, in practice they can also give rise to unfairness. For example, if the wrong-doing director is also a majority shareholder who ratifies their wrong-doing by passing an ordinary resolution. The director in this case has used their majority power as a shareholder unfairly to right a wrong. The same applies where a number of directors together constitute a majority shareholding at general meetings. Protection is therefore available to the minority shareholder in certain situations.

5.8.2 Statutory protection

Minority shareholders have little direct power within the company, as they cannot be certain of passing any resolutions at a general meeting without the backing of other shareholders. But these minority shareholders are by no means powerless. They have all of the rights of shareholders mentioned at **5.6.3** above (subject to minimum shareholdings in certain cases), and these may be useful in protecting the position of a minority shareholder within the company.

In particular there is the right not to be unfairly prejudiced (see **5.6.3.14** above). Where a director is also the majority shareholder, such a person should not use their majority at a general meeting to sanction an abuse by them in their capacity as a director. They cannot use it to sanction their own misdemeanours. Using a majority in this way may amount to 'unfair prejudice' to other shareholders, and those other shareholders may obtain a remedy by petitioning the court.

Other statutory rights include the right for holders of at least 5% of the voting shares to circulate a written resolution (see **5.6.3.7** above), requisition a general meeting (see **5.6.3.11** above) or to circulate a written statement at a general meeting (see **5.6.3.8** above) and to petition the court to wind up the company (see **5.6.3.15** above).

In addition there is further power, if the shareholder holds more than 25% of the company's shares, to prevent a special resolution from being passed, since a 75% majority is required for such resolutions (CA 2006, s 283(1)).

5.8.3 Shareholders' agreement

We have seen that shareholders may enter into a shareholders' agreement and, by so doing, will be bound contractually to act in accordance with the terms of that agreement. This can be used to give minority shareholders protection they would not otherwise have at a shareholders' general meeting (see **5.6.2.2** above).

5.8.4 Ratification

The right of the majority to pass an ordinary resolution to ratify wrong-doing in the company cannot be exercised where the approval of that action would be illegal or requires a special resolution under the CA 2006. For example, approving a dividend payment out of capital is prohibited by s 830 of the CA 2006, and amending the articles must be done by a special resolution under s 21 of the Act.

5.8.5 Amendments to the articles

We saw at **4.4.2.2** above that amendments to the company's articles must be 'bona fide for the benefit of the company as a whole', and that they may be challenged if they are made with the intention of discriminating against minority shareholders.

5.8.6 Derivative claim

In certain limited circumstances under the CA 2006, a minority shareholder is permitted to bring a 'derivative claim' in the company's name for a wrong committed *against the company*. This right is available, for example, where wrong-doing directors control the board and refuse to take action on behalf of the company. The minority should in this case have the right to take action on behalf of the company to protect the company. Such a claim is thus an exception to the rule in *Foss v Harbottle* (see **5.8.1** above).

It is essential to note that if the minority shareholder wishes to make a claim in respect of a wrong committed against *them* rather than against the company, they must do so in a personal claim (eg, under s 33 of the CA 2006); a derivative claim would be inappropriate.

Prior to the CA 2006, the procedure for bringing a derivative claim was a matter for the common law, and such a claim could be brought for 'fraud on the minority'. It was a very complex, uncertain and costly procedure, and as such was a significant barrier to a minority shareholder enforcing the company's rights. The procedure under ss 260 to 264 of the CA 2006 must now be used instead of the common law procedure, and seeks to address some of the previous concerns.

A claim may be brought by any shareholder under s 260(3) of the CA 2006 for an actual or proposed act or omission involving negligence, default, breach of duty or breach of trust by a director. There is no need to demonstrate any actual loss suffered by the company, or indeed any benefit gained by the directors.

A derivative claim will comprise two stages:

(a) a preliminary stage to decide whether the applicant is entitled to bring a derivative claim;

(b) then, if successful, the hearing of the claim itself.

The preliminary stage involves the applicant obtaining the permission of the court to bring a derivative claim (CA 2006, s 261(1)). It also has two stages. The court must first consider the claim, and must dismiss it under s 261(2) unless the applicant shows a prima facie case for giving permission. Only if this prima facie case is established will the court move on to the second stage and hold a full hearing to decide whether to grant permission for the derivative claim to continue or not (CA 2006, s 261(4)). The aim behind this two-step preliminary process is to weed out any frivolous or vexatious claims, or claims without merit.

Section 263 of the CA 2006 sets out the rules which a court must take into consideration at the full permission hearing, in deciding whether or not to allow the shareholder to bring the derivative claim. These include:

(a) whether or not the shareholder is acting in good faith in bringing the claim;

(b) the importance a director (who is under a duty to promote the success of the company under s 172 of the CA 2006) would place on continuing the claim; and

(c) whether authorisation or ratification of the wrong by the company would be likely.

The court must also have particular regard to any evidence put before it as to the views of shareholders who have no personal interest in the matter (CA 2006, s 263(4)).

The court must refuse permission under s 263(2) if:

(a) a person acting in accordance with the director's duty under s 172 of the CA 2006 (duty to promote the success of the company) would not seek to continue the claim; or

(b) the act or omission forming the basis of the claim has been authorised or ratified by the company. Under s 239 of the CA 2006, the ratification must be passed by the shareholders without the votes of the director concerned (assuming the director is a shareholder) or a person connected to them (eg, their wife or civil partner).

Only if successful at the permission stage will the derivative claim proceed to a full trial of the issues raised (eg, the breach of duty by the director). If this claim is successful, it will result in a remedy being awarded to the company and not the shareholder, as a derivative claim is being brought on behalf of the company.

In *Kiani v Cooper* [2010] EWHC 577 (Ch), permission to proceed with a derivative claim under s 261 of the CA 2006 was granted to a shareholder where the director in question had failed to produce evidence supporting his defence to allegations of breach of fiduciary duty.

By contrast, see *Zavahir v Shankleman* [2016] EWHC 2772 (Ch) for an example of when permission to proceed was not granted.

5.9 TYPES OF SHAREHOLDER

There are different types of shareholder whom you will come across in practice when dealing with private limited companies. An overview of the main types follows.

5.9.1 Single member company

We saw at **3.7** above that it is possible to form a limited company with just one shareholder under s 7 of the CA 2006. This type of company is called a single member company. The rules which apply to the single shareholder are identical to those that apply to a company with more than one shareholder. However, there will be certain differences in practice, reflecting the ease with which decisions can be taken in a single member company. The differences are noted where relevant in this part of the book.

A note must be made of the fact that the company is a single member company in the company's register of members (see **5.4.1** above).

5.9.2 Different classes of share

It is possible to have more than one type of share in a company, eg ordinary shares and preference shares. In such a case, the rights of the shareholders to a dividend, to vote and to a surplus on a profitable winding up of the company will vary. The rights of these different shareholders will be set out in the company's articles (see **9.6** below).

5.9.3 Joint shareholders

As with other types of property, it is possible to own a share jointly. In other words, more than one shareholder may own one shareholding, be that one or more shares. Under s 113(5) of the CA 2006, the register of members must state the names of each joint holder, but need set out just one address which will be valid for all the shareholders.

5.9.4 Corporate shareholder

As a separate legal person it is perfectly possible for a company to own shares in another company. In fact it is very common in practice for a group of related companies to come into being as a business grows, and also for certain companies to invest in other unrelated companies in order to make money.

The key difference between a corporate shareholder and a human shareholder is that a company cannot, of course, take decisions on its own and cannot turn up to shareholders' general meetings. In order to get round these difficulties, the CA 2006 requires a corporate shareholder to appoint a human to act on its behalf at general meetings. This may either be a proxy (see **5.6.3.5** above) or a corporate representative.

A corporate representative is appointed under s 323(1) of the CA 2006 by a resolution of the board of directors of the company owning the shares. The representative will then be allowed to exercise the same powers the company could exercise if it were an individual shareholder (CA 2006, s 323(2)), including the right to speak, vote (on a show of hands or poll) and appoint a proxy.

It is possible to appoint more than one representative.

5.9.5 Public company

A public company shareholder, particularly of a company which is publicly traded on the stock market, has additional rights over a private company shareholder, but is also subject to greater responsibilities to reflect the fact that these companies can offer shares to the public and their importance to the UK's economy.

5.10 SHAREHOLDER POWER

The power a shareholder wields in a company is dependent on the number of voting shares they hold in the company. **Table 5.1** below provides a summary of some of the key thresholds of shareholder power, and what that allows the shareholder with that shareholding to do.

Table 5.1 Key thresholds of shareholder power

Shareholding	*What shareholders can do*	*Restrictions*
100%	pass all resolutions at will	legality
75%	pass special resolution	weighted voting rights (if in articles) unfair prejudice petition (if wrong-doing)
over 50%	pass ordinary resolution	weighted voting rights (if in articles) unfair prejudice petition (if wrong-doing)
over 25%	block special resolution	
10%	demand poll vote	
5%	circulate a written resolution requisition a general meeting circulate a written statement	
any shareholder	vote (if voting shares) receive notice of general meetings receive dividend receive a share certificate have name on register receive a copy of accounts inspect minutes, registers and key contracts ask court for general meeting restrain breach of directors' duties bring unfair prejudice petition bring winding-up proceedings	see above if declared subject to articles (if restrictions on transfers) if company solvent

CHAPTER 6

OFFICERS OF THE COMPANY

LEARNING OUTCOMES

After reading this chapter you will be able to:

- identify the officers involved in a company
- understand the role of each of the different officers
- explain the powers and duties of a company director
- identify the legal rules which affect the company's officers.

6.1 INTRODUCTION

The officers of a company are the key persons involved in the running of the company who have responsibilities and liability for acting on its behalf. They include the company secretary, the directors and the managers of the company (CA 2006, s 1173(1)). The auditors of the company are also officers of the company (CA 2006, s 487(1)). It is, though, the directors who are the most important of all. We shall now consider the officers of the company in turn.

6.2 COMPANY SECRETARY

A private company is not required to have a company secretary (CA 2006, s 270(1)) and smaller private companies formed under the CA 2006 generally do not have them. Nonetheless, in practice some will do so, either because the company was formed before 1 October 2009, when a company secretary was compulsory, or to ensure that there is a dedicated person to deal with the company's legal administrative requirements (particularly with larger private companies).

The company secretary is an officer of the company by virtue of s 1121 of the CA 2006.

It is possible to appoint either a human or a company to act as company secretary. In the case of a corporate company secretary, the secretary will act through a human authorised by that company. It is also possible for more than one secretary to be appointed at the same time, and these persons will be known as joint company secretaries.

There is no need for a company secretary to have their identity verified (see **3.11** above).

6.2.1 Functions

If a company secretary is appointed, it is for the directors of that company to decide exactly what the company secretary should be required to do. The functions of a company secretary are not prescribed and can vary enormously, but generally they will centre around the administration of the company.

The duties are likely to be influenced by the size of the company and whether or not the company secretary works for the company full time. The full-time company secretary of a large company may be the head of an administration department. In a small company, they may well hold this post as an 'extra' on top of other full-time duties, such as a director. Alternatively, a professionally qualified person, such as a solicitor or an accountant, may be the company secretary. However, the secretary of a private company does not have to possess any specific qualifications.

The duties commonly assigned to a company secretary are:

(a) to write up the minutes of board meetings and general meetings;
(b) to keep up to date the company's internal registers; and
(c) to send the necessary returns to the Registrar of Companies.

The company secretary has apparent authority on behalf of the company to make contracts connected with the administrative side of the company's business, for example to order routine office supplies. Usually, though, the company secretary will have actual authority to enter into contracts of this type under the terms of their appointment (in the appointing board resolution or in their service contract). However, a company secretary has no apparent authority to enter into trading contracts on the company's behalf, for example to borrow money in the company's name.

If no company secretary is appointed then the duties normally performed by them will usually be taken on by others in the company. If there is a requirement in the CA 2006 for a company secretary to perform an act then it may in this case be performed either by the directors themselves, or by someone authorised specifically or generally by the directors (CA 2006, s 270(3)(b)).

6.2.2 Appointment

If appointed when the company is first registered, the first secretary of the company will be named on the statement of proposed officers on Form IN01. The company must confirm on Form IN01 on behalf of the secretary that they consent to act as such. The secretary automatically takes office when the certificate of incorporation is issued (CA 2006, s 16(6)(b)).

Subsequently, if any change occurs, the new company secretary will be appointed by the board of directors passing a board resolution. Usually this power will be expressly stated in the company's articles, although there is none in the model articles for private companies as these articles are most suited for small private companies where no company secretary is likely.

Under s 276(1)(a) of the CA 2006 the company must notify the Registrar of Companies within 14 days of the appointment of a secretary on Form AP03 for a human secretary and Form AP04 for a corporate secretary (copies available on the Companies House website at <www.gov.uk/government/organisations/companies-house>).

In addition, every company that has a company secretary must keep a register of its secretaries (CA 2006, s 275(1)) which contains the required particulars (CA 2006, s 275(2)). This register must therefore be updated whenever a secretary is appointed to the company.

Section 279A of the CA 2006 allows private companies to elect not to keep their own register of secretaries, and alternatively they can ensure that the necessary information is filed and kept up-to-date on the central register for the company held at Companies House.

The register must be available for inspection by the shareholders without charge (or for others on payment of a fee) at the company's registered office (CA 2006, s 275(3) and (5)) (or SAIL under s 1136 of the CA 2006). If this is not done, a criminal offence is committed by the company and every officer in default (CA 2006, s 275(6)).

In the case of a secretary who is a human, the particulars that are required to be entered in the register are details of the secretary's name and address for service of documents, which may simply state 'the company's registered office' (CA 2006, s 277(1) and (5)).

In the case of a corporate secretary, the particulars that are required to be entered in the register are:

(a) for a UK company, details of the corporate name, the company's registered or principal office and its registration number; and

(b) for a non-UK company, the legal form and law which governs it, together with details of its register and registration number (if relevant) (CA 2006, s 278(1)).

The Economic Crime and Corporate Transparency Act 2023 (ECCTA) will remove the requirement for a company to maintain a register of secretaries as well as the right of a company to elect to keep its register of secretaries centrally at Companies House.

ECCTA will also repeal ss 275–278 and s 279A and replace them with a new s 279G of the CA 2006 requiring a company to notify Companies House of the date of the appointment or departure of a company secretary within 14 days. For the appointment of a new secretary, s 279G requires a statement by the company:

- *setting out the required information on the secretary (contained in new s 279J (individual secretary) and s 279K (corporate secretary));*
- *confirming the secretary has consented to act as a secretary.*

These amendments are expected to come into force by 2027.

6.2.3 Terms and remuneration

The directors decide the contractual terms on which the company secretary is to hold office, and they fix the amount of the company secretary's remuneration.

6.2.4 Removal from office

The directors have the power to remove the company secretary from office at any time. The consequences of such removal will depend upon the terms of the contract fixed by the directors at the time of the company secretary's appointment, but they may include compensation for breach of contract and give rise to statutory employment law claims.

Of course, a secretary can also resign from their position.

Under s 276(1)(a) of the CA 2006 the company must notify the Registrar of Companies within 14 days of the resignation or removal of a secretary on Form TM02 (a copy is available on the Companies House website at <www.gov.uk/government/organisations/companies-house>). In addition, the register of secretaries (see **6.2.2**) must be updated whenever a secretary leaves the company.

The Economic Crime and Corporate Transparency Act 2023 will repeal s 276(1)(a) and replace it with a new s 279G(1)(b) of the CA 2006 requiring a company to notify Companies House of the date of the departure of a company secretary within 14 days.

This amendment is expected to come into force by 2027.

6.2.5 Change in details

Under s 276(1)(b) of the CA 2006 the company must notify the Registrar of Companies within 14 days of any change in the particulars for a company secretary kept in the register of secretaries (see **6.2.2**), on Form CH03 for a human secretary and on Form CH04 for a corporate secretary (copies available on the Companies House website at <www.gov.uk/government/organisations/companies-house>). In addition, the register of secretaries must be updated whenever a secretary's required particulars change.

The Economic Crime and Corporate Transparency Act 2023 will repeal s 276(1)(b) and replace it with a new s 279H of the CA 2006 requiring a company to notify Companies House of any changes to the information required on a company secretary within 14 days. Under a new s279I, if there is a change in details of the company secretary between the application for registration of a new company and incorporation then a notification must be made to Companies House within 14 days of incorporation. This amendment is expected to come into force by 2027.

6.2.6 Public companies

In contrast to a private company, a public company must have a company secretary (CA 2006, s 271).

The company secretary of a public company has to be qualified as specified in s 273 of the 2006 Act. This includes having the requisite knowledge and experience, and, for example, having been a secretary of a public company for three out of the last five years or being a solicitor, barrister, chartered accountant, or chartered secretary. There are other recognised qualifications set out in s 273.

You can find out more on the role of company secretaries, particularly in public companies, including publicly-traded companies, from the Chartered Governance Institute (CGI) website at <http://www.cgi.org.uk>.

6.3 DIRECTORS

Every private company must have at least one director (CA 2006, s 154(1)), and every public company must have at least two (CA 2006, s 154(2)). The directors of a company are the people who manage the company on a day-to-day basis. They take business decisions and make contracts on the company's behalf. The company exists as a legal person, but being an artificial person it needs human agents to act on its behalf. These are the directors, and as such they have a considerable amount of power within the company structure. As a result, various safeguards are usually built into the company structure, both by statute and by the articles, in order to protect members. These subject the directors to a large number of restrictions and controls which are covered in **Chapter 7**. Generally, the directors, like the shareholders, are protected from personal liability by the fact of the company being a separate legal person with its own liability, but there are various exceptions to this in light of the controls placed on directors.

The directors collectively are known as the board of directors and take decisions on behalf of the company through a forum known as the board meeting which will be examined at **6.5** below.

6.3.1 Types of directors

There are a number of different types of director who may be involved in the running of the company. Despite the differences in terminology and responsibility, in the eyes of the law they are generally all subject to the same legal controls on their activities. By s 250(1) of the CA 2006 the term 'director' whenever used in the CA 2006 is defined to include any person occupying the position of director by whatever name called.

6.3.1.1 Executive directors

This is a director who has been appointed to an executive office within the company. Such a director is the typical director of a small private company who will generally spend all or most of their time working on the day-to-day business of the company. An executive director will be an employee of the company and have a service contract with it (which may be written or verbal) under which, in return for a salary and possibly benefits, the director agrees to work for the company (eg see art 19 of the model articles for private companies). Such directors often have an official title, such as Chief Executive or Managing Director, Finance Director or Sales Director.

Chief Executive/Managing Director

The board of directors usually have the power to delegate their powers, including by appointing a Chief Executive or Managing Director, to whom they generally give authority to run the company on a day-to-day basis (see **6.5.1 below**). In other words, the Chief Executive may be given power to act as if they were the whole board of directors. The term Chief Executive has become more popular as a title for someone who would otherwise be called a Managing Director – it apparently appeals more to be called a chief rather than a manager!

The board will fix the terms of the Chief Executive's service contract, including the level of remuneration the director is to receive. The Chief Executive will be formally appointed as a director of the company with specific powers as granted by the company's articles. For example, although not specifically mentioned by name, under art 5 of the model articles for private companies the directors may delegate their powers to such person on such terms as they think fit. This of course allows the directors tremendous flexibility to give a Chief Executive whatever powers they wish.

A company with unamended Table A articles will have the right under art 84 specifically to appoint a 'Managing Director' with such powers as the board choose to grant the director.

6.3.1.2 Non-executive directors

A non-executive director (also known as a NED) does not participate in the day-to-day running of the business. Their principal role is to attend and vote at board meetings. A NED is not an employee and would not have a contract of employment with the company. Their payment would be in the form of directors' fees.

In a private company there are often no NEDs at all. If they are appointed they may, for example, also be shareholders in a small family company with no business experience who do not wish to take an active role in running the company. Sometimes they are appointed for their experience, and may therefore be called upon to offer their advice on the running of the company, particularly if the other directors who are the entrepreneurs who set up the company have little prior management or business experience.

In practice NEDs are more relevant to public companies, particularly to publicly-traded companies. For example, a specified number of NEDs must be appointed to the boards of directors of public companies which are listed on the Main Market of the London Stock Exchange, in accordance with a set of rules known as the UK Corporate Governance Code. This is because such companies are the very biggest in the UK and allow members of the public to invest their money directly in them. The NEDs of these companies must usually be independent and are intended to act as dispassionate judges of how the business and the executive directors of the company are functioning. The aim is to help prevent some of the outrageously poor decision-making which, for example, occurred on the boards of directors of UK publicly-traded banks and other financial institutions leading up to the global financial crisis in 2007/8.

It is very important to note, however, that even though a NED might only attend the company's board meetings, the provisions of the CA 2006 relating to directors apply equally to executive directors and to NEDS. Thus, a NED can still be liable to the company, for example, for breach of their director's duties (*Equitable Life v Bowley* [2003] EWHC 2263).

6.3.1.3 Chairperson

The directors usually have the power in the articles to appoint one of themselves as the chairperson (sometimes known as 'chairwoman', 'chairman' or 'chair') (eg, art 12 of the model articles for private companies). In private companies the chairperson, if appointed, will lead the directors' board meetings and shareholders' general meetings (eg, arts 12 and 39 respectively of the model articles for private companies). The powers of the chairperson are determined by the company's articles. In a private company with unamended model articles the chairperson has no special powers other than their casting (that is deciding) vote in the event of an equal vote for and against a board resolution (art 13). Even this may not be granted by the articles if it gives too much power to the chairperson. The main task for the chairperson then is to take charge at company meetings. The chairperson is appointed by the board passing a board resolution, and they may be removed from their position by the board at any time.

The chairperson of a public company, particularly a publicly-traded one, has a much more important role to play and will be the figurehead of the company in its dealings with shareholders and outsiders.

6.3.1.4 Shadow directors

A person is a shadow director if that person gives directions or instructions to the directors of a company and those directors are accustomed to act in accordance with that person's directions or instructions (CA 2006, s 251(1)). A shadow director is therefore a person who has not been formally appointed by the company as director but who ultimately influences the decisions of the directors.

Sometimes people seek to avoid the onerous duties imposed on directors by not being formally appointed as directors, even though they are running the company on a daily basis. Designating such people as shadow directors prevents them from having all the benefits of running the company without shouldering any of the legal responsibilities which protect both the company and its shareholders. Many of the provisions of the CA 2006 that apply to directors also apply to shadow directors. Section 223(1) of the CA 2006 sets out provisions that may require shareholder approval, which also apply to shadow directors, for example ss 190–196 requiring shareholder approval for certain contracts with the company in which directors have an interest (see **7.12.1** below). Furthermore, s 170(5) of the CA 2006 makes it clear that the directors' duties under ss 171–177 of the Act apply to shadow directors to the extent that they are capable of applying.

In the case of *Secretary of State for Trade and Industry v Deverell* [2000] 2 All ER 365, the Court of Appeal held that a shadow director was anyone, other than a professional adviser, who exercises real influence in the corporate affairs of a company but who does not necessarily give directions or instructions on every matter decided by the directors. There is no need to show that the directors surrendered their discretion, or that the shadow director was trying to conceal their own influence. However, the directors must act on the instructions or directions regularly over time.

In *Ultraframe (UK) v Fielding* [2005] EWHC 2506 (Ch), the Court of Appeal held that a person becomes a shadow director only when the directors act on the instructions given. The mere act of giving instructions is not enough. The case also confirmed that the fact that a company's directors are obliged to act in accordance with the instructions of a major lender of money to the company does not automatically make the lender a shadow director. It is not necessary that all of the directors acted in accordance with the shadow director's directions but that a majority of them did (*In the matter of Coroin Ltd*, Ch D, 5 March 2012).

A person advising in a professional capacity does not become liable as a shadow director (CA 2006, s 251(2)).

6.3.1.5 De facto directors

A 'de facto' director includes a person who has never been appointed as a director of a company but nevertheless performs the functions of a director, or a person appointed under a defect or who stays on after their term has expired. Case law has held that such a person may fall within the definition of a 'director' under s 250(1) of the CA 2006 (see **6.3.1** above) and under the IA 1986 (eg, *Re Hydrodam (Corby) Ltd* [1994] 2 BCLC 180). There may be an overlap between a shadow director and a de facto director.

In *Smithton Ltd v Naggar and others* [2014] EWCA Civ 939, the Court of Appeal noted a number of points that assist in determining whether a person is a de facto director:

- The question is whether they have assumed responsibility to act as a director.
- The question whether or not they acted as a director must be determined objectively. It does not matter whether the individual thought they were acting as a director.
- Whether the company considered the individual to be a director and held them out as such, and whether third parties considered that they were a director, are, however, relevant factors.
- The court must look at the acts in their context and determine their cumulative effect.
- The fact that a person is consulted about directorial decisions, or is asked for approval, does not in general make them a director because they are not making the decision.

The Supreme Court, in a majority opinion in the case of *Holland v The Commissioners for HMRC* [2010] UKSC 51, has held that an individual director of a corporate director of another company is not a de facto director of that other company, and could therefore not be held personally liable for the unlawful payment of a dividend.

A person appointed, but with some defect in their appointment, would have their acts validated as far as third parties are concerned by s 161 of the CA 2006.

6.3.1.6 Alternate directors

An alternate director is someone who attends board meetings in place of a director, ie a stand-in director. The ability to send a substitute to board meetings is governed by the articles of the company. The model articles for private companies do not contain any provision for the appointment of alternate directors, so if this was desired a special article to that effect would need to be added. Table A contains a specific power under art 65 to allow for alternate directors.

If directors are permitted to appoint alternate directors, the articles usually allow them to appoint another director of the company as their alternate, in which case that other director will have their own vote plus the absent director's vote (ie they would have two votes as opposed to the usual one for each director). An alternate director would also be given notice of all meetings, and may attend and vote in the same way as the appointing director.

6.3.1.7 Corporate director

It is possible to have a corporate director of a company (*Holland v The Commissioners for HMRC* [2010] UKSC 51). A corporate director is a company that acts as a director. In practice, of course, for this system to work a human must act on behalf of the corporate director. However, because of s 155(1) of the CA 2006, which requires every company formed under the CA 2006 to have at least one human appointed as a director, a corporate director can be appointed only in private companies with at least two directors or in a public company.

The Small Business, Enterprise and Employment Act 2015, which received Royal Assent in March 2015, has inserted a new s 156A into the Companies Act 2006. This provision requires every director to be a human and prohibits corporate directors. A new CA 2006, s 156B allows the Secretary of State for DBT to make regulations setting out exceptions to this ban on corporate directors. The most recent Government proposals will permit corporate directors but only if all directors of the corporate director of a company are themselves human. At the time of writing, it is unclear when these provisions will be brought into force as the Government has repeatedly delayed introducing them. The reader is advised to check the DBT website for further information.

An individual who is appointed to act on behalf of a corporate director may, assuming the legal tests are met, be a shadow director or a de facto director. However, a de facto directorship will not arise where the individual is merely discharging their duties as the corporate director (*Holland v HMRC*, **6.3.1.5** above).

6.3.2 Appointment of directors

The first directors of a company will be those persons named as directors in the statement of proposed officers (see **3.10.1** above). They will automatically become directors on the date of incorporation (CA 2006, s 16(6)(a)).

Subsequently, directors may be appointed in accordance with the procedure in the articles, although it is necessary first to check that there are no statutory or articles restrictions on whether a person is eligible to be a director.

Section 167M of the CA 2006 states that an individual must not act as a director unless their identity has been verified. Further information on the verification procedure can be found at **3.11** above. *This verification system currently operates voluntarily and is expected to become fully compulsory by the end of 2026.*

6.3.2.1 Statutory restrictions

A director must be at least 16 years old when they take office, otherwise the appointment will be void (CA 2006, s 157). The current Government does not intend to use powers under s 158 of the CA 2006 to allow for exceptions to the minimum age requirement.

A director disqualified under the Company Directors Disqualification Act (CDDA) 1986 will commit a criminal offence under s 13 of that Act if they act as a director of a company during the period of the disqualification. Further, an undischarged bankrupt cannot act as a director of a company (CDDA 1986, s 11). For example, a director of Supergroup, the company that owns the Superdry clothing brand, had to resign when he was made bankrupt in 2015, following a demand from the tax authorities.

There is a power under s 1184 of the CA 2006 for the Secretary of State for DBT to prevent someone from being a director of a UK company if that person is subject to restrictions under foreign law. The idea is that if a person is disqualified from being a director under foreign law, they should not be able to be one in the UK.

6.3.2.2 Restrictions in the articles

The company's articles may provide for the ineligibility of a director. Article 18 of the model articles for private companies, in addition to some of the reasons given in **6.3.2.1** above, prevents a person from holding office who is likely to be physically or mentally incapable of acting as a director in certain circumstances. Under Table A, art 81, a person cannot be (or continue as) a director if they are of unsound mind, or if they are absent from board meetings for more than six months without permission.

6.3.2.3 Procedure for appointment

The procedure for appointing a new director is a matter for the company's articles. This will usually involve passing either an ordinary resolution of the shareholders in general meeting, or a board resolution of the existing directors.

A private company using model art 17 may appoint a director using either of the two methods mentioned above without any special conditions. It is usually simpler for a new director to be appointed by the existing board, as there is then no need to call a shareholders' general meeting or organise the passing of a shareholders' written resolution. However, which method is used will depend on the company concerned. If the existing directors are also all shareholders then a directors' resolution would be the normal way to appoint further directors; if the shareholders are different from the directors then a shareholders' resolution may be more appropriate, as ultimately the shareholders own the company.

A company that still has unamended Table A articles may also appoint a new director using the two methods outlined above. However, if an appointment is made by the existing directors under Table A, art 79, such an appointee can hold office only until the next AGM (see **8.7.1** below), at which point they may remain as a director only if reappointed by the shareholders passing an ordinary resolution. Alternatively, if the new director is to be appointed by the shareholders under Table A, art 78, there are additional conditions relating to approval and notice in arts 76 and 77 which must also be complied with.

We saw at **5.6.3.9** above that the shareholders may remove a director by ordinary resolution. If at the same time the shareholders pass an ordinary resolution to appoint a new director at that general meeting, 'special notice' of that resolution must be given by the proposing shareholder(s) to the company, as required by s 168(2) of the CA 2006 (see **6.10.3** below).

The company must make a statement on behalf of a person seeking appointment as a director, indicating their consent to act as a director (CA 2006, s 167(2)(b)). For the first director or directors of the company this is set out on Form IN01 (see **3.9.1** above). For directors appointed after incorporation, the company must sign the statement on Form AP01 (if an individual) or on Form AP02 (if a corporate director) (copies of which may be found on the Companies House website at <www.gov.uk/government/organisations/companies-house>). Thus a person cannot be appointed to office against their will.

The appointment of a new director (after incorporation) must be notified to Companies House on Form AP01 (if an individual) or on Form AP02 (if a corporate director) within 14 days of that person becoming a director (CA 2006, s 167(1)(a)). In addition, the register of directors must be updated, assuming it is being kept (see **6.9.1** below).

Under s 1079B of the CA 2006, as soon as reasonably practicable after the notification of appointment of a new director has been made, the Registrar of Companies must send information on the roles and duties of a director to that director.

A new director will usually become an employee of the company; consequently, there will also usually be formalities to be satisfied relating to the director's service contract (see **6.8** below).

The Economic Crime and Corporate Transparency Act 2023 (ECCTA) will repeal s 167(1) and (2) and replace them with a new s 167G of the CA 2006 requiring a company to notify Companies House of the date of appointment of a director together with a statement by the company:

- *setting out the required information on the director (contained in new s 167J (individual director) and s 167K (corporate director));*
- *confirming that the director has consented to act as a director;*
- *if an individual director, that their identity has been verified in accordance with the procedure in new s 1110A;*
- *that the director is not disqualified as a director or otherwise ineligible for the role.*

ECCTA will also remove the need for a company to keep a register of directors.

This amendment is expected to come into force by 2027.

6.3.2.4 Owning shares

It is not necessary for a director to own shares in the company. However, particularly in small companies the shareholders, as owners of the company, will want to manage their company too, and so will be appointed as directors. If this happens the individual has two separate roles, and when acting as a director will be subject to the same rules and liability as a director who does not own shares in the company.

6.3.2.5 Number of directors

We saw at **6.3** above that a private company must have at least one director. However, a company may have more, depending on the articles. The model articles for private companies (art 11) assume that there are two directors, as this is the minimum number required for valid board meetings to be held (known as the 'quorum'). Although if a company with model articles has just a sole director then that director can still validly take decisions because of art 7(2).

It is possible to set a different minimum number of directors if required (eg if it is felt that there should be three directors). Either a special article to this effect should be included on formation of the company, or the existing articles should be changed by special resolution of the members under s 21 of the CA 2006.

6.4 NATURE OF OFFICE

The nature of the relationship between the directors of a company and their company is complicated. In legal terms it is a multi-layered relationship, drawing on different sets of legal principles.

First, directors are agents of their company. Under agency law the company as a separate legal person is the principal and the directors are its agents, given both actual and apparent authority to bind the company. This becomes particularly relevant when considering possible liability for directors' acts on behalf of the company (see **7.13.1**).

The directors are also in a fiduciary relationship with their company. Although not trustees of the company's property, they are in a trustee-like position and owe special duties to their company. For example, because of this fiduciary relationship, the directors must show the utmost good faith in their dealings with the company. This is most relevant when considering directors' duties (see **6.6** below).

Some directors will be employees of the company. Usually this will apply only to the executive directors of the company who have a service contract and are paid a salary. The relationship between these employee directors and their company will therefore also be governed by employment law and the contract of employment between them. We consider this further at **6.8** below.

These overlapping sets of rules demonstrate how important the role of a director is in practice. They also help to explain why directors are subject to so many duties and responsibilities, as we shall see in **Chapter 7**.

6.5 DIRECTORS' POWERS

The directors are responsible for the management of the company and are given powers in this regard by the company's articles. Article 3 of the model articles for private companies is typical, in that it states that the directors are responsible for the management of the company and can exercise all the company's powers. There is a similar provision in art 70 of Table A.

The directors usually exercise these powers by passing resolutions (decisions) at a meeting of the board of directors of the company, known more usually as a board meeting or (as in the model articles for private companies) as a directors' meeting. The term 'board meeting' is used in this book as it is more widely used in practice.

The directors generally act jointly. For example, art 7 of the model articles for private companies states that the general rule as to decision-making by directors is that it may be done by a majority decision at a board meeting. Ultimately this is a matter for the articles, and art 7 goes on to say that a decision may also be taken in accordance with art 8 where the board can exercise their powers unanimously without a meeting being held, so long as all directors indicate to one another that they share a common view on a matter. In practice, therefore, this method of decision-making could be as informal as a text message to the other directors.

The practical impact of the directors' management role as stated in the company's articles is that the shareholders do not generally get involved in the day-to-day running of the company. Once the directors have been given a certain power, that power then belongs to the board and it cannot generally be exercised by the shareholders instead. This means that the shareholders cannot usually overrule the board or retrospectively alter one of the board's decisions.

We saw at **5.7** above that the shareholders usually become involved only when the CA 2006 requires them to take a decision at a general meeting and that decision cannot be taken by the directors (eg, a decision to change the company's articles). Also, some decisions of the directors need approval by the shareholders in a general meeting before they can take effect. For example, before the directors can enter into a so-called substantial property transaction under s 190(1) of the CA 2006 between the company and one of its own directors, the company's shareholders must first pass an ordinary resolution (see **7.12.1** below). The shareholders therefore hold a power of veto, because if it the ordinary resolution is not passed, the contract cannot be entered into. The payment of dividends under the model articles for private companies is another example (see **9.8** below).

Usually this arrangement works smoothly. If, however, the shareholders dislike the way the directors are running the company, they may exercise certain powers. There is normally the power to direct the directors what to do by special resolution expressly mentioned in the articles (eg, in art 4 of the model articles for private companies or in art 70 of Table A). The power under art 3 of the model articles for private companies, enabling the directors to exercise all the powers of the company, is made specifically subject to the remaining articles, so art 4 will have supremacy. In practice this power would be used only exceptionally. Alternatively the shareholders may change the articles by special resolution under s 21 of the CA 2006 in order to take certain powers from the board. Both these decisions require a 75% shareholder majority, which demonstrates the seriousness with which the directors' general power of management of the company is taken. There is a further power for shareholders to remove directors by ordinary resolution (over 50% of votes in favour) under s 168(1) of the CA 2006.

There are various procedural requirements that need to be met to ensure that board meetings and decisions taken by the directors at them are valid. These will be set out in the company's articles and vary from company to company. We cover these requirements in detail in **Chapter 8** below.

6.5.1 Delegation of powers

Generally, directors are required to exercise their powers jointly by acting as a board (see art 7 of the model articles for private companies). However, it is usual to find certain provisions in the articles of a company which enable directors to delegate some, if not all, of their functions. This is done for practical reasons where there is more than one director. It allows a specified director or directors to act on behalf of the whole board in the name of commercial expediency. Requiring the whole board to convene and agree a decision to buy a new computer for the office receptionist is unnecessarily restrictive, inefficient and burdensome.

Article 5 of the model articles for private companies is one example of the power to delegate. It is drafted in extremely wide terms. It allows the directors as a board to decide to delegate any of their powers:

(a) to such person or committee;

(b) by such means;

(c) to such an extent;

(d) in relation to such matters; and

(e) on such terms;

as they think fit.

Article 5 even allows the board to grant the director delegated the power to delegate further to another person if required. Clearly such a power gives the directors tremendous flexibility. There is also a right of delegation under art 72 of Table A; and although it is also very wide, it is couched in more general language.

If the board decide to appoint a Chief Executive or Managing Director (see **6.3.1.1** above), the board will, at the same time, decide which powers are to be delegated to that person. It is common to give the Managing Director the ability to make day-to-day decisions on behalf of the company, more radical and important issues (such as the purchase of another business, or borrowing large amounts of money) being reserved to the board as a whole. The Managing Director may be given all or any of the powers of the board, but these may be varied or withdrawn at any time by the board.

Directors may also delegate their functions to other executive directors, and even to ordinary employees of the company should the company's circumstances so require.

If a director is unable to attend a board meeting, the director may (depending on the articles) appoint an alternate director to go in their place (see **6.3.1.6** above). This involves delegating the first director's powers to the alternate director for the duration of the alternate's appointment.

6.5.2 Authority of directors

The ability of a director to bind a company in a contractual relationship with a third party is based on the director's position as agent of the company. There are two types of authority: actual authority, and apparent (also known as ostensible) authority.

Directors will bind the company if they act with either actual or apparent authority. If they exceed this authority, they will not bind the company. They will be personally liable for breach of warranty of authority to any third party with whom they were dealing. They will also be personally liable on the contract to the third party, as they would have failed to tie the company into the contractual obligation.

Actual authority is where the principal (the company) gives the agent (the director) specific prior consent to the agent's actions. Apparent authority is where the agent (the director) acts without the principal's (the company) prior consent but still binds the principal (the company) in the contract with the third party. That is, the principal (the company) is estopped from denying the agent's (the director) authority. In *Freeman and Lockyer (A Firm) v Buckhurst Park Properties (Mangal) Ltd* [1964] 2 QB 480, Lord Diplock explained the difference between actual and apparent authority in the following terms:

> An 'actual' authority is a legal relationship between principal and agent created by a consensual agreement to which they alone are the parties. ... To this agreement the third party is a stranger; he may be totally ignorant of the existence of any authority on the part of the agent. Nevertheless, if the agent does enter into a contract pursuant to the 'actual' authority, it does create contractual rights and liabilities between the principal and the third party.
>
> An 'apparent' authority, on the other hand, is a legal relationship between the principal and the third party created by a representation, made by the principal to the third party, intended to be and in fact acted on by the third party, that the agent has authority ... To the relationship so created the agent is a stranger.

Actual authority may be express or implied. Express actual authority is given where, for example, the board of directors pass a board resolution authorising one of their number to enter into a contract on behalf of the company. An example of implied actual authority may be found in the case of *Hely-Hutchinson v Brayhead Ltd* [1968] 1 QB 549. There was a chairman whom the other directors allowed to act as if he were the Managing Director. The Court of Appeal held that he had implied actual authority to act as Managing Director. There was no actual appointment as a Managing Director, but the other directors let the chairman take on the role and were happy for this to continue.

Apparent authority is based on a representation, by words or conduct, to the third party by the company that the person in question (eg, the director) is acting with the company's authority. Apparent authority cannot arise by the agent's own actions, only by those of the company. In effect, the basis of apparent authority is that the company is estopped from denying the agent's authority to bind the company in a contract with the third party. Without this, an 'agent' who acted without authority would not bind the company but would bind themselves alone to the third party.

The Court of Appeal considered apparent authority in *Pharmed Medicare Private Ltd v Univar Ltd* [2003] 1 All ER (Comm) 321. The Court of Appeal held that the company was bound by the contract in question. When a company puts forward an employee as someone with whom the seller can contract, and the company honours the contracts so made, then that employee has apparent authority to make further contracts. In *Bank of Baroda v Shah (Dilip)* [1999] WL 851947, the Court of Appeal held that a representative of the bank had apparent authority to release Mr Shah from his personal guarantee of a loan made to his company. In *Mahomed v Ravat Bombay House (Pty)* [1958] (4) SA 704, the claimant was held to be entitled to rely on the apparent authority of a single director. In *Racing UK Ltd v Doncaster Racecourse Ltd* [2004] EWHC 2813, a Doncaster Council-owned company was held to be bound by a contract entered into by someone who had apparent authority to act on behalf of the company. In effect, the company was bound because it failed to correct the mistaken impression upon which the claimant had entered into the contract. The theme throughout these cases is that the courts found that a plausible representative of a company had apparent authority to third parties, in the absence of information from the company to correct this impression. However, in *Criterion Properties v Stratford UK Properties LLC* [2004] UKHL 28, the House of Lords held that an improper agreement entered into without the knowledge of the other directors was unenforceable against the company, as the director in question had neither actual nor apparent authority.

As can be seen from the above cases, the board of directors may give authority not just to other directors but to non-directors, employees who work for the company, in order to allow those individuals to enter contracts on behalf of the company.

6.6 DIRECTORS' DUTIES

Once appointed, directors are subject to an array of legal duties and responsibilities because of the special position they hold in relation to their company. These duties play a significant role in determining how a director can and cannot act. We examine the most important duties in **Chapter 7**.

6.7 DIRECTORS' ANNUAL RESPONSIBILITIES

Directors have a number of responsibilities which they must perform on an annual basis.

6.7.1 Company accounts

A company must keep adequate accounting records under s 386(1) of the CA 2006, otherwise it commits an offence. It is the directors' responsibility to ensure that full accounts are produced for each financial year (CA 2006, s 394).

These accounts must give a 'true and fair view of the state of affairs of the company as at the end of the financial year' (CA 2006, s 396(2)). The directors must not approve the accounts unless they are satisfied that they give a true and fair view of the assets, liabilities, financial position, and profit and loss of the company (CA 2006, s 393(1)).

The form and content of company accounts are prescribed by ss 396–413 of the CA 2006, and are also governed by standards set by the accountancy profession and contained in Financial Reporting Standards (FRSs).

By s 415 of the CA 2006, every company must prepare a directors' report for each financial year to accompany the accounts. The accounts, directors' report and, if required, auditors' report (see **6.12.1** below) must be circulated to every shareholder in accordance with s 423(1) of the CA 2006. This is the directors' responsibility.

Section 417 of the CA 2006 requires the directors' report to include a business review which contains a balanced and comprehensive review of the development and performance of the company's business, the risk and uncertainties faced, and the position of the business at the end of the financial year. This does not apply to 'small' companies.

Under s 441 of the CA 2006, companies must also file the accounts and directors' report for each financial year at Companies House. However, so-called 'micro-entities', 'small' and 'medium-sized' companies may file an abbreviated version of the year-end accounts (Small Companies (Micro-Entities' Accounts) Regulations 2013 (SI 2013/3008), CA 2006, s 444 and s 445 respectively).

A micro-entity is defined in s 384A of the CA 2006 as one which satisfies at least two of the following requirements:

(a) annual turnover: not more than £1 million;

(b) balance sheet total: not more than £500,000;

(c) number of employees: not more than 10.

A small company is defined in s 382(3) of the CA 2006 as one which satisfies at least two of the following requirements:

(a) annual turnover: not more than £15 million;

(b) balance sheet total: not more than £7.5 million;

(c) number of employees: not more than 50.

A medium-sized company is defined in s 465(3) of the CA 2006 as one which satisfies at least two of the following requirements:

(a) annual turnover: not more than £54 million;

(b) balance sheet total: not more than £27 million;

(c) number of employees: not more than 250.

The time limit for filing accounts is nine months from the end of the accounting reference period for a private company (CA 2006, s 442(2)).

Under the Economic Crime and Corporate Transparency Act 2023, the authority for a 'micro-entity' having to submit accounts will change to a new s 443A rather than s 444 as currently. This amendment is expected to come into force by the end of 2027.

6.7.2 The confirmation statement

Every company must submit a confirmation statement to the Registrar of Companies once in every 12-month period. The directors are responsible for doing this within 14 days after the company's 'confirmation date' (the date to which the confirmation statement is made up) (CA 2006, s 853A(1) and (3)). A company's first confirmation date is the anniversary of the date of its incorporation. Subsequently, it is the anniversary of the previous confirmation date (CA 2006, s 853A(5)). A failure to submit the confirmation statement on time is a criminal offence.

The confirmation statement (Form CS01) is designed to ensure that the information on the company at Companies House is kept up to date. A copy of the confirmation statement may be found on the Companies House website at <www.gov.uk/government/organisations/

companies-house>. The form includes a statement that all information required to be delivered by the company pursuant to CA 2006, s 853A(1)(a) has been delivered or is being delivered with this statement. The information required includes the address of the registered office, the registered email address, details of the company's main business activities, details of the directors and the company secretary (if any), details of persons with significant control (PSCs), details of issued share capital, and details of the shareholders. All this information is kept at Companies House and is available to anyone who chooses to make a company search.

Under s 853BA of the CA 2006, the company must make a statement (on the confirmation statement) that the intended future activities of the company are lawful.

It may be submitted in paper form or electronically. Companies House encourages companies to file the form electronically. This is reflected in the fee payable when submitting the confirmation statement: this is £34 for electronic submission and £62 for a paper form.

6.7.3 Dividends

The directors in managing the company have the power to recommend payment of a dividend (a share of profits) to the company's shareholders if there are sufficient distributable profits available (see **9.8** below).

6.8 DIRECTORS' SERVICE CONTRACTS

Where a director works for the company as an executive director, they are usually also an employee of the company. Although a contract may be oral, it is always advisable for a director and the company to draw up a written contract of employment, often called a (director's) service contract.

6.8.1 Contracts awarded by the board

The board of directors will be empowered under the company's articles to enter into a service contract with a director on behalf of the company. For example, art 3 and art 19 of the model articles for private companies and Table A, art 84 permit the board to do this. The board will decide the terms of each service contract, including the director's responsibilities, any authority the director is to have to act on behalf of the board (see **6.5** above), and the amount of salary and benefits to be paid.

When a service contract is being discussed and voted upon at a board meeting, if the director who is to be awarded the service contract has already taken up office, although a formal declaration to the board of a personal interest will not normally be necessary due to s 177(6) of the CA 2006 (see **7.9.4** below), the director will often be prevented under the articles from voting and counting in the quorum for that board meeting for reasons of fairness. As a member of the board the director would have to decide on behalf of the company what the terms of their own contract should be, including the amount of remuneration. As an individual, however, the director will of course want the best possible terms for themselves. This gives rise to a conflict of interest, so the articles often disqualify a director in this position from participating in the decision to award the contract (see **8.4.3** and **8.4.4** below).

However, this restriction, if it applies in the articles, may create a problem where there are only two directors and one (or both of them) is to be granted a service contract. If the quorum for board meetings is two, the restriction in the articles will mean that only one director can validly participate and so the meeting would not be quorate. In other words, no valid decision could be taken. The problem may be overcome by changing the articles (by special resolution of the shareholders) to allow directors to vote whenever they have an interest in a matter with their company (including in relation to their own service contracts). This may be undesirable, though, as a protection against potential abuse by a director has been removed for good. An alternative might be for the shareholders to pass an ordinary resolution at a general meeting, *temporarily* to relax the rules on directors voting and counting in the quorum just for this particular board resolution. The articles will often allow this, eg art 14 of the model articles for private companies and Table A, art 96.

6.8.2 Guaranteed-term contracts

Sometimes the board of directors will think it appropriate to award a director a guaranteed-term contract, under which the director is contractually guaranteed to be employed for a specified period of time. For example, one of the directors may, by their service contract, be appointed for a guaranteed period of 10 years. The main advantage for the director of this type of contract is that it offers job security for the period of time concerned; if the company breaches the contract by removing the director from their job before the 10-year guaranteed term has elapsed, the director will be able to claim damages. The starting point for calculating damages would be the salary the director would have received over the whole 10-year period had they not been dismissed. If, for example, the director was earning £100,000 a year and was removed after one year, the starting point for damages would be £900,000!

Such contracts are potentially a big financial risk for the company. The CA 2006 consequently provides protection to the shareholders of the company – who, it should be remembered, are the owners of the company and may not be the directors themselves – by allowing them to veto certain guaranteed-term contracts between the company (negotiated by the board) and the individual directors. Where the company is proposing to enter into a service contract with a director for a guaranteed term of longer than two years, it must obtain the prior consent of the shareholders by ordinary resolution at a general meeting (CA 2006, s 188).

If the directors of the company call a shareholders' general meeting to ask them to pass such a resolution, a memorandum setting out the proposed service contract in question must be available for inspection by members at the meeting itself and for 15 days prior to the meeting at the registered office. If a written resolution of the shareholders is to be used instead of holding an actual meeting, the memorandum of the proposed service contracts must be sent out to members with the written resolution itself (CA 2006, s 188(5)). This ensures that the shareholders have full information regarding the contract before deciding whether to vote for its approval or not.

If the approval of the shareholders is not obtained under s 188 of the CA 2006, the service contract will still be effective, save for the clause stating that the director is to be employed for a guaranteed term. Instead of that director's job being guaranteed for a specified period of time, the contract would then be capable of termination on reasonable notice. All the rest of the terms of the contract decided upon by the directors will be valid and enforceable against the company, but the guaranteed-term element will not. Therefore, if the director concerned were to be dismissed in breach of contract, their damages would be based not on the guaranteed period of time stated in the contract, but on the period of time deemed by the court to be 'reasonable notice'.

A service contract is defined in s 227(1) of the CA 2006 to include a contract under which the director undertakes to perform services personally for the company. Under s 227(2) of the CA 2006, this may be within or outside the scope of the ordinary duties of a director. The definition includes not just the usual employment contract but also more informal letters of appointment and contracts for services, ie a consultancy contract.

6.8.3 Inspection of service contracts

Under s 228 of the CA 2006, copies of all directors' service contracts (or a written memorandum if the contract is not in writing) must be kept at the registered office, or its single alternative inspection location (SAIL) under s 1136 (see **8.11.4**), for inspection by the company's shareholders under s 229 of the 2006 Act. This applies to all directors' service contracts. It is not limited to those requiring approval by the shareholders because the service contract is for a guaranteed term exceeding two years.

The copies must be kept for inspection for one year after the contracts expire (CA 2006, s 228(3)).

A shareholder also has the right to request a copy of the contract under s 229(2) of the CA 2006.

By s 230 of the 2006 Act, these provisions also apply to shadow directors (see **6.3.1.4** above).

6.9 NOTIFICATION REQUIREMENTS

There are various requirements under the CA 2006 requiring information to be collated on the directors of a company. The primary purpose of gathering this information is to ensure that the shareholders of the company and interested outsiders can search it to discover key facts about those managing the company. This may, for example, then influence whether a person wishes to become involved with a company.

6.9.1 The register of directors

Every company must keep a register of directors (CA 2006, s 162(1)) containing the required particulars (CA 2006, s 162(2)). It must be available for inspection by the shareholders without charge (or for others on payment of a fee) at the company's registered office (or SAIL under s 1136 of the Act). If this is not done, a criminal offence is committed by the company and every officer in default (CA 2006, s 162(6)).

Section 167A of the CA 2006 allows private companies to elect not to keep their own register of directors, and alternatively they can ensure that the necessary information is filed and kept up-to-date on the central register for the company held at Companies House. The company must notify the Registrar of Companies of the election (CA 2006, ss 167A(3) and 167B(1)). During the time that this election not to have a register of directors is in force, the company must notify the Registrar of Companies as soon as is reasonably practicable of any information that otherwise would have gone into the register of directors (CA 2006, s 167D(2) and (3)). This election can be withdrawn and the register of directors reactivated following the procedure in CA 2006, s 167E.

In the case of a director who is a human, the required particulars that must be entered in the register are details of the director's name, address for service of documents (which may be 'the company's registered office'), country of usual residence, nationality, business occupation (if any) and date of birth (CA 2006, s 163(1) and (5)).

In the case of a corporate director, the required particulars that must be entered in the register are details of the corporate name, registered or principal office, for an EEA company the register in which the company file is kept and its registration number, and for a non-EEA company the legal form and law which governs it, together with details of its register and registration number (if relevant) (CA 2006, s 164).

This register must be updated whenever a director joins or leaves the board, or if a director's required details change.

The Economic Crime and Corporate Transparency Act 2023 (ECCTA) will remove the need for a company to maintain a register of directors as well as the right of a company to elect to keep its register of directors centrally at Companies House.

ECCTA will repeal ss 162–164 and ss 167A, 167B, 167D and 167E and replace them with a new s 167G of the CA 2006 requiring a company to notify Companies House of the date of the appointment or departure of a director within 14 days. For an appointment of a new director, s 167G requires a statement by the company:

- *setting out the required information on the director (contained in new s 167J (individual director) and s 167K (corporate director));*
- *confirming the director has consented to act as a director;*

- *if an individual director, that their identity has been verified in accordance with the procedure in new s 1110A;*
- *that the director is not disqualified as a director or otherwise ineligible for the role.*

A notification must also be sent within 14 days if the director's details change (new s 167H).

These amendments are expected to come into force by 2027.

6.9.2 The register of directors' residential addresses

Every company must also keep a register of directors' residential addresses (CA 2006, s 165(1)), which unsurprisingly states the usual residential address of each of the directors (CA 2006, s 165(2)). This applies to human directors only, not corporate directors.

Section 167A of the CA 2006 allows private companies to elect not to keep their own register of directors' residential addresses, and alternatively they can ensure that the necessary information is filed and kept up-to-date on the central register for the company held at Companies House. This information will not be available for public inspection. The company must notify the Registrar of Companies of the election (CA 2006, ss 167A(3) and 167B(1)). During the time that this election not to have a register of directors' residential addresses is in force, the company must notify the Registrar of Companies as soon as is reasonably practicable of any information that otherwise would have gone into the register of directors' residential addresses (CA 2006, s 167D(2) and (3)). This election can be withdrawn and the register of directors' residential addresses reactivated following the procedure in CA 2006, s 167E.

The register of directors' residential addresses is *not* open to inspection. This is to protect directors at serious risk of violence or intimidation (see **3.9.2** above).

If the director's residential address is the same as their service address as already provided (see **6.9.1** above), this fact may be stated in the register rather than entering the full address again (CA 2006, s 165(3)).

Failure to keep a register of directors' residential addresses is a criminal offence committed by the company and every officer in default (CA 2006, s 165(4)). This register must therefore be updated whenever a human director joins or leaves the board, or when an existing human director's address changes.

The Economic Crime and Corporate Transparency Act 2023 (ECCTA) will remove the need for a company to maintain a register of directors' residential addresses as well as the right of a company to elect to keep its register of directors' residential addresses centrally at Companies House.

ECCTA will also repeal s 165 and ss 167A, 167B, 167D and 167E and replace them with a new s 167G of the CA 2006 requiring a company to notify Companies House of the usual residential address of a director on their appointment within 14 days (or should this address change under a new s 167H).

These amendments are expected to come into force by 2027.

6.9.3 Companies House

We saw at **6.3.2.3** above that details of the first director or directors of a company must be included on Form IN01, and that thereafter Form AP01 or AP02 must be submitted to Companies House within 14 days of the appointment of a human or corporate director respectively.

In addition, any change in the required particulars of a director contained in the register of directors or register of directors' residential addresses must be notified within 14 days of the change (CA 2006, s 167(1)(b)), using Form CH01 for a human director and Form CH02 for a corporate director (copies available on the Companies House website at <www.gov.uk/government/organisations/companies-house>).

Whenever a director leaves office, the Registrar of Companies must be informed within 14 days by sending a Form TM01 for a human director or Form TM02 for a corporate director (copies available on the Companies House website at <http://www.companieshouse.gov.uk>).

The Economic Crime and Corporate Transparency Act 2023 will repeal s 167 and replace it with a new s 167H requiring changes to the information on individual and corporate directors to be notified to Companies House within 14 days. In addition, under a new s 167I, any changes to the information on proposed directors made after an application to incorporate a new company is submitted and before it is incorporated must be notified to Companies House within 14 days of the date of incorporation. Under this provision, a company must also make a notification to Companies House if a proposed director does not become a director on incorporation. These changes are expected to come into force by 2027.

6.9.4 Company stationery

We saw at **3.18.2** above that under powers contained in s 82 of the CA 2006, the Secretary of State for DBT has made the Company, Limited Liability Partnership and Business (Names and Trading Disclosures) Regulations 2015 (SI 2015/17). Under reg 26 of the Regulations, all company business letters must contain the names of either all the directors or none of the directors. This does not apply where a director's name is mentioned only in the text of the letter or as a signatory. It therefore applies to the situation where a director's name is included, for example, as part of the headed notepaper.

6.10 TERMINATION OF DIRECTORSHIP

There are a number of ways in which a director may leave office and cease to be a director. This may be done in accordance with provisions in the articles, or pursuant to certain statutory powers. A company director's departure from office will usually be voluntary, but on occasion it can happen against the director's wishes.

6.10.1 Resignation

A director may resign at any time by giving notice to the company. This is envisaged by art 18(f) of the model articles for private companies and by Table A, art 81(d). If the director is subject to an employment contract then the director must take account of any notice periods or other procedures in order to avoid liability for breach of contract.

6.10.2 Removal by the board of directors

Sometimes, power is given to the board of directors in the articles to dismiss a fellow director by majority vote at a board meeting. In exercising this power the directors must act bona fide in the best interests of the company. In other words, the power must be used for proper reasons, for example where there has been gross negligence by the director or a failure to perform the director's duties over time. There is no such power in either the model articles for private companies or Table A.

6.10.3 Removal by shareholders under the CA 2006

Shareholders of a company have the right to remove a director from office at any time by passing an ordinary resolution, and this right cannot be taken from them by anything contained in the director's service contract (CA 2006, s 168(1)). This right also cannot be taken away by the articles (although the articles may provide for additional methods of removal).

Any shareholder wanting to propose a resolution to remove a director must give the company 'special notice' (CA 2006, s 168(2)). Pursuant to s 312(1) of the Act, special notice means that the shareholder must give formal notice to the company (at its registered office) of their intention to propose the resolution at least 28 clear days before a general meeting. (If it is intended to appoint a replacement director at the same meeting, special notice must be given of this appointment as well.) A written resolution of the shareholders cannot be used in this case (CA 2006, s 288(2)(a)).

6.10.3.1 Co-operative board of directors

If the board of directors are happy to see their colleague face the threat of removal by the shareholder's resolution and no general meeting has been called to discuss other matters, they can respond to the s 168 notice given by the shareholder(s) and call a meeting in the usual way (CA 2006, s 312(2)). Note that this can happen only if a majority of directors on the board vote in favour of calling the meeting. If, for example, there are only two directors, and one votes in favour of calling the meeting and the one under threat of removal votes against, then in the absence of a chairperson with a casting vote voting in favour (this second vote to overcome deadlock depends on there being such a provision in the articles), the meeting will not be called and the procedure at **6.10.3.2** below will have to be followed.

An ordinary resolution must be passed by the shareholders under s 168(1) of the CA 2006 to remove a director from office. So if the board of directors do decide to call a general meeting for this purpose, only 14 clear days' notice of the meeting is required from the company to the shareholders. The fact that it is held within 28 clear days of the notice being served does not prevent the shareholder's special notice from being valid and the resolution for removal must be voted upon. This is because the shareholder will be deemed to have given proper notice in these circumstances under s 312(4) of the CA 2006. This provision prevents the directors from trying to frustrate the attempt by the shareholder to have the resolution voted upon by holding a shareholders' meeting within the 28-day period and then preventing the shareholders from considering the resolution because at least 28 days' notice was not given before the meeting as required by s 312(1) of the 2006 Act.

The meeting will then be held and the resolution voted upon. Only a majority of the shareholder votes (over 50%) cast at the meeting is needed to pass the resolution and remove the director. If that majority threshold is not reached, the director will remain in office.

If a general meeting has already been called to consider other issues and the shareholder(s) subsequently serve(s) the s 168 notice to have the ordinary resolution considered at the general meeting, the board of directors may agree by a majority to add the resolution to the agenda of the meeting (remember that the director under threat of removal will vote against this), but only if they have time to give at least 14 clear days' notice before the meeting by an advertisement in a newspaper or by other means allowed by the articles (CA 2006, s 312(3)).

6.10.3.2 Unco-operative board of directors

The reality is more usually that the directors are unwilling to call a general meeting in response to being served a s 168 notice because they do not support the removal of one of their fellow directors and hope to prevent a vote on the resolution. In this case the shareholder(s) can force the directors to call a general meeting and have the resolution considered under s 303 of the CA 2006 (see **5.6.3.11** above), provided they own at least 5% of the shares in the company and serve a notice on the directors in the form required by s 303. Under s 304(1)(a) of the CA 2006, the directors have 21 days from receipt of this notice to call a general meeting. That general meeting, at which the resolution to remove the director will be considered, must be held not more than 28 days after the date on which the meeting was called (CA 2006, s 304(1)(b)).

However, if the directors are being really obstructive they may still not do as they are supposed to under s 304 of the CA 2006 and may refuse to call the meeting. If this happens, the shareholder(s) who requisitioned the meeting (or any of them with over 50% of the voting rights of all those who requested the meeting) may call the general meeting themselves (CA 2006, s 305). The meeting must then be held not more than three months after the date on which the directors became subject to the requirement to call the meeting (CA 2006, s 305(3)). Usually, though, since the shareholders now have control, they will want to hold the meeting as quickly as possible and will give 14 clear days' notice (as allowed under s 305(4) of the CA 2006).

The meeting will now be held and the resolution finally voted upon. Only a majority of the shareholder votes (over 50%) cast at the meeting is needed to pass the resolution and remove the director. If that majority threshold is not reached, the director may remain in office.

6.10.3.3 Director's rights

Whenever the company receives special notice of a resolution to remove a director under s 168 of the CA 2006, the board must ensure that a copy of the notice is sent to the director concerned immediately under s 169(1) of the Act. That director then has the right to make written representations to the company, and the company must circulate them to shareholders (CA 2006, s 169(3)). The director may also speak at the meeting, whether or not the director is also a shareholder (CA 2006, s 169(2)).

6.10.3.4 Protection?

Before giving special notice to the company for the removal of a director under s 168 of the CA 2006, the shareholder(s) should check the company's articles to see whether or not they contain a so-called *Bushell v Faith* clause (from the case of the same name, [1970] AC 1099). This is a special article giving directors who are also shareholders weighted voting rights on a resolution for their removal. For example, the director might have 10 times the usual votes on such a resolution. Provided the director is also a shareholder of the company, this will usually prevent the other shareholder(s) from being able to remove the director from their position. The shareholder(s) wishing to remove a director should check whether it might be possible to remove *the Bushell v Faith* clause by passing a special resolution under s 21 of the CA 2006 at a general meeting, or whether the director has also been given weighted voting rights for this too, in which case the director cannot be removed from office against the director's will.

Even if there is no such special article, the shareholder proposing the ordinary resolution should also check the director's service contract (which is open to inspection at the registered office, see **6.8.3** above) to check the amount of compensation which might be payable for breach of contract. It could be very expensive for the company to get rid of the director, particularly where the director concerned has been given a long fixed-term contract.

6.10.3.5 Effect of removal

If a director is removed from the board then the director automatically loses any executive role that that person might occupy within the company, if the executive role is dependent on that person being a director. However, the now ex-director still retains any accrued employment rights, including those arising under their service contract. This service contract between the ex-director and the company is not rendered invalid by that person's removal as a director; it is still binding on both parties, and the company has prima facie breached its obligations under the contract by preventing the director from performing their duties and earning a salary. This therefore may entitle the ex-director to make a claim against the company for wrongful dismissal.

In addition, the ex-director may have a claim for unfair dismissal, or even possibly redundancy, depending on the particular facts. In *Cobley v Forward Technology Industries plc* [2003] EWCA Civ 646, the director in question had been removed from the board of directors and had his service contract terminated in accordance with its terms. The Court of Appeal held that the termination of the service contract was for 'some other substantial reason' under s 98(1)(b) of the Employment Rights Act 1996, and therefore the director's dismissal was not an 'unfair dismissal' under the 1996 Act.

The issue of employment rights applies only to a director who is employed by the company, ie an executive director. If the ex-director were a non-executive director, that person's duties would usually have been confined to attending the board meetings; that person would have had no job within the company. Therefore, normally, the ex-director could not have a claim for breach of any employment rights.

If a director is removed from the board, the officers of the company are under an obligation to notify the Registrar of Companies, and must delete that person's name from the register of directors and the register of directors' residential addresses (see **6.9.1** to **6.9.3** above).

The Economic Crime and Corporate Transparency Act 2023 will remove the requirement for a company to maintain a register of directors and a register of directors' residential addresses. On removal from the board, a notification to Companies House will have to be made within 14 days. This amendment is expected to come into force by 2027.

6.10.4 Removal by shareholders under the articles

Under Table A, art 73, but *not* under the model articles for private companies, directors must retire by rotation. At the first AGM of the company, all the directors are required to retire from office but will automatically be reappointed unless a resolution to the contrary is passed by the shareholders. At each subsequent AGM, one-third of the total number of directors must retire from office and be subject to re-election (or a number as near to one-third as can be achieved). It is thus open to the shareholders to remove a director from the board when that person's position as director is subject to confirmation in this way. This is therefore a much easier way to remove a director than using s 168 of the CA 2006 (see **6.10.3** above). Nevertheless, it is important to note that under Table A, art 84, executive directors, including Managing Directors, are exempt from the requirement to retire by rotation.

This power is generally not needed in a small private company where the composition of the shareholders and the directors is largely the same, and this explains why it was omitted from the model articles for private companies when the CA 2006 came into force. The power is included in the model articles for *public* companies, though.

6.10.5 Protecting a director from dismissal

There are various ways to protect a director before matters get to the stage of a resolution to dismiss them. The possibilities include:

(a) a *Bushell v Faith* clause (see **6.10.3.4** above) to give the director weighted voting rights if a resolution to dismiss that person is put forward at a general meeting (plus possibly a secondary clause giving weighted rights on a resolution to remove the *Bushell v Faith* clause itself from the articles), but depending on the wording of the clause it may now be harder to 'entrench' such rights under the CA 2006 than was the case previously (see **4.4.3** above);

(b) a fixed-term service contract of long duration and without a break clause, so that the director might have to be paid significant compensation if they were to be dismissed as a director (subject to shareholder approval for a fixed-term contract over two years, see **6.8.2** above);

(c) a shareholders' agreement (see **5.6.2.2**) under which the parties to the agreement, if the directors were also shareholders, could agree not to vote against specified directors on a motion to dismiss any of those directors; or

(d) making sure that if the director has made a loan to the company which is outstanding, it is expressed to be repayable if the director loses their position, as this would act as a financial disincentive to dismiss the director.

6.10.6 Disqualification of directors by the court

The court has a discretionary power to disqualify a person from being a director under the CDDA 1986. The period of disqualification ranges from two years up to 15 years. The director's previous behaviour and the seriousness of the current offence will be relevant in determining the length of disqualification.

The grounds for disqualification under the CDDA 1986 are:

(a) conviction of an indictable offence (s 2);
(b) persistent breaches of companies legislation (s 3);
(c) fraud in a winding up (s 4);
(d) on summary conviction for a filing or notice default (s 5);
(e) being an unfit director of insolvent companies (s 6) (see **6.10.6.1** below);
(f) disqualification after investigation (s 8);
(g) fraudulent or wrongful trading (s 10);
(h) a breach of competition law (s 9A); and
(i) being subject to an asset freeze under the Sanctions and Anti-Money Laundering Act 2018.

A director is expected to have a prudent businessperson's sense of reality (*In the matter of Queens Moat Houses plc; sub nom Secretary of State for Trade and Industry v Bairstow* [2005] 1 BCLC 136). In *Bairstow*, the director was held not to have been dishonest but had failed to guard against the publication of seriously misleading financial information, and could not rely on his ignorance of accountancy. He was thus disqualified as a director by the court.

The primary aim is to protect the public from the future activities of such persons. In *Re Sevenoaks Stationers Ltd* [1990] 3 WLR 1165, the tariff for disqualification was suggested to be:

(a) 2–5 years for not particularly serious offences;
(b) 6–10 years for serious offences not meriting the top bracket; or
(c) 11–15 years for particularly serious cases.

In *Vintage Hallmark plc* [2006] EWHC 2761, two directors were disqualified for 15 years each. They had sought money from investors, even though the directors knew that the business had liabilities of £52 million but assets of only £5 million.

In *Official Receiver v Stern (No 2)* [2002] 1 BCLC 119, Mr Stern was found to have made unauthorised drawings from the companies concerned, to have traded at risk of the creditors and to have paid off his own guarantee when the company was insolvent. The Court of Appeal confirmed his disqualification for 12 years.

A director was disqualified for 10 years where he had failed to keep accounting records, pay customers and had made false statements to the company's liquidator (*Secretary of State for Trade and Industry v Vandevivere* [2005] Lawtel AC0108520).

In *Kotonou v Secretary of State for Business, Enterprise and Regulatory Reform* [2010] EWHC 19 (Ch), a director appealed against a disqualification for eight years. His company's creditors were owed £1.7 million, which included a debt to the Crown of £570,000 for PAYE and National Insurance. He had drawn an excessive salary from his company and allowed it to fund a debt in paying money to another company without good cause. He had also previously been a director of a company which had gone into creditors' voluntary liquidation. His appeal was rejected, not surprisingly.

At the other end of the scale, a director who was held to have breached his fiduciary duties to the company and ignored statutory obligations concerning the filing of accounts and returns was disqualified for two years (*Secretary of State for Trade and Industry v Goldberg* [2003] EWHC 2843).

Breach of a disqualification order will have serious consequences. In *R v Seager; R v Blatch* [2009] EWCA Crim 1303, S, who had participated in the running of six companies after having been disqualified, was made subject to a confiscation order for £941,272 under s 71 of the Criminal Justice Act 1988. B, who had previously given an undertaking to the court not to engage in the running of companies without leave of the court, was made subject to a confiscation order of £356,249 under s 6(4) of the Proceeds of Crime Act 2002. The basis of the sums was the turnover of the company. The Court of Appeal held that confiscation proceedings following breach of a disqualification order were on the same basis as for any crime (*R v May (Raymond George)* [2008] 1 AC 1028). The Court held that the basis to be used should be the personal benefit received by the individuals concerned (and not the profits made by the company), and made an order in that lesser amount in respect of B and quashed the order in regard to S as there was no evidence as to what that amount might have been.

Section 3 above will be amended to include persistent non-compliance with company filing obligations and identity verification requirements (see ***3.11*** *above). A new ground for disqualification will apply to directors subject to an asset freeze under sanctions legislation (CDDA 1986, s 11A). At the time of writing, it is not clear when these new provisions will be brought into effect.*

6.10.6.1 Unfit director of insolvent companies

Disqualifications under s 6 of the CDDA 1986 are the most common.

The factors to be taken into account in deciding unfitness under s 6 are set out in Sch 1 to the CDDA 1986. These include:

(a) any misfeasance on the part of the director;
(b) the extent of the director's responsibility for voidable transactions;
(c) the extent of the director's responsibility for failure to comply with Companies Act regulations;
(d) the extent of the director's responsibility for insolvency;
(e) the extent of the director's responsibility for failure to supply goods which have been paid for (in full or in part); and
(f) the extent of responsibility for preferences, or transactions at undervalues.

The basic question is whether there has been a breach of the 'common standard of commercial morality'. This might include:

(a) failure to keep books and records;
(b) failure to file returns;
(c) paying excessive amounts of directors' remuneration;
(d) recklessly trading whilst insolvent; or
(e) purchasing stock before liquidation in the knowledge that it would be of no use to anyone but the present trade. The company then goes into liquidation and the directors repurchase the stock from the liquidator at a knock-down price.

Other negative points which may arise include:

(a) trading on 'Crown monies', ie not paying VAT, PAYE or National Insurance Contributions to the Government, and using the money as working capital; and
(b) 'reckless trading whilst insolvent', which does not mean that a wrongful trading action has to be established.

Positive points that would count in a director's favour are:

(a) employing qualified financial staff;
(b) taking professional advice;
(c) regular budgets; and

(d) a large personal financial commitment to the company.

In *In the matter of Uno plc & World of Leather plc; sub nom Secretary of State for Trade and Industry v Gill* [2004] EWHC 933, the directors had continued to trade and take customer deposits for the furniture which the company sold. However, the directors had tried to find a buyer for some of their shops. They had also taken legal and accountancy advice. They were not found to be unfit under s 6 of the CDDA 1986.

6.10.6.2 Effects of disqualification

When a disqualification order has been made against an individual, they may not without leave of the court:

(a) be a director; or

(b) be concerned in any way in the promotion, formation or management of a company.

Section 169A of the CA 2006 makes it clear that disqualification of a director means that they cease to hold the office of director.

Under s 13 of the CDDA 1986, contravention of a disqualification order is a criminal offence and is punishable by up to two years' imprisonment. By s 15, if someone is involved in management of a company in breach of a disqualification order, they also become personally liable for the relevant debts of the company.

It is possible for a disqualified director to apply for leave to act as a director during their period of disqualification (CDDA 1986, s 17). In *In re Gibson Davies Ltd* [1995] BCC 11, Sir Mervyn Davies said:

> On an application under section 17 ... the court must be satisfied that there is a need to make the order and, more importantly, that if the order is made the public will remain adequately protected.

In *In the matter of China Worldwide Jazz*, Lawtel, 6 June 2003, the court granted leave to act. The basis was that the director had not been dishonest and that the business was a profitable one (and was therefore unlikely to go insolvent). Such permission is often qualified by requiring the presence on the board of someone professionally qualified, eg an accountant, to keep an eye on the errant director. There could also be a requirement to accept personal liability for debts of the company.

In *Re Amaron Ltd* [1997] 2 BCLC 115, Neuberger J did not allow the application. This was a case in which the applicant had allowed the company to trade while insolvent and to retain money owed to creditors in order to fund continued trading.

6.10.7 Disqualification of directors under the articles

It is usual for the articles of a company to provide that in certain circumstances a person is automatically disqualified from acting as a director. Article 18 of the model articles for private companies provides that a director shall automatically cease to hold office in a variety of situations, for example if they become bankrupt or if they are mentally ill, or if a doctor's written opinion is given to the company that the director is physically or mentally incapable of acting as a director and may remain so for more than three months.

Article 18(e), which automatically disqualifies a director where a court makes an order restricting that person's rights due to mental health problems, has now been removed. Companies which adopt the model articles on or after 23 April 2013 will therefore no longer have this provision in their model articles.

6.11 MANAGERS

A manager is an officer of the company by virtue of s 1173(1) of the CA 2006. In this context we do not mean a Managing Director or any other type of director but

> any person who in the affairs of the company exercises a supervisory control which reflects the general policy of the company for the time being or which is related to the general administration of the company is in the sphere of management. (*Re a Company* [1980] Ch 138)

The key consequence of a manager being an officer of a company is that that person could be held to be in a fiduciary relationship with the company and therefore owe it fiduciary duties (see **6.4** above).

6.12 AUDITORS

The auditors are officers of the company by virtue, for example, of s 487(1) of the CA 2006, which refers to their holding office. Their role is limited to the company's finances.

6.12.1 Functions

We saw at **6.7** above that the directors of every company must prepare accounts for each financial year (CA 2006, s 394).

There is a general duty on every company to appoint an auditor to review those accounts independently every year (CA 2006, s 485 for a private company). The main duty of the auditor is, under s 495(1) of the Act, to prepare a report on the accounts to be sent to a private company's shareholders. This report must state whether in the auditor's opinion the accounts have been prepared properly and give a true and fair view of the company (CA 2006, s 495(3)).

The auditor must ensure that those who have put up the money for the business (the shareholders) are not defrauded or misled by those in charge of the company's finances, ie the directors. If an auditor qualifies their report in any way, that person is warning the members that there may have been some unethical business dealings, or even fraud.

Notice of all general meetings must also be sent to the auditor, and that person then has a right to attend and speak at any such meeting, although they do not have a right to vote (CA 2006, s 502).

A small company (see **6.7.1** above) with a balance sheet total of not more than £7.5 million and a turnover of not more than £15 million in that financial year is exempt from the statutory audit requirements (CA 2006, s 477). To benefit from the exemption the directors have to declare on the balance sheet, under s 475(3) of the CA 2006, that the directors acknowledge their responsibility to keep accounting records that comply with the CA 2006, and the shareholders must not have exercised their right under s 476 of the CA 2006 to call for an audit.

Shareholders holding not less than 10% of the issued share capital may require the company to have its accounts audited by lodging a written notice at the registered office during the financial year in question, but not more than one month before the end of the financial year (CA 2006, s 476).

Companies which do not trade, ie so-called dormant companies, may also file abbreviated accounts and are exempt from audit under s 480 of the CA 2006.

6.12.2 Appointment

If a company must have an auditor, it must appoint someone who is qualified (a certified or chartered accountant) and independent (not connected with anyone involved in the company) (CA 2006, ss 1212–1215). Usually a firm of accountants is appointed to be the company's auditor, which means that any qualified member of that firm at the date of the appointment may undertake the audit.

Under s 485(1) of the CA 2006, an auditor must be appointed for each financial year of the company unless the directors resolve that audited accounts are unlikely to be required. For a private company the directors will usually appoint the very first auditor of the company (CA

2006, s 485(3)); thereafter the shareholders will usually have the power to appoint the auditor by ordinary resolution (CA 2006, s 485(4)).

The appointment must be made before the end of a 28-day period after circulation of the accounts until the equivalent period in the following year. Under s 487 of the CA 2006, an auditor of a private company is deemed to be re-appointed automatically unless:

(a) the auditor was appointed by the directors (as with the first auditor);
(b) the articles require re-appointment;
(c) 5% of the shareholders give notice under s 488 of the CA 2006;
(d) the shareholders resolve that that person should not be re-appointed; or
(e) the directors have resolved that no audited accounts will be required.

6.12.3 Terms and remuneration

The terms on which the auditor holds office and the auditor's fee for doing so will be a matter for negotiation between the auditor and the company. The directors approve the contract with the first auditor; in subsequent years the approval of members is necessary (CA 2006, s 492).

6.12.4 Liability of auditors

The leading case on the liability of auditors is *Caparo v Dickman* [1990] 2 AC 605. The House of Lords held that auditors conducting an annual audit did not owe a duty of care either to the shareholders or to potential investors, ie potential shareholders. Foreseeability alone was not enough to impose such a duty; there would also have to be proximity between the relevant parties, otherwise the auditors would have an unlimited duty of care. There may be liability in other circumstances, for example where auditors make a statement about the reliability of the accounts to purchasers of a company (eg *Peach Publishing Ltd v Slater & Co* [1996] BCC 751 and *Electra Private Equity Partners v KPMG Peat Marwick* [2001] 1 BCLC 589). In *Equitable Life v Ernst & Young* [2003] EWCA Civ 1114, the insurance company failed in its attempt to sue its auditors for their alleged failure to point out problems in the company's allocation of resources to deal with future liabilities.

Auditors can be sued if they fail to spot a fraud against the company. However, in *Moore Stephens v Rolls Ltd* [2009] UKHL 29, it was the company itself, through its owner and director Mr S, which had been used to defraud several banks. The liquidator of the company claimed for these losses, for which the company had successfully been sued by the banks. It was held that the company was in effect a party to the fraud and could not claim against the auditors.

The whole issue of auditor liability was thrown up by the Enron financial scandal in the United States in late 2001, which resulted in immense liability for the auditors in question, to the extent that that firm of auditors, Arthur Andersen, was subsequently dissolved. As a result of concern by auditors that their liability was unlimited and to avoid another collapse, there are provisions in the CA 2006 to deal with this situation. Essentially, shareholders of a company can agree to limit the liability of their auditors by passing an ordinary resolution (CA 2006, ss 532–538). However, no limitation is able reduce the auditors' liability to less than an amount which would be fair and reasonable in all the circumstances. Any such agreement also has to be disclosed in the annual accounts or directors' report. The agreement can relate to acts or omissions in the course of the audit for one financial year only.

There is a power in s 535 of the CA 2006 for the Government to make regulations about agreements limiting an auditor's liability, though none have yet been made.

There are two criminal offences which auditors may commit under s 507 of the CA 2006. These are knowingly or recklessly either including misleading material, or omitting required statements under the CA 2006.

In light of the scandalous failure of auditors (amongst others) to detect problems in financial services companies which were involved in the global financial crisis of 2007/08 and more recent high-profile collapses of companies such as Carillion (the outsourcing company) with the loss of 9,000 jobs and over £7 billion in debts, the Government has decided to replace the regulator overseeing auditors and increase its powers by establishing a new body, the Auditing, Reporting and Governance Authority (ARGA). It is not clear when ARGA will be up and running as the necessary legislation has not yet been put before Parliament and has been repeatedly delayed.

6.12.5 Removal from office and resignation

The auditor may be removed from office at any time by the shareholders (CA 2006, s 510). The procedure under s 511 of the CA 2006 is exactly the same as that required for the removal of a director, ie an ordinary resolution is required, of which special notice has been given by the proposing shareholder to the company (see **6.10.3** above). Shareholders must hold a general meeting. A written resolution cannot be used to achieve this. The consequences of removal (eg, whether compensation is payable) are dependent upon the terms of the contract between the company and the auditor (CA 2006, s 510(3)).

An auditor may resign from office by notice in writing sent to the registered office (CA 2006, s 516).

Under s 519 of the CA 2006, an auditor who ceases to hold office for any reason must deliver a statement to the company of the circumstances connected with the cessation. This is particularly useful in the very rare situation where the company's finances are particularly questionable and the auditor resigns for this reason. An example of this happened with a publicly-traded company, TUI Travel PLC, the leisure travel company, in January 2011. The auditors, KPMG, resigned after discovering a £117m black hole in the accounts. They stated in unusually strong terms in their resignation letter that their relationship with the company was becoming 'increasingly strained', stating further that 'we are not confident that in the future we could carry out an audit of the company to the appropriate standard, but others may be able to do so'. The statement must be filed with the Registrar of Companies. In certain circumstances either the auditor, or the company or both have an obligation to inform the appropriate audit authority, which is currently the Professional Oversight Board of the Financial Reporting Council (CA 2006, ss 522 and 523).

The FRC is due to be replaced by a new regulatory body, ARGA, the Auditing, Reporting and Governance Authority by 2028, although the necessary legislation has yet to be laid before Parliament.

CHAPTER 7

CONTROLS ON DIRECTORS

LEARNING OUTCOMES

After reading this chapter you will be able to:

- identify the content and application of the duties which apply to company directors
- understand the consequences of a breach of duty
- explain how to avoid such a breach
- identify other legal controls on directors' behaviour.

7.1 INTRODUCTION

We have already seen that a company is a separate legal person in its own right, but that since it is an artificial rather than a human person, others must act on its behalf. We saw in **Chapter 6** that the directors of a company are its most important officers, and that in managing the company's business on a daily basis they have extensive powers to run the company. However, it is the shareholders rather than the directors of a company who own it; and although a director of a company may also be one of its shareholders, there is no reason why these persons should not be different. Therefore whole series of controls are placed on the directors of the company to ensure that the company, and ultimately the shareholders' investments in the company, are properly protected. We examine these controls in this chapter, as well as the liability which arises.

7.2 DIRECTORS' GENERAL DUTIES

The directors of a company have duties imposed on them by law. These duties seek to hold the directors to account for the way in which they run the company. They seek to protect the company by regulating the directors' behaviour. If any of the directors breaches any of these duties then they will incur liability and action may be taken against them. The directors must therefore comply with all of these duties at all times to avoid this risk of liability.

Before the CA 2006 came into force, directors were subject to duties which derived principally from equitable principles but also from common law rules. The duties of directors therefore evolved through decisions of the courts. The courts have long held directors to be in a fiduciary relationship with their company and to owe it fiduciary duties. They have considered directors to be analogous to trustees, namely, in a special position of trust in relation to their company. The fiduciary duties imposed on directors therefore arose out of equitable principles, for example the directors had to act at all times in good faith in the interests of the company. Directors were also subject to the common law duty of skill and care.

The CA 2006 brought about radical change to directors' duties. The previous equitable and common law duties were codified and reformed in ss 171–181 of the Act. Seven separate general duties are set out in ss 171 to 177 (see **7.3 to 7.9** below). Section 170(3) of the CA 2006 states that these general duties are:

> based on certain common law rules and equitable principles as they apply in relation to directors and have effect in place of those rules and principles as regards duties owed to a company by a director.

The new duties have therefore replaced the previous duties.

Nevertheless, s 170(4) of the CA 2006 goes on to provide that:

> the general duties shall be interpreted and applied in the same way as common law rules or equitable principles, and regard shall be had to the corresponding common law rules and equitable principles in interpreting and applying the general duties.

In other words, the CA 2006 general directors' duties will be interpreted in accordance with the previous case law on directors' duties. Section 178 also states that the remedies for breach of the general duties will be the same as under the corresponding equitable principles or common law rules. In addition, it was made clear in government-prepared Explanatory Notes to the CA 2006 that it is intended that the CA 2006 general duties should also take account of future changes in the law regarding relevant equitable principles and the common law.

More than one duty may apply to the directors in any one situation (CA 2006, s 179(1)), and therefore the directors must comply with all of them.

7.2.1 Who owes the duties?

The duties apply to all directors of the company. We saw at **6.3.1** above that a 'director' is defined by s 250(1) of the CA 2006 to include any person occupying the position of director by whatever name called. This will include both executive and non-executive directors (*Commonwealth Oil and Gas Co Ltd v Baxter* [2007] Scot CS CSOH 198), and de facto directors.

The duties apply to shadow directors as well, where they are capable of applying.

7.2.2 To whom are the duties owed?

Directors owe their duties to the company (CA 2006, s 170(1)) rather than to the shareholders, creditors or other directors of the company. This means that the company itself (acting through the board of directors) must take action against a director for breach of these duties (see **7.10** below) as any wrong is committed against the company itself. However, we also saw at **5.8.6** above that in limited circumstances the shareholders may bring a derivative action on behalf of the company to enforce the company's rights.

In very exceptional cases the directors might owe a duty to shareholders as well as to the company where, for example, they agreed to act as agents for the shareholders, or if they assumed responsibility for giving advice to the shareholders on their shareholdings, but this would seem to be relevant only in small family companies (*Platt v Platt* [1999] 2 BCLC 745) and does not arise in the ordinary course of running a company.

A director may also owe duties to the creditors of their company rather than to the shareholders if the company is insolvent or approaching insolvency (see **7.13.10** below). This is explicitly acknowledged in the duty to promote the success of the company (see **7.4** below) in s 172(3) of the CA 2006.

7.3 DUTY TO ACT WITHIN POWERS

Under s 171 of the CA 2006:

> A director of a company must—
>
> (a) act in accordance with the company's constitution, and
>
> (b) only exercise powers for the purposes for which they are conferred.

This general duty is a codification of the fiduciary duty that a director must use their powers for a proper purpose, and must act within the powers conferred by the company's memorandum and articles of association.

Section 17 of the CA 2006 defines a company's constitution to include its articles of association. This duty will be therefore be breached if a director acts outside the powers given in the articles. For example, the company's articles may only permit a director acting on their own to enter into a contract worth less than £1,000. If a director enters into a contract worth £2,000, they will have breached their duty to the company under s 171(a) of the CA 2006.

As regards the requirement in s 171(b) above, the courts would ascertain objectively the purpose for which the power was conferred and then consider whether that was the director's substantial or primary purpose in exercising the power (*Howard Smith Ltd v Ampol Petroleum Ltd* [1974] AC 821). Many of the cases involve deciding whether directors have properly exercised powers under the constitution to issue new shares in the company. If, for example, the directors issued the new voting shares to themselves as shareholders, or to 'friendly' shareholders in order to prevent other shareholders taking control of the company, this duty would usually be breached. This would be the case even if the directors believed this action was in the best interests of the company (*Howard Smith Ltd v Ampol Petroleum Ltd*). A breach of this duty may also arise, though, in relation to the exercise of other powers, such as the power to call general meetings (*Pergamon Press Ltd v Maxwell* [1970] 1 WLR 1167) or the power to enter contracts on behalf of the company (*Lee Panavision Ltd v Lee Lighting Ltd* [1992] BCLC 22).

7.4 DUTY TO PROMOTE THE SUCCESS OF THE COMPANY

Section 172 of the CA 2006 sets out the most important duty of the director of a company. It requires the director

> to act in the way he considers, in good faith, would be most likely to promote the success of the company for the benefit of its members as a whole ...

This duty is based primarily on the previous fiduciary duty to act in good faith in the best interests of the company (*Re Smith and Fawcett Ltd* [1942] Ch 304).

In considering the s 172 duty, directors must have regard to various factors set out in s 172(1) of the Act. This list is not exhaustive, however. The factors are:

(a) the likely consequences of any decision in the long term,

(b) the interests of the company's employees,

(c) the need to foster the company's business relationships with suppliers, customers and others,

(d) the impact of the company's operations on the community and the environment,

(e) the desirability of the company maintaining a reputation for high standards of business conduct, and

(f) the need to act fairly as between members of the company.

A subjective rather than an objective test is applied to this duty. This means that the duty does not require a director to act in a way which a court would consider is most likely to promote the success of the company for the shareholders as a whole, but rather in a way which the director honestly considers would do so (*Re Southern Counties Fresh Food Ltd* [2008] EWHC 2810). In other words, there might be action which is more likely to promote the company's success, but this will not result in a breach of duty by a director if the director honestly considered that the director's own act was most likely to promote the company's success. In *Madoff Securities International Ltd v Raven & Others* [2013] EWHC 3147 (Comm) (18 October 2013), it was stated that a director may legitimately defer to his fellow directors' views if he thinks they believe they are acting in the best interests of the company, even if he is not himself in agreement. As board decisions are taken by majority decision, a director is not in breach of the duty merely because he would have decided differently on his own. The effect of this test in practice therefore makes it very difficult to challenge directors' decision-making. If the quality of decision-making is poor it will still not usually amount to a breach of this duty, provided the director or directors concerned honestly believed their decision was most likely to promote the company's success.

The need for the directors to take into account the various factors mentioned above is intended to ensure that the directors think of the impact of their decisions beyond the company and its shareholders alone. However, in practice, having regard to these factors, although compulsory, is thought unlikely to result in a greater risk of liability for the directors, because these factors are to be considered with regard to promoting the success of the company *for the benefit of its members* (ie shareholders) as a whole. Nonetheless, in order to prove that the factors were considered, board minutes may well refer to the s 172(1) factors having been taken into account; and if any factors are particularly relevant on the facts then greater reasoning should be perhaps be included in the board minutes. If a decision is particularly controversial (eg, closing down part of the company's business) then it may be worth addressing all of the factors in the board minutes.

The meaning of 'success' in s 172 of the CA 2006 is not entirely clear, but it seems that for a commercial company this would usually mean a long-term increase in the company's value for its shareholders.

It also should be noted that this duty is not limited to board resolutions or other decisions taken by the whole board; it applies to all decisions taken by any director.

A review of the implementation of this duty was carried out as part of the Government's review of the introduction of the CA 2006. A report released in late 2010 stated that more clarity and guidance was needed to increase understanding and awareness of the effect of the s 172 duty.

7.5 DUTY TO EXERCISE INDEPENDENT JUDGMENT

Under s 173 of the CA 2006, a director must exercise independent judgment. This is a restatement of the previous fiduciary duty that a director must not fetter their own discretion (ie restrict the exercise of the director's independent judgment). This duty seeks to ensure that directors act independently in their decision-making rather than contracting it out. So, for example, a director could not enter into an agreement with another person (such as a shareholder who appointed them) that they would vote in a particular way at a board meeting.

This is not a blanket requirement, however, as s 173(2) of the CA 2006 provides:

> This duty is not infringed by [the director of a company] acting—
>
> (a) in accordance with an agreement duly entered into by the company that restricts the future exercise of discretion by its directors, or
>
> (b) in a way authorised by the company's constitution.

This protects the right of the directors to enter into a contract on behalf of the company that may in the future require the directors to act in a particular way, provided it is done in good faith in the interests of the company (*Fulham Football Club Ltd v Cabra Estates plc* [1994] 1 BCLC 363).

There is also no prohibition on directors taking advice, eg legal or financial advice.

It was held in *Madoff Securities International Ltd v Raven & Others* (above) that there was no breach of this duty where directors of a company acted in deference to the superior skill and knowledge of a fellow director who was a financial expert, described as a 'titan of Wall Street'. This was the case even though it subsequently transpired that the director was a financial fraudster who embezzled billions of dollars and was sentenced to 150 years in prison in the US. It would, however, be a breach of duty for a director to allow themselves to be dominated, bamboozled or manipulated by a dominant fellow director where this involved a total surrender of their responsibility.

7.6 DUTY TO EXERCISE REASONABLE CARE, SKILL AND DILIGENCE

Section 174 of the CA 2006 provides:

> (1) A director of a company must exercise reasonable care, skill and diligence.
>
> (2) This means the care, skill and diligence that would be exercised by a reasonably diligent person with—
>
> (a) the general knowledge, skill and experience that may reasonably be expected of a person carrying out the functions carried out by the director in relation to the company, and
>
> (b) the general knowledge, skill and experience that the director has.

This codifies the previous common law duty of care and skill (*Gregson v HAE Trustees Ltd* [2008] EWHC 1006).

The s 174 general duty seeks to ensure that directors carry out their functions sufficiently carefully and competently. The duty will therefore be breached if the director is incompetent or negligent and falls below the required standard of behaviour.

The precise standard of care, skill and diligence which must be demonstrated under s 174 of the CA 2006 needs some analysis. The required standard set out in s 174(2) is adopted from case law on the old common law duty (such as *Norman v Theodore Goddard* [1991] BCC 14 and *Re D'Jan of London Ltd* [1994] BCLC 561) which was itself based on a test used in s 214(4) of the IA 1986 to judge the offence of wrongful trading by directors under insolvency law (see **7.13.10.1** below).

The test is in two parts. The first part, s 174(2)(a) of the CA 2006, sets out the minimum standard required of a director. It is an objective requirement that must be met if the director is to avoid being in breach of this duty. The particular standard will vary depending on the particular functions and responsibilities of the director, and the circumstances of the company. For example, all Managing Directors/Chief Executives of small private companies which are profitable will generally be held to the same minimum standard of competence. The standard applicable to a director of a profitable company will change if it experiences financial difficulties (*Roberts v Frohlich* [2011] EWHC 257 (Ch), a case in which directors of a property development company were found to have breached this duty).

Section 174(2)(b) of the CA 2006 sets out the second part of the test. This is the subjective element, in that it looks at the knowledge, skill and experience of the individual director concerned. If (and only if) the individual director possesses a higher standard of general knowledge, skill or experience than that reasonably expected under part (a) of the test, the director will be judged by that higher standard. For example, if a director has specialist knowledge, such as if they were also a qualified accountant, they would probably be held to a higher standard than the objective standard.

Directors cannot simply escape liability under this duty by arguing that they have delegated their responsibilities lawfully to another director or person. They must exercise their powers of supervision adequately, and whether this requirement has been met will depend on the facts of each particular case (*Re Barings plc No 5* [2000] 1 BCLC 523).

A director who is completely inactive – as may occur in family companies when spouses, children or other relatives are appointed as directors of the company – will be in breach of this duty and may be held liable for wrongs committed by the company. In *Lexi Holdings plc (In administration) v Luqman* [2009] 2 BCLC 1, the Court of Appeal held that two directors were in breach of their duty of skill and care to the company by allowing another director (their brother) to commit a fraud on the company, involving the embezzlement of £60 million over a period of years, through their inactivity. It will also be a breach of duty for a director to allow themselves to be dominated or manipulated by a fellow director resulting in them handing over decision-making to that director (*Madoff Securities International Ltd v Raven & Others* (above)).

An executive director (see **6.3.1.1** above) would normally have a written contract of employment. This will usually contain express terms requiring a duty of skill and care to the company. If the director's behaviour falls below the required standard there will therefore also be a right for the company to seek damages for breach of contract.

7.7 DUTY TO AVOID CONFLICTS OF INTEREST

Section 175 of the CA 2006 sets out the director's general duty to avoid conflicts of interest with the director's company. Section 175(1) states:

> A director of a company must avoid a situation in which he has, or can have, a direct or indirect interest that conflicts, or possibly may conflict, with the interests of the company.

Section 175(2) provides:

> This applies in particular to the exploitation of any property, information, or opportunity (and it is immaterial whether the company could take advantage of the property, information or opportunity).

This has replaced the former fiduciary duties that a director must not, unless given consent by the company, put themselves in a position where the director's personal interests and the director's duty to the company conflict (*Aberdeen Railway Co v Blaikie Bros* (1845) 1 Macq 461), and that a director must not make a profit from being a director unless the company authorises it (*Regal (Hastings) Ltd v Gulliver* [1967] AC 134). The CA 2006 has made some important changes to the previous law.

Section 175(1) of the CA 2006 states the general 'no conflicts' fiduciary duty. Section 175(2) codifies the 'no profits' duty. Note that some case law treats the 'no profits' duty as an example of the 'no conflicts' rule rather than as a separate duty.

Section 175(1) and (2) of the CA 2006 are couched in very wide terms. Merely having an indirect conflict in a 'situation' with the company, or a possible conflict or even a possible indirect conflict, is enough to trigger the prohibition, and this emphasises the importance of the nature of the fiduciary relationship between a director and the director's company. There are, however, some important exclusions which will prevent a conflict from amounting to a breach of this director's duty:

(a) *Under s 175(3), for conflicts arising under a transaction or an arrangement with the company.* This would cover, for instance, a contract made between the company on the one hand and the director on the other. These are excluded because such 'transactional' conflicts are dealt with elsewhere in the CA 2006. For example, there are more specific provisions under ss 177 and 182 of the Act, requiring a director to declare their interest in a proposed or existing transaction or arrangement with the company respectively (see **7.9** below). In addition there are further restrictions in the CA 2006 regulating substantial property transactions with directors (see **7.12.1** below), and loans, quasi-loans and credit transactions with directors (see **7.12.2** below).

(b) *Under s 175(4), if the board of directors authorise the matter giving rise to the conflict (and meet the applicable conditions), there will be no breach of this duty* (see **7.11.1** below).

(c) *Under s 175(4), if the situation cannot reasonably be regarded as likely to give rise to a conflict of interest.*

An example of the relevance of the duty under s 175 of the CA 2006, particularly s 175(2), may be seen with regard to so-called corporate opportunities. These are business opportunities, such as new trading contracts, into which the company might enter. There will be a prima facie breach of s 175 of the CA 2006 if a director has obtained information about new business opportunities as a result of being a director in the company, and then uses that information for their personal advantage, eg by entering into the contract in their own name rather than in the company's name (*Cook v Deeks* [1916] 1 AC 554). This will be seen as a breach of the fiduciary relationship between the director and the company. In *Aerostar Maintenance International Ltd v Wilson* [2010] EWHC 2032 (Ch), a director breached his fiduciary duties by setting up a new company which took an aircraft maintenance contract he had originally been negotiating on behalf of the other company for which he worked as a director.

In *Regal (Hastings) Ltd v Gulliver* (above) the company owned a cinema. Regal set up a subsidiary company to buy two further cinemas. The directors of Regal invested money in the subsidiary company after Regal decided not to invest the necessary money itself. On the sale of both companies to a third party, the directors were found to be in breach of their fiduciary duty when they made a profit on the sale of their shares in the subsidiary. They were ordered to pay their profit back to their company, Regal, because they obtained the opportunity to invest only because they were directors of Regal. This was the case even though Regal itself had not wanted to make the investment in the subsidiary. An example under the CA 2006 where s 175 was not found to have been breached may be seen in *Kleanthous v Paphitis* [2011] EWHC 2287 where directors, having failed to persuade their company to buy a chain of lingerie shops, set up a company to buy it and eventually sold it for £10 million. There was no breach as the directors had made full disclosure to the board and no objections were raised.

A director cannot simply resign and then take the opportunity post-resignation. In *Industrial Development Consultants Ltd v Cooley* [1972] 2 All ER 162, a director had resigned from the company by feigning illness in order to take for himself a lucrative contract for consultancy services. He was found liable to his company for breach of his fiduciary duty and had to hand over to the company his profit on the contract. Similarly in *CMS Dolphin Ltd v Simonet* [2001] 2 BCLC 704, a director of his company was also liable when he set up a competing company and poached his former company's clients. In both these cases the director planned to leave the company to exploit opportunities which rightfully belonged to the company.

Contrast this with *Island Export Finance v Umunna* [1986] BCLC 460, where the director in question had resigned some time before the business opportunity arose. The director was therefore not liable to his former company for breach of the general duty as there was no breach of the fiduciary relationship.

The extent of s 175 is demonstrated in the case of *Towers v Premier Waste Management Ltd* [2011] EWCA Civ 923. A director of Premier, Mr Towers, borrowed some equipment from one of the company's customers for his personal use without disclosing his personal interest to the board. The Court of Appeal found he had breached his duty under s 175 (and s 176 – see **7.8** below) even though there was no bad faith, no actual conflict and the absence of a quantifiable loss to the company. Towers was ordered to pay rental costs to the company.

If a director does breach this duty, the director will be obliged to account to the company for any profit made unless the director's actions are authorised by the company, eg by the directors under s 175(4) of the CA 2006 (see **7.11.1** below).

7.8 DUTY NOT TO ACCEPT BENEFITS FROM THIRD PARTIES

Under s 176(1) of the CA 2006:

(1) A director of a company must not accept a benefit from a third party conferred by reason of—

(a) his being a director, or

(b) his doing (or not doing) anything as director.

There is an important exception under s 176(4):

(4) This duty is not infringed if the acceptance of the benefit cannot reasonably be regarded as likely to give rise to a conflict of interest.

For example, s 176 would cover corporate hospitality given to a director. There may be provisions permitting such benefits in the articles, and there is also a right for the shareholders to approve the giving of such benefits (see **7.12** below). Care should also be taken that receipt of a benefit, including corporate hospitality, does not amount to an offence under the wide-ranging Bribery Act 2010, punishable by an unlimited fine and up to 10 years' imprisonment. An example of a breach of s 176 can be found in *Towers v Premier Waste Management Ltd* [2011] EWCA Civ 923 (see **7.7** above).

7.9 DUTY TO DECLARE INTEREST IN PROPOSED TRANSACTION OR ARRANGEMENT WITH COMPANY

Section 177 of the CA 2006 provides:

(1) If a director of a company is in any way, directly or indirectly, interested in a proposed transaction or arrangement with the company, he must declare the nature and extent of that interest to the other directors.

This replaces the former equitable principle that a director must disclose to the company any interest in a transaction with that company, otherwise it would be voidable at the instance of the company or the company could make the director account for any profit (*Aberdeen Railway Co v Blaikie Bros* (1845) 1 Macq 461).

7.9.1 Aim of section 177

The aim of s 177 of the CA 2006 is to ensure that the board of directors (who will act on behalf of the company) have full disclosure of a possible conflict of interest before deciding whether to enter into the transaction with one of their own directors. The board of directors need to be aware that the director concerned, when acting on behalf of the company as a decision-maker, also has a vested interest in a personal capacity, because clearly this may affect their judgment when acting for the company. Let us assume that the director is selling a piece of land to the company. In the usual course of events the company will want to buy the land at the cheapest price possible and the director, in their personal capacity, will want to sell at the highest price possible. This will usually give rise to a conflict of interest. What this section therefore typically means in practice is that before a company enters into a contract with the director, the director must made a declaration that they have an interest in the contract, what that interest is and what the extent of it is. If the director does not do this, the contract may be challenged.

7.9.2 How is the declaration made?

If it has to be made, the declaration must be made before the company enters into the contract (CA 2006, s 177(4)). Under s 177(2)(a) it may be made at a directors' board meeting; or under s 177(2)(b)(i) it may be made by notice to the directors in writing, which can be done outside of a board meeting. If made in writing, the declaration must comply with the requirements of s 184 of the CA 2006, namely, it must be in paper or electronic form and be sent by hand, post or, if agreed by the recipient, by electronic means to all of the other directors. The declaration may also be made orally, eg at the board meeting.

Section 177(2)(b)(ii) of the CA 2006 allows for the declaration to be made by way of a general notice. This would be relevant in a situation where a declaration would have to be made by a director about an interest which arises repeatedly over time. This might occur in one of two situations:

(a) *Under s 185(2)(a) of the CA 2006, if the director of the company has an interest in another company.* For example, if the director was also a director or a shareholder of another company, and both companies were to contract with one another on a regular basis, then the director would have to declare their interest (being a director or shareholder in the other company) under s 177 of the CA 2006 each time. By giving a general notice in accordance with s 185 of the CA 2006, the director would usually need to make only one declaration which would be valid for all subsequent contracts between the two companies.

(b) *Under s 185(2)(b) of the CA 2006, if the director made a general notice regarding the director's connection with a specified person.* For example, the director might give general notice in accordance with s 185 of the CA 2006 declaring the director's connection with their spouse. This would then mean that once the general notice had been given, the director would not have to make a declaration every time the company entered into a contract with their spouse.

In order to make this general notice under s 185 of the CA 2006, the notice must:

(a) be given to the other directors at a board meeting or read at the next board meeting after it was given (s 185(4)); and

(b) state the nature and extent of the director's interest in the company or the nature of his connection with the specified person (s 185(3)).

7.9.3 Impact of making the declaration

The impact of making the declaration will be set out in the company's articles. Therefore the obligation to make a declaration under s 177 and its effect on the running of the company as set out in the articles are two separate issues. Remember that the articles may vary from company to company, so the impact of the declaration will not always be the same. For a company which has model articles for private companies, the basic rule is that under art 14(1) the director who made the declaration cannot vote as a director regarding the contract, nor form part of the quorum (minimum number of directors required) for a board meeting. For example, having declared an interest in a contract for the sale of land by the director to the company, that director cannot vote on the board resolution approving the contract, nor count in the quorum for that board meeting. There are, however, certain exceptions. See **8.4.3** and **8.4.4** below for further information.

7.9.4 Exceptions to duty to declare interest

Section 177(5) of the CA 2006 does not require a director to declare their interest when that director is not aware of the interest or the transaction or arrangement in question. Section 177(6) does not require the declaration of an interest which cannot reasonably be regarded as likely to give rise to a conflict of interest, of which the directors are already aware or ought reasonably to be aware, or if it involves the director's service contract the terms of which have been or will be discussed at a board meeting. Note that if one of the last two exceptions mentioned applies and the company has unamended model articles, the director concerned will still not be able to vote or count in the quorum on the matter under discussion as art 14 of the model articles of private companies is still applicable.

A declaration does not need to be made where there is just one director of a company whose articles require only one director (Explanatory Notes to the CA 2006, para 352). This is a decided improvement over the position prior to the CA 2006. In *Neptune (Vehicle Washing Equipment) Ltd v Fitzgerald* [1996] Ch 274 the court held that a single director obliged to make a declaration had to have a 'statutory pause for thought' or, if someone else was present, make the declaration out loud. (During the case it came to light that the director concerned was in the habit of taking business decisions while in the toilet.)

7.9.5 Duty to declare interest in existing transaction or arrangement with company

Section 177 of the CA 2006 (see **7.9.1 to 7.9.4** above) deals with directors' interests in a *proposed* transaction or arrangement with the company; under s 182 of the CA 2006, a director must declare any interest in an *existing* transaction or arrangement with the company. This declaration would therefore have to be made, for example, when there was already a contract in existence and the director subsequently became interested. This might happen if there was an existing contract between the company of which they were a director and another company, and the director became a shareholder of the second company.

If required to be made, this declaration must be made as soon as is reasonably possible (CA 2006, s 182(4)). By s 182(2), it must be made at a board meeting or by notice in writing in accordance with s 184 of the CA 2006, or it is possible to make a general notice if required in accordance with s 185 of the CA 2006 (see **7.9.2** above).

The same exceptions apply as for the s 177 declaration (see **7.9.4** above) (CA 2006, s 182(5) and (6)).

Under s 187(1) of the CA 2006, the requirements under s 182 also apply to shadow directors, but with some amendments.

7.10 CONSEQUENCES OF A BREACH OF A DIRECTOR'S DUTY

The first point to note is that, as mentioned at **7.2.2** above, the directors owe their general duties to the company and not to the shareholders. This means that it is the company which is the proper claimant and which must take action against the director for breach of a general duty, because the wrong is committed against the company. The decision to take action on behalf of the company would usually be taken by majority vote of the board of directors. In certain circumstances the shareholders may bring a derivative action on behalf of the company to enforce the company's rights (see **5.8.6** above).

The consequences of a breach (or threatened breach) of one of the director's duties in ss 171 to 177 of the CA 2006 are the same as if the corresponding equitable principles or common law rules applied (CA 2006, s 178). This means that breaches of all the general duties will be determined by equitable principles, except the duty to exercise reasonable care, skill and diligence under s 174 of the CA 2006 which will be determined by the common law.

The remedies for the company for a breach of all duties (with the exception of the s 174 duty) are (as appropriate):

(a) the requirement for the director to account for profits (*Cook v Deeks* [1916] 1 AC 554; *Regal (Hastings) Ltd v Gulliver* [1967] AC 134);
(b) the requirement for the director to return company property (*JJ Harrison (Properties) Ltd v Harrison* [2001] EWCA Civ 1467);
(c) payment of equitable compensation by the director (*Gwembe Valley Development Co Ltd v Koshy* [2003] EWCA Civ 1048);
(d) rescission of a contract; and
(e) an injunction against the director (usually when the breach is threatened).

The aim of these remedies is not to compensate the company for the breach of duty by the director but to confiscate any profit made by the director in breach and give it to the company (*Murad v Al-Saraj* [2005] EWCA Civ 959).

Requiring a director to account for profits is the most important remedy. It has a deterrent function, seeking to put off directors from breaching their duties rather than to compensate the company for any loss (*Murad v Al-Saraj*). In practice it can be quite difficult for a court to identify the relevant profits arising from the breach of duty.

For breach of s 174 of the CA 2006 (the director's duty to exercise reasonable care, skill and dliligence – see **7.6** above), the primary remedy will be common law damages awarded against the director for negligence (*Lexi Holdings plc (In administration) v Luqman* [2009] 2 BCLC 1).

Only failure by a director to make a declaration under s 182 of the CA 2006 is a criminal offence, which is punishable by a fine (CA 2006, s 183(1)).

In *Gardner v Parker* [2004] EWCA Civ 781, the Court of Appeal rejected a shareholder's claim for loss due to the decrease in the value of his shares caused by a breach of duty of a director.

7.11 AVOIDING LIABILITY FOR BREACH OF A DIRECTOR'S DUTY

There are a number of ways in which a director may avoid liability for breach of one the general duties in ss 171 to 177 of the CA 2006.

7.11.1 Authorisation for s 175

This applies only to the general duty under s 175 of the CA 2006 to avoid conflicts of interests (see **7.7** above). Section 175(4) provides that there will be no breach of this duty if the board of directors authorise the matter giving rise to the conflict. In other words, the board may absolve what would otherwise amount to a breach of s 175. Where a director acts in accordance with the provisions of the articles, the director will not be liable for breach of the s 175 duty (CA 2006, s 180(4)(b)).

For a private company, authorisation may be given provided the company's articles do not prevent it (CA 2006, s 175(5)(a)). For a public company, the articles must specifically permit the directors to authorise the matter. There is no such provision in the model articles for private companies. The directors will take such a decision by passing a board resolution at a board meeting of the company. However, the director in question cannot vote or count in the quorum (CA 2006, s 175(6)).

Section 180(1)(a) of the CA 2006 confirms that where authorisation is given, the transaction cannot be set aside.

7.11.2 Section 180 of the CA 2006

Where authorisation is obtained for the duties under s 175 of the CA 2006 to avoid conflicts of interest (see **7.11.1** above) or s 177 to declare an interest in a proposed transaction or arrangement (see **7.9** above) then there is no need for shareholder approval unless required by the articles or other enactment. This merely confirms that, subject to the articles, approval by the directors alone is possible.

7.11.3 Ratification

Under s 239(1) of the CA 2006 the shareholders may ratify conduct of the director which amounts to a breach of a director's duty, as well as negligence, default and breach of trust. If the shareholders ratify the director's conduct then the company cannot subsequently take action against the director for the breach. In effect the company is sanctioning the director's behaviour.

The decision must be taken by a shareholders' resolution (CA 2006, s 239(2)). This may be an ordinary resolution at a general meeting, or a written resolution of the shareholders. If the director is also a shareholder, the director's votes and those of any shareholder 'connected' with the director (see **7.12.1.3** below) will be disregarded, but they do form part of the quorum (CA 2006, s 239(4)). Alternatively, if the resolution is proposed as a written resolution then the director and any persons connected to the director will not be eligible to participate (CA 2006, s 239(3)). The voting restrictions do not apply if the matter is decided by unanimous consent (CA 2006, s 239(6)(a)).

Section 239 of the CA 2006 maintains the rules regarding acts which cannot be ratified (*Franbar Holdings Ltd v Patel* [2008] EWHC 1534 (Ch)). Ratification is not possible if done unfairly or improperly, or if it is illegal or oppressive towards a minority (*North-West Transportation Co Ltd v Beatty* (1887) 12 App Cas 589). If there is improper ratification, aggrieved shareholders might bring an action for unfair prejudice under s 994 of the CA 2006 (see **5.8.6** above).

7.11.4 Relief by the court

Under s 1157(1) of the CA 2006, a court may relieve a director of liability where it has found them to be liable for negligence, default, breach of duty or breach of trust. The conditions for such relief are that the director acted honestly and reasonably, and considering all the circumstances they ought fairly to be excused. The director may even apply to the court for relief before a claim is made (CA 2006, s 1157(2)).

In *Lexi Holdings plc (In administration) v Luqman* [2009] 2 BCLC 1, an application under the forerunner to s 1157 was refused, on the basis that the directors' inactivity was of itself unreasonable.

In *Bhullar v Bhullar* [2017] EWHC 407 (Ch) the court found that the director concerned had not acted dishonestly but had acted unreasonably and so should not be relieved of liability.

7.11.5 Insurance

The basic position in s 232(1) of the CA 2006 is that a provision which purports to exempt a director from liability to the company is void. Further, any attempt to indemnify the director against liability may be done only in accordance with the provisions of the Act (CA 2006, s 232(2)). Section 233 does allow a company to purchase insurance for any of its directors to cover the risk of liability arising through negligence, default, breach of duty or breach of trust.

7.12 OTHER CONTROLS IMPOSED ON DIRECTORS

Those duties mentioned in **7.3** to **7.9** above are the general duties which apply to all directors. In addition, a whole series of specific controls are imposed on directors, primarily under the CA 2006, with which they must comply or the company can take action against them. The need for these controls again emphasises the special role of directors in relation to their company. You will see from what follows that certain actions are forbidden altogether, and that other things may be done only with the consent of the shareholders.

7.12.1 Substantial property transactions

Sections 190 to 196 of the CA 2006 govern arrangements known as substantial property transactions (SPTs).

If a director in their personal capacity, or someone 'connected' to the director, buys something from or sells something to the company, the consent of the shareholders by resolution is necessary if the asset being bought or sold is of a 'non-cash' nature and is deemed to be 'substantial' (CA 2006, s 190(1)).

This is therefore another example of the CA 2006 seeking to control situations where directors have an actual or a potential conflict of interest with their company. An SPT involves a contract directly or indirectly between the director and the company, where there is the risk that the director will be conflicted when acting for the company in deciding the terms of the contract. For example, the director may be the other party to the contract, and so there will obviously be a question mark over the director's impartiality when acting for the company. We have already seen how this interest in the contract gives rise to a requirement for disclosure by way of a declaration under s 177 of the CA 2006 (see **7.9.5**) . However, because of the very nature of an SPT contract, and the amount of money involved, greater protection for the company is thought necessary. Therefore the shareholders have a veto over whether the company should enter an SPT.

7.12.1.1 Requirements

Various requirements must be met under s 190 of the CA 2006 before a matter will constitute an SPT. These are that there must be:

(a) an arrangement (also referred to in the CA 2006 at times as a 'transaction');
(b) between the company and:
  (i) one of its directors, or
  (ii) a person 'connected' with such a director, or
  (iii) one of its holding company directors, or
  (iv) a person 'connected' with a holding company director;
(c) involving the acquisition of a 'non-cash' asset;
(d) that is 'substantial'.

If these are all established then there will be an SPT and approval by the shareholders is needed.

7.12.1.2 Arrangement

The requirement for an 'arrangement' in s 190(1) of the CA 2006 will usually involve a contract between the parties, for example a contract to buy land or a contract to buy a business. However, to ensure the company is fully protected and to prevent unscrupulous directors trying to evade the need for shareholder approval, this definition also covers looser arrangements. For example, it includes an understanding or agreement which is not contractually binding on the parties (*Re Duckwari plc* [1999] Ch 253). For the remainder of this discussion we shall assume there is a proper contract involved.

7.12.1.3 Parties

There are four different possibilities, as set out at **7.12.1.1** above, of which we shall discuss the first two.

The simplest example would be the first mentioned – a contract between the company and the director directly. See **Figure 7.1** below.

Figure 7.1 Contract between the company and one of its directors

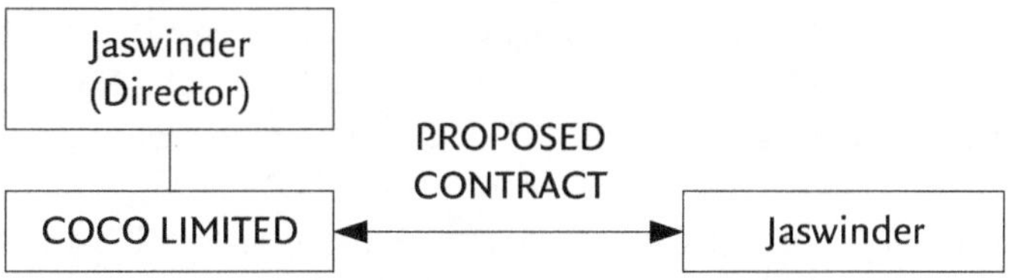

However, s 190 of the CA 2006 also extends to a contract between the company on the one hand and a person connected with a director on the other. 'Connected persons' are defined in ss 252 to 256 of the Act, and we shall now examine this definition.

Persons connected to a director

The reason for extending the restrictions to persons connected to the director is to prevent abuse. It would otherwise be all too easy for a director to circumvent the rules regulating them by involving someone close to the director but who is not legally a director themselves. This might be a member of the director's family, or even a company which the director controlled.

The following are the most commonly occurring 'connected persons' under s 252(2) of the CA 2006:

(a) *Members of the director's family* (CA 2006, s 252(2)(a)). This includes under s 253(2) a director's:
  (i) spouse or civil partner;
  (ii) partner (of whatever gender) with whom the director lives in an 'enduring family relationship';
  (iii) children and step-children;
  (iv) partner's (under (ii) above) children or step-children if they are under 18 years old and live with the director;
  (v) parents.

  Therefore, for example, a contract between the company and the husband of a director of that company would initially be caught under s 190 of the CA 2006. See **Figure 7.2** below.

Figure 7.2 Contract between the company and a director's spouse

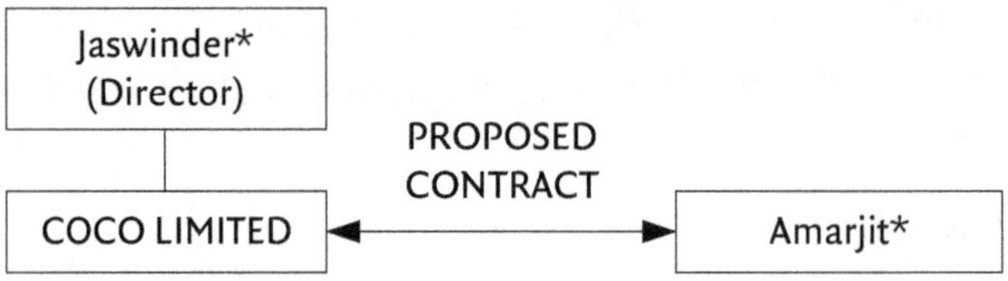

*Jaswinder and Amarjit are married.

  The definition of members of the director's family does not extend to the director's siblings, grandparents, grandchildren, uncles, aunts and cousins, and so these relatives are not 'connected persons'. A contract with these individuals falls outside s 190 of the CA 2006.

(b) *A body corporate connected to the director* (CA 2006, s 252(2)(b)). This catches contracts between the director's company and certain other companies in which the director is a shareholder.

  Section 254 of the CA 2006 defines those bodies corporate (ie companies) with which a director is connected. It is a complex definition. For our purposes the most important part is that if the director and persons connected with the director own at least 20% of the voting shares in the company then that company will be a body corporate connected to the director, and therefore a person connected to that director for the purposes of s 190 of the Act.

  In **Figure 7.3** set out below, the contract between ABC Limited and XYZ Limited is, from ABC's point of view only, prima facie caught under s 190 of the CA 2006. This is because there is a contract between ABC Limited and a person connected with Daisy, a director of ABC Limited. The person connected is XYZ Limited, because Daisy owns over 20% of the voting shares in the company (CA 2006, ss 252(2)(b) and 254(2)). We shall be able to ascertain definitively that this is a SPT only if the contract is for the acquisition of a non-cash asset that is substantial. Note that this contract is not an SPT for XYZ Limited.

Figure 7.3 Contract between the company and a company connected to the director

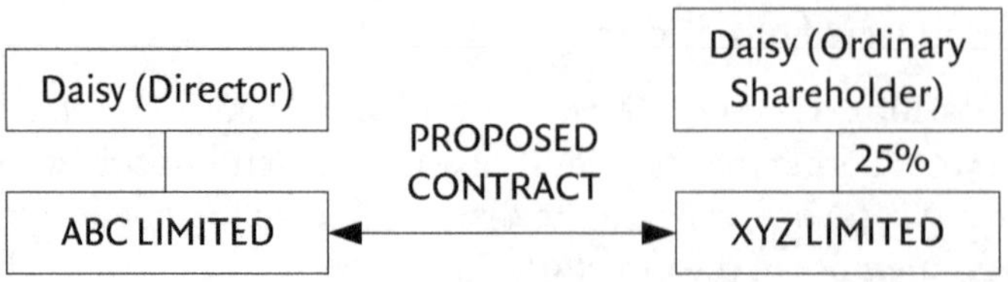

  In **Figure 7.4** following, the contract between ABC Limited and XYZ Limited is again prima facie caught under s 190 of the CA 2006. This is because there is a contract between ABC Limited and a person connected with Daisy, a director of ABC Limited. The person connected is again XYZ Limited, because Daisy and a person connected with her (Caroline, her civil partner) own 30% (ie over 20%) of the voting shares in the company (CA 2006, ss 252(2)(b) and 254(2)). In other words, to establish whether the 20% threshold has been reached, the shareholdings in the other company of all persons connected to the director must be added up. Daisy alone does not reach the 20% threshold, but when her shareholdings are added to those of a connected person she does. Note that it is not necessary for the director to have a shareholding in the other company, provided the 20% threshold is met. For example, if Caroline herself owned 30% of the shares in XYZ Limited, the contract would still be caught (CA 2006, s 254(2)).

Figure 7.4 Contract between the company and a company connected to the director due to family ownership

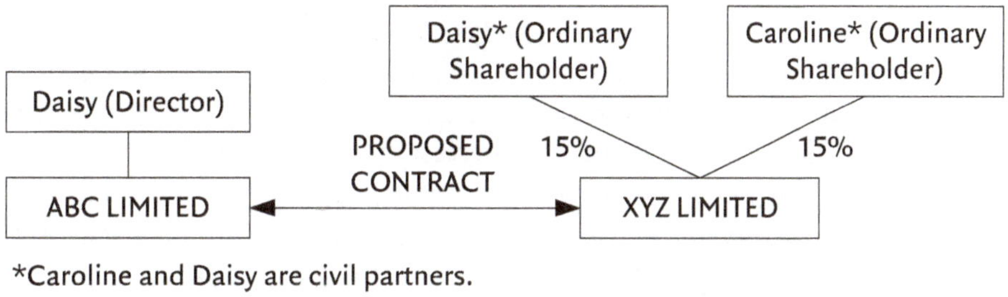

In **Figure 7.5** set out below, the contract between ABC Limited and XYZ Limited is not caught by s 190 of the CA 2006. It will not be an SPT. This is because there is not a contract between ABC Limited and a person connected with Daisy, a director of ABC Limited. XYZ Limited is not a person connected because Daisy does not own over 20% of the voting shares in the company, and Craig is not a person 'connected' to her. Craig is Daisy's brother and so falls outside the definition of 'family member' in s 253 of the CA 2006. Similarly, the fact that Craig owns over 20% of the shares himself is irrelevant because he is not a director of ABC Limited. Remember that the restrictions under s 190 of the CA 2006 seek to control a director's behaviour with regards to that company.

Figure 7.5 Contract not caught by the s 190 restrictions

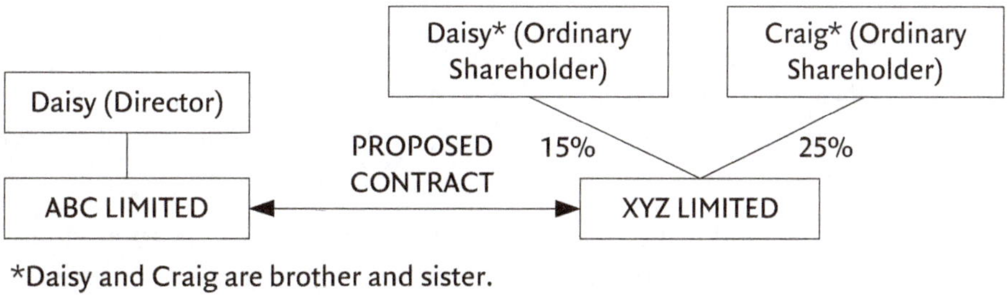

Therefore, whenever the company proposes entering a contract with a director or a member of the director's family, or with a company in which the director or the director's family owns shares, it is essential to check whether that contract falls within s 190 of the CA 2006.

Note that a reference to a 'director' under these provisions will cover a shadow director too (CA 2006, s 223(1)(b)).

7.12.1.4 Acquisition of a non-cash asset

If there is a contract between the correct parties, the next stage under s 190(1) of the CA 2006 is to check that the contract relates to the acquisition of a non-cash asset (NCA).

An NCA is defined in s 1163 of the Act. It means, 'any property or interest in property, other than cash'. In other words, if the contract between the company and the director or a connected person is for cash, for example a loan, then it is not a SPT within s 190. This is because loans are regulated elsewhere in the CA 2006 (see **7.12.2** below). An NCA covers assets such as land, machinery, shares and even property rights, such as a lease and certain security such as a mortgage or fixed and floating charges (see **11.4** below). So, for example, a contract for the sale or purchase of land, or a lease or mortgage, between the company and the director or a connected person would usually fall within s 190 of the CA 2006.

7.12.1.5 Substantial NCA

Under s 190(1) of CA 2006, the contract between the relevant parties must be for a *substantial* NCA. This is defined in s 191 of the Act. There are three separate thresholds we need to consider:

(a) If the value of the NCA is £5,000 or less, it is not 'substantial' and the transaction will not be a SPT (CA 2006, s 191(2)). This is a 'de minimis' provision and therefore excludes minor contracts between the director and the company. Remember, however, that in this case the director is still subject to their other duties, eg the duty under s 177 to make a declaration of their interest in the contract.

(b) If the value of the NCA is over £5,000 but not more than £100,000, it will be 'substantial' only if its value exceeds 10% of the company's asset value (CA 2006, s 191(2)(a)).

In this category there are therefore two possible outcomes:

(i) either the value of the NCA exceeds 10% of the asset value, in which case it will be an SPT, or

(ii) the value of the NCA is 10% or less of the asset value, in which it will not be an SPT.

Clearly a comparison has to be made between the value of the NCA, for example the land being bought, and the company's asset value. The company's asset value is usually the figure for its net assets in its accounts.

Let us assume that the NCA is land and is being bought by the company from a director for the price of £100,000. The company's asset value as defined is £1,000,000. The calculation is

$$\frac{£100{,}000}{£1{,}000{,}000} \times 100 = 10\%$$

In this case the land equals exactly 10% of the company's asset value. Consequently, this is *not* a SPT because it does not *exceed* 10% of the asset value as required.

(c) If the value of the NCA is over £100,000 it will always be 'substantial' (CA 2006, s 191(2)(b)).

The value should be determined at the date the contract is entered into (CA 2006, s 191(5)). Also, the value of a series of contracts will be aggregated, ie added together, to see if the thresholds have been met (CA 2006, s 190(5)). This prevents directors avoiding the controls by splitting one contract into two or more contracts of lesser value.

If the NCA is substantial under the thresholds described above then there will be an SPT under s 190(1), and the impact will be as explained at **7.12.1.6** below. If it is not substantial, there will be no SPT and s 190 does not apply. Ordinarily such a contract will then be a matter for the board of directors, without shareholder involvement.

7.12.1.6 Effect of being an SPT

Under s 190(1) of CA 2006, the SPT must be approved by shareholder resolution. This approval may be given by ordinary resolution at a general meeting, or by way of written resolution. The approval may be given before the contract is entered into, or the contract may be made conditional on subsequent approval by the shareholders.

7.12.1.7 Exceptions

Section 190 of the CA 2006 does not apply to a director's entitlements under a service contract with the company, or to payments to a director for loss of office (see **7.12.3** and **7.12.4** below) (CA 2006, s 190(6)).

Approval by the shareholders under s 190(1) is not required in the following cases:

(a) where the company is a wholly-owned subsidiary of another company;

(b) a contract between a company and a director in their capacity as a shareholder of the company (s 192(a)). Note that this exception does not exclude all transactions between the company and one of its directors just because the director is also a shareholder. It will only exempt contracts which the director enters in the character of a shareholder, for example the payment of dividends because that contract is entered with them as a shareholder rather than as a director. Another example is when a company enters into contracts to buy back some of its shares from its shareholders (see **9.5** below), including with a shareholder who is also a director of the company;

(c) a contract between a holding company and one of its subsidiaries (s 192(b)(i));

(d) a contract between two wholly-owned subsidiaries of the same holding company (s 192(b)(ii)); and

(e) if the company is in administration or being wound up (and is insolvent) (s 193(1)).

7.12.1.8 Breach of section 190

Under s 195(2) of the CA 2006, if shareholder approval is not obtained where it is necessary, the contract is voidable by the company unless certain conditions apply, eg where restitution of property or money is no longer possible.

Also, under s 195(3), a director who was party to the contract, a person connected to such a director and any other director who authorised the contract become liable to indemnify the company for any loss it has suffered, and to account to the company for any gain they have made.

It is possible for the shareholders to ratify the failure to obtain shareholder approval by shareholders' resolution (ordinary resolution at a general meeting, or written resolution) within a reasonable period of time (CA 2006, s 196).

Examples of SPTs under the forerunner to s 190 of the CA 2006 may be found in *British Racing Drivers' Club Ltd v Hextall Erskine & Co (A Firm)* [1996] 3 All ER 667, *Demite Ltd v Protec Health Ltd* [1998] BCC 638 and *Re Duckwari plc (No 3); Duckwari plc v Offerventure Ltd (No 3)* [1999] 1 BCLC 168.

7.12.2 Loans to directors

Section 197(1) of the CA 2006 requires a shareholders' resolution to approve a loan to a director of its company or its holding company. This approval is also required for the giving of a guarantee or provision of security by the company to a third party who gives a loan to a director. This ensures that the shareholders can veto any director borrowing money from the company or using the company to obtain a loan.

Before approval is given, under s 197(3) of the CA 2006 a memorandum must be drawn up which sets out the nature of the transaction, the amount of the loan, its purpose and the extent of the company's liability under any transaction connected with the loan (s 197(4)). The memorandum must be made available at the company's registered office for not less than 15 days ending on the day of the general meeting and at the meeting itself (s 197(3)(b)). If the resolution is to be passed by written resolution, a copy of the memorandum must be sent to all eligible shareholders with the resolution or before it is sent out (s 197(3)(a)).

Approval is also required where the loan or security arrangements are entered into with a person connected with a director (see **7.12.1.3** above) and the company is either a public company or a company associated with a public company (CA 2006, s 200(1) and (2)). By s 256(b) of the Act, an associated company includes one which is a subsidiary of another. For example, if a private company was a subsidiary of a public company, these restrictions would apply to the private company as well as to the public company.

7.12.2.1 Quasi-loans and credit transactions

There are also restrictions on what are known as 'quasi-loans' (defined in s 199(1) of the CA 2006) made to a director and on 'credit transactions' (defined in s 202(1)) made to a director. These controls apply to a public company or a company associated with a public company, which could therefore include a private company (see **7.12.2** above). For both types of arrangement, prior shareholder approval is required as with a loan (CA 2006, ss 198(3) and 201(3)). The same conditions as apply to a loan, including the conditions concerning the memorandum, apply here.

A quasi-loan arises where the company meets some financial obligation of the director on the understanding that the director will reimburse it later, for example where a director uses a company credit card to pay for personal items and will reimburse the company at a future date. A credit transaction arises where, for example, the company provides the director with goods or services and the director pays the company for these in instalments over time.

In the case of both a quasi-loan and a credit transaction, the restrictions extend to where these arrangements are made to a connected person of a public company or a company associated with a public company (CA 2006, ss 200(2) and 201(2)).

7.12.2.2 Exceptions

There are certain exceptions where the loans, quasi-loans and credit transactions do not require shareholder approval but may be entered into by a resolution of the board of directors. These exceptions include:

(a) loans and quasi-loans up to £10,000 for whatever reason (s 207(1));
(b) credit transactions up to £15,000 for whatever reason (s 207(2));
(c) loans, quasi-loans and credit transactions up to £50,000 for the director's or other person's expenditure for the company's business (s 204);
(d) loans, quasi-loans and credit transactions to fund a director's defence against proceedings for alleged breach of duty, negligence, default or breach of trust (s 205), or against investigations by regulatory authorities (s 206);
(e) loans, quasi-loans and credit transactions made between certain group companies (s 208).

7.12.2.3 Breach

Under s 213(2) of the CA 2006, if shareholder approval is not obtained where it is necessary, the contract is voidable by the company unless certain conditions apply, eg where restitution of property or money is no longer possible.

Also, under s 213(3) of the CA 2006, a director who was party to the contract, a person connected to such a director and any other director who authorised the contract become liable to indemnify the company for any loss it has suffered and to account to the company for any gain they have made.

It is possible for the shareholders to ratify the failure to obtain shareholder approval by shareholders' resolution (ordinary resolution at a general meeting, or written resolution) within a reasonable period of time (CA 2006, s 214).

7.12.3 Service contract

We saw at **6.8.2** above that under s 188 of the CA 2006, if the board of directors wish to enter into a service contract with a director for a fixed term in excess of two years then the prior approval of the shareholders is necessary, otherwise the fixed term is ineffective and the contract is terminable on reasonable notice.

7.12.4 Payment for loss of office

When a director leaves office the board may wish to pay the departing director a non-contractual 'payment for loss of office', for example as an expression of appreciation for service rendered. The board cannot do so without first obtaining the approval of the shareholders by resolution (ordinary resolution at a general meeting, or written resolution) (CA 2006, s 217(1)).

A memorandum containing particulars of the payment must be drawn up (s 217(3)). It must be made available at the company's registered office for not less than 15 days ending on the day of the general meeting and at the meeting itself (s 217(3)(b)). If the resolution is to be passed by written resolution, a copy of the memorandum must be sent to all eligible shareholders with the resolution or before it is sent out (s 217(3)(a)).

Payments to past directors (CA 2006, s 215(1)) and to persons connected to directors (s 215(3)(a)) are also caught.

Section 221 of the CA 2006 includes an exemption for small payments, ie those having a total value of less than £200.

Note that this requirement for shareholder approval applies only to non-contractual payments. It does not apply under s 220(1) of the CA 2006 to contractual payments for loss of office (included in a service contract for example). It also does not extend to payment of compensation for breach of contract, for unfair dismissal, for redundancy or pension for past service. These are payments to which the director is legally entitled, and such payments can be made by the directors without needing to consult the shareholders.

The civil consequences of a breach of these provisions are set out in s 222 of the CA 2006.

7.13 DIRECTOR'S LIABILITY

The controls that we have considered so far in this chapter are generally effective because the directors will wish to avoid the potential liability which arises (see **7.10** and **7.12** above). Usually in these cases any wrong is committed against the company, and so it is for the company to decide whether to take action or not. A director may be subject to further liability, though, by virtue of being a director, and this liability may extend to the company or to outsiders.

7.13.1 Agency

We saw at **6.5.2** above that a director is an agent of their company. Contracts made by the directors in the company's name are made on behalf of the company and the company will be party to the contract, not the directors. This means that directors are not personally liable for breach of contract by the company even if it was their actions which caused the breach. Nonetheless, liability can still arise for directors in two situations.

7.13.1.1 Exceeding actual authority

A company is bound by a contract made on behalf of the company by a director (as agent) who was acting outside the director's actual authority but within the director's apparent authority (see **6.6.2** above). This is nevertheless unauthorised behaviour by the director. The director is therefore liable to indemnify the company for any loss it has suffered, and to account to the company for any profit the director has made. The shareholders may ratify any such breach of authority, however, in accordance with s 239 of the CA 2006 (see **7.11.2** above).

7.13.1.2 Breach of warranty of authority

Where a director purports to act on behalf of the company but is acting outside the scope of the director's actual and apparent authority, the director will not bind the company by their actions. The director will be personally liable to the third party on the contract for breach of warranty of authority.

This liability is based on the assumption that the director has impliedly warranted to an outsider that the director has the authority to enter into the contract. If the director has exceeded their powers, or those of the board of directors or of the company, then the director has broken that warranty and is liable accordingly to the third party.

Section 40(2) of the CA 2006 provides that an outsider dealing with a company is not bound to check on the powers of the directors or of the company. Section 40(1) also provides that, as regards an outsider, the power of the directors to bind the company shall not be limited by the company's constitution; in other words, the outsider is not affected by any such restraints inside the company if the outsider is acting in good faith.

7.13.2 Torts

The basic rule is that any tort committed by the company does not usually give rise to liability for the directors even if they caused the tort to be committed. Again this is because the directors are acting as agents, and it is the principal – the company – which will be responsible. However, there are situations in which a director may incur personal liability. A director may be liable in tort as a director if the director:

(a) commits a tort separate from that of the company (*Standard Chartered Bank v Pakistan National Shipping Corporation (No 2)* [2003] 1 All ER 173, where the director in question committed the tort of deceit);

(b) voluntarily assumes personal responsibility for the tort by creating a special relationship between the director and the third party (*Williams v Natural Life Health Foods Ltd* [1998] 1 WLR 830); or

(c) procures or induces the company to commit a tort where the director acts beyond the director's constitutional role in the company (*MCA Records Inc v Charly Records Ltd* [2003] 1 BCLC 93).

7.13.3 Debts

Generally directors have no liability whatsoever for any debts they incur on the company's behalf. This is another demonstration of the company's separate legal personality and the fact that directors act as agents of the company. If a director is also a shareholder in a company which goes into insolvent liquidation, the worst that can happen to that director is that the director loses their job as director, together with the salary that goes with it. The director will also lose whatever money the director invested in the company when they bought shares.

A director may, however, be personally liable for debts incurred by engaging in misconduct. For example, in *Contex Drouzbha v Wiseman and another* [2007] EWCA Civ 120, a director was found liable for his company's debts because of his fraudulent misrepresentation in entering a contract with a supplier when he knew that his company would be unable to pay for the goods. The threshold for liability in these circumstances is high, and here it involved fraud.

Also, if directors have personally guaranteed a loan to the company and the company defaults under the terms of that loan, the lender may enforce the guarantees against the personal assets of the directors. If need be, directors will even be required to sell their homes to repay the company's debt, or may be declared bankrupt if they do not have sufficient assets. Unlike the example in the previous paragraph, this is not punitive liability imposed on the directors for committing a wrong; it is an example of personal contractual liability. The directors will have freely entered into the contract (the guarantee) in a personal capacity in order to ensure that the lender will lend the money to the company. If they are subsequently called on to pay up under the guarantee, this is precisely what the directors have agreed to do.

7.13.4 Failure to maintain company records

Under various provisions of the CA 2006, all directors (and other officers) of the company are required to maintain proper, up-to-date records both at Companies House and internally (the company records). These include minutes of meetings, registers and copies of certain contracts, memoranda and financial records. By s 1135 of the CA 2006, the relevant information may be kept in hard copy or electronic form (capable of being printed out whenever required). Failure to keep proper records renders those in default (including directors) liable to a fine (s 1135(3)). In the case of a failure to keep proper accounting records, the directors in default (and other officers) may be sentenced to up to two years' imprisonment (CA 2006, s 389).

In addition, there are specific offences which will be committed for failure to keep a particular register up to date, or a particular document at the company's registered office or SAIL, or for failure to file a required document with Companies House, eg under s 113(7) of the CA 2006 in relation to the register of members. Usually all directors in default (and other officers) will be liable for a fine.

The Economic Crime and Corporate Transparency Act 2023 will remove the requirement of companies to keep registers except for the register of members. In their place, requirements will be placed on the company to ensure that the relevant information (eg a change in the directors or company secretary) is notified to Companies House. A failure to do this will result in an offence being committed, for which the directors can be fined. This new offence is expected to come into force by 2027.

7.13.5 Liability for financial records

The directors are subject to a range of possible liability regarding their responsibilities for the company's accounts and related reports (see **6.7.1** above). This liability can be both civil and criminal. For example, under s 463 of the CA 2006, directors are liable to compensate their company in certain circumstances for any loss suffered by it as a result of any untrue or misleading statement in the required directors' report. It is also a criminal offence under ss 415 and 419 of the Act not to comply with the statutory requirements regarding the preparation of the directors' report.

7.13.6 Liability for share capital transactions

The directors of a company may be liable for breaches of the statutory rules seeking to protect the company's share capital; for example, if there is prohibited financial assistance (CA 2006, s 680(1); see **9.4** below), or if a required directors' statement is unreasonably given for a redemption or buy-back of shares out of capital (CA 2006, s 715; see **9.5** below). These offences are punishable by up to two years' imprisonment and a fine.

7.13.7 Liability for health and safety breaches

The directors (and other officers) may be criminally liable for breaches of health and safety legislation committed by the company (Health and Safety at Work, etc Act 1974, s 37). Unlimited fines may be imposed, and imprisonment of up to two years. A director may also be disqualified as a director.

Where the company's actions have led to death of an individual (eg, an employee or a customer) and management failure is to blame, the directors may be prosecuted for the common law offence of gross negligence manslaughter.

The Corporate Manslaughter and Corporate Homicide Act 2007 (CMCHA 2007) (see **2.3.5** above) may be used only against a company. Originally, the first successful prosecution of a company under the CMCHA 2007 (against Cotswold Geotechnical (Holdings) Ltd, following the death of an employee) also involved the prosecution of one of the directors for gross negligence manslaughter. The prosecution against the director was stopped due to his ill-health.

7.13.8 Bribery

A maximum prison sentence of 10 years and/or an unlimited fine may be imposed on directors under the Bribery Act 2010 for four criminal offences relating to bribery. This Act, which came into force on 1 July 2011, is a concern for company directors because of the very wide definition and reach of the offences (including overseas), the penalties and the strict liability involved. The first prosecution under the Bribery Act 2010 was launched by the Serious Fraud Office in 2013. Two directors, Gary West and Stuart Stone, connected to Sustainable Agroenergy plc were convicted and sentenced to four and six years' imprisonment respectively, in December 2014, for breaches of ss 1 and 2 of the Bribery Act 2010.

7.13.9 Political donations

If a company makes a donation to a political party under Part 14 of the CA 2006 without shareholder approval (where required), the directors will be personally liable under s 369(2) of the Act to reimburse the company to the amount of that donation.

7.13.10 Financial difficulties

Although we have seen that the directors of a company are not usually liable for the debts of a company (**7.13.3** above), they may be personally liable on the insolvency of a company if their behaviour falls below the required standard.

7.13.10.1 Wrongful trading

A director may be liable for wrongful trading under s 214 of the IA 1986. A wrongful trading action may be brought by a liquidator only after the company has gone insolvent, or (from 1 October 2015) by an administrator where the company has gone into insolvent administration (IA 1986, s 246ZB). If at some time before the winding up the director knew, or ought to have known, that there was no reasonable prospect that the company would avoid insolvent liquidation, the director may be found guilty of wrongful trading and have to make a contribution to the company's assets. All directors must therefore show some level of financial understanding and diligence, and take advice if their company is in financial difficulties.

When looking at whether a director knew, or ought to have known, that the company could not avoid insolvent liquidation, both subjective and objective tests are applied (IA 1986, s 214(4)). That is:

(a) What did this particular director know?

(b) And what would a reasonable director have known in the circumstances?

Matters such as the size of the business, the director's function (eg, a finance director is expected to have a greater degree of competence on accountancy matters than other directors), etc are looked at. In practice, the liquidator seeks overwhelming evidence of insolvency about which any director should have been aware. This might be evidence showing:

(a) insolvency on a balance sheet basis;

(b) creditor pressure;

(c) late filing of accounts;

(d) any qualification on the accounts by the auditors;

(e) the practice of paying the creditors only when they issue proceedings or statutory demands; or
(f) numerous judgments against the company.

Section 214(3) of the IA 1986 provides a defence. This is that the director took every step with a view to minimising a potential loss to the company's creditors after the director became aware that the company had no prospects of avoiding insolvent liquidation. It would certainly include taking professional advice, both legal and accountancy, minimising further goods taken on credit, rigorous collection of debts, and drawing up management accounts (possibly daily) to establish the financial position of the company. It does not usually include resigning.

If wrongful trading is established then a director may be ordered to make a personal contribution for the loss that the director has caused by their actions. In this case, the personal contribution is compensatory rather than punitive.

Precautions that a director may wish to take to protect themselves from an accusation of wrongful trading include:

(a) keeping an accurate record of their own activities, including board meetings;
(b) being satisfied that the financial records kept are sufficient;
(c) seeking professional advice at the earliest sign of financial problems in the company;
(d) raising with the board financial concerns when these start to become evident; and
(e) possibly resigning (but the director might be liable whether or not the director remained on the board).

For an example of a case of wrongful trading, see *Rubin v Gunner* [2004] EWHC 316. The directors had continued to pay themselves salaries after a date when there was no reasonable prospect of the company avoiding insolvent liquidation. They could not therefore use the defence in s 214(3) of the IA 1986. They were held liable to make a contribution to the assets of the company, and thereby in effect to the creditors of the company. In *Bangla Television Ltd (in liquidation) v Bangla TV Ltd* [2009] EWHC 1632 (Ch), two directors who transferred assets of the company to another company for £250,000, which was not in fact paid, were made liable under s 214 of the IA 1986 to contribute £250,000 to the liquidation, on the basis of joint and several liability.

7.13.10.2 Fraudulent trading

The offence of fraudulent trading under s 213 of the IA 1986 is not limited to directors but also applies to any persons knowingly party to such action (see IA 1986, s 213(2)). A fraudulent trading claim may be brought by a liquidator of the company or (from 1 October 2015) by an administrator where the company has gone into insolvent administration (IA 1986, s 246ZA).

In order for fraudulent trading to be established, it must be shown that the business of the company was carried on with intent to defraud creditors. Basically, the directors must have known that creditors would not be paid. The case of *In re Patrick and Lyon Ltd* [1933] Ch 786 suggests that 'real moral blame' must be established before fraudulent trading can successfully be proceeded against.

In *Morphitis v Bernasconi* [2003] BCC 540, the Court of Appeal held that it was not enough that a creditor had been defrauded for a director to run foul of s 213 of the IA 1986. Rather, the company actually had to have been run with the intent to defraud creditors, which demands a higher standard of proof.

In practice, fraudulent trading actions are rare due to the difficulty of establishing intent, and are only used against persons engaged in criminal conduct (see *R v Nigel Garvey* [2001] EWCA Crim 1365, where the accused was sentenced to four years' imprisonment). Liquidators tend to rely on wrongful trading (**7.13.10.1** above), which achieves substantially the same recovery of assets for the creditors.

If fraudulent trading is established, the directors may be made liable to make such personal contribution to the company's assets as a court thinks proper.

In *Bank of India v Christopher Morris* [2005] EWCA Civ 693, the Court of Appeal looked again at s 213. It held that s 213 of the IA 1986 attracted only civil liability and was not a penal provision. Thus, there was a liability under s 213 to pay 'compensation' in cases where the company which traded fraudulently was being wound up. The Court pointed out that criminal punishment for fraudulent trading was dealt with separately, in what is now s 993 of the CA 2006.

7.13.10.3 Misfeasance

A liquidator or creditor may bring proceedings against directors of the company after liquidation if misfeasance has occurred under s 212 of the IA 1986. Basically, misfeasance is any breach of any fiduciary or other duty of directors. If misfeasance is established then, under s 212(3) of the 1986 Act, directors may be ordered to repay any money or personally contribute to the assets of the company to compensate for their misfeasance. In *ED Games Ltd* v *Cipolletta* [2009] EWHC 223 (Ch), the court upheld the liquidator's claim under s 212 of the IA 1986 seeking a contribution to the company's losses from a director of the company, which owed £900,000 including a substantial VAT payment.

In *Whalley (Liquidator of MDA Investment Management Ltd) v Doney* [2003] EWHC 227, the sole director of an insolvent company was found liable for misfeasance under s 212 of the IA 1986. He had sold the business just prior to liquidation, and part of the proceeds were channelled to another of his companies.

7.13.11 Environmental legislation

Directors may also face potential civil and criminal liability under environmental legislation (for example under the Environmental Protection Act 1990). In 2021 a company director was sentenced to 2 years and 3 months imprisonment and fined £72,000 for allowing toxic waste to be illegally dumped in a former quarry.

7.13.12 Sole director

Section 231 of the CA 2006 requires a company with a sole shareholder (a single-member company) who is also a director, which enters into a contract otherwise than in the ordinary course of business and where the contract is not in writing, to produce a written memorandum of the terms of the contract or record them in the first board meeting following the making of the contract. If the company fails to do this then every director or other officer in default commits an offence and is subject to a fine.

7.13.13 Disqualification

We saw at **6.10.6** above that a director may be disqualified as a director under the CDDA 1986. Any director who is guilty of acting while disqualified causes themselves to be personally liable for the company's debts incurred during the period when they did so act (CDDA 1986, s 15). They are also liable to a fine or imprisonment (CDDA 1986, s 13).

7.13.14 Liability for dividends

Directors who authorised the payment of a dividend to shareholders may be liable to repay the money to the company if the payment was illegal (eg, if there were insufficient distributable profits), even though they did not benefit from it personally (*Bairstow v Queens Moat Houses plc* [2000] 1 BCLC 549).

7.13.15 Competition law

If a director is guilty of a cartel offence under the Enterprise Act 2002, which seeks to prevent anti-competitive behaviour such as price-fixing, the director may be imprisoned for up to five years and/or given an unlimited fine. However, fines imposed on the company under the Competition Act 1998 for anti-competitive behaviour cannot be reclaimed from the directors (*Safeway Stores Ltd v Twigger* [2010] EWCA Civ 1472).

CHAPTER 8

COMPANY DECISION-MAKING

LEARNING OUTCOMES

After reading this chapter you will be able to:

- determine who takes a decision on behalf a company and at what forum
- explain the different methods by which a decision of the company directors can be taken
- explain the different ways in which the company's shareholders can take decisions
- understand the legal rules governing the holding of directors' and shareholders' meetings
- identify the procedural rules affecting company decision-making and the use of electronic communication.

8.1 INTRODUCTION

We have seen that the company, being an artificial person, needs humans to take decisions on its behalf. The two categories of decision-maker for the company are the shareholders as owners and the directors managing the company. In this chapter we examine the mechanics of decision-making by companies – the detailed rules deciding who takes a decision for the company, the meetings at which decisions are taken, the various ways of taking the decision and the administrative requirements to ensure the decision is taken properly. This area is of the utmost importance for the corporate lawyer, for although it is always their client who takes the decision affecting the company and its business, it is the lawyer who must ensure that the decision is taken in a manner which complies with the law, and who must be prepared to explain to the client why the steps taken are necessary.

How decisions are taken by a company is governed by the CA 2006, the company's articles of association, the common law and sometimes even the personal preferences of the people running the company. As relevant rules will be contained in the company's articles, these will of course vary from company to company. Therefore it is essential for the lawyer advising a company to obtain the most up-to-date set of articles before proceeding. In this chapter we consider decision-making predominantly from the point of view of a company with unamended model articles for private companies (see **4.3.1** above), but from time to time reference will be made to some common amendments which are made to the model articles.

It is also worth pointing out at the outset that particular care must be taken with company decision-making in two cases. First, when there is a single-member company, because decision-making in such a case may be streamlined significantly as compared to decision-making in a company with two or more shareholders. The second is where one individual is both a shareholder and a director of a company. Difficulties may arise, as that same person must act in two separate capacities, and differently, under the law, depending on whether that person is acting as a shareholder or as a director, and it is easy to confuse the two roles.

What follows is a consideration of the law and practice of decision-making affecting private companies limited by shares only. The rules are more complex for public companies and publicly-traded companies, and beyond the scope of this book.

8.2 WHO TAKES THE DECISION?

It is the directors who have the powers to manage the company on a daily basis (see **6.5** above), and many decisions affecting the company may be taken by a decision of the board of directors alone. For instance, the directors on their own have the power to change the location of the company's registered office under s 87(1) of the CA 2006. We have also seen (at **6.5.1** above) that the board of directors may even delegate their decision-making power to just one of their number under principles of agency law.

But we have also come across instances when the shareholders of the company are involved in taking decisions. The CA 2006 reserves a number of decisions affecting the company to the shareholders. These are the most important decisions impacting upon the company, and reserving these decisions to the shareholders recognises the reality that it is the shareholders and not the directors who own the company. Some of the decisions shareholders are required to take under the CA 2006 are:

(a) amending the company's articles by special resolution (s 21(1); see **4.4.1** above);
(b) approving a substantial property transaction ('SPT' – see **7.12.1** above) by ordinary resolution (s 190(1));
(c) approving a director's service contract for a fixed term over two years (see **6.8.2** above) by ordinary resolution (s 188(2));
(d) approving compensation to a director for loss of office (see **7.12.4** above) by ordinary resolution (s 217(1));
(e) authorising directors to allot shares (when required) (see **9.3.2** below) by ordinary resolution (s 551(1));
(f) disapplying shareholders' pre-emption rights (when required) (see **9.3.3** below) by special resolution (ss 569(1), 570(1), 571(1));
(g) approving a contract to buy back the company's shares (see **9.5.3.1** below) by ordinary resolution (s 694(2));
(h) approving payment to buy back the company's shares out of capital (see **9.5.3.2** above) by special resolution (s 716(1));
(i) ratifying a director's breach of duty (see **7.11.2** above) by ordinary resolution (s 239(2));
(j) authorising political donations by ordinary resolution (s 366(1));
(k) deciding to register the (private) company as a public company (see **12.4.3** below) by special resolution (s 97(1)(a));
(l) removing a director of the company against their will (see **6.10.3** above) by ordinary resolution (s 168(1));

(m) removing an auditor of the company (see **6.12.5** above) by ordinary resolution (s 510(2));

(n) changing the company's name by special resolution, provided no other procedure is set out in the articles (see **3.20.4**) (s 77(1)).

Further, in the articles it is usually provided that the shareholders can:

(o) direct the board of directors how to act (see **6.5** above) by special resolution (eg, art 4(1) of the model articles for private companies/Table A, art 70).

The shareholders also have powers to pass a resolution to wind up the company under the IA 1986, and the company's articles may require shareholder resolutions in situations where they are not required under the CA 2006.

Some of these shareholder resolutions, if passed, take effect straight away. For example, a special resolution to change the company's articles takes effect immediately it is passed. Whilst the directors must attend to some administrative formalities afterwards, they do not play any role in the decision-making process. By contrast, some of these shareholder resolutions merely give *permission* for the transaction to proceed. In such cases a decision of the directors to enter the relevant contract or to perform the act will also be required, usually after the shareholders have approved the transaction. For example, if the board of directors decide that they want the company to enter a contract with one of their directors and this amounts to an SPT, the directors usually first go to the shareholders and get approval under s 190(1) of the CA 2006 by an ordinary resolution. Assuming the shareholders give their permission for the SPT, the directors must then pass their own resolution at a directors' meeting to approve the terms of the contract and authorise signatories for the company before the contract can be entered into and become legally binding. In other words, a decision of both the shareholders and the directors is required.

Thus, some decisions may be taken by the directors alone, some by the shareholders alone and some require both to participate. The question then is which decision is taken in each of these different ways. This depends on the decision being made, and how that decision is treated under the rules both in the CA 2006 and the company's own articles.

It is also worth noting at the outset that, in practice, where a decision must be taken by the shareholders, usually it will be the directors who start the decision-making process. The directors may, for example, in running the business decide that it is in the company's best interests to remove a particular restriction in the articles. Because of s 21 of the CA 2006, this is not a change the directors are allowed to make themselves. The directors will need to call the shareholders together and ask them to decide whether to approve the change by voting on a special resolution. If the required number of shareholder votes is obtained for the resolution, it will pass and the change will take effect. If not, the articles will remain as they are and the directors must continue to live with the restriction. It is therefore usually the directors who start the ball rolling, as this is what they have been appointed, and paid, to do. It would only be in extremely rare circumstances that the shareholders would use their powers (eg, under art 4(1) of the model articles for private companies/Table A, art 70) to tell the directors what decisions they should be taking.

8.3 INTRODUCTION TO DIRECTORS' DECISION-MAKING

8.3.1 Decisions by the board of directors

The rules regarding directors' decision-making are found predominantly in the company's articles of association. In the discussion that follows, we consider a private company with the model articles for private companies.

Directors generally take decisions collectively as a board, except where they have delegated their specific decision-making powers to an individual director such as the Chief Executive/

Managing Director. The board may take decisions either at a board meeting (also known as a 'directors' meeting'), or by written resolution (without holding a board meeting).

The decision taken by the directors at a board meeting is known as 'board resolution', and a decision taken by written resolution is known as a 'directors' written resolution'. Frequently in practice, the term 'board resolution' is used to refer to both types of decision.

8.3.2 A sole director

A company can have just one director (CA 2006, s 154). How the director takes decisions is a matter for the articles. Article 7(2) of the model articles for private companies allows a sole director to take decisions however the director wishes. However, a sole director must still comply with requirements of the CA 2006 and keep a written record of decisions taken (minutes) for 10 years (CA 2006, s 248(2)). As mentioned at **7.9.4** above, a sole director does not have to make a declaration of interest. Where a company which should have more than one director currently only has a sole director, the director must make any necessary declarations of interests in writing (see **7.9.5** above) (CA 2006, s 186).

8.4 BOARD MEETING

If the directors of the company choose to take a decision by holding a board meeting rather than by passing a directors' written resolution, there are certain procedural rules which must be complied with which will predominantly be contained in the company's articles.

8.4.1 Calling a board meeting

Article 9(1) of the model articles for private companies permits any one of the directors to call a board meeting, or to authorise the company secretary (if there is one) to do so at any time. Meetings do not just occur automatically; someone must call them (although board meetings at fixed intervals are permitted – see **8.4.2** below). Calling a meeting simply involves summoning all the directors to meet together so they may take decisions on behalf of the company.

8.4.2 Notice

When a director calls a board meeting, the director must give the other directors notice of the meeting before it takes place (model articles for private companies, art 9(1)). In other words, the director must give the other directors advance warning of the proposed meeting. Such notice must be reasonable (*Re Homer District Consolidated Gold Mines, ex parte Smith* (1888) 39 Ch D 546).

What amounts to reasonable notice will depend upon the circumstances and the particular company. With a small private company, board meetings are often held at very short notice – a few minutes' or even a moment's notice would suffice, provided it gave all the directors a reasonable opportunity to attend and that this was the usual notice period. For larger companies (where the directors may be in different places) longer notice will be more normal. There is no need for notice to be given where the directors have previously decided that board meetings are to be held at fixed intervals, eg the first Monday of every month at 9am or every Wednesday at 5pm.

There is no need for notice of a board meeting to be in writing (model articles for private companies, art 9(3)). Notice may be given orally (*Browne v La Trinidad* (1887) 37 ChD 1 (CA)). It is possible for the articles to require notice to be given in writing, though.

Under art 9(2) of the model articles for private companies, the notice must specify the proposed date, time and place of the meeting, and the means of communication if the directors are not all going to be in the same place. For example, under the model articles for private companies, telephone calls, video calls (via Skype for example), even text messaging or instant messaging are all possible means of holding the meeting, provided the directors can communicate to the others any information or opinions they have (model articles for private companies, art 10(1)). Although there is no need to specify the business of the meeting (*La Compagnie de Mayville v Whitley* [1896] 1 Ch 788 (CA)), common sense would usually dictate that an agenda should be included with the notice, together with any necessary documents that it would be helpful to review in advance of the meeting.

Notice must be given to each director wherever the director is (model articles for private companies, art 9(3)), although this may be waived by the individual director in accordance with art 9(4). Many companies (eg, those using Table A, art 88) do not require notice to be given to directors who are overseas.

If notice is not given to all directors in accordance with the articles, the director(s) not given notice seem to have the right to demand that another meeting be held within a reasonable time (*Browne v La Trinidad* (1887) 37 ChD 1 (CA)).

8.4.3 Quorum

All directors, their alternates (see **6.3.1.6** above) and the company secretary (if any) may attend the board meeting. Professional advisers such as lawyers and accountants may also attend certain meetings, particularly if the company is undertaking a complex transaction. However, only directors or their alternates may form part of the quorum.

The quorum for a board meeting is the minimum number of directors who are required by the company's articles to be present for valid decisions to be taken at that meeting. The quorum is therefore a device, in the interests of fairness, to ensure that a minimum number of eligible people is present at a meeting before decisions may be taken.

The quorum for a board meeting with the model articles for private companies is two directors (art 11(2)). There is no provision to allow for the appointment of alternates. For a company using Table A, art 89, the quorum is also two directors, but alternates may be appointed. In both cases the directors themselves may decide to fix a different number for the quorum, although for the model articles for private companies this number must not be less than two (art 11(2)). Instead of these articles, there may well be a special article for the quorum which varies these rules. In this case the special article's quorum requirements must be met; for example, the article may provide for a quorum of two directors at all times, and the directors have no discretion to change it but the shareholders do. A meeting at which the quorum is present is known as 'quorate'.

Not all directors who attend a board meeting necessarily count in the quorum. Directors who have a personal interest in a matter (see **7.9 above**) may be prevented from counting in the quorum under the articles. For example, art 14(1) of the model articles for private companies prevents directors who are interested in an actual or a proposed transaction or arrangement with the company (say, a contract) from forming part of the quorum unless a specified exception in art 14(3) applies. Table A, art 95 has the same effect, subject to exceptions in Table A, art 94. If a director cannot form part of the quorum, they are still entitled to attend the board meeting (*Hayes v Bristol Plant Hire* [1957] 1 All ER 685).

How will the board know if a director has such an interest which prevents the director from forming part of the quorum? We saw at **7.9** above that a director must make a declaration to the company of their interest, under s 177 of the CA 2006 for an interest in a proposed transaction or s 182 of the CA 2006 for an interest in an existing transaction with the company, or by a general notice under s 185 of the CA 2006. The declaration may be made in writing or at the board meeting (see **7.9.2** above).

As mentioned above, there are certain exceptions for a company using art 14 of the model articles for private companies. In other words, in some circumstances a director may form part of the quorum even though the director has an interest in a matter. For example, if the director's interest cannot reasonably be regarded as likely to give rise to a conflict of interest (art 14(3)(b)) then the director may still form part of the quorum. Also, if the conflict of interest (giving rise to the declaration) arose from one of three permitted causes set out in art 14(4) then again the director may still form part of the quorum. These permitted causes include:

(a) a guarantee given by or to a director for an obligation of the company; and

(b) a contract with the director and the company to buy shares in the company.

So, depending on the matters being decided at the meeting, one or more of the company's directors may be prevented from forming part of the quorum. If there are still sufficient directors at the meeting who can form the requisite quorum then the meeting can proceed nonetheless. For example, if there are three directors of a company with unamended model articles for private companies and one director cannot form part of the quorum, provided the other two attend there will be a valid quorum and decisions can be taken.

If, however, as a result of a director or directors being excluded from the quorum under the articles there are insufficient directors who can make up the quorum, there will be a problem. Say that a company with unamended model articles for private companies has just two directors and one of them cannot form part of the quorum due to a personal interest; there will be only one director left who is able to count in the quorum. As the minimum number required is two directors under art 11(2), a valid meeting cannot be held and no decision regarding the contract involving the personal interest can be taken.

What is the solution here? Note that the model articles for private companies do not allow for the directors to exercise their discretion under art 11 to change the quorum from two directors to one director (art 11(2)). For a company with the model articles for private companies a solution is found in art 14(3). This provision permits the shareholders of the company to pass an ordinary resolution disapplying art 14(1) *temporarily*, thus allowing the director to form part of the quorum for board meetings relating to that contract. This power also exists for Table A companies under art 96.

It is also possible for the directors to call a shareholders' general meeting to remove this restriction permanently by passing a special resolution under s 21 of the CA 2006 to alter the articles. For example, a special article could be adopted which would always allow a director to form part of the quorum (and vote) regardless of the contract in which they are interested. This might be more suitable for small companies where the directors are also the shareholders.

In both cases the owners of the company, the shareholders, have the right to decide whether to relax the rules for those managing the company, the directors. If the resolution is passed, the board meeting can then be held as a quorum can now be achieved.

Even where one of these possible courses of action is adopted by the company and directors are allowed to participate at board meetings irrespective of their personal involvement, they must still remember to declare any personal interest to the other directors, as this requirement cannot be dispensed with.

A director may not have to be physically present with other directors to form a quorum. This ultimately depends on the articles. For example, under art 10 of the model articles for private companies, a director may participate in a meeting anywhere so long as the director can communicate information and opinions to the other directors and vice versa.

8.4.4 Voting

Once a quorum has been established, the directors can turn to the agenda for the board meeting and the decisions that need to be taken. Decisions will be taken by the directors voting for or against a board resolution. The rules for voting are found in the articles and may be supplemented by case law, depending on the circumstances.

As with the quorum, there may be restrictions in the company's articles on directors voting on matters where they have a personal interest in the outcome of the vote, eg a director voting on a contract between the company and the director or another company in which the director is a shareholder. For a company with model articles for private companies the restrictions in art 14 (see **8.4.3** above) also apply to voting. In Table A restrictions on directors voting are contained in art 94. However, if the exceptions under these provisions apply then the director will be able to vote.

In practice this means that a director of a company with model articles for private companies or Table A, who has a personal interest in a matter being decided upon by the board, cannot either form part of the quorum or vote on the matter unless an exception applies or a resolution is passed to relax the rules. For example, a director who is seeking to buy shares from their company has an interest in this contract which must be declared under the CA 2006. Nonetheless, the director may still count and form part of the quorum and vote on the resolution to allot the shares to them because art 14(4)(b) of the model articles for private companies or Table A, art 94(c) permits the director to do so.

For a company with model articles for private companies or Table A, each director has one vote at a board meeting and all resolutions may be passed by majority vote (model articles for private companies, art 7(1); Table A, art 88). If there is an equal number of votes for and against a resolution there is deadlock and the negative view will prevail, which means that the resolution is defeated unless the chairperson has a casting vote (see **8.4.5** below).

If the directors are physically present at the board meeting, voting will usually take place by a show of hands (raising a hand) or by oral assent or dissent (saying 'yes' or 'no'). Under art 10 of the model articles for private companies, voting may be more flexible, taking place using electronic means – by phone or video call, or even by text or instant messaging. This provision is much wider than its counterpart in Table A which does not permit these methods.

8.4.5 Chairperson

The board of directors may, if the power exists in the company's articles, appoint one of their number to be the chairperson. The chairperson has control of the agenda and the meeting. This power may be found in art 12(1) of the model articles for private companies and Table A, art 91, but there is no need for a chairperson to be appointed under these provisions. A special article may require there to be a chairperson, or may not allow one to be appointed.

A chairperson of a small private company, if one is appointed, will have a potentially important role to play in two main situations. First, if there is any dispute over the ability of a particular director to vote and count in the quorum on any issue, it is the chairperson who must decide this, and their decision is final (model articles for private companies, art 14(6); Table A, art 98).

Secondly, if a vote on a board resolution is deadlocked, with as many votes for the resolution as against, the chairperson may, if the articles grant it, have a casting vote. This is a second vote for the chairperson, exercisable *only* where there is deadlock. This means that the chairperson will determine the outcome of the resolution with their casting vote. Article 13(1) of the model articles for private companies and Table A, art 88 have such a casting vote for the chairperson. The model articles also go further and grant this casting vote to a director who chairs the meeting without formally being appointed as chairperson. Article 13(2) of the model articles for private companies does exclude the casting vote, though, if the chairperson is prevented from voting or counting in the quorum under art 14.

In practice, because of the power which the casting vote gives the chairperson at board meetings, this right is often excluded from the articles (see **8.7.7.4** below).

8.4.6 Administration

Minutes must be recorded for every board meeting and kept for 10 years, otherwise an offence is committed by every officer of the company in default (CA 2006, s 248). Minutes do not record verbatim what was said by the directors at the meeting but are a record in overview form of the decisions made at the meeting. Increasingly they also record the reasons for the decisions (particularly because of the directors' duty under s 172 of the CA – see **7.4** above). Section 1135(1) of the CA 2006 requires minutes to be kept in hard-copy or electronic form, and if kept electronically they must be capable of being reproduced in hard copy.

The articles may contain supplementary provisions regarding the minutes. For example, art 15 of the model articles for private companies requires them to be in writing, so an audio recording of the meeting would be insufficient.

The minutes are open to inspection by the directors (*Conway v Petronius Clothing Co* [1978] 1 WLR 72), but usually not by the shareholders (*R v Mariquita and New Grenada Mining Company* (1859) 1 El & El 289). They may become visible to shareholders under a shareholders' agreement (see **5.6.2.2** above) or in litigation, eg where there is a petition for unfair prejudice under s 994 of the CA 2006 (see **5.6.3.14** above).

If the minutes of the meeting are signed by the chairperson, they are evidence of the proceedings at that meeting (CA 2006, s 249(1)). Unless the contrary is proved, where minutes are prepared in accordance with s 248 of the CA 2006 the meeting is deemed duly held, all proceedings are deemed to have taken place and all appointments are deemed validly made (CA 2006, s 249(1)).

Minutes must be kept by a sole director as well (see **8.3.2** above).

Depending on the decisions reached by the directors, further administrative requirements may need to be fulfilled, eg filing requirements for forms in accordance with the CA 2006 (see **8.11** below). The directors will also be responsible for dealing with the administration arising out of shareholders' general meetings (see **8.11** below).

8.5 DIRECTORS' WRITTEN RESOLUTIONS

A directors' written resolution is an alternative way for directors to take decisions without having to call and hold a board meeting. It is also the way in which a company with a sole director will take decisions. It is permitted if the articles allow for this form of decision-making (eg model articles for private companies, art 8(2); Table A, art 93).

Under art 8(1) of the model articles for private companies, all eligible directors must agree to the proposed resolution. An eligible director is one who would have been able to vote at a board meeting if one had been held (model articles for private companies, art 8(3)). Thus, directors who are unable to vote at a board meeting because of a personal interest cannot take part in a decision by written resolution. A copy of the proposed resolution should be sent to every eligible director; and if each director then signs their copy of the resolution, or gives other written consent, and returns it to the company, the resolution is validly passed. This is subject to one condition, that there are sufficient eligible directors to have formed a quorum if a meeting had been held (model articles for private companies, art 8(4)). This means that written resolutions cannot be used to circumvent quorum problems.

The advantage of this form of decision-making is it allows for great flexibility, in that the copies of the resolution do not need to be signed (eg an e-mail will do) and the decisions of the directors do not need to be taken simultaneously; the resolution will become effective when the last eligible director expresses their consent.

It should also be noted that art 8 of the model articles for private companies goes further than just permitting written resolutions; it allows decisions to be taken unanimously by the directors when they indicate to each other *by any means* that they share a common view on a matter. This embraces electronic technology in all its forms. In practice, though, a company will be well advised to ensure there is a written record of its directors' decisions, as this may be important in the future should a dispute or financial difficulties arise. A company may amend the model articles in order to restrict the ways in which this 'by any means' method may be used.

There is no requirement under the CA 2006 to keep copies of written resolutions (or unanimous board decisions taken other than at a board meeting), as s 248 of the CA 2006 (see **8.4.6** above) applies only to a board meeting. This is therefore a matter for the articles. Article 15 of the model articles for private companies requires that a written record of every written resolution or unanimous board decision be kept for 10 years. If the articles do not contain such a provision, for the reasons stated above it is nonetheless advisable to retain written records for possible future use.

8.6 INTRODUCTION TO SHAREHOLDERS' DECISION-MAKING

We saw at **8.2** above that the most significant decisions affecting the company must be taken by the shareholders as owners. The complexity of shareholder decision-making depends on the type of company, the decision being taken, the number of shareholders and how contentious or otherwise the decision is. Private companies are accorded much more flexibility and are subject to looser regulation than public companies. A private company with just one shareholder can take decisions more easily than a private company with two or more shareholders.

We shall now consider how it is that the shareholders of a private company take decisions. We first address the position of a company with more than one shareholder, and then that of the single-member company. In doing so we do not consider private traded companies under the CA 2006 as these are extremely rare. Note that the explanations below for private companies will not always be accurate for private traded companies.

The shareholders of a private company with more than one shareholder will normally take decisions in one of two ways:

(a) by passing a resolution at a shareholders' general meeting; or
(b) by a shareholders' written resolution.

They are mutually exclusive. Each will be considered in turn.

8.7 SHAREHOLDERS' GENERAL MEETINGS

There are two different types of shareholders' meeting at which shareholders may take their decisions:

(a) an annual general meeting (AGM); and
(b) a general meeting (GM).

8.7.1 The AGM

An AGM is a shareholders' meeting held once every year, at which certain key information is provided and key decisions are taken. There is no requirement under the CA 2006 for private companies to hold an AGM. Nonetheless, the AGM is still of importance to a significant number of private companies. This is because the CA 2006 does not prevent a private company from having an AGM if its articles so require. Companies formed under the CA 2006 will generally not have provisions requiring an AGM to be held in order to keep decision-making as flexible as possible, but private companies formed before 1 October 2007 were required by law to hold an AGM every year (unless they passed a special type of resolution to suspend this requirement). Although some private companies formed before 1 October 2007 have now taken advantage of the CA 2006 and changed their articles to remove the need for an AGM, many have not and still have articles which specify that an AGM must be held.

The AGM may be useful for private companies where the shareholders are not all directors. This is because it provides those shareholders who are not on the board with an opportunity to question the directors at least once a year, particularly on the strategy of the company and the company's finances. Also, directors of companies with unamended Table A articles will have to retire by rotation at an AGM (Table A, art 73), and shareholders could take this opportunity to remove a director from office.

Section 336(1) of the CA 2006 does require a *public* company to hold an AGM every year, in the six months after its accounting reference date (the end of its financial year).

8.7.2 The GM

Every shareholder meeting which is not an AGM will be a GM. Companies formed under the CA 2006 will hold GMs only, unless they decide to include a provision in their articles requiring an AGM. Such GMs will be held as and when they are required in order for the shareholders to decide on matters which require their approval under the CA 2006 or the company's articles.

Before the CA 2006 came into force GMs were known as 'extraordinary general meetings' (EGMs). Many older companies' articles still refer to EGMs rather than GMs, and this term is still used by some of these companies. It is also commonly used by public companies to distinguish this meeting from an AGM. There is nothing to prevent a GM from being called an EGM, and no particular consequence in practice. Both terms simply mean that it is a meeting of the shareholders which is not an AGM. It is suggested, though, that the term 'general meeting' (and thus 'GM') be used to refer to meetings for companies formed under the CA 2006, as this is the terminology used in the CA 2006 itself.

Please note that in what follows below, 'GM' is used to refer to both a GM and an AGM unless otherwise stated.

8.7.3 Calling general meetings

Shareholders meetings, both GMs and AGMs, do not just happen, they must be called. As with a board meeting (see **8.4**), this is simply a way of inviting the shareholders to attend the meeting to exercise their voting rights. A meeting may be called in a number of ways, but the normal way is for the directors to do this.

8.7.3.1 The directors

Under s 302 of the CA 2006, the directors may call a GM. This is far and away the most common way by which a GM is called. This reflects the principle that it is the directors who run the company on a day-to-day basis, and they will decide what the company should be doing. If one of those decisions requires shareholder approval, eg under the CA 2006, then it makes sense that it is the directors who will want to call the shareholders to a meeting. A GM may be called at any time (except an AGM for a public company, which must be called so that it is held within the six-month time limit after the end of the financial year – see **8.7.1** above).

The directors must pass a board resolution to call a GM (*Browne v La Trinidad* (1887) 37 ChD 1). They must therefore either hold a board meeting and pass a board resolution by a majority vote (see **8.4** above), or sign a directors' written resolution (see **8.5** above) and then send out a notice to the shareholders. The form of the notice is explained at **8.7.4** below.

Note that on a board resolution just to call a GM, the restrictions under model articles for private companies, art 14 on quorum and voting at the board meeting (see **8.4.3** and **8.4.4** above) do not apply, because this decision is seen as purely procedural, one in which no director has a personal interest, in order to get the shareholders together to exercise their votes.

8.7.3.2 The shareholders

Alternatively, the shareholders themselves may call a GM under s 305(1) of the CA 2006. In order to do so, they must first make a request requiring the board of directors to call the GM under s 303 of the CA 2006. The shareholders may make this request only if they together own at least 5% of the paid-up share capital of the company with voting rights (in most small private companies this will simply be a 5% shareholding in the company) and meet other conditions set out in s 303 of the Act. The directors then have 21 days to pass a board resolution to call the GM, to be held not more than 28 days after the notice has been sent (CA 2006, s 304(1)). If the board fail to do this, the shareholders can step in and call the GM, and reclaim their reasonable expenses (CA 2006, s 305).

It is very important to note that this power is used only very rarely by shareholders in practice. Most companies operate consensually, with the directors taking the lead. This power is likely to be used by the shareholders only if there is a dispute with the directors of the company and they are refusing to call a GM.

8.7.3.3 The court

The court may order a GM to be held under s 306 of the CA 2006 if it is impracticable to call it in the usual way. Again, this is not the normal way of calling meetings. The fact that court proceedings are necessary means that it is used only rarely. For example, in *Re El Sombrero Ltd* [1958] Ch 900, where two directors and minority shareholders were refusing to attend meetings to prevent the majority shareholder owning 90% of the company's shares from holding a GM to dismiss them as directors. A more recent example can be found in *Schofield v Jones* [2019] EWHC 803 (Ch).

The application to court may be made by any director or shareholder with voting rights, or the court may order a GM to be held on its own initiative (CA 2006, s 306(2)).

8.7.3.4 The auditors

Under s 518 of the CA 2006, the company's auditors (see **6.12** above) have the right to call a meeting on their resignation if the auditors attach a statement of circumstances under section 519 of the CA 2006 to the notice of resignation and they wish to explain the circumstances of their resignation to the shareholders. This would arise only exceptionally in practice, if the auditors had strong concerns about the financial management of the company.

8.7.4 Notice of general meetings

Those calling a GM must give advance warning (ie notice) of that meeting to the shareholders so that they can make plans to attend the meeting and consider how they will exercise their voting rights on the votes being proposed.

8.7.4.1 To whom is notice given?

Notice of a GM must be given to all shareholders of the company and to every director, to the personal representative of a deceased member and to the trustee in bankruptcy of a bankrupt member (CA 2006, s 310). The company's articles may make alternative provision (s 310(4)), for example some companies exclude giving notice to shareholders resident overseas. Notice must also be given to the auditors (s 502(2)(a)).

8.7.4.2 How must notice be given?

Notice must be given either in hard-copy form (on paper), or electronically (eg by e-mail or fax) or via a website, or by a combination of these methods (CA 2006, s 308).

If in hard-copy form, the notice must either be handed to the shareholders (and others) personally, or be sent by post. For shareholders and directors it will normally be posted to the address which appears on the register of members or directors (CA 2006, ss 1143(1) and 1144(2), Sch 5, Part 2).

Alternatively, notice may be given by electronic means (CA 2006, Sch 5, Part 3) or by publication on the company's website (Sch 5, Part 4), subject to meeting the applicable conditions.

8.7.4.3 Content of notice

A notice of a GM under the CA 2006 must include:

(a) the time, date and place of the meeting (s 311(1));
(b) the general nature of the business to be dealt with (although this provision may be amended by the articles) (s 311(2));
(c) with reasonable prominence, a statement of rights to appoint a proxy (s 325(1));
(d) the full text of any special resolution proposed at the meeting (s 283(6)(a)).

The statement of proxy ((c) above) informs the recipient shareholder that if they are unable to attend or do not wish to attend the meeting, the shareholder is entitled to appoint someone else in their place (known as a proxy), and that person has the right to attend the GM and exercise the shareholder's right to speak and vote (CA 2006, s 325). The proxy need not be a member of the company.

The requirement regarding the special resolution ((d) above) means that, at the GM itself, no amendment may be made to the wording of any such resolution (*In the matter of Uniq PLC* [2011] EWHC 749 (Ch)). However, in the case quoted it was held to be permissible for a mistake in the resolution to be corrected by reading the wording of the resolution with an accompanying circular to shareholders, so that as a matter of construction the resolution could be read as if the error had not been made.

There is no similar requirement to include the full text of an ordinary resolution being proposed at the meeting; in the case of an ordinary resolution, the requirement is that sufficient detail must be given to enable members to decide whether or not it is an issue on which they have a view and for which they would wish to attend. It is, though, common practice to include the full text of ordinary resolutions to assist the shareholders in their decision-making. It is also possible for there to be an amendment to an ordinary resolution at the meeting, provided the change is not so radical that it would make the notice of the meeting ineffective (*Betts v MacNaghten* [1910] 1 Ch 430).

If the shareholders choose to take advantage of their rights under s 314(1) of the CA 2006 to require a statement to be circulated concerning business to be decided upon at the meeting (see **5.6.3.8** above), this must usually be circulated with the notice of the GM (CA 2006, s 315(1)).

In addition, further information may be sent with the notice of GM, for example where a director is protesting their removal under s 169 of the CA 2006 or where a compensation payment is proposed for a director's loss of office under s 217 of the CA 2006.

There is no prescribed format for a notice of a GM.

8.7.4.4 Length of notice

The shareholders (and those others entitled) of a private company (which is not traded) must be given at least 14 'clear' days' notice of a GM (CA 2006, s 307(A1) and (1), and s 360).

'Clear' days means that the day on which the notice is given and the day on which the meeting is held are not be counted in the number of days' notice (CA 2006, s 360). In other words, there must be at least 14 days' notice which starts to run on the day after the notice of the GM is given, and the meeting must then be held on the next day after the 14 days have expired. For example, if notice of a private company's GM is given to all those entitled to it on 1 July, 2 July then becomes the first of the 14 days for which notice of the meeting is required. The fourteenth of the 14 days is 15 July, and thus the GM can validly be held on 16 July. In other words, the meeting can take place 16 days from the date the notice of the GM is first given. Also be aware that the notice period includes weekends and bank holidays (unless the articles say otherwise, which usually they do not).

Where a company has unamended Table A articles, those articles may extend this notice period (CA 2006, s 307(3)). For such a company, the required notice period varies according to the type of resolution and meeting (Table A, art 38). All resolutions to be passed at an AGM and a special resolution to be passed at a GM require at least 21 clear days' notice; 14 clear days' notice will apply only if ordinary resolutions alone are to be passed at a GM, except where a director is to be appointed by the shareholders for which 21 clear days' notice is needed.

In addition to the minimum 14 clear days' notice period, it is usually necessary under s 1147 of the CA 2006 to add a further 48 hours before the GM can be held, unless the company's articles state otherwise. This is because s 1147 provides that a document (including a notice of a GM) is deemed to have been received by the intended recipient 48 hours after it was sent by post or electronically. This provision saves the company from having to check that every shareholder (and others entitled) has received the notice of the GM. The model articles for private companies and Table A do not vary this.

This means that if notice of a private company's GM is sent by post to all those entitled to it on 1 July, 3 July is the day on which the recipients are deemed to have received it. The date of 4 July then becomes the first of the 14 days for which notice of the meeting is required, as the date of receipt is not counted. The fourteenth of the 14 days is 17 July, and thus the GM can validly be held on the next day, 18 July. In other words, the meeting can take place 18 days from the date the notice of the GM is first given.

The minimum notice period applicable to the GMs for public companies and traded companies is more complex (see CA 2006, ss 307 and 307A).

8.7.4.5 Short notice

As an alternative to waiting the full notice period before a GM can be held, it is possible for the shareholders of a company to agree to hold a GM on short notice (CA 2006, s 307(4)). Short notice means any notice period less than the usual notice period required, which is the 14 clear days required for private companies. It means that the GM may, for example, be held on the same day that the notice of the meeting is given. Short notice is therefore a device to speed up decision-making by shareholders, who would otherwise have to wait two and a half weeks for the GM.

As the notice period is a protection for the shareholders, it will be for them to decide whether to allow the GM to be held on short notice. Under s 307 of the CA 2006, a two-stage test must be met before short notice can be given:

(a) a majority in number of the shareholders must agree to holding the meeting on short notice (CA 2006, s 307(5)); and

(b) those shareholders must hold at least 90% of the voting shares in the private company (CA 2006, s 307(5)(a) and (6)(a)). This 90% threshold may be increased by the articles to 95% (CA 2006, s 307(6)(a)), which applies to many companies formed before the CA 2006 came into force.

A 'majority in number' means that more of the shareholders must be in favour of short notice than against.

EXAMPLE 1

For a company with three shareholders, the agreement of at least two of the shareholders is therefore necessary.

> **EXAMPLE 2**
>
> For a company with two shareholders, short notice can happen only with the agreement of both of them.

It does not matter what percentage the minority owns, even if it is the required 90%. If, for example, a company had six shareholders, one of whom owned 90% of the shares and supported short notice, and five of whom each owned 2% and who were against short notice, then short notice would not be possible because the sole supporter does not constitute a majority in number; four of the shareholders would need to agree.

Provided there is a majority of shareholders in favour, those shareholders must own the required percentage of voting shares. If two out of three shareholders support short notice but they own only 75% of the shares, short notice is not possible.

If short notice is purportedly used without complying with the statutory and article requirements, the decisions taken at the GM will be invalid (*Schofield v Schofield*, Court of Appeal (Civil Division), 25 February 2011).

It should be noted that there are some circumstances in which short notice cannot be used, eg the removal of a director under s 168 of the CA 2006 (see **6.10.3** above).

Short notice is useful where the shareholders are in agreement on the matters to be decided at a GM as it speeds up the whole process. An alternative to short notice would be for the shareholders to use a written resolution (see **8.9** below).

8.7.4.6 Invalid notice

It is essential that notice be given in the proper form to all those entitled to it, because the basic rule is that if this is not done then any resolutions purportedly passed at the meeting may be invalid (CA 2006, s 301(a)). A deliberate decision not to send a notice to a shareholder can also amount to a breach by a director of s 171(b) of the CA 2006 for exercising their powers for an improper purpose (see eg *Re OS3 Distribution Ltd (sub nom Watchstone Group PLC v Quob Park Estate Ltd)* [2017] EWHC 2621 (Ch)). However, if notice is accidentally not given to a person entitled to it, the resolutions passed at the meeting are still valid (CA 2006, s 313(1)). See *In the matter of Halcrow Holdings Ltd* [2011] EWHC 3662 (Ch) for an example. This provision will not of course assist the company where there is any suggestion that the 'mistake' was deliberate, eg if a dissenting shareholder has not been given notice in a deliberate attempt to exclude them from the meeting.

8.7.5 Quorum

The quorum is the minimum number of shareholders who are required to attend the GM in order for resolutions to be passed validly at that GM. Subject to the company's articles, s 318(2) of the CA 2006 fixes the quorum for GMs at two, unless the company in question is a single-member company (see **8.10** below) in which case the quorum is one (CA 2006, s 318(1)).

The quorum of a company with more than one shareholder cannot normally be reduced to one, because generally one person cannot constitute a 'meeting' (*Sharp v Dawes* (1876) 2 QBD 26 (CA)). However, in exceptional circumstances the court may reduce the quorum to one under s 306 of the CA 2006. This would arise, for example, where a shareholder refuses to attend a GM so that no decisions can be taken (*Re El Sombrero Ltd* [1958] Ch 900).

The quorum may, however, be increased to any figure thought appropriate for that company, by the shareholders amending the articles by special resolution. In a small private company, the statutory quorum of two is usually suitable. In a two-person company this prevents one shareholder from being able to take decisions on their own, thereby acquiring too much power. In a larger company, the members may feel that it is inappropriate to validate a meeting when only two shareholders are present, and a larger number may be specified in the articles as the quorum. For companies with the model articles for private companies or Table A the quorum is two.

If a shareholder sends a proxy to the meeting in their place (see **8.7.4.3** above), the proxy counts as part of the quorum (CA 2006, s 324(1)). However, generally, there must be at least two people physically present in the room for there to be a 'meeting'. So one person who attends as a shareholder themselves and who is also a proxy for another shareholder cannot, on their own, fulfil the requirement of a quorum of two (*Re Sanitary Carbon Co* [1870] WN 233).

A GM must be quorate when it starts, and must remain quorate throughout the meeting. If too few people are present at the start of the meeting, or if someone has to leave and the meeting ceases to be quorate, the chairperson will adjourn the meeting to a later date (model articles for private companies, art 41(1); Table A, art 41). A further attempt will then be made to hold a quorate meeting.

Directors are also permitted to attend a GM (model articles for private companies, art 40(1); Table A, art 44) but they cannot vote unless they are also shareholders. Auditors may also attend (CA 2006, s 502(2)). The chairperson of the meeting has a discretion to allow other people to attend the GM under art 40(2) of the model articles for private companies.

8.7.6 The chairperson

The chairperson at a GM will usually be the same person as is appointed to be the chairperson for board meetings (eg model articles for private companies, art 39; or Table A, art 42). If there is no power in the articles, the chairperson may be elected by an ordinary resolution at a GM (CA 2006, s 319(1)). Subject to the articles, a proxy may be chairperson (CA 2006, s 328(1)).

The chairperson's task is to preside at meetings and to keep order. For example, they will determine whether a quorum is present, take items in turn from the agenda and decide whether proposed amendments to ordinary resolutions may be allowed. They will declare whether a particular resolution has been passed or defeated. The chairperson's statement on this is conclusive, unless the vote was on a show of hands and a poll is subsequently demanded (CA 2006, s 320) or unless their declaration is clearly bad on the face of it (*Re Caratal (New) Mines Ltd* [1902] 2 Ch 499). For example, if 10 shareholders are present at the meeting, each of whom holds 10 shares in the company, and on a show of hands nine of them vote for the resolution and one votes against it, but the chairperson declares that the resolution is defeated, that is a ruling which is clearly bad on the face of it.

For a discussion of the chairperson's casting vote, see **8.7.7.4** below.

8.7.7 Voting

Once a quorum has been declared, the shareholders may take decisions by voting on resolutions at the GM (CA 2006, s 281(1)(b)). Certain considerations need to be borne in mind, as follows.

8.7.7.1 How does voting take place?

Shareholders may vote at general meetings in one of two ways:

(a) on a show of hands; or
(b) on a poll vote (CA 2006, ss 282 and 283).

If a vote is taken on a show of hands, every shareholder has one vote (s 284(2)). If a poll vote is taken, each shareholder has one vote for every share they own (s 284(3)). A proxy may vote in either case, exercising the same number of votes as the shareholder they represent (s 285). These rules may be varied by the company's articles (ss 284(4) and 285(5)).

> **EXAMPLE**
>
> A company has issued 100 shares. It has three shareholders.
>
> Two shareholders each hold 20 shares (20% each).
>
> One shareholder holds 60 shares (60%).
>
> An ordinary resolution has been proposed at a GM. The one 60% shareholder is in favour of the resolution. The two 20% shareholders are against it.
>
> If all shareholders are present at the GM then on a vote on a show of hands the resolution would be defeated by 2:1; but on a poll vote the resolution would pass because the shareholder in favour has 60% of the votes and the two against only 40%. The ordinary resolution (which requires over 50% in favour) would pass by 60% to 40%.

Initially, all votes will be taken on a show of hands for administrative convenience, as most decision-making in small private companies is consensual; but as the example above shows, this method can clearly be disadvantageous to shareholders holding a majority of votes. If, therefore, the result of the show of hands is not unanimous, a poll vote may be demanded (CA 2006, s 321(1)). The right to a poll vote may be completely excluded in the articles only for a vote at a GM to appoint a chairperson or adjourn the meeting (s 321(1)).

If the vote is a poll vote, it is taken in writing with one vote per share, usually immediately (*R v Chillington Iron Co* (1825) 29 ChD 159); but votes cast in advance of the meeting may also be included in a poll vote, subject to the articles of the company (CA 2006, s 322A).

The articles will specify who can ask for a poll vote, and a proxy has the same right as the shareholder they represent in this regard. The only restriction on this is that the articles cannot be amended so that more than five members or holders of more than 10% of the company's shares must request a poll in order for one to be held (CA 2006, s 321).

Under art 44 of the model articles for private companies, a poll vote must be taken if requested by:

(a) the chairperson; or

(b) the directors; or

(c) any two shareholders;

(d) or any shareholder(s) holding at least 10% of the shares.

Therefore, under the model articles for private companies, the only shareholder or proxy who has no right to a poll vote is a single shareholder who owns less than 10% of the company's shares. If the shareholders wanted to amend this to allow any single shareholder to insist on a poll being held, they could do so by passing a special resolution to change the articles. Clearly, there would be little point in a shareholder with a very small percentage of the shares asking for a poll vote if they were the only shareholder who wished to overturn the result of the vote on a show of hands. Such a shareholder's right to demand a poll may be important, however, where they hold the few votes that could affect the outcome of the vote.

8.7.7.2 Proxies

A proxy is a person who attends a GM in place of a shareholder of the company (CA 2006, s 324). The proxy must vote in accordance with the wishes of the shareholder who appointed the proxy (CA 2006, s 322A). If a member wants to send a proxy to a meeting rather than attend personally, they must formally appoint a person as their proxy by depositing notice in writing at the registered office (model articles for private companies, art 45). The company cannot insist on more than 48 hours' notice prior to a GM of the appointment of a proxy (CA 2006, s 327).

A proxy may be appointed for one meeting, or for several meetings. The appointee may be told whether to vote for or against particular resolutions by the shareholder who appoints them, or they may be required to attend the meeting, hear the arguments put forward and vote in whatever manner they feel appropriate.

A shareholder could ask another shareholder of the company to attend the meeting as their proxy, or they might ask a complete outsider to stand in for them.

We have seen that a proxy can vote on a show of hands and if there is a poll (CA 2006, s 285). They have the same right as their appointer to request that a poll be taken. A proxy can also speak at a GM. Therefore, a shareholder may wish to appoint a proxy not only where the shareholder is unable to attend GMs, but also where they feel that a proxy might be more articulate or persuasive when speaking on a particular issue.

Section 324(2) of the CA 2006 also allows a shareholder to appoint different proxies for different shares.

We saw at **8.7.4.3** above that every notice of a GM must inform the shareholders clearly of their right to appoint proxies under s 324 of the CA 2006 and under any wider rights in the articles (CA 2006, s 325). It is an offence committed by every officer of the company if the information is omitted (s 325(4)).

A proxy may even be chairperson of a GM (CA 2006, s 328), subject to the articles.

If it is intended to terminate a proxy's authority, the company must have received notice of that intention before the start of the relevant GM (CA 2006, s 330). If the articles specify more than 48 hours' notice then that provision is void under s 330(6).

8.7.7.3 Resolutions

A resolution is the decision which the shareholders will take at a properly convened GM. There are three types of resolution which may be passed:

(a) an ordinary resolution;

(b) a special resolution; and

(c) an extraordinary resolution.

Each of these is examined in further detail below.

Ordinary resolution

An ordinary resolution is passed if a simple majority of the members voting at the meeting are in favour of it (CA 2006, s 282). Thus, the resolution will be passed if, on a show of hands, a majority in number of the members present vote for the resolution (s 282(3)). In other words, it will be passed if more people vote in favour of it than against it. We saw, though (**8.7.7.1** above), that a poll vote may be called if the show of hands produces an unfair result. To pass an ordinary resolution on a poll vote, it must be passed by a simple majority (ie more than 50%) of the voting rights cast by those entitled to vote in person, by proxy or (if the articles allow it in accordance with s 322A of the CA 2006) in advance (s 282(4)).

It is important to note that an ordinary resolution will be passed by a simple majority of the shares of *those who vote*; it does not require over 50% of all the votes in the company, the principle being that if a shareholder does not turn up to the meeting or appoint a proxy, the shareholder loses their vote.

EXAMPLE

A company has issued 100 shares.

The company has five shareholders and each owns 20 shares (20%).

If all five shareholders are present at a GM, or send a proxy, any three of them can pass an ordinary resolution because between them they will have 60% of the votes (ie 60 out of 100), which is the minimum required here to reach the threshold of more than 50%.

> However, if only three shareholders turn up to the meeting and the other two do not send proxies in their place, any two of those shareholders present would between them hold over 50% of the votes (ie 40 out of 60), and thus could pass an ordinary resolution.

Sometimes the CA 2006 does not expressly refer to an 'ordinary resolution'. Instead it simply refers to 'a resolution of the company' or 'a resolution of the members'. Under s 281(3) of the CA 2006, where those terms are used and it is not stated what type of resolution it is, it will be an ordinary resolution unless the company's articles require a higher voting majority.

We saw at **8.2** above some examples of when ordinary resolutions are required under the CA 2006. Note that the articles may require an ordinary resolution to be passed as a special resolution (see below) (CA 2006, s 282(5)).

Special resolution

A special resolution requires at least a 75% majority for it to be passed (CA 2006, s 283(1)). This means that, on a vote on a show of hands, at least 75% of the number of shareholders, or their proxies, present vote in its favour (s 283(4)). On a poll vote, 75% of the votes cast by those entitled to vote in person, by proxy or (if the articles allow it in accordance with s 322A of the CA 2006) in advance must be in favour of the resolution (s 283(5)).

It is important to note that a special resolution will be passed by a 75% majority of the shares of *those who vote*; it does not need 75% of all the votes in the company. Note also that the required majority is 75%, not *over* 75%.

> **EXAMPLE**
>
> A company has issued 100 shares.
>
> The company has 10 shareholders and each owns 10 shares (10%).
>
> If all 10 shareholders are present at a GM, or send a proxy, any eight of them can pass a special resolution because between them they would have 80% of the votes (ie 80 out of 100) which here is the minimum required to hit the 75% threshold.
>
> However, if only eight shareholders turn up to the meeting and the other two do not send proxies in their place, any six of those shareholders present would between them hold 75% of the votes (ie 60 out of 80), and thus could pass a special resolution.

We saw at **8.2** above some examples of when special resolutions are required under the CA 2006. Remember also that there are specific conditions for special resolutions, regarding the content of the notice of the GM (see **8.7.4.3** above).

Extraordinary resolution

An extraordinary resolution is not mentioned in the CA 2006. It was a form of shareholder decision provided for in the CA 1985. However, its existence has been preserved for those companies which retain this method of decision-making in their articles (Companies Act 2006 (Commencement No 3, Consequential Amendments, Transitional Provisions and Savings) Order 2007 (SI 2007/2194), Sch 3, para 23). The majority required is the same as for a special resolution (above). It is not a valid method for decision-making for companies formed under the CA 2006.

Which resolution to use?

Shareholders can act by ordinary resolution (simple majority), unless they are required to use some other sort of resolution either by statute or by the company's articles. We saw at **8.2** above that the CA 2006 insists that for certain decisions only a certain type of resolution is adequate, eg a special resolution is needed to change the company's articles. Therefore, for these amendments to be made validly, a special resolution must be used.

Where, however, the CA 2006 or the articles specify that an ordinary resolution may be used, it is open to the shareholders to change the articles to require a special resolution to be used instead (CA 2006, s 282(5)). The two exceptions to this are removal of a director against their will and the removal of the company's auditors. These rights may be exercised by a simple majority of the shareholders under the CA 2006, and they are rights which cannot be taken away (CA 2006, ss 168 and 510 respectively).

8.7.7.4 Deadlock

If on a poll vote for an ordinary resolution the votes are 50% in favour and 50% against, the resolution has not passed as there is no simple majority (over 50% in favour) as required by s 282 of the Act. The question then arises whether the chairperson of the GM has a casting vote to decide the outcome. There are two different situations.

Companies formed under the CA 2006 are not allowed, by virtue of the definition of 'ordinary resolution' in s 282 of the CA 2006, to use a casting vote to break a deadlocked vote on an ordinary resolution. For companies formed before 1 October 2007, if they had a casting vote for the chairperson at GMs (as, for example, was found in Table A, art 50) then this is still valid. In exercising the power in this case, the chairperson should cast their vote as a fiduciary rather than as an individual; in other words, for what is best for the company rather than for their personal position.

8.7.7.5 Interests

Generally, there are no restrictions on the way in which a shareholders exercise their voting rights. When voting at shareholders' GMs they need only have regard to their own self-interest and need not consider whether they are acting in the interests of the company because shareholders are not fiduciaries of the company (*Pender v Lushington* (1877) 6 ChD 70). It is after all the shareholders who have invested their own money in the company. On the other hand, as we have seen at **6.4** above, because of their fiduciary relationship with a company, there are at times significant restrictions on how a director can vote at board meetings. If a shareholder is also a director, when exercising votes at a GM *as a shareholder*, the shareholder is allowed to ignore those duties to the company which the shareholder is obliged to take into account when exercising their vote *as a director* at a board meeting (*North-West Transportation Co Ltd v Beatty* (1887) 12 App Cas 589).

There are some exceptions to this general rule when the votes of a shareholder who is involved in a matter to be voted on at a GM are ignored. They include votes by a director who is also a shareholder, and persons connected to the director, on an ordinary resolution under s 239 of the CA to ratify a director's breach of duty (see **7.11.2** above) (CA 2006, s 239(4)). Similarly, when a company wants to buy back its shares and the shareholders vote on the ordinary resolution to approve the contract and, if required, on the special resolution to approve a buy-back out of capital. Votes on the shares to be bought back are ignored (CA 2006, ss 695 and 717) (see **9.5** below).

8.8 UNANIMOUS AGREEMENTS

If all shareholders are present at a meeting and unanimously give their consent to a proposal, it does not matter that no formal resolution was put to the vote (*Wright v Atlas Wright (Europe) Ltd* [1999] BCC 163, which concerned approval of a director's long-term service contract). Cases such as *Re Duomatic Ltd* [1969] 2 Ch 365 have taken this concept further and held that all that is required is the unanimous consent of the shareholders who have a right to vote. There is no need to convene a shareholders' meeting at all. An example of this is *Euro Brokers Holdings Ltd v Monecor (London) Ltd* [2003] BCC 573, where the Court of Appeal held that an informal meeting of the only two shareholders was valid. The principle was also followed in *Deakin v Faulding (No 2)* [2001] 98 (35) LSG 32. However, this does not allow shareholders to take decisions which would be unlawful under the CA 2006, and it may not be valid for certain resolutions, such as those required to reduce a company's capital (*Re Barry Artist* [1985] 1 WLR 1305), or to dismiss a director or the company's auditors.

The common law position on informal meetings is preserved by s 281(4)(a) of the CA 2006.

It should be noted that this approach would not normally be recommended as a way of taking decisions. There are established procedures under the CA 2006 which, if followed, mean that the resolutions passed will be legally binding on the company. The common law position can be uncertain, and there is a risk that any decisions purportedly taken will be found to be invalid.

8.9 SHAREHOLDERS' WRITTEN RESOLUTIONS

In **8.7** above we examined the situation where the shareholders take their decisions at a validly convened GM. The other main way in which the shareholders of a company can take valid decisions is by passing a validly proposed written resolution. This method of decision-making does not require a GM to be held. It is therefore a very common way for private companies, particularly smaller ones, to take shareholder decisions. Indeed, for many private companies it will be used as the usual shareholder decision-making mechanism rather than holding a GM. This is because the written resolution procedure does not require any shareholders to meet face to face, and so is quicker than a meeting called on full notice, involves less administration and is more cost-effective.

8.9.1 When may it be used?

Public companies cannot use the shareholders' written resolution procedure (CA 2006, s 281(2)).

Private limited companies are always permitted to use the written resolution procedure instead of a GM, except in two circumstances:

(a) a GM must be called to dismiss a director (CA 2006, ss 168(1) and 288(2); see **6.10.3**); and

(b) a GM must be called to dismiss the company's auditors (CA 2006, ss 510(2) and 288(2); see **6.12.5**).

This is to allow the director and the auditors the right to speak at a GM in order to defend themselves.

Just as it is the board of directors who will usually call a GM, in normal circumstances it is the board's responsibility to initiate the written resolution procedure (CA 2006, s 291(1)). There is, however, a right under s 292(1) of the Act for the shareholders to require a written resolution to be circulated among the shareholders, together with a statement of not more than 1,000 words about the resolution (CA 2006, s 292(3)). This will in practice be used sparingly – primarily in situations where there is a fundamental disagreement or dispute between the board and some of the shareholders. In order for this right to be used, the shareholder(s) requisitioning the written resolution must together own at least 5% of the voting shares in the company (unless a lower percentage is specified in the articles) (CA 2006, s 292(4) and (5)). In addition, the request must identify the resolution, be in hard-copy or electronic form, be effective if passed, be authenticated (eg, signed) by the person(s) making it and must not be defamatory, vexatious or frivolous (CA 2006, s 292(2) and (6)). The company must circulate the resolution and statement within 21 days of the requirements under s 292 of the Act being met (CA 2006, s 293(1) and (3)).

8.9.2 Circulation

A written resolution proposed by the directors or the requisitioning shareholders must be circulated to all 'eligible members' (CA 2006, ss 291(2) and 293(1) respectively) and to the auditors (s 502(1)).

An 'eligible member' is defined as a shareholder who would have been entitled to vote on the 'circulation date' of the written resolution (CA 2006, s 289(1)). The 'circulation date' is the date on which a resolution is first sent to an eligible member (s 290). If a shareholder transfers their shares to a new shareholder on the circulation date, the shareholder who is eligible is the one who owned the shares at the time the first copy of the resolution was circulated (s 289(2)).

The written resolution may be circulated to the eligible members in one of two different ways:

(a) Separate copies may be sent to each eligible member at the same time by the directors (s 291(3)(a)) or by requisitioning shareholders (s 293(2)(a)). Thus, if there were four shareholders of a company, four separate copies of the resolution would be prepared and one sent to each shareholder.

(b) Alternatively, just one copy of the resolution may be prepared, and this same copy is then sent to each shareholder in turn by the directors (s 291(3)(b)) or by requisitioning shareholders (s 293(2)(b)). So, in our example, the same copy of the resolution would be sent out four times, to each of the four shareholders

Circulation may be effected in hard-copy or electronic form, or by using a website (CA 2006, ss 291(3) and 293(2) respectively). The non-hard copy methods may be used only if the requirements relating to electronic communication with shareholders have been complied with (CA 2006, ss 298 and 299).

For an example of where the purported circulation of a written resolution was held to be invalid, see *Re Sprout Land Holdings Ltd* [2019] EWHC 806 (Ch).

8.9.3 Agreement

As no meeting is held when a written resolution is proposed, there is no physical voting, such as a show of hands or a poll vote, to determine its success or failure. A written resolution is passed by the shareholders. In other words, a decision is taken by them if sufficient eligible members agree to the written resolution by a certain deadline.

8.9.3.1 How to agree

The shareholder's agreement to the written resolution is shown by the company receiving an authenticated document from the eligible member, identifying the resolution and indicating the member's agreement (CA 2006, s 296(1)). When the written resolution is sent out by the directors it must contain a statement under s 291(4) of the Act informing the shareholder how to signify agreement. (There is a similar provision under s 293(4) of the CA 2006 for a resolution sent out at the request of requisitioning shareholders.)

The aim behind the CA 2006 is to provide as much flexibility to private companies as possible. Therefore, agreement may be signified by a physical signature on a piece of paper containing the resolution, but it might also be given electronically without a physical signature.

8.9.3.2 Requisite majority

What would be passed as an ordinary resolution at a GM is passed as a written resolution using the written resolution procedure if eligible members representing a simple majority (more than 50%) of the total voting rights of all the eligible members agree to the resolution (CA 2006, s 282(2)).

What would be passed as a special resolution at a GM is passed as a written resolution using the written resolution procedure if eligible members representing a majority of at least 75% of the total voting rights of all the eligible members agree to the resolution (CA 2006, s 283(2)).

Under the written resolution procedure, the eligible members' voting rights are calculated on the basis of one vote per share (as opposed to one vote per person), unless the company's articles provide otherwise (CA 2006, s 284(1) and (4)).

Note that the written resolution (whether passed by a simple majority or by a 75% majority) will be passed as soon as the required majority of eligible members have agreed to it (CA 2006, s 296(4)). For example, assume that there is a company with four shareholders, each owning 25% of the voting shares. They are all eligible members. The board of directors of circulate a written resolution (which would be an ordinary resolution if at a GM) on 1 January. On 2 January, two shareholders agree to the written resolution. On 4 January, a third shareholder agrees to the written resolution. The resolution is now passed, as the 'over 50%' threshold has been met even though the fourth shareholder has not yet indicated whether they agree.

8.9.3.3 Deadline for agreement

A proposed written resolution must be passed before the end of 28 days beginning on the circulation date (see **8.9.2** above), or the period specified in the articles if different, otherwise it will lapse (CA 2006, s 297(1)) and any agreement signified by an eligible member after this date is ineffective (CA 2006, s 297(2)). Therefore there only is a limited window during which agreement may be given and the requisite majority to pass the resolution may be obtained. This is to ensure that decisions affecting the company are not left outstanding for long periods of time. Of course the shareholders may reach agreement well within the 28-day limit, and usually they will want to take the decision as soon as possible.

When the written resolution is sent out by the directors, the statement it must contain under s 291(4) of the Act (see **8.9.3.1** above) must also include the date by which the resolution must be passed if it is not to lapse. (There is a similar provision under s 293(4) of the CA 2006 for a resolution sent out at the request of requisitioning shareholders.)

8.10 SINGLE-MEMBER COMPANY

A single-member company, ie a company with just one shareholder, may take decisions in three different ways:

(a) by passing a resolution at a GM in the usual way (CA 2006, s 301);

(b) by passing a written resolution in accordance with the rules explained at **8.9** above; or

(c) simply taking an informal decision without a GM or a written resolution (the equivalent of the unanimous agreement for a company with more than one shareholder – see **8.8** above).

If a GM is held, the quorum for such meetings is one by virtue of s 318(1) of the CA 2006. If the decision is taken without a GM or written resolution, the sole member must provide details of the decision to the company where it is one that could have been taken at a GM (s 357(2)), otherwise an offence is committed by the shareholder (s 357(3)). This ensures that the company has proof of the decisions made informally by the sole shareholder which would otherwise be recorded if they were taken at a GM or by written resolution. Decision-making in such companies will usually be done in this informal way, particularly as it is likely that the sole shareholder will also be the sole director of the company.

8.11 POST-DECISION REQUIREMENTS

Whether the decision of the directors or shareholders is taken at a meeting or by written resolution (or by unanimous consent where permitted), various statutory requirements are imposed on the company to keep certain information about the decision and to file it with Companies House, in order that those involved with the company and members of the public will have access to the most up-to-date details on the company's make-up and key decisions. After certain decisions have been taken, new documents will also have to be issued to shareholders or contracts will have to be executed.

8.11.1 Filing

The CA 2006 requires the filing of one or more of a form, a shareholders' resolution and a related document, depending on the particular decision taken. Note that a company will file only what the law requires it to file.

8.11.1.1 Resolutions

Under ss 29 and 30 of the CA 2006, copies of all special resolutions, and equivalent written resolutions and decisions taken by unanimous consent, must be sent to the Registrar of Companies at Companies House. This must be done within 15 days of their being made (s 30(1)) otherwise an offence is committed by the company and every officer in default (s 30(2)).

In addition, the CA 2006 may require copies of other resolutions to be sent to Companies House. For example, an ordinary resolution passed by the shareholders to give the directors authority to allot new shares (s 551(9)) (see **9.3.2** below) and an ordinary resolution passed by the shareholders to allow the company to send information by publication on a website (Sch 5, para 10). Usually, though, copies of ordinary resolutions are not sent to the Registrar.

By s 355(1) of the CA 2006, a company must keep records of all resolutions passed otherwise than at a GM (eg, written resolutions) and any details provided by a sole member in accordance with s 357 of the Act (see **8.10** above). These records must be kept for a minimum of 10 years (s 355(2)) at the company's registered office or SAIL (s 358(1)) (see **8.11.4** below), otherwise an offence is committed by every officer in default (s 355(3)).

8.11.1.2 Forms and information

Various forms may need to be completed and sent to the Registrar of Companies in accordance with the requirements of the CA 2006, depending on the decision made. There may be a time limit imposed for submission. The main forms covering decisions dealt with in this Part are:

Form AA01: for a change of accounting reference date (s 392)

Form AD01: for a change of registered office (s 87)

Form AD02: notification of SAIL within 14 days (see **8.11.4** below) (s 358)

Form AP01: for appointment of an individual director within 14 days of appointment (s 167)

Form AP02: for appointment of a corporate director within 14 days of appointment (s 167)

Form AP03: for appointment of an individual company secretary within 14 days of appointment (s 276)

Form AP04: for appointment of a corporate company secretary within 14 days of appointment (s 276)

Form CH01: for change of an individual director's details within 14 days of change (s 167)

Form CH02: for change of a corporate director's details within 14 days of change (s 167)

Form CH03: for change of an individual company secretary's details within 14 days of change (s 276)

Form CH04: for change of a corporate company secretary's details within 14 days of change (s 276)

Form MR01: for particulars of a mortgage or charge within 21 days of creation (s 859D) (see **11.10**)

Form MR04: for satisfaction of a mortgage or charge (s 859L)

Form NM01: for a change of company name by special resolution (s 78)

Form NM04: for a change of company name by the articles (s 79)

Form PSC01: for notification of an individual PSC within 14 days after entry in the PSC register (s 790VA)

Form PSC02: notification of a Relevant Legal Entity PSC within 14 days after entry in the PSC register (s 790VA)

Form PSC04: for change of a PSC's details within 14 days after entry in the PSC register (s 790VA)

Form PSC07: notification of ceasing to be a PSC within 14 days after entry in the PSC register (s 790VA)

Form SH01: return of allotment of shares within one month of allotment (s 555)

Form SH03: return of purchase of own shares within 28 days of purchase (s 707)

Form SH06: for notification of cancellation of shares on purchase within 28 days of cancellation (s 708)

Form SH19: reduction of share capital within 15 days of resolution (s 644)

Form TM01: for termination of appointment of a director within 14 days of termination (s 167)

Form TM02: for termination of appointment of a company secretary within 14 days of termination (s 276)

Where no deadline is set by the CA 2006 for submission, the form should be submitted as soon as possible as the change may not take effect until this has been done.

Copies of all of these forms may be found on the Companies House website, <www.gov.uk/government/organisations/companies-house>.

A fee is payable when submitting certain forms, including for Forms MR01 (£24 paper/£15 electronic), NM01 and NM04 (£30/£20/same day £83) above.

A change in the company's registered email address (s 853CB) can only be made online through the Companies House website.

ECCTA will repeal s 167 and s 276. The new authority for notifying Companies House of the:

- *appointment and termination of a director will be a new s 167G;*
- *change in a director's details will be new ss 167H–167I;*
- *appointment and termination of a company secretary will be a new s 279G;*
- *change in a company secretary's details will be new ss 279H–279I;*
- *an individual or Relevant Legal Entity becoming or ceasing to be a PSC will be s 790LA; and*
- *change in a PSC's details will be s 790LC.*

The content of these forms will be amended by Companies House once the relevant ECCTA provisions are brought into force, which is expected to take place by 2027.

8.11.1.3 Documents

On occasion, following a decision taken by the shareholders or directors, the CA 2006 requires a document to be filed at Companies House (usually with an accompanying resolution) and/or retained at the company's registered office or SAIL (see **8.11.4** below) for inspection. For example, if a special resolution to amend the company's articles is passed by the shareholders under s 21 of the CA 2006, a copy of the amended articles must be filed at Companies House not later than 15 days after the special resolution is passed (s 26(1)), along with the special resolution.

In other cases certain documents must be kept and made available for inspection by shareholders and sometimes others, including a director's service contract (or written memorandum of its terms) under s 228 of the CA 2006 (see **6.8.2** above) for at least one year after the end of the contract (ss 228(3) and 229(1)). A contract to buy back the company's shares must be kept for at least 10 years and made available for inspection (s 702). A company must also keep available for inspection a copy of any charge over the company's property (s 877).

A number of the provisions of the CA 2006 require shareholder approval of contracts. Although obtaining this consent is essential, the contract will not be entered into by the shareholders. Once permission has been given by the shareholders, it still remains for the directors to resolve to enter the contract and authorise its execution. In these cases the contract will thus need to be signed after the shareholders' meeting. Examples include an SPT (see **7.12.1** above), a director's service contract (see **6.8.2** above) and a contract for the buy-back of shares (see **9.5** below).

Lastly, whenever there is a transaction involving shares in the company, consideration must be given to the share certificate which documents ownership of the company. If shares are sold or given away, or there is a transmission of shares (see **9.9** and **9.10**), a new share certificate must be issued to the new shareholder and the previous owner's share certificate must be destroyed. If a company allots new shares to existing or new shareholders (see **9.3** below), it must issue new share certificates for the new shares; and if a company buys back its own shares (see **9.5** below) then the share certificates of the previous owners must be destroyed and new ones issued if they retain any shares in the company.

8.11.2 Registers

We have seen that a company is obliged by the CA 2006 to maintain certain registers in respect of its activities. There are others we shall also come across later in this chapter and in Part II. These registers must be updated following changes to the information in them in light of the decisions made by the board and the shareholders. A failure to do so will result in an offence being committed.

The main registers are the register of members (see **5.4** above), the PSC register (see **5.5** above), the register of directors (see **6.9.1** above), the register of directors' residential addresses (see **6.9.2** above) and the register of secretaries (see **6.2.2** above). It is important to note that one decision may result in a change to more than one of the registers. For example, a change of company name under s 78 of the CA 2006 will result in the name having to be changed in all of the company's registers. A resolution to change the place of storage and inspection of certain records from the company's registered office to a SAIL will result in all the registers having to be moved to the new location. The appointment of a new director who also buys shares in the company will mean that the registers of members, directors and directors' residential addresses will have to be updated.

It is also worth noting that a change in some of the information in the registers does not require a formal decision to have been taken by the board of directors or by the shareholders. If a director marries and changes her surname, this information will have to be updated in the registers of directors and directors' residential addresses.

Under s 128B of the CA 2006, private companies may elect not to keep their own registers of members, PSCs, directors, directors' residential addresses and secretaries; and alternatively they can ensure that the necessary information is filed and kept up-to-date on the central register for the company held at Companies House in electronic form. All shareholders must agree for this election to be valid, and the Registrar of Companies must be notified using Forms EH01–EH05 (one for each register). If a change occurs to the information held on the central register (such as the appointment of a new director), the company must file the usual form for such a change and this will update the electronic version.

The Economic Crime and Corporate Transparency Act 2023 will remove the requirement for a company to keep a register of directors, directors' residential addresses, company secretaries and the PSC register. It will also remove the right of a company to elect to keep its registers centrally at Companies House. This will repeal s 128B. The effect of these changes will be that companies will only need to maintain a register of members and that the company should keep its own register rather than relying on Companies House keeping it centrally for the company. These amendments are expected to come into force by 2027.

8.11.3 Minutes

Minutes must be kept for all proceedings of GMs (CA 2006, s 355(1)(b)) for at least 10 years (s 355(2)) at the company's registered office or SAIL (s 358(1)), otherwise an offence is committed by every officer of the company in default. The minutes will not record verbatim what was said at the GM but are a record in overview form of what happened at the meeting, including any decisions made and follow-up action to be taken. Section 1135(1) of the CA 2006 requires minutes to be kept in hard-copy or electronic form, and if kept electronically must be capable of being reproduced in hard copy. The articles may contain supplementary provisions regarding the minutes. There are, however, none in the model articles for private companies.

The minutes are open to inspection free of charge by the shareholders (s 358(3)), who may request a copy subject to payment of a fee (s 358(4)). The fee prescribed by the Companies (Fees for Inspecting and Copying of Records) Regulations 2007 (SI 2007/2612) is 10 pence per 500 words and the company's reasonable costs of delivery.

If the minutes of the meeting are signed by the chairperson they are evidence of the proceedings at that meeting (s 356(4)). Unless the contrary is proved, where minutes are prepared the GM is deemed duly held, all proceedings are deemed to have taken place and all appointments are deemed validly made (s 356(5)).

Minutes of a GM of a single-member company (if held) must also be kept (see **8.10** above), as must minutes of directors' board meetings (see **8.4.6** above).

In small private companies, the proceedings of board meetings and GMs will be extremely predictable as most decision-making will be uncontroversial. This is because the directors will have discussed their plans with the shareholders informally first, or be the only shareholders themselves, so they know in advance what the outcome of any vote will be. Thus the usual method is to prepare draft minutes in advance. It often falls to the trainee solicitor to do this. Once the meeting has been held, the minutes will be signed.

8.11.4 Single alternative inspection location

We have seen that certain registers (except those kept on the public register at Companies House), documents and other records, such as minutes of meetings, must be kept by the company. Ordinarily this will be at the company's registered office, but under the Companies (Company Records) Regulations 2008 (SI 2008/3006, made under s 1136 of the CA 2006) the company may choose to keep these records at a so-called 'single alternative inspection location' (SAIL). The company may make this decision by a board resolution of the directors.

The records which may be kept at the SAIL include:

(a) the register of members;
(b) the PSC register;
(c) the register of directors;
(d) the register of secretaries;
(e) the register of debenture holders;
(f) the register of charges;
(g) directors' service contracts kept under s 228 of the CA 2006;

(h) contracts relating to a purchase by a company of its owns shares kept under s 702 of the CA 2006;
(i) a charge document kept under s 877 of the CA 2006;
(j) resolutions passed otherwise at GMs, minutes of GMs and decisions of sole shareholders under s 357 of the CA 2006.

There is no legal requirement for a company to maintain a register of debenture holders or charges. However, some companies may choose to keep these.

The SAIL must be one location and be notified to the Registrar of Companies, originally on Form AD02 and on Form AD03 if the SAIL is changed.

The Economic Crime and Corporate Transparency Act 2023 will remove the requirement of a company to keep a register of directors, directors' addresses, secretaries and the PSC register. This change is expected to take effect by 2027.

8.12 JOINT DECISION-MAKING

We have seen that both the directors and the shareholders may take decisions in a variety of ways in order to effect change in the company. We now need to consider how the two decision-making bodies interact.

If a decision is a matter for the board alone, eg a decision to change the company's registered office, then only a board meeting will need to be held and a board resolution passed to make the change. Once this has been done, the necessary administration must be attended to. The shareholders have no involvement whatsoever.

If, however, the decision requires the shareholders' involvement, eg an ordinary resolution to approve an SPT (see **7.12.1** above), the situation is more complex. Assuming that the normal pattern of events is followed, in this case the directors would have to call and hold a board meeting. At that board meeting the directors will resolve to approve the draft terms of the contract. Following this their principal aim would be to get the shareholders to make their decision on the required shareholders' resolution, eg the SPT ordinary resolution under s 190 of the CA 2006, before the contract is signed. The decision for the board is therefore whether to call a GM or to circulate a written resolution. Whichever method they choose, they must pass a board resolution at the board meeting to effect that choice. In other words, the directors will pass a board resolution either to call a GM, or to circulate a written resolution.

If the directors decide to circulate a written resolution, it is then a matter of waiting for a response from the shareholders. Once the requisite majority has been attained (assuming that enough shareholders vote in favour), the directors can then proceed to deal with the outstanding matters. In the case of an SPT, this would involve passing a board resolution either at a new board meeting or a reconvened board meeting to enter the contract, and authorising signatories to the contract on behalf of the company. A reconvened board meeting will occur where the board meeting at which it was resolved to circulate the written resolution was adjourned (in other words, put on hold) rather than formally closed (ended). If the board meeting was closed after the resolution was passed to circulate the written resolution then a new one must be called in order to have a valid meeting to deal with the requirements once the shareholders have approved the SPT. The board has a choice, therefore:

(a) either to leave the first meeting adjourned and then reconvene it, ie in effect reactivate it when required; or
(b) hold two board meetings.

You will come across both in practice and nothing really turns on the choice.

Alternatively, if the directors decide to call a GM, having passed the necessary board resolution, they will send out the necessary notice of a GM instead of a written resolution. The shareholders will then hold their GM after the minimum notice period has elapsed (remembering that the 14 clear days' notice may be truncated if short notice can be obtained). The shareholders will then vote for or against the resolution, eg the SPT ordinary resolution under s 190 of the CA 2006. Once approval has been given, the directors will either reconvene their original board meeting (if it was adjourned) or hold a second board meeting to enter the contract, and authorise signatories on behalf of the company.

A simplified flowchart of the decision-making process is set out in **Figure 8.1** below. In it:

BM = Board Meeting

BR = Board Resolution

OR = Ordinary Resolution

SHs = Shareholders

WR = Written Resolution

Figure 8.1 Decision-making process

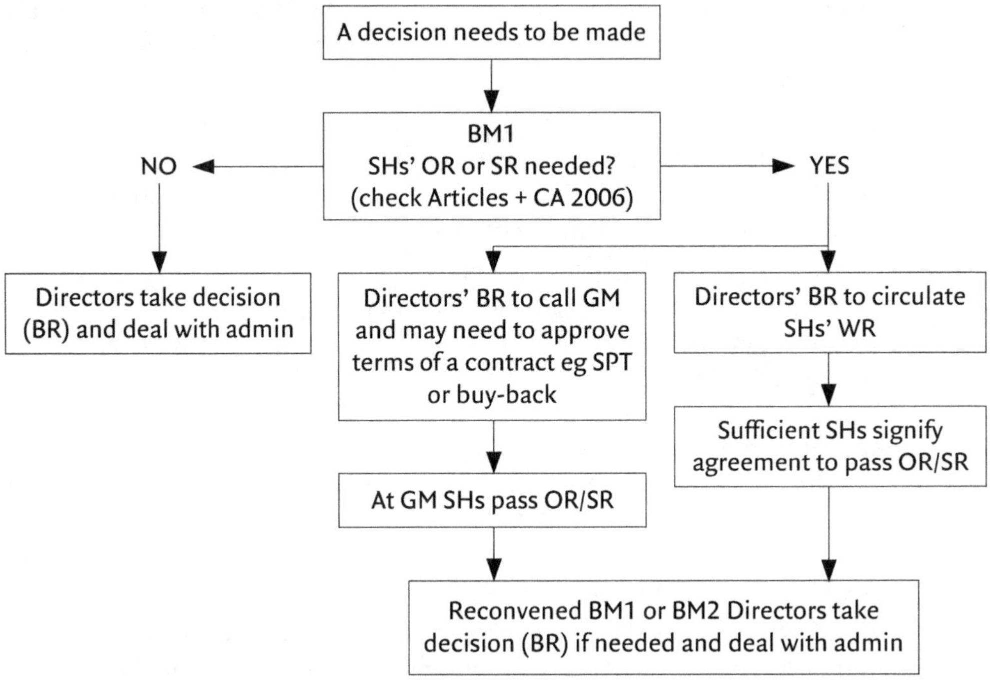

8.13 ELECTRONIC COMMUNICATION

Under the CA 2006, a company may send to and receive from its shareholders notices and other documents concerning GMs. In summary, this may be done as follows.

8.13.1 E-mail

Individual shareholders need to give their consent to be contacted by the company by e-mail or other electronic means rather than by post (CA 2006, Sch 5, Part 3, para 6).

A shareholder is still entitled to receive documents in hard-copy form, if they so request within 21 days of receiving the electronic communication (CA 2006, s 1145). This must be provided free of charge.

Electronic communication *from the shareholder* to the company is also allowed, subject to the company's consent (CA 2006, s 333 and Sch 4).

8.13.2 Websites

The shareholders may pass a resolution authorising the use of a company website for communication, or the articles may so provide. If either is the case, the individual shareholders are required to opt out of using the website rather than to opt in (CA 2006, Sch 5, Part 4, para 10).

Companies need to tell shareholders when they post new shareholders' documents on the website. There would therefore also need to be consent from the shareholders for e-mail communication (CA 2006, s 309).

CHAPTER 9

FINANCING A COMPANY I – SHARES

LEARNING OUTCOMES

After reading this chapter you will be able to:

- explain the maintenance of capital principle
- understand the various ways in which use of the company's share capital is controlled
- explain the law and procedure for a company issuing new shares
- understand the law and procedure for the transfer and transmission of shares between shareholders
- identify sources of finance for a company.

9.1 INTRODUCTION

We saw at **1.8** to **1.10** above that there are a number of different types of company. In this book we consider only companies limited by shares. The members of these companies own the company through their ownership of shares, and in the case of private companies limited by shares will be given a share certificate as evidence of title. They are therefore known as 'shareholders'. In this chapter we examine some of the most important issues which surround shares and share ownership, both for the company and the shareholders.

9.2 MAINTENANCE OF SHARE CAPITAL

The maintenance of share capital is one of the main principles of company law. In *Aveling Barford v Perion Ltd* [1989] BCLC 626, Hoffmann J said that

> a company cannot, without the leave of the court or the adoption of a special procedure, return its capital to its shareholders. It follows that a transaction which amounts to an unauthorised return of capital is ultra vires and cannot be validated by shareholder ratification or approval.

Capital must generally be maintained, as it is the fund to which the creditors look for payment of debts owed to them. In other words, paid-up share capital must not be returned to its shareholders, and their liability in respect of capital not paid up on shares must not be reduced.

The principle has the following consequences:

(a) a company must not generally purchase its own shares (CA 2006, s 658);
(b) a public company may not generally give financial assistance to anyone for the purposes of buying the company's shares;
(c) dividends must not be paid out of capital (only out of distributable profits);
(d) if a public company suffers a serious loss of capital, a general meeting must be called to discuss the problem; and
(e) a subsidiary may not be a member of its own holding company, and any allotment or transfer of shares in a holding company to its subsidiary is void.

After shareholders have paid for their shares, the money produced constitutes the company's capital. Creditors will expect this fund to be available to meet the company's debts, and because the liability of the shareholders of the company is limited, this capital sum should not be diminished. The impact of this on the shareholders of the company is that, having bought their shares in the company, they cannot normally hand their share certificate back to the company in exchange for the consideration they originally provided. If they want to realise their investment, they must sell their shares to another investor. The company cannot generally reduce its share capital by exchanging shareholders' shares for valuable consideration.

Like all principles, there are exceptions to this one, so that a company may:

(a) reduce its share capital with the consent of the court (or, if a private company, by passing a special resolution) under ss 641–648 of the CA 2006;
(b) buy back (CA 2006, s 690) or redeem (ss 684–689) its own shares;
(c) purchase its own shares under a court order made under s 994 of the CA 2006 to buy out an unfairly prejudiced minority, or under ss 98–99 to buy out a minority on the conversion of a public company to a private company; or
(d) return capital to shareholders, after payment of the company's debts, in a winding up.

For the record, the principle of maintenance of capital also applies to the sums received when:

(a) redeemable shares are redeemed by the company (the money being paid in to the capital redemption reserve); or
(b) shares are issued at a premium (the money being paid in to the share premium account).

9.3 ISSUING SHARES

The allotment of new shares is often known as 'equity finance'. In return for issuing shares, the company will receive cash (or property) which it may then use for the company's business. This contrasts with the other main way in which companies raise finance: borrowing money ('debt finance') (see **Chapter 10**). Note also that the allotment of shares is different from a transfer of existing shares, where an existing shareholder sells or gives their shares to another person (see **9.9** below).

When a company wants to raise equity finance by allotting new shares, the board (usually with the advice of accountants or bankers) will determine the price and number of shares to allot. However, solicitors advise on the statutory and procedural requirements for the allotment to take place lawfully, as well as preparing the relevant documents.

An allotment is effected by the board receiving an application from a person who wants to buy shares from the company ('the subscriber'), resolving to allot shares to that person, issuing them with a share certificate and entering that person's name on the company's register of members.

However, the CA 2006 (or related secondary legislation) may require the board to obtain various resolutions from the shareholders before they resolve to allot the shares, since an allotment will potentially affect each existing shareholder's shareholding as a percentage of ownership of the company. An allotment may make an important difference to the existing shareholders' voting strength on ordinary and special resolutions. It may also mean reduced dividends for the existing shareholders, since the profits available for distribution as dividends will have to be split among a greater number of shares.

The resolutions under the CA 2006 concern the need for the directors to have authority to allot shares (CA 2006, s 549) and the statutory pre-emption rights, ie a right of first refusal given to existing shareholders (CA 2006, ss 561 and 565). There may also be restrictions under the articles (see **9.3.1**).

It should be noted that the two words 'allotting' and 'issuing' are often used interchangeably. Strictly speaking, shares are *allotted* to someone (ie allocated) when that person has the unconditional right for their name to be entered onto the company's register of members (CA 2006, s 558). They may then be said to have been *issued* by the company when the name of the shareholder has actually been entered on the company's register of members (*Re Heaton's Steel and Iron Co, Blyth's case* (1876) 4 ChD 140). The terms 'issuing' and 'allotting' are frequently used, however, to describe the whole process by which a shareholder takes shares in a company.

9.3.1 Share capital

The share capital is the amount of money which a company raises by issuing shares. Before the CA 2006 came into force, companies were required to have what was known as an 'authorised share capital'. This was a 'ceiling' on the number of shares which the company could allot. It was abolished from 1 October 2009; but for pre-1 October 2009 companies, the limit in the authorised share capital clause (which used to be stated in the company's memorandum (see **3.14** above)) was not removed but automatically transferred to the articles, where it operates as a restriction on the company which may be amended or removed if required (CA 2006, s 28). If the company has adopted new articles since 1 October 2009, this will usually not be a problem, as the new articles would not normally include such a provision; but if the provision still exists, the articles may need to be amended in order for the company to issue the shares it wishes. This amendment is by ordinary resolution rather than the usual special resolution to amend the articles (under the transitional provisions in SI 2008/2860, Sch 2, para 42).

For companies formed under the CA 2006, there is no automatic limit on the maximum number of shares. Instead, a company is simply required to make a statement of capital and initial shareholdings when the company was incorporated on Form IN01. For example, a new company is often formed with 100 ordinary shares of a nominal value (par value) of £1 each, and this information would be included in the statement of capital. This therefore represents the company's share capital.

In order for a company to raise additional finance by issuing more shares, it must follow the procedure under the CA 2006 and in its articles. In some cases the shareholders will need to give their prior approval to issuing more shares above the amount with which the company was formed. However, a private company with only one class of shares may be able to take advantage of a simplified procedure (CA 2006, ss 549–551).

Although rare, it is possible for a CA 2006 company to include a restriction in its articles on the number of shares which it can issue. If this is the case and the company wishes to raise money by issuing shares in excess of this limit, then the company can only proceed if the shareholders first agree to remove this limit by changing the articles by passing a special resolution under s 21 of the CA 2006.

Whenever new shares are issued by the company, it will have to submit a new statement of capital to reflect the new number of shares.

9.3.2 Directors' power to issue shares

The board will often want to allot shares in the company at the first board meeting of a new company, and may subsequently wish to issue more shares to raise additional finance. When issuing new shares, a company will fall into one of two categories under the CA 2006: either (i) a private company with just one class of shares and no requirements in its articles; or (ii) all other companies (eg private companies with more than one class of shares and public companies).

Private companies with one class of share

Under the 2006 Act, the directors of a private company automatically have authority to allot its shares, provided the company has only one class of shares and there is nothing to the contrary in the articles (s 550). If a pre-1 October 2009 company wishes to make use of the power given under s 550, it has to pass an ordinary resolution of the shareholders in order to do so. Once it has done so, this power exists permanently (Companies Act 2006 (Commencement No 8, Transitional Provisions and Savings) Order 2008 (SI 2008/2860), Sch 2, para 43).

All other companies

The directors can issue shares in the company only if they have authority to do so. This authority must be given specifically, either in the articles (by a special article), or by ordinary resolution of the shareholders at a GM or by written resolution (CA 2006, ss 549–551). Where a new company is formed, it is useful if the authority is contained in a special article so that the matter does not have to be considered at a GM or by written resolution. If an ordinary resolution is required, this is one of the exceptional ordinary resolutions which must be filed with the Registrar of Companies (CA 2006, s 551(9)).

In whatever way the necessary authority is given, it must state the number of shares the directors are authorised to allot. Authority may be given for the directors to allot just one batch of shares, or it may be given generally, allowing them to issue any number of shares up to the amount of the nominal capital. It must also give the period of time for which the authority is to last, which cannot normally be longer than five years, although this may be renewed at any time for a period not longer than five years (CA 2006, s 551(3)). The directors' power to allot shares may be revoked by the shareholders at any time by the passing of an ordinary resolution.

Unusually, an ordinary resolution is sufficient to remove this authority even if the authority was originally given by the articles (which normally require a special resolution for any amendment). Any such ordinary resolution is one of the exceptional ordinary resolutions which must be filed with the Registrar of Companies (CA 2006, s 551(9)).

Under s 555 of the CA 2006, a return of allotments must be filed with Companies House within one month, as must a modified statement of capital (s 555(3)). Both of these are contained on Form SH01. By filing this form the statutory requirements are met. This ensures that the public record always gives an up-to-date view of the company's capital. This applies to both categories of company discussed above.

9.3.3 Statutory pre-emption rights

Even where directors have the authority to issue shares, they cannot necessarily allot them to whomsoever they choose. Sections 561 and 565 of the CA 2006 provide that where shares are being issued in exchange for cash (and not for anything else), those shares must first be offered to the existing shareholders of the company. The number that each current shareholder is offered is dependent upon the percentage of the shares they currently hold. The offer to the existing shareholders must remain open for at least 14 days, and only if the present shareholders decline to take up the shares can they be offered elsewhere.

If pre-emption rights apply, as they usually do on an allotment of new shares, and the directors do not wish to allot the shares to the existing shareholders in accordance with their current shareholdings, they should first check the articles to see whether the statutory pre-emption rights have been removed. If not removed by the articles, a special resolution is necessary to dispense formally with the need to offer the shares to the present shareholders.

Pre-emption rights may be disapplied (ie excluded) in various ways under the CA 2006. Depending on the method used, the pre-emption rights may be dispensed with either generally or for just one particular issue of shares.

Where shares are issued wholly or partly for non-cash consideration (say, a piece of land), s 561 of the CA 2006 has no application (s 565). In such a case, there would be no need to disapply statutory pre-emption rights, as there would not be any pre-emption rights in the first place. (Although the articles should be checked carefully as these may include pre-emption rights even where the consideration is non-cash.)

9.3.3.1 Private company

Under s 569 of the CA 2006, a private company *with only one class of shares* may disapply the statutory pre-emption rights by a special resolution of the shareholders, or by a provision in the articles. The advantage to this section is that the disapplication may be indefinite. This will be the usual method of disapplication for a small private company. As there is no provision for disapplication in the model articles for private companies, a company with these articles would need to pass a special resolution to take advantage of s 569 of the CA 2006.

There are, however, other possible methods of disapplication under the CA 2006 for a private company:

(a) A private company may disapply the statutory pre-emption rights in s 561 of the CA 2006 by including a special article either generally or in relation to particular allotments (s 567).

(b) Under s 568 of the CA 2006, pre-emption provisions in the articles will override the statutory provisions in s 561 of the Act, though the notice provisions in s 562 still apply unless they too have been excluded in the articles.

(c) Under s 570 of the CA 2006, a private company may also disapply the statutory pre-emption rights under s 561 by a special resolution of the shareholders or by a provision in the articles where the directors are authorised generally to allot shares under s 551 of the Act. This disapplication lasts only as long as the s 551 authority itself. This is usually not as advantageous for a private company as the s 569 option above.

(d) A private company may disapply the statutory pre-emption rights under s 561 by a special resolution of the shareholders (CA 2006, s 571) for a specified allotment of shares. Along with notice of the GM called to pass such a special resolution (or the written resolution), directors must send to all shareholders a written statement setting out their reasons for proposing the special resolution, the consideration which the company is to receive and their justification of this amount. This method is usually not as advantageous for a private company as the s 569 option above.

9.3.3.2 Public company

Under s 568 of the CA 2006, pre-emption provisions in the articles will override the statutory provisions in s 561 of the CA 2006.

A public company may also disapply the statutory pre-emption rights under s 561 by a special resolution of the shareholders, or by a provision in the articles, under s 570 of the CA 2006 where the directors are authorised generally to allot shares under s 551 of the Act. This disapplication lasts only as long as the s 551 authority.

A public company may alternatively disapply the statutory pre-emption rights under s 561 by a special resolution of the shareholders (s 571) for a specified allotment of shares.

9.3.4 Procedure

There are two separate procedures that may be used to allot shares in the company. Which one is to be followed depends on whether shareholder approval is required.

9.3.4.1 Shareholder approval needed

(a) A board meeting must be called by any director on reasonable notice.

(b) Directors must check:

  (i) whether any restrictions in the articles need to be revoked;

  (ii) whether they have authority to allot the shares, under the articles or under the CA 2006, or whether the shareholders first need either to amend the articles or to pass an ordinary resolution authorising the allotment; and

  (iii) whether they are obliged to offer the shares to current shareholders first (pre-emption rights).

(c) If the articles need to be amended to remove a restriction on the number of shares which can be issued and/or authority is needed and/or pre-emption rights need to be disapplied, the directors will need to pass a board resolution to call a GM or propose written resolutions for the shareholders to agree. Fourteen clear days' notice is required for the GM in the usual way. Notice in writing must be sent to all shareholders, and short notice may be consented to by the shareholders.

(d) The GM will then be held and the resolutions passed if the requisite majority vote in favour.

(e) The directors will then call a second board meeting (or the first board meeting will be reconvened) and the directors will pass a board resolution to allot the shares.

  They will resolve to issue the shares to those persons who have made written application for them. Private companies are not in general permitted to offer their shares to members of the public (see **12.2.1** below). Therefore, it is necessary that the offer to buy comes from the prospective shareholders and that that offer is accepted by the company.

(f) If the company has a seal, the directors will resolve to seal the share certificates, which will be sent to the new shareholders, and will instruct the secretary to enter the name of the new shareholders on the register of members. They will also instruct the secretary to notify the Registrar of Companies on Form SH01 that new shares have been issued.

9.3.4.2 Shareholder approval not needed

(a) A board meeting must be called by any director on reasonable notice.

(b) Directors must check:

  (i) whether they have authority to allot the shares, under the articles or under the CA 2006; and

  (ii) whether they are obliged to offer the shares to current shareholders first (pre-emption rights).

(c) Assuming no shareholder approval is needed for authority and pre-emption rights need not be disapplied, the directors will only need to pass a board resolution to allot the shares. No shareholder involvement is required and so no GM is needed.

The board will resolve to issue the shares to those persons who have made written application for them.

(d) If the company has a seal, the directors will resolve to seal the share certificates, which will be sent to the new shareholders, and will instruct the secretary to enter the name of the new members on the register of members. They will also instruct the secretary to notify the Registrar of Companies on Form SH01 that new shares have been issued.

9.3.5 Payment for shares

A prospective shareholder must normally pay for shares in cash. The prospective shareholder may provide non-cash consideration only if the company, ie the board, agrees. If consideration in kind is acceptable to the directors, they must send a return to the Registrar, and must also send a statement of capital (CA 2006, ss 555–557).

9.3.6 Partly-paid shares

When the directors of a company decide to issue shares, they will expect the prospective new shareholder to pay for those shares. For example, if a prospective new shareholder offers to buy 100 £1 shares at £1 each, the directors will expect the prospective new shareholder to pay the company £100 (or they may agree to accept assets worth £100 in payment for the shares). Throughout this book, it has been assumed that company shares are fully paid. However, the directors may agree to issue shares partly paid, which means that although the full price of the shares must be paid eventually, it does not have to be paid immediately. For example, the directors might issue 100 £1 shares on the basis that 50p per share is payable on issue and the remaining 50p per share is payable six months later.

9.3.7 Issue at a premium

The nominal value of each share, as stated in the statement of capital, is also known as the par value. Depending on their market value, the shares may be issued for a price greater than their nominal value. If this happens, the excess amount of consideration paid above the nominal value of the shares must be recorded in a separate share premium account (CA 2006, s 610). It is treated as share capital, and thus is subject to the requirement that this fund must be maintained.

Section 610 specifies the permitted uses for the share premium account. For example, paying up bonus shares will still be permitted. However, some existing uses will not be allowed in future (eg to pay off expenses incurred in the company's formation).

9.3.8 Issue at a discount

Shares may not be issued for less than their nominal value (CA 2006, s 580). If this happens, the shareholder is obliged to pay the amount of discount to the company with interest (CA 2006, s 580(2)).

9.3.9 Redenomination of share capital

Under ss 622–628 of the CA 2006, a company is able to redenominate its shares into a different currency by passing an ordinary resolution. If the exchange rate between the currencies produces an unacceptable value per share then the company's share capital may be reduced by up to 10% by the passing of a special resolution. The amount of the reduction is transferred to a 'redenomination reserve', to be used for paying bonus shares. Alternatively, it will be possible to increase the new value of the shares by using distributable reserves for that purpose.

9.4 FINANCIAL ASSISTANCE BY A PUBLIC COMPANY FOR THE PURCHASE OF SHARES

If someone wants to buy shares in the company but cannot afford to do so without a loan, that person may ask the company itself to lend them the necessary money. Alternatively, that person may ask a financial institution such as a bank to do so, and the bank may then ask the company to guarantee the loan. The general rule is that a *public* company cannot give a prospective or an actual shareholder any financial assistance to enable them to purchase shares in the company (CA 2006, s 678). Section 678(1) of the Act deals with financial assistance given before, or at the time of, the acquisition, whereas s 678(3) deals with financial assistance given after the event.

'Financial assistance' means a gift, loan, indemnity, guarantee, assignment or other transaction by which the acquirer is directly or indirectly put in funds (CA 2006, s 677). Any other transaction may amount to assistance if it materially reduces the company's assets, eg the payment by the target company of the legal fees of a bidder company on a takeover. In *Chaston v SWP Group plc* [2003] All ER (D) 179, the Court of Appeal held that payment by a target company of the fees of accountants retained by the purchaser to produce a report amounted to unlawful financial assistance. In *Harlow v Loveday* [2004] EWHC 1261, a loan given to purchase shares was held to be financial assistance. In *Dyment v Boyden and Others* [2004] EWCA Civ 1586, the Court of Appeal was asked to consider the forerunners to both s 678(1) and (3) of the CA 2006. It held that the claimant failed to show that any financial assistance was given by the company before or at the same time as the acquisition of B's shares, as required under s 678(1). The judge at first instance had therefore not erred in dismissing that claim. On the second aspect of the case, the company's entry into the lease in question was 'in connection with' the acquisition by the claimant of B's shares. However, it was not 'for the purpose of' that acquisition, so did not fall within s 678(3).

Section 678(2) of the CA 2006 exempts from s 678(1) two categories of transactions:

(a) those where the principal purpose was not the giving of financial assistance; or
(b) those where the financial assistance was incidental to some larger purpose.

However, these provisions are vague and difficult to rely on (see *Brady v Brady* [1989] AC 755). In that case, a bona fide arrangement to split a family company into two new businesses was held by the House of Lords not to be saved by what is now s 678(2) of the CA 2006. The deal in question was to divide a family company's assets between two new companies, so that the brothers who ran the family businesses could go their separate ways. Although the arrangement involved the existing company giving financial assistance, it was held at first instance to be incidental to the larger purpose of the rearrangement and to fall within what is now s 678(2)(b) of the 2006 Act. The House of Lords disagreed and thus severely restricted the use of this provision.

There are also specific commonsense exceptions to s 678 of the CA 2006 in ss 681 and 682, such as the payment of a dividend to shareholders.

The prohibition on financial assistance does not apply to private companies (unless the financial assistance involves a public company).

The provision of financial assistance by the company may be useful where a new shareholder wishes to join the company, and the current shareholders and directors are keen that they should do so. It is also useful where one shareholder wishes to leave the company and the other shareholders want to buy that shareholder out rather than have someone new involved in the business. However, if the person seeking financial help from the company is also a director of the company, the company must comply with the restrictions which apply to loans to directors too (see **7.12.2** above).

More recent cases on financial assistance tend to consider in detail the commercial context of the transaction in order to decide whether or not it is financial assistance 'for the purposes of acquiring shares'. This is not very helpful to the lawyer trying to advise a client, as general lessons often cannot be drawn from a particular decision. In *MT Realisations Ltd (in liquidation) v Digital Equipment Co Ltd* [2003] EWCA Civ 494, the comment was made that

> the authorities provide useful illustrations of the variety of fact situations in which the issue can arise, but it is rare to find an authority on s [678] which requires a particular result to be reached on different facts.

In *MT Realisations* the Court of Appeal held that the matters in question did not amount to financial assistance. The facts concerned inter-company loans which were payable on demand, and secured by fixed and floating charges. There was therefore no option but to repay the loans or allow the creditors to enforce their security. This meant that there was no 'assistance', as the company had no choice in the matter.

Some examples of the pervasive nature of the financial assistance problem are set out below. In these scenarios, P plc is proposing to buy the shares of S plc from V plc, the parent company of S plc. Will s 678(1) and (3) of the CA 2006 prohibit the following?

EXAMPLES

(a) S agrees to lend P £3 million so that the deal can go ahead. When P has taken over S, P can repay the money to V from the profits it makes from S's business.

This is direct financial assistance and therefore caught. Section 677(1)(c)(i) covers loans.

(b) P borrows the £3 million from Global Bank. It plans to repay the money to Global Bank from the profits it expects to make from S's business after the takeover.

This is permitted and not financial assistance.

(c) P wants to borrow £3 million from Global Bank. S guarantees the loan so that the deal can proceed. The deal goes ahead, P makes money from the deal, the loan to Global Bank is paid off and the guarantee is not called upon. It has not cost S anything.

This is caught. Section 677(1)(b)(i) of the CA 2006 includes security for a loan. The purpose of the loan is to provide financial assistance.

(d) P owes S £1 million. S waives the debt, and P can go ahead with the purchase of S.

Waiving the debt would seem to be a gift under s 677(1)(a) of the CA 2006, hence it is financial assistance.

(e) P wants to borrow £3 million from Global Bank. S lets Global Bank look at its up-to-date accounts, not just the published ones. Global Bank is happy with the accounts and agrees to lend £3 million to P.

This is assistance, but it is not financial assistance and therefore is not caught by ss 677 and 678 of the CA 2006.

Barclays Bank PLC, a public company, and so subject to the prohibition under the CA 2006, was charged with financial assistance in relation to an attempt to save the bank from nationalisation by the UK Government during the financial crisis in 2008. John Varley and Roger Jenkins, two former senior executives of Barclays, have also been charged with providing unlawful financial assistance. They are due to stand trial in 2019 and face up to 10 years' imprisonment if found guilty.

9.5 BUY-BACK OF SHARES BY THE COMPANY

If a shareholder wanted to sell their shares in a private limited company, they would have two options:

(a) find a third party to buy them (transfer of shares (see **9.9** below)); or

(b) ask the company itself to buy the shares back from the shareholder (known as a 'buy-back of shares', or a 'purchase by the company of its own shares').

If the private limited company bought back the shares, it would obviously have to pay the shareholder for them. However, the shares would immediately become worthless in the company's hands. This is because s 706(b)(i) of the CA 2006 provides that the bought-back shares are usually treated as cancelled, ie they cease to exist. So from the company's point of view, buying back the company's shares amounts to a return of money from the company to the shareholder. The money would leave the company permanently, and the company would receive nothing of financial value in return.

For that reason, the directors should consider carefully whether the proposed buy-back of shares makes commercial sense for the company (especially given their duty under s 172 of the CA 2006 to promote the success of the company – see **7.4** above).

9.5.1 Commercial considerations

The directors might spend the company's existing cash on buying back a shareholder's shares (or sell some of the company's assets to generate the cash to buy back the shareholder's shares). However, the company might have cash-flow problems, and would not even have gained anything of financial value through the buy-back. If the company borrows money to pay for the buy-back, the result may be even worse. The company will still be spending its money on the buy-back without getting anything of financial value in return, but will also be saddled with a debt which it eventually must repay, as well as paying interest in the meantime.

The directors may therefore consider issuing new shares to someone else, in order to raise funds to buy back the first shareholder's shares. From a commercial point of view, this has the advantage that issuing shares raises cash for the company but costs it nothing, unlike borrowing money.

So why would a private limited company ever buy back shares, given that it seems so financially unattractive? There are two fairly common scenarios:

(a) The first typically arises in companies where the directors are the main or only shareholders. One of the directors is in serious dispute with the others. The others want that director to resign from the board. The director refuses to resign unless someone agrees to buy their shares for a fair price. The other directors are unwilling or unable to buy the director's shares (by a transfer of shares, see **9.9** below). However, they are prepared to arrange for the company itself to buy the director's shares. They consider that a buy-back is a price worth paying for that person to cut their ties with the company, both as director and as shareholder.

(b) The second fairly common scenario is the family-owned and family-run business, where a family member wants to extract their investment from the business (eg, on retirement). The directors may be sympathetic to this request, and arrange for the company to buy back their shares. In this scenario, there is less likely to be a strong commercial case for the company buying the person's shares. The board should therefore consider particularly carefully whether the buy-back is compatible with their duty to the company under s 172 of the CA 2006.

Buy-backs are used much more commonly in publicly-traded companies as a means of:

(a) returning surplus cash to shareholders (instead of paying a dividend);

(b) reducing the number of shares in issue to increase the earnings per share (eg, profit per share) as this can increase the company's attractiveness to investors; and

(c) increasing the value of the existing shares.

One example is BHP Billiton PLC, the global mining company which is publicly traded on the London Stock Exchange, which bought back a staggering US$10 billion of shares in the first quarter of 2011.

So far we have covered some commercial considerations for a company which is being asked to buy back shares. However, the company's directors must give equally careful thought to the legal considerations.

9.5.2 Legal considerations

When a company makes a profit, that profit belongs to the company under the principle of separate legal personality. The shareholders cannot simply treat it or other of the company's assets as if they were their own. However, in recognition of the fact that it is the shareholders who have invested their money in the company, and therefore who own it, the shareholders ultimately receive the company's accumulated profits, in two ways:

(a) during the company's lifetime whenever it pays a dividend; and

(b) by winding up the company while it is still solvent, selling everything it owns and splitting up the proceeds among the shareholders.

Potentially, a buy-back threatens this, because rather than the company using the shareholders' investment to make and accumulate profits, and ultimately pay them to the shareholders, the company would be giving away some of those profits and getting nothing in return. Thus the shareholders would be missing out on profits which they might ultimately have expected to receive, either by way of dividend or on a solvent winding up.

If the buy-back was on a greater scale, it might involve spending not only all the profits of the company plus the proceeds of any share issue to fund the buy-back, but also some of the company's existing share capital (the original money invested by the shareholders). In this scenario the company is also giving away some of the very investment which enabled it to trade and make profits in the first place. This means:

(a) that 'lost' investment could not work to make future profits for the shareholders;

(b) potentially, the company's funds might be so depleted that the company could go into insolvent liquidation (in which case the shareholders would probably lose all their investment as the company's assets would be used to pay off its creditors).

The company's creditors may also be concerned about a proposed buy-back representing the expenditure of some of the company's existing share capital because:

(a) it could increase the company's chances of becoming insolvent;

(b) if the company became insolvent, it would own less than the original investment which is available as a pool of money for creditors. Thus the creditors would be likely to get back less of their money from the company than before the buy-back.

For these reasons a company is subject to the principle of maintenance of capital. That is, the principle that a company should not return its existing share capital to its shareholders, or should only do so subject to procedures designed to protect the shareholders and creditors. See further **9.2** above.

Of course, the company's existing share capital is not an easily identifiable separate pile of cash. All the company's wealth, including its existing share capital and its profits, is embodied in its assets. One of these assets will be cash, but the rest may take other physical forms (eg, stock in the warehouse, factory premises) or even intangible form (eg, a valuable registered trademark). However, if a company has total net assets of (say) £100, and its existing share capital is £40, if the company gives away £70, that must represent expenditure of some of its existing share capital.

9.5.3 Procedure

Note that there is a distinction between a buy-back of shares on a stock market (a so-called 'market purchase', s 693(4) of the CA 2006) and a buy-back not on a stock market (known as an 'off-market purchase', s 693(2) of the CA 2006). In this book we deal only with 'off-market' purchases, as these are the type carried out by private companies. Section 701 of the CA 2006 deals with 'market' purchases carried out by publicly-traded companies.

There is also a distinction under the CA 2006 between a private company paying for the buy-back out of distributable profits and the fresh issue of shares on the one hand, and a buy-back out of capital on the other. We consider the differences below.

9.5.3.1 Buy-back out of profit or fresh issue of shares

Procedurally this is a simpler form of buy-back, because the company is not touching its existing share capital. Note that there is an alternative to this procedure for a buy-back of small amounts, as explained at **9.5.3.3** below.

A company may buy back its own shares from its shareholders out of distributable profits or the proceeds of a fresh issue of shares (CA 2006, s 692(2)), provided the following conditions are satisfied:

(a) the articles of the company must not forbid this (s 690(1));

(b) the shares must be fully paid (s 691(1)); and

(c) when the shares are bought by the company, it must pay for them at the time of purchase (s 691(2)).

When a company buys back a shareholder's shares, it enters into a contract with the shareholder. This contract must be approved by the shareholders passing an ordinary resolution at a GM, or a shareholders' written resolution (CA 2006, s 694(2)). The directors must therefore first hold a board meeting to pass a board resolution either to call a GM, or to circulate a written resolution.

On the shareholders' vote, if the ordinary resolution at the GM would not have passed without the votes relating to shares being bought back, the ordinary resolution will be ineffective (CA 2006, s 695(3)). Alternatively, a shareholder having their shares bought back is excluded from participating in a written resolution (CA 2006, s 695(2)).

A copy of the contract, or a summary of it, must be available for inspection for no fewer than 15 days before the GM and at the GM (or be sent with the proposed written resolution or before it is circulated) (CA 2006, s 696(2)).

Assuming the ordinary resolution is passed, the directors will hold a second board meeting (or reconvene the earlier adjourned board meeting) and pass a board resolution to enter into the contract to buy back the shares.

The directors will also attend to the administration, which will include paying for the shares and sending Form SH03 (Return of purchase of own shares) and Form SH06 (Notice of Cancellation of Shares) to Companies House, both with details of the shares bought back and both within 28 days (CA 2006, ss 707 and 708). A copy of the contract, or a summary of it, must be available for inspection for 10 years after purchase of the shares, at the company's registered office or SAIL (see **8.11.4** above). The register of members must be altered to reflect the change, and any share certificates dealt with.

The effects of a buy-back are, after the shares are cancelled:

(a) the company does not become the holder of its own shares;

(b) the issued share capital of the company is decreased;

(c) voting control between the shareholders may have been altered;

(d) a capital redemption reserve will need to be created, or increased if one already exists; and

(e) the share premium account is reduced, if a premium paid on buy-back or redemption has been financed out of a fresh issue of shares.

See also **Table 9.4** below.

9.5.3.2 Buy-back out of capital

If the cost of the buy-back is such that it uses up all the company's distributable profits (and the proceeds of any share issue intended to fund the buy-back), some of the company's existing share capital may be used (CA 2006, s 709) but various additional conditions must be satisfied (s 713) because this goes against the 'maintenance of capital' rule. Note that there is an alternative to this procedure for a buy-back of small amounts, as explained at **9.5.3.3** below, and where the buy-back is for the purposes of an employees' share scheme, as explained at **9.5.3.4** below.

A company may buy back its own shares out of capital subject to the company's articles not prohibiting it (CA 2006, s 709(1)). All of the conditions for a buy-back out of distributable profits must be met (see **9.5.3.1**), as well as some specific to a buy-back out of capital. Therefore:

(a) the shares must be fully paid (s 691(1));

(b) when the shares are bought by the company, it must pay for them at the time of purchase (s 691(2)); and further

(c) the directors must make a statement of solvency, stating that the company is solvent and will remain so for the next 12 months (s 714) after the buy-back out of capital. The directors should not make such a statement without careful thought, because if the company is wound up within one year of their statement and proves to be insolvent, both the seller of the shares and the directors of the company may be required to contribute to the financial losses of the company (IA 1986, s 76). In addition, directors face criminal sanctions for making such a statement without having reasonable grounds (CA 2006, s 715). The statement by the directors must be made no sooner than one week before the GM (CA 2006, s 716(2)).

The amount of capital which may be used is limited and is called the 'permissible capital payment' (PCP) (CA 2006, ss 710–712). The auditors must produce a report for the directors that the PCP is in order and that they do not know of anything that would make the statement unreasonable (s 714(6)).

The buy-back contract must be approved by the shareholders passing an ordinary resolution at a GM, or a shareholders' written resolution (CA 2006, s 694(2)). Further, a special resolution or written resolution must be passed by the shareholders to approve the payment out of capital (CA 2006, s 716(1)). The directors must therefore first hold a board meeting to pass a board resolution to attend to the auditor's report and statement, and either call a GM or circulate a written resolution. As all directors must make the statement, in practice this resolution must be passed by all directors.

On the shareholders' votes, if the ordinary and special resolutions at the GM would not have passed without the votes relating to shares being bought back, the resolutions will be ineffective (CA 2006, ss 695(3) and 717(3)). Alternatively, a shareholder having their shares bought back is excluded from participating in a written resolution (CA 2006, ss 695(2) and 717(2)).

A copy of the contract, or a summary of it, must be available for inspection for no fewer than 15 days before the GM and at the GM (or be sent with or before the written resolution is circulated) (CA 2006, s 696(2)). Further, the auditors' report and directors' statement must be made available at the GM only, or be sent with the proposed written resolution or before it is circulated (CA 2006, s 718(2)).

Assuming the ordinary and special resolutions are passed, a notice must be placed in the *London Gazette*, and also either in an appropriate national newspaper or in a written notice to every creditor, in accordance with s 719 of the CA 2006, within the week following the passing of the resolutions, to allow for dissenting shareholders or any creditor of the company to make an application to court under s 721 to cancel the buy-back out of capital. The court has wide powers. However, it does not seem to be the appropriate route for an 'unfair prejudice' petition, which should instead be brought under s 994 of the CA 2006 (see **5.6.3.14** above). No later than the day on which the first of these notices is published, a copy of the auditors' report and directors' statement must be filed at Companies House (CA 2006, s 719(4)). The report and statement must be made available at the registered office for five weeks after the special resolution is passed (CA 2006, s 720(1) and (2)).

Assuming a court application is not made, the directors will hold a second board meeting (or reconvene the earlier adjourned board meeting) and pass a board resolution to enter into the contract to buy-back the shares. This must be done no earlier than five weeks after and no later than seven weeks after the date of the special resolution to approve the buy-back out of capital (CA 2006, s 723(1)).

The directors will also attend to the administration, which will include paying for the shares, sending a copy of the special resolution to Companies House within 15 days (CA 2006, ss 29 and 30), and sending Form SH03 (Return of purchase of own shares) and Form SH06 (Notice of Cancellation of Shares), both with details of the shares bought back and both within 28 days (ss 707 and 708). A copy of the contract, or a summary of it, must be available for inspection for 10 years after purchase of the shares, at the company's registered office or SAIL (see **8.11.4** above). The register of members must be altered to reflect the change, and any share certificates dealt with.

See also **Table 9.5** below.

9.5.3.3 Buy-back of a small amount

A private company can pay for a buy-back with cash even if this does not amount to distributable profits or even if it is capital, provided the company's articles authorise this and the amount does not exceed the lower of:

(a) £15,000; or

(b) 5% of the company's share capital,

in a financial year (CA 2006, s 692(1ZA)(b)).

The 5% figure is based on the total nominal value of the company's issued share capital, ie it excludes any premium (DBT Guidance, 'Simple Guide to the Buyback Regulations 2013', available online at www.gov.uk).

In addition there is no special procedure to follow for such buy-backs. It is not necessary to follow the procedures set out at **9.5.3.2** above. The buy-back contract will simply require a shareholders' ordinary resolution as at **9.5.3.1** above. The aim is to reduce the administrative burden on private companies for what are small buy-backs. These provisions came into force in April 2013. This means that many private companies will not currently have authority in their articles to use this power. Before they can take advantage of this procedure, such companies will first need to obtain shareholder approval to amend their articles.

9.5.3.4 Buy-back for the purposes of an employees' share scheme

Section 723A of the CA 2006 allows a private company to pay for a buy-back out of capital for or pursuant to an employees' share scheme under a simplified regime from that set out at **9.5.3.2** above. Such a buy-back only requires a special resolution of the shareholders supported by a solvency statement. There are other procedural and practical advantages as well. Employee share schemes seek to reward employees of a company by allowing them to own shares in their company and participate in what hopefully is its success, hence the reason for allowing a simplified procedure for this type of buy-back.

9.5.3.5 An alternative to buy-back out of capital – reduction of capital

As can be seen, the extra procedural requirements under the CA 2006 for a buy-back out of capital are burdensome, including the time and cost involved in preparing the necessary reports, the cost of advertising the buy-back, and delaying the buy-back to give the creditors and dissenting shareholders a chance to seek a court order halting the buy-back.

However, as an alternative to a buy-back out of capital, ss 641–644 of the CA 2006 and the Companies (Reduction of Share Capital) Order 2008 (SI 2008/1915) allow a private limited company only to re-classify some of its existing share capital as distributable profits, so that the proposed payment to the shareholders will no longer represent expenditure of existing share capital. This tactic avoids the extra cost and delay involved in buying back shares at a price which does represent expenditure of existing share capital.

The re-classification process involves a 'reduction of share capital' rather than a buy-back of shares. That is, the company's existing share capital is treated as reduced, and the amount by which it is reduced creates a reserve which is treated as distributable profits.

So in practice, once a private limited company has worked out how much the buy-back will cost, it should establish whether this price would represent expenditure of the company's existing share capital. If it would, rather than using the procedure for this buy-back out of capital (as set out in **9.5.3.2** above), the company can consider using this 'reduction of share capital' process to stop the proposed price representing expenditure of existing share capital. In practice, because this is a new procedure, it is still unclear whether private companies are using this method rather than the procedure for the buy-back out of capital. It is becoming increasingly popular as it is cheaper, quicker, less complicated administratively and does not involve the threat of court proceedings.

As you might by now expect, the procedure involves meeting a number of conditions, as follows:

(a) The company's articles must not prohibit the reduction of the company's share capital (CA 2006, s 641(6)).

(b) The directors must make a solvency statement (CA 2006, s 642(1)), stating that the company is solvent and will remain so for the next 12 months (s 643(1)) after the reduction of capital. The directors face criminal sanctions for making such a statement without having reasonable grounds for doing so (s 643(4)) as well as liability for breach of s 172 of the CA 2006 (the duty to promote the success of the company – see **7.4** above) and s 174 of the CA 2006 (the duty to exercise reasonable care, skill and diligence – see **7.6** above) (see *LRH Services Ltd (In Liquidation) v Trew and Others* [2018] EWHC 600 (Ch)).

(c) The shareholders must approve the reduction of capital by passing a special resolution at a GM or a shareholders' written resolution (CA 2006, s 641(1)(a)). The directors must therefore first hold a board meeting to attend to the solvency statement, and then pass a board resolution either to call a GM or to circulate a written resolution. The solvency statement by the directors must be made no sooner than 15 days before the GM (s 642(1)(a)) and be made available to the shareholders at the GM (s 642(3)), or be sent with the proposed written resolution or before it is circulated (s 642(2)).

Assuming the special resolution is passed, the directors will hold a second board meeting (or reconvene the earlier adjourned board meeting) to attend to the administration. This will include paying for the shares, signing a statement of compliance that the 15-day time period was met and made available to the shareholders (see above) (s 644(5)), sending a copy of the special resolution to Companies House within 15 days (ss 29 and 30), and sending Form SH19 and the solvency statement within 15 days (s 644(1)). The reduction of share capital will take place on registration of these documents (s 644(4) and s 641(5)). The register of members, and possibly the PSC register, must be altered to reflect the change, and any share certificates dealt with.

The Economic Crime and Corporate Transparency Act 2023 (ECCTA) will remove the requirement for a company to maintain a PSC register. Under a new s 790LA of the CA 2006, a company will be required to notify Companies House of a person who becomes or ceases to be a PSC within 14 days. The requirement to maintain a register of members will be retained when the relevant ECCTA provisions come into force, but it will no longer be possible for a company to maintain this register centrally at Companies House. It will have to keep its own register of members. These changes are expected to come into force by 2027.

9.5.3.6 Working out if capital is required

The crucial issue is how to work out whether the proposed buy-back price would involve expenditure of existing share capital.

A company has three methods of raising the funds to buy back a person's shares:

(a) use its existing cash (or sell some of its existing assets to provide cash);

(b) borrow money; and

(c) issue new shares.

The company may use just one of these methods, or a combination. It is important to realise that you cannot tell whether the buy-back represents a buy-back out of the company's existing share capital simply by looking at the method used to raise the funding for the buy-back. Instead, you have to ask how much the total cost of the buy-back will be as a proportion of the company's existing wealth.

To illustrate this, consider the balance sheet of Newco Limited (Newco) below, using the notes which follow to assist you in your understanding.

In order to calculate whether a buy-back will represent the use of a company's existing share capital, you need to take the following three steps:

Step 1: Ascertain how much it will cost the company to buy the shares back.

Step 2: Add together the company's 'distributable profits' (the figure in the Profit/(Loss) Reserve), and the money (if any) which the company expects to make from issuing shares to fund the buy-back.

Step 3: If the amount in Step 1 is greater than the amount produced by Step 2, by definition the buy-back will represent the use of the company's existing share capital. This is because your calculation has shown that even spending money representing all of the company's distributable profits, and spending all the proceeds of issuing new shares, will not be enough to pay for the buy-back.

NEWCO LIMITED
Balance Sheet as at [date]

	£	£	£
FIXED ASSETS			
Premises		60,000	
Plant and Machinery		70,000	
			130,000
CURRENT ASSETS			
Stock	40,000		
Debtors	40,000		
Cash	20,000		
	100,000		
CURRENT LIABILITIES			
Creditors	10,000		
Overdraft	50,000		
	(60,000)		
NET CURRENT ASSETS			40,000
TOTAL ASSETS LESS CURRENT LIABILITIES			170,000

CREDITORS: amounts falling due after 1 year		
Debenture		(75,000)
NET ASSETS (*Note 1*)		95,000
CAPITAL AND RESERVES (*Note 2*)		
Share Capital (*Notes 3 and 4*)	40,000	
Share Premium (*Notes 3 and 4*)	20,000	
Profit/(Loss) Reserve (*Note 5*)	35,000	
		95,000

Notes:

1. The net assets figure (£95,000) in Newco's balance sheet is the total existing wealth of Newco. That is because the net assets figure is the total of everything Newco owns, after deducting everything it owes.
2. The information on Newco's balance sheet below the net assets figure does not represent 'extra assets'. Instead, it tells you where Newco's existing wealth came from.
3. The 'Share Capital' line (£40,000) and the 'Share Premium' line (£20,000) tell you how much of Newco's existing wealth represents money which the shareholders invested in the company in exchange for the issue of shares. That is, the aggregate of the 'Share Capital' figure and the 'Share Premium' figure (£60,000) is Newco's existing share capital for the purposes of the CA 2006 provisions on buy-back.
4. The accounting reason for the breakdown as between the 'Share Capital' figure and the 'Share Premium' figure is simply to show how the company's existing share capital is broken down as between:
   (a) the total nominal or 'par' value of all the shares issued by Newco (this is the 'Share Capital' figure – £40,000); and
   (b) the total of all the premiums over and above the nominal value which Newco has charged when issuing shares (this is the 'Share Premium' figure – £20,000).
5. By contrast, the 'Profit/(Loss) Reserve' (£35,000) shows how much of Newco's existing wealth represents the profit which Newco has made over its entire history but not yet given to the shareholders by way of dividends. The CA 2006 refers to this figure as Newco's 'distributable profits'.

Now apply this to an example. Newco's board of directors are proposing to arrange for Newco to buy back some shares for a total price of £30,000. The board intend to raise the necessary funds by borrowing £15,000 from a bank, and generating £15,000 by issuing shares.

Applying the three steps above:

Step 1: Ascertain how much it will cost Newco to buy the shares back, ie £30,000.

Step 2: Add together the company's 'distributable profits' (the figure in the Profit/(Loss) Reserve) (£35,000) and the money Newco expects to make from issuing shares to fund the buy-back (£15,000), ie £50,000.

Step 3: If the amount in Step 1 is greater than the amount produced by Step 2, by definition the buy-back will represent the use of the company's existing share capital.

Here the amount in Step 1 (the cost of the buy-back) is only £30,000. This is not greater than the amount produced by Step 2 (£50,000 = 'distributable profits' + proceeds of issuing fresh shares). Thus Newco's buy-back will not represent a buy-back out of Newco's existing share capital for the purposes of the CA 2006.

9.5.3.7 What happens to the shares bought back?

Depending on the type of procedure used and the source of the money to pay for the shares, the options are different.

For a buy-back out of distributable profits only, under s 724 of the CA 2006 the shares can either be cancelled, and so will no longer exist and reduce the company's issued share capital, or they can be held in treasury. Treasury shares are not cancelled but are kept in reserve. In other words they can, for example, be resold at a later date by the company to other shareholders. Treasury shares must comply with the provisions of ss 724–732 of the CA 2006.

For a buy-back out of capital, buy-back of a small amount and a buy-back financed by the fresh issue of shares, under s 706(b) of the CA 2006 the shares must be cancelled and cannot be held in treasury.

9.6 CLASSES OF SHARES

A company may decide to create different classes of shares. Usually some shares will be described as ordinary shares, but there may be more than one class of ordinary shares within the company. For example, two different classes of ordinary shares may carry different voting rights or dividend rights.

In any one company, the rights attaching to a share are dependent on the articles of that company. If no separate rights attach to a particular class of shares, the common law rule is that all shares are to rank equally (*Birch v Cropper* [1889] 14 App Cas 525 (HL), *Scottish Insurance Corp Ltd v Wilsons & Clyde Coal Co Ltd* [1949] AC 462). See also s 629 of the CA 2006.

The different classes of shares and the rights attaching to them must be included on the statement of capital which is lodged at Companies House when the company is formed (as part of Form IN01) and whenever the number of issued shares changes. The statement of capital is simply part of the relevant Companies House forms. The rights attaching to each class of shares must be specified each time a statement of capital is filed, eg 'ordinary shares, voting rights (one vote per share), right to dividend, right to capital'.

Types of shares may include those discussed in **9.6.1** to **9.6.4** below.

9.6.1 Ordinary shares

These carry the primary voting rights of the company, the right to a dividend if declared, and rights to participate in a surplus in a winding up.

If no differences between shares are expressed, it is assumed that all shares have the same rights. If, for example, the statement of capital states that the capital of the company is to be £100 divided into 100 shares of £1 each, the shares all have the same, unrestricted rights. It is unnecessary to classify them as *ordinary shares* since there are no others. But there is no objection to doing so.

A company may, at its option, attach special rights to different shares, for example as regards dividends, return of capital or voting (or less often the right to appoint a director).

A not uncommon example of classes of shares is ordinary shares with voting rights, and ordinary shares without voting rights (often distinguished as 'A' ordinary shares).

9.6.2 Preference shares

A preference share is any share having priority over the ordinary shares. The priority might be in relation to capital or dividends, or (usually) both. There are no other *implied* differences between preference and ordinary shares, though there are often express differences between them.

The preferential dividend may be cumulative, or it may be payable only out of the profits of each year. The dividend will generally be a fixed one, ie it is expressed as a fixed percentage of the par value of the share. It is not a right to compel the company to pay the dividend if it declines to do so. This issue is likely to arise if the company decides to transfer available profits or reserves, or makes a provision in its accounts for a liability or loss instead of using the profits to pay the preference dividend.

Preference shares often exist in a company's structure for historical reasons. For example, they are often created in the financing of a management buy-out of a company, so that the institutions which provided the finance can have first bite at the profits of the company. In due course, those shares will be sold on to new investors. However, preference shares do not usually carry a vote.

In many ways, preference shares are an alternative to lending money to the company, ie loans. Their attraction is that preference shareholders will be entitled first to any profits of the company at a fixed rate, and that the dividend is usually paid quarterly. Preference shares are usually redeemable, so the investor may exchange the shares for cash at some stage in the future (see **9.6.4**).

There are four kinds of preference shares:

(a) cumulative;
(b) non-cumulative;
(c) participating; and
(d) convertible.

'Cumulative' means that the preference shareholder has to be paid any missed dividends as well as the current dividend, if the preference share dividend has not been paid on a preceding occasion. This ranks before payment of dividends to the ordinary shareholders. 'Non-cumulative' therefore means that if there are insufficient profits to pay a dividend in one year then the unpaid dividend will not be paid in future years.

Participating shareholders have a further right to participate in profits or assets, in addition to the fixed preference rights. For example, if the ordinary shareholders are paid a dividend above a specified amount, this could trigger a right to an additional payment to the preference shareholders.

Convertible preference shares may be exchanged for ordinary shares at a specified price and after a specified date.

The rights of a preference shareholder will turn on the articles of the company (or possibly on the terms of the issue, depending on the facts).

9.6.3 Non-voting shares

These are not common in private companies but may occur in public companies, eg to enable existing shareholders to retain control of the company by allowing new investors to buy only non-voting shares.

9.6.4 Redeemable shares

Section 684 of the CA 2006 allows a private company to issue redeemable shares, provided it is not forbidden to do so by its articles. If the company is a public company, it must be so authorised by its articles. In order to prevent a company being left with no share capital as a result of redemptions, s 684(4) forbids the issue of redeemable shares when the company has no issued non-redeemable shares.

If the directors decided to issue redeemable shares, they would need to ensure that a special article was included in the company's articles, setting out details of the terms and conditions of issue. For example, shares may be redeemable at the option of the shareholder, or of the company or of either.

The articles must also provide for the terms and manner of the redemption. The directors of a private company can decide the conditions of redemption if they are authorised by an ordinary resolution of the members or by the articles (CA 2006, s 685(1)). Generally, redeemable shares have to be redeemed from distributable profits, but *private* companies may redeem out of capital if so permitted by their articles (CA 2006, s 687), upon the passing of a special resolution and the directors making a declaration of solvency.

Redeemed shares are treated as being cancelled. A notice must be sent to the Registrar of Companies within one month of the shares being redeemed, along with an amended statement of capital (CA 2006, ss 688 and 689). Form SH02 covers both requirements.

Redeemable shares are sometimes used by venture capital investors to ensure a straightforward exit route from the company when they invest in it. They will usually want an easy exit from the company after three to five years, at which point they can extract their investment and gains, and go on to their next project.

9.7 OFFERING SHARES TO THE PUBLIC

Offering shares for sale in a company has the potential for fraud. Thus, private companies are in general prohibited from offering their shares to the investing public at large (Financial Services and Markets Act 2000, s 75(3); Financial Services and Markets Act 2000 (Official Listing of Securities) Regulations 2001 (SI 2001/2956), reg 3(a); CA 2006, ss 755–760). A private company may therefore not be listed on the Stock Exchange (FCA Handbook, UK Listing Rules).

Offering shares to the public in contravention of the prohibition against doing so is not a criminal offence, but the court may order re-registration of the private company as a public company, or may make a remedial order which could include repurchase of the shares by the company (CA 2006, ss 757–759). Sections 755–760 of the CA 2006 do allow a private company to offer securities to the public as part of the process of re-registering as a public company.

For more information on public companies which can offer shares to the public, see **1.9.3** above.

9.8 DIVIDENDS

Initially, it is the directors who must decide whether or not to pay a dividend to shareholders. They are permitted to recommend the payment of a dividend (an income payment on shares) only if there are 'profits available' (CA 2006, s 830). To ascertain whether there are profits available, the directors must deduct from all the realised profits of the company to date all the realised losses to date. If there is any profit left after doing this, that money is available to pay a dividend. The directors may uncover this information by looking at the latest set of audited accounts. This means that even if the company has not made a profit this year, it may still be able to pay a dividend if the profits from previous years are sufficient.

If a dividend is paid when there are insufficient profits available for the purpose, the directors who authorised the payment are jointly and severally liable to the company for the full amount. Any shareholder who has received the dividend must refund it to the company if they know or have reasonable grounds for believing that the payment is unauthorised.

Directors of a company who authorise the payment of dividends otherwise than out of distributable profits may be personally liable to repay those dividends to the company, whether or not they themselves were shareholders (*Bairstow v Queens Moat Houses plc* [2000] 1 BCLC 549). An example of a company that mistakenly paid out dividends when it had insufficient distributable profits is the betting firm, Betfair. It announced in August 2014 that it should not have paid certain dividends to shareholders over the period 2011–13.

The power to declare a dividend is determined by the articles of the company. Under art 30(2) of the model articles for private companies, the directors decide whether it is appropriate to pay a dividend to shareholders. If they decide that the company has sufficient funds, they will recommend the amount of the dividend. The shareholders in a GM will actually declare the dividend under art 30(1) of the model articles for private companies. The shareholders cannot vote to pay themselves more than the directors have recommended, although they could decide that a smaller amount was more appropriate (eg see art 30(3) of the model articles for private companies). The form of a dividend is usually that shareholders receive, for example, 5p in the pound, which means that for every £1 share they hold, they receive 5p.

If a dividend is paid unlawfully, there is no obligation on the shareholder to repay it, unless the shareholders knew or had reasonable grounds to believe that the payment had been made improperly (CA 2006, s 847) (*It's a Wrap (UK) Ltd (In liquidation) v Gula* [2006] BCC 626).

9.9 TRANSFER OF SHARES

Shares are transferred if the shareholder who owns them, sells them or gives them to another person.

9.9.1 Procedure for transfer

The seller or donor of the shares ('the transferor') should complete and sign a stock transfer form, which they should then give to the buyer or recipient ('the transferee') (CA 2006, ss 770–772). There is no need for the transferee to sign the stock transfer form. There is also no need for the signature of the transferor to be witnessed. The transferor should hand the share certificate to the transferee too.

If the shares are being sold for more than £1,000, the buyer must pay stamp duty (currently charged at 0.5% rounded up to the nearest £5) on the stock transfer form. If the shares are a gift, no stamp duty is payable. The minimum stamp duty is £5.

The transferee needs to send the share certificate and stock transfer form to the company.

The company should send the new shareholder a new share certificate in their name within two months, and should also ensure that their name is entered on the register of members within the same time period (CA 2006, s 771).

The change in the composition of the membership of the company is notified to the Registrar of Companies on the confirmation statement CS01.

9.9.2 Restrictions on transfer

The ability of the shareholders of a company to transfer their shares to whomever they choose will be governed by the articles of the company. Under art 26 of the model articles for private companies, directors have an absolute discretion in this matter and may refuse to place a name on the register of members. Alternatively, shareholders may be permitted under a special article to transfer their shares without restriction only to other shareholders of the company, or to members of their own family. A further option is that shareholders may be allowed to consider transferring their shares to people who are not already shareholders of the company only if they first offer those shares to the other shareholders at a fair value, and those shareholders reject this offer.

Unless they are given power under the articles, the directors cannot refuse to place a new shareholder's name on the register of members. If they wrongly refuse to do so, their decision may be challenged by an application to the court for an order for rectification of the register (CA 2006, s 125). If directors are given some discretion in this matter, they must make a decision within a reasonable time, which will be not more than the two-month period within which they are obliged to deliver the new share certificate. If directors exercise their discretion and refuse to register a new shareholder, the court generally will not interfere with that decision unless the transferee can show that the directors did not act in good faith. If the directors properly exercise their power to refuse to register the name of the transferee, the transferee has no claim for damages or for rescission of the contract: the transferor remains the legal owner of the shares, their name continues to appear on the register of members, and they hold the shares on trust for the transferee. In any event, there is a longstop time limit of 10 years, after which claims cannot be made (CA 2006, s 128).

9.10 TRANSMISSION OF SHARES

Transmission is the automatic process by which, when a shareholder dies, their shares immediately pass to the shareholder's personal representatives (PRs), or if a shareholder is declared bankrupt, the shareholder's shares automatically vest in their trustee in bankruptcy.

When either event happens, the PRs or the trustee are entitled to any dividend declared on the shares, but they cannot exercise the votes which attach to the shares as they are not members of the company (model articles for private companies, art 27).

The PRs of a deceased shareholder must produce to the company a grant of representation to establish their right to deal with the shares as PRs of the estate, but they then have a choice:

(a) They may elect to be registered as shareholders themselves. In such a case, the entry on the register of members does not show that they hold the shares in a representative capacity. This choice is subject to the articles of the company, which may give the directors a discretion to refuse to place any name on the register of members. The directors cannot prevent the PRs from acquiring the shares by transmission in their capacity as PRs, but they can prevent their being registered as shareholders if the articles give them the power to refuse registration. If the PRs are registered as shareholders of the company, they can then transfer the shares in the usual way (see **9.9.1**), either passing them to the beneficiary under the deceased member's will or selling them to a third party for the benefit of the deceased member's estate.

(b) They can transfer the shares directly to the ultimate beneficiary or to a third party in their representative capacity. There is no need for the PRs to be registered as shareholders in order to do this. This choice is also subject to the articles of the company.

A trustee in bankruptcy has the same choice, ie the trustee may elect to be registered as a shareholder and then sell the shares, or the trustee can sell them directly in the trustee's representative capacity. The trustee must produce the court order concerning their appointment in order to establish their right to deal with the shares.

9.11 SERIOUS LOSS OF CAPITAL

Under s 656 of the CA 2006, the directors of a *public* company are obliged to call a general meeting within 28 days from the earliest date on which any director knew that the company had suffered a serious loss of capital. The date of the meeting must be fixed for not more than 56 days ahead. A serious loss of capital is where the net assets are worth less than half the called-up share capital. This happened to Southern Cross Healthcare Group plc in June 2011. By December 2011 the company, which ran hundreds of care homes, was in such financial difficulties that it was being wound up.

9.12 OTHER WAYS OF SELLING SHARES

The following methods will apply to public companies, particularly publicly-traded companies. They will not apply to private companies.

9.12.1 A placing

Here, new shares are created. The company's broker will sell them direct to a range of investors, usually at a slight discount on the market price.

9.12.2 Placing and open offer

This mechanism preserves the basic principle of pre-emption rights, but does so indirectly. Thus, the new shares are created and sold to financial institutions, usually at a small discount.

However, the existing shareholders have the right to take up the new shares at the same price, referred to as a 'claw back' feature. So only those new shares that the existing shareholders do not want will end up with the financial institutions.

9.12.3 A vendor placing

A vendor placing occurs when a purchaser is able to buy 'Target Co' (ie buy the share capital of Target Co) without paying cash. The mechanism is that the purchaser issues new shares in itself and uses these to raise money to fund the acquisition.

The results are:

(a) the vendor receives cash and gives Target Co shares to the purchaser;

(b) the purchaser receives the Target Co shares and gives its own newly-issued shares to the placees; and

(c) the placees have bought shares in the purchaser for cash.

See **Figure 9.1** below.

Figure 9.1 A vendor placing

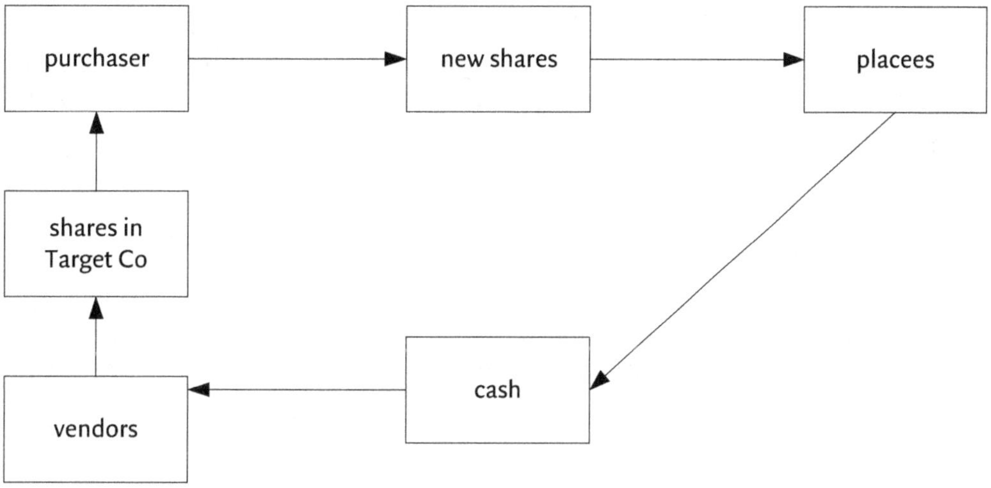

9.13 WHERE DOES THE MONEY COME FROM?

9.13.1 Shareholders and directors

We have seen that it is possible to set up a company with just £1 of equity finance. We have also seen (at **9.3** above) that those involved with the running of the company – the shareholders and directors – may inject further equity finance into their companies by buying shares which the company issues. Initially, a significant amount of the company's capital is usually provided by the individuals who will run the company. This may be in the form of both debt and equity finance. It may also be possible for the persons setting up or running the company to encourage family or friends to provide some finance.

9.13.2 Banks

For many small companies, their primary source of outside finance is debt finance from their 'high street' bank, such as Barclays or HSBC. The banks can provide overdraft facilities, or term loans or revolving credit facilities for the needs of the company (see **Chapter 10** below).

9.13.3 Venture capital

Where significant amounts of outside finance are required, venture capitalists may become involved. These are businesses, insurance companies, pension funds, banks or wealthy individuals looking for investment in companies which have the potential for fairly rapid growth, in the hope that after a few years such companies will float on the London Stock Exchange as publicly-traded companies. This will enable the venture capitalist to sell its investment and realise a substantial capital gain. This investment may comprise just equity, or debt finance or a combination of the two.

Typical features of venture capital include the following:

(a) The investment will be in ordinary shares in the company. The shareholding taken will be a substantial stake in the company, but not normally a majority stake since such a surrender of control would usually be unacceptable to the individuals already running the company.

(b) Part of the investment may be in the form of debt finance.

(c) The venture capitalist may require that there are management changes in the company, including a seat on the board for its own representatives.

(d) Before investing, the venture capitalist will carry out a thorough investigation into the company's business, finances, management and future prospects.

In 2025, venture capital firms such as 3i (website <http://www.3i.com>) had invested approximately £9 billion in over 9,000 companies (predominantly in technology, healthcare and financial and consumer services) across the UK.

The British Private Equity & Venture Capital Association (BVCA) represents the venture capital industry in the UK, and you can find out more about venture capitalists from its website <www.bvca.co.uk>.

9.14 SUMMARIES AND CHECKLISTS

9.14.1 Allotment of shares

Tables 9.1 and **9.2** following set out the requirements that must be met by companies wishing to allot shares, depending on whether the individual company was or was not incorporated under the CA 2006. For filing, etc see **9.14.2** below.

Table 9.1 Requirements for allotment of shares by companies incorporated under the CA 2006 (on or after 1 October 2009)

<table>
<tr><th>Do any constitutional restrictions need to be revoked?</th><th>Do the directors need a new authority to allot?</th><th>Do any pre-emption rights for the existing shareholders need to be disapplied?</th></tr>
<tr>
<td>Not a major problem for CA 2006 companies as there is no authorised share capital in the memorandum. But, to be sure, check articles for any upper limit on size of allotment: if too low, remove by SR.

[NB: it is unusual for the Articles to impose an upper limit on the number of shares that the company may allot. The model articles do not contain such a limit.]</td>
<td>Check whether authority already exists in the articles or in a shareholders' resolution.

1. If it does exist, check the number of shares covered and the duration of the authority.

2. If it does not exist or the number of shares covered is inadequate/duration has expired, then:

A. Private company with one class of shares does not need authority to allot

Section 550 gives authority unless there is a prohibition in the articles, so:
• check articles for restrictions on directors' authority to allot and if a restriction exists:
– remove it by SR; or
– pass an OR under s 551 to grant a new authority to allot.

[The model articles do not contain such restrictions and they are rare.]

B. All other companies
• pass an OR under s 551 to grant a new authority to allot.</td>
<td>Check whether statutory rights apply (requiring allotment in proportion to existing holdings).

They are irrelevant, so do not apply, when:
(a) there is an allotment of shares which are not equity securities (s 561);
(b) there is non-cash consideration (s 565);
(c) it is a private company only: articles state that the statutory regime does not apply (a general exclusion) (s 567);
(d) articles impose their own pre-emption regime (s 568).

1. If the statutory regime applies consider:
• following the regime; or
• disapplying it by SR; or
• [whether articles allow directors or members to disapply it; or
• asking members to waive their statutory pre-emption rights.]

2. If articles impose their own pre-emption regime, consider disapplying that regime (the articles themselves will explain how).</td>
</tr>
</table>

Table 9.2 Requirements for allotment of shares by companies incorporated before 1 October 2009

Do any constitutional restrictions need to be revoked?	*Do the directors need a new authority to allot?*	*Do any pre-emption rights for the existing shareholders need to be disapplied?*
Check authorised share capital (ASC) clause in the **memorandum**. If **too low**, remove it by OR. (The usual way to do this is to revoke the ASC clause by OR.[1] While it is possible to amend such a restriction, most solicitors revoke the ASC clause completely.) AND Check the **articles** for any upper limit on the size of allotment. If **too low**, remove the article by SR. [NB: Although the memorandum will always have an ASC clause, it is highly unusual for the articles also to impose an upper limit on the number of shares that the company may allot. Table A does not contain such a limit.]	Check whether authority already exists in the articles or in a shareholders' resolution. 1. If it **does** exist, check the number of shares covered and the duration of the authority. 2. If it **does not** exist or the number of shares covered is inadequate/duration has expired, then: **A. Private company with one class of shares (s 550)** • pass OR to activate directors' powers under s 550.[2] This gives directors authority to allot subject to any restrictions in the articles, so: Check articles for restrictions on directors' authority to allot. If such a restriction exists: • remove it by SR; or • pass an OR under s 551 to grant a new authority to allot. [These are rare. Table A does not contain such a restriction.] **B. All other companies (s 551)** • pass an OR under s 551 to grant a new authority to allot.	Check whether statutory rights apply (requiring allotment in proportion to existing holdings). They are irrelevant so do not apply when: (a) there is non-cash consideration (s 565); (b) there is an allotment of shares which are not equity securities (s 561); (c) it is a private company only: articles state that statutory regime does not apply (a general exclusion) (s 567); (d) articles impose their own pre-emption regime (s 568). **1. If the statutory regime applies consider:** • following the regime; or • disapplying it by SR; or • [whether articles allow directors or members to disapply it; or • asking members to waive their statutory pre-emption rights.] **2. If articles impose their own pre-emption regime,** consider disapplying that regime (the articles themselves will explain how).

[1] Under the transitional provisions in SI 2008/2860, Sch 2, para 42.
[2] Under the transitional provisions in SI 2008/2860, Sch 2, para 43.

9.14.2 Filing requirements

Table 9.3 below sets out the filing requirements for all companies.

Table 9.3 Filing requirements for all companies (whether incorporated under the CA 2006 or incorporated before 1 October 2009)

Copies of resolutions to be sent to Companies House within 15 days	All SRs. Any OR removing effect of authorised share capital limit in a 1985 Act company.[1] Any OR providing that the directors of a 1985 Act company with a single class of shares are to have the powers provided by s 550.[2] Any s 551 OR granting directors authority to allot (s 551(9)). Any SR disapplying pre-emption rights (ss 29– 30).
Company forms to be sent to Companies House	Return of allotment and statement of capital (Form SH01) within one month of the allotment (s 555). Possibly Form/s PSC01 (for an individual becoming a PSC) Form/s PSC02 (for a company becoming a PSC) Form/s PSC04 (for a change in the percentage bands for being a PSC) Form/s PSC07 (for a person or company ceasing to be a PSC) (s 790VA).
Entries in company's own registers	Entry of new member/amendment of existing member's details in register of members (s 113). Must be done within 2 months (s 554). Entry of new member/amendment of existing member's details in PSC register (if relevant thresholds met – see **5.5** above) (s 790M). *The Economic Crime and Corporate Transparency Act 2023 will remove the requirement for a company to maintain a PSC register. This is expected to happen by 2027.*
Preparation and allocation of share certificates	Prepare share certificates within 2 months of allotment (s 769).

[1] Under the transitional provisions in SI 2008/2860, Sch 2, para 42(3).
[2] Under the transitional provisions in SI 2008/2860, Sch 2, para 43(3).

9.14.3 Buy-back of a company's own shares

Table 9.4 Buy-back of a company's own shares, otherwise than from capital (not de minimis amounts)

References are to the CA 2006.

Timing	*Procedure*	*Deadline (if applicable)*
Before BM	Check no limit on s 690 power.	
	Prepare accounts to ascertain available profits and confirm shares are fully paid (s 691(1)).	
BM	Board meeting to resolve: • to decide method of finance • approve draft terms of purchase • call GM/propose WRs	
	Contract or memorandum of terms made available to members.	if WR used: circulated with WR if GM: at registered office for at least 15 days before GM (s 696)
WR	**WR:** Circulate WR (OR to authorise buy-back contract) with contract. Holder(s) of shares being bought are not eligible to vote (s 695(2)).	
alternatively		
GM	**GM:** Pass OR to authorise buy-back contract (s 694). Resolution is invalid if vote is passed on the strength of votes derived from the shares being bought (s 695(3)). Such votes should not be cast. Contract must be available at GM.	
After GM/WR	Keep minutes/written resolutions	for 10 years (s 355)
Completion BM	Board meeting resolves to enter into the contract and [1/2] director/s are authorised to execute the buy-back contract.	
After completion	File return of purchase of own shares (s 707) and notice of cancellation of shares (s 708)	within 28 days of completion
	Keep copy of contract at registered office	for 10 years (s 702(3))
	Cancel the shares, update register of members and PSC register (if required – see **5.5** above). *The Economic Crime and Corporate Transparency Act 2023 will remove the requirement for a company to maintain a PSC register. This is expected to happen by 2027.*	

Table 9.5 Buy-back of a company's own shares, from profits and capital (not de minimis amounts and employee share schemes)

References are to the CA 2006.

Timing	*Procedure*	*Deadline (if applicable)*
Before BM	Check no limit on s 690 and s 709 powers.	
	Prepare accounts to ascertain available profits and confirm shares are fully paid.	No earlier than 3 months before the directors prepare the statement of solvency (s 712(7)).
BM	Board meeting to resolve: • to decide method of finance • approve terms of statement of solvency and auditors' report • approve terms of purchase • call GM/propose WRs.	
	Contract or memorandum of terms made available to members (s 696(2)).	if WRs used: circulated with WRs if GM: at registered office at least 15 days before GM
	Statement of Solvency and Auditors' Report (SS and AR)	signed no earlier than 1 week before GM/passing of WR (s 716(2))
WRs	**WR:** Circulate WR (ss 694, 717 and 718; see below) with contract, SS and AR. Holder(s) of shares being bought are not eligible to vote (s 695(2) and s 717(2)).	
alternatively		
GM	**GM:** (s 694, 716 and 718) Pass • OR to authorise contract • SR to authorise payment out of capital Contract, SS and AR must be at the meeting or circulated with WR. Resolution is invalid if vote is passed on the strength of votes derived from shares being bought (s 695(3) and s 717(3)). Such votes should not be cast.	
After GM/WR	Keep minutes/written resolutions	for 10 years (s 355)
	Creditors' and dissenting members' right to object	lasts for 5 weeks after SR (s 721)
	Keep SS and AR at the company's own registered office	for 5 weeks from date of SR (s 720)
	Place notices in *London Gazette* and national newspaper/to creditors	within 1 week of SR (s 719(1) and (2))
	File the SS and AR at Companies House	before first publication (s 719(4))
	File SR	within 15 days of GM/WRs (s 29(1)(a) and s 30(1))
Completion (BM)	Directors resolve to enter into contract and authorise [1/2] director/s to sign. Payment out of capital takes place	 between 5 and 7 weeks after SR (s 723)

After completion	File return of purchase of own shares and notice of cancellation of shares	within 28 days of completion
	Keep copy of contract at registered office Cancel the shares, update register of members and PSC register (if required – see **5.5** above). *The Economic Crime and Corporate Transparency Act 2023 will remove the requirement for a company to maintain a PSC register. This is expected to happen by 2027.*	for 10 years

9.14.4 Procedure for transfer of shares

(a) Give share certificate and transfer form to transferee.
(b) Buyer pays stamp duty (no stamp duty on a gift).
(c) Apply to company for registration.
(d) Board consider whether to refuse registration (if the articles give them this power).
(e) Board resolve to issue and seal new share certificate (if company has seal).
(f) Update register of members.

9.14.5 Procedure on death/bankruptcy of shareholder

(a) Shares pass automatically by transmission to personal representative/trustee in bankruptcy.
(b) Personal representative/trustee in bankruptcy may either:
    (i) have themselves entered on the register; or
    (ii) transfer shares to some other person.

Note: Both of these are subject to any restrictions on transfer which may be contained in the articles.

CHAPTER 10

FINANCING A COMPANY II – DEBT

LEARNING OUTCOMES

After reading this chapter you will be able to:

- identify the main sources of debt finance for a company
- compare the different types of loan a company can take
- understand the role of debt securities
- compare debt and equity finance.

10.1 INTRODUCTION

Debt finance is the money a company raises by borrowing. It is an alternative to equity finance (see **Chapter 9**). Companies in the UK borrow billions of pounds every year. A company may have to borrow money for a number of reasons, for example to fund the start up of its operations (particularly where finance from shareholders is limited), to fund expansion of its business (eg to build a new factory, or buy another business or company), or to help it through temporary cash-flow or longer-term financial difficulties. So debt finance will often be required by a company to help it commence trading once it has been formed, and thereafter during its trading life.

There are two main types of debt finance: loans and debt securities.

A loan arises when a company borrows money from banks or other lenders (such as its directors or shareholders). There are many types of loan, but the main ones include a bank overdraft, a term loan and a revolving credit facility, and we consider each of these later in this chapter. As an alternative, or in addition to taking out a loan, a company may issue debt securities to investors. These are IOUs which are issued by the company to the investor in return for a cash payment. These IOUs have to be redeemed (ie repaid) by the company at an agreed future date. We cover these briefly at **10.8** below.

With both loans and debt securities, therefore, the company borrows money, either from a bank or from an investor, which it will eventually have to repay. In this book we concentrate primarily on lending by banks.

A company must be able to borrow the money. A company formed under the CA 2006 has unrestricted objects unless specifically restricted by the company's articles of association (CA 2006, s 31(1)). The model articles for private companies do not place any restriction on borrowing. A company will therefore have an implied power to borrow money, unless expressly excluded by placing a restriction in the company's articles (*General Auction Estate and Monetary Co v Smith* [1891] 3 Ch 432). If the company has amended model articles or bespoke articles, these should be checked for any restrictions.

For a company formed before 1 October 2009, the objects of the company were set out in its old-style memorandum of association, and on that date became part of its articles. If the company's articles have not been updated to take account of the CA 2006, the memorandum must be checked to see that there is no restriction on the company borrowing (see **4.6.1.2** above).

For both types of company, if there are any restrictions preventing the company from borrowing money, the company's shareholders must pass a special resolution under s 21 of the CA 2006 to amend the articles.

Further, the directors must have the authority to act on behalf of the company and borrow money. For a company with model articles for a private company, the directors' authority would flow from art 3; and for a company formed before 1 October 2009 with an unamended Table A, this authority would stem from art 70. If the company has amended or bespoke articles, they must be checked to see that, for instance, they do not require the shareholders' prior approval for borrowing over a certain level.

A private company is able to borrow money from the moment its certificate of incorporation is issued. A private company which converts into a public company must, under s 761 of the CA 2006, first obtain its trading certificate (see **12.4.2.2** below).

A company will often have to offer a lender security over its property in return for receiving the money. With it, the lender will still get its money back even if the borrowing company defaults on the loan and cannot repay it. The taking of security over a company's assets is discussed at **10.11** below and in **Chapter 11**.

10.2 EQUITY FINANCE OR DEBT FINANCE?

The company has a choice as to the way in which it raises the finance it needs. The major difference between equity finance (the company raising funds by issuing shares) and debt finance (the company raising funds by borrowing money) is that, as we have seen in **Chapter 9**, equity finance is tightly controlled by the CA 2006. In contrast, there is not much legislation directed toward debt finance (such legislation as there is mainly concerns debentures (see **10.10** below) and the granting of security by companies). Instead, the law of contract applies. Debt finance can therefore be a more flexible source of funds for the company than equity finance. In practice most companies raise money through a combination of debt and equity finance, as each method has its advantages and disadvantages (see further **10.12** below).

10.3 LOANS

As noted above, there is little legal control on loans between the lender (usually a bank) and the borrower (the company) apart from contract law. As with any contract, there will be negotiations between the parties over the terms of that contract. The terms will be agreed on the basis of usual market practice, the purpose and length of the loan, the background and finances of the company, the relative bargaining power of the parties – usually it will be the company (as borrower) that needs the bank more than the bank needs the company – and general economic conditions. As a lawyer you will not be involved in agreeing the commercial terms but in negotiating the legal documentation (the loan agreement and supporting documents) once the commercial terms have been settled.

There is no legal requirement for a company to give the lender security for a loan. However, if the lender has security then the loan (which is said to be 'secured') can be more easily recovered if the company defaults and is unable to repay, consequently a lender may require security as a condition of making the loan. If security is not given, the loan is said to be 'unsecured'. A company will pay a higher rate of interest for an unsecured loan, as the risk that the lender will not get repaid is greater than it would be if the loan was secured.

There are many different types of loan; here, we concentrate on the three main types:

(a) an overdraft;

(b) a term loan; and

(c) a revolving credit facility.

In each case the agreement between the borrowing company and the lender is governed by contract law as clarified by the common law. A company will choose one type of loan over another on the basis of the purpose for which it needs the loan and the typical features of each type.

10.4 OVERDRAFT FACILITY

Most small and medium-sized companies rely heavily on overdraft facilities. An overdraft facility is a contract between the company and its bank which allows the company to go overdrawn on its current account. It is a form of temporary loan used to cover everyday business expenses when there is no other source of money available. The company becomes the debtor of the bank for the amount of the overdraft. The maximum amount of the overdraft will be agreed with the bank in advance, but the amount used or owed by the company may vary on a day-to-day basis.

If an overdraft has not been agreed in advance, the bank is not bound to meet any withdrawal not covered by funds in the account. Therefore a company attempting to withdraw money in excess of the funds in its account may be regarded as making an offer, which the bank accepts by meeting the drawing (ie providing the money). There then exists a contract in regard to the overdraft.

An overdraft is known as an 'uncommitted' facility. This means that it will usually be payable on demand. In other words, at any time a bank may demand that the overdraft be repaid by the company immediately; no notice need be given. 'On demand' means that the borrower is given enough time to effect the mechanics of payment, but not enough time to go and raise the money (*Bank of Baroda v Panessar* [1986] 3 All ER 751). In practice the bank will not demand repayment of the overdraft unless the company is in financial difficulties.

The company will have to pay a fee for the overdraft facility. Interest is also charged by reference to the bank's base rate (which is the rate at which the bank is prepared to lend to its customers with the best credit rating). It is charged on a compound basis, ie any unpaid interest is added to the capital and interest is charged on the total amount. This practice will be implied in overdraft contracts unless the parties have agreed otherwise (*Kitchen v HSBC Bank plc* [2000] 1 All ER (Comm) 787).

The advantages of an overdraft for the company are therefore that it is a flexible source of finance and relatively few formalities are required to arrange it (usually there will be a letter from the bank setting out its terms and conditions which the company must accept if it wants the overdraft). The disadvantages are that it may be called in at any time by the bank, and it is a relatively expensive way to borrow as it usually unsecured.

If security is taken over an existing overdraft account, the parties should be advised that money paid into an overdraft account (a credit) is treated as discharging the debt incurred first unless the parties have agreed otherwise – the rule in *Clayton's case* (1816) 35 ER 781. Under the Insolvency Act 1986 (IA 1986), security may be held to be invalid if it is in respect of monies advanced to the borrower *before* the security was put in place (IA 1986, ss 239 and 245). So, the rule in *Clayton's case* determines whether the outstanding balance on the account is new money advanced after the security was granted, in which case the security is valid (*Re Thomas Mortimer Ltd* [1964] 3 WLR 427 (Note); *Re Yeovil Glove Company Ltd* [1965] Ch 148).

10.5 TERM LOANS

The second type of loan is a term loan. This is where a company borrows a fixed amount of money, usually from a bank, for a specified period, ie a 'term', at the end of which it all must be repaid. Interest is also payable at regular intervals. Short-term loans are usually for up to one year; medium-term loans are usually for one to five years; and long-term loans are usually for more than five years. Term loans are typically used by a company to purchase a capital asset, such as land, a building or machinery.

Term loans may be secured or unsecured (although they are usually secured), and they may be bilateral or syndicated. A bilateral loan is between two parties, the company and one lender, usually a bank. A syndicated loan is between the company and a number of different lenders who jointly provide the money the company wants to borrow. A syndicated loan is used where the loan amount is high, and therefore the risk of lending to the company is shared between a number of banks rather than falling on one alone.

The contract for a term loan may be called a 'loan agreement', or a 'credit agreement' or a 'facility agreement'. The terms are used interchangeably.

A term loan may allow the borrowing company to draw down (ie take out) the loan all in one go, or to take it in instalments at, or by, agreed dates. The advantage of taking the money in instalments is that this will reduce interest payments.

The loan will usually be available to the borrower only for a short period (or periods if instalments are agreed) of time, known as the 'availability period', and it will not be available thereafter even if the company has not borrowed the full amount. The company will not usually be compelled to take the full amount of the loan if it decides it does not need all of the instalments.

The advantages of a term loan for a company are that it gives it greater certainty than an overdraft which is on demand, and the borrower has greater control. The disadvantages are the time and expense in negotiating and agreeing all the legal documentation for such a loan, and the fact that once repaid the money cannot then be reborrowed by the company.

10.6 REVOLVING CREDIT FACILITY

The third type of loan is a revolving credit facility. Here, a bank agrees to make available a maximum amount of money to the company throughout the agreed period of the facility. The company can borrow and repay amounts during the lifetime of the facility. Crucially, it is also able to reborrow amounts that it has already repaid, so long as it does not exceed the overall maximum figure (hence 'revolving'). The 'facility' part of the name of this type of loan indicates that it is an amount of money made available to a company which does not necessarily have to be taken up. Such loans therefore share characteristics of both overdrafts and term loans. They are useful for companies whose income is not evenly distributed throughout the year. Interest is also payable at regular intervals.

Revolving credit facilities may be secured or unsecured (although they are usually secured), and they can be bilateral or syndicated (see **10.5** above). The contract for a revolving credit facility is usually called a 'facility agreement'.

The advantages of a revolving credit facility for a company are that it is a very flexible means of borrowing money, and it is possible to reduce the total amount of interest payable by reducing borrowings. The disadvantages are the time and expense in negotiating and agreeing all the legal documentation for such a loan, and the higher fees that are charged.

10.7 CONTRACTUAL TERMS

Both a term loan and a revolving credit facility usually involve complex contracts which require a lot of negotiation between lawyers for the bank(s) and the company. A basic overview of some of the more important clauses which will be found in both types of loan is set out below. The term 'facility agreement' is used to cover both types of contract.

10.7.1 Payment of money to the borrower

The initial clauses of the facility agreement will set out:

(a) the amount of the loan;

(b) the currency (eg £, $ or €);

(c) the type of loan (if it is to be a term loan or revolving credit facility); and

(d) the availability period(s) during which the loan can be taken (for a revolving credit facility this is almost the entire length of the facility).

Both a term loan and a revolving credit facility are 'committed' facilities. In other words, once the loan agreement has been signed, the bank must provide the company with the loan monies when it requests them. A 'commitment' fee will be payable by the company for this reason.

In the unlikely event that the lender refused to lend in breach of the facility agreement, the company would be entitled to damages. If the company was able to obtain the same loan elsewhere then the damages would be nominal. However, if the loan was to have been at a low rate of interest that is not obtainable elsewhere, the damages could be substantial. They may be regarded as damages for loss of expectation, to compensate the borrower for not being in the position that they should have been in (see *Robinson v Harman* (1848) 1 Exch 850). There is also a reasonableness factor to be taken into account in deciding the damages (see *Ruxley Electronics & Construction v Forsyth* [1996] 1 AC 344). Specific performance is usually refused where damages are an adequate remedy.

10.7.2 Repayment and pre-payment

Unlike an overdraft, the bank cannot demand repayment of a term loan or revolving credit facility whenever it wishes. It can do so only in accordance with the terms of the facility agreement, ie when there has been an event of default (see **10.7.6** below).

The facility agreement will set out the agreed repayment schedule for the loan. It may provide for repayment:

(a) of the whole loan in one go at the end of the term (a 'bullet' payment); or

(b) in equal instalments over the term of the loan ('amortisation'); or

(c) in unequal instalments with the final instalment being the largest ('balloon repayment').

Repayments in instalments will give the lender early notice should the company have difficulty in making repayments, if the company defaults on a payment. Repayments for a revolving credit facility will be repaid at the end of each interest period but can be reborrowed, whereas for a term loan they will be spread out more evenly throughout the period of the loan.

In a term loan, the company may in addition be granted an option in the facility agreement to repay earlier than the agreed repayment schedule. This is known as 'pre-payment of the loan'. The advantage to the company is that it can reduce future interest payments as the outstanding loan amount will be reduced. The borrowing company would have to give notice of an intended prepayment, and will be able to do so only on an agreed date (usually on the last day of a period for which interest is calculated). The reason for this is that banks themselves will usually borrow at least some of the money which they lend. If they accepted prepayment from the borrowing company on another date, they could find that they have to pay interest to another bank without having the income (from the company paying interest).

It is usual to require that any prepayments are applied in reverse order to their maturity, ie they are applied to the last scheduled repayment first, and then the next to last. This has the effect of shortening the period of the loan.

10.7.3 Interest rates

The interest rate payable for the loan is a matter of agreement between the parties. There is no statutory control of the interest rate applicable to companies. It will be expressly stated in the facility agreement. It may be fixed for the period of the loan, or it could be variable, ie a 'floating' rate. Floating rate loan agreements commonly provide for the interest rate to be altered at specified intervals, eg three or six months, by reference to a formula which is intended to maintain the lender's profit on the loan. The reason for this is that the base interest rate for sterling is reviewed every six weeks by a committee of the Bank of England, and may be altered up or down. At the time of writing the base rate has reached levels not seen since 2008 as a result of a return of high inflation caused by the pandemic, Brexit and the illegal Russian invasion of Ukraine.

The money which the bank lends may be its own money, from its depositors, or may be borrowed from other banks. In the case of a large loan, it will be at least partly borrowed from other banks. The interest rate in such a case will be set according to a formula in the facility agreement, so that the company pays the lender an interest rate which allows the lender to repay the interest on its own borrowings and to make a profit. It will consist of three parts:

(a) mandatory costs (which a bank must pay to regulatory bodies such as the Bank of England);

(b) the interest rate at which banks borrow from one another (eg LIBOR, the London Interbank Offered Rate, which may be found at <www.theice.com/iba/libor>); and

(c) the margin, which is the lender's profit.

Lenders will often want to impose default interest, ie an increased interest rate, if scheduled payments are missed. However, the law on penalty clauses could cause problems. Contract law allows the courts to strike down a provision which constitutes a penalty clause as opposed to a clause for liquidated damages. One indicator of a penalty clause is where the breach is failure to pay a sum, and the sum stipulated to be paid under the contract is greater than the sum actually owed (see *Bridge v Campbell Discount Co Ltd* [1962] 1 All ER 385). In *Jeancharm Ltd (t/a Beaver International) v Barnet Football Club Ltd* [2003] EWCA Civ 58, it was held that default interest may not constitute a penalty. The condition to this was that the rate had to be such as only to compensate the lender for its additional funding costs and the increased credit risk of lending to a defaulting borrower. In that case, however, a 5% a week rate represented a yearly interest rate of 260%. The Court of Appeal held that such a sum did not amount to a genuine pre-estimate but was a penalty clause in the sense of *Dunlop Pneumatic Tyre Co v New Garage* [1915] AC 79. Such default interest clauses in a facility agreement must therefore be drafted very carefully, in accordance with current jurisprudence.

10.7.4 Express covenants

The facility agreement will include a series of covenants given by the company to the bank. A covenant is a contractual promise to do or not to do something. The function of covenants is to try to ensure that the company conducts its business within agreed limits so that the lender has every chance of being repaid in full.

Covenants tend to fall into three categories:

(a) those that relate to the provision of information on the company;
(b) those that relate to the financial performance of the company; and
(c) those dealing with non-financial matters.

The restrictions on the financial performance of the company are put in place to ensure that the company stays solvent and is not too dependent on debt. So, for example, the company will be required by the lender to pay all debts as they fall due. The borrower will also usually be obliged to seek equity finance for new ventures (see **Chapter 9**), as opposed to further debt finance.

Covenants on the following matters are also commonly included, again to ensure that there will be sufficient money to repay the loan:

(a) *Limitation of dividends*. The company must ensure that dividends and other distributions to shareholders do not exceed a specified percentage of the net profits.
(b) *Minimum capital requirements*. The company must ensure that current assets exceed current liabilities by a specified amount of money or a specified percentage.
(c) *No disposal of assets, or change of business*. The company must not dispose of assets without the lender's consent, or change the scope or nature of the business.
(d) *No further security over the assets*. The company must not create any further security over the whole, or any part, of the undertaking without the lender's consent (a 'negative pledge' clause, see **Chapter 11**).
(e) *Information on the company's business*. This would include annual accounts, interim financial statements, communications sent to shareholders and such other information as the lender may require.

The final form of the covenants will depend on negotiations between the parties, but remember that the lender has the money and the company needs the money, so the commercial strength is on the lender's side. However, the lender will not wish to run the borrower's business by remote control, so the lender will leave the company reasonable commercial latitude. One reason for this is the risks of the bank being found liable as a shadow director of the borrowing company.

In *re a Company (No 005009 of 1987)* [1989] BCLC 13, it was held that there was a triable issue as to whether a bank had become a shadow director of an insolvent company in the context of s 214 of the IA 1986 for the offence of wrongful trading by directors (see **7.13.10.1** above). It seems unlikely that the lender could be so liable unless it stepped outside the normal lender–customer relationship. In that case, the borrower had reached its overdraft limit. The lender commissioned a report on the financial affairs of the company, which included steps that should be taken by the borrower's management. The company then implemented these steps. Advisers are protected under s 251 of the IA 1986 from liability as a shadow director, but there is a difference between advising and instructing. In *Secretary of State for Trade and Industry v Deverell* [2000] 2 All ER 365, the Court of Appeal held that a shadow director was anyone, other than a professional adviser, who exercised real influence in the corporate affairs of a company.

One way round this problem is for the lender in such a situation to make continuation of the loan conditional on certain steps being taken by the company. The company then has the choice of taking a new loan on those conditions, or looking elsewhere.

As a matter of general commercial common sense, a lender will monitor the company's current account very closely. This will provide good information on how the borrower is progressing financially. It will also give early warning of any problems.

10.7.5 Implied covenants

As with any contract, terms may be implied into the facility agreement, for example by trade usage such as the bank's right to charge compound interest. The court's power to imply terms is limited. A contractual term would be implied only if it were necessary to give efficacy to the contract (see *Thames Cruises Ltd v George Wheeler Launches Ltd* [2003] EWHC 3093). In any event, the court could not imply a term that was inconsistent with an express term of the contract. This should not be a problem with facility agreements drawn up by legal advisers.

10.7.6 Events of default

The facility agreement will contain 'events of default'. If the company breaches any of these terms, the lender may terminate the agreement if it so wishes. Such events include failure to pay any sum due (be it interest or repayment of capital), commencement of an insolvency procedure and breach of other obligations under the facility agreement. Another possible event of default is cross-default, where the company fails to meet some other indebtedness or financial payment due, ie has defaulted on a loan to another lender. The rationale is that this is the first sign of financial trouble for the company which may well affect the second lender.

10.8 DEBT SECURITIES

Debt securities are the other main form of debt finance. They are financial instruments issued to investors by a company to raise money. The company sells the debt securities to investors for cash, which the company promises to repay on the agreed date, typically with interest. In other words, debt securities are basically just a type of IOU issued by the company. Like shares, once issued, they can usually be sold on by the initial investors. It is therefore really only publicly-traded companies (see **1.9.3.1** above) that would use debt securities.

There are many different types of debt security, but the main types are as follows:

(a) *Commercial paper*. These are short-term debt securities which have to be repaid (this is also known as 'mature') by the company within 12 months of being issued to investors. This therefore offers an alternative to short-term borrowing from a bank. Commercial paper is not usually traded on the London Stock Exchange.

(b) *Bonds*. These are medium to long-term debt securities which will mature over a year after the company has issued them to investors. Usually bonds are admitted to the London Stock Exchange to facilitate trading in them by investors. They are sometimes called 'notes' instead.

(c) *EMTN programme*. This is the Euro Medium-Term Note programme. It is another way for a company to issue debt securities. Once established, the programme allows the company to issue to investors notes (IOUs) of varying lengths (usually anything up to 30 years) in a series of different issues over time. It therefore can be more flexible and efficient for the company than issuing separate bonds or commercial paper over time. Again, notes issued under an EMTN programme will be traded on the London Stock Exchange.

Before the company issues debt securities it may have to grant security to guarantee repayment of the amounts it has borrowed. Debt securities may therefore be secured or unsecured.

10.9 OTHER SOURCES

There are other sources of debt finance for a company, for example where it utilises short-term trade credit. This arises where the company arranges to pay its suppliers a number of days after their invoices have been received (eg, 30 days) and not on delivery of the goods.

A company may also use debt factoring to raise money. This is where a company sells its trade debts (ie money owed to the company) to a collection agency. The agency pays the company a proportion of the debts assigned to it. The agency now owns the debts, and seeks to get as much back as possible from the debtors and make a profit in the process.

10.10 DEBENTURES

A debenture is not a separate type of debt finance. It is a term used to describe different types of debt finance. It has more than one meaning. Under the common law it is defined as 'a document which either creates a debt or acknowledges it' (*Levy v Abercorris Slate and Steel* (1887) 37 Ch 260). Section 738 of the CA 2006 also contains a partial definition of a 'debenture', which includes 'debenture stock, bonds and any other securities of a company, whether or not constituting a charge on the assets of the company'. The CA 2006 definition does not replace the common law definition but merely provides further clarification.

The meaning of 'debenture' is therefore very wide. It includes debt securities (see **10.3** to **10.8** above). The significance of the definition is that certain rights are given to the holder of a debenture under the CA 2006. For example, under s 423(1) of the CA 2006, a company must send a copy of the company's accounts to every debenture holder.

In practice, 'debenture' is most commonly used in a narrower sense simply to refer to a document which gives security for the repayment of a loan. This might be just a separate contract granting the security, or a more comprehensive contract containing both the loan and security for it.

10.11 SECURED DEBT

A lender with security may claim the secured assets of the company if the company fails to meet its obligations under the facility agreement. If the company becomes insolvent, secured creditors are therefore in a much stronger position than unsecured creditors, who generally do not have any rights of priority to the company's assets.

Unsecured debts are governed by the equality (*pari passu*) principle, which means that the unsecured debts are all reduced pro rata if there are insufficient funds to pay all the company's debts. Security allows the lender to avoid this principle. For this reason, most borrowing by a company will involve the company giving security over its assets. We examine taking security further in **Chapter 11**.

10.12 COMPARISON OF DEBT AND EQUITY FINANCE

10.12.1 For the investor

10.12.1.1 The relative risk of the investment

It is generally perceived that buying shares in a company is a more risky investment than lending money to a company. If the company is in financial difficulties then it will not declare a dividend, as it can do so only if it has distributable profits, and even then the payment of a dividend is usually discretionary. The shareholder will also lose the capital value of their shares if the company goes insolvent – in other words, the shares the shareholder bought are worthless. However, with loans, the interest payments are a contractual liability of the company which must be met, and therefore will be paid before dividends. Also, a loan will often be secured over the company's property and there may be personal guarantees from the directors. This security means that a lender is much more likely to be repaid their loan than a shareholder their investment in the shares, if the company goes insolvent.

10.12.1.2 Involvement in the company

A shareholder as owner of the company has certain rights within the company (see **5.6** above), including the right to attend GMs and to vote, and as such can influence the direction of the company. A lender is merely a creditor of the company without any ownership rights, and therefore has no say whatever in the way the company is run provided the company sticks to the term of the facility agreement.

10.12.1.3 Income

A shareholder has no guaranteed income from their investment in shares of the company. A dividend will be paid by the company only if the directors decide to recommend one, and they may do so under the CA 2006 only if the company is sufficiently profitable. In contrast, a lender to the company must be paid the agreed rate of interest by the company at the agreed times specified in the debenture itself. Such interest is a debt owed by the company, and it must be paid regardless of whether the company makes a profit. If it fails to do so the company will be in default, and the lender may demand repayment of the loan and enforce its security.

10.12.1.4 Repayment of capital

Generally, a shareholder's capital is not repaid by the company unless the company is wound up and the company comes to an end (although a shareholder may recoup their investment by selling their shares to a third party). In contrast, a lender will agree with the company a date for repayment of the capital sum loaned, and this date will be stated in the debenture. On that date the company must repay the loan or it will be in default.

10.12.1.5 Restrictions on sale

If a shareholder wishes to sell their shares in order to realise their capital investment in the company, the transfer of their shares is governed by the articles, and in a private company these usually restrict the shareholder's choice. For example, art 26(5) of the model articles gives the directors of a company total freedom to refuse to register a new shareholder. If a lender wishes to realise their capital earlier than the repayment date agreed, the lender may sell their debenture to whomsoever they choose. No restriction in the articles will affect the lender's right to sell.

10.12.1.6 Capital value of the investment

The value of a private company's shares may increase or decrease, depending on the company's fortunes. Many shareholders make such an investment hoping for capital appreciation rather than income by way of dividend.

The capital value of a debenture generally remains constant, being the value of the loan. There is usually no possibility of capital appreciation or depreciation with this type of investment. The purpose of an investment in this form is the receipt of income in the form of regular interest payments by the company.

10.12.2 For the company

As we have seen, the major difference between a company raising equity finance (by selling its shares) and raising money by debt finance (by the company borrowing money) is that equity finance is tightly controlled by the CA 2006 (see **Chapter 9**). Debt finance is predominantly a matter of contract law, and may therefore be a more flexible way for the company to raise money.

10.12.2.1 Payment of income

The company is able to pay a dividend to its members only if there are sufficient available profits (see **9.8** above). Even if the company is sufficiently profitable, the directors usually have complete discretion as to whether a dividend should be paid (depending on the type of share).

Debt interest must be paid in accordance with the terms of the facility agreement, whether or not the company has profits available. If there are no profits, the company must use capital to make the interest payment. If the company fails to make a payment of interest, the lender is entitled to enforce the terms of the debenture by the appointment of a receiver or an administrator.

10.12.2.2 Tax treatment of income payments

The payment of a dividend is not a deductible expense for the company. It is simply a distribution of profit, after it has paid corporation tax.

Payment of debenture interest, as it is incurred for the purposes of the trade, is a normal trading expense of the company, and so is deductible by it in computing trading profit before its corporation tax is assessed.

10.12.2.3 Involvement of investor

If a person buys shares in the company and has their name entered on the register of members, they are then a shareholder of the company and have certain rights as an owner. That person might thus have a degree of influence over the way in which the company is run. Problems might arise if that shareholder's views were not in accordance with those of the directors and other shareholders.

A lender generally cannot interfere in the way the company is run. If the company complies with the terms of the debenture, the lender can take no action to influence company policy.

10.12.2.4 Repayment of capital

The company generally does not have to repay to shareholders the capital which they have invested until the company ceases in business and is wound up. Therefore, this is not a matter which the directors of the company usually need consider.

Loan capital, however, must be repaid at some date in the future (possibly on demand). Consequently, the directors of the company must make provision for this and ensure that funds are available to repay the loan whenever it falls due.

10.12.2.5 Cost – debt finance

The cost of debt is relatively easy to establish. Put simply, it is the interest rate charged by the lender to the borrowing company. The rate will depend on commercial factors such as the security offered by the company, how much is borrowed, how long it is borrowed for, the company's creditworthiness and general economic conditions.

The tax system favours debt financing because interest, unlike dividends, is tax deductible. In assessing the cost of borrowing, the tax savings have to be taken into account.

10.12.2.6 Cost – equity finance

The cost of equity is harder to pin down. It constitutes the likely returns to the new shareholder, including dividends (if paid), capital appreciation (if made) and share buybacks (if made). These returns are the cost to the existing shareholders, as their share of future dividends or capital growth is decreased by the presence of an extra shareholder. Dividends are not deductible for corporation tax purposes.

10.12.2.7 Existing capital structure

If the company already has a lot of debt (technically described as having a high 'gearing'), it may be able to obtain more finance only in the form of equity finance (ie, by a fresh issue of shares).

Gearing is the ratio (ie, a comparison) of borrowings to shareholder funds (in effect, share capital and retained profits). High gearing means a greater burden of borrowings and the greater possibility of insolvency if trading conditions worsen.

10.12.2.8 Existing restrictions

The articles may restrict the company's ability to borrow.

The terms of existing facility agreements may restrict the taking of new loans or debt, at least without the existing lender's consent.

10.12.2.9 Availability and cost of debt

Are banks prepared to lend money to the would-be borrowing company? If so, at what cost?

10.12.2.10 Conclusion

Ultimately, whether debt or equity finance, or a combination of the two, is the best option to raise new money for a company turns on a variety of factors. In fact, in recent years equity finance has been much the preferred source of new money by UK companies, mainly because interest rates have been historically high.

10.13 WHERE DOES THE MONEY COME FROM?

10.13.1 Shareholders and directors

As with equity finance (see **9.13** above), debt finance may be provided by those directly involved with running the company, the shareholders and directors. In addition, it may be possible for the persons setting up or running the company to encourage family or friends to provide some finance.

10.13.2 Banks

For many small companies, their primary source of debt finance is their high street bank, such as Barclays or HSBC. The banks are able to provide overdraft facilities, or term loans or revolving credit facilities for the needs of the company. The high street banks have specialist departments dealing with lending to companies and other businesses. You can find more information, for example, on HSBC's website at <http://www.business.hsbc.co.uk>.

10.13.3 Venture capital

In addition to equity finance, part of the investment by venture capitalists (see **9.13.3**) may be in the form of debt finance.

10.13.4 Other sources

Increasingly innovative ways are being developed to allow for lending to companies without going through the traditional channels, ie banks. One example is Kuflink, which is an online marketplace that allows investors to lend directly to businesses or individuals in the UK. More information is available from the website <http://www.kuflink.com>. This source of finance is increasing in popularity.

CHAPTER 11

TAKING SECURITY

LEARNING OUTCOMES

After reading this chapter you will be able to:

- explain why companies give security to lenders
- differentiate between the types of security a company can give
- understand the key legal and procedural issues surrounding a company taking security
- explain the importance of registration of security
- understand the priority of competing charges.

11.1 INTRODUCTION

We looked in **Chapter 10** at how a company can raise funds by borrowing money (known as debt finance). In this chapter we look at why and how a company creates security over its assets, the different types of security, the process of registering security and the problems that result from a failure to do so.

11.2 WHY GRANT SECURITY?

The ideal situation with debt finance is one in which the company repays the lender the borrowed amounts on time out of profits it has made from running the business. However, we saw in **Chapter 10** that usually a lender will not rely on this and will require security over the company's assets in return for making the loan, in order to increase its chances of being repaid if the company should get into financial difficulties. If the company fails to repay the loan as agreed then the lender can seize the secured assets, sell them and pay itself out of the proceeds of sale. This may be done in priority to any claims on outstanding sums made by unsecured creditors of the company. Taking security is therefore advantageous for the lender, and often a prerequisite for a loan, as it lowers the risk of its not being repaid (even if it does not entirely eliminate that risk).

The company may benefit too from giving security, as the lender will usually allow the company to borrow money at a rate that is lower than would otherwise be the case. The downside for the company is that it must accept restrictions on the use of the asset or assets it has given as security. The reality is, however, that the company's need for the loan will outweigh any restrictions imposed.

11.3 INITIAL CONSIDERATIONS

11.3.1 Sources of law

The creation of security by a company is predominantly a matter of contract law, thus the type and extent of security and the terms on which it is granted are generally determined by agreement between the parties after negotiations. There are, though, important provisions affecting security in legislation, for example in the CA 2006 regarding debentures and the process and effect of registration of security by a company. Important rules affecting security are also included in the Insolvency Act 1986 (IA 1986), and are covered in greater detail when considering corporate insolvency in **Chapter 19**. The Law of Property Act 1925 (LPA 1925) is relevant too, particularly where land is involved. The common law also has an important rule to play in clarifying the underlying contract law and statutory provisions.

11.3.2 Terminology

Rather unhelpfully for the new student of this area of law, there is no consistency in the use of terminology for describing the security which a company may grant.

The CA 2006 uses 'charge' as an umbrella term for most types of security, and in s 859A(7) specifically states that '"charge" includes mortgage'. In contrast, the LPA 1925 uses the term 'mortgage' as the umbrella term for security in that Act, defining this (s 205(1)(xvi)) to 'include any charge or lien on any property'. Further complicating matters, the IA 1986 defines 'security' as 'any mortgage, charge, lien or other security'.

We also saw at **10.10** above that the word 'debenture' has different meanings. In its practical business usage it means an agreement pursuant to which a company gives security to a lender (often together with the terms of the loan).

It is important, therefore, initially to check very carefully which legislation you are working with, and thus the precise meaning of the rules you are applying. Furthermore, when considering a contractual document granting security, it is essential to read the agreement carefully and not just to rely on its name, to ensure that you have correctly identified the type of security it covers.

11.3.3 Initial considerations for the company

As well as ensuring that the company has the power to borrow (see **10.1** above), the directors must make sure that the company has the power to grant security over its assets before entering into any security contracts on the company's behalf, otherwise they will be acting outside their authority and in breach of duty.

A company formed under the CA 2006 has unrestricted objects, unless specifically restricted by the company's articles of association (s 31(1)). The model articles for private companies do not place any restriction on granting security. A company will therefore have an implied power to grant security for any borrowing. If the company has amended model articles or bespoke articles, these should be checked for any restrictions.

For a company formed before 1 October 2009, the objects of the company were set out in its old-style memorandum of association, and on that date became part of its articles. If the company's articles have not been updated to take account of the CA 2006, the memorandum must be checked to see that there is no restriction on the company granting security.

For both types of company, if there are any restrictions preventing the company from granting the security, the company's shareholders must first pass a special resolution under s 21 of the CA 2006 to amend the company's articles.

The directors should also ensure that they have the necessary authority to enter into any security contract on the company's behalf. For a company with model articles for a private company, the directors' authority would flow from art 3; and for a company formed before 1

October 2009 with an unamended Table A, this authority would come from art 70. If they are amended or bespoke articles, they must be checked for any restrictions on the directors acting in this situation.

11.3.4 Initial considerations for the lender

The lender should make sure that there are no restrictions on the company granting security, and that the directors have the authority to act on behalf of the company in the transaction and that the people the lender is dealing with have actually been properly appointed as directors of the company. It should do this by inspecting the articles of the company, searching the company's records at Companies House and requesting copies of relevant board resolutions.

The lender should also search the company's records at Companies House to see if any charges have been registered already against the company's property, and so ensure that there is sufficient value in that property to provide adequate security for the proposed loan. Under s 859I of the CA 2006, the Registrar of Companies must include a certified copy of the instrument creating the charge in the register, which is open to inspection by any person.

From the register, the lender will be able to discover:

(a) the date of creation of any existing charge;
(b) the amount secured;
(c) which property is the subject of the charge; and
(d) who holds that charge (ie who can enforce the charge).

If the lender is proposing to take a charge over land held by the company, it should also conduct a search at Land Registry to check the company's title to the land and to see if any pre-existing charges have been registered. Similarly at the Intellectual Property Office, if a charge is to be taken over intellectual property rights such as a trade mark.

A lender should also conduct a 'winding-up search' by telephone at the Companies Court to check that no insolvency proceedings have been commenced against the company.

11.3.5 What assets may be secured?

Virtually all assets that a company might own may be offered as security for its borrowings. For example, a company may grant security over:

(a) its land, whether freehold or leasehold, and over its fixtures and fittings;
(b) its tangible property, such as machinery, computers and stock;
(c) its intangible property, such as money in a bank account, debts owed to it, any shares it owns in other companies and intellectual property rights.

11.4 TYPES OF SECURITY

There is a number of different types of security which a company may give for a loan. These are, principally, mortgages, fixed charges and floating charges, although other types exist too, as we shall see at **11.4.3** below.

11.4.1 Mortgages

This is the highest form of security. A lender would seek to take a mortgage over high-quality assets owned by the borrowing company, such as land, buildings, machinery, aircraft and ships, and even shares it owns in other companies. A mortgage, with the exception of land, involves the transfer of legal ownership from the mortgagor (the company) to the mortgagee (the lender); and although the mortgage gives the lender the right to immediate possession of the property, this is held in reserve and exercised only if the borrowed money is not repaid, ie if the company defaults. The title will be transferred back to the company when the borrowings have been repaid. A separate mortgage must be created over each asset. A mortgage taken over land is actually, 'a charge by deed expressed to be by way of legal mortgage' (LPA 1925, s 87). The rights of the mortgagee arise under the LPA 1925. These include the key rights to take possession of the land and to sell it.

11.4.2 Charges

This is a form of security which does not transfer legal ownership from the chargor (the company) to the chargee (also known as the charge holder) (the lender) and does not give the chargee the right to immediate possession of the property. A charge does, however, give the lender important rights over the asset should the company fail to repay the money borrowed. These are explained below. There are two different types of charge a company may grant:

(a) a fixed charge; and
(b) a floating charge.

11.4.2.1 Fixed charges

A fixed charge may be taken over property such as machinery and shares owned by the company in other companies, and to this extent it is an alternative to a mortgage. A company must create a separate fixed charge over each asset. It is also possible to create more than one fixed charge over the same asset. The effect of the charge is that the lender has control of the asset. For example, the company will not be permitted to dispose of the asset (eg, sell it) without the charge holder's consent. The charge holder will also require the company to keep the asset in good condition.

If the company gets into financial difficulties and goes into receivership or liquidation, the fixed charge holder will have the right to sell the asset and be paid out of the proceeds of the sale (to repay the outstanding amount of any borrowings) before any other claimants, such as unsecured creditors of the company, can claim the proceeds. This right of first claim over the proceeds makes a fixed charge a significant form of security for a lender.

11.4.2.2 Floating charges

Some assets belonging to a company are not suitable for a fixed charge because the company needs to sell them as part of doing business, eg stock. If these assets were subject to a fixed charge, the company would need the charge holder's consent each time it wanted to sell any of them. Clearly this would be both unworkable and unwarranted, as selling its stock is what the company must do on a daily basis in order to operate its business and make money.

A floating charge is the solution to this problem. In *In re Panama, New Zealand and Australian Royal Mail Company* (1870) LR 5 Ch App 318, the court allowed the creation of an equitable charge over the company's undertaking (ie business) and stock. A floating charge therefore secures a group of assets, such as stock, which is constantly changing. It is possible to create more than one floating charge over the same group of assets.

The three basic features of a floating charge were identified in *Re Yorkshire Woolcombers Association Ltd; Houldsworth v Yorkshire Woolcombers Association Ltd* [1903] 2 Ch 284, as being:

(a) an equitable charge over the whole or a class of the company's assets, eg stock;
(b) the assets subject to the charge are constantly changing; and
(c) the company retains the freedom to deal with the assets in the ordinary course of business until the charge 'crystallises'.

The assets subject to the floating charge are therefore identified generically, such as 'stock' or 'the undertaking', rather than specifying individual items as with a fixed charge, such as 'the public house, "The Old Vic", at Albert Square, Walford, London'. Note that it is possible to take a floating charge even over all of the company's undertaking, which would be over all of the assets which make up the business run by the company.

It is the company's freedom to deal with the assets in particular which distinguishes the floating charge from other types of security.

A further characteristic of the floating charge is that on the occurrence of certain events, the floating charge will automatically *crystallise* over the assets charged. This will happen if:

(a) the company goes into receivership;

(b) the company goes into liquidation;

(c) the company ceases to trade; or

(d) any other event occurs which is specified in the charge document (the contract for the floating charge made between the company and the lender).

All of these events will prevent the company repaying, or make it less likely that it will be able to repay, the outstanding borrowings. On crystallisation the company can no longer deal with the assets covered by the charge. In effect the floating charge turns into a fixed charge (see **11.4.2.1** above).

11.4.2.3 Advantages of floating charges

One advantage of a floating charge from the company's viewpoint is that it allows it to deal with the secured assets on a day-to-day basis. Another is that, as a form of security which can attach to assets unsuited for a fixed charge or mortgage, it allows the company to maximise the amount that it is able to borrow. It is also advantageous that a floating charge may be taken over the whole of a company's business.

11.4.2.4 Disadvantages of floating charges

As a general rule, a fixed charge will take priority over a floating charge over the same assets. For example, say that a fixed charge was granted over a factory owned by the borrowing company to a first lender, and then a second, different lender was granted a floating charge by the same company over the whole of its undertaking (which would include the factory). If the company went insolvent and the factory was sold, the fixed charge holder (the first lender) would have priority over the proceeds of sale; only if there was money left over after the first lender's debts had been paid off in full would that go to the floating charge holder (the second lender).

A disadvantage of a floating charge from the viewpoint of the holder (the lender) is that the company is allowed to deal with the assets. Thus, the company could sell its existing stock and not purchase new stock to replace it. So a floating charge over stock would be of little value in those circumstances. One solution to this problem is for the lender to take fixed charges over other assets of the company too.

A further disadvantage is that certain other creditors have the right to claim money from the proceeds of sale of the assets covered by the floating charge if the company goes insolvent before the charge holder itself gets the money. These include so-called 'preferential' creditors, who take priority over the holder of a floating charge but not over the holder of a fixed charge. Preferential creditors include employees of the company as regards certain outstanding wages of and certain pension contributions. Following the court's decision in *Bloom and others v Pensions Regulator (Nortel, Re)* [2010] EWHC 3010 (Ch), certain other pension payments will be treated as an expense of the administration and therefore paid before the charge holder. In some cases an additional amount of money from the sale of assets covered by the floating charge are 'ring-fenced' for unsecured creditors of the company. This money will be deducted before the floating charge holder is paid.

Furthermore, in certain circumstances, under s 245 of the IA 1986 a floating charge is automatically void and a liquidator or an administrator of an insolvent company can set it aside. This would have the effect of removing the floating charge holder's priority over unsecured creditors of the company (see **19.5.4** below).

11.4.2.5 Book debts

Book debts are, put simply, money which is owed to the company by its debtors. As an asset of the company they may be charged. There has been much confusion over the years as to the type of security which could be taken over them. As book debts vary over time, they are suitable for charging by way of a floating charge; but it may be that they can also be secured by a fixed charge. The House of Lords' decision in *National Westminster Bank plc v Spectrum Plus Limited and Others* [2005] UKHL 41 clarified the difference, and held that book debts could be secured by a fixed charge where the charge holder had control over both the debts and the proceeds once they were paid. This might arise, for example, where the charge holder allowed the company to collect the book debts, but then the company had to pay over the money to the charge holder to settle part of the debt owed by the company. If, on the contrary, the company was able to use the proceeds from the book debts for its business purposes then this would indicate a floating charge.

It is also important to note there that merely calling a charge 'fixed' would not prevent the court from holding it to be floating, and vice versa. The court will look to the substance of the charge and its commercial effect, rather than relying on a description of the charge.

11.4.3 Other security

There are also other types of security or security-like agreements into which a company may enter. These include the following.

11.4.3.1 Guarantee

Strictly, guarantees are not a form of security, but their effect is potentially the same as they offer a lender another source for repayment for a loan if the company itself cannot repay it from its income. Director-shareholders are sometimes required by a lender personally to guarantee a loan to their company. Usually only company money can be used to pay company debts because of the principles of separate legal personality and limited liability (see **2.3** above). However, if the directors give personal guarantees for a loan, they will have to pay the lender whatever amount is outstanding if, for some reason, the lender is unable to recover the loan in full from the company, eg because the company is insolvent. Director-shareholders who do give personal guarantees in this way risk the loss of their personal assets if the company fails, possibly even loss of their homes. A director-shareholder who cannot pay the sum they guaranteed from their own resources may therefore even face personal bankruptcy.

A lender may require the director-shareholders of the company personally to guarantee a loan to the company particularly, but not exclusively, where the company is a small company, or where it is a new company.

11.4.3.2 Pledge

A pledge arises where an asset is physically delivered to serve as security until the debtor has paid their debt. There is a right to sell the asset to settle the debt owed, provided the creditor gives sufficient notice. What is sufficient notice varies according to the circumstances, but it may be agreed by the parties.

11.4.3.3 Lien

A lien is the right to physical possession of the debtor's goods until the debt is paid. There is no right to sell the assets to settle the debt owed. Liens may arise under the common law, in equity or by statute.

A common law lien arises by law and permits the creditor to retain possession of a company's assets until a debt is paid. For example, a garage mechanic has the right to retain one of the company's vans until any repairs have been paid for by the company.

A statutory lien is imposed by statute. For example, a lien arises under s 41 of the Sale of Goods Act 1979. An unpaid seller of goods to a company which are still in their possession may keep them until they have been paid.

11.4.3.4 Retention of title

Under retention of title, in a sale of goods the buyer does not get title to the goods until he pays the full price to the seller. If the buyer defaults then the goods are repossessed by the seller. This is an interest retained by the creditor. Such a clause is not registrable (see **31.8.7**).

11.5 KEY TERMS IN A CHARGING DOCUMENT

11.5.1 Security

This is one of the most important clauses in a charging document. The security might be in the form of a fixed charge or a floating charge, or might be a combination of the two, eg a fixed charge on anything owned by the company over which it is possible to take a fixed charge, and a further floating charge over the whole of the company's undertaking. The specific assets subject to each charge will also be listed.

11.5.2 Representations and warranties

The borrowing company will have to make a series of contractual statements relating to the assets which it is charging. This will be done with the intention of getting the company to reveal all relevant information about the assets. For example, the company will have to warrant that the property is free from any other charge. If there is another charge already over the asset then the company must disclose this or it will breach the contract and also give the lender the right to terminate the loan agreement.

11.5.3 Covenants

The borrowing company will have to make a series of covenants (contractual promises) relating to the assets which it is charging. The covenants will seek to ensure that the value of the assets is maintained by the company, for example by stipulating that the company will conduct proper maintenance and arrange adequate insurance.

11.5.4 Enforcement and powers

The agreement will set out the circumstances in which the security becomes enforceable, for example if the loan payments are not made on time, if provisions of the charging document are breached or if the company gets into financial difficulty.

It will also set out the lender's powers, including the power to sell the assets which are the subject of the charge free from restrictions imposed under the LPA 1925 (which apply to land and other property such as goods), in order to recover the debt due.

The lender will want to have expressly stated its power to appoint an administrator, for example if it is a qualifying floating charge holder (QFCH). If it is a QFCH, the lender will be empowered to appoint an administrator without petitioning the court (see **further 19.7.1.6 below**).

11.6 PROCEDURAL MATTERS FOR ISSUE OF DEBENTURE

It will usually be the directors' decision whether to borrow money in the company's name, and it is they who will negotiate with the lender the terms on which the loan is to be made, including the provision by the company of any security. A resolution of the board of directors will therefore usually be sufficient to authorise both the borrowing by the company and the grant of any security.

However, there may be problems over the ability of the directors to vote and count in the quorum on the resolution to borrow and grant security, particularly where the directors have been asked to guarantee the loan personally. The articles may prevent any director who has a personal interest (possibly all directors) from being involved in the decision to borrow (see **8.4.3 and 8.4.4** above). It may therefore be necessary to call a GM or circulate written resolutions, either to suspend any prohibition in the articles by ordinary resolution or to change the articles by special resolution.

Once the directors have resolved to enter into the loan and grant security, the contracts will be signed in accordance with the CA 2006, which will usually entail signature by two directors or a director and a witness. The directors will also affix the company seal (if the company has one).

11.7 REGISTRATION

The registration regime for charges created by a company under the CA 2006 operates on the basis of a voluntary system of registration. The company or a person 'interested in the charge' may decide to register it. However, because of the consequences of a failure to register a charge in the required time period (for example, the security may become void (see **11.7.1** below)), in practice there is a huge incentive to register.

The CA 2006 specifies that a 'charge' created by a company may be registered. Very limited guidance as to what this means is provided in s 859A, which states that it does include mortgages. There is therefore uncertainty over the full extent of the new regime given the wide range of possible security. Certainly as before, in addition to mortgages, fixed and floating charges over land, ships, aircraft, machinery, book debts, shares and intellectual property will be registrable. It may also be the case that solicitors will attempt to register other types of security previously thought not registrable, such as contractual liens and pledges, out of an abundance of caution. Only time will tell. However, guarantees will not normally need to be registered.

Once the company has formally entered into the agreement containing the charge with the charge holder (be it in a separate document or in a debenture (ie with the loan agreement)), the company or any person interested in the charge will have to deliver:

(a) a s 859D statement of particulars to Companies House (s 859A(2)); and
(b) a certified copy of the instrument creating the charge (s 859A(3)).

A 'person interested in the charge' includes the charge holder. The charge holder is included because it is they who will suffer if the charge is not registered (see **11.7.1** below). Previous practice was for the charge holder's solicitors to deliver the necessary documentation on the company's behalf. This is expected to continue.

The s 859D statement of particulars will in the vast majority of cases be Form MR01 (see **11.10** below or find it on the Companies House website at <www.gov.uk/government/organisations/companies-house>). You will see that there is, as always, very useful guidance on the form itself regarding how to complete it.

The documentation can be submitted in paper form or electronically. There is currently a £24 fee for paper registration and a £15 fee for electronic registration of Form MR01.

A critical point to note is that Form MR01 and the charging document must be submitted to Companies House within 21 days beginning with the day after the day on which the charge was created (CA 2006, s 859A(2) and (4)), together with the fee. There are consequences if registration is not made (see **11.7.1** below) or is made late (see **11.7.2** below).

Once the documents have been delivered, and assuming everything is in order, the Registrar of Companies must register the charge (CA 2006, s 859A(2)). The Registrar must allocate a 12-digit unique reference code to the charge and make a note on the register, and include the certified copy of the charge on the register (CA 2006, s 859I(2)). The Registrar must also give the person who delivered the documents a certificate of registration (CA 2006, s 859I(3)), which (under s 859I(6) of the CA 2006) is conclusive evidence that the charge is properly registered. The Form MR01 and the certified copy of the charging document will be put on the company's file, which is available for public inspection. This information will be particularly useful for future lenders to the company.

If the required documents are correctly delivered on time, the charge will be fully valid against another creditor of the company, or an administrator or a liquidator of the company if it should get into financial difficulties.

A copy of the charging document and Form MR01 should be kept available for inspection (CA 2006, s 859P) at its registered office or SAIL (see **8.11.4** above) (CA 2006, s 859Q). Failure to do this is a criminal offence, but it does not affect the validity of the charge in any way.

If a fixed charge is taken over land then this must also be registered at Land Registry. In other words, a charge involving land must be registered twice – at Companies House and at Land Registry.

If such a charge is not registered at Land Registry, a buyer of the land in question takes free from the fixed charge, even if they actually knew of its existence. The position of a buyer is governed solely by what is apparent from Land Registry documents, even if the fixed charge over the land has been registered at Companies House.

There are also separate registers for charges over specialist assets, such as ships, aircraft and intellectual property rights.

Note that the above describes the position for companies established under English law. Different rules apply to overseas companies with a registered establishment in the UK.

11.7.1 Failure to register at Companies House

Failure to register the charge renders the charge void against a liquidator or an administrator of the company, and also against the company's other creditors (CA 2006, s 859H(3)).

This means in practice that another creditor (ie lender) who registers a charge over the same asset later will take priority over the charge holder of the charge that was not registered. The liquidator or administrator must ignore the original charge in determining how much creditors get and in what order, if the company goes insolvent. This would be disastrous for the original charge holder, of course, as it would lose its priority over the proceeds of sale of the asset. If the failure to register was due to the solicitor's mistake, it could well lead to a claim for negligence.

The security remains valid against the company itself, although the money secured by the charge becomes payable immediately (CA 2006, s 859H(4)).

11.7.2 Late or inaccurate delivery

If the 21-day period for delivery of the required documents is missed (note that weekends and bank holidays are included in the 21 days), or if the details supplied on the form are inaccurate, the same consequences apply as are explained at **11.7.1** above.

There is a limited power under s 859F of the CA 2006 for the court to extend the 21-day period if the failure to deliver the required documents was accidental or due to inadvertence, or if it would not prejudice the position of other creditors or shareholders of the company. If an application is successful, the charge will have priority only from the date of actual registration, and it may therefore lose priority due to the delay if other charges have been registered in the meantime.

In addition to the court's power to order an extension of time, it has power under s 859M to allow rectification of any statement or notice delivered to the Registrar for any inaccurate details, and to order the replacement of a document on the register under s 859N if, for example, the charging document was defective or the wrong document was sent.

An example of registration under the previous law being granted out of time is *Re Chantry House Developments plc* [1990] BCC 646. In this case, a building society was given permission to register a mortgage out of time. There were no other secured lenders. It was held that 'the failure to register was accidental and it was just and equitable to allow late registration to give the building society security that it had contracted for'.

11.7.3 Redemption of the loan

When the loan secured by a registered charge is repaid by the company to the lender, a person with an interest in the registration of the charge (such as a director of the company) may, but is not obliged to, complete, sign and send Form MR04 to the Registrar of Companies at Companies House. In practice, this will be done to ensure the company's file is up to date. The Registrar will include a statement of satisfaction on the company's file. This form should be used even if the charge was registered before 6 April 2013 (the date the new registration regime came into force).

If any entries were made against land at Land Registry, these should now be removed.

11.7.4 Release of charge/sale of property

If, instead of the loan being paid off, the lender decides to release the company's property from the charge or allows the company to sell the asset covered by the charge, a person with an interest in the registration of the charge (such as a director of the company) must complete, sign and send Form MR05 to the Registrar of Companies at Companies House. The Registrar will include a statement, either of release of charge or that the property no longer belongs to the company, on its file.

If any entries were made against land at Land Registry, these should now be removed using Form DS1.

11.8 REMEDIES OF THE DEBENTURE HOLDER

See **19.7.1 below** on administration.

11.9 PRIORITY OF CHARGES

We have seen that more than one charge may attach to the same company asset. Consequently, the priority of creditors over the proceeds of sale of that asset should the company go insolvent (in other words, which creditor gets its money first) is a very important matter. The order of priority is fixed by law.

It is a complex area, but to simplify considerably, provided the charges are all registered properly under s 859A of the CA 2006:

(a) A fixed charge or mortgage will take priority over a floating charge over the same asset, even if the floating charge was created before the fixed charge or mortgage.

(b) If there is more than one fixed charge and mortgage over the same asset, they have priority in order of their date of creation (and not their date of registration).

(c) If there is more than one floating charge over the same asset, they have priority in order of their date of creation (and not their date of registration).

11.9.1 Subordination

It is possible for creditors to enter into an agreement between themselves to alter the order of priority of their charges. This is known as subordination and the agreement is known as a deed of priority; it is executed by the creditors concerned and sometimes the company. This might happen, for example, if the holder of a fixed charge allowed a bank to have priority for its floating charge, without which priority the bank would not advance new funds to allow the borrower to continue to trade.

11.9.2 Negative pledge

We saw at **11.9** above that a floating charge ranks behind a later fixed charge or mortgage over the same asset, provided that later fixed charge or mortgage is properly registered. In order to prevent this from happening, it is usual to include in the floating charge documentation what is called a 'negative pledge' clause. This clause prohibits the company from creating later charges with priority to the floating charge (ie fixed or mortgage) without the floating charge holder's permission. If a subsequent lender takes a charge over the same asset and has actual knowledge of the negative pledge clause then the subsequent lender will be subordinate to the original charge holder (*English and Scottish Mercantile Investment Company Ltd v Brunton* [1892] 2 QB 700).

In practice, therefore, the existence of a negative pledge clause is identified by completing a section of Form MR01 sent to Companies House (see **11.7** above), and the clause itself will be included in the certified copy of the charging document which is delivered to the Registrar. It is important to note that constructive knowledge by the subsequent charge holder may not be enough. There is still uncertainty on this point as it has not been tested in the courts under the CA 2006. However, if the subsequent charge holder conducts a search of the company's records at Companies House (as will usually be the case as part of checking the company's suitability) then it will come across the certified copy of the charging document containing this clause. The subsequent charge holder will therefore have the required *actual* knowledge and will not have priority over the floating charge. It is also possible that the subsequent charge holder will be liable for the tort of inducing breach of contract (*Swiss Bank Corp v Lloyds Bank Ltd* [1979] 2 All ER 853).

In order to protect itself from being in such a situation, the agreement for the subsequent charge should contain a covenant (contractual promise) by the company to the effect that there are no earlier charges which are subject to a negative pledge clause. If this is not true, the company will be in breach of that agreement and it may be terminated immediately.

In accordance with Sections 859A and 859J of the Companies Act 2006.

MR01
Particulars of a charge

Companies House

Go online to file this information
www.gov.uk/companieshouse

A fee is be payable with this form
Please see 'How to pay' on the last page.

✓ **What this form is for**
You may use this form to register a charge created or evidenced by an instrument.

✗ **What this form is NOT for**
You may not use this form to register a charge where there is no instrument. Use form MR08.

For further information, please refer to our guidance at: www.gov.uk/companieshouse

This form **must be delivered to the Registrar for registration within 21 days** beginning with the day after the date of creation of the charge. If delivered outside of the 21 days it will be rejected unless it is accompanied by a court order extending the time for delivery.

You **must** enclose a certified copy of the instrument with this form. This will be scanned and placed on the public record. **Do not send the original.**

1 Company details

For official use

Company number

Company name in full

→ **Filling in this form**
Please complete in typescript or in bold black capitals.

All fields are mandatory unless specified or indicated by *

2 Charge creation date

Charge creation date d d m m y y y y

3 Names of persons, security agents or trustees entitled to the charge

Please show the names of each of the persons, security agents or trustees entitled to the charge.

Name

Name

Name

Name

If there are more than four names, please supply any four of these names then tick the statement below.

☐ I confirm that there are more than four persons, security agents or trustees entitled to the charge.

06/16 Version 2.1

MR01
Particulars of a charge

4 **Brief description**

Please give a short description of any land, ship, aircraft or intellectual property registered or required to be registered in the UK subject to a charge (which is not a floating charge) or fixed security included in the instrument.

Please submit only a short description If there are a number of plots of land, aircraft and/or ships, you should simply describe some of them in the text field and add a statement along the lines of, "for more details please refer to the instrument".

Please limit the description to the available space.

Brief description

5 **Other charge or fixed security**

Does the instrument include a charge (which is not a floating charge) or fixed security over any tangible or intangible or (in Scotland) corporeal or incorporeal property not described above? Please tick the appropriate box.

☐ **Yes**

☐ **No**

6 **Floating charge**

Is the instrument expressed to contain a floating charge? Please tick the appropriate box.

☐ **Yes** Continue

☐ **No** Go to **Section 7**

Is the floating charge expressed to cover all the property and undertaking of the company?

☐ **Yes**

7 **Negative Pledge**

Do any of the terms of the charge prohibit or restrict the company from creating further security that will rank equally with or ahead of the charge?
Please tick the appropriate box.

☐ **Yes**

☐ **No**

8 **Trustee statement** ❶

You may tick the box if the company named in Section 1 is acting as trustee of the property or undertaking which is the subject of the charge.

☐

❶ This statement may be filed after the registration of the charge (use form MR06).

9 **Signature**

Please sign the form here.

Signature

Signature

X X

This form must be signed by a person with an interest in the charge.

MR01
Particulars of a charge

Presenter information

You do not have to give any contact information, but if you do, it will help Companies House if there is a query on the form. The contact information you give will be visible to searchers of the public record.

Contact name

Company name

Address

Post town

County/Region

Postcode

Country

DX

Telephone

Certificate

We will send your certificate to the presenter's address if given above or to the company's Registered Office if you have left the presenter's information blank.

Checklist

We may return forms completed incorrectly or with information missing.

Please make sure you have remembered the following:

- ☐ The company name and number match the information held on the public Register.
- ☐ You have included a certified copy of the instrument with this form.
- ☐ You have entered the date on which the charge was created.
- ☐ You have shown the names of persons entitled to the charge.
- ☐ You have ticked any appropriate boxes in Sections 3, 5, 6, 7 & 8.
- ☐ You have given a description in Section 4, if appropriate.
- ☐ You have signed the form.
- ☐ You have enclosed the correct fee.
- ☐ Please do not send the original instrument; it must be a certified copy.

Important information

Please note that all information on this form will appear on the public record.

How to pay

A fee of £23 is payable to Companies House in respect of each mortgage or charge filed on paper.

Make cheques or postal orders payable to 'Companies House.'

Where to send

You may return this form to any Companies House address. However, for expediency, we advise you to return it to the appropriate address below:

For companies registered in England and Wales:
The Registrar of Companies, Companies House,
Crown Way, Cardiff, Wales, CF14 3UZ.
DX 33050 Cardiff.

For companies registered in Scotland:
The Registrar of Companies, Companies House,
Fourth floor, Edinburgh Quay 2,
139 Fountainbridge, Edinburgh, Scotland, EH3 9FF.
DX ED235 Edinburgh 1
or LP - 4 Edinburgh 2 (Legal Post).

For companies registered in Northern Ireland:
The Registrar of Companies, Companies House,
Second Floor, The Linenhall, 32-38 Linenhall Street,
Belfast, Northern Ireland, BT2 8BG.
DX 481 N.R. Belfast 1.

Further information

For further information, please see the guidance notes on the website at www.gov.uk/companieshouse or email enquiries@companieshouse.gov.uk

This form is available in an alternative format. Please visit the forms page on the website at www.gov.uk/companieshouse

This form has been provided free of charge by Companies House. 06/16 Version 2.1

CHAPTER 12

PUBLIC COMPANIES

LEARNING OUTCOMES

After reading this chapter you will be able to:

- explain what a public company is and how it is formed
- compare the advantages and disadvantages of becoming a public company
- understand the differences between public and private companies.

12.1 WHAT IS A PUBLIC COMPANY?

A public company is defined by s 4(2) of the CA 2006. It is a company limited by shares or by guarantee and having a share capital, which has complied with the requirements of the CA 2006 to enable it to be registered or re-registered as such. As we saw at **1.9.3** above, public companies are far less numerous in practice, and usually far larger in size than their private counterparts.

How a company can achieve this public company status is explained at **12.4** below.

12.2 ADVANTAGES OF PUBLIC COMPANY STATUS

Why would an entrepreneur set up a public company rather than a private company?

12.2.1 Ability to offer shares to the public

Under s 755 of the CA 2006, it is prohibited for a private company to offer its shares to the public. The main reason for registering or re-registering as a public company, therefore, is to enable a company to offer its shares to the public. This provides a company with a new source of finance (the consideration received for the shares) and opens up new opportunities for raising finance which might otherwise be unavailable to the company.

If s 755 is breached, a court has the power to re-register the offending private company as a public one under s 758 of the Act. If the company does not meet the requirements to become a public company, however, the court either may order that the company is wound up (s 758), or it may make a remedial order under s 759 of the Act. The remedial order seeks to put a person affected by a breach of s 755 back into the position they were in before the breach. The court has wide-ranging powers to achieve this. The application to court for a s 758 or s 759 order may be made by a shareholder or creditor of the offending company, or by the Secretary of State for DBT.

12.2.2 Prestige

A secondary reason for a company to register or re-register as a public company is to benefit from the prestige conferred by the letters 'plc' ('public limited company'). Public limited companies are generally larger in size and enjoy a higher profile in the business world in the UK. They are also subject to tighter regulation than private companies, which means they may offer more protection to shareholders. Some companies therefore opt for public company status even if they have no immediate plans to offer shares to the public. Subsidiaries of public companies are often public companies too, for the same reason.

12.2.3 Publicly-traded company

Only a public limited company can become listed on the Main Market of the London Stock Exchange or quoted on AIM. This is because such companies offer shares to the public at large. If a private company is growing fast and needs to access the huge pool of money available from the public, it will often seek to become publicly traded, and therefore must first become a public company (see **1.9.3.1** to **1.9.3.3** above for further information on publicly-traded companies).

12.3 POTENTIAL DISADVANTAGES OF PUBLIC COMPANY STATUS

As noted at **12.2.1** above, public company status brings with it the financial advantage of being able to offer shares to the public, and a certain element of commercial respectability. However, these advantages mean (in theory at least) that any public company may be owned by members of the public who have little day-to-day involvement in the company's business, and who therefore require greater statutory protection than the owners of a private company who typically are more involved in the running of their companies, often as directors. For this reason, public companies are much more strictly regulated than private companies. This will add to the cost of running the company, and may restrict what it wishes to do and how it seeks to operate. **Table 12.1** below summarises the main differences between the regulation of public limited companies and that of private limited companies.

Table 12.1 Regulation of public companies compared to private companies

	Public company	*Private company*
Accounts	Must file with Companies House within 6 months after end of accounting reference period (CA 2006, s 442(2)(b)).	Must file within 9 months after end of accounting reference period (CA 2006, s 442(2)(a)).
	Must file full accounts with Companies House (CA 2006, ss 446 and 447; ss 384 and 467). Accounts must be laid before a GM no later than 6 months after end of accounting reference period (CA 2006, s 437).	Requirements to file full accounts may be relaxed for micro-entities, small and medium-sized companies (CA 2006, ss 444 and 445). No requirement to do so. *The Economic Crime and Corporate Transparency Act 2023 will change the authority for micro-entities' filing requirement to a new s 443A.*
Administration	Must hold an Annual General Meeting (AGM) every year (CA 2006, s 336).	No requirement to hold an AGM unless articles require it (SI 2007/2194, Sch 3, para 32(11)).
	The requisite percentage for holding a GM on short notice is 95% (CA 2006, s 307(6)(b)). Cannot use the written resolution procedure (CA 2006, s 288).	The requisite percentage for holding a general meeting on short notice is 90% (CA 2006, s 307(6)(a)). Can use the written resolution procedure (CA 2006, s 288).

	Public company	*Private company*
Directors	Minimum of 2 (CA 2006, s 154(2)).	Minimum of 1 (CA 2006, s 154(1)).
	Restrictions apply on voting for the appointment of more than one director in just one resolution (CA 2006, s 160).	No equivalent restriction applies.
	A public company may make a quasi-loan and a credit transaction with one of its directors only provided prior shareholder approval has been obtained (CA 2006, ss 198 and 201).	The need for shareholder approval for quasi-loans and credit transactions with a director will be required only if the private company is 'associated with a public company', as defined in CA 2006, s 256 (CA 2006, ss 198(1) and 201(1)).
Financial assistance	Prohibited (CA 2006, s 678), subject to CA 2006, ss 681 and 682. See **Chapter 9**.	Generally permitted. Restrictions apply to private companies which are subsidiaries of public companies.
Secretary	A secretary is required (CA 2006, s 271). Section 273 sets out the qualifications required.	A secretary is not compulsory (CA 2006, s 270(1)). If a company chooses to have one, there are no qualification requirements.
Share capital	The company must have allotted share capital at least up to the value of the authorised minimum [currently £50,000 – the CA 2006, s 763 permits a euro equivalent to this amount, set at €57,100 (SI 2009/2425)] to register (CA 2006, s 761) or re-register (CA 2006, s 91(1)). The company must maintain this as its minimum share capital (CA 2006, ss 650 and 662).	No restriction on allotted share capital.
	Each share allotted must be paid up to at least one-quarter of its nominal value together with the whole of any premium on it (CA 2006, s 586).	No equivalent restriction applies. Shares may be allotted nil paid, partly paid or fully paid.
	Section 561 pre-emption rights on allotment may be disapplied under s 570 or s 571 by special resolution, or excluded and replaced by articles conferring a corresponding right under s 568.	Section 561 pre-emption rights on allotment may be disapplied under s 569 (by special resolution or provision in the articles), under s 570 or 571 by special resolution, or excluded under s 567 (by provision in the articles).

	Public company	Private company
	Restrictions apply on consideration for allotment of shares (ss 585, 587 and 598).	These sections do not apply.
	Valuer's report required to value non-cash consideration for the allotment of shares (s 593).	No equivalent requirement applies.
	GM required in the event of a serious loss of capital (s 656).	No equivalent requirement applies.
	Charges on own shares are void, subject to certain exceptions (s 670).	Subject to certain requirements in s 670(2), charges on own shares are permitted.
	May redeem and purchase shares out of distributable profits or the proceeds of a fresh issue, but not out of capital (ss 687 and 692).	May redeem and purchase shares out of distributable profits, the proceeds of a fresh issue, or out of capital (ss 687 and 692).
Shareholders	Must disclose certain information to the company under DTR 5 of the Disclosure and Transparency Rules, the UK version of the Market Abuse Regulation and CA 2006, Part 22.	No equivalent restrictions apply.
Takeovers of another company	Subject to the City Code on Takeovers and Mergers.	Typically not subject to the Takeover Code (but it may apply in very limited circumstances).

Furthermore, if the public company becomes a publicly-traded company then it will become subject to yet further regulation. Additional restrictions may apply under the CA 2006, as will a whole series of additional statutory and regulatory rules. A public company quoted on AIM becomes subject to the AIM Rules, which may be found on the London Stock Exchange's website at <http://www. londonstockexchange.com>. A public company listed on the Main Market of the London Stock Exchange is subject to the Financial Services and Markets Act (FSMA) 2000 and a variety of rules, including those in the FCA's Handbook (particularly the UK Listing Rules, the Prospectus Regulation Rules, and the Disclosure Guidance and Transparency Rules, which may be found on the FCA's website at <www.handbook.fca.org.uk/handbook>) and the UK Corporate Governance Code (which is available at <http://www.frc.org.uk>).

New Prospectus Rules: Admission to a Regulated Market (PRMs) will replace the Prospectus Regulation Rules in early 2026.

12.4 ACHIEVING PUBLIC COMPANY STATUS

A company may achieve public company status in two ways:

(a) by registering as a public company on original incorporation; or

(b) by registering as a private company on original incorporation then re-registering as a public company.

The procedures under (a) and (b) ensure that the resulting public company complies with the CA 2006 requirements relating to a public company's articles, name and share capital.

12.4.1 Incorporation of a company

Under s 9 of the CA 2006, the following must be sent to the Registrar of Companies to incorporate any company, private or public:

(a) memorandum of association (in the form set out in Sch 1 to the Companies (Registration) Regulations 2008 (SI 2008/3014));

(b) an application for registration (Form IN01) containing:

   (i) a statement that the subscribers wish to form the company for lawful purposes (as required by s 9(2)(e));

   (ii) a statement of the intended appropriate registered email address of the company (as required by s 9(5)(aa));

   (iii) a statement of share capital and initial shareholding (content requirements set out in s 10),

   (iv) a statement of initial significant control (content requirements set out in s 12A),

   (v) a statement of the proposed first officers of the company (content requirements set out in s 12),

   (vi) a statement of the intended registered office,

   (vii) copy articles of association (unless the new model articles for public companies are adopted unamended), and

   (viii) a statement of compliance that all requirements of the CA 2006 have been met (further requirements set out in s 13); and

(c) a registration fee.

The Economic Crime and Corporate Transparency Act 2023 will require additional statements in the application for registration once the relevant provisions have been brought into force:

(i) of each of the subscribers to the memorandum of association's forename, surname and address for service of documents (as required by new ss 9(3A) and 9A); and

(ii) that none of the subscribers to the memorandum of association is disqualified under the directors disqualification legislation (as required by a new s 9(4)(e)).

These changes are expected to come into force by 2027.

12.4.2 Registration as a public company on original incorporation

In addition to sending the documents referred to at **12.4.1** above to the Registrar of Companies, the following extra requirements apply if it is wished to register the company as a public company on original incorporation:

(a) *Articles.* The articles must be in a form suitable for a public company. Under s 20 of the CA 2006, on registration of a public company a default set of model articles will apply, save to the extent that they are excluded or modified. These public company model articles may be found in Sch 3 to the Companies (Model Articles) Regulations 2008 (SI 2008/3229). The new model articles for a public company limited by shares are more comprehensive than those for a private company and are laid out as shown in **Table 12.2** following.

   Note that as with a private company, a public company may adopt unamended model articles, amended model articles or bespoke articles (see **4.3** above).

(b) *Name.* The company name must end with 'public limited company' or the Welsh equivalent (CA 2006, s 58), or with the abbreviation 'plc' or its Welsh equivalent 'ccc' (s 58(2)). Note that the rules relating to the company name as set out at **3.5** above apply equally to public companies.

(c) *Allotted share capital.* The allotted share capital of the company must be not less than the 'authorised minimum' (CA 2006, s 761(2)). Currently the authorised minimum is £50,000 (s 763). In addition, each share allotted must be paid up to at least one-quarter of its nominal value together with the whole of any premium on it (s 586). See further **12.4.2.2** below.

12.4.2.1 Certificate of incorporation

If the company meets all the requirements set out at **12.4.1** and **12.4.2** above, it will be able to obtain a certificate from the Registrar of Companies that the company has been registered as a public company on original incorporation. However, although this certificate of incorporation will prove that the public company exists (CA 2006, s 15(1)), and details of the company will now be recorded at Companies House, the public company needs to obtain one other certificate before it can commence business – a trading certificate.

Table 12.2 Model articles for a public company limited by shares

Article numbers	*Subject*
1	defined terms
2	the limitation of the liability of members
3–6	directors' powers and responsibilities
7–19	decision-making by directors, including general rules for voting, and use of alternate directors
20–24	appointment of directors, including retirement by rotation
25–27	alternate directors
28–33	organisation of general meetings
34–40	voting at general meetings, including demanding a poll and procedure on a poll vote
41	restrictions on members' rights
42	class meetings (for the holders of different classes of shares)
43–45	shares, including – issuing different classes of shares, – payment of commission on subscription for shares, and – company not bound by less than absolute interests
46–49	share certificates
50–51	shares not held in certificated form, share warrants
63–68	transfer and transmission of shares, both certificated and uncertificated
69	consolidation of shares
70–77	dividends and other distributions
78	capitalisation of profits
79–84	means of communication, company seals, no right to inspect accounts, and provisions for employees on cessation of business
85–86	indemnity and insurance for directors

12.4.2.2 Trading certificate

A company which has been registered as a public company on original incorporation must not begin business or exercise any borrowing powers until it has a trading certificate, issued under s 761 of the CA 2006, confirming that the company has met the *allotted share capital* requirements of the CA 2006 (see **12.4.2** above at (c)). The certificate is proof that the company is able to trade and borrow. To obtain this certificate, an application must be made (accompanied by a statement of compliance) on Form SH50 (available on the Companies House website <www.gov.uk/government/organisations/companies-house>) to the Companies Registrar under s 762 of the 2006 Act.

The allotted share capital requirements are that the company must have allotted shares at least up to the value of the authorised minimum (CA 2006, s 761), which, as stated in **12.4.2** above, is currently £50,000 (s 763) or the euro equivalent (currently €57,100 under the Companies

(Authorised Minimum) Regulations 2009 (SI 2009/2425)). Each allotted share must be paid up to at least one-quarter of its nominal value together with the whole of any premium on it (CA 2006, s 586).

What does this mean in practice? If 50,000 shares with a nominal value of £1 each are allotted at nominal value with no premium, the minimum consideration which must be paid to the company is one-quarter of the nominal value of each share, that is 0.25p per share, making a total minimum payment of £12,500 for 50,000 shares. If, however, the shares are allotted for, say, £3 each, then each share has a premium (the amount by which the price exceeds the nominal value) of £2. This premium must be paid to the company together with a minimum of a quarter of the nominal value of each share, which is £2 plus 0.25p, that is £2.25 per share, making a total minimum payment of £112,500 for 50,000 shares.

12.4.3 Re-registration as a public company

A company which has registered as a private company on original incorporation (by complying with the requirements detailed at **12.4.1** above) may re-register as a public company pursuant to ss 90–96 of the CA 2006. The company must pass a special resolution at a GM or by written resolution, meet the specified conditions and submit an application in a prescribed form to the Registrar of Companies (s 90(1)).

12.4.3.1 Resolution

The special (or written) resolution must:

(a) approve the re-registration of the company (s 90(1)(a));

(b) alter the company's name so that it is in a form suitable for a public company. Section 58(1) of the CA 2006 requires that the name must end with 'public limited company' or 'plc' (or the Welsh equivalent – s 58(2)); and

(c) alter the articles so that they are in a form suitable for a public company. It is probable that the existing private company articles will require substantial amendment; it is often easier to adopt an entirely new set of articles rather than to amend the existing articles. If the company is re-registering as a public company as a preliminary step to becoming a publicly-traded company in the immediate future, it may be appropriate to adopt a set of articles suitable not only for a public company but also for a public company whose shares are traded on a stock market. In this case the articles will probably disapply the public company model articles in their entirety and will be bespoke.

12.4.3.2 Share capital requirements

The resolution deals with the requirements as to a public company's articles and name. What about the share capital requirements of a public company? These are dealt with by s 90(2) of the CA 2006. *At the time the shareholders pass the special resolution* (see **12.4.3.1** above) the company must have satisfied certain conditions as to its share capital, namely, that the company must have allotted shares at least up to the value of the authorised minimum (s 91(1)(a)), which is currently £50,000 (s 763) or the euro equivalent (currently €57,100) and that each allotted share must be paid up to at least one-quarter of its nominal value together with the whole of any premium on it (s 91(1)(b)).

These requirements reflect those which must be satisfied when a company originally incorporated as a public company applies for a trading certificate (see **12.4.2.2** above). A trading certificate therefore is not required for a private company which re-registers as a public company; the certificate of incorporation is all the company needs.

Note that s 91(1)(c) and (d) of the CA 2006 provide some further requirements as to shares which have been allotted in consideration of an undertaking by a person to perform work, for example for the company. Note also that some shares may be disregarded for the purposes of satisfying the share capital requirements (see CA 2006, s 91(2), (3) and (4)).

12.4.3.3 Application for re-registration

The special resolution must be delivered to the Registrar of Companies, together with an application for re-registration on Form RR01 (available on the Companies House website <www.gov.uk/government/organisations/companies-house>) which has been signed by a director, the company secretary or a person authorised by the directors under s 270 or s 274 of the CA 2006. If the existing private company does not have a company secretary, one must be appointed and details included in the application. This is because under s 271 of the CA 2006, a public company must have a company secretary, whereas this is not a requirement for a private company (see **6.2** above). The application must be accompanied by the fee for re-registration (currently £71, together with £30 for any change of name (the change of name fee does not arise if it is just 'Limited' changing to 'PLC'; the fee will arise only if the name change is more substantial); currently re-registration cannot be done electronically, only by using paper forms) and the following documents:

(a) the revised articles (CA 2006, s 94(2)(b));

(b) a balance sheet prepared not more than seven months before the application, containing an unqualified report by the company's auditors (CA 2006, s 94(2)(c) and s 92(1)). If the company's accounting reference date is within this seven-month period, this requirement may be met by the end of year balance sheet; if not, then an interim balance sheet must be prepared and must be audited, which can prove time-consuming and expensive. The auditors must also provide a written statement regarding the level of the company's net assets (as revealed by the balance sheet) in comparison to the company's called-up share capital and undistributable reserves (CA 2006, s 92(1)(c));

(c) a valuation report on any shares which have been allotted for non-cash consideration between the date of the balance sheet (referred to at (b) above) and the date the special resolution was passed (CA 2006, s 93(1)(a) and s 93(2)(a)). This ensures that a private company seeking to re-register is brought into line with the general requirement under s 593 of the CA 2006 that public companies seeking to allot shares for non-cash consideration must have such consideration valued before allotting the shares; and

(d) a statement of compliance in the prescribed form (CA 2006, s 90(1)(c)(ii)). This forms part of Form RR01.

12.4.3.4 Certificate of re-registration on incorporation as a public company

If the Registrar of Companies is satisfied with the application, the Registrar will issue the company with a certificate of re-registration on incorporation as a public company (CA 2006, s 96). The private company becomes a public company, and the revised articles and change of name will take effect on the issue of this certificate, which is proof of public company status.

12.4.3.5 Trading disclosures

The Companies (Trading Disclosures) Regulations 2008 (SI 2008/495), made under s 82 of the CA 2006, which set out the requirements for a company to identify itself at certain locations (including any place of business), on certain documents (including letters and order forms) and on its websites (see **3.18.2** above), apply equally to public companies. Breach of these requirements may result in a fine for the company and any officer of the company who is in default. The company must therefore update its websites and order new signs and company documentation, which will reflect its new identity, in advance of re-registration to ensure that it is able to meet these requirements with effect from the date the certificate of incorporation on re-registration is issued.

12.5 PRACTICAL DIFFERENCES BETWEEN PUBLIC AND PRIVATE COMPANIES

In addition to the legal differences between a private and a public company (see **Table 12.1** above) there are some important practical differences.

In a private company the directors and shareholders are often substantially the same persons, which generally allows for quicker decision-making and more streamlined administration. In a public company there will usually be a significant difference in personnel between the shareholders (who may well include specialist institutional investors such as banks, pension funds and insurance companies) and the directors (whose position is more like that of employees who are paid to manage the business). The directors of a public company will therefore need to spend more time communicating with the shareholders to inform them of their strategy for the company, and company administration is generally more onerous as the short-cuts for private companies are usually not available.

In a private company the shareholders usually cannot sell their shares easily because the articles of association tend to contain restrictions on transfer (often in the form of directors' power of veto on the registration of the transfer, such as art 26(5) of the model articles for private companies limited by shares – see **9.9.2** above) and because of difficulties of valuation, given that there is no ready market for these shares. In a public company there is less likely to be any restriction on transfer as there is usually a broader range of shareholder. If the public company has its shares admitted to the Main Market of the London Stock Exchange or AIM, there can be no restriction on the transfer of shares.

A private company may, or may not, choose to pay dividends to its shareholders in any given year in which it makes a profit. However, a public company, particularly one which is publicly traded, needs to have a record of paying dividends every year when it is profitable in order to encourage investors to buy shares in that company.

PART III

RUNNING A BUSINESS IN PARTNERSHIP

When a business is run by a partnership, the relationships between the key players are less formalised than within companies.

This Part considers how and on what terms a partnership may be established, the ongoing implications of being in partnership, both as regards fellow partners and as regards debts of the business, and how a partner may retire from or break up the partnership.

This Part is also applicable to a partnership formed by two or more companies to undertake a joint venture.

CHAPTER 13

THE START OF A PARTNERSHIP

LEARNING OUTCOMES

After reading this chapter you will be able to:

- identify when a partnership exists and what it is
- explain the formalities for setting up a partnership.

13.1 INTRODUCTION

Where two or more persons wish to establish a business relationship between themselves without becoming a company, partnership is only one of a number of possibilities. Other possibilities include the relationships of employer and employee, principal and agent, franchisor and franchisee.

The chapters which follow deal with the law of partnerships. The principal Act is the Partnership Act 1890 ('PA 1890'), though partnership as such existed long before this Act. The Act was drafted to deal with a collection of human beings who were in business together, in effect regulated by a contract, written or oral. One of the main advantages of partnership is a lack of formality which was an even more important advantage in the past, as formation of a new company in the nineteenth century used to be very difficult.

Where there are documents governing relations within a partnership (and there is no obligation to have such documents), that documentation can be kept away from the public gaze as there are no disclosure requirements for partnerships, but there are such requirements for companies.

13.2 WHAT IS A PARTNERSHIP?

13.2.1 Definition

A partnership arises where two or more persons agree that they will run a business together and actually do so. The term 'partnership' therefore describes no more than a business relationship based on an agreement (ie contract). The agreement may be oral or in writing, or may even be implied by conduct. A partnership need not necessarily be recognised as such by the parties since the existence of a partnership depends on whether or not the definition contained in s 1 of the PA 1890 applies. By this section, 'partnership is the relation which subsists between persons carrying on a business in common with a view of profit'. An example of s 1 is the case of *Khan v Miah* [2000] 1 WLR 2123, where the House of Lords held that the partnership in that case had commenced, even though the restaurant in question had not opened before the partnership between the parties had broken down. In *Young v Zahid* [2006] EWCA Civ 613, a partner in a law firm who was paid only a fixed salary, and not a share of the profits, was held to be a 'partner' under s 1. In other words, in both cases, the s 1 definition decided when the partnership commenced, not any agreement to the contrary between the parties. In *Rowlands v Hodson* [2009] EWCA Civ 1042, a solicitor who had sold her interest in the partnership to a successor, but who had retained a supervisory role in order to satisfy Law Society requirements, was held to be a partner and to be liable, therefore, for the debts of the partnership.

There must be more than mere agreement or setting up a partnership to form a partnership (*Ilott v Williams & Others* [2013] EWCA Civ 645). There must be the 'carrying on a business in common'. This means that two or more persons share responsibility for the business and for decisions which affect the business; in effect, that there are two or more proprietors. In contrast, an employer and their employee may be running a business together, but this will not mean that they are partners. The employee must accept the decisions and instructions of their employer, and they have no right to interfere.

It is important to realise at the outset that the partnership does **not** have a separate legal existence. In contrast, a company does have such a separate legal existence.

A partnership may be created:

(a) for a specific purpose or for a pre-determined period of time; or
(b) so as to continue without reference to duration – a partnership 'at will'.

The 'persons' in partnership would usually be people, but they could be two or more companies. This might be the case where companies form a joint venture, often specifically to take on a new project.

In order to be able to identify a particular relationship as being a partnership, it is necessary to appreciate the fundamental characteristics of a partnership.

13.2.2 Fundamental characteristics

Typical rights and responsibilities of partners which are fundamental to the relationship include:

(a) the right to be involved in making decisions which affect the business;
(b) the right to share in the profits of the business;
(c) the right to examine the accounts of the business;
(d) the right to insist on openness and honesty from fellow partners;
(e) the right to veto the introduction of a new partner; and
(f) the responsibility for sharing any losses made by the business.

Theoretically, any or all of these fundamental characteristics may be varied or excluded by the agreement governing the relationship, although at some point variations or exclusions could go as far as to deny the existence of the partnership.

13.3 SETTING UP A PARTNERSHIP

Since the existence of a partnership is established by applying the definition to the relationship (which may be based on an oral agreement), it follows that there is no necessary formality. However, a written agreement is invaluable as evidence of the relationship and of its terms. It is also useful for the partners to have a written 'constitution' to which they may refer. It may, amongst other things, provide solutions to possible disagreements or disputes and thus perhaps avoid future litigation. Indeed in *Ham v Ham & Another* [2013] EWCA Civ 1301, the Court of Appeal criticised poorly drafted partnership agreements and stated that it was to be hoped that in future those preparing partnership agreements would take note of the anxiety, expense and delay caused by imprecise drafting. That particular case, which arose out of one of the partners leaving, could have been avoided if the partnership agreement had clearly addressed the issue. It also helps in ensuring that the undesired aspects of the PA 1890 have been in fact avoided. Typical terms of a partnership agreement are considered in **Chapter 14**.

13.4 FORMALITIES REQUIRED BY STATUTE

13.4.1 Business names

Where ss 1192–1206 of the CA 2006 apply, there are controls over the choice of partnership name (ss 1193, 1194), and requirements as to revealing the names and business address of the partners (s 1201). These controls and requirements will not apply, however, if the name of the partnership business consists simply of the names of the partners, because the Act itself will not then apply. For example, if Paula Jones and Alan Burns commence business in partnership, the following business names will not be subject to the Act: 'Jones and Burns', 'P Jones and A Burns', 'Paula Jones and Alan Burns'. Conversely, if they choose one of the following business names, they will be subject to the Act: 'P Jones', 'Jones, Burns & Co', 'JB Services'.

If the Act applies, certain words or expressions forming part of the business name will require the written approval of the Secretary of State for Business, Energy and Industrial Strategy (and possibly the prior approval of another relevant body). These include words or expressions contained in the Company, Limited Liability Partnership and Business Names (Sensitive Words and Expressions) Regulation 2014 (SI 2014/3140). In addition, prescribed information must appear on all stationery (s 1202) and on a notice at any place of business to which customers or suppliers have access (s 1204). This information consists of the names of the partners and (for each partner) an address in Great Britain for service of documents. Non-compliance with the obligations is an offence punishable by a fine, and the partners will be unable to enforce contracts if the other party can show that that party was prejudiced by the non-compliance (ss 1205, 1206).

In some partnerships, it would be unrealistic to comply with the legislation requirements for stating partners' names on stationery. There is no limitation on the size of a partnership. It is provided, therefore, that the partnership may instead include on its stationery a statement that a full list of partners is available at the principal place of business (s 1203).

13.4.2 Other statutory obligations

Other statutory obligations which may arise at the start of a partnership are not peculiar to partnerships and may arise at the start of any business. These include obligations concerning income tax (or corporation tax, where the partners in a joint venture are companies), VAT and National Insurance. A partnership will have the additional obligation, in this context, of notifying HMRC of the identity of the partners.

13.5 THE LAW OF PARTNERSHIP AND ITS USE IN JOINT VENTURES

Partnership may be a suitable vehicle for a group of individuals to engage in a business venture together because of the informal nature of partnerships, the commercial secrecy that is possible, and the ability for the partners to claim tax relief for start-up losses. However, these attributes can also serve to make partnership a suitable vehicle for two or more companies which wish to combine forces to start a new venture together, perhaps in a new country or in a new field of technology. Although the partners are companies, not human beings, the law is still the same, primarily the PA 1890, even though the Act was not drafted with that situation in mind. This situation of 'old' law being used for a 'new' factual situation is a recurring theme in English law. You will come across this type of situation throughout your legal career.

CHAPTER 14

THE PARTNERSHIP AGREEMENT

LEARNING OUTCOMES

After reading this chapter you will be able to:

- understand the role, content and format of a partnership agreement
- understand the legal rules governing key elements of a partnership
- explain the methods of leaving a partnership.

14.1 INTRODUCTION

Section 24 of the PA 1890 contains a number of provisions concerning the running of the partnership that will be implied into a partnership agreement in the absence of express provision. However, the Act is rather limited in scope and inevitably cannot do more than treat all partners equally. The length of a partnership agreement will depend on the imagination and thoroughness of the partners and their advisers. The following range of topics gives some idea of the possible provisions of a comprehensive agreement, although there will always be scope for additional provisions. Do not forget that the Partnership Act is over 130 years old and cannot be expected to meet modern business practices, so many of its terms will need to be varied by the agreement between the parties.

14.2 COMMENCEMENT DATE

The existence of a partnership is established when the statutory definition in s 1 of the PA 1890 is satisfied. The date specified in the agreement will not necessarily be correct therefore, but it is desirable to specify a date from which the parties regard their mutual rights and responsibilities as taking effect.

14.3 NAME

The name of the partnership should be stated since this means that it is fixed and any partner can insist as a matter of contract on there being no change to it. The firm name may be different from the business (or trading) name (see **3.5.7** above), in which case both names should be stated in the agreement.

14.4 FINANCIAL INPUT

Each partner is likely to be putting capital into the business, whether this is the result of borrowing or from their own resources. This is one of the ways in which the partnership will finance the purchase of assets needed to run the business. The agreement should state how much capital each partner is contributing and, possibly, deal with the question of future increases in contributions, if such increases are anticipated.

14.5 SHARES IN INCOME PROFITS/LOSSES

Partners may be content to share income profits of the business equally. Indeed, if there is no evidence of contrary agreement, this will be the effect of the PA 1890 which will imply such a term. Any losses may also be shared equally. Again, this will be implied by the PA 1890 if there is no evidence of contrary agreement. In practice, the circumstances will often suggest that a different, more detailed, basis for division of profits is appropriate. The partnership agreement may provide for various possibilities in dividing profits, including the following.

14.5.1 Salary

Salaries of differing fixed amounts might be appropriate before any surplus profit is divided between the partners. Their purpose is to ensure that certain factors are reflected in the partners' incomes. These factors might include different amounts of time devoted to the business (eg allowing for a part-time or even a sleeping partner) and the different degrees of skill and experience of the partners.

14.5.2 Interest

Interest (at a specified rate) might be allowed on partners' capital contributions, again before any surplus profit is divided between the partners. This is simply to reward partners in proportion to their contribution to the financing of the partnership.

14.5.3 Profit-sharing

A suitable ratio in which the profits remaining after salaries and interest on capital are to be shared should be stated. If salaries and interest on capital have achieved sufficient 'fine tuning', then equal shares may be appropriate. On the other hand, the longer-serving partner or partners may negotiate for a higher share to reflect, for example, seniority in the business.

Any provisions of this kind in the agreement should also state what is to happen in the event of a loss. In particular, are salaries and interest on capital still to be awarded, thus exacerbating a loss?

14.6 DRAWINGS

One source of future ill-feeling and possible dispute between partners is the amount of money that they each withdraw from the business from time to time in respect of their shares of the profits. One partner may be conservative, wishing to maintain a healthy bank balance for the partnership, while another is more cavalier in their attitude. Often a partnership agreement will state a monthly limit on how much each partner can withdraw, perhaps with provision for periodic review. The clause may also stipulate the consequences of exceeding the stated limit.

In a joint venture agreement between companies, the way in which losses or profits are dealt with will be a key consideration.

14.7 SHARES IN INCREASES/DECREASES IN ASSET VALUES

If a fixed asset of the partnership (such as premises) is sold, realising an increase or a decrease in its value, how is this to be shared between the partners? If the assets are revalued, without the disposal, to show their current value in the accounts (eg in anticipation of a new person joining the partnership), how is this increase/decrease to be reflected in the value of each existing partner's share in the business, as shown in the accounts? Partners may be content to share these increases/decreases equally and, as with income, this will be the effect of PA 1890 which will imply such a term if there is no agreement to the contrary. However, as with income, there may be circumstances where the partners would agree a different basis for division. In particular, if there is disparity in capital contributions, the partner who contributes the greater share of the capital may feel that they should receive the greater share of any gain. The basis for division of increases (or decreases) in asset values is sometimes known as the 'asset-surplus sharing ratio'. As with all aspects of any agreement, this provision will be a matter for negotiation and the other partners may feel that, if interest on capital is to be allowed (as in **14.5.2**), this provides sufficient recognition of the disparity in contributions.

14.8 PLACE AND NATURE OF BUSINESS

The agreement may contain clauses which describe the premises at which the business will be carried on, the geographical area of its operations and the nature of the business which will be carried on. Once agreed, any change would need the unanimous consent of the partners.

14.9 OWNERSHIP OF ASSETS

A partnership asset is an asset where beneficial ownership rests with all the partners, although not necessarily in equal shares. Many disputes have arisen over the factual question of what is a partnership asset and what belongs to a partner individually. This may arise as a result of the partnership being formed where certain assets which are to be used by the business (eg freehold premises or a lease of premises) already belong to one of the persons who is becoming a partner and there is no clear agreement as to what was intended as to ownership. That partner could have continued to own the asset personally (allowing the firm the use of the asset) or the asset could have become partnership property, either by its value representing a capital contribution from that partner or by that partner receiving payment from the others. Equally, a dispute may arise over an asset which has been acquired during the partnership where there was no clear agreement (either express or implied) as to the partners' intentions as to ownership.

In many instances no dispute will arise because there will be evidence of what was intended. Title deeds may indicate who was the owner, but these need not be conclusive since one partner may have legal title in their sole name whilst holding as trustee for all the partners beneficially so that the asset is in fact a partnership asset. The accounts of the partnership should reveal what capital contributions have been made and should correspondingly record what are the assets of the partnership, but these may not be conclusive evidence. To avoid the possibility of there being a dispute over the available evidence or no clear evidence, the agreement should stipulate what are the assets of the partnership (eg by referring to a list contained in a schedule to the agreement).

If there is a dispute, what circumstances are likely to trigger it? The dispute may arise on dissolution when it becomes necessary to establish how much each partner is entitled to receive. The value of an asset owned by just one partner will not be shared. It may be that a profit is made out of a particular asset. A profit on an asset owned by just one partner will not be shared. Any or all of the partners may incur liability to capital gains tax or inheritance tax by reference to a particular asset and wish to claim certain reliefs. Liability to tax and the availability or amount of certain reliefs will depend on whether the asset is or is not a partnership asset.

For an unusual problem on partnership property, see *Don King Productions Inc v Warren (No 1)* [2000] Ch 291, where the property was contracts relating to boxing.

14.10 WORK INPUT

The PA 1890 will imply a term into a partnership agreement, in the absence of contrary agreement, that all partners are entitled to take part in the management of the business, albeit without any obligation to do so. There is no implication that a partner must devote their full time and attention to the business. Wilful neglect of the business (as opposed to a degree of laziness) may mean that the other partners are entitled to be compensated for the extra work undertaken by them.

The agreement should set out the degree of commitment expected of each partner. The term might require the partner to work in the business full-time or part-time or even not work at all (being a dormant or sleeping partner). To express these degrees of work with precision in terms of fixed hours of work may well be inappropriate, particularly for full-time working partners. Often the agreement will be expressed in more general terms so that, for example, a full-time working partner 'must devote their whole time and attention to the business'. In order to reinforce this rather widely expressed obligation, often there is further provision to the effect that such partners must not be involved in any other business whatsoever during the partnership. This absolute bar is enforceable and does not fall foul of the public policy issues which may make such covenants in restraint of trade void after termination of the relationship of the partners (see **14.17**).

Inevitably, there must be qualifications to the main statement as to the amount of work required of a partner. There must be provisions dealing with holiday entitlement, with sickness and with any other reasons for being absent from work, such as maternity (or even paternity). The 1890 Act offers no guidance as to what would be implied here in the absence of express provision.

14.11 ROLES

Partners may have differing functions within the partnership so that not only must the agreement describe the amount of work input but also each partner's function. For example, a sleeping partner's role might be defined as being limited to attending meetings of the partners and the agreement would state that they have no authority to enter into contracts on behalf of the partnership. The agreement might state that a particular partner (with limited experience) only has authority to make contracts within specified limits, thereby partly defining their role.

Whatever is agreed along these lines is binding between the partners. Any partner who ignored any such restriction would be acting in breach of contract. The question of whether any contract made by them in breach of the partnership agreement would be enforceable against the firm by the third party depends on the application of s 5 of the PA 1890 which is considered in **Chapter 16**.

14.12 DECISION-MAKING

Unless the agreement provides to the contrary, all partnership decisions will be made on the basis of a simple majority (where each partner has one vote), except that decisions on changing the nature of the business or on introduction of a new partner require unanimity. However, it may be that the agreement should be more detailed, perhaps describing certain decisions which may be made by any partner on their own (such as routine sales and purchases of stock). Other decisions may require a simple majority (such as hiring staff) and certain decisions may require unanimity (such as borrowing money). In this context, it is important to appreciate that anything contained in the agreement (eg type of business) is a term of the contract between the partners and therefore cannot be altered without the consent of all parties to the contract (ie all partners would have to consent). That consent might be built into the contract itself, in that the agreement might contain provision for altering its terms (eg that a change in the type of business is to be effective if agreed by a majority of the partners).

In a joint venture between companies, a decision-making mechanism will need to be included in the agreement.

14.13 DURATION

14.13.1 Dissolution by notice

How long is the partnership to last before it may be dissolved either by just one partner who wishes to leave or by all the partners wishing to go their separate ways? If there is no provision in the agreement, the partnership can be dissolved at any time by any partner giving notice to the others. This is a partnership at will. A partnership cannot be a 'partnership at will' under s 26 if there is any limitation placed on a partner's right to terminate the agreement by them alone giving notice (see *Moss v Elphick* [1910] 1 KB 846). The notice of dissolution can have immediate effect and need not even be in writing unless the agreement itself was by deed. Although having the advantage of allowing each partner freedom to dissolve the whole partnership at any time and for any reason, a partnership at will has the corresponding disadvantages for the firm as a whole of insecurity and instability. Frequently, therefore, a partnership agreement will restrict the right of partners to dissolve the partnership.

A somewhat unusual example of a partnership at will occurred in *Byford v Oliver* [2003] All ER (D) 345. This case concerned the heavy metal band, 'Saxon'. Over the 20 years of its existence, the line-up of the band had changed but the claimant had been there throughout that time. It was held that he owned the name and goodwill of the band, not the defendants. The claimant would therefore have been entitled to register the name 'Saxon' as a trade mark, but the defendants were not.

Section 32 of the PA 1890 defines the basis on which partnerships of any type are to be dissolved, subject to alternative agreement between the partners.

14.13.2 Other solutions

One possible provision is that any notice of dissolution must allow a minimum period (of, say, six months) before taking effect. This at least gives time to settle what should happen on the dissolution (eg, some partners might negotiate the purchase of the interest of another in order to continue the business).

Another possibility is to agree a duration of a fixed term of a number of years. This provides certainty but is inflexible in committing each partner to the partnership for a certain duration. A fixed-term agreement can also be criticised if it fails to provide for what should happen if partners wish to continue after the expiry of their fixed term. However, this can be dealt with by providing that the partnership will continue automatically on the same terms after the fixed term except that thenceforth it will be terminable by, say, three months' notice.

Yet another possible provision is that the partnership is to continue for as long as there are at least two remaining partners, despite the departure of any partner by reason of retirement (see **14.14**), expulsion (see **14.15**), death or bankruptcy. This provision has the merit of providing some degree of security and stability whilst allowing individuals the flexibility of being able to leave. In case the departure of a partner might present financial problems for the others in buying out the departing partner's share, ancillary provisions can be included delaying payment to the outgoing partner so they are, in effect, forced to lend money to the partnership.

14.13.3 Death and bankruptcy

Under s 33 of the PA 1890, unless there is contrary agreement, the death or bankruptcy of a partner will automatically cause dissolution of the entire partnership. Therefore, it is appropriate to add a further provision that on the death or bankruptcy of a partner the remaining partners will automatically continue in partnership with one another on buying out the deceased or bankrupt partner's share in the business.

Again, with a joint venture between companies, the agreement will need to provide a mechanism for unwinding the joint venture if one party goes insolvent.

14.13.4 Court order

Situations may arise where a partner is 'locked into' a partnership by an agreement which contains no provision allowing them to dissolve the partnership or even to retire. To deal with this, s 35 of the PA 1890 provides that, on certain grounds, the court can make an order for dissolution. This effectively enables the partner to break their agreement with the other partners without being liable for breach of contract. If none of the grounds in the Act are satisfied, the partner has no escape without being liable for breach of contract.

14.14 RETIREMENT

In the context of partnership law, the word 'retirement' does not mean being eligible to collect the old age pension. It means leaving the partnership, perhaps to follow other business opportunities. The PA 1890 provides for retirement but only for a partnership at will by dissolving the partnership under s 26.

It is easy to assume that a partner must have the right to retire from the partnership when they please. Yet the agreement may contain provisions on duration which will have the effect of preventing retirement other than by the partner acting in breach of contract (such as a fixed term with no get-out provisions). Even if there is no provision on duration, strictly a partner's exit route is by dissolving the entire partnership by giving notice. It would then be for the others to re-form the partnership if they could reach agreement with the outgoing partner for the purchase of their share.

It is usually desirable therefore to have express provision governing the question of when a partner can retire (without dissolving the partnership so far as the others are concerned) and of payment for the departing partner's share by the others (see **14.16**).

14.15 EXPULSION

Expulsion of a partner is analogous to retirement, save that expulsion happens at the instigation of the other partners while retirement is a voluntary act of the outgoing partner. It amounts to terminating the contract (the partnership agreement) with the outgoing partner without their consent. It is an important sanction for breach of the agreement or for other stipulated forms of misconduct. As with retirement, the PA 1890 does not provide for the possibility of a partner being expelled by the others without their consent. There should therefore be provision in a partnership agreement for the possibility of expulsion. The agreement should state on what grounds the right to expel is to be exercisable and how it will be exercised (eg by a unanimous decision of the other partners with immediate effect). As with a retirement clause, the expulsion clause should also deal with the question of payment for the outgoing partner's share.

14.16 PAYMENT FOR OUTGOING PARTNER'S SHARE

Where a person ceases to be a partner by reason of retirement, expulsion, death or bankruptcy and others continue in partnership together, the remaining partners will need to pay for the outgoing partner's share in the business. To avoid any need to negotiate the terms of the purchase at the time, the agreement should contain the appropriate terms. If the agreement is silent on this and a settlement cannot be agreed at the time, s 42 of the PA 1890 becomes relevant. Under this section, if a person ceases to be a partner and others continue in partnership but there is delay in final payment of the former partner's share, then the former partner or their estate is entitled to receive either interest at 5% on the amount of their share or such share of the profits as is attributable to the use of the outgoing partner's share.

The terms that may be appropriate for inclusion in the partnership agreement will depend on the circumstances, but they should deal with the following:

(a) Whether there is to be a binding obligation on the partners to purchase the outgoing partner's share, or whether they are merely to have an option to purchase. Apart from the question of certainty as to what will happen, these alternatives have differing tax implications. In order to obtain business property relief for inheritance tax, an option to purchase is preferable.
(b) The basis on which the outgoing partner's share will be valued.
(c) Provision for a professional valuation if the partners cannot reach agreement between themselves.
(d) The date on which payment will be due (or dates, if payment by instalments is agreed).
(e) An indemnity for liabilities of the firm if these were taken into account in the valuation.

14.17 RESTRAINT OF TRADE FOLLOWING DEPARTURE

14.17.1 Competition

There will be no implied term preventing an outgoing partner from setting up in competition with the partnership or joining a rival business or even poaching the employees of the partnership to work in a rival business. There should always be a provision limiting an outgoing partner's freedom to compete with the firm to protect the business connections of the continuing firm (broadly to preserve its customers and its employees) and to protect its confidential information. The drafting of such clauses is critically important because a restraint of trade clause which is held to be unreasonable will be void as a matter of public policy. However, courts are more likely to uphold a restraint of trade clause when it is to protect the purchaser of a business, rather than to restrict the activities of an individual partner departing from a continuing business.

14.17.2 Drafting a non-competition clause

One type of clause commonly used to restrain an ex-partner's activities is a clause which seeks to prevent the person from being involved in any way in a competing business. The key issues to address in drafting such a clause (a non-competition clause) are:

(a) What is the clause aiming to protect? There must be a legitimate interest; this will usually be the firm's business connections, its employees and/or its confidential information.
(b) Is the clause reasonable, as drafted, for the protection of that interest? It must be limited as to its geographical area and as to its duration, and both the area and the duration must not be greater than is reasonable for the protection of the legitimate interest in question.

Suppose, for example, that the partnership of X, Y and Z carries on business as double glazing installers throughout Cheshire and North Wales, where all three partners are fully involved throughout the area. Their agreement contains a clause stipulating that, on leaving the partnership, a partner will not work in any way in the building trade for 10 years in England or Wales. This clause will be void because it is unreasonably wide on all three aspects. If the clause had stipulated that, on leaving the partnership, a partner would not work in the business of double glazing installation for 12 months throughout Cheshire and North Wales, this might be valid and enforceable.

14.17.3 Other forms of restraint of trade

Other forms of restraint of trade clauses may also be considered. A 'non-dealing clause' seeks to prevent the former partner from entering into contracts with customers or former customers or employees of the partnership which they have left. A 'non-solicitation clause' merely seeks to prevent them from soliciting contracts from such customers or employees. Both types of clauses are less restrictive of the former partner's freedom to continue their trade and therefore more likely to be held enforceable, provided that the effect of the clause is limited to what is reasonable for the protection of the firm's legitimate interest.

14.18 ARBITRATION

To avoid the expense, delay and adverse publicity arising out of litigation between partners, the agreement may provide that certain disputes should be referred to arbitration. Usually the disputes in question will be described as those arising out of the interpretation or application of the agreement itself rather than disputes over the running of the business.

CHAPTER 15

Partners' Responsibilities

LEARNING OUTCOMES

After reading this chapter you will be able to:

- understand the duty of utmost good faith between partners
- explain further legal and contractual responsibilities imposed on partners.

15.1 INTRODUCTION

Although a partner has no definable role other than under the terms of the partnership agreement (which may be express or implied), the partner does have certain responsibilities towards the partner's fellow partners and correspondingly certain rights against the partner's fellow partners which arise as a result of the existence of the partnership relationship.

15.2 UTMOST GOOD FAITH

By common law, partnership is a relationship onto which is imposed a duty of the utmost fairness and good faith from one partner to another. Particular applications of this principle, contained in ss 28–30 of the PA 1890, are that:

(a) partners must divulge to one another all relevant information connected with the business and their relationship;

(b) they must be prepared to share with their fellow partners any profit or benefit they receive that is connected with or derived from the partnership, the business or its property without the consent of the other partners; and

(c) they must be prepared to share with their fellow partners any profits they make from carrying on a competing business without the consent of the other partners.

EXAMPLES

In negotiating to sell to the partnership business premises owned by them, a partner must not suppress information which will affect the valuation. The doctrine of caveat emptor does not apply to partners' dealings with one another.

If a customer of the firm asks a partner to do some work for cash in their spare time, the cash belongs to the partnership unless the other partners choose to allow the partner to keep it.

If a partner sets up a competing business in their spare time, the profits of that business belong to the partnership unless otherwise agreed.

> If the partnership owns a lease of its business premises which contains an option to purchase the freehold, a partner who exercises the option in their own name must allow their fellow partners to share in the profit that they make.

In *Broadhurst v Broadhurst* [2006] EWHC 2727, a partner was held to be in breach of his duties of utmost good faith under ss 28 and 29 of the PA 1890. The errant partner in a car dealing business had not remitted all the sale proceeds for a consignment of cars into the accounts of the business. He had also caused cars to be impounded abroad and therefore not to be imported into the UK in good time.

15.3 FURTHER RESPONSIBILITIES IMPLIED BY THE ACT

Further responsibilities that may be enforced by the partners against one another are:

(a) the responsibility for bearing a share of any loss made by the business (the particular share depending upon the terms of their agreement) (PA 1890, s 24(1));

(b) the obligation as a firm to indemnify fellow partners against bearing more than their share (as above) of any liability or expense connected with the business (PA 1890, s 24(2)).

15.4 CONTRACTUAL RESPONSIBILITIES

Most of the responsibilities of a partner to the partner's fellow partners derive from the terms of their partnership agreement and may be express or implied.

CHAPTER 16

Liability for the Firm's Debts

LEARNING OUTCOMES

After reading this chapter you will be able to:

- explain when a partnership will be liable for its debts
- identify against whom the debts will be enforceable
- explain what happens if a partner is unable to pay their share of partnership debts.

16.1 INTRODUCTION

Transactions which may affect a partnership generally involve contracts. Contracts may be made by all of the partners acting collectively (eg they all sign a lease of business premises) or by just one of the partners. Some or all of the partners may seek to deny that they are liable on the contract (or for breach of it). In such cases, it is necessary first to identify whether the firm itself is liable and then, if the firm is liable, to identify which individuals are liable. These matters are governed by the following sections of the PA 1890. They are based on agency principles and are explained in the text which follows:

> **5 Power of partner to bind the firm**
>
> Every partner is an agent of the firm and his other partners for the purpose of the business of the partnership; and the acts of every partner who does any act for carrying on in the usual way business of the kind carried on by the firm of which he is a member bind the firm and his partners, unless the partner so acting has in fact no authority to act for the firm in the particular matter, and the person with whom he is dealing either knows that he has no authority, or does not know or believe him to be a partner.
>
> **6 Partners bound by acts on behalf of firm**
>
> An act or instrument relating to the business of the firm and done or executed in the firm-name, or in any other manner showing an intention to bind the firm, by any person thereto authorised whether a partner or not, is binding on the firm and all the partners.
>
> Provided that this section shall not affect any general rule of law relating to the execution of deeds or negotiable instruments.
>
> **7 Partner using credit of firm for private purposes**
>
> Where one partner pledges the credit of the firm for a purpose apparently not connected with the firm's ordinary course of business, the firm is not bound, unless he is in fact specially authorised by the other partners; but this section does not affect any personal liability incurred by an individual partner.
>
> **8 Effect of notice that firm will not be bound by acts of partner**
>
> If it has been agreed between the partners that any restriction shall be placed on the power of any one or more of them to bind the firm, no act done in contravention of the agreement is binding on the firm with respect to persons having notice of the agreement.

Remember that a partnership has no legal existence separate from that of the partners (unlike a company). So when the PA 1890 refers to the 'firm', it means the partners.

Under s 5, the act has to be in the usual course of the firm's business. In *Hirst v Etherington* [1999] Lloyd's Rep PN 938, the debt incurred by one partner in a solicitors' firm was held not to have been entered into in the usual course of the firm's business. His partner was therefore not also liable on the debt.

16.2 WHEN WILL THE FIRM BE LIABLE?

It should be noted that s 5 deals with a partner's authority. There is no equivalent provision for companies in the CA 2006.

16.2.1 Actual authority

The firm will always be liable for actions which were actually authorised. An action may be actually authorised in various ways:

(a) The partners may have acted jointly in making the contract; clearly they are not then at liberty to change their minds.

(b) Express actual authority: the partners may have *expressly* instructed one of the partners to represent the firm in a particular transaction or type of transaction. For example, one of the partners may have the function, under their agreement, of purchasing stock for the business. That partner is then acting with actual authority and the firm is bound by any contract that the partner makes within the scope of that authority.

(c) Implied actual authority: the partners may have *impliedly* accepted that one or more partners have the authority to represent the firm in a particular type of transaction. If all the partners are actively involved in running the business without any limitations being agreed between them, it will be implied that each partner has authority, for example, to sell the firm's products in the ordinary course of business. Alternatively, authority may be implied by a regular course of dealing by one of the partners in which the others have acquiesced.

16.2.2 Apparent (ostensible) authority

The firm may be liable for actions which were not actually authorised but which may have appeared to an outsider to be authorised. This liability derives from application of the principles of agency law, based on the fact that each partner is an agent of the firm and of their fellow partners for the purposes of the partnership business. Thus, even though as between the partners there is some express or implied limitation on the partner's authority, the firm will be liable by application of s 5 where:

(a) the transaction is one which relates to the type of business in which the firm is apparently engaged (ie 'business of the kind carried on by the firm' per s 5);

(b) the transaction is one for which a partner in such a firm would usually be expected to have the authority to act (ie 'in the usual way' per s 5);

(c) the other party to the transaction did not know that the partner did not actually have authority to act; and

(d) the other party deals with a person whom they know or believe to be a partner.

It can be seen that points (c) and (d) relate to the knowledge or belief of the third party who has dealt with the partner. It will be a subjective test as to whether these conditions are satisfied. On the other hand, points (a) and (b) call for an objective test of what would appear to an outsider to be the nature of the firm's business and what authority one would expect a partner in such a firm to have.

EXAMPLE 1

At a partner's meeting of the firm of A B & Co, it is decided that the firm should enter into a contract for the purchase of new premises at 21 High Street and a contract for the sale of their present business premises at 13 Side Street. Both written contracts are duly signed by all of the partners. The firm is bound by these contracts because they were actually authorised by means of the partners acting together. Note that the result would be the same if one partner had been instructed to sign the contract on behalf of the firm.

EXAMPLE 2

Without consulting his fellow partners, C, the senior partner of C, D & Co seizes an unexpected opportunity to purchase new business premises at 12 High Street and to sell the firm's present business premises at 31 Side Street by signing a written contract for each on behalf of the firm. Although undoubtedly connected with the firm's business, the firm is not bound by the contract because C was not actually authorised and, because a third party would not normally expect that one partner would have authority to make such a major contract on his own, there is no apparent authority. However, C is personally liable to the third party under the contract.

EXAMPLE 3

E, a partner in E F Plumbers, has placed several unconnected orders on credit in the name of the firm without consulting her partner F. In each case, the supplier has assumed that E was authorised to make the contract on behalf of her firm. The orders were:

(a) a quantity of copper piping;
(b) a jacuzzi and luxury bathroom suite;
(c) a brand-new van with 'E F Plumbers' printed on the side;
(d) a quantity of roofing felt and heavy timber.

In the first three instances, each contract is apparently connected with the business and so it would only be necessary to resolve whether a single partner would usually be expected to have the authority to make the contract. The order for the van may be too major for there to be apparent authority, but the other two contracts would seem to be binding on the firm. The contract for the roofing felt and timber has no apparent connection with the firm's business and therefore it is likely that the firm would not be bound unless there were special facts (eg some representation by the firm and not just by E) which led the supplier to believe that E had the authority to make this contract.

EXAMPLE 4

J K Hairstylists are visited by Morris, a salesman for a manufacturer of a new range of shampoos for salon use. After an inspection of his products, Morris hears J and K discussing their merits and J being adamant that the firm should stick with its present supplier and order nothing from Morris.

Ignoring this deadlock with his partner, K orders a supply from Morris. Although K would have had apparent authority to make such a contract if Morris had not been aware of their discussion, in fact Morris has reason to believe that K had no authority to make the contract and so the firm is not liable.

See the case of *JJ Coughlan v Ruparelia* [2003] EWCA Civ 1057 for an example of when the other partners will not be liable in contract (see **16.2.4** for the facts of this case).

In *Bourne v Brandon Davis* [2006] EWHC 1567 (Ch), it was held that musicians in a pop group could not have their performing rights assigned *en bloc* by another member of the group without their consent. The rights were personal to each of them and not 'the business of the partnership', so s 5 did not apply.

16.2.3 Personal liability

In any of the above instances, the partner who has acted will be personally liable to the other party under the contract. Also, if the partner who has acted has done so without actual authority but has made the firm liable by virtue of their apparent authority, then the partner is liable to indemnify the partner's fellow partners for any liability or loss which they incur. This is on the basis that the partner has broken the partner's agreement with their fellow partners by acting without actual authority. See also **16.3**.

16.2.4 Tortious liability

Only liability in contract has been considered so far. Occasionally the firm (as well as the partner in question) is liable for some act of a partner which is tortious by nature, for example, negligence. The position here is governed by s 10, which makes the firm liable for any wrongful act or omission of a partner who acts in the ordinary course of the firm's business or with the authority of the partner's partners.

The text of ss 10 and 12 of the PA 1890 is as follows:

> **10 Liability of the firm for wrongs**
>
> Where, by any wrongful act or omission of any partner acting in the ordinary course of the business of the firm, or with the authority of his co-partners, loss or injury is caused to any person not being a partner in the firm, or any penalty is incurred, the firm is liable therefor to the same extent as the partner so acting or omitting to act.
>
> **12 Liability for wrongs joint and several**
>
> Every partner is liable jointly with his co-partners and also severally for everything for which the firm while he is a partner therein becomes liable under either of the two last preceding sections.

The House of Lords held in *Dubai Aluminium Co Ltd v Salaam* [2002] 3 WLR 1913 that s 10 covers all types of wrongdoing, including a dishonest breach of trust or fiduciary duty, and is not limited to common law torts. However, in *JJ Coughlan v Ruparelia* [2003] EWCA Civ 1057 the Court of Appeal held that ss 5 and 10 did not make the other partners liable for breach of contract and deceit arising out of a fraudulent investment scheme. The solicitor in question was found liable but his partners were not. The making of the agreement in question by the partner was not 'an act for carrying on in the usual way business of the kind carried on by the firm' under s 5, as would have been needed to make the other partners liable in contract. They were also not liable in the tort of deceit under s 10 as the scheme was not 'in the ordinary course of the business of the firm'.

16.3 AGAINST WHOM CAN THE FIRM'S LIABILITIES BE ENFORCED?

16.3.1 Potential defendants

The person who is seeking to enforce a liability of the firm under the principles considered in **16.2**, or who is seeking to claim damages for breach of such a contract, will want to know who can be sued. The range of potential defendants may be quite extensive:

(a) The partner with whom the person made the contract can be sued individually because there will be privity of contract between them on which the potential claimant can rely. This will only be a real problem for that partner if they have acted without authority in entering the contract.

(b) The firm can be sued. In fact, any claim should be commenced against the partnership as such, if it has a name and if it is 'appropriate' to do so: CPR Part 7, Practice Direction

7A, 7.3. All those who were partners at the time when the debt or obligation was incurred are jointly liable to satisfy the judgment (PA 1890, ss 9 and 17, Civil Liability (Contribution) Act 1978, s 3).

(c) Any person who was a partner at the time when the debt or obligation was incurred can be sued individually. However, it is unlikely that a creditor would sue only one partner in this way, but any partner who is so sued is entitled to claim an indemnity from the remaining partners so that the liability is shared between them.

(d) Although generally someone who left the firm before the debt or obligation was incurred or who has joined the firm since that time is not liable (PA 1890, s 17), such a person may be sued or made liable for a judgment against the firm as a result of:
   (i) 'holding out' (see **16.3.3**); or
   (ii) failure to give appropriate notice of retirement (see **16.3.4**); or
   (iii) a novation agreement (see **16.3.5**).

In the case of *Dubai Aluminium Co Ltd v Salaam* [2002] 3 WLR 1913, partners in a partnership were held liable for the fraudulent act of their partner who acted dishonestly but in the ordinary course of business of that partnership, a law firm. Section 1(1) of the Civil Liability (Contribution) Act 1978 states that:

> (1) ... any person liable in respect of any damage suffered by another person may recover a contribution from any other person liable in respect of the same damage (whether jointly with him or otherwise).

Section 2 states:

> (1) Subject to subsection (3) below, in any proceedings for contribution under section 1 above the amount of the contribution recoverable from any person shall be such as may be found by the court to be just and equitable having regard to the extent of that person's responsibility for the damage in question.

16.3.2 Suing in the firm's name

In practice, the most appropriate way of proceeding if court action is necessary is to sue the partners as a group of persons in the firm's name (see **16.3.1(b)**). This has the merit that if judgment is obtained against the partners in the firm's name, this can be enforced against the partnership assets and also potentially against assets owned personally by any of the persons who were partners at the time that the debt or obligation was incurred (or who were liable as if they were partners (see **16.3.1**)).

EXAMPLE

'Hot Pots' are distributors of potatoes for the catering industry. Originally, the firm consisted of A, B and C as partners. In December, two weeks after A had retired from the firm, Hot Pots agree to purchase the entire crop of Farmer Giles's potatoes in the coming year at a price which is fixed. As a result of ideal growing conditions, there is a glut of potatoes and the contract price turns out to be much higher than the market price at the time of delivery. Hot Pots cancel the order and Farmer Giles sues for breach of contract. Before judgment is obtained against the firm, B retires and D joins the firm. Once judgment is obtained against Hot Pots it can be enforced against the assets of the partnership and/or the assets of B personally and/or the assets of C personally. It could not be enforced against the assets of A, unless there was a 'holding out' (see **16.3.3**) or a failure to give appropriate notice of retirement (see **16.3.4**), or against the assets of D unless there was a novation agreement (see **16.3.5**).

16.3.3 Persons liable by 'holding out'

Where a creditor of a partnership has relied on a representation (or 'holding out') that a particular person was a partner in that firm, the creditor may be able to hold that person liable for the firm's debt (PA 1890, s 14). This would be so even though it transpires that the person has never been a partner or, perhaps, had been a partner but had retired before the contract was made. The representation in question may be oral (eg where the person is described as a partner in conversation), in writing (eg on headed notepaper) or even by conduct (eg in a previous course of dealing). The representation may be made by the person themselves or, provided it is made with the person's knowledge, by another person.

In *Sangster v Biddulphs* [2005] EWHC 658 (Ch), the test relied on for liability under s 14 was that from *Nationwide Building Society v Lewis* [1998] Ch 482. This was that for liability there had to be (a) holding out, (b) reliance thereon, and (c) the consequent giving of credit to the firm.

EXAMPLE 1

A has retired from the firm of 'Hot Pots', leaving B and C to carry on the business. After A's retirement B and C wrote to Farmer Giles on some of the firm's old headed notepaper offering to purchase his entire crop of potatoes at a fixed price. On the notepaper, A's name still appears as a partner and Farmer Giles has observed this and relied upon it. If A knows that the firm is using up the old stock of notepaper without removing his name, this may operate as a representation with his knowledge that he is a partner. Conversely, if he stipulated that the old notepaper should be destroyed on his retirement, but B and C have failed to do this, then any such representation is not made with his knowledge and he is not liable.

EXAMPLE 2

Varying the facts of Example 1, the contract between 'Hot Pots' and Farmer Giles for the purchase and sale of potatoes was made orally when B and C met Farmer Giles on his farm and the contract was subsequently confirmed on the old notepaper. Since the contract was already made before Farmer Giles saw the notepaper, he cannot have relied on the notepaper as containing any representation and therefore cannot hold A liable.

EXAMPLE 3

Again varying the facts of Example 1, Farmer Giles in fact knew that A had retired when goods were ordered on the old notepaper; because of his knowledge of the retirement, he cannot have relied on the notepaper as containing any representation and therefore cannot hold A liable.

16.3.4 Persons liable by failure to notify leaving

The firm's debts can be enforced against all those who were partners at the time when the debt or obligation was incurred (see **16.3.1**). Although a person may retire from a partnership, they remain liable on those contracts already made. The terms for the purchase of the partner's share in the business should include a provision whereby the purchasing partner(s) indemnify the partner against liability for any such debts which were taken into account in valuing the partner's share (see **14.16**).

A separate point arises under s 36 of the PA 1890. Where a partner leaves the partnership (eg on retirement or expulsion), the partner must give notice of their leaving since otherwise the partner may become liable for the acts of their former partner or partners done after the partner leaves the firm, if the creditor is unaware of the fact that the partner has left. The notices which the partner should give are prescribed by s 36 and consist of:

(a) actual notice (eg by sending out standard letters announcing the partner is leaving) to all those who have dealt with the firm prior to the partner leaving (s 36(1)); and

(b) an advertisement in the *London Gazette* (or, for Scotland, the *Edinburgh Gazette*) as notice to any person who did not deal with the firm prior to the date of that partner's retirement or expulsion (s 36(2)).

A creditor who was unaware of the partner's leaving and who can establish that the type of notice appropriate to the creditor (as above) was not given, will be able to sue the former partner for the firm's debt, in spite of the fact that he has ceased to be a partner. The principle on which s 36 is based, unlike that on which s 14 is based, does not depend on the creditor having relied on some representation at the time of the transaction. Rather the creditor is given the right to assume that the membership of the firm continues unchanged until notice of the prescribed type (as above) is given. It follows that, if the creditor was never aware that the person had been a partner, no notice of any sort will be required since that creditor cannot be assuming the continuance of that person in the partnership (s 36(3)).

If the reason for ceasing to be a partner is death or bankruptcy (rather than retirement or expulsion), no notice of the event is required. The estate of the deceased or bankrupt partner is not liable for events occurring after the death or bankruptcy.

EXAMPLE 1

If, in the 'Hot Pots' examples (see **16.3.2** and **16.3.3**) Farmer Giles had dealt with 'Hot Pots' previously, he is entitled to assume that A remains a partner until he receives actual notice of his retirement. If Farmer Giles has not heard that A has retired, he will be able to sue A, as well as the others, on the contract for the potatoes.

EXAMPLE 2

If Farmer Giles has never dealt with 'Hot Pots' previously, but was aware that A was a member of the firm, he will be able to assume that A remains a partner unless the fact of A's leaving is advertised in the *London Gazette*. Therefore, if A's retirement has not been so advertised and Farmer Giles has not heard that A has retired, he will be able to sue A, as well as the others, on the contract for the potatoes. Where the retirement has been so advertised there is no requirement that Farmer Giles was aware of the advertisement or even that he had heard of the London Gazette! The advertisement operates as deemed notice to Farmer Giles.

EXAMPLE 3

If Farmer Giles has never dealt with 'Hot Pots' previously and was not aware that A was a member of the firm, he cannot hold A liable to him on the basis of s 36 even if A fails to give any notice of A's retirement.

16.3.5 Liability under a novation agreement

A novation agreement in this context is a tripartite contract involving the creditor of the firm, the partners at the time the contract with the creditor was made and the newly constituted partnership. The partnership may change because one partner leaves and/or a new partner joins. Under this contract of novation, it may be agreed that the creditor will release the original partners from their liability under the contract and instead the firm as newly constituted will take over this liability.

It may be that a retiring partner will be released from an existing debt whilst substituting an incoming partner. This is clearly advantageous to the retiring partner whilst disadvantageous to the incoming partner, and the latter will usually agree to this only as part of the broader package of terms on which they are taken into partnership. It may be that a partner retires and no new partner joins. In this case, in order to ensure that the novation is contractually binding, either there must be consideration for the creditor's promise to release the retiring partner from the liability or the contract must be executed as a deed.

A novation agreement, which, as described, is a tripartite agreement releasing a retiring partner from an existing debt, should not be confused with an indemnity in relation to existing debts. Such an indemnity is a bipartite agreement between the retiring partner and the other partners. Since the firm's creditors will not be party to this agreement they are not bound by it and can still sue the retired partner. It would then be for the indemnifying partners to meet the liability and thus protect the retired partner from it.

EXAMPLE

In the example in **16.3.2**, the incoming partner D was not liable to Farmer Giles. If Farmer Giles, the partners in 'Hot Pots' and D had entered into a novation agreement as described above, then in fact D would be liable to Farmer Giles.

16.4 WHAT IF A PARTNER CANNOT PAY?

16.4.1 Non-payment generally

A creditor can sue the firm as a group of persons or can sue individually any of the persons who are liable as partners. If the creditor has obtained judgment against a partner individually and that partner cannot pay, the creditor is then at liberty to commence fresh proceedings in order to obtain judgment against the firm. Even if the firm cannot pay out of its assets, either because it cannot raise the cash to do so or because its assets in total are insufficient to meet its liabilities in total, judgment against the firm can be enforced against the private assets of any person liable as a partner. If the claim of the creditor cannot be satisfied in any of these ways, it follows that the firm is insolvent and all of the individuals liable as partners are also insolvent, so that insolvency proceedings are likely to follow.

16.4.2 Insolvency

Insolvency is considered in **Chapters 19** and **20**. The law on insolvency of a partnership and of its partners individually is governed by the Insolvent Partnerships Order 1994 (SI 1994/2421) (as amended by SI 2002/1308) and the Insolvency Act 1986. The provisions are complex, but the main point is that, although a partnership is not a person in its own right, nevertheless an insolvent partnership may be wound up as an unregistered company or may avail itself of the rescue procedures available to companies, such as a 'voluntary arrangement' with creditors or an 'administration order' of the court (see **19.7**). A partnership is not governed by the laws on bankruptcy which relate to individuals. Thus, the partnership may be subject to a winding-up order and the individual partners may be subject to bankruptcy orders.

With a partnership joint venture involving companies, the agreement will need to provide a mechanism to unwind the joint venture in the event that one party may be heading for insolvency.

16.5 SUMMARY

The key question is:

Where a contract has been made by a partner (X), is the firm (and therefore all the partners and possibly other persons) liable in relation to that contract?

The path to the answer is:

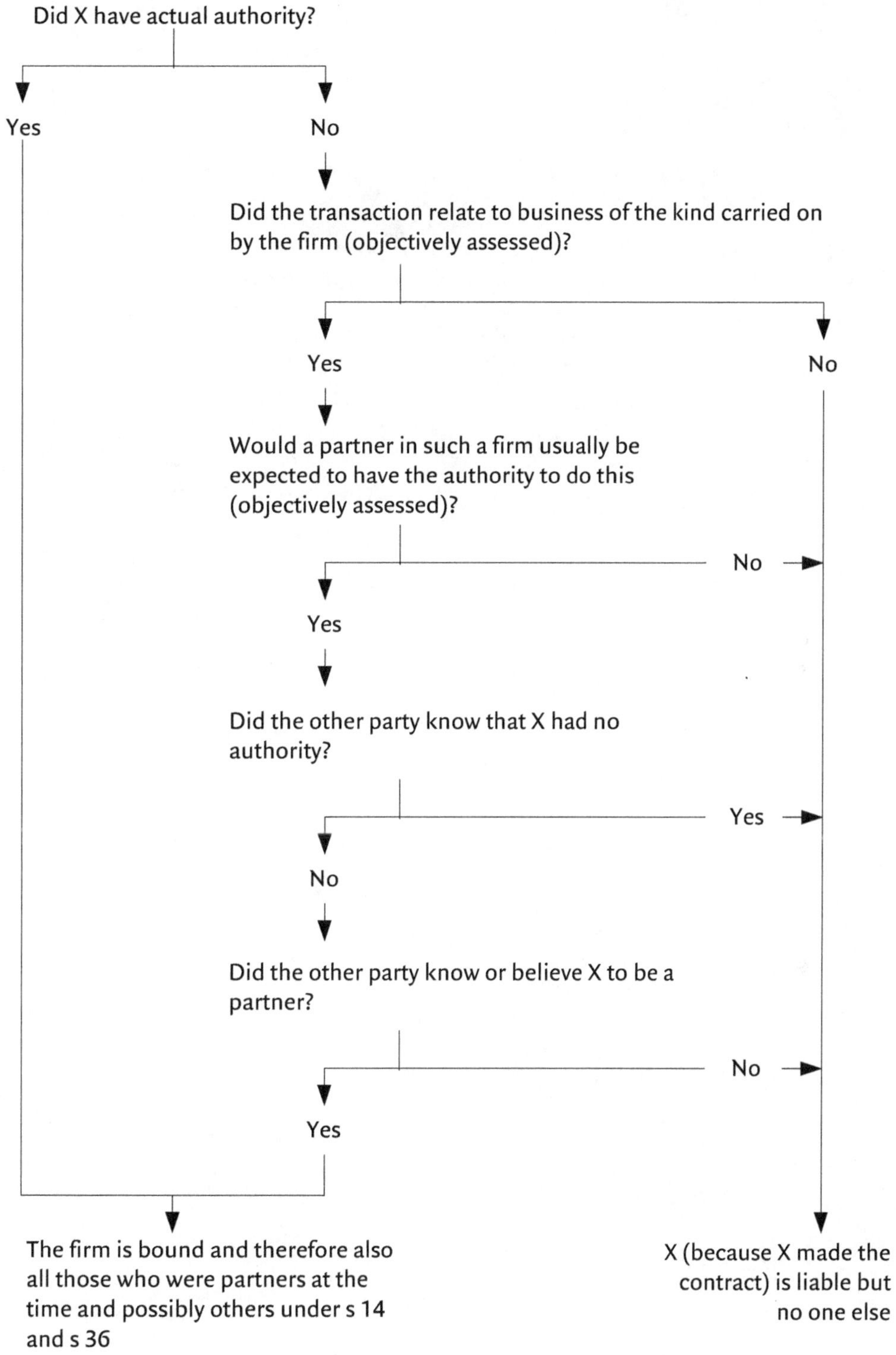

CHAPTER 17

DISSOLUTION

LEARNING OUTCOMES

After reading this chapter you will be able to:

- identify the circumstances in which a partnership comes to an end
- explain how the partnership assets are divided up on dissolution
- understand how the firm is wound up.

17.1 INTRODUCTION

Dissolution is when a partnership ends. It may be by agreement between the partners, it may be where one partner is in a position to insist (contrary to the wishes of the other(s)) or it may be by circumstances which had not been anticipated. One of the main implications of dissolution is the question of what happens to the business and its assets. Should one or more of the partners take over the business by paying off the other(s)? The circumstances for, and the consequences of, dissolution should be dealt with in a partnership agreement, but failing that, the Partnership Act 1890 (PA 1890) provides the details.

17.2 WHEN DOES DISSOLUTION OCCUR?

Dissolution of a partnership means that the contractual relationship joining all of the current partners comes to an end. It may be that some of the partners in fact succeed to the business and continue in a new partnership with one another. For example, if one of the partners retires and the others continue in partnership, strictly one partnership is dissolved and a new one formed.

Under ss 32–35 of the PA 1890, a partnership is expressed to be dissolved on the occurrence of any one of several events, although most of these provisions may be excluded by agreement (see **17.3**).

17.2.1 Notice

A notice of dissolution may be given by any partner to the other or others (PA 1890, ss 26 and 32). This notice need not state any reason for the dissolution and can have immediate effect. It need not even be in writing unless the partnership agreement was by deed. A partnership which is terminable under s 26 is known as a 'partnership at will'.

17.2.2 Expiry of fixed term

A partnership dissolves on the expiry of a fixed term for which the partners have agreed to continue in partnership, unless their agreement provides for continuance after the fixed term has expired (PA 1890, s 32). This must be taken to give effect to what the partners intended in agreeing a fixed duration. If the partners in fact continue their relationship after the fixed term has expired (and hence after the original partnership has dissolved), they will be presumed to be partners on the same terms as before except that their new partnership is a partnership at will and its terms must be consistent with that type of partnership (s 27).

17.2.3 Charging order over partner's assets

A notice of dissolution may be given by the other partners to a partner whose share in the partnership assets has been charged under s 23 by order of the court as security for the payment of that partner's private debt (PA 1890, s 33).

A judgment creditor of a partner in their private capacity may use s 23 as a means of enforcing the judgment. The creditor is not permitted to make any direct claim on the partnership assets even though the partner will be joint owner of those assets. The effect of a charging order under s 23 is that the creditor of that partner has an indirect claim by becoming the chargee of the partner's share in those assets. The creditor's charge may also entitle them to receive the partner's share of the profits of the partnership. At this stage, the other partners have the right to pay off the creditor and then look to their partner for recompense. If this does not happen, then, in order to enforce the charge (and hence the indirect claim on the partnership assets), the creditor may obtain an order of the court for the sale of the partner's share in the assets. If such a sale is ordered the most likely buyers are the other partners, but if they do not wish to purchase the share an outsider may do so. This will not make the outsider a partner in the firm since they are merely the owner of a share in the assets. Since this situation is likely to be unsatisfactory from the other partners' point of view, they have the right just mentioned to give notice of dissolution of the partnership.

17.2.4 Death or bankruptcy

Death or bankruptcy will automatically terminate the partnership (PA 1890, s 33) so that the personal representatives of the deceased or the trustee in bankruptcy of the bankrupt can collect for the former partner's estate the amount to which the former partner was entitled for their share.

With a joint venture between companies, the agreement will need to provide a mechanism for unwinding the joint venture if one party goes insolvent.

17.2.5 Illegality

Where it is illegal to carry on the business of the partnership, the partnership will dissolve (PA 1890, s 34). This situation might arise where the partnership business consists of the sale of alcohol and the partnership loses its licence to sell alcohol or where the partnership business is that of a solicitors' practice and one of the partners is struck off the Roll of Solicitors. The provisions of s 34 cannot be excluded even by a written partnership agreement, in contrast to ss 32–33 which can be excluded by agreement.

17.2.6 Court order for dissolution

The court has power (PA 1890, s 35) to order dissolution on various grounds, one of which (the 'just and equitable' ground) provides the court with such a wide discretion that it effectively makes the other, more specific, grounds unnecessary. Broadly, the other grounds are designed to cover circumstances where one partner ought to leave (eg on account of their conduct) but they are unwilling to do so and the others cannot expel them because their agreement failed to provide for this. Cases under s 35 are unusual because most partnerships, whether governed by an express or an implied agreement, can be dissolved without court intervention. This may be because there is nothing in their agreement to prevent a partner from giving notice to dissolve the partnership. Even if this is prevented by their agreement, the partners may be able to negotiate dissolution, for example where one partner will leave and be paid for their share, allowing the others to re-form in partnership.

On occasions, however, there will be a partnership agreement which would prevent dissolution unless all of the partners agreed. For example, the agreement may state that the partnership will continue for a long fixed term, or even for the joint lives of the partners. In such cases, unless the agreement provides for an unhappy partner to retire or for a troublesome partner to be expelled, it may be necessary to apply to the court for an order for dissolution. The order effectively breaks the partnership agreement without any partner being liable to the others for breach of contract.

17.3 EXPRESS TERMS ON DISSOLUTION

17.3.1 Restrictions on dissolution

Generally, it will be inappropriate to leave the question of duration and dissolution to be governed by the PA 1890. The partners will not want the insecurity of a partnership at will, nor will they want the death or bankruptcy of one partner to cause a dissolution of the partnership between the survivors. Usually, therefore, it will be appropriate for the partnership agreement to exclude at least these possibilities and to make express provision as to the duration of the partnership (see **14.13**).

17.3.2 Purchase of outgoing partner's share

If dissolution occurs where one partner leaves (by retirement, expulsion, death or bankruptcy) and the others are to continue as partners, the agreement should contain provisions allowing for the remaining partners to purchase the share of the former partner and fixing the terms of the purchase. If the agreement does not contain such provisions, it may be possible for the parties involved to negotiate terms for the outgoing partner's share to be purchased by the continuing partners. Inevitably, it may be some time after the partner has left that a price is settled and the others agree to purchase. If the agreement does not deal with the question of payment for the use of the former partner's share in the assets since the former partner left, the former partner will be entitled to receive, at the former partner's option, either interest at 5% per annum on the value of the former partner's share, or such sum as the court may order as representing the share of profits made which is attributable to the use of the former partner's share (PA 1890, s 42). The purchase agreement can exclude this entitlement (see **14.16**).

17.4 THE BUSINESS, ITS GOODWILL AND OTHER ASSETS FOLLOWING DISSOLUTION WITHOUT CONTINUING PARTNERS

17.4.1 Disposal of the business

Sometimes dissolution occurs where the partners cannot reach agreement as to some of the partners carrying on with the business and purchasing an outgoing partner's share. Then it will be necessary for there to be a disposal of the business and for the proceeds of sale to be used to pay off creditors and then to pay to the partners the amount to which they are entitled. This disposal of a business may be by sale as a going concern or, if a buyer cannot be found, by breaking up the business and selling its assets separately. This position is reinforced by s 39 of the PA 1890, which gives every partner the right to insist on a disposal and payment as above, if necessary by application to court for the business and affairs of the firm to be wound up.

17.4.2 Goodwill

There is a serious financial disadvantage to the partners if the business is not purchased as a going concern but is broken up with the assets being sold separately. A valuable asset of any successful business is its goodwill. Goodwill can be described as the benefit of the business's reputation and connections and the benefit of having its own momentum so that profits will continue to be earned because the business is established.

A common basis for valuing goodwill is to take a number (perhaps two) of years' profit. For example, if the business generated £25,000 and £30,000 profit in the previous two years, the goodwill of the business might be valued at £55,000. Another approach to understanding the meaning of goodwill is to consider a person who is contemplating either purchasing an established business as a going concern or setting up a new business. In either instance, the cost would include the purchase of the necessary tangible assets like premises, equipment, stock, etc, but if purchasing an established business the buyer will have to pay for the benefit of its being established and already making a profit. This payment (of whatever amount is negotiated) is for goodwill. It can be seen therefore that, in the context of dissolution of partnership, the question of someone (whether it be continuing partners or an outsider) taking over the business as a going concern (and therefore paying for goodwill) is of considerable financial significance to a partner who is leaving.

Financial considerations apart, one other aspect of selling goodwill is worth considering at this point. The buyer of goodwill is likely to insist on the seller(s) entering into a covenant in restraint of trade for the protection of the goodwill which the buyer is purchasing. If the seller was free to become involved immediately in a competing business, the benefit of having purchased (effectively) an established set of customers might be seriously undermined. Therefore, in return for the financial benefit of selling their share in the goodwill, an outgoing partner will have to accept the limitations imposed on their future activities by a covenant in restraint of trade. It should be remembered that a covenant in restraint of trade will be valid only if it is reasonable in the circumstances (see **14.17**).

However, courts are more likely to uphold a restraint of trade clause when it is to protect the purchaser of a business, rather than to restrict the activities of an individual partner departing from a continuing business.

17.5 DISTRIBUTION OF PROCEEDS FOLLOWING SALE OF THE BUSINESS OR ITS ASSETS

Unless there is agreement to the contrary, the proceeds of sale of the business or its assets will be used in the following sequence (PA 1890, s 44). First, creditors of the firm (ie anyone with a claim against the firm except for the partners themselves) must be paid in full. If there is a shortfall so that the firm is insolvent, the partners must pay the balance from their private assets, sharing the loss in accordance with their partnership agreement. Secondly, partners who have lent money to the firm must be repaid, together with any interest to which they are entitled. Thirdly, partners must be paid their capital entitlement. Finally, if there is a surplus, this will be shared between the partners in accordance with their partnership agreement. For an example of the problems of dissolution, see *Hurst v Bryk* [2000] 2 All ER 193, where the partner who did not want the partnership to be disolved was still liable for his share of the partnership debts under s 44.

17.6 FOLLOWING DISSOLUTION, WHO WINDS UP THE FIRM'S AFFAIRS?

Each partner (except a bankrupt partner) has continuing authority to act for the purposes of winding up the firm's affairs (PA 1890, s 38). It may be that there is no need for any person outside the partnership to become involved in the dissolution. On the other hand, if there is a dispute between the partners, or if the assets are in jeopardy, any partner (or the trustee in bankruptcy of a bankrupt partner or the personal representatives of a deceased partner) may apply to the court for the appointment of a person (even one of the partners) as receiver to deal with the assets or as receiver and manager to conduct the business in addition to the above, perhaps with a view to selling the business as a going concern. The receiver or receiver and manager is an officer of the court and will be entitled to receive remuneration for their services from the partnership assets, although not from the partners' personal money.

CHAPTER 18

Limited Liability Partnerships

LEARNING OUTCOMES

After reading this chapter you will be able to:

- explain how an LLP is formed
- explain the legal rules governing an LLP during its lifetime
- understand the advantages and disadvantages of running a business as an LLP.

18.1 INTRODUCTION

Limited liability partnerships (LLPs) were created by the Limited Liability Partnerships Act 2000 (LLPA 2000) in response to pressure from professional firms for more protection from liability than was possible with existing partnership law. An LLP is, in effect, a hybrid between a partnership under the PA 1890 and a limited company under the CA 2006. The main users of the LLP structure are professional firms. There is a set of regulations on applying the CA 2006 to LLPs, the Limited Liability Partnerships (Application of the Companies Act 2006) Regulations 2009 (SI 2009/1804).

Partners in an LLP ('members') have full limited liability. The LLP is a corporate body with a separate identity from the members. The provisions under the IA 1986 and CDDA 1986 are applied to LLPs.

An LLP is required by s 8 of the LLPA 2000 to have at least two 'designated members' who are responsible for sending documents to Companies House.

An LLP is registered by sending an incorporation document to Companies House, but there is no need to send a copy of any partnership agreement or other constitutional document. This document is known as Form LL IN01 and is generally equivalent to that used for a company (Form IN01). It must contain (LLPA 2000, s 2(2)):

(a) the name of the LLP;

(b) the country where the registered office is situated;

(c) an 'appropriate' registered office address;
(d) an 'appropriate' registered email address;
(e) the name and address of each member of the LLP;
(f) the identities of the designated members; and
(g) a statement of initial PSCs.

Form LL IN01 also contains a statement that the requirements of s 2(1)(a) have been complied with, that two or more of the partners must have subscribed their names to the incorporation form.

A fee is payable to Companies House to incorporate an LLP. The cost is £50 using Companies House software and £71 if submitting paper documents. A same-day incorporation service costing £78 is available for Companies House software users only.

If satisfied with the information provided in Form LL IN01, Companies House will issue a certificate of incorporation. The name of an LLP has to end with the words 'limited liability partnership' or 'LLP', or their Welsh equivalents. The rules on registration of names are similar to those for companies (see **3.5** above).

There is no management structure imposed on an LLP, that is, there is no equivalent of the model articles for a company. Implied terms which would apply in the absence of contrary agreement are provided by regulations (see **18.7**).

Members will owe a duty to the LLP as a body corporate in common law, but it seems unclear whether they owe a duty of good faith to each other.

Members are agents of the LLP, under s 6 of the LLPA 2000 (see **16.1** above) which is equivalent to s 5 of the PA 1890 .

The relationship between the members is set out in s 5 of the LLPA 2000, which is equivalent to s 24 of the PA 1890 (see **14.1** above).

An LLP has no share capital and therefore there are no requirements to maintain share capital. There are no directors and shareholders. There are just 'members'. The members are free to decide upon management and decision processes.

There is no restriction on membership numbers, though there have to be at least two members to constitute an LLP. The LLP structure is open to any type of business (LPPA 2000, s 2(1)(a)).

The LLP itself can be liable for, eg, torts and debts, but the members have limited liability.

An LLP has to file annual accounts, which are then a public document.

The provisions relating to wrongful and fraudulent trading also apply to the members of an LLP (Limited Liability Partnerships Regulations 2001, SI 2001/1090 ('LLP Regulations 2001'), reg 5).

An LLP cannot convert into a limited company directly, but the business itself could be incorporated.

For tax purposes, an LLP is to be treated as an ordinary partnership, that is, the partners will be liable to income tax under the ITTOIA 2005 for their share of profits, and to capital gains tax on gains made on the disposal of partnership assets.

Overall, LLPs are a curious mix of the law of partnership and the law of companies. For example, in *Feetum v Levy* [2005] EWCA Civ 1601, the Court of Appeal looked at the rule in *Foss v Harbottle* (1843) 2 Hare 461, which is a case that deals with the rights of shareholders (see **5.3**). The Court held that, on the facts in question, the rule did not stop members of an LLP from challenging the appointment of an administrative receiver to the partnership (see **18.6**).

In July 2001, the accountancy firm of Ernst and Young became an LLP. Pricewaterhouse Coopers became an LLP on 1 January 2003. Most LLPs are professional firms, for example solicitors, accountants and surveyors.

The limited liability partnership has a legal personality separate from that of its members. Thus, it is the limited liability partnership that carries the duties and liabilities of the business which are owed to outsiders. Unlike the position with a partnership, the existence of the LLP is separate from that of its members. So, a partnership will cease to exist if there are not two or more members, ie partners. This is not the case with an LLP. It continues to exist as a separate legal entity until it is dissolved.

The Economic Crime and Corporate Transparency Act 2023 (ECCTA) will introduce a number of changes to the law affecting LLPs, including requiring the verification of the identity (see ***3.11*** *above) of all LLP members, PSCs and people who deliver required documents to the Registrar on behalf of the LLP. If that party is a company then all of its directors must have their identity verified. The system for checking identities does not, at the time of writing, yet extend to LLPs. It is expected to come into force by the end of 2026.*

18.2 FORMALITIES

The LLP must have its name on the outside of its place of business. Similarly, its business stationery must mention its name, its place of registration and its registration number, and the address of the registered office (CA 2006, s 82(1), (2)). It must always have a registered office, as it is an address for service of official documents (LLPA 2000, Sch, para 6).

Entering into contracts and executing other documents is much the same for LLPs as for companies. Thus, a contract may be made on behalf of an LLP by anyone acting with express or implied authority. So, a document is executed on behalf of an LLP by that document being signed by two members of the LLP, or by applying the common seal of the LLP, if it has one.

An LLP can change its name at any time. There is no procedure prescribed in legislation for doing so. This should be a matter addressed in the LLP partnership agreement. If it is not then the default rules apply (see **18.7**), and the consent of all the members is needed (LLP Regulations 2001, regs 7 and 8).

Every LLP must send to the Registrar an annual confirmation statement (CA 2006, s 853A). This covers the following items:

(a) the address of the registered office;
(b) the names and addresses of the members of the LLP;
(c) the identity of the designated members, if not all members are designated; and
(d) the address where the register of debenture holders is kept, if it is not the registered office.

Under s 853BA, the LLP must also confirm that its activities are intended to be lawful (made on the confirmation statement).

The appropriate form is a variation of the standard form for companies. It must be signed by a designated member (see **18.8**) who certifies that the return is accurate.

Changes to the membership of an LLP must be notified to the Registrar of Companies as they occur (LLPA 2000, s 9(1)(a)).

18.3 AUTHORITY OF A MEMBER TO BIND THE LLP

Every member of an LLP is the agent of the LLP (LLPA 2000, s 6(1)). Section 6(2) provides for limitations to be placed on a member's actual authority. So, an LLP is not bound if the member has no authority to act for the LLP in that matter and the third party in question knows that fact. The LLP agreement, if there is one, should provide for limits on the authority of members. However, this still leaves open the question of apparent authority. The extent of the apparent authority will be determined by the nature of the business concerned, and therefore what constitutes the 'normal course' of that business. Apparent authority is dependent upon the representations which the LLP makes to the third party or, more likely, the mistaken impressions which the LLP fails to correct (see **6.5.2**).

The member will cease to be the agent of the LLP whenever they cease to be a member of that LLP.

18.4 OWNING PROPERTY AND THE GRANTING OF CHARGES

An LLP can issue debentures and grant fixed or floating charges. Every LLP must keep a copy of every charge requiring registration at its registered office (CA 2006, s 859P). These must be open for inspection by any creditor or member of the LLP without payment of a fee.

The LLP is required to register charges with the Registrar in the same way that a company is so required. An amended version of the form for companies is used for registration of charges for an LLP. As with companies, there is a power of the court to rectify omission of registration of a charge (CA 2006, s 859M).

18.5 NEW MEMBERS

The LLP is incorporated with its first members. Thereafter, any person may become a member with the agreement of the existing members. As with a traditional partnership, being a member of an LLP is a matter of contract. Any LLP agreement therefore needs to make provision for new members joining the LLP.

18.6 EFFECT OF LIMITED LIABILITY

If the LLP becomes insolvent, both the LLP and the members will be subject to the IA 1986 regime with regard to the liquidation of companies. Thus, there is the possibility of the member being found liable for misfeasance, fraudulent trading or wrongful trading (see **7.13.10.3**, **7.13.10.2** and **7.13.10.1** respectively). The member may therefore be required to contribute to the assets of the insolvent LLP in the same way that a company director can be, under the equivalent provisions for companies (but see **18.10** re protection of members' personal assets). The Company Directors Disqualification Act 1986 also applies to members of an LLP.

It seems that members of an LLP do not have as great a problem with restrictions on their right of action as do members of a company (see **5.8.1**). Thus, the Court of Appeal held in *Feetum v Levy* [2005] EWCA Civ 1601 that the rule in *Foss v Harbottle* did not prevent members of an LLP from challenging the appointment of administrative receivers.

18.7 THE LLP AGREEMENT

Section 5(1) of the LLPA 2000 provides that the mutual rights and duties of an LLP and its members are governed by an agreement between the members, or in the absence of an agreement by the provisions of the LLP Regulations 2001. The Regulations provide a set of 'default rules'. These rules adopt some of the provisions contained in ss 24–30 of the PA 1890, with appropriate modifications. The matters covered by the default rules are as follows, with references to the PA 1890 for comparison:

(a) sharing in capital and profits (PA 1890, s 24(1));
(b) indemnity to members (s 24(2));
(c) right to take part in management (s 24(5));
(d) no entitlement to remuneration (s 24(6));
(e) introduction of a new member and voluntary assignment of a member's interest (s 24(7));

(f) ordinary matters connected with the business to be decided by majority (s 24(8));

(g) books and records to be available for inspection by any member (s 24(9));

(h) each member to render true accounts and full information to any member (s 28);

(i) obligation to account to the LLP for any profits made from a competing business without consent (s 30);

(j) obligation to account to the LLP for any private benefit derived without consent from use of LLP property (s 29(1)); and

(k) no majority power to expel without express agreement as to such power (s 25).

18.8 DESIGNATED MEMBERS

At least two of the members of the LLP must be 'designated members' (LLPA 2000, ss 2(1)(a), 8(2)). The original two designated members will be the subscribers to the incorporation document. One possibility is that all members of the LLP will be designated members. Alternatively, the LLP may specify named members as the designated members in addition to, or in place of, the original subscribers (LLPA 2000, s 8(4)(b)).

The responsibilities of the designated members are contained in the LLPA 2000, the CA 2006 and the IA 1986. Broadly, designated members have powers equivalent to directors in a company. However, they also have the duties and responsibilities of being a member of the LLP.

Designated members must:

(a) sign and file the annual accounts with the Registrar (CA 2006, s 444(6));

(b) appoint, remove and remunerate auditors (CA 2006, s 485(4));

(c) file the confirmation statement (CA 2006, s 853A);

(d) send notices to the Registrar, for example concerning a member leaving or joining the LLP (LLPA 2000, s 9(1));

(e) send a statement of release of a charge to the Registrar (CA 2006, s 859L);

(f) apply for a change of name of the LLP (LLPA 2000, Sch, para 5(2)(b));

(g) apply to strike off the LLP from the register (CA 2006, s 1003); or

(h) wind up the LLP or apply for a voluntary arrangement (IA 1986, s 89(1)).

All the functions of a designated member must be carried out consistent with the core fiduciary obligation owed by every member to the LLP itself, ie an obligation of loyalty and promoting the best interests of the LLP (see **18.9**). The designated members will also owe a duty to the LLP of reasonable care and skill.

18.9 THE DUTIES AND RESPONSIBILITIES OF MEMBERS

Many LLPs will have a written agreement. However, this will not be the only source of the duties and responsibilities of the members. As a member is in the position of agent with the LLP as principal, the member will owe a fiduciary duty to the LLP. There are also the default rules to be considered.

The member's duties to the LLP will include:

(a) a duty to account for any money received on behalf of the LLP;

(b) a duty not to apply LLP monies improperly;

(c) fiduciary duties, for example a duty of good faith towards the LLP;

(d) duties on members as a whole, for example to prepare financial accounts which give a true and fair view of the LLP's financial position;

(e) duties on individual members, for example to give the auditors such information as they require from the member; and

(f) duties to the member's co-members, for example a duty to render true accounts and full information on matters concerning the LLP.

18.10 CAPITAL AND PROFITS

Funding for a business comes either from debt or equity, ie borrowing or shares. With an LLP, the equity is the members' capital which they have contributed to the business. Default rule 1 provides that members are entitled to share equally in the capital and profits of the LLP, in the absence of contrary agreement. The default rules do not deal with losses, as it is the LLP itself which bears any losses, just as a company does. In other words, this is where limited liability applies and benefits the members of the LLP. The only thing that the member has at risk is the contributions the member has made to the LLP's finances, ie the member's capital and any profits due to the member, and loans from the member which the LLP cannot repay.

18.11 MANAGEMENT AND DECISION-MAKING

Default rules 3 and 4 provide that every member may take part in the management of the LLP, and that no member is entitled to remuneration for doing so. These rules are adapted from s 24(5) and (6) of the PA 1890. The LLP agreement can depart from these rules and the members can create any management structure that is desired.

Default rule 6 is adapted from s 24(8) of the PA 1890 and provides that ordinary matters of the LLP are to be decided by a majority of the members. No change in the nature of the business of the LLP can be made without the consent of all members.

18.12 CESSATION OF MEMBERSHIP AND ITS CONSEQUENCES

A person may cease to be a member of an LLP by giving reasonable notice to the other members (LLPA 2000, s 4(3)). There is no equivalent provision to this in a traditional partnership. The bankruptcy of a member does not automatically cause a termination of membership of the LLP, unless the LLP agreement so provides. Also, a member cannot be expelled or be required to retire, unless the LLP agreement deals with this (default rule 8, which adopts s 25 of the PA 1890).

If a person ceases to be a member, the LLP must notify the Registrar within 14 days.

It seems that under the default rules, there is no automatic right for a lending member to be repaid their capital. This is therefore a matter that should be addressed in the LLP agreement.

In its decision in *Tiffin v Lester Aldridge LLP* [2012] EWCA Civ 35, the Court of Appeal held that a fixed-share partner of an LLP who had limited profits and voting rights was a member and not an employee of the LLP under the LLPA 2000, s 4(4). This meant that statutory employment rights accorded to employees, such as the right to bring a claim for unfair dismissal and to a redundancy payment, were not available to such a person. Contrast this with the decision in *Williamson & Soden Solicitors v Briars* [2011] UKEAT 0611_10_2005, where a solicitor paid a profit share rather than a salary, and not having invested in the equity of the firm, was held to be an employee rather than a member.

18.13 ADVANTAGES AND DISADVANTAGES OF AN LLP

Advantages

(a) limited liability and separate legal personality (like a company);

(b) a flexible organisational structure: the members can decide what they want;

(c) the ability to grant fixed and floating charges over its assets; security needs to be registered with the Registrar of Companies;

(d) the ability to appoint an administrator.

Disadvantages

(a) the requirement to file accounts with the Registrar of Companies, which will then be public documents;

(b) the potential 'clawback' provisions in the event of an insolvency;

(c) the transfer of a personal interest in an LLP is more complex than transferring shares (but a transfer can be less problematic with an LLP that with an ordinary partnership structure as LLP membership can be assigned);

(d) an LLP cannot convert into a limited company.

18.14 APPLICATIONS OF AN LLP

The LLP structure has been primarily of interest to professional partnerships, eg solicitors, accountants and engineers. An LLP could also be used in the context of joint ventures or in project finance.

PART III SUMMARY

RUNNING A BUSINESS IN PARTNERSHIP

Topic	*Summary*
Definition	A partnership is 'the relation which subsists between persons carrying on a business in common with a view of profit'. There must be two or more persons for a partnership, and whether a partnership exists is a question of fact. A written agreement is *not* required, although most partnerships have one.
Liability	Partners have unlimited liability for a partnership's debts. A partnership is not a separate legal entity from its partners and one partner can be liable for all of a partnership's debts.
Registration	There is no registration process to form a partnership and no obligation to make accounts public. A partnership is usually referred to as a 'firm' to distinguish it from a company.
Duration	Most partnerships are 'at will': a partnership has no set duration and will continue until dissolved, unless otherwise agreed.
Regulation	The main statute regulating partnerships is the Partnership Act 1890 (PA 1890). Partners can regulate their affairs as they wish so long as this is not inconsistent with the PA 1890. The PA 1890 has, in s 24, rules which will regulate the partners and their business, unless varied by agreement.
Management and decisions	The PA 1890 allows all partners to take part in managing the business and for decisions to be taken by a majority. However, in certain situations, unanimity is required. These are: a change in business; introducing a new partner; altering the partnership agreement; and expelling a partner.
Duty of good faith	Partners must act in good faith towards each other. They must disclose information about the business to each other (s 28); account for any benefits gained from using partnership property or its name (s 29); and account for any profits made from a competing business (s 30).
Finance	Partnerships can be financed by the partners, bank borrowing and retention of profits. Partners can invest by way of capital or lending. Capital investment can be in the form of assets or cash. This capital is a debt owed to the partner, usually repaid only on dissolution or the departure of the partner. There is no entitlement to any interest on capital unless agreed. A loan made by a partner is like a bank loan, save that the PA 1890 stipulates a 5% interest rate unless otherwise agreed.

Topic	Summary
Sharing capital and profits	Partners share equally in capital and profits unless otherwise agreed. Where capital is provided in varying amounts, it is implied that this will be repaid in proportion to these amounts. There is no such implication for profits and losses: partners share them equally unless otherwise agreed.
Drawing and salary	Profits are calculated annually but partners may take out money periodically against expected profits: these are called drawings. Some partners receive a salary, which is seen as an appropriation of profit, so is not a deductible expense of the business for tax purposes.
Actual authority	A partnership is bound by the acts of a partner acting within the partner's authority. Express actual authority is where authority has been given by the partnership. Implied actual authority can arise from a course of dealing or where the authority arises naturally from an express authority.
Apparent authority	A firm is also bound where a third party can rely on apparent authority, defined in s 5. Here, a partner must act in the usual way for carrying on the business of the kind carried on by the firm. The third party can rely on this *unless* the partner has no authority to act on the particular matter and the third party either (a) knows the partner has no authority; or (b) does not know or believe them to be a partner. Where a firm is bound by a partner acting beyond authority, it can require the partner to indemnify the firm for any liabilities incurred.
New and retiring partners: liability	A new partner is not liable to creditors for anything done before joining. However, the partner can agree with the other partners to pay a share of existing debts. A retiring partner remains liable for debts incurred whilst the partner was a partner but not those incurred after the partner's departure. This may not, however, be the case if it appears to a third party that the retiree is still a partner or the retiree holds themselves out to still be a partner. To avoid this, retiring partners should give formal notice of their departure to existing customers and suppliers. A notice in the *London Gazette* provides similar notice to any new customers of the firm. The partner should also ensure removal of their name from the firm's stationery.
Dissolving a partnership	A partnership can be dissolved at any time by notice from one or more partners, unless its agreement states otherwise. Similarly, the death or bankruptcy of a partner will dissolve the partnership unless otherwise agreed. Partners may also agree that the partnership will expire at the end of an agreed period or venture.
Court dissolution	A court can dissolve a partnership on a number of grounds: where a partner becomes permanently incapable of performing their role; where a partner's conduct prejudicially affects the business or makes it unreasonable for the other partners to carry on working with them; where the business can only be carried on at a loss; or where it is felt just and equitable to dissolve the firm.

Topic	Summary
Winding up a partnership's affairs	Where a firm is dissolved, its affairs are wound up. Its assets and liabilities are calculated, and debts owed to creditors are paid first. Then, advances made by partners are repaid, followed by capital and, finally, a division of any remaining amounts according to the profit-sharing ratio. If the partnership has made losses, these have to be met in the following order: from profits; from capital; and then from contributions from partners according to the profit-sharing ratio.

PART IV

INSOLVENCY

This Part first considers the insolvency of a company. An insolvent company may be put into liquidation, a process by which all assets are recovered and then distributed in an order laid down by statute between the creditors. This is broadly equivalent to the bankruptcy of an individual. However, liquidation differs fundamentally from bankruptcy, in that at the end of the liquidation the company is dissolved and ceases to exist. Consideration is also given in this Part to alternative processes applicable to companies that may enable the company potentially to survive the insolvency, ie, company voluntary arrangements (CVAs), administration and (albeit more briefly) receivership; both administrative receivership and Law of Property Act receivership (which is also known as fixed charge receivership). In addition, the changes and new insolvency procedures brought in by the Corporate Insolvency and Governance Act 2020 are considered. This was an Act that was passed as a direct result of the Covid-19 pandemic and as an attempt to assist in mitigating the economic fallout from that situation, but some provisions are permanent and so are now embedded into insolvency law.

Lastly, we consider the implications of the insolvency of an individual (a 'debtor'). The debtor who is unable to pay their debts is faced with the possibility of bankruptcy (or, if they have very limited assets, a debt relief order), as a result of which virtually all their assets are taken and shared between their other creditors. At the end of the bankruptcy, the debtor is largely freed from outstanding claims and is able to start afresh. As with companies, alternatives are also considered, such as individual voluntary arrangements (IVAs) in which creditors may accept payment which is delayed, and which is normally less than their full entitlement.

You will find the following websites useful to check statistics and to obtain the details of the latest practices and procedures:

The Insolvency Service:
<http://www.gov.uk/government/organisations/insolvency-service>

Companies House:
<http://www.gov.uk/government/organisations/companies-house>

Department for Business and Trade
<http://www.gov.uk/government/organisations/department-for-business-and-trade>

You will also find a useful glossary of insolvency terminology in the summary at the end of Part IV.

Note: The law is accurate as at 1 May 2025, but readers should be aware that insolvency is very much a fast-moving area of law, so it is important to keep up to date with both actual and potential changes.

CHAPTER 19

CORPORATE INSOLVENCY

LEARNING OUTCOMES

After reading this chapter you will be able to:

- explain how to assess the insolvency of a company
- understand the process for and the effect of liquidation
- describe how to preserve and increase the company's assets
- describe how to distribute company assets on liquidation
- list and explain the alternatives to liquidation.

19.1 INTRODUCTION

The law relating to corporate insolvency is mainly contained in the Insolvency Act 1986 (IA 1986). The IA 1986 has been subject to a number of amendments in the last 39 years, and subsequent Acts in this area have been passed which have developed the law, but it still remains the root piece of legislation for this area of law. The detailed rules for implementing the law are contained in the Insolvency Rules 2016 (SI 2016/1024) (IR 2016), which came into force on 6 April 2017.

The basic aims of corporate insolvency law (in no particular order) are to:

- protect creditors of the company;
- balance the interests of competing groups of creditors;
- promote corporate rescues; and
- control or punish the directors.

With this is mind, there are several mechanisms available to the companies, the creditors and other interested parties. In this chapter we are going to look at the following:

(a) *Liquidation* – which ultimately brings the company to an end and divides up the assets (see **19.3**, **19.4** and **19.10**).

(b) *Administration and company voluntary arrangements* – both of which aim to rescue the company (**see 19.7**).

(c) *The moratorium and restructuring plan* – both of which are new corporate rescue procedures introduced by the Corporate Insolvency and Governance Act (CIGA) 2020 (see **19.7**).

(d) *Receivership* – an option for secured creditors to recover what is owed solely to them (**see 19.8**).

The latest statistics for each procedure can be found on the Insolvency Service website at <http://www.gov.uk/government/organisations/insolvency-service>

It should be noted that many of the procedures are also available for limited liability partnerships (LLPs), with appropriate modifications, which are beyond the scope of this chapter.

The Department for Business and Trade (DBT) is particularly keen to encourage managed risk-taking and entrepreneurship, by providing mechanisms to help companies in difficulties to get back on their feet, so it is expected that the possibility of rescuing a company will always be explored, before taking the radical step of bringing a company to an end by liquidation.

Throughout this chapter, references to a liquidator, administrator, supervisor of a voluntary arrangement, monitor or administrative receiver mean a Licensed Insolvency Practitioner.

19.2 WHEN IS A COMPANY INSOLVENT AND HOW IS THIS PROVED?

Before we look at insolvency procedures, it is important to be aware of the situations when a company's solvency is relevant. For example:

(a) insolvency is usually a prerequisite for insolvency proceedings (see **19.3** and **19.7**);

(b) the duties owed by the directors depend on whether or not the company is or was insolvent (see **7.13.10**);

(c) past transactions of the company may be investigated, if the company was insolvent at the time or shortly after the transactions were made (see **19.5**);

(d) some company procedures, such as buy-back out of capital, may be undertaken only if the company is solvent (see **9.5.3.2**).

The test for insolvency used for most of the procedures in this chapter is contained in the IA 1986, ss 122 and 123, and is based on the company's ability or otherwise to pay its debts (IA 1986, s 122(1)(f)).

A company is deemed unable to pay its debts if:

(a) a creditor owed more than £750 has served a formal written demand on the company (a 'statutory demand'), waited three weeks and has not been paid or come to an arrangement with the company (IA 1986, s 123(1)(a));

(b) a creditor has obtained judgment against the company *and* attempted to execute the judgment (by sending court officials to recover assets or cash from the company), and the debt is still unsatisfied in full or in part (IA 1986, s 123(1)(b));

(c) it can be proved to the court that the company cannot pay its debts as they fall due (often known as the 'cash flow test' – see **Example 1** below) (IA 1986, s 123(1)(e));

(d) it can be proved to the court that the company's assets are less than its liabilities (often known as the 'balance sheet test' – see **Example 2** below) (IA 1986, s 123(2)).

EXAMPLE 1 – THE CASH FLOW TEST

Debtor Ltd owes £35,000 to Creditor Ltd and this sum is now two months overdue. Creditor Ltd has been telephoning and e-mailing regularly to chase the payment, and Debtor Ltd has been forced to admit, in an e-mail, that it cannot pay any of this sum until it receives payment from some of its debtors, who are themselves late paying.

Creditor Ltd would be able to show that Debtor Ltd is cash-flow insolvent under the IA 1986, s 123(1)(e), using the e-mail as evidence.

EXAMPLE 2 – THE BALANCE SHEET TEST

LMN Ltd has the following assets and liabilities listed on its balance sheet:

Assets	*Value*	*Liabilities*	*Value (in £000)*
Factory/offices	£600,000	Bank loans	(£900,000)
Debtors and cash	£20,000	Outstanding interest on loans	(£25,000)
Machinery/ equipment	£30,000	Creditors	(£75,000)
Total	£650,000		(£1,000,000)

If the figures are accurate, it should be possible to prove to the court that the company is balance sheet insolvent under the IA 1986, s 123(2). However, in practice this test is little used, as it is difficult for the creditor to obtain the information, and easy for the debtor company to prove that the figures are out of date or subject to re-valuation.

In addition, the Supreme Court decision in *BNY Corporate Trustee Services Ltd v Eurosail-UK 2007-3BL PLC* [2013] UKSC 28 sets out the complex arguments that can exist for the balance sheet insolvency test.

In fact, it is usually easier to use the statutory demand ((a) above) or unsatisfied judgment ((b) above), as they are both deemed evidence of insolvency and the creditor does not have to provide additional evidence (which may be difficult to obtain) to prove that the debtor is actually insolvent.

19.2.1 What are the insolvent company's options?

The directors of a company that is or may be insolvent must be very careful to take all steps they can to remedy the situation. In particular, reference should be made to the provisions set out in s 172(3) of the Companies Act 2006. They should usually take professional advice as soon as possible and need to be alert to the possibility that one or more creditors may serve statutory demands or sue, making the need for action even more pressing. If they do not take all steps, they may be personally liable on liquidation or administration (see **7.13.10**) and may be subject to disqualification (see **6.10.6**). The directors have several options, as outlined below:

(a) To take steps (together with the members of the company) to put the company into liquidation themselves (see **19.3.2**).

(b) To talk to their creditors, to see if they will wait for payment or come to a compromise.

(c) To enter into a formal arrangement with their creditors, called a company voluntary arrangement (CVA). This may be an arrangement to pay the creditors less than the full amount owed, or for them to wait longer to be paid. A CVA may allow the company to avoid liquidation (see **19.7.3**).

(d) To appoint an administrator to take over the running of the company and, possibly, to return it to solvent trading or sell it as a going concern (see **19.7.1**). Again, this may allow the company to avoid liquidation and provide a better result for creditors overall.

(e) To utilise the moratorium procedure created by CIGA 2020 as a 'breathing space' (see **19.7.4**).

(f) To enter into a restructuring plan created by CIGA 2020 (see **19.7.5**).

(g) To enter into a scheme of arrangement pursuant to the Companies Act 2006 (see **19.7.6**).

19.2.2 What are the unpaid creditor's options?

The options of an unpaid creditor often depend on whether it has security or not.

19.2.2.1 Unsecured creditor

The options of an unsecured creditor would be to:

(a) serve a statutory demand for a debt in excess of £750 (IA 1986, s 123(1)(a)), wait three weeks and then present a petition to the court to put the company into liquidation;

(b) sue the company, obtain judgment, attempt to execute the judgment (IA 1986, s 123 (1)(b)) and then present a petition to the court to put the company into liquidation;

(c) suggest a CVA, although this is a process driven by the company through its directors (see **19.7.3**);

(d) apply to court to put the company into administration (see **19.7.1**).

Generally, an unsecured creditor will prefer one of the rescue mechanisms in (c) or (d), as it is likely to receive little or nothing if the company goes into liquidation. However, the issue of a statutory demand or the commencement of court action may encourage the debtor company to find the money to pay that particular creditor, rather than another, if it possibly can, which may solve the problem for that creditor.

It should also be noted that, despite some considerable discussion in the insolvency profession, the minimum debt required to serve a statutory demand and thus potentially trigger a winding up petition remains at the very low figure of £750, and there are no imminent plans to increase that.

19.2.2.2 Secured creditor

As well as the options listed in **19.2.2.1** above, the secured creditor *may* have the following *additional* options, depending on the type of security it has:

(a) To appoint an administrator out of court (see **19.7.1.6**).

(b) To appoint an LPA receiver (see **19.8.1**).

(c) If the security for the debt was created before 15 September 2003, to appoint an administrative receiver (see **19.8.2**).

It should also be noted that the secured creditor must be very careful not to take any steps which may result in the loss of security. For example, a statutory demand should only be served for the unsecured element of any debt. It is always better to rely on the options created by the security itself.

19.3 WHAT IS LIQUIDATION?

Liquidation, also known as a 'winding up', is the most common form of insolvency procedure. Liquidation is the end of the road for a company; it ceases to exist.

The basic steps are:

(a) Liquidation proceedings are commenced.

(b) A liquidator is appointed.

(c) The liquidator collects the company's assets and may review past transactions.

(d) The liquidator distributes the assets in the statutory order to the creditors.

(e) The company is dissolved.

There are three types of liquidation:

(a) *Compulsory liquidation* (CL) – commenced against an *insolvent* company by a third party.

(b) *Creditors' voluntary liquidation* (CVL) – commenced by an *insolvent* company, usually in response to creditor pressure.

(c) *Members' voluntary liquidation* (MVL) – commenced by a *solvent* company that wishes to cease trading or is possibly also dormant.

19.3.1 Compulsory liquidation

Compulsory liquidation is normally a result of a hostile process initiated against the company's wishes. In a CL, the company is insolvent. The process is commenced by the presentation at court of a winding-up petition. The petitioner must be able to prove one or more of the grounds in the IA 1986, s 122 (see **19.3.1.1** below). This is not a decision to be taken lightly by the creditor, as they must pay a substantial deposit to cover the costs of the Official Receiver (who is always the initial liquidator) and also a fee to the court. These deposits and fees are updated regularly and should be checked before filing the petition. The current fees may be found at <www.gov.uk/government/publications/fees-in-the-civil-and-family-courts-main-fees-ex50> (Civil and Family Court Fees – Leaflet EX50) and in the Insolvency Proceedings (Fees) (Amendment) Order 2022 (SI 2022/929). It is important to ensure the correct fee is paid as these do change reasonably regularly. At the time of writing, the combined fee plus deposit to commence compulsory winding up proceedings is £2,943.00.

19.3.1.1 Grounds for compulsory liquidation

The most common ground on which a petition for liquidation may be founded is that the company is unable to pay its debts (IA 1986, s 122 (1)(f)). As we saw at **19.2**, there are four ways in which this may be proved:

(a) By statutory demand (IA 1986, s 123(1)(a)).

(b) By unsatisfied judgment (IA 1986, s 123(1)(b)).

(c) By the cash flow test (IA 1986, s 123(1)(e)). There are a number of indicators that a court may take into account in assessing whether a company is unable to satisfy the cash flow test. These include:

  (i) the creditor having demanded money and the company (without reasonable excuse) having failed to comply with that demand; and

  (ii) the company admitting it cannot pay the debt (eg, in open correspondence).

(d) By the balance sheet test (IA 1986, s 123(2)).

The courts will consider all relevant factors and may dismiss the petition if the debtor company can show that it may recover its financial position or if the debt is disputed in any way by the debtor company. The Court of Appeal set out the relevant law in this area in the case of *Tallington Lakes Ltd v Ancasta International Boat Sales Ltd* [2012] EWCA Civ 1712. In general terms, if the debtor company is able to establish a genuine and substantial dispute, the petitioning creditor will be injuncted and prevented from proceeding with the petition. For a Court of Appeal decision on this area, see *Misra Ventures Ltd v LDX International Group LLP* [2018] EWCA Civ 330 where the Court dismissed an injunction to restrain the presentation of a winding-up petition on the basis that there was inadequate material before it to justify finding that there was a dispute via a cross claim of substance. Each case is, of course, decided on its own facts, but, generally, if some evidence of a dispute is established, the court will find in favour of the debtor company. There are some very limited exceptions to this, for example see *Lacontha Foundation v GBI Investments Ltd* [2010] EWHC 37 (Ch), in which the High Court set out guidelines for assessing whether the winding-up order should be made, even when the debt is disputed. Of course, if the petitioning creditor has a judgment already, it will be very difficult for the debtor company to succeed in arguing that there is a dispute unless it is also able to have the judgment set aside.

If the winding-up petition is accepted and the winding-up order is made, the Official Receiver (OR), a civil servant and court official employed by the Insolvency Service, will automatically become liquidator. They must decide whether it is appropriate for the creditors to appoint an insolvency practitioner as liquidator in their place. Obviously, no private practice insolvency practitioner will be willing to act unless there are sufficient assets within the company to pay their fees.

In general terms, if more than 50% in value of creditors formally seek a private practice insolvency practitioner to be appointed, then their wishes should prevail. In certain circumstances as well, the OR may decide that it is appropriate for an alternative private practice liquidator to be appointed rather than the case remaining with the Insolvency Service.

- Note: There were some temporary provisions created by CIGA 2020 and related statutory instruments which made the process of putting a company into compulsory liquidation more onerous for a creditor. However, those provisions no longer remain in force, and the winding up practice and procedure is as it was prior to the temporary measures placed in force during the pandemic, with the £750 minimum debt level remaining.

19.3.2 Voluntary liquidation

There are two types of voluntary liquidation, creditors' voluntary liquidation and members' voluntary liquidation. Both are voluntary in the sense that the directors and members of the company initiate the process, rather than a creditor, but only the MVL is truly voluntary, in that the members and directors control the process from start to finish. It is important to remember that the members and directors of a company may not be the same persons. In small private companies, they may be, of course. Directors undertake the day-to-day management of the company and this would include managing situations when financial issues raise their head. Hence, it is often appropriate to talk of directors initiating formal insolvency processes, but the members also have their part to play at the outset as the owners of the company.

19.3.2.1 Creditors' voluntary liquidation

A CVL is initiated by the directors of the company and is then taken forward by the creditors of the company. However, whilst the CVL procedure is voluntary (in that the directors are not being forced to recommend liquidation), it is usually the result either of outside creditor pressure or of professional advice to the directors that the company is insolvent. Directors are usually unwilling to put the company into liquidation, as they always think that better times are around the corner. However, the threat of potential actions against them for misfeasance and fraudulent or wrongful trading usually concentrates their minds (see **7.13.10**).

19.3.2.2 Members' voluntary liquidation

This is available only to a solvent company. The directors have to swear a statutory declaration that the company is solvent and must take appropriate advice before doing so. They are liable to a fine, or even imprisonment, for making the declaration without reasonable grounds (IA 1986, s 89(4)). If the company is not solvent, then the CVL (**19.3.2.1** above) should be used instead.

A solvent company may want to wind itself up for a number of reasons, for example:

(a) the company is small and the directors (who are the only shareholders) all want to retire; or

(b) a group of companies has become unwieldy and some of the companies within it are no longer operational.

CASE EXAMPLES OF LIQUIDATIONS

1. Blackpool Airport Limited went into CVL in October 2014, following several years of trading at a loss. The company owed more than £35 million on liquidation, with assets of less than £600,000.
2. Ilkeston Town Football Club went into CL in 2010, after HMRC issued a winding-up petition. Despite vociferous argument and offers of monthly payments, the court concluded that the company was clearly insolvent and granted the petition.

> Many other football clubs have also faced insolvency actions in recent years, of course, including a number of high-profile ones, with Bolton Wanderers FC going into administration at the end of the 2018/19 season and Wigan Athletic FC suffering a similar fate in 2020. In general terms, for football clubs, the aim is to avoid liquidation and seek alternative rescue mechanisms to enable the club to survive and continue to operate as a professional body. This happened after long and difficult processes for both Bolton Wanderers and Wigan Athletic. However, the well-publicised case of Bury Football Club demonstrated that sometimes these rescue procedures are simply not possible and Bury was expelled from the English Football League in 2019.

19.4 THE LIQUIDATION PROCESS AND THE EFFECT ON THE COMPANY AND ITS DIRECTORS

19.4.1 Liquidation process

The process of liquidation is relatively straightforward and is similar for compulsory and voluntary liquidations. It can last for a few months, or for a number of years. The detail is set out in the flowchart at **19.10.1** below.

19.4.2 Powers and duties of the liquidator

The powers and duties of the liquidator are broadly the same for compulsory and voluntary liquidations (IA 1986, Sch 4 (as amended)). This Schedule to the Insolvency Act 1986 contains a list of statutory powers that liquidators used to be able to exercise with sanction of the court or creditors. Following the introduction of the Small Business, Enterprise and Employment Act 2015, a liquidator no longer needs sanction before exercising any of the powers set out in Parts 1–3 of Sch 4. Such powers include the following:

(a) To collect in the assets and distribute them in accordance with the statutory order (see **19.6**).

(b) To sell assets.

(c) To use the company bank account.

(d) To appoint agents.

(e) To litigate on the company's behalf and defend litigation on the company's behalf.

(f) To carry on the company business.

(g) To do all of the things necessary to facilitate winding up.

(h) To investigate past transactions of the company (see **19.5**) and the conduct of the directors (see **7.13.10**).

Additional duties are imposed on the Official Receiver in CLs, to ensure that matters are investigated thoroughly and that a report is presented to the creditors and (if necessary) to the court (see IA 1986, s 132).

The liquidator will also review the actions of the directors as, if a director has transferred property after the winding up has begun, or in anticipation of it up to one year beforehand, the director may be liable for the offence of fraud under the IA 1986, s 206 (see the example below). Other recovery actions also exist for the liquidator or administrator, and these are considered at **19.5** below.

> **CASE EXAMPLE**
>
> In *R (on the application of BERR) v Lowe* [2009] EWCA Crim 194, the director pleaded guilty to the offence in IA 1986, s 206(1)(b) of fraudulently removing the company's property during winding-up proceedings (he had transferred company property to another company he owned after the commencement of winding-up proceedings by HMRC) and was made subject to a confiscation order under the Proceeds of Crime Act 2002, s 6(6) and s 7(3).

Also, if it appears to the liquidator during the course of a MVL that the company is insolvent, the liquidator must convert the liquidation to a CVL (IA 1986, s 95).

19.4.3 Effects of liquidation

The main effects of liquidation are that:

(a) the directors' powers cease, and the liquidator takes over the running of the company (IA 1986, ss 91 and 103); and

(b) in a CL the directors' appointments are terminated (*Measures Brothers Ltd v Measures* [1910] 2 Ch 248).

19.4.4 The end of the liquidation

The liquidation concludes when:

(a) the liquidator sells the available assets;

(b) they distribute the money to the creditors (see **19.6**);

(c) the liquidator is released;

(d) the accounts are forwarded to Companies House and the court; and

(e) three months later the company is dissolved by the Registrar of Companies.

19.5 PRESERVING AND INCREASING THE COMPANY'S ASSETS

When financial pressures exist or when liquidation or administration is looming on the horizon, it is quite common for the directors (and others) to consider dispersing assets away from the company's ownership, to keep them out of the hands of the liquidator or administrator.

As liquidators and administrators have a duty to maximise the funds available to the creditors, if possible, and not to do anything which would decrease them, there are various powers in the IA 1986 that allow them to investigate the company's affairs and the actions of the directors prior to liquidation and/or administration. We shall look briefly at the powers to investigate, and sometimes to set aside certain transactions, namely:

(a) Transactions at an undervalue.

(b) Preferences.

(c) Extortionate credit transactions.

(d) Floating charges.

(e) Transactions defrauding creditors.

See **19.5.1** to **19.5.5** below.

In pursuing such actions, the aim is to challenge any transactions that are voidable and therefore return assets or cash to the company for the benefit of the creditors.

There are further powers to investigate the conduct of the directors, which may allow the liquidator or administrator to obtain a financial contribution to the company assets from the individual directors personally. Liquidators or administrators may investigate:

(a) fraudulent trading; and

(b) wrongful trading.

On *liquidation only*, the liquidator may also disclaim onerous transactions (IA 1986, s 178) and investigate misfeasance (IA 1986, s 212).

See **7.13.10** for details.

19.5.1 Transactions at an undervalue

Only a liquidator or an administrator is able to pursue a transaction at an undervalue (IA 1986, s 238(1) and (2) (as amended)). It is not a remedy which may be pursued by creditors generally.

EXAMPLE OF A VOIDABLE TRANSACTION AT AN UNDERVALUE

Cars Ltd, a car auctioneer, has been finding the recession difficult and has numerous creditors pressing for outstanding payments which it cannot meet.

It allows the directors to transfer their company cars into their own names, so they can keep them even if the company comes to an end.

Six months later the company goes into administration, and the administrator applies to have the transfers set aside, so the cars can be returned to the ownership of the company.

19.5.1.1 What is an undervalue?

An undervalue (IA 1986, s 238(4)) is either:

(a) a gift; or

(b) a transaction where the company received consideration (in money or money's worth) significantly lower in value than it provided. For example, a company sells a large amount of its own office furniture to the wife of one of the directors for £500. She immediately sells it on to a hotel chain for £5,000. In short, the company is not receiving what it should for its assets, and the director's wife has benefited to the detriment of the general body of creditors.

Is granting security a transaction at an undervalue? This was considered at length in the case of *Re MC Bacon Ltd* [1990] BCLC 324, when it was decided that the granting of security does not change the value of the company's assets and therefore cannot reduce their value. So, the granting of security is unlikely to be a transaction at an undervalue.

19.5.1.2 How far back can the liquidator or administrator go?

The transaction must occur within the 'relevant time'. The 'relevant time' is two years ending with the onset of insolvency (IA 1986, s 240(1)(a)). The onset of insolvency varies depending on the procedure involved. For a CL this will be the date of presentation of the petition, and for a CVL it will be the date it formally enters into liquidation. For administration, it will be the date when the company files a Notice of Intention to Appoint an Administrator or the date when it actually goes into administration (whichever is the earlier).

19.5.1.3 Does the company have to have been insolvent at the time?

When the transaction was entered into, the company must have been insolvent at the time or become insolvent as a result (IA 1986 s 240(2)). This is presumed for a connected person (see IA 1986, s 249 for the definition of a 'connected person' – broadly, a director or their spouse or any other closely related family member defined as an 'associate' (see IA 1986, s 435)). The presumption may be rebutted.

The liquidator/administrator will have to produce evidence of insolvency at the time or as a result, by referring to balance sheets, correspondence, court proceedings, etc.

19.5.1.4 Is there a defence?

There is a defence (IA 1986, s 238(5)) if the transaction was entered into in good faith, for the purpose of carrying on the business and when it was made there were reasonable grounds for believing it would benefit the company.

Obviously, it would be up to the directors to produce evidence of the circumstances at the time, such as board minutes, meetings with banks, legal advisers and accountants, to show that they were acting in the interests of the company and not their own interests.

19.5.1.5 What orders may be made?

If a transaction at an undervalue is proved, the transaction will be voidable at the discretion of the court and a number of orders may be made by the court (IA 1986, s 241). These include returning property to the company (s 241(1)(a)), returning proceeds of sale to the company (s 241(1)(b)) and the discharge of any security (s 241(1)(c)).

19.5.2 Preferences

19.5.2.1 What is a preference?

A preference arises where one person is 'preferred' by the company, in that it has been paid ahead of other creditors or been put in a better position on insolvent liquidation or administration (IA 1986, s 239(4) (as amended)). The definition makes it clear that:

(a) the person preferred must be the company's creditor, surety or guarantor (otherwise there can be no preference);

(b) the person preferred must have been put in a better position on liquidation or administration than they would have been in had the event not occurred; and

(c) the company *must have desired to prefer* the creditor/guarantor/surety (IA 1986, s 239(5)) (see **19.5.2.2** below).

Examples of a preference include:

(a) making an unsecured creditor secured;

(b) paying one unsecured creditor before other unsecured creditors;

(c) allowing a supplier of goods to change its terms and conditions to include a retention of title clause where none existed previously; or

(d) allowing a creditor to enter judgment against the company when the company has a good defence to the claim.

EXAMPLE OF A VOIDABLE PREFERENCE

Greenveg Ltd delivers organic food boxes nationally. When its only van breaks down and is irreparable, Greenveg decides to borrow the money for a new van from Bob, one of the two directors, rather than from the bank, so that it does not have to pay interest.

Over the following months, the business suffers and starts to lose money. Management accounts show the company is probably insolvent. Both directors decide that they should repay the loan to Bob, while they still have enough cash to do so.

Eighteen months later the company goes into CVL. The liquidator applies to set aside the repayment as a voidable preference, so that the loan repayment can be returned to the company.

19.5.2.2 Desire to prefer

The company must have desired to prefer the creditor (IA 1986, ss 239(5) and (6)). The courts have said that desire to prefer is stronger than intention, and that a desire means that the company should 'positively wish' to put somebody in a better position.

CASE EXAMPLE ON 'DESIRE TO PREFER'

In *Re MC Bacon Ltd* [1990] BCLC 324, the bacon retailer was in financial difficulty and approached the bank for an increased overdraft. The bank agreed, subject to taking a floating charge. The company then went into liquidation and the liquidator argued the charge was a preference. Discussing whether there was a desire to prefer, Millet J said:

> A man is not to be taken as desiring all the necessary consequences of his actions. Some consequences may be of advantage to him and be desired by him; others may not affect him and be matters of indifference to him; while still others may be positively disadvantageous to him and not be desired by him but be regarded by him as the unavoidable price of obtaining the desired advantages ... the company [must] positively wish ... to improve the creditor's position.

He concluded that the company had granted the charge so that it could try to keep the company going, and not with a desire to put the bank in a better position on insolvent liquidation, and so the transaction could not be a preference.

Desire to prefer is presumed if the preference is in favour of a connected person (see IA 1986, s 249 for the definition of a connected person, as set out above). This presumption may be rebutted.

19.5.2.3 How far back can the liquidator or administrator go?

If a preference is given to a person who is *connected* (IA 1986, s 249) with the company then the time period is two years, ending with the onset of insolvency (IA 1986, s 240(1)). For the definition of 'onset of insolvency', see **19.5.1.2**.

If a preference is given to someone who is *unconnected* then the relevant time is six months, ending with the onset of insolvency.

19.5.2.4 Does the company have to have been insolvent at the time?

The company must have been insolvent at the time of the preference or must have become so as a result (IA 1986, s 240(2)), but there is no presumption of insolvency if the preference is to a connected person (which is different to the position for a transaction at an undervalue recovery action).

19.5.2.5 Orders

The orders that may be made are the same as for transactions at an undervalue (see **19.5.1.5**).

19.5.3 Extortionate credit transactions

A liquidator or an administrator may apply to reopen credit transactions made within three years from when the company went into liquidation (IA 1986, s 244(2)).

They may apply only if the credit transaction was *extortionate*. This is defined in IA 1986, s 244(3). Basically, payments must be 'grossly exorbitant', or the transaction must 'grossly contravene ordinary principles of fair dealing'.

There is very little case law on this area as it is quite rare in practice, since it is extremely hard to show that the payments are 'grossly exorbitant'.

19.5.4 Floating charges

19.5.4.1 What types of floating charges may be avoided?

A floating charge may be:

(a) voidable as a preference (see **19.5.2**); and/or

(b) an invalid floating charge and automatically void (see **19.5.4.2** and **19.5.4.3**) (IA 1986, s 245).

19.5.4.2 Invalid floating charges

There does not have to be an application by an insolvency office holder under IA 1986, s 245. If the criteria are fulfilled, the floating charge is automatically invalid. In practice, the office holder will write to the floating charge holder stating that the office holder believes the floating charge to be invalid. Usually, the next step is that the floating charge holder will either seek to enforce the charge and force the liquidator into injunctive proceedings or, more commonly, seek a declaration from the court that the floating charge is valid.

The section is primarily designed to invalidate floating charges which have been created for *no* consideration. The section *does not* apply to fixed charges.

19.5.4.3 How far back can the liquidator or administrator go?

If the floating charge is given to a person who is *connected* with the company, then the time period is two years, ending with the onset of insolvency (IA 1986, s 245(5)). For the definition of 'onset of insolvency', see **19.5.1.2**.

If the floating charge is given to someone who is *unconnected* then the relevant time is 12 months, ending with the onset of insolvency. (Remember the definition of a 'connected person' from IA 1986, s 249.)

19.5.4.4 Does the company have to have been insolvent at the time?

If the floating charge is given to an unconnected person, the company must have been insolvent at the time of the charge or must have become so as a result (IA 1986, s 245(4)). There is no need to show insolvency if the transaction is with a connected person.

EXAMPLE OF AN INVALID FLOATING CHARGE

ABC Ltd has an unsecured overdraft of £50,000 at the bank; and the bank, upon hearing that the company is in financial difficulty, requires a floating charge to secure the overdraft. It does not change the overdraft limit or provide any fresh lending. ABC Ltd goes into insolvent liquidation seven months later.

This floating charge will be automatically invalid if the liquidator can show that ABC Ltd was insolvent at the time it was given. This is because no consideration was provided by the bank at the time the security was given. The consideration occurred earlier, when the overdraft limit was agreed. The bank will become an unsecured creditor.

19.5.5 Transactions defrauding creditors

There are also powers in IA 1986, s 423 to set aside transactions defrauding creditors. This section is much wider than the other sections we have already looked at. Basically, any 'victim' of such a transaction may make an application, with the leave of the court. Liquidators and administrators may also make an application, and it is also appropriate in the personal insolvency arena (see **20.5.4**).

19.5.5.1 What is a transaction defrauding creditors?

A transaction is one to defraud creditors if it is at an undervalue (IA 1986, s 238, see **19.5.1**) *and* the purpose of the transaction was to:

(a) put assets beyond the reach of someone in relation to any claim they might make; or
(b) prejudice the interests of someone in relation to any claim they might make (IA 1986, s 423(3)).

A classic example is a company engaged in litigation which sees that a substantial judgment will be awarded against it at the end of the day. As a result of this, it siphons off assets to third parties so that the judgment may not be enforced.

19.5.5.2 Orders

The orders that may be made by the court are similar to those under IA 1986, s 241 (see **19.5.1.5**) (IA 1986, s 425).

There is no time limit in IA 1986 for transactions defrauding creditors, so in practice, as it is so hard to prove the intention to defraud, s 423 tends to be used only when the time limit for transactions at an undervalue has expired. For a very recent case which considered the breadth of s 423, see *El-Husseiny v Invest Bank PSC* [2025] UKSC 4. There, the appellant attempted to argue that s 423 could not apply as the property that was transferred belonged to a corporate vehicle and not himself. The Supreme Court disagreed and concluded that s 423 is sufficiently wide to apply when a debtor causes their company to transfer the company's assets at an undervalue, thereby resulting in the diminution of the value of the debtor's shares. If this was not the case, it would prejudice a creditor's ability to enforce a judgment against a debtor.

19.6 DISTRIBUTING THE COMPANY'S ASSETS IN A LIQUIDATION

During the course of the liquidation, a liquidator (whether it be voluntary or compulsory) will ask creditors to send them details of their debt on a standard form. This is called 'proving the debt'. The liquidator will then approve or reject the proof of debt and will rank it in the liquidation. There are some exceptions to this procedure for 'small debts', which are defined as sums that do not exceed £1,000, when the acceptance procedure is much more straightforward.

Once all the assets have been collected in and realised, a liquidator must pay the assets in the following order (subject to fixed charges – see **19.6.1** below) (IA 1986, ss 175, 176ZA and 176A):

(a) Expenses of the winding up (the liquidator's and their professional advisers' fees).

(b) Preferential debts (which rank and abate equally – see **19.6.4** below).

(c) Monies secured by floating charges by order of priority (subject to ring fencing – see **19.6.3**).

(d) Unsecured creditors (which rank and abate equally – see **19.6.4** below).

(e) If there is any surplus, it is distributed amongst shareholders.

19.6.1 What about fixed charges?

Fixed charges will usually have been paid out already, when the asset to which they were fixed was sold. If there is a surplus, this will be paid to the liquidator. If there is a shortfall, the fixed charge holder may try to recover this shortfall as an unsecured creditor.

19.6.2 What are preferential debts?

There are a few categories of preferential debts in the IA 1986, ss 175, 386 and Sch 6, and also those created on 1 January 2015 by the Banks and Building Societies (Depositor Preference and Priorities) Order 2014 (SI 2014/3486), but the most common are as follows:

(a) Wages and salary of employees for work done in the four months before the insolvency date (IA 1986, Sch 6, para 9), up to a maximum of £800 per person (Insolvency Proceedings (Monetary Limits) Order 1986 (SI 1986/1996), art 4).

(b) Holiday pay due to any employee whose contract has been terminated, whether that termination takes place before or after the insolvency date (IA 1986, Sch 6, para 10).

Until comparatively recently, employees were the only type of preferential creditor in cases of insolvent liquidation, but from 1 December 2020, legislation via the Finance Act 2020 was brought in to enable HMRC to join them as secondary preferential creditors. This move up the rankings further displaces unsecured creditors and, given that HMRC is usually one of the largest creditors in these situations, there are obvious implications for UK businesses.

Being a secondary preferential creditor means HMRC is only to be a preferred creditor in relation to certain types of taxes – in this case the taxes collected by a business on its behalf, such as PAYE and VAT. HMRC will remain an unsecured creditor for corporation tax and any other taxes owed directly by a company.

19.6.3 What is ring fencing?

Before distributing assets to the holders of floating charges created on or after 15 September 2003 (IA 1986, s 176A), the liquidator must set aside ('ring fence') the prescribed part for unsecured creditors.

The prescribed part is calculated as a percentage of the value of the company's property which is subject to floating charges, with 50% of the first £10,000 of net floating charge realisations plus 20% of anything thereafter, up to the increased limit of £800,000 made by the Insolvency Act 1986 (Prescribed Part) (Amendment) Order 2020. That Order amended the Insolvency Act 1986 (Prescribed Part) Order 2003 to increase the prescribed part cap from £600,000 to £800,000 and came into force on 6 April 2020.

Lenders with floating charges should note that the Order will not apply to floating charges created before 6 April 2020 (a 'grandfathered floating charge') provided no floating charge is created after 6 April 2020 which ranks equally with or in priority to the grandfathered floating charge.

Secured creditors are not allowed to have access to the ring-fenced fund for any unsecured portion of their debts (*Re Airbase (UK) Ltd v HMRC* [2008] EWHC 124 (Ch)).

19.6.4 What does rank and abate equally mean?

If debts or creditors rank and abate equally, this means that all the creditors in a particular category (eg, preferential creditors) will share the money available. Since there may not be enough for every creditor in that category to be paid in full, each will receive the same percentage of their original debt.

SIMPLE EXAMPLE OF A FINAL DISTRIBUTION BY LIQUIDATOR WITH NO SECURED CREDITOR INVOLVED

Debts		*Funds available to liquidator (assets)*
Owed to HMRC	£45,000	£100,000
Costs of liquidation	£10,000	
Owed to preferential creditors	£15,000	
Owed to business creditors	£120,000	

Calculation showing how the assets are shared out

Funds available to liquidator	£100,000
Less costs and expenses (paid in full)	(£10,000)
Less preferential creditors (paid in full)	(£15,000)
Amount remaining for unsecured creditors	£75,000

Unsecured creditors amount to £45,000 + £120,000 = £165,000

75,000/165,000 = approx. £0.46

Unsecured creditors receive approximately 46p for every £1 they are owed.

This example illustrates the fact that anyone issuing a winding-up petition as a creditor should bear in mind that they alone will not receive the assets of the company. The assets will be distributed according to the statutory order and equally amongst all of a particular class of creditors, if there is not sufficient to pay them in full. Unsecured creditors are highly unlikely to receive more than a few pence in the pound in a normal insolvent liquidation, as the majority of the assets are usually subject to security.

19.7 ALTERNATIVES TO LIQUIDATION

The company (and, sometimes, the creditor) may try to avoid liquidation by using one of the following procedures:

(a) Administration (IA 1986, Sch B1) (see **19.7.1** and **19.7.2** below).

(b) Company voluntary arrangements (CVAs) (IA 1986, Part I) (see **19.7.3** below).

(c) The moratorium procedure (CIGA 2020, s 1, inserting a new Part A1 into the IA 1986) (see **19.7.4** below).

(d) The restructuring plan procedure (CIGA 2020, s 7 and Sch 9, inserting a new Part 26A (ss 901A–910L) into the Companies Act 2006 (see **19.7.5** below).

(e) Schemes of arrangement (CA 2006, ss 895–901) (see **19.7.6** below).

(f) Informal agreements with creditors.

The procedures are not mutually exclusive, and, for example, an informal agreement may be followed by a CVA, or an administrator may arrange a CVA. In addition, the new moratorium procedure (at (c) above) may be a precursor for a subsequent CVA or administration. We shall look in more detail at the first two options, and then also analyse the two new procedures (c) and (d) brought in by CIGA 2020. Finally, we shall then briefly consider option (e). As for option (f), this is a non-statutory and non-binding solution, so clearly there is always a risk that one or more creditors may choose to invoke winding up or other procedures. It is not necessary to consider it in any further detail, therefore.

19.7.1 Administration

Administration is a procedure which allows an independent insolvency practitioner, the administrator, to run, reorganise and possibly sell, as a going concern, a company that is suffering financial problems. The main advantage of this procedure is that the administrator has the benefit of a moratorium (freeze on creditor actions) (see **19.7.1.4**), which allows them to operate virtually unhindered by creditors at the outset of the process. This moratorium must not be confused with the separate moratorium procedure created by CIGA 2020 (see **19.7.4** below).

The latest regime for administration was implemented on 15 September 2003. This revised regime in effect replaces administrative receivership (see **19.8.2**) for charges coming into existence on or after that date, and radically changes the form of administration in place before that date. The reasons for the reform were twofold:

(a) Administrative receivership was seen to be too slanted toward the interests of the secured creditor who appointed the administrative receiver. This was at the expense of other creditors, and hampered the 'rescue' of a company in financial difficulty.

(b) The old model of administration was unwieldy, expensive and often of indeterminate duration.

Administrative receivership still exists for charges created before 15 September 2003 but will become less important as time passes of course (see **19.8.2**).

19.7.1.1 The purposes of administration

IA 1986, Sch B1, para 3(1) states that the administrator has to perform their duties with the object of:

(a) rescuing the company as a going concern; *or*
(b) achieving a better result for the company's creditors as a whole than would be likely if the company were wound up (without first being in administration); *or*
(c) realising property in order to make a distribution to one or more secured or preferential creditors (IA 1986, Sch B1, para 3(1)).

The administrator must start by aiming for objective (a) and move down the list only if the alternative is not reasonably practicable, or if objective (b) is better for the creditors as a whole and objective (c) will not unnecessarily harm them (IA 1986, Sch B1, para 3(3) and (4)).

The administrator has to perform all their duties in the interests of the company's creditors as a whole (IA 1986, Sch B1, para 3(2)).

19.7.1.2 The administration process

There are two routes into administration:

(a) By court order, made in an open hearing, upon a formal application to court (the *court route*) (IA 1986, Sch B1, para 10) by one of the persons set out in IA 1986, Sch B1, para 12(1).
(b) By the filing at court of a prescribed series of documents (the *out-of-court route*), by:
    (i) the company (para 22(1));
    (ii) its directors (para 22(2)); or
    (iii) the holder of a *qualifying floating charge* (see **19.7.1.3**) over the company's assets (para 14).

19.7.1.3 What is a qualifying floating charge?

A qualifying floating charge (QFC) is one where the charge document:

(a) states that para 14 of Sch B1 to the IA 1986 applies to it and–
    (i) purports to empower the holder of the floating charge to appoint an administrator of the company, or
    (ii) purports to empower the holder of the floating charge to make an appointment which would be the appointment of an administrative receiver within the meaning given by s 29(2) of the IA 1986; *and*
(b) is a QFC which, on its own or with other security held by the same lender, relates to the whole, or substantially the whole, of the company's property (para 14(3)).

SAMPLE CLAUSE IN A QFC

12.1 Subject as provided below, if:

12.1.1 the Debenture Holder has demanded payment of any money or discharge of any obligation secured by this Deed; or

12.1.2 the Company so requests in writing at any time,

and at any time thereafter the Debenture Holder may appoint any one or more persons to be a Receiver of all or any part of the Charged Assets, and/or may appoint any one or more persons to be Administrators of the Company under paragraph 14 of Schedule B1 to the Insolvency Act 1986. ...

(Source: *Encyclopaedia of Forms & Precedents*)

19.7.1.4 The statutory moratorium

Whichever route is used, there will be a statutory moratorium throughout the administration (IA 1986, Sch B1, paras 42 and 43). This moratorium restricts the ability of third parties to enforce their rights without the consent of the administrator. It also prevents the commencement of any other insolvency procedures, such as the presentation of a winding-up petition.

This gives the administrator vital breathing space to assess the state of the company's finances and to investigate the possibility of selling the company on as a going concern, thus protecting some, or even all, of the employees' jobs.

19.7.1.5 The court route

The court may make an administration order only if it is satisfied that:

(a) the company is or is likely to become unable to pay its debts (as defined in IA 1986, s 123); and

(b) the administration order is reasonably likely to achieve the purpose of administration, typically that administration would achieve a better result for the company's creditors than would liquidation.

As soon as reasonably practicable after making the application, the applicant must notify:

(a) any person who has appointed (or is entitled to appoint) an administrative receiver of the company;

(b) any qualifying floating charge holder (QFCH) who may be entitled to appoint an administrator; and

(c) such other persons as may be prescribed by the IR 2016.

> **CASE EXAMPLE OF APPOINTMENT BY THE COURT**
>
> In *In the Matter of Redman Construction Ltd* [2004] All ER (D) 146 (Jun), the company was in financial difficulty and a winding-up petition had been presented by a creditor. The company applied to the court for an administration order on the basis that it had several large contracts in the pipeline and that the creditors would receive considerably more on administration than on liquidation.
>
> The court agreed that purpose (b) of IA 1986, Sch B1, para 3(1) (see **19.7.1.1**) was likely to be achieved and granted the order.

19.7.1.6 Out-of-court route – appointment by a QFCH

The out-of-court route allows lenders with a QFC easily to appoint administrators. The administrator has a duty to all the creditors, in comparison with receivers, who have, in practical terms, a duty only to their appointer.

If there is another QFCH whose charge would have priority, then the lender cannot appoint an administrator until it has given two business days' written notice of its intention so to appoint. This allows the holder of the prior charge to consider whether to appoint an administrator itself. An interim moratorium exists whilst the other QFCH deliberates on their options.

The floating charge in question must be enforceable. In other words, the floating charge holder must be entitled under the loan agreement to enforce its security, for example, because of late payment by the borrower or other events of default as defined in the charge document itself. This is sometimes called a 'trigger event'.

It is not possible for a QFCH to appoint an administrator out-of-court under IA 1986, Sch B1, para 14 where there is a provisional liquidator or an administrative receiver already appointed or the company is already being wound up, but only if it is being wound up by a creditors' voluntary liquidation (CVL) or there is an administrator already proposed by the company or directors.

Notice of appointment has to be filed at court by the lender together with various documents. The notice must include a statutory declaration by the lender to the effect that:

(a) the lender is the holder of a QFC in respect of the company's property;
(b) the floating charge has become enforceable; and
(c) the appointment is in accordance with IA 1986, Sch B1.

Once these documents have been filed at court (and the other parts of Sch B1, para 18 are complied with) the administration begins.

It should be noted that an 'old' floating charge, ie, one created before 15 September 2003, which complies with the para 14(3) conditions (see **19.7.1.3**) will enable the lender to choose between appointing an administrator and appointing an administrative receiver (see **19.8.2**). In practice, it is the administration process that is almost always utilised these days.

19.7.1.7 Out-of-court route – appointment by the company or directors

This procedure is intended to make corporate rescue easier. The directors, or the company, will need to give notice to any QFCHs. The QFCH will agree or will appoint an alternative administrator. The moratorium comes into effect immediately the notice of intention to appoint is filed at court. However, if it is the company which appoints, the first step will be to call a general meeting (see **8.6–8.9**) to seek the members' approval (see **8.2**). If it is the directors who appoint, they will need to pass a board resolution to that effect.

The first stage of appointment is that a notice of intention is served on:

(a) the court;
(b) any QFCH; and
(c) any lender entitled to appoint an administrative receiver (IA 1986, Sch B1, para 26).

The directors must also file a statutory declaration that:

(a) the company is unable to pay its debts;
(b) the company is not in liquidation; and
(c) the restrictions in paras 23 to 25 do not apply (eg, there has been no administration within the previous 12 months) (IA 1986, Sch B1, para 27(2)).

In practice, what this means is that if a compulsory winding-up petition has been issued, the company or directors cannot utilise the out-of-court administration route but have to make an application to court for the right to appoint an administrator in substitution for the compulsory winding-up petition to continue.

CASE EXAMPLE OF A FAILED APPOINTMENT OUT-OF-COURT BY THE COMPANY

In *Blights Builders Ltd, Re* [2006] EWHC 3549 (Ch), [2007] 3 All ER 776, Ch D, the company had only one director and shareholder, who died. The company was found to be insolvent. The executors used the votes attached to their shares to appoint administrators under IA 1986, Sch B1, para 22. They then gave notice to a floating charge holder under para 26(1), who gave them permission to proceed.

Unfortunately, the executors were unaware that another creditor had already issued a winding-up petition, and so the appointment of the administrators was declared invalid under para 25(a).

19.7.1.8 Administration process

Once the administration has been started, the main moratorium comes into effect and protects the company whilst the administrator tries to rescue it.

The administrator will put forward their proposals. The creditors may seek further details, or may amend the proposals (IA 1986, Sch B1, para 53(1)(b)). It is important to remember that the administrator may have been appointed by the directors (see **19.7.1.7** above), and the creditors may regard the administrator as the directors' 'stooge'. So, ultimately, the creditors always have the 'final say' on decisions. There have been a number of instances where the administrator has been replaced at the request of creditors and an appropriate majority has supported that request. The proposals will be approved if a majority (in value) of creditors present and voting vote in favour of them (as long as those voting against the proposals are not more than 50% (by value) of creditors who are unconnected to the company).

The effects of the administration order are that:

(a) the company is managed by the administrator;
(b) the directors' powers cease, though they are still in office;
(c) the moratorium continues;
(d) the administrator controls the company's assets (but does not own them); and
(e) the administrator carries out the administrator's proposals, which have been approved by the creditors.

19.7.1.9 Powers and duties of an administrator

The administrator has statutory powers under IA 1986, Sch B1, and IR 2016, for example to:

(a) remove and appoint directors (para 61);
(b) call a meeting of creditors or members, if required (para 62);
(c) apply to the court for directions (para 63);
(d) pay money to a creditor (para 65), but only with the court's permission if it is to an unsecured creditor;
(e) pay money to any party if it is likely to assist the administration (para 66);
(f) deal with property that is subject to a floating charge (para 70);
(g) deal with property subject to a fixed charge, subject to the permission of the court (para 71); and
(h) deal with property that is the subject of a hire-purchase agreement (para 72).

Like a liquidator, the administrator also has the power to investigate past transactions of the company and, if necessary, apply to have them set aside or challenged (see **19.5**) so that they can swell the assets available for the creditors. The administrator can also commence fraudulent or wrongful trading proceedings to seek recoveries against directors personally for the benefit of creditors.

In addition to these powers, the administrator has the power to do anything necessary or expedient for the management of the affairs, business and property of the company. They are required to exercise these powers for the purpose of the administration (IA 1986, Sch B1, para 3) (see **19.7.1.1**).

19.7.1.10 End of the administration

The administration may be ended (IA 1986, Sch B1):

(a) automatically after one year from the date the administration took effect – this may be extended in certain circumstances (para 76);
(b) on application by the administrator to the court, under para 79, if:
    (i) they think the purpose of administration cannot be achieved in relation to the company,
    (ii) they think the company should not have entered administration,
    (iii) a creditors' meeting requires them to make an application, or
    (iv) they think that the purpose of administration has been sufficiently achieved in relation to the company;

(c) by termination where the object has been achieved (for an administrator appointed by the out-of-court route) (para 80);

(d) by the court ending the administration on the application of a creditor (para 81);

(e) by the court converting the administration into a liquidation, in the public interest (para 82);

(f) by the administrator converting the administration into a CVL (para 83);

(g) by the administrator dissolving the company where they believe there is no property which might permit a distribution to creditors (para 84); and

(h) when the administrator resigns (para 87), is removed (para 88), ceases to be qualified (para 89) or is replaced by those who appointed the administrator in the first place (paras 92, 93, 94).

CASE EXAMPLE OF AN ADMINISTRATION

HMV, which went into administration in January 2013, managed, via a restructuring deal involving the closure of shops, the renegotiation of leases and the loss of some jobs, to exit administration in April the same year.

By April 2015, the company had regained market share to such an extent that it was Britain's biggest music retailer. However, as has been well reported, it once again fell into administration at the end of 2018 and was the subject of a further insolvency rescue.

Many other retailers have, as has been widely reported, fallen into one or other formal insolvency procedure in the preceding two years, and this is a trend that is likely to continue. In March 2021, Jessops, Britain's 86-year-old specialist camera retailer, filed a notice of intention to appoint administrators for the third time since 2013. The chain is currently owned by the *Dragon's Den* entrepreneur, Peter Jones, who bought it in 2013. There was a second administration in 2019. It was stated that the latest procedure was commenced with a view to considering a CVA process. The business still trades online and from a very limited number of locations.

Another major retailer to suffer in recent years is Debenhams, which has been through a CVA process; administration and also liquidation in recent years. The brand has continued to trade online following its acquisition by Boohoo.

The difficulties facing many commercial retailers was one of the reasons for the new insolvency rescue measures referred to earlier in this chapter and considered later.

19.7.2 'Pre-pack' administration

Pre-packaged administration occurs when a company is placed into administration and almost immediately its assets and business are sold by the administrator, often to the management of the insolvent company. The unsecured creditors are not consulted and are unlikely to be paid many, if any, of their debts. The name of the new business is often close to that of the insolvent company. The justification often given at this stage is that the jobs of the employees are more likely to be saved by using this 'pre-pack' route. This procedure has faced substantial criticism in recent years.

As from 1 January 2009, administrators were bound by an additional Statement of Insolvency Practice, SIP 16 ('SIP'), issued by the Joint Insolvency Committee. This strives to satisfy the unsecured creditors that their interests have been considered, by requiring the administrator to disclose to them various information, including:

(a) the source of the administrator's introduction;

(b) the extent of the administrator's involvement prior to their appointment;

(c) any valuations of the business or the underlying assets;

(d) the alternative courses of action which were considered;

(e) why it was not appropriate to keep the business trading and sell it as a going concern;

(f) whether efforts were made to consult major creditors; and

(g) the identity of the purchasers and any connections they have to the former management.

Since the original version of this SIP was approved, there has been a review of whether further regulation or legislation was necessary to control pre-packs, as they are viewed with great suspicion by unsecured creditors. In January 2013 the Government announced that it would not formally legislate but would instead investigate ways of improving transparency and confidence using the present system. In June 2014 it published the Graham Review, which recommended further amendments to SIP 16 and, amongst other things, self-regulation by the industry to improve transparency and disclosure, particularly where there are closely connected parties involved in the sale and purchase. The revised SIP 16 was then effective from 1 November 2015. However, with creditor dissatisfaction remaining, the Government passed the Administration (Restrictions on Disposal etc to Connected Persons) Regulations 2021 (SI 2021/427) which came into force on 30 April 2021. These Regulations place more onerous and additional requirements on pre-packs involving connected parties, and SIPs 13 and 16 have been updated with the sole purpose of adapting them to align with the new legislative requirements in the Regulations.

CASE EXAMPLE OF AN LLP PRE-PACK ADMINISTRATION

Old, established, Manchester-based law firm, Cobbetts, announced in February 2013 its intention to appoint administrators after several years of difficulties and significant reductions in profits. Within 24 hours, national firm DWF announced its intention to acquire most of the profitable parts of Cobbetts' business after a pre-pack arrangement was confirmed. DWF announced its intention to honour all training contracts and absorb most of the Cobbetts staff into its existing premises. Many professional services firms trade as LLPs, and several who have found themselves in financial difficulties have utilised the pre-packaged administration as a rescue procedure and preserved jobs as a result.

19.7.3 Company voluntary arrangements (CVAs)

A CVA is a potential rescue mechanism and is therefore an alternative to liquidation. In reality, it is also an alternative to administration/administrative receivership (see **19.7.1** and **19.8**) as a CVA will require the support of anyone entitled to appoint a receiver/administrator. It may even develop out of an administration, and so is a fairly flexible procedure.

19.7.3.1 What is a CVA?

A CVA is:

(a) a written agreement dealing with the financial affairs of the company, and which binds all the relevant parties (usually the company and all its creditors), provided the statutory procedures are followed. It is sometimes referred to as a 'statutory contract';

(b) likely to involve agreeing with the creditors that they will either:

  (i) wait longer to be paid; or

  (ii) accept payment of only part of their debt; or

  (iii) a combination of the two.

(c) a relatively easy and comparatively low-cost procedure;

(d) available to directors, liquidators and administrators;

(e) typically used where the underlying business of the company is sound, but the company has hit a cash-flow problem. This could be because it has lost a key customer, or because a customer has itself become insolvent owing the company substantial sums of money, or simply because the company cannot afford to pay all of its suppliers at once.

Thus, the aim of a CVA is to prevent a liquidation, and to do so more cheaply than an administration.

In a CVA, the creditors are unlikely to be paid in full, but they still are likely to be paid more than they would be if the company went into liquidation. Part of the reason for this is that CVA is a less complex process with little court involvement, and therefore less costly than administration or liquidation. However, there is no guarantee that administration and/or liquidation will be avoided, as even with a CVA, trading may continue to falter and cash-flow problems may worsen, leading to a more serious financial situation and, ultimately, administration or liquidation.

19.7.3.2 The CVA process

The process is set out in brief in the flowchart at **19.10.2**.

The key points to note for a CVA are as follows:

(a) No moratorium on enforcement for creditors exists in the same way as under the administration process. It used to be possible to have a moratorium on actions by the creditors in the case of 'small companies', as defined by CA 2006, s 382, but this provision was repealed by the Corporate Insolvency and Governance Act 2020.

(b) For larger companies there was never a moratorium in any event. This may be overcome by putting the company into administration first, to take advantage of the statutory moratorium (see **19.7.1.4** above), but this would significantly increase costs and remove one of the main benefits of CVA – the fact that it is relatively inexpensive. It is probably the lack of the availability of the moratorium to all sizes of companies, as opposed to just small companies, that means that the CVA procedure is not utilised as often as administration to undertake company rescue. However, with the passing of CIGA 2020, a company could potentially use the moratorium created by that Act (see **19.7.4** below) to gain the breathing space from creditor action whilst embarking on the creation of a CVA proposal for approval.

(c) Proposals must be approved by a majority of 75% or more in value of the creditors. A CVA must also pass a second test in that it must also have been approved by 50% or over of non-connected creditors. It is for the convenor or chair of the meeting to decide if a creditor is connected or not. So, all unsecured creditors get an opportunity to vote on whether to approve, reject or modify a CVA proposal. Secured creditors cannot vote, except in relation to any part of their debt that is unsecured.

(d) All unsecured creditors who would have been entitled to vote are bound by the proposal as regards past debts but not as regards future debts (IA 1986, s 5, as amended by the Insolvency Act 2000). The CVA does not affect the rights of secured creditors and preferential creditors, unless they agree.

CASE EXAMPLES OF CVA

1. Tragus Group, owner of the Café Rouge restaurant chain, agreed a CVA with its creditors in June 2014, allowing it to reduce its debt burden from £354 million to £91 million. Approval was given by over 80% of the creditors, many of whom were landlords of the restaurants.

2. Portsmouth Football Club, which became the first premier league club (as it was then) to go into administration in 2010, negotiated a CVA with its creditors later that year. HMRC, which claimed it was owed £12 million, was not able to block the CVA as it did not own 25% of the debt, but it applied to the High Court to have the CVA cancelled on the basis that it was unfair; HMRC was not happy that some football-related creditors, including the players, were going to receive 100% of what they were owed under special Football Association rules, while HMRC and other unsecured creditors were going to receive only 20p/£. The High Court disagreed with HMRC and allowed the CVA to go ahead, saving the club from probable liquidation. However, by February 2012 the club was once more in administration, and, after lengthy negotiations, it was sold to the Supporters Trust in 2013.

3. Eighty-eight-year-old high street retailer, British Home Stores (BHS) managed in March 2016 to agree a CVA with the approval of more than 95% of its creditors, including significant reductions in rents due. Unfortunately, a matter of weeks later, in late April 2016, the company appointed administrators. The company blamed the failure of a last-minute rescue deal and the inability to sell properties in the number and at the value required. After frantic, unsuccessful, attempts by the administrators to find a buyer, the company went into liquidation at the beginning of June 2016.

As has been mentioned before in respect of the retail sector, in recent years, a significant number of 'retail' CVAs have taken place and caused considerable press and media interest. Landlords of many of the stores in these retail failures have been concerned at the way the process has been conducted, and this has been one of the themes of recent times. The first major court challenge was the case of *Discovery (Northampton) Ltd v Debenhams* [2019] EWHC 2441 (Ch), where the landlords were defeated on all bar one of their grounds of challenge. The only successful challenge was in respect of the terms of the CVA which required the landlords to waive and release any rights to forfeit (ie, the right to take back possession) that existed under their leases in respect of any events associated with the terms of the CVA. The applicant landlords argued that the terms of a CVA could not limit or release a landlord's right to forfeit a lease held by a company subject to a CVA in this way. The court agreed and ordered that the terms of the CVA be amended to remove reference to the forfeiture restraint provisions.

Since that decision there have been further challenges by commercial retail landlords to the CVA process, notably in the case of *Lazari Properties 2 Ltd and others v New Look Retailers Ltd, Butters and another* [2021] EWHC 1209 (Ch) where the court once again rejected all challenges pursued by the landlords on the grounds of jurisdiction, material irregularity and unfair prejudice. Although the landlords were given permission to appeal to the Court of Appeal, the case was settled on the eve of that hearing on confidential terms and so the above first instance decisions remain as settled law.

For a more recent example of a successful creditor challenge to a CVA, however, see *Re Mizen Design/Build Ltd* [2023] EWHC 127 (Ch).

19.7.4 The moratorium created by CIGA 2020

New procedures and measures to rescue companies in financial distress as a result of the Covid-19 pandemic were introduced by CIGA 2020, which came into force on 26 June 2020, including a new standalone moratorium. This is not to be confused with the moratorium created by the administration process (see **19.7.1.4** above). These provisions are permanent ones created by CIGA 2020. As at the end of March 2025, 60 moratoriums had been obtained. It is fair to say that it was expected that there would have been a greater uptake of this procedure than has been the case.

In this moratorium, a company is protected from various creditor actions in respect of pre-moratorium debts but must continue to pay its moratorium debts in full. The company's directors remain in control, but an independent monitor (who is a qualified insolvency practitioner) has oversight throughout and can terminate the moratorium in various circumstances.

During this moratorium:

- creditors cannot petition for the winding up of the company;
- no winding-up or administration proceedings or process can be progressed;
- no right of forfeiture can be exercised in relation to premises occupied by the company;
- subject to some exceptions, there can be no enforcement of security over the company's property;
- there can no repossession of goods;
- subject to some exceptions, no 'legal process' can be issued or continued against the company.

A fundamental requirement is that the company must be, or likely to become, unable to pay its debts. No application can be made if the company has entered into a moratorium in the previous 12 months. In addition, some companies are not eligible for the procedure, including insurance companies, banks, or companies that are party to sizeable capital markets arrangements. This is sometimes called the 'financial services' exception.

Provided there is no outstanding winding-up petition against the company and the company is an English company, the directors can obtain a moratorium by filing the relevant documents at court. The directors must confirm that the company is or is likely to become unable to pay its debts.

Also, the proposed monitor must confirm that, in their view, it is likely that a moratorium for the company would result in the rescue of the company as a going concern.

Most pre-moratorium debts are made subject to the 'payment holiday'. Debts that remain payable in the moratorium fall into two categories: pre-moratorium debts that are excluded from the payment holiday; and moratorium debts.

Pre-moratorium debts that are excluded from the payment holiday are:

- the monitor's remuneration or expenses;
- goods or services supplied during the moratorium;
- rent in respect of a period during the moratorium;
- wages or salary arising under a contract of employment;
- redundancy payments;
- debts or other liabilities arising under a contact or other instrument involving financial services.

Pre-moratorium debts excluded from the payment holiday and moratorium debts must be paid in full during the moratorium, and confirmations that these debts have been paid have to be filed at court to support any extension to the moratorium period.

The monitor is required to terminate the moratorium if they consider that the company is unable to pay these debts.

The initial period of the moratorium is 20 business days beginning with the business day after the moratorium comes into force, which is the date of the filing of the documents at court or the court order, but it can be extended for a further 20 business days without creditor consent on the filing at court of certain documentation. Further, if the creditors (those who are not going to be paid during the moratorium because of the payment holiday) consent to an extension, the moratorium can be extended by the directors for a period of up to one year.

Alternatively, the directors can make an application to court after the 15th business day of the initial moratorium period for an extension of the period. The court will consider whether the extension is in the interests of the pre-moratorium creditors and whether the court considers that the rescue is likely.

The monitor is an officer of the court and must be an insolvency practitioner and has various duties to undertake. For the first judicial consideration of the moratorium regime, see *Re Corbin & King Holdings Ltd* [2022] EWHC 340 (Ch).

The monitor must bring the moratorium to an end by filing a notice at court if:

- they think that the moratorium is no longer likely to result in the rescue of the company as a going concern;
- they think that the objective of rescue has been achieved;
- they are unable to carry out their functions as the directors have not provided them with the relevant information;
- the company is unable to pay moratorium debts which have fallen due or pre-moratorium debts for which the company does not have a payment holiday.

19.7.5 The restructuring plan created by CIGA 2020

This was a new, flexible court-supervised restructuring tool introduced in 2020. The restructuring plan draws upon features of the existing Companies Act 2006 scheme of arrangement procedure (which remains available, see **19.7.6** below) but includes features which are new to the UK. There are a number of similarities to the US Chapter 11 bankruptcy proceedings.

A restructuring plan is an 'arrangement' or 'compromise' between the company and its creditors (including secured creditors) and/or shareholders – and can be proposed by any of them. It has a number of enhancements on the existing scheme of arrangement procedure, notably, the 'cross-class cram down' provisions, as further discussed below.

To be eligible to use the restructuring plan, a company need not be insolvent but must:

- have encountered (or be likely to encounter) financial difficulties that are affecting (or will/may affect) its going concern status; and
- propose to eliminate, reduce, prevent or mitigate the effect of those financial difficulties through the use of this procedure.

There is no requirement that a company establish its Centre of Main Interests in England to be eligible. Rather, it must simply establish a 'sufficient connection' to the English jurisdiction. It is expected that the test of 'sufficient connection' will be aligned with the jurisdiction test for schemes – a relatively low bar which has, historically, enabled a significant number of non-English companies to establish jurisdiction under the English courts to implement a restructuring.

Procedurally, a restructuring plan is very similar to a scheme, with both requiring court sanction. Typically, directors of a company, in conjunction with insolvency practitioners and restructuring lawyers, will prepare a restructuring plan proposal and apply to court for approval to convene meetings of the company's creditors and members. As stated above, creditors and shareholders may also make such a proposal, although this is likely to be more difficult since third parties will almost certainly not have the relevant and detailed information compared to the company itself.

A wide range of restructuring options can be implemented within a restructuring plan, and several well known public companies have used this new procedure to good effect. Soon after the implementation of CIGA 2020, we saw a solvent recapitalisation in the Virgin Atlantic case, a combination of debt-for-debt and debt-for-equity swaps in the PizzaExpress plan and a solvent wind-down in the Deep Ocean matter. As at the end of March 2025, 36 companies had a restructuring plan registered at Companies House, and the procedure is now being utilised by mid market companies and not just viewed as an option for large Plcs.

Implementation of a restructuring plan involves two court hearings. At the first hearing (called 'the convening hearing'), when deciding whether to convene creditor and member meetings, the court will consider whether:

- the company meets the eligibility criteria;
- the creditor classes have been formulated correctly;
- there are any creditors who do not have a genuine economic interest in the outcome and therefore should be excluded from voting; and
- there are any jurisdictional issues.

Creditors can, if they wish, make representations at this hearing. If the court is satisfied that the convening conditions have been satisfied, it will make an order convening the creditor and member meetings. The company then sends to all creditors and members notice of the meetings and documentation outlining the restructuring plan and its effect on them. Separate class meetings will then be held, and votes recorded. Subject to voting thresholds being met (as detailed below), a second hearing is held ('the sanctioning hearing') to decide whether the court, at its absolute discretion, sanctions the proposed plan.

There are some key features to this process:

(a) *Voting thresholds.* A restructuring plan requires the approval of 75% in gross value of debt or equity that votes in each class of creditors or members. This is unlike the scheme of arrangement, which requires an overall majority in number threshold.

(b) *Cross-class cram down.* Cross-class cram down is a new concept to insolvent restructuring in this country. It enables a dissenting class of creditors to be 'crammed down' so as to prevent hold-out creditors blocking otherwise viable plans. Thus it adds a new level of flexibility. Cross-class cram down will be available where:

    - the court is satisfied that no member of the dissenting class(es) would be any worse off under the plan than they would be in the event of the 'relevant alternative';
    - at least one class that would benefit from the 'relevant alternative' has voted in favour of the plan; and
    - the court is prepared to sanction the plan.

    The 'relevant alternative' will be whatever the court considers the most likely to occur in relation to the company should the plan not be sanctioned by the court. In practice, this will be the alternative of liquidation.

A good example of the cross-class cram down procedure is found in the Virgin Active restructuring as dissenting landlords found their objections to the process overruled. See *Virgin Active Holdings Ltd & Ors, Re* [2021] EWHC 1246 (Ch). In *Re Houst Ltd* [2022] EWHC 1941 (Ch), judgment was handed down in relation to the sanction of the first Part 26A restructuring plan to be proposed by a small–medium enterprise (SME). The decision is also an interesting one for other reasons, notably the cram down of HMRC as a dissenting creditor.

However, in *Re Great Annual Savings Company Ltd* [2023] EWHC 1141 (Ch), HMRC successfully resisted a cram down. The judge refused to sanction the Plan, on the grounds that (a) he was not persuaded that HMRC would be no worse off under the Plan than in the relevant alternative; and (b) the Plan did not, in his view, result in a fair distribution of the restructuring surplus. The judgment addresses a number of issues surrounding Restructuring Plans generally and is an important decision when considering the possible use of this procedure by SMEs, in particular where a cram down of HMRC is sought. The attitude and approach of HMRC to restructuring plans is important to consider, as it is often a key creditor.

In 2025, we have seen a trend to a more supportive approach by HMRC to proposals than perhaps seemed to be the case in earlier years.

In January 2024, the Court of Appeal upheld a challenge launched by dissenting creditors to overturn Adler's Restructuring Plan previously approved by the High Court under Part 26A of the Companies Act 2006 (*Strategic Value Capital Solutions Master Fund LP and others v AGPS BondCo PLC* [2024] EWCA Civ 24). In his judgment concerning the first-ever appeal of a Restructuring Plan, Lord Justice Snowden created important authority which helps to define the boundaries of RPs, including, in particular, the application of the *pari passu* principle.

19.7.6 Schemes of arrangement

Schemes of arrangement (CA 2006, ss 895 – 901) are similar to CVAs, in that they involve a compromise with creditors, but they are not an insolvency procedure as such, as they may be undertaken at any stage in the lifetime of a company.

They are more expensive and cumbersome than CVAs, as two court hearings are required as well as meetings of creditors and shareholders. Schemes of arrangement tend to be used to restructure large companies with complex capital structures, sometimes before take-over, and often include a 'debt-for-equity' swap, in which creditors are given shares in exchange for their debts. It should be emphasised that this restructuring option still exists post-CIGA 2020, and many comparisons can be drawn with the new restructuring plan, although the operation of the cross-class cram down is a fundamental difference. It will be interesting to see the interaction of these two procedures moving forward.

19.8 OPTIONS ONLY FOR SECURED CREDITORS – RECEIVERSHIP

Creditors who lend to companies will usually take security (see **Chapter 11**). Such creditors may be able to appoint a receiver. Technically we should not refer to a 'receiver' but to the full title, which is an 'administrative receiver'. There has to be a loan involved for receivership to be a relevant course of action, and a receiver is usually appointed when the company is not complying with the terms of the charge holder's loan agreement.

Receivership is not really an insolvency procedure, as a receiver may be appointed by a charge holder whenever the charge allows it to. The company does not need to be insolvent, although it often will be. The receiver will be an insolvency practitioner, unless the appointment is of a Law of Property Act Receiver (see **19.8.1**).

The task of the receiver is to take possession of the charged property and deal with it for the benefit of the charge holder only (in contrast to an administrator, who deals with the company's assets for the benefit of all the creditors), which will usually mean selling it. After this has been done, the receiver has no further interest in the company (though if they are appointed under a floating charge, they do also have a duty to pay preferential creditors (IA 1986, s 40)).

19.8.1 Law of Property Act (LPA) Receivers

A *fixed charge holder* may appoint a receiver to enforce its security. This type of receiver was traditionally appointed under the Law of Property Act 1925 (LPA), with the powers contained in that Act, and so is often referred to as an 'LPA Receiver'. However, these days, the fixed charge holder would normally have express power to appoint in the charge document, and the powers and duties of the receiver would also be set out in that document.

An LPA Receiver is usually appointed with a view to selling the charged property so that the debt to the charge holder can be repaid.

An LPA Receiver does not have to be a Licensed Insolvency Practitioner, and, indeed, they are often a surveyor or other suitable qualified professional.

19.8.2 Administrative Receivers

Administrative Receivers may be appointed under s 29 of the IA 1986, by a *floating charge holder* who has a floating charge over the company's undertaking. However, since implementation on 15 September 2003 of the reforms brought in by the Enterprise Act 2002, administrative receivership may be used only for floating charges created before that date (IA 1986, ss 72A–72H). (There are some exceptions which are not relevant here.)

These older charges will become increasingly less important with time. The route that may be used for floating charges created on or after 15 September 2003 is administration (see **19.7.1**). The following two sections (**19.8.2.1** and **19.8.2.2**) are included for background information only.

19.8.2.1 Events triggering the appointment of an administrative receiver

The loan documentation will specify the events that will enable the lender to appoint an administrative receiver. They might include:

(a) failure to meet a demand to pay capital or interest;

(b) presentation of a winding-up petition;

(c) presentation of a petition for administration or a CVA (see **19.7**);

(d) the levying of distress or execution against the company's assets;

(e) failure to comply with restrictions in the loan documentation, eg, by granting a new charge over assets;

(f) the company ceasing to trade;

(g) the assets being in jeopardy; or

(h) the inability of the company to pay its debts.

19.8.2.2 Procedure for administrative receivership

The administrative receiver essentially takes over the running of the company, purely with a view to selling the charged assets, paying their own costs and repaying the charge holder. Once they have done that, they will resign. The relevant legislation is set out in IA 1986, ss 42–49.

19.8.3 The effect of administrative receivership

In theory, once the administrative receiver has completed their work, they return the company to the management of the directors, who may continue to run the business.

In practice, however, this process is very frequently followed by liquidation, as there are often few useful assets left in the business once the charge holder has been paid.

19.9 'PHOENIX' COMPANIES

Section 216 of the IA 1986 prohibits the re-use of a company's name (or a similar name) where the company has gone into insolvent liquidation. This is to counter the threat of an unscrupulous trader putting one company into liquidation and then transferring the assets to a new one using the same name, possibly operating on the same premises with the same staff, the debts of the old company having been left behind (see *Re Lightning Electrical Contractors Ltd* [1996] 2 BCLC 302, *R (on the application of Griffin) v Richmond Magistrates Court* [2008] EWHC 84 (QB)). The new company has risen from the ashes like the fabled phoenix, hence the name of the problem.

The directors in question may be held personally liable for the debts of the new company under IA 1986, s 216, unless they obtain the consent of the court to be directors of the new company, and they may also be liable to criminal penalties.

There are limited exceptions to the general rule that a successor phoenix company cannot re-use the original registered name or trading name of a previous company that has gone into insolvent liquidation, which are set out at rr 22.4, 22.6 and 22.7 of IR 2016. These provisions address what are known as 'the three excepted cases'.

The first exception is possibly the most important exception to re-using a company name in a phoenix company. Where a NewCo (the successor company) acquires the whole, or substantially the whole, of the business of an insolvent company, under arrangements made by an insolvency practitioner acting as its liquidator, or administrator, the successor company may, for the purposes of s 216 of the IA 1986, give notice under this rule to the insolvent company's creditors.

This second exception involves the directors of the successor phoenix company applying to court for permission (or 'leave' as the court calls it) to re-use the name of the insolvent company. The application to court must be made no later than 7 days from the date on which the company went into liquidation, and leave must be granted by the court no later than 6 weeks from that date.

The third exception allows a company to re-use the name of an insolvent company that is otherwise prohibited if:

(a) it has been known by that name for the whole of the period of 12 months ending with the day before the liquidating company went into liquidation; and

(b) it has not at any time in those 12 months been dormant within the meaning of s 252(5) of the Companies Act 2006.

The Court of Appeal decision of *PSV 1982 Ltd v Langdon (Re Discovery Yachts Ltd)* [2022] EWCA Civ 1319 raised some interesting preliminary issues for the court to consider in connection with a director acting in contravention of ss 216 and 217 of the Insolvency Act (IA) 1986. For an example of a case where the defendants successfully invoked the non-dormancy defence, see *Maxima Creditor Resolutions Ltd v Fealy and Barrett* [2024] EWHC 2694 (Ch).

19.10 SUMMARIES

The flowcharts set out at **19.10.1 and 19.10.2** below summarise the liquidation procedure and the CVA procedure respectively.

19.10.1 Summary of liquidation procedure

Compulsory Liquidation	*Voluntary Liquidation*	
	Creditors	*Members*
Petition under IA 1986, s 122 (creditor, company or directors) filed at court and served on company. **Start of winding up**	Directors agree by a majority that the company is insolvent and needs to be placed into liquidation.	Directors make statutory declaration of solvency.
Company cannot dispose of assets (IA 1986, s 127).	Members pass special resolution to liquidate the company and may consider nominating a liquidator. Directors' powers effectively cease. **Start of winding up**	Members pass special resolution to start liquidation and ordinary resolution to appoint liquidator. Directors' powers cease (IA 1986, s 91(2)). **Start of winding up**
Petition advertised in *The Gazette*.	Resolution advertised in *The Gazette*.	

Compulsory Liquidation	*Voluntary Liquidation*	
	Creditors	*Members*
Court hearing. If winding-up order made Official Receiver appointed as liquidator and directors' powers cease.	The directors of the company must, before the end of the period of 7 days beginning with the day after the day on which the company passes a resolution for voluntary winding up, make out a statement in the prescribed form as to the affairs of the company; and send the statement to the company's creditors. They must also in accordance with the rules seek a nomination from the company's creditors for a person to be the liquidator. The previous physical meeting of creditors under the 1986 Rules has been abolished under the 2016 Rules and is replaced by creditors considering the appointment of a liquidator by the company either holding a virtual meeting or seeking that decision by the new deemed consent procedure.	
Official Receiver advertises order in *The Gazette* and notifies Registrar.	Appointment of liquidator advertised in *The Gazette* and Registrar notified.	Appointment of liquidator advertised in *The Gazette* and Registrar notified.
Liquidator investigates and reports to creditors and asks for details of debts.	Liquidator investigates and reports to creditors and asks for details of debts.	Liquidator investigates and reports to creditors and asks for details of debts.
Creditors may appoint alternative liquidator (IA 1986, s 139).		
Liquidator collects in assets and realises if necessary, and then distributes in the statutory order.		
Final accounts sent to creditors and/or members.		
Final return filed with court and Registrar.	Final return filed with Registrar.	
Company dissolved after three months.		

19.10.2 Summary of CVA procedure

Directors may take advice from insolvency practitioner.

↓

Directors make written proposal to creditors and identify insolvency practitioner who will supervise the arrangement (the 'nominee').

↓

Nominee may call meeting of creditors under the 'Decision Procedure' in IR 2016 and may also call a meeting of members.

↓

Proposals require the approval of 75% or more in value of creditors (excluding secured) taking part in the Decision Procedure. This must not include more than 50% of connected creditors.

↓

All creditors (except secured and preferential who disagree) are bound, even if they did not take part in the Decision Procedure (IR 2016 and IA 1986, s 5, as amended by IA 2000).

↓

Nominee becomes 'supervisor' and reports to court on approval.

↓

Directors remain in office and run company, but supervisor checks implementation of proposals.

↓

At the end of the CVA, supervisor makes final report to creditors and members.

CHAPTER 20

PERSONAL INSOLVENCY

LEARNING OUTCOMES

After reading this chapter you will be able to:

- explain how to assess the insolvency of an individual
- understand the process for and the effect of bankruptcy
- describe how to preserve and increase the bankrupt's assets
- describe how to distribute the bankrupt's assets on bankruptcy
- list and explain the alternatives to bankruptcy.

20.1 INTRODUCTION

The term 'bankruptcy' applies to individuals, not to companies or limited liability partnerships. However, individual partners in a partnership can be made bankrupt (although, interestingly enough, the partnership itself is subject to the winding-up regime). Individuals may find themselves insolvent and, possibly, bankrupt for many reasons, for example:

- cash-flow problems, such as borrowing too much and being unable to make the repayments;
- losing their jobs;
- being part of an unsuccessful business or partnership which fails;
- being a director of a company and incurring personal liability in some way, eg, by giving a personal guarantee.

The law relating to bankruptcy is mainly contained in the Insolvency Act 1986 (IA 1986) and the Enterprise Act 2002, and its aim is to encourage entrepreneurship by allowing honest bankrupts to be discharged after one year with a clean slate, while punishing reckless bankrupts by imposing restrictions on their activities for up to 15 years.

The detailed rules for implementing the law are contained in the Insolvency Rules 2016 (SI 2016/1024) (IR 2016), which came into force on 6 April 2017.

We shall look at the bankruptcy process and also consider some of the other options available to insolvent individuals, including the statutory 'breathing space' regime that came into force on 4 May 2021.

20.2 WHEN IS AN INDIVIDUAL INSOLVENT?

Just as for companies, it is important to be able to identify when an individual is in financial difficulties and may actually be insolvent. The IA 1986 contains two tests (IA 1986, s 267(2)) based on whether the individual is able to pay their debts:

(a) The debt (or debts) is payable immediately and the debtor does not have sufficient funds to do this, even though the debtor may be able to at some point in the future (see Example (a) below).

(b) The debt (or debts) is payable at some specified point in the future and the debtor has no reasonable prospect of being able to pay (see Example (b) below).

EXAMPLES

(a) David throws a lavish 40th birthday party; the following week he is made redundant. When the invoice for the catering arrives, payable immediately, he has no funds in his bank account to pay. He has no credit cards or other means of borrowing, as he has been bankrupt before. There is a possibility he might be able to borrow from an old friend, but the friend needs to sell some paintings first and has no buyers at the moment.

(b) Geraint buys an expensive set of lounge furniture for £7,500 on a special deal: 'Buy and take home now – no payment for two years!' After 18 months, Geraint loses his job, and he is forced to claim benefits. He knows he will not receive enough to make the payment on the sofa in six months, and the sofa is already rather tatty and cannot be returned.

20.2.1 How can a creditor prove the debtor is insolvent?

An unpaid creditor may get fed up with waiting to be paid and try to make a debtor bankrupt. The creditor must first prove that the debtor is *insolvent*, without necessarily knowing much, if anything, about the debtor's personal affairs. The courts have provided three relatively easy ways in which to do this (IA 1986, s 268):

(a) Serve a statutory demand (a formal, written demand) on the debtor for a liquidated debt of £5,000 or more (either pre- or post- judgment) *and* wait three weeks to see whether the debtor pays the demanded sum or applies to court to set aside the statutory demand.

(b) Serve a statutory demand on the debtor in respect of a liability to pay the creditor a sum of £5,000 or more on a future date *and* wait three weeks to see whether the debtor shows a reasonable prospect of being able to pay the sum when it falls due or applies to court to set aside the statutory demand.

(c) Obtain a court judgment for a debt of £5,000 or more *and* attempt execution of that judgment debt (ie, send enforcement officials to recover assets or cash from the debtor) and that execution fails.

It should be recognised that the statutory demand route set out in (a) above, either pre or post a judgment having been obtained, is the most common method by which the bankruptcy process is commenced. However, if the situation set out in (c) above occurs, there is an automatic right to commence bankruptcy action without the need to go down the statutory demand route.

For the avoidance of doubt, it should be stressed that the previous (but now no longer operative) temporary provisions regarding company winding-up proceedings created by the Corporate Insolvency and Governance Act 2020 never applied to personal insolvency practice and procedure, which is totally unaffected by that Act.

20.2.2 What are the insolvent debtor's options?

Many debtors bury their heads in the sand, ignoring bills and final demands, only to find that matters are taken out of their hands by one or more disgruntled creditors who serve statutory demands or sue for the debt. However, this does not have to be the case; the insolvent debtor does have some options. The debtor may:

(a) apply online for their own bankruptcy, to show the courts that they are doing their best to sort out things for themselves;

(b) talk to his creditors, to see if they will wait for payment or come to a compromise;

(c) enter into a formal arrangement with all their creditors, called an individual voluntary arrangement (IVA). This may be an agreement to pay the creditors less than the full amount owed, and/or for the creditors to wait longer (probably years) to be paid. An IVA may allow the debtor to avoid bankruptcy completely;

(d) apply for a debt relief order (DRO);

(e) from 4 May 2020, apply under the Debt Respite Scheme for a breathing space from creditor action for up to 60 days.

There are advantages and disadvantages to each of these options, and we shall explore these later in the chapter (see **20.7.1–20.7.4**).

20.3 WHAT IS BANKRUPTCY?

Bankruptcy is a judicial process during which all the assets of the bankrupt are passed to a third party, called the trustee in bankruptcy, who pays as many of the debts as possible in a statutory order. Eventually, even if the debts have not been paid in full, the bankrupt will usually be discharged, free from almost all of the debts, and can start afresh. There are some limited exceptions in terms of assets not passing to the trustee in bankruptcy. It is worth noting that student loans are one of those debts specifically excluded, and they remain payable even after the bankrupt has been discharged (Higher Education Act 2004, s 42, as amended).

The vast majority of bankrupts obtain automatic discharge after one year (IA 1986, s 279). The remaining bankrupts could have their bankruptcy suspended and/or also be subject to a bankruptcy restriction order (BRO) or bankruptcy restriction undertaking (BRU) which may restrict their activities for several years (see **20.4.6.2**).

CASE STUDY

Joseph, who has been running a moderately successful graphic design business for 20 years as a sole trader, has been diagnosed with a serious wasting disease which means that he finds it very difficult to work with his hands. He is the main designer and is struggling to do the work the clients require.

Unfortunately, Joseph refuses to accept the situation and tries to carry on, incurring large debts to photographers, and to his stationery suppliers and landlord. Eventually, he misses a vital deadline for his main client, who refuses to pay for the job, as he is entitled to do.

One of the photographers gets fed up with ringing Joseph to ask for payment and serves a statutory demand for £10,000. Joseph cannot satisfy the demand, as his business account is overdrawn, and he cannot borrow anything, as he has no assets to use as security – he rents his business premises, his business assets are just computers, which are virtually worthless, as they are over three years old, and his family home is subject to a large mortgage and, in the current market, may even be worth less than the mortgage.

Joseph puts the demand in a drawer and tries to forget about it.

After three weeks, the photographer presents a bankruptcy petition to the court.

20.4 THE BANKRUPTCY PROCESS

Bankruptcy is commenced by the presentation to the court of a petition or by the debtor making an online application. The latter was a new procedure that commenced in April 2016 (see **20.4.2**). A petition may be presented by one or more of the creditors, or by various other parties listed in IA 1986, s 264. Here we are going to concentrate on creditor petitions. If the petition or debtor application is successful, a bankruptcy order is made.

20.4.1 Creditor's petition

A creditor may present a petition to the court (IA 1986, s 264) if the debtor owes the creditor £5,000 or more (this must be a liquidated, ie, known, sum which is unsecured). The creditor must also be able to claim that the debtor is unable to pay the debt or has little prospect of being able to pay it. This will be presumed if the creditor has followed one of the methods set out in IA 1986, s 268 to show insolvency (see **20.2.1**), and, as stated, this is most commonly evidenced by there being an unsatisfied statutory demand.

Creditors owed less than £5,000 cannot present a petition on their own but may join together, provided the total amount owed to all the petitioners is not less than £5,000.

The petition should be presented to the debtor's local county court hearing centre (provided it has bankruptcy jurisdiction). However, government departments, including HM Revenue and Customs (HMRC), present all petitions in London.

This is not a decision to be taken lightly by the creditor, as they must pay a substantial deposit to cover the costs of the trustee in bankruptcy and also a fee to the court. These deposits and fees are updated regularly and should be checked before filing the petition. The current fees may be found at <www.gov.uk/government/publications/fees-in-the-civil-and-family-courts-main-fees-ex50> (Civil and Family Court Fees – Leaflet EX50) and in the Insolvency Proceedings (Fees) (Amendment) Order 2022 (SI 2022/929). It is important to ensure the correct fee is paid as these do change reasonably regularly. At the time of writing, the combined fee plus deposit to make someone bankrupt is £1,843.00.

The creditor must also arrange for the petition to be served personally on the debtor; although if the debtor is elusive, the creditor may ask the court for permission to serve another way, such as by pushing the petition through the letterbox at the debtor's home address. This is called obtaining an order for substituted service.

20.4.2 Debtor's application

Since 6 April 2016, a debtor is no longer to petition the court to be made bankrupt. Instead, a debtor must now apply online to an adjudicator appointed by the Secretary of State who will make a bankruptcy order if appropriate. The adjudicator is not a judge but an employee of the Insolvency Service and has authority to make a bankruptcy order. The ground for the application is that the debtor is unable to pay their debts (IA 1986, s 263H). The fees payable can currently be found in the Insolvency Proceedings (Fees) Order 2016 (SI 2016/692). As well as a court fee, an adjudicator's deposit has to be paid as security for the payment of the official receiver's administration fee. At the time of writing, the combined fee is £680.00. These fees were not increased in 2022 when the creditor petition fees and deposit increased, as set out above.

If the statutory requirements are satisfied, the adjudicator must make a bankruptcy order against the debtor, or refuse to make such an order, within 28 days from the application, unless further information from the debtor is required. If the adjudicator requests further information (IA 1986, s 263L) the adjudicator has 42 days from the date of the application to make an order. If the adjudicator does not respond to the debtor before the end of this period, the application is deemed refused.

20.4.3 The Role of the Official Receiver

When a bankruptcy order is made by the court or the adjudicator, the Official Receiver (OR) (who is a civil servant employed by the Insolvency Service and officer of the court) initially takes control of the debtor's property. They, or their department, will:

(a) ask the debtor for a statement of affairs and investigate, if necessary;

(b) take steps to protect property;

(c) possibly, dispose of perishable goods or those going down in value.

The OR will act as the trustee in bankruptcy from the moment a bankruptcy order is made, but, just as for a compulsory liquidation order, there is the possibility of creditors seeking the appointment of a trustee in bankruptcy from the private sector under similar procedures.

20.4.4 The role of the trustee in bankruptcy

The bankrupt's estate vests automatically in their trustee in bankruptcy (IA 1986, s 306). The trustee's function is to collect and, if necessary, sell the bankrupt's assets, so that they may be distributed to the creditors in accordance with IA 1986, s 328 (see **20.6**). The trustee then applies for their release.

The trustee has wide-ranging powers to investigate the debtor's affairs and may scrutinise and in some cases set aside or challenge transactions the debtor has entered into prior to the bankruptcy (see **20.5**). In a number of respects these mirror the corporate recovery provisions that were set out in **Chapter 19**, but not absolutely.

20.4.5 What happens to the bankrupt's property?

The bankrupt's estate vests in the trustee and is defined in IA 1986, s 283. It includes most of the bankrupt's real and personal property. However, the bankrupt is able to keep some assets which are needed for day-to-day living, such as:

(a) tools of any trade; and

(b) clothing and furniture, unless it is of high value, in which case the trustee has power to sell the asset and replace it with something cheaper (see IA 1986, s 308).

For a leading case analysing the 'tools of the trade' provisions, see *Birdi v Price & Another* [2018] EWHC 2943 (Ch) where HHJ Eyre QC clarified what constitutes tools of the trade for the purposes of s 283(2)(a) of the Insolvency Act 1986. In particular, he stated that regard should be had to the purpose of s 283(2)(a), which is to enable a debtor to achieve rehabilitation as a useful and productive member of society.

Also, the bankrupt is entitled to retain any salary they make; but the trustee may apply for an income payments order if the salary exceeds a sum sufficient to meet the reasonable needs of the bankrupt and their family (IA 1986, s 310). This payments order can last for up to three years, even if the bankrupt has been discharged from their bankruptcy by then. The order must, however, be obtained prior to the discharge of bankruptcy. It is also possible to obtain these payments by way of an income payments agreement, which has the same effect as a formally obtained court order.

CASE STUDY

As Joseph did not respond to the statutory demand and could not make any payments, the court granted the bankruptcy order against him.

His creditors sought and obtained the appointment of an insolvency practitioner as trustee in bankruptcy in place of the OR.

Most of Joseph's assets have vested in the trustee, but he has been allowed to keep the stationery, computers, etc he has been using to run his business, so that he can try to carry on earning a living.

> He has also been allowed to keep his clothes and most of the furniture in his family home, although the trustee has insisted on the sale of some valuable antiques which had been left to Joseph by his father. The trustee has allowed him to replace these items with cheap flat-pack equivalents.

20.4.5.1 Special rules for the matrimonial home

If the debtor owns their own home, their interest in that home passes to the trustee. However, there may be other legal or equitable interests in the house, for example:

(a) The house may be held in joint names.

(b) The spouse/partner may have an equitable interest arising from a trust (eg where the spouse/partner contributed to the purchase price).

(c) The spouse may also have a right of occupation under the Family Law Act 1996 and related legislation.

(d) Minor children (under 18) may live with the bankrupt in the bankrupt's home, which may give the bankrupt (and the spouse/partner) a right of occupation.

In these situations, the debtor cannot be evicted from their home immediately, so the trustee cannot sell it without a court order. The court will consider the interests of creditors; the conduct and needs and financial resources of the spouse/civil partner or former spouse/former civil partner; the needs of the children (if any) and all relevant circumstances. During this time, the bankrupt may be able to arrange for their spouse/partner to buy the bankrupt's share of the property, or to find alternative accommodation. The thrust of the legislation, though, is that if there are competing interests, then, after one year of the bankruptcy, the interests of the creditors are paramount (IA 1986, s 335A).

20.4.5.2 What happens after three years?

After three years the matrimonial home re-vests in the bankrupt (IA 1986, s 283A) unless the trustee has done one of the following:

(a) realised the interest (usually, sold the house);

(b) applied for an order of sale or possession in respect of the house;

(c) applied for a charging order over the house; or

(d) entered an agreement with the bankrupt regarding the bankrupt's interest in the house (eg, the bankrupt can keep the interest in the house, but will owe more in the bankruptcy).

This means that the bankrupt does not have years of uncertainty, wondering whether the trustee might decide to sell the family home many years later because it has gone up in value.

20.4.6 What is the effect of bankruptcy on the bankrupt?

When a bankruptcy order is made, the individual who is party to that order is subjected to a number of restrictions and disabilities. These are partly designed to protect creditors by preventing the bankrupt from getting into financial difficulties again but are also designed to stop the dishonest or negligent bankrupt from repeating inappropriate behaviour.

20.4.6.1 Restrictions applying as soon as the bankruptcy order is made

Restrictions on business activities

A bankrupt is allowed to retain the tools of their trade (see **20.4.5**) and a vehicle, of modest value, but it is a criminal offence for a bankrupt to obtain credit of more than a prescribed amount (currently £500 in total) without disclosing their bankruptcy. Practically, this may make it extremely difficult for the bankrupt to carry on their business.

The following is a list of some of the other automatic business restrictions effective as soon as the bankruptcy order is made. The bankrupt cannot:

(a) act as a director of a company or be (directly or indirectly) involved in the management, promotion, or formation of a company, unless the court grants permission to act in such a capacity (Company Directors Disqualification Act 1986 (CDDA 1986), s 11). Breach of this prohibition is a criminal offence (CDDA 1986, s 13). Company articles usually provide that the director immediately ceases to hold office as a director (see model articles for private companies, art 18). (Similar rules apply to members of a limited liability partnership (Limited Liability Partnerships Regulations 2001 (SI 2001/1090, reg 4(2)).)

(b) trade under a different name from the one in which the bankruptcy order was made, without disclosing to all those who trade with that person under the new name that they are an undischarged bankrupt (IA 1986, s 360(1)(b)); and

(c) continue in partnership (Partnership Act 1890, s 33 provides for automatic dissolution), unless the partnership agreement provides otherwise. The bankrupt's share in the partnership will have to be realised. It is common to find a provision in the partnership agreement by which the bankrupt immediately and automatically ceases to be a partner, and the other partners have an option to buy the bankrupt out, rather than completely dissolving the firm.

Personal disabilities

The following is a brief list of some of the other things bankrupts cannot do during the period of bankruptcy until the order is discharged:

(a) Obtain credit of the prescribed amount (currently £500) or more (whether by themselves or jointly with another), without informing the lender that they are an undischarged bankrupt (IA 1986, s 360(1)(a)). Obtaining credit includes taking possession of goods under a hire-purchase agreement (IA 1986, s 360(2)).

(b) Practise as a solicitor without the leave of the Solicitors Regulation Authority (Solicitors Act 1974, s 15). Other professions generally have similar restrictions.

The main practical effect of these restrictions for the average bankrupt is that it is difficult to obtain a bank account and impossible to obtain a credit card, and the bankrupt may have to conduct their financial affairs mainly using cash. This can, of course, cause problems for employees whose salary is usually paid straight into a bank account.

Though a bank will not allow a bankrupt to maintain a normal current account, it is possible to have a bank account, as long as it is one that does not allow an overdraft, or the provision of credit. This will enable wages to be paid into a bank account and for cash withdrawals to be made, provided there are sufficient funds. It also allows for electronic payments to be made from the account, again assuming there are sufficient funds available.

UK Finance (formerly the British Bankers Association), the trade association for the UK banking sector, has stated that it wishes to act to improve access to bank accounts for bankrupts. This was prompted by changes to the law which means that if account holders withdraw funds, the banks will be protected from recovery action by trustees if they have not received specific notice that the monies in the bank account were part of the bankrupt's estate. This change will undoubtedly ease a lot of the difficulties that bankrupts have previously encountered which have, in the past, resulted in them making highly unsatisfactory and irregular arrangements with third parties (often family and friends) holding monies received by way of wages for the bankrupt and processing any bills and payments for the bankrupt from their own account. The Government is also concerned that those who have had financial difficulties in the past should as far as possible have the opportunity for financial rehabilitation. Therefore, the position now is that, in the UK, after being declared bankrupt, individuals can still open and use bank accounts, though they may be limited to basic accounts. These accounts do not typically offer overdrafts or credit facilities. Whilst bankrupts do not need to inform the Official Receiver about a new bank account (unless specifically asked), they must report any funds in the account exceeding reasonable living expenses.

20.4.6.2 Additional restrictions that may be imposed on culpable bankrupts

A significant minority of bankrupts are considered to be 'culpable' and to have caused the bankruptcy by their own dishonesty, negligence, or recklessness. Bankruptcy restriction orders (BROs) are intended to protect the public from these bankrupts.

Such orders will be made by the court and will last from two to 15 years. Even when an IVA (see **20.7**) comes into effect after bankruptcy, it will not affect any BRO which has been made.

The bankrupt may avoid court proceedings by agreeing to the restrictions and signing a bankruptcy restriction undertaking (BRU), but the effect is the same as a BRO.

Here are a few examples (from a long list) of the restrictions that apply automatically to an individual subject to a BRO or a BRU (IA 1986, Sch 4A). A number of these also, of course, apply to an undischarged bankrupt. The individual cannot:

(a) act as receiver or manager of a company's property on behalf of a debenture holder (IA 1986, s 31);

(b) obtain credit above the prescribed limit (currently £500) without disclosing that they are subject to a BRO (IA 1986, s 360);

(c) trade in a name other than that under which that person was made bankrupt (IA 1986, s 360);

(d) act as an insolvency practitioner (IA 1986, s 390);

(e) act as a company director (CDDA 1986, s 11(1));

(f) act as a Member of Parliament in either House (this does not apply if the individual is merely bankrupt) (IA 1986, s 426A); or

(g) act as a member of a local authority (again, this does not apply if the individual is merely bankrupt) (Local Government Act 1972).

This is consistent with the policy of allowing 'accidental' bankrupts to be discharged with a clean slate after one year but keeping control over the activities of those bankrupts who are deemed 'culpable'. The high profile case of the tennis player, Boris Becker, is a good example of the use of some of these provisions, and, in addition, criminal proceedings were successfully completed against him resulting in a custodial sentence.

CASE STUDY

During Joseph's period of bankruptcy, it becomes apparent that he had been neglecting his affairs more than it first appeared. He has not been paying VAT or PAYE Income Tax and National Insurance to HMRC, and he has built up significant debts to them. This is viewed particularly seriously by the insolvency authorities, and in view of the fact that Joseph has been bankrupt before, he is told that there will be a hearing to consider a BRO.

Joseph is advised to avoid court proceedings and to agree to a BRU, which results in him signing a BRU lasting for five years, starting on the date of his discharge from bankruptcy.

20.5 PRESERVING AND INCREASING THE BANKRUPT'S ASSETS

The trustee has a duty to creditors to increase the fund available to pay them, if possible, and to do nothing that might reduce whatever money is available. Therefore, the trustee has various powers that allow investigation of the bankrupt's affairs prior to bankruptcy. In this section we look briefly at the powers to:

(a) disclaim onerous property;

(b) set aside transactions at an undervalue;

(c) set aside preferences;

(d) set aside transactions defrauding creditors; and

(e) avoid extortionate credit transactions.

The aim of these powers is to make sure that the trustee does not retain assets that will reduce in value and tries to swell the assets by clawing back money that the bankrupt, intentionally or otherwise, has put out of reach of their creditors.

CASE STUDY

Whilst investigating Joseph's affairs, the trustee discovers that four years ago Joseph transferred ownership of a holiday cottage in Cornwall, worth about £165,000, to his wife, and two months ago he repaid a debt of £5,000 to an old friend from university.

The trustee suspects that the transfer of the property may be a transaction at an undervalue (see **20.5.2** below) and that the debt payment may be a preference (see **20.5.3** below). Consequently, he investigates further, as he may be able to have the cottage ownership transferred to him and may be able to reclaim the £5,000, thus increasing the assets available to the creditors by approximately £170,000 (£165,000 (the cottage) + £5,000 (the debt)).

20.5.1 Onerous property

The trustee may disclaim onerous property, such as land burdened with onerous covenants or unprofitable contracts (IA 1986, s 315). In practice, this is often an action around a lease that the bankrupt is subject to and potentially a number of future years. A disclaimer ends all the bankrupt's rights and liabilities in respect of the property in question, and discharges the trustee from any personal responsibility for that property. Any person who suffers loss as a result of a disclaimer by the trustee in bankruptcy may prove in the bankruptcy for their loss. Such people are, however, unsecured creditors. To prevent third parties from having to wait a long time to find out whether a trustee intends to disclaim, any person who has an interest in property previously owned by the bankrupt is entitled to serve written notice on the trustee in bankruptcy requiring the trustee to disclaim the property within 28 days, failing which the trustee loses the power to do so (IA 1986, s 316).

20.5.2 Transactions at an undervalue

20.5.2.1 What is an undervalue?

An undervalue is either:

(a) a gift; or

(b) a transaction where the bankrupt received consideration (in money or money's worth) significantly lower in value than that which they provided (IA 1986, s 339(3)).

Any such transaction is caught by this provision, including, potentially, a property adjustment order on divorce, as long as the bankrupt received no consideration, or significantly less consideration than they gave. Although in a clean-break divorce, the person benefiting from the order is usually taken to have given consideration by giving up their right to the other marital assets (see *Haines v Hill* [2007] EWCA Civ 1284). In practice, trustees in bankruptcy do not challenge property adjustment orders made in matrimonial proceedings unless collusion or other nefarious behaviour is evidenced by the parties to the order.

EXAMPLE OF A POSSIBLE TRANSACTION AT AN UNDERVALUE

Aasif, who has been running a small building firm for many years, realises that the business is in financial trouble as he has no new contracts at all. The business owns a beautiful flat on Poole Harbour, worth at least £500,000, and which Aasif has always used for entertaining clients. Aasif does not want to lose the flat, so he transfers it into the name of his daughter, and she in return promises to come in to work once a month for six months to try to drum up new business for him.

20.5.2.2 How far back may the trustee go?

The trustee may investigate transactions up to five years before the presentation of the bankruptcy petition (IA 1986, s 341). This is a longer time period than exists for the similar corporate recovery provision (see **19.5.1.2**).

20.5.2.3 Does the bankrupt have to have been insolvent at the time?

There is no need to prove the debtor was insolvent at the time (or as a result of the transaction), unless the transaction was more than two years before the petition (IA 1986, s 341(2)). Even if the transaction was more than two years before the petition, insolvency may be presumed if the transaction was in favour of an 'associate' (broadly, a close relative or business associate, as defined by IA 1986, s 435). This presumption may be rebutted.

CASE STUDY

Joseph's trustee is not able to establish that the transfer of the cottage was a transaction at an undervalue, as Joseph is able to prove he was not insolvent at the time or as a result of the transaction.

20.5.3 Preferences

20.5.3.1 What is a preference?

An arrangement is a preference if it places a creditor, surety, or guarantor in a better position than they would have been in otherwise on bankruptcy, and the debtor intended (at least partly) to do this (IA 1986, s 340). For example, if the debtor has borrowed money from a friend and, facing imminent bankruptcy, he then repays that friend in order to ensure that the friend does not lose money, that would be a preference.

Where the preference is in favour of an associate (as defined by IA 1986, s 435), there is a presumption that the debtor intended to prefer that person. This presumption may be rebutted.

20.5.3.2 How far back may the trustee go?

The trustee in bankruptcy may make an application to set aside any 'preference' made within the six months prior to the bankruptcy petition (IA 1986, s 341(1)), or within two years prior to the petition if the preference is in respect of an associate (IA 1986, s 435).

20.5.3.3 Does the bankrupt have to have been insolvent at the time?

The trustee must prove that the debtor was insolvent at the time or became insolvent as a result of the preference being granted (IA 1986, s 341(2)).

> **CASE STUDY**
>
> Joseph's trustee is able to establish that the payment to Joseph's friend was a preference, because he obtains a copy of an e-mail sent to the friend saying that Joseph would make the repayment now, while he still could, as his creditors were 'baying for blood' and he felt he could be made bankrupt 'at any time'. On investigation of his finances, it is clear that he was already technically insolvent.

20.5.4 Transactions defrauding creditors

This is a recovery action that applies to both corporate and personal insolvency and can be found at IA 1986, s 423. The applicability of this section to corporate insolvency is discussed at **19.5.5**.

Where a transaction has been made at an undervalue deliberately for the purpose of making the debtor's property unavailable to pay creditors, any 'victim' of the transaction, or the trustee or supervisor of a voluntary arrangement, may make application to have the transaction set aside (IA 1986, s 424). It can even be utilised by a creditor pre-insolvency as an asset recovery tool if that creditor is a 'victim' of the transaction. If a creditor wants to take action post-insolvency as a victim, rather than allow the insolvency practitioner to take the action, then permission of the court must be sought.

This provision has no time limit in the IA 1986, so even a transaction which took place many years ago could be set aside on this basis. However, the greater the time that has elapsed between the transaction and the bankruptcy, the weaker is the evidence that the aim of the transaction was to avoid the asset in question being used to pay creditors.

Motive is essential here. The trustee must show that the purpose of the transaction was to put assets beyond the reach of creditors. The provision is therefore rarely used by trustees unless the time limit for an application under IA 1986, s 339 has expired (see **20.5.2.2**).

20.5.5 Extortionate credit transactions

The trustee is able to apply to set aside or vary the terms of any credit provided to the bankrupt within the three years prior to the bankruptcy order, if the credit terms are 'extortionate' (IA 1986, s 343). This means that the terms require 'grossly exorbitant' payments or have 'grossly contravened ... fair dealing'.

Individuals with low incomes often do find themselves attracted to loan sharks, who lend small sums at very high interest rates. The rates often increase drastically if the debtor is late with any repayments. However, the section has not been used widely and there is no case law, probably because it is so hard to prove that the interest rate is 'grossly exorbitant'.

20.6 DISTRIBUTING THE BANKRUPT'S ASSETS

Once the trustee has taken control of the bankrupt's assets and finalised investigations and proceedings to set aside antecedent transactions, the assets must be converted into money and distributed to the creditors.

Secured creditors, of course, may sell the charged assets themselves, pay their debt and pass any surplus to the trustee. If the asset does not produce sufficient funds, the secured creditor will have to claim the balance as an unsecured creditor, along with everyone else.

The assets must be distributed in accordance with the statutory order set out mainly in IA 1986, s 328, as follows:

(a) *The costs of the bankruptcy.* The first items to be paid are the expenses incurred as a result of the bankruptcy, including the professional charges of the trustee in bankruptcy and any professional advisers appointed by the trustee, for example solicitors. *then*

(b) *Preferential debts.* If there is insufficient money available to pay all preferential debts (see **20.6.1**), they rank and abate equally (see **20.6.2**). *then*

(c) *Ordinary unsecured creditors.* If funds are insufficient to pay all debts in this category, they rank and abate equally. *then*

(d) *Postponed creditors.* These are debts to the spouse or civil partner (IA 1986, s 329).

20.6.1 What are preferential debts?

Schedule 6 to the IA 1986 contains a list of debts that are designated as 'preferential debts'. They include:

(a) accrued holiday pay owed to employees; and

(b) wages of employees due in the last four months before the bankruptcy order (subject to a current maximum amount of £800 per employee (Insolvency Proceedings (Monetary Limits) Order 1986 (SI 1986/1996))).

As is to be expected, employees in a personal insolvency situation are not as common as in corporate insolvency. However, a sole business owner or partner who goes bankrupt may have had employees on the payroll.

Up until the end of November 2020, employees were the only type of preferential creditor in cases of persons who were or had been trading prior to their bankruptcy, but, from 1 December 2020, legislation via the Finance Act 2020 was brought in to enable HMRC to join them as secondary preferential creditors. This move up the rankings further displaces unsecured creditors and, given that HMRC is usually one of the largest creditors in these situations, there are clear implications for other creditors of businesses in terms of the potential amount to be recovered.

Being a secondary preferential creditor means that HMRC is only to be a preferred creditor in relation to certain types of taxes – in this case the taxes collected by a business on its behalf, such as PAYE and VAT.

20.6.2 What does 'rank and abate equally' mean?

This means that each creditor in a particular category (eg, preferential, and unsecured creditors) will share the money available. Since there may not be enough for every creditor in that category to be paid in full, each will receive the same percentage of their original debt.

CASE STUDY

At the end of the bankruptcy, Joseph's trustee has the following assets and liabilities (the matrimonial home has been sold, and no money remained after payment of the mortgage and sale costs):

Assets		*Liabilities*	
Antique furniture	£10,000	Trustee's costs and expenses	£10,000
Quoted shares	£8,000	Owed to 4 employees for last month's wages	£2,400
Preference repayment	£5,000	Business creditors	£20,000
		HMRC	£8,000
		Overdraft	£15,000
Total	£23,000	Total	£55,400

The assets would be distributed as follows:

Assets	£23,000	
Less costs of trustee	(£10,000)	
Less preferential debts	(£10,400)	(assuming the HMRC monies owed are VAT and PAYE)
Total remaining for unsecured creditors	£2,600	

Unsecured creditors and the bank overdraft (totalling £35,000) rank and abate equally, so:

2,600/35,000 = approx. £0.07

Unsecured creditors will receive approximately 7p for every £1 they are owed.

20.6.3 Discharge

When the bankruptcy order is discharged, the bankruptcy comes to an end. The effect of this is that the bankrupt is released from most of their previous debts (IA 1986, s 281) (see **20.3** for an example of debts that are not released) but may still be subject to a BRO or BRU (see **20.4.6.2**). Discharge occurs automatically after one year (IA 1986, s 279) unless it is suspended, as stated below.

At this point, the realisation and distribution of the assets of the bankrupt may not be complete. Any property which has vested in the trustee in bankruptcy remains so and is not returned to the debtor (other than the special rules for the realisation of the matrimonial home, where particular time periods exist – see **20.4.5.2**), and the debtor is still required to assist the trustee with their task of the realisation of assets.

Automatic discharge may be suspended if the bankrupt is unco-operative or dishonest during the bankruptcy period, but this is more likely to be dealt with by way of a BRO or BRU. Sometimes suspension and a BRO action are both pursued.

20.7 ALTERNATIVES TO BANKRUPTCY

It is not inevitable that the individual facing financial difficulties will become bankrupt. There are some alternatives, and it is better to consider these sooner rather than later or the creditors may start proceedings themselves.

The main options are:

(a) an individual voluntary arrangement (IVA) (see **20.7.1** below);

(b) negotiation with creditors (see **20.7.2** below);

(c) for the debtor with minimal assets and income, a debt relief order (DRO) (see **20.7.3** below); and

(d) the 'breathing space' regime (see **20.7.4** below).

20.7.1 Individual voluntary arrangement

An IVA may arise as follows:

(a) A debtor may take advice and try to instigate an IVA themselves. To do this, the debtor requires professional assistance, so they must find an insolvency practitioner who is willing to assist them in drawing up proposals and to supervise their implementation if they receive the approval of creditors. The insolvency practitioner is known initially as the debtor's 'nominee'. It will clearly be difficult to find a nominee if there are no assets at all from which to pay their fees.

(b) Alternatively, the debtor's trustee in bankruptcy may apply for an IVA during the bankruptcy process.

20.7.1.1 IVA procedure

(For the purposes of this analysis, we shall assume that the debtor is male.)

Once they have found someone willing to be their nominee, the debtor must prepare a statement of affairs for that nominee and should immediately apply to the bankruptcy court for an interim order (IA 1986, s 253). This has the effect of stopping any other proceedings being taken against the debtor while their creditors consider the debtor's proposals. While the interim order is in force (usually for 14 days, but it may be extended) no bankruptcy petition may be presented or proceeded with unless the leave of the court is obtained. No other proceedings, execution or other legal process may be commenced or continued against the debtor or their property. The interim order thus creates a moratorium. It is possible (but rare) to proceed with an IVA proposal without applying for an interim order. If this procedure is adopted, then no statutory moratorium applies.

The nominee will prepare a report for the court advising whether there are any realistic proposals to be made and therefore whether it is worth calling a meeting of creditors. If a meeting of creditors is called and the meeting approves the proposals (by 75% or more majority in value, of which at least 50% in value of creditors who are not 'associates' of the debtor agree), then the proposal will be passed. Effectively, therefore, two votes take place. It is for the convenor or chair of the meeting to decide if a creditor is an associate of the debtor. Every ordinary, unsecured creditor who had notice of the meeting and was entitled to attend and vote is bound by the decision of the meeting, whether or not they actually did attend and vote. Preferential and secured creditors are not bound by the voluntary arrangement unless they agree to it (IA 1986, s 258).

If the creditors approve the proposed voluntary arrangement, the nominee (now called a 'supervisor') will implement the proposals. If the debtor fails to comply with the arrangement, or if it transpires that the creditors were persuaded to accept the debtor's proposal by means of false or misleading information, the supervisor or any creditor who is party to the voluntary arrangement may petition for the debtor's bankruptcy. This is particularly relevant where it is discovered that the debtor has made transactions at an undervalue (see **20.5.2**) or preferences (see **20.5.3**) immediately prior to the voluntary arrangement, as only a trustee in bankruptcy has the power to apply to the court to set aside these transactions and recover the money which can be used to pay creditors. A supervisor has no power to do this.

20.7.1.2 Advantages for the debtor in a voluntary arrangement

If a debtor manages to reach a voluntary arrangement with their creditors, the debtor avoids the stigma of bankruptcy, the accompanying bad publicity, and the trauma of, possibly, a public examination in open court. The debtor also avoids the various disabilities and disqualifications which follow from being declared bankrupt (see **20.4.6**). A voluntary arrangement is suitable only if the debtor has the means to make a reasonable offer of payment to their creditors. The insolvency practitioner will be able to advise on the likely acceptability of the proposals.

20.7.1.3 Advantages for the creditor

If the debtor is insolvent (as they frequently will be) then creditors, particularly ordinary unsecured creditors, will have to accept that they are unlikely to be paid the amount due to them in full. They may feel that if they accept a voluntary arrangement proposed by the debtor, they will recover a higher percentage of the debt due to them (because the costs involved in a voluntary arrangement may be lower than in a full bankruptcy), or that they will be paid sooner (because the full bankruptcy process can be extremely lengthy). Creditors will also need to judge for themselves whether the debtor can be relied upon to honour the arrangement. They can always seek advice as to whether to instigate bankruptcy proceedings should the debtor prove to have deceived them in the information provided or to be untrustworthy.

20.7.1.4 The Straightforward Consumer IVA Protocol (the Protocol)

Many debtors are consumers with large credit card debts. In this situation the lenders will usually follow the Protocol, which has been approved by the British Bankers' Association. It aims to balance the conflicting interests of the consumer (to free themselves from as much debt as possible), the lender (to recover as much as possible) and the supervisor (to charge as appropriate for the time spent) and contains standard terms on issues such as fees for insolvency practitioners and levels of return for creditors. The latest version of the Protocol was published in April 2021 and can be found at <www.gov.uk/government/publications/individual-voluntary-arrangement-iva-protocol/iva-protocol-2021>. However, this should not be used after 30 June 2025 when a new Protocol will have been brought in, which at the time of writing can be found at <www.gov.uk/government/publications/individual-voluntary-arrangement-iva-protocol/iva-protocol-2025>.

In addition, in June 2022 the IVA Standing Committee issued new guidance to insolvency practitioners to support the Straightforward Consumer IVA protocol for existing and new protocol compliant individual voluntary arrangements. The guidance was produced in light of the cost of living crisis.

EXAMPLE OF AN IVA

Narinder, who used to have a good job in the City, has been steadily building up huge credit card debts following his redundancy. He has been using one card to pay off another and opening new cards; but he can no longer do this, as he has reached his limit on all the cards and cannot apply for any more.

Narinder recently managed to get a fairly well-paid job (although after paying his living expenses he still did not have enough income to pay even the minimum monthly payments on the cards) and consulted an insolvency practitioner about what he should do.

The insolvency practitioner advised that Narinder should seek to implement an IVA and offered to act as his nominee. The creditors have now agreed to accept monthly payments for five years, at which point they will write off any remaining debts. They have reserved the right under the terms of the proposal to review the payments if Narinder's income improves.

20.7.2 Negotiation with creditors

An individual who recognises they are in financial difficulties should always talk to their creditors as soon as possible. Many creditors will be prepared to listen to suggestions, as they know they are unlikely to recover all their debts if the individual becomes bankrupt. This is particularly important if the family home is mortgaged and there are difficulties paying the mortgage, or if the individual's business is in trouble.

However, any agreement with one or more creditors is unlikely to be binding on third parties and will not stop other creditors from starting proceedings themselves. It is partly for that reason that the new breathing space regime was created in 2021 (see **20.7.4** below).

20.7.3 Debt relief order

Debt relief orders (DROs) were an addition to the insolvency procedures for individuals and became available on 6 April 2009 (Tribunals, Courts and Enforcement Act 2007, s 108 and Sch 17).

The DRO is made by the Official Receiver following an online application, and from April 2024 there is no longer any administrative fee to pay for such an application. It is available only to those debtors whose liabilities and assets are small. The relevant qualifying criteria were increased in June 2024. Further, from April 2024, the £90 fee for applying for a DRO has also been abolished, and these combined changes have resulted in a considerable increase in the number of DROs being seen.

The current key criteria are that the debtor must *not*:

(a) have total unsecured liabilities exceeding £50,000;
(b) have total gross assets exceeding £2,000 and not own a car worth £4,000 or more (unless it has been specially adapted because the debtor has a disability);
(c) have disposable income exceeding £75 per month, after deduction of normal household expenses;
(d) have been the subject of a DRO in the preceding six years; and
(e) be subject to another formal insolvency procedure.

The effects are that the debtor will be:

(a) protected from enforcement action by most of their creditors;
(b) free of the debts at the end of the DRO period (usually 12 months);
(c) obliged to co-operate with the Official Receiver and provide information; and
(d) expected to make arrangements to pay their creditors if their financial situation improves.

During the DRO the debtor is under the same restrictions that apply during a BRO/BRU (see **20.4.6.2**), and these restrictions may be extended for up to 15 years by a debt relief restrictions order (DRRO) or a debt relief restrictions undertaking (DRRU) if the debtor is seemingly dishonest or culpable.

20.7.4 Debt Respite Scheme (Breathing Space)

The Debt Respite Scheme (Breathing Space Moratorium and Mental Health Crisis Moratorium) (England and Wales) Regulations 2020 (SI 2020/1311) came into force on 4 May 2021. Essentially, this gives debtors time to seek to consider if other formal debt solutions are appropriate without having creditors breathing down their necks.

Guidance and further information on this scheme can be found at: <www.gov.uk/government/publications/debt-respite-scheme-breathing-space-guidance/debt-respite-scheme-breathing-space-guidance-for-creditors>.

There are two types of moratorium created by these Regulations. A breathing space moratorium, which lasts for up to 60 days, and a mental health crisis breathing space moratorium, which lasts as long as the treatment continues for the debtor, plus 30 days. Once effective, a creditor must stop all action relating to that debt and apply the protections set out in the Regulations. If a creditor has commenced legal proceedings these must be put on hold, including enforcement action.

A debtor can apply to a debt advice provider who is authorised by the Financial Conduct Authority (FCA) to offer debt counselling for advice and a breathing space moratorium. The charity debt sector has been very involved in the implementation of this process.

To qualify, the debtor must:

- be an individual living in England or Wales (includes sole traders);
- owe a qualifying debt to a creditor;
- not have a debt relief order or an individual voluntary arrangement or be an undischarged bankrupt;

- not already have had a breathing space in the previous 12 months.

The debt advice provider must be satisfied that the debtor cannot pay some or all of their debt as it falls due and consider the debtor would benefit from a debt solution.

All personal debts are likely to be qualifying debts with a few exceptions. It includes joint debts even if only one debtor applies, and business debts owed by sole traders who are not registered for VAT.

The Insolvency Service will maintain the electronic service that the debt advice providers will use, will send out the notification to creditors and maintain a register of persons whose debts are in a breathing space and the date it ended or was cancelled in the last 15 months.

Once notified, a creditor will need to identify all debts owed by the debtor and advise the debt advisor of any debts not included on the notification. In addition, the creditor will need to:

- stop all interest and charges for the duration of the breathing space;
- stop any enforcement or recovery action to recover the debt;
- stop contacting the debtor to request payment.

If proceedings have been commenced, then the court must be told in writing forthwith to enable it to stay bankruptcy proceedings and enforcement.

A creditor has 20 days to challenge a moratorium if it considers that the debtor has enough funds to pay their debts as they fall due, but the creditor will need evidence to support this application. If the debt advisor, after consideration, does not cancel the moratorium, the creditor can apply to the County Court for it to be reviewed.

The case of *Kaye v Lees* [2023] EWHC 152 (KB) was the first example of a creditor successfully challenging the imposition of a moratorium against them. The case provides guidance to both creditors and debtors regarding the way the courts will construe these Regulations. As stated in that case, the court will intervene to prevent debtors taking advantage of them by applying for successive moratoria, and, to rely on the mental health breathing space scheme, debtors will need to provide conclusive medical evidence that they are receiving mental health treatment. If debtors who are not suffering from a mental health disorder are simply trying to use the Regulations to avoid payment, then this case demonstrates that the court will cancel the moratorium if it unfairly prejudices the creditor. Following that judgment, the High Court handed down a further judgment in this long-running litigation. This time, the court revisited the injunction preventing the defendant from seeking a mental health crisis moratorium (*Kaye v Lees* [2023] EWHC 758 (KB)).

There has been a considerable use of the breathing space regime since its introduction, but note that the second part of the process (the statutory debt repayment scheme) is not yet in force.

20.8 SUMMARIES AND CHECKLISTS

20.8.1 Summary of bankruptcy procedure

(a) Petition by creditor to court or application by debtor to the adjudicator.
(b) Court hearing (if appropriate) and bankruptcy order made.
(c) Official Receiver appointed and automatically becomes the trustee in bankruptcy.
(d) Bankrupt's property vests in trustee.
(e) Statement of affairs submitted to Official Receiver.
(f) Creditors may be able to appoint a trustee in bankruptcy to replace the Official Receiver.
(g) Trustee collects assets and investigates past conduct.
(h) Trustee distributes assets.

(i) Bankrupt discharged (automatically one year after bankruptcy order made unless suspension ordered).

(j) A BRO or BRU may remain in place for up to 15 years.

20.8.2 Summary of IVA procedure

(a) Proposal – by debtor or trustee in bankruptcy.

(b) Nominee appointed.

(c) Interim order – to prevent other creditor actions.

(d) Creditors vote on proposals – 75% or more in value (including at least 50% of creditors who are not associates of the debtor) required for approval and to bind all unsecured creditors.

(e) Supervisor appointed – nominee becomes supervisor and implements proposals.

(f) If proposals carried out by the debtor, the IVA is complete, and the debtor is released from it.

PART IV SUMMARY

INSOLVENCY

Topic	*Summary*
Terminology and regulation	The term 'insolvency' is a generic term used when referring to both companies and individuals. 'Liquidation' and 'administration' are the main terms relating to companies, and 'bankruptcy' applies to individuals. The principal law relating to these areas is found in the Insolvency Act 1986, although several subsequent Acts are also relevant, notably the Enterprise Act 2002, the Small Business, Enterprise and Employment Act 2015 and the Corporate Insolvency and Governance Act 2020. In April 2017, a new set of supporting Insolvency Rules became operative.
Insolvency regimes	There are a number of insolvency regimes which can be used to deal with companies in financial difficulties: company voluntary arrangements; administration; liquidation; and receivership (strictly speaking the correct term is administrative receivership). The Corporate Insolvency and Governance Act 2020 also introduced two new permanent corporate rescue regimes, namely the moratorium and the restructuring plan.
Company voluntary arrangements (CVAs)	CVAs allow a company's directors to make a proposal to creditors. The proposal will be some alternative means of dealing with the company's financial difficulties as opposed to liquidation or administration. An insolvency practitioner, the *nominee*, reports to court on the proposal's viability. Creditors representing more than 75% in value of the company's debts must approve the proposal. A CVA must also pass a second test in that it must also have been approved by 50% or over of non-connected creditors. If approved, all creditors, whose rights remain, save secured and preferential creditors, are bound by the CVA.
Administration	This is aimed at saving companies in financial difficulties or at least securing a better return to creditors. Administration may be commenced by a company in difficulties, its directors or a qualifying floating chargeholder. Other creditors may also seek an administration order by petitioning the court.
Administration process	The procedure is based on the appointment of an administrator, whose role is to achieve the aims referred to above. The administrator is given statutory powers to deal with the company's property and, effectively, run the company during the period of administration. As with CVAs, creditors' decisions will be sought to ensure matters are carried out correctly.
Administration moratorium	The advantage of an administration is that it creates a moratorium on creditor actions, providing the administrator with a 'breathing space' to carry out their duties.

Topic	Summary
Liquidation	Liquidation is also known as 'winding up'. This is the most common insolvency procedure, and it results in the distribution of assets to creditors and the eventual dissolution of the company. There are different types of liquidation, depending on the company's financial position and who commences proceedings.
Members' voluntary liquidation	This is available only where a company is solvent. The directors make a statutory declaration of solvency. The members pass a special resolution to wind up the company and an ordinary resolution to appoint a liquidator. The liquidator gathers in and realises the company's assets, then distributes them to the company's creditors who, given the company's solvency, should be paid their debts in full.
Creditors' voluntary liquidation	Where a company is insolvent, its members and directors may decide to place the company in liquidation and to appoint a liquidator. A decision-making procedure then takes place at which creditors have the ability to appoint their chosen liquidator in proportion to the value of their debt. The liquidator then, as in a members' voluntary liquidation, gathers in and realises the company's assets, before distributing them to creditors.
Compulsory liquidation	Liquidation can also be commenced by a creditor. This is brought about by court order rather than company resolutions. A creditor may petition for liquidation on the grounds that the company is unable to pay its debts. If the petition is successful, the Official Receiver is appointed. Creditors may then seek to appoint an insolvency practitioner in the OR's place to be liquidator. Again, this liquidator is charged with realising assets and distributing them to creditors.
Statutory order of payment	Administrators and liquidators are required to pay out assets in a particular order. First, the expenses of the winding up; secondly, preferential debts; thirdly, monies secured by floating charges; and then unsecured creditors. Following these, interest on preferential and unsecured debts is paid before, finally, any remaining surplus is paid to shareholders. An element of a company's assets is 'ring-fenced' for unsecured creditors.
Receivership	Where a creditor has a fixed charge over a company's assets, then it will be entitled to appoint a receiver to realise these assets if the company becomes insolvent. Prior to September 2003, floating chargeholders could appoint an administrative receiver, who had wide powers. The ability to do so is now reserved to specialised situations for all charges created since 15 September 2003, with administration being the main procedure available to floating chargeholders and the one utilised by them.
Moratorium (under the Corporate Insolvency and Governance Act 2020)	In this moratorium, a company is protected from various creditor actions in respect of the majority of its pre-moratorium debts. The company's directors remain in control of the company, but an independent monitor (who must be an insolvency practitioner) oversees the process throughout the period of the moratorium and can terminate it in various circumstances if it is not working. This procedure may be a precursor to an application for another corporate rescue procedure.

Topic	Summary
The Restructuring Plan	The Restructuring Plan is a powerful and flexible new court-supervised restructuring process. In some respects, this procedure is similar to a Scheme of Arrangement under Part 26 of the Companies Act 2006. Unlike a Scheme, however, a Restructuring Plan can be imposed on a dissenting class of creditors, which is called a cross-class cram down.
Past transactions	Liquidators and administrators are able to take action to overturn certain antecedent transactions in order to claw back assets. These include: • transactions at an undervalue • preferences • extortionate credit transactions • certain floating charges • transactions defrauding creditors. The basic premise behind these rights is that creditors should not be prejudiced where a company, prior to insolvency, has caused assets to be diverted from the creditors who would be entitled to them on insolvency.
Bankruptcy	Bankruptcy is commenced by a petition to the court by a creditor or an online application by the debtor themselves. An order will be made if it is proved a debtor is unable to pay their debts. Where an order is made, all the bankrupt's property – save for tools of the trade, clothing, and furniture – will vest in a trustee in bankruptcy, who will initially always be the Official Receiver (an employee of the Insolvency Service). The trustee's job is to convert the property into money and use that money to pay the bankrupt's debts. Similar provisions (in the main) to those applicable to corporate insolvency allow the trustee in bankruptcy to seek to recover assets where particular antecedent transactions have taken place (see the consideration of this area above).
Discharge	A bankruptcy order is discharged automatically one year after the date of order unless a specific application is made to suspend this or make the bankrupt subject to further restrictions.
Individual voluntary arrangements (IVAs)	An IVA is an alternative to a bankruptcy order. A debtor works with an insolvency practitioner (initially called a 'nominee') to draw up proposals to be made to creditors. A statement of affairs is prepared, and an interim order sought from the court. This prevents proceedings being brought against the debtor – usually for 14 days – whilst creditors consider the debtor's proposals. If 75% or more in value of creditors (including at least 50% of creditors who are not associates of the debtor) approve the proposals at a meeting, then every ordinary, unsecured creditor with notice of the decision-making process will be bound. The nominee then becomes the supervisor of the IVA and carries out the proposals.
Debt relief orders	A debt relief order is available for debtors with relatively small debts and little in the way of assets.
Breathing space	The Debt Respite Scheme (Breathing Space) was a new personal insolvency option that commenced in May 2021, and it gives an individual with problem debt issues the right to legal protections from their creditors for a period of time. There are two types of breathing space: a standard breathing space and a mental health crisis breathing space.

PART V

TAXATION

Any business that is run with a view to making a profit should be structured in the light of the tax issues relevant to that business. These issues affect the operation of the business itself, and also the personal financial affairs of those involved in running the business. In the case of a sole trader, this link is obvious, but also applies to the partners in a partnership, the shareholders (and other investors) in a company, and the employees of a business (in whatever form it operates).

The rationale behind, and the operation of, income tax, capital gains tax, inheritance tax and value added tax are discussed in ***Legal Foundations***, and the impact of those taxes, along with that of corporation tax, is considered further in Part V.

Part V begins (**Chapter 21**) with a description of the method of calculating the trading profits of a business (whether unincorporated or a company) and goes on to analyse how profits are taxed in the context of a company (**Chapters 22** and **23**), a sole trader (**Chapter 24**) and a partnership (**Chapter 25**). **Chapter 26** considers the taxation of employees and company directors. Part V concludes with a description of the taxation of savings and investment income (interest and dividends) in **Chapter 27**, an analysis of the capital tax issues relevant to individuals when they dispose of their business interests (**Chapter 28**) and an overview of the tax considerations in the choice of business medium (**Chapter 29**). It does not deal with provisions relating to trustees or personal representatives.

A summary of the key themes contained in Part V, and of the main rates and allowances for 2025/26, is reproduced at the end of Part V for ease of reference.

The text of Part V is drafted on the assumption that all individuals and companies concerned in a business are UK-resident for tax purposes, and is only intended as a brief introduction to some of the major taxation provisions.

CHAPTER 21

Calculation of Trading Profits of a Business

LEARNING OUTCOMES

After reading this chapter you will be able to:

- explain the process for calculating a business's trading profits for tax purposes
- understand the detail of the elements that make up the trading profit calculation
- appreciate how the trading profit calculation can lead to an overall trading profit or trading loss.

21.1 INTRODUCTION

21.1.1 The nature of trading profits

A business may make two kinds of profit: income and capital. In so far as profits are recurring by nature (eg trading, rent, interest), they are likely to form income profits. This chapter concentrates on the calculation of trading profits (which are likely to form the largest source of income profits for most businesses). The way in which trading and other income profits are taxed depends on the format of the business being carried on.

21.1.1.1 Sole trader

A sole trader's income profits form part of their 'total income' for the purposes of income tax (see Step 1 of the income tax calculation described in ***Legal Foundations***).

21.1.1.2 Company

A company's income profits (along with its capital profits) are charged to corporation tax (see Step 1 of the corporation tax calculation described in **Chapter 22**).

21.1.1.3 Partnership

The income profits made by a partnership are divided amongst the partners and charged either to income tax (in the case of individual partners) or to corporation tax (in the case of corporate partners).

21.1.1.4 Relevant legislation

The way in which each business format is taxed is considered in more detail in **Chapters 22** and **23** (in relation to companies), **Chapter 24** (in relation to sole traders) and **Chapter 25** (in relation to partners).

The way in which trading profits are calculated is broadly the same for both income tax (relevant to sole traders and individual partners) and corporation tax (relevant to companies). However, the rules for income tax and corporation tax are contained in different statutes. To calculate trading profits for the purposes of income tax, reference should be made to the Income Tax (Trading and Other Income) Act 2005 (ITTOIA 2005). The ITTOIA 2005 contains provisions on 'Trading Income' in Part 2; this covers various items but the key one is 'profits of a trade'. The corporation tax code is contained in the Corporation Tax Act 2009 (CTA 2009) where Part 3 also contains rules for 'Trading Income', and in the Corporation Tax Act 2010 (CTA 2010).

21.1.2 The accounting period of a business

A business must prepare accounts for an accounting period (usually of 12 months) to show the profit (or loss) made by its trade. Although the profit and loss account for the accounting period will be used as a starting point for ascertaining the figure which is taxable, some adjustment will usually be required as some of the expenses likely to be shown in the profit and loss account (such as entertainment of customers) are not generally allowed as deductions for tax purposes and the calculation must be revised to satisfy the tax rules prior to submission to His Majesty's Revenue and Customs (HMRC).

21.1.3 Method of calculation of trading income

For tax purposes, the trading profits or trading loss of a business for an accounting period are calculated in the following way:

chargeable receipts (see **21.2**)
LESS
any deductible expenditure (see **21.3**)
LESS
any capital allowances (see **21.4**)
EQUALS
trading profit (or trading loss).

With effect from 2024/25, the default method by which most unincorporated businesses calculate their trading income for income tax purposes is the so-called 'cash basis'. This effectively taxes the difference between money received and money paid during the accounting period. There are some advantages for smaller businesses in following this simpler method of record keeping and calculation. However, it is thought that larger or more complex businesses are likely to opt out. Added to which, the cash basis does not apply for companies. Given that this method of taxing trading income is of limited application, it will not be considered further in this book.

21.2 CHARGEABLE RECEIPTS

To be chargeable, receipts of the business must derive from its trade and be income rather than capital in nature (ITTOIA 2005, Part 2; CTA 2009, Part 3, Ch 6).

21.2.1 Trade

Despite the frequency with which 'trade' appears in all the major tax statutes, it does not have a full statutory definition (beyond, for example, the rather unhelpful references in the Income Tax Act 2007, s 989, and the CTA 2010, s 1119, which confirm that '"trade" includes any venture in the nature of trade'). Many cases have had to address the issue, but each turns on its own facts and so none provides a conclusive test. As a general guideline, however, Lord Reid's comments in the case of *Ransom (Inspector of Taxes) v Higgs* [1974] 1 WLR 1594 may be helpful:

> As an ordinary word in the English language 'trade' has or has had a variety of meanings or shades of meaning. Leaving aside obsolete or rare usage it is sometimes used to denote any mercantile operation but it is commonly used to denote operations of a commercial character by which the trader provides to customers for reward some kind of goods or services.

Receipts of the trade are those which derive from the trading activity rather than from circumstances not directly connected with the trade. Most receipts of the trade, such as money received from sales of goods and services, are easily identified, but some are less so. For example, a sum received on cancellation of a trading contract as compensation would be a receipt of the trade, but a gratuitous sum received on termination of a trading relationship as a token of personal appreciation would not.

21.2.2 Income

There are no clear-cut rules to determine when a receipt is income in nature rather than capital (despite the large amount of case law on the subject). As a general rule, however, if something is purchased for the purpose of resale at a profit (such as stock), the money received from the resale will be of an income nature. In contrast, receipts of a capital nature will generally derive from the sale of an asset which was purchased for the benefit or use of the business on a more or less permanent basis rather than for resale. For example, a trader who purchases some trading premises and who eventually (perhaps many years later) sells them receives a sum of a capital nature.

Some receipts will arise from types of transactions which are different from the sale of goods or services, so that the above principles have to be applied by analogy. For example, a sum received as compensation for cancellation of a contract for the sale of goods is of an income nature because it represents what would have been an income profit if the goods had been sold.

21.3 DEDUCTIBLE EXPENDITURE

In calculating taxable trading profits there must be deducted from chargeable receipts of the trade any expenditure which is of an income nature, which has been incurred 'wholly and exclusively' for the trade and deduction of which is not prohibited by statute (ITTOIA 2005, s 34; CTA 2009, Part 3, Ch 4).

21.3.1 Expenditure of an 'income nature'

(a) If expenditure on an item is incurred for the purpose of enabling the trader to sell that item at a profit, it is of an income nature. Therefore the expense to a trader of buying their stock is of an income nature and deductible from chargeable receipts in calculating trading profits. Conversely the expense to the trader of buying their premises (buying a permanent asset for their business) is of a capital nature and not deductible (but see **21.4**).

(b) A further relevant (and sometimes more appropriate) test is whether the expenditure has the quality of recurrence, rather than being once and for all expenditure. All expenditure on general overheads like electricity, telephone charges, staff salaries and rent has this quality of recurrence in the sense that the type of expenditure is likely to be incurred repeatedly. Also, interest paid on borrowing (eg on an overdraft) for business purposes will generally qualify as being expenditure of an income nature. Expenditure on the purchase of long-term assets of the business (like premises and furniture) will not recur in the foreseeable future in that the asset has been acquired for the on-going benefit of the trade, and so is not of an income nature.

21.3.2 'Wholly and exclusively for the purposes of the trade'

To be deductible, the expenditure must also have been incurred wholly and exclusively for the purposes of the trade (ITTOIA 2005, s 34; CTA 2009, s 54). Expenditure which has a dual purpose cannot be wholly and exclusively for one purpose. For example, when a taxpayer pays for a meal in a restaurant when working away from home, the greater cost of the meal compared with eating at home was not incurred wholly and exclusively for business purposes; the cost of the meal had a dual purpose which included satisfying a person's basic need to eat (*Caillebotte v Quinn* [1975] 1 WLR 731). Similarly, when a barrister purchases clothing suitable for wearing in court, the greater cost of that clothing compared with casual clothing was not incurred wholly and exclusively for business purposes; the cost of the clothing had a dual purpose, including satisfying a person's basic need to be clothed (*Mallalieu v Drummond* [1983] 2 AC 861). In fact, despite this principle which has been clearly established in case law, HMRC allows some expenses to be apportioned so that part is deductible; for example, where a taxpayer works from home, part of the cost of heating and lighting the home will be deductible for tax purposes (and a right to apportion an identifiable proportion of an expense where that proportion is incurred wholly and exclusively for the purposes of the trade is now included in ITTOIA 2005, s 34(2)).

21.3.3 Common examples of deductible expenditure

Although any given item of expenditure must be checked to confirm that it is of an income nature and incurred wholly and exclusively for the purposes of the trade, the following common examples of expenditure by a business will usually be classed as deductible:

(a) salaries;
(b) rent on premises;
(c) utility charges (eg gas, electricity, and telephone bills);
(d) stock (ie items purchased for resale);
(e) business rates;
(f) stationery/postage.

21.4 CAPITAL ALLOWANCES

As described in **21.3** above, expenditure on capital items cannot, in principle, be deducted from chargeable receipts when calculating trading profits for an accounting period because it is not of an income nature. This can cause severe cash flow problems for a business that needs to invest in expensive capital items to help produce the goods or services in which it deals. To help alleviate this problem, legislation exists to allow a specified amount of the cost of certain capital items or activities to be deducted each year in calculating trading profits. The principal category covered by the legislation is plant and machinery (although allowances may also be available for other specified expenditure, such as 'research and development' and 'buildings and structures'). Under the Capital Allowances Act 2001 (CAA 2001), where expenditure is incurred on certain assets or activities, a percentage of the capital expenditure will be allowed as a deduction in calculating trading profits in a given accounting period. These deductions are known as capital allowances.

21.4.1 Plant and machinery

For most businesses, the most common form of capital allowance claimed will be those for plant and machinery.

21.4.1.1 Definitions

'Plant and machinery' is not defined in the CAA 2001. In *Yarmouth v France* (1887) 19 QBD 647, it was said that plant includes whatever apparatus is used by the businessperson for carrying on their business; this includes all goods and chattels which they keep for permanent use in their business but not, for example, stock in trade. Examples of plant and machinery are office equipment, computers, tools and manufacturing equipment.

21.4.1.2 The allowance (CAA 2001, ss 52–59)

At present, for most qualifying assets, the taxpayer is allowed, in each 12-month accounting period of ownership of the asset, to deduct a 'writing down allowance' of up to 18% of the reducing balance of the cost of the asset in calculating their trading profits. (Note: there are special rules for calculating the capital allowances given for expenditure on certain types of assets (see **21.4.1.6**).) The reduced balance of the cost at the end of each accounting period is also known as the 'written-down value' of the asset. It is possible to claim part only of the maximum permissible allowance, but all of the examples that follow assume the taxpayer will take full advantage of the allowances available each year.

EXAMPLE

A printer, who owns no other machinery or plant, purchases a new printing press for £500,000. Starting in the accounting period of purchase, and assuming no further purchases (and ignoring the annual investment allowance, for which see **21.4.1.5**), the capital allowances are as follows:

Year 1 – 18% of £500,000 = £90,000	writing down allowance, leaving £410,000 as the written-down value of the asset
Year 2 – 18% of £410,000 = £73,800	writing down allowance, leaving £336,200 as the written-down value of the asset
Year 3 – 18% of £336,200 = £60,516	writing down allowance, leaving £275,684 as the written-down value of the asset

etc.

Suppose that the chargeable receipts of the trade less other deductible expenses amount to £1 million each year. This means (following deduction of the writing down allowance) that his trading profit from this source is as follows:

Year 1: £910,000 (£1 million less £90,000 writing down allowance)

Year 2: £926,200 (£1 million less £73,800 writing down allowance)

Year 3: £939,484 (£1 million less £60,516 writing down allowance).

21.4.1.3 Sale of assets

If, in due course, the item of plant and machinery is sold, it will be necessary to compare the written-down value of the asset at the time of sale with the actual sale price in order to assess whether the sale produces a 'profit' or a 'loss' when comparing these figures. If a 'profit' results, this may (subject to pooling – see **21.4.1.4**) be the subject of a 'balancing charge' and form a chargeable receipt in the accounting period in which the sale takes place; if a 'loss' results, there may be a 'balancing allowance' (ie a deduction from chargeable receipts in that period). The purpose of a balancing charge or a balancing allowance is to ensure that the taxpayer has had tax relief for precisely the amount by which the asset diminished in value.

Suppose that the printer in the Example, at the beginning of Year 4, sells the printing press for £300,000. If so, they have made a 'profit' of £24,316 compared with its written-down value (£275,684) and the £24,316 will form part of their chargeable receipts in Year 4.

21.4.1.4 Pooling

In practice, traders will often own more than one item of plant and machinery. To avoid a calculation being required every time an item is sold, all expenditure on plant and machinery is, in general, 'pooled' together and the writing down allowance is given each year on the balance of expenditure within the whole pool. This is expressed in s 55 of the CAA 2001 as being an allowance on the amount by which the 'available qualifying expenditure' ('AQE') exceeds the 'total of any disposal receipts' ('TDR'). If an asset is sold, the sale proceeds are deducted from the value of the pool; generally, therefore, no balancing allowance or charge should occur until the trade is discontinued and the whole pool sold.

EXAMPLE

Bob, a sole trader, has an existing pool of machinery and plant with a written-down value of £80,000. He sells some machinery for £20,000:

	£
Written-down value of pool at the start of the accounting period (AQE)	80,000
Less: disposal value (TDR)	20,000
	60,000
Less: writing down allowance (on £60,000) for the year of 18%	10,800
Value of pool carried forward to the next accounting period	49,200

If Bob sells the business in the following accounting period and the value agreed for the assets in the pool is, say, £50,000 a balancing charge of £800 will be included as a chargeable receipt when calculating Bob's trading profit for the final accounting period of the business under his ownership.

If the written-down value of the pool being used for an accounting period is ever £1,000 or less, the trader has the option of claiming a writing down allowance big enough to eliminate the pool (and so avoid having to submit accounts showing very small writing-down allowances for years to come).

21.4.1.5 Annual investment allowance (CAA 2001, ss 51A–51N)

Historically, from time to time, various additional capital allowances have been given in the first year of ownership of an asset in certain circumstances. Under the current scheme, every ongoing business receives an annual investment allowance ('AIA') of a maximum of £1,000,000 so that the first £1,000,000 of 'fresh' qualifying expenditure on plant and machinery incurred in an accounting period will be wholly deductible (in effect a 100% allowance).

(A group of companies will receive only one AIA for the group in each accounting period but can allocate it within the group as it sees fit.)

EXAMPLE 1

Riz, a sole trader, owns a manufacturing business. In her current accounting period, she buys some machinery for £170,000. The written-down value of her existing pool of plant and machinery is £80,000.

In the current accounting period, she is entitled to the following capital allowances:

	£	£
AIA – entire £170,000 spent on new machinery:		170,000
Writing down allowance:		
Written-down value of pool	80,000 x 18% =	14,400
Total capital allowances for the accounting period		184,400

(The written-down value of the pool for the next accounting period will be £65,600 (£80,000 less £14,400).)

EXAMPLE 2

Tom, a sole trader, owns a manufacturing business. In his current accounting period during 2025, he buys a machine for £1,300,000. The written-down value of his existing pool of plant and machinery is £200,000.

In the current accounting period, he is entitled to the following capital allowances:

	£	£
AIA – first £1,000,000 spent on the machine:		1,000,000
Writing down allowance:		
On remaining value of the machine	300,000	
Written-down value of pool	200,000	
	500,000 x 18% =	90,000
Total capital allowances for the accounting period		1,090,000

(The written-down value of the pool for the next accounting period will be £410,000 (£500,000 less £90,000).)

21.4.1.6 Full expensing and special first year allowance

Periodically, over recent years, the Government has used the incentive of short-term generous capital allowances to encourage investment. For example, in the wake of the Covid-19 pandemic, for a time companies investing in new plant and machinery were able to claim a 'super-deduction' of 130%.

The current scheme of 'first year allowances' applies to expenditure on or after 1 April 2023. A company is able to claim a first year allowance of 100% (full expensing) on qualifying expenditure on the provision of new plant and machinery for the year in which that expenditure was incurred. It should be noted that the plant and machinery in question must be 'new', so assets which are used or second-hand do not qualify.

Expenditure by companies on assets which would normally attract the special rate of 6%, such as long-life assets (see **21.4.1.7**), receive a special first year allowance of 50%.

The amount that can be claimed as a first year allowance is uncapped. On disposal of the asset, a balancing charge is applied equal to 100% of the disposal value where full expensing has been claimed (or 50% in the case of the special first year allowance).

21.4.1.7 Special rules for particular types of assets

(a) Short-life assets (CAA 2001, ss 83–89)

If a business thinks an asset will have a useful working life of less than eight years, an election can be made (within two years after the end of the accounting period in which the expenditure was incurred) to treat the asset as a short-life asset. The detail of the rules on short-life assets is beyond the scope of this book, but they allow a short-life asset to be kept in its own pool so that a disposal of it triggers an immediate balancing allowance or charge.

(b) Long-life assets and integral features (CAA 2001, s 33A and ss 90–104E)

Long-life assets are defined as those with an expected working life, when new, of at least 25 years. Again, these rules are complex, but their general effect is to give a less generous writing down allowance (of 6%) for long-life assets.

'Integral features' covers plant and machinery that is integral to a building (such as escalators, electrical and lighting equipment, and air conditioning systems). Like long-life assets, such integral features only qualify for a 6% writing down allowance (and are also pooled with them in a separate 'special rate pool').

Both long-life assets and integral features are eligible for the AIA.

EXAMPLE

Samuel, a sole trader, owns a high street fashion store. In his current accounting period during 2025, he replaces escalators to the first floor at a cost of £1,070,000. He has no existing pool of integral features.

In the current accounting period, he is entitled to the following capital allowances:

	£	£
AIA – first £1,000,000 spent on escalator		1,000,000
Writing down allowance:		
Remaining value of escalator	70,000 x 6% =	4,200
Total capital allowances for the accounting period		1,004,200

(The written-down value of the special rate pool for the next accounting period will be £65,800 (£1,070,000 less £1,004,200).)

21.4.2 The interrelation of capital allowances and capital gains legislation

Some capital assets (eg plant and machinery) may qualify both for capital allowances and be chargeable assets for the purposes of capital gains legislation. If so, special rules apply to determine exactly how any rise or fall in the value of the asset on its disposal will be taxed. The rules are designed to ensure that where capital allowances have been claimed an adjustment is made so that only the 'true' gain or loss on the disposal of the asset is used in the capital gains calculation.

EXAMPLE

Some plant and machinery is acquired in Year 1 for £20,000. Two years later, it has a written-down value of £13,448.

(a) If it is then sold for £13,448, there will be no balancing capital allowance or charge, and no gain or loss created for capital gains purposes.

(b) If, instead, it is sold for £12,000, there will be a balancing capital allowance of £1,448, but no gain or loss created for capital gains purposes.

(c) If, instead, it is sold for £15,000, there will be a balancing charge of £1,552 for capital allowances purposes, but no gain or loss created for capital gains purposes.

(d) Finally, if it is sold for £22,000, there will be a balancing charge of £6,552 for capital allowances purposes (to reflect the difference between the written-down value of £13,448 and the acquisition value of £20,000) plus a capital gain of £2,000 to reflect the rise in value above and beyond the original acquisition value.

Scenario (c) and, particularly, scenario (d) are unlikely to occur frequently in practice because machinery and plant tends to decrease in value and so is unlikely to be sold for more than its written-down value.

21.5 ILLUSTRATION OF TRADING PROFIT CALCULATION

Kevin, a sole trader, runs a business that makes and sells ceramic tiles. In the business's most recent accounting period, the sales from tiles totalled £1 million. Deductible expenditure was £300,000, broken down as follows:

Wages	£80,000
Materials	£140,000
Rent	£40,000
General overheads (telephone, electricity, advertising etc)	£40,000

The business has a pool of general plant and machinery with a written-down value at the start of the accounting period of £100,000. Kevin also buys a new kiln for £200,000 during the accounting period.

Calculation of trading profits:	£
Chargeable receipts (sales)	1,000,000
Less	
Deductible expenditure	300,000
Less	
Capital allowances:	
On the kiln – entire £200,000 (within AIA)	200,000
On the pool – £100,000 x 18% writing down allowance	18,000
Trading profit	482,000

The written-down value of the pool of plant and machinery carried forward to the next accounting period will be £82,000 (£100,000 less the £18,000 writing down allowance claimed this year).

21.6 TRADING LOSSES

The calculation of chargeable receipts, less deductible expenditure, less available capital allowances may produce a negative figure – ie a trading loss rather than a trading profit. In such a situation there will be no trading income from the accounting period of the loss to be taxed. In certain circumstances, relief is given for the trading loss for tax purposes – see **Chapters 22** and **24** for further details.

CHAPTER 22

TAXATION OF COMPANIES I – CORPORATION TAX

LEARNING OUTCOMES

After reading this chapter you will be able to:

- explain the steps to calculate corporation tax and when it is payable
- understand when a company can claim relief for a trading loss
- appreciate the corporation tax treatment of goodwill and dividends
- understand how corporation tax interacts with other taxes.

22.1 INTRODUCTION

Companies pay corporation tax rather than income tax or capital gains tax. This difference between companies on the one hand and individuals (whether sole traders or partners) on the other is not as fundamental as it might appear because, in calculating the company's profits chargeable to corporation tax, income profits are broadly calculated on the principles applicable to income tax and capital gains are broadly calculated on the principles applicable to capital gains tax.

A company is liable to pay corporation tax on its income profits and capital gains and the method of calculation is dealt with in detail at **22.2–22.6**. In short, it involves the following steps:

Step 1: Calculate income profits (see **22.2**)
Step 2: Calculate chargeable gains (see **22.3**)
Step 3: Calculate total profits; apply reliefs available against total profits (see **22.4**)
Step 4: Calculate the tax at the appropriate rate(s) (see **22.5**)

Corporation tax is one of the taxes subject to the 'general anti-abuse rule' ('GAAR') introduced by the Finance Act 2013. The GAAR is an addition to the many existing specific anti-avoidance rules and is designed to allow HMRC to counteract 'abusive' tax avoidance schemes intended to exploit loopholes in the legislation governing the rules for calculating corporation tax.

22.2 STEP 1: CALCULATE INCOME PROFITS

A company's income profits chargeable to corporation tax will be calculated under the rules of the appropriate part of the CTA 2009, most notably:

Part 3 – Trading Income

Part 4 – Property Income

Parts 5 and 6 – Loan Relationships

This chapter concentrates on trading income.

22.2.1 Trading income

It will be necessary to calculate the trading income (whether a trading profit or a trading loss) for an accounting period using the rules considered in **Chapter 21**, ie:

chargeable receipts
LESS
any deductible expenditure
LESS
any capital allowances
EQUALS
Trading profit (or trading loss).

22.2.1.1 Chargeable receipts

Examples of chargeable receipts for a company will usually be very similar to those of other businesses, ie money received for the sale of goods and services (for further details see **21.2**).

22.2.1.2 Deductible expenditure

The rules described at **21.3** apply to a company. Examples of deductible expenditure with particular relevance in the context of a company are:

(a) Directors'/employees' salaries or fees and benefits in kind. Occasionally there may be a problem over deductibility if a director is paid a salary that is excessive as remuneration for their services. If the salary is paid for personal reasons and not wholly and exclusively for the purposes of the trade, then it will not be deductible. It has been held (in *Copeman v William J Flood and Sons Ltd* [1941] 1 KB 202) that a substantial salary paid to a director who performed minimal duties should be apportioned into two parts; that part which was reasonable for the duties performed would be deductible in calculating the company's taxable profits and the other excessive part would not. It is unlikely that this problem would arise over a salary paid to a director who works full-time for the company where the salary would be fully deductible for corporation tax purposes.

(b) Contributions to an approved pension scheme for directors/employees. These are fully deductible.

(c) Payment to a director/employee on termination of employment. Where a payment is made to a director/employee by way of compensation for loss of office or employment, this will qualify as a deductible expense under the normal rules. Where a payment is made in return for a director's/employee's undertaking not to compete with the company's business following termination of their office or employment, such a payment is deductible under specific provisions (Income Tax (Earnings and Pensions) Act 2003 (ITEPA), s 225, and see **26.3**).

(d) Interest payments on borrowings. These will generally be deductible under the loan relationships rules (see **27.2.2**), although there are limits on the amount of interest payments which can be deducted by listed companies.

22.2.1.3 Capital allowances

In calculating its trading profit, a company may also deduct capital allowances claimed on expenditure on machinery and plant and on other qualifying assets. These are available by way of writing down allowances in the way described in **21.4.1**, and the annual investment allowance, and balancing charges or allowances also work similarly. Full expensing and the special first year allowance (see **21.4.1.6**) are only available to companies.

22.2.2 Trading losses brought forward

The company may be able to reduce its trading profit by claiming relief for a loss previously suffered in the trade and 'carried forward' under the CTA 2010, s 45 (see **22.7**).

22.2.3 Other income

Any income from other sources must be added (eg property income or interest received from investments). (For the corporation tax treatment of goodwill and other intellectual property, see **22.8**.)

22.3 STEP 2: CALCULATE CHARGEABLE GAINS

A company's gains chargeable to corporation tax will be calculated using the same broad principles as for capital gains tax, but with important modifications. The stages to calculate the gain within Step 2 are as follows:

Stage 1: Identify a chargeable disposal (see **22.3.1**).

Stage 2: Calculate the gain (or loss) (see **22.3.2**).

Stage 3: Apply reliefs (see **22.3.3**).

Stage 4: Aggregate remaining gains/losses.

Any gain remaining after the application of reliefs forms part of the company's total profits for the purposes of corporation tax (Taxation of Chargeable Gains Act 1992 (TCGA 1992), s 8 and CTA 2010, s 4).

22.3.1 Stage 1: identify a chargeable disposal

22.3.1.1 General principles

A chargeable disposal by a company can arise on a disposal of chargeable assets by way of either sale or gift. Chargeable assets for corporation tax purposes are defined broadly as for capital gains tax and the most common examples in the context of a disposal by a company are likely to include land and buildings and shares held in other companies (although if the disposal proceeds form part of the company's income stream (eg regular sales of land as part of a property developer's trade) they will normally form part of the company's income profits rather than its chargeable gains – see TCGA 1992, s 37). Special rules apply to disposals of goodwill and intellectual property (see **22.8**).

22.3.1.2 Plant and machinery

The position for plant and machinery is complicated by the fact that capital allowances may be available in relation to the expenditure incurred on it. If this is the case, the plant and machinery will not benefit from the usual capital gains exemption for 'wasting assets' (assets with a predicted working life of 50 years or less). In practice, however, plant and machinery is unlikely to increase in value and so a chargeable capital gain will not arise (and any decrease in value will have been deducted from trading profits (income) under the capital allowances regime so no allowable capital loss will arise either). For further details on the interaction of the capital allowances and capital gains legislation, see **21.4.2**.

22.3.2 Stage 2: calculate the gain (or loss)

22.3.2.1 Method of calculation

The procedure to follow in order the calculate the gain (or loss) on a chargeable disposal involves the following calculation.

Proceeds of disposal (or market value in the case of a gift or sale at an undervalue)

LESS

Costs of disposal

= Net proceeds of disposal

LESS

Other allowable expenditure (initial and subsequent expenditure)

= Gain (before indexation) or Loss

LESS

Indexation allowance

= Gain (after indexation)

If a company sells an asset at an undervalue, a decision must be made as to what figure to use for the proceeds of disposal. If the sale is merely a bad bargain, the actual sale price will be used, but if there is a gift element then the market value of the asset will be used. If the company sells to a 'connected person', the sale will be deemed to take place at market value. A company is connected with a person if that person controls the company (either alone or with others connected to that person). A company is connected to another company if they are both controlled by the same person, or by a combination of that person and others connected with that person (TCGA 1992, s 286(5); and see also **28.3.3**).

If the disposal of the asset leads to a loss (ignoring indexation, for which see below), that capital loss can be deducted from the other chargeable gains made by the company in its accounting period, but not from its income profits. Any unused loss can be carried forward to be deducted from the first available chargeable gains made by the company in subsequent accounting period(s) (until the loss is absorbed).

22.3.2.2 The indexation allowance

The indexation allowance is used when calculating the gain on an asset which has been owned for any period between 31 March 1982 and the date of disposal. The purpose of the indexation allowance is to remove inflationary gains from the capital gains calculation so that a smaller gain is charged to tax. Tables published by HMRC express the relevant inflation information as an indexation factor for ease of calculation. The indexation allowance is calculated by multiplying the initial and subsequent expenditure by the indexation factor that covers the period from the date the expenditure was incurred (or 31 March 1982 if later) to the date of disposal of the asset (or 31 December 2017 if earlier). Once the allowance has been calculated, it is deducted from the 'gain (before indexation)' to give the 'gain (after indexation)'.

There are several other features of indexation to note:

(a) The allowance is applied to initial and subsequent expenditure but not to the costs of disposal. If different items of expenditure are incurred at different times, different indexation factors will have to be used for each item of expenditure.

(b) Where a company disposes of an asset which it owned on 31 March 1982, special rules are applied. The aim of these rules is to exclude from the tax calculation the part of the gain that accrued before 31 March 1982, so that no tax is paid on that part of the gain. The indexation allowance for such assets will be based on the market value of the assets on 31 March 1982, rather than actual expenditure.

(c) The indexation allowance can be used to reduce the gain to zero, but cannot be used to create or increase a loss.

(d) If there has been overall deflation between the date of the expenditure and the date of disposal, no indexation allowance is available on that expenditure.

EXAMPLE

Smallco Ltd acquired some premises in June 2012 for £100,000 and sold them in January 2025 for £250,000. The incidental costs of disposal (legal and land agent fees) were £5,000 and the incidental costs of acquisition (legal and surveyor's fees) were £3,000. In August 2014, the company extended the premises at a cost of £30,000. Assume the indexation factor for the period between June 2012 and 31 December 2017 is 0.2 and that for the period between August 2014 and 31 December 2017 it is 0.12.

	£	£
Proceeds of disposal		250,000
Less incidental costs of disposal		5,000
= Net proceeds of disposal		245,000
Less initial expenditure:		
Acquisition cost	100,000	
Incidental costs of acquisition	3,000	103,000
Less subsequent expenditure		30,000
= Gain (before indexation)		112,000
Less indexation allowance:		
On initial expenditure	(103,000 x 0.2)	20,600
On subsequent expenditure	(30,000 x 0.12)	3,600
= Gain (after indexation)		87,800

22.3.3 Stage 3: apply reliefs

The range of reliefs available to companies is smaller than that available to individuals. Examples of some of the reliefs available to a company are described below (other reliefs of less general application are considered in other titles in this series).

22.3.3.1 Roll-over relief on the replacement of qualifying business assets (TCGA 1992, ss 152–159)

This relief is designed to encourage companies to expand and thrive by allowing the corporation tax due on the disposal of a 'qualifying asset' to be effectively postponed when the consideration obtained for the disposal is applied in acquiring another qualifying asset by way of replacement.

(a) Conditions for the relief to apply

(i) Qualifying assets

The principal qualifying assets for the purposes of the relief are land and buildings, although more exotic assets, such as ships, satellites and spacecraft, also qualify. The company must use the asset in its trade (as opposed to holding it as an investment).

(Note:

(a) company shares are *not* qualifying assets;

(b) goodwill and other intellectual property is subject to a separate roll-over relief (see **22.8**);

(c) although *fixed* plant and machinery is a qualifying asset, a sale of such an asset will rarely produce a gain (as most depreciate in value) and any roll-over relief when acquiring such assets will be restricted if they are wasting assets (TCGA 1992, s 154). What constitutes 'fixed' plant and machinery is, in itself, not straightforward. There is no statutory definition, so each case turns on its own facts, but claims are unlikely to succeed if the item in question is moveable and intended to be so to enable changes in the layout of the workplace.)

Provided both the asset disposed of and the asset acquired fall within the definition of qualifying assets, they do not need to be the same type of asset. For example, it is possible to sell a qualifying ship, and roll-over the gain into the purchase of qualifying buildings.

(ii) Time limits

For the relief to apply, the disposal and acquisition must take place within certain time limits. The replacement asset must be acquired within one year before or three years after the disposal of the original asset, unless an extended period is allowed by HMRC.

EXAMPLE

If a company disposes of a qualifying asset at the start of January 2025, a replacement qualifying asset would need to be acquired at some point in the period stretching from the start of January 2024 to the end of December 2027.

(b) Application of the relief

If a qualifying asset is disposed of and, within the time limits, the consideration from the disposal is applied in acquiring another qualifying asset to be used in the company's trade, then any liability to corporation tax arising from the disposal can be postponed (at least until the disposal of the replacement asset) by rolling-over the gain (after allowing for any indexation) on the disposal of the original asset into the acquisition cost of the replacement asset. This means that the gain (after allowing for any indexation) is notionally deducted from the acquisition cost of the replacement asset to give a lower acquisition cost for use in subsequent corporation tax calculations. Thus a later disposal of the replacement asset may produce a gain that comprises both the rolled-over gain and any gain on the replacement asset itself (TCGA 1992, s 153 contains restrictions on the relief if part only of the value of the consideration on the disposal of the original asset is used to acquire the new asset).

EXAMPLE

In September 2025 Mediumco Ltd sells some premises that it has owned since 2006 for £70,000. It makes a gain (after indexation) of £30,000. Six months later, the company buys some more premises for £80,000. If the company claims roll-over relief on the replacement of qualifying assets:

(a) the company will not pay any corporation tax in respect of the gain realised on the disposal of the original premises (as it has been effectively postponed by being rolled-over);

(b) for the purposes of future corporation tax calculations the replacement premises will be treated as being acquired for £50,000 (£80,000 less £30,000).

Imagine that the company then sells the new premises in 2028 for £125,000. The calculation of its gain will be:

	£	
Proceeds of disposal	125,000	
Less		
Adjusted acquisition cost	50,000	(without the effect of roll-over it would be 80,000)
Gain before indexation	75,000	(without the effect of roll-over it would be only 45,000)

Provided the qualifying conditions were met, the gain from the 2028 sale (after indexation) could itself be rolled-over.

(Note: The roll-over relief contained in TCGA 1992, ss 152–159 is also available to individuals in a slightly different form – see **28.4.1**.)

22.3.3.2 Exemption for disposals of substantial shareholdings (TCGA 1992, Sch 7AC)

A company's gains on the disposal of shares it owns in another company are completely exempt from corporation tax if the conditions of the relief are met. In outline, for disposals after 1 April 2017, these are:

(a) the disposing company must have owned at least 10% of the ordinary shares in the other company for a continuous period of at least 12 months beginning not more than six years before the date of disposal;

(b) the company in which the shares are owned has been a trading company throughout the 12-month period of ownership.

The structure of the relief allows the disposing company to dispose of its shareholding in the other company in more than one 'batch', provided the time limits are met.

EXAMPLE

Y Ltd has owned 10% of the ordinary shares in Z Ltd for five years. In January 2025, Y Ltd sells half its shareholding in Z Ltd. The gain on this disposal is exempt. In June 2025, Y Ltd sells the remainder of its shares in Z Ltd. This disposal is also exempt because, although Y Ltd did not own 10% of Z Ltd at the time of the June 2025 disposal, it had owned 10% of the shares for at least 12 months in the six-year period leading up to the June 2025 disposal.

Additional rules apply to disposals involving groups of companies. Although the exemption will benefit companies that make a gain on the disposal of a substantial shareholding, it will be a disadvantage when a loss is made as that loss will not be deductible for capital gains purposes.

22.4 STEP 3: CALCULATE TOTAL PROFITS; APPLY RELIEFS AVAILABLE AGAINST TOTAL PROFITS

A company's income profits and any capital gains will be added together to produce the company's total profits for that period. Certain reliefs are then available at this stage (as opposed to others which must be applied within Step 1 or Step 2 as appropriate). The main examples of reliefs that can be applied against total profits are as follows.

22.4.1 Qualifying donations to charity (CTA 2010, ss 189–217)

Donations to charity meeting the conditions in Part 6 of the CTA 2010 are deductible from total profits.

22.4.2 Certain trading loss reliefs

Relief for a trading loss under CTA 2010, s 37 (carry-across/carry-back relief), s 39 (terminal carry-back relief) and s 45 (carry-forward relief) is given against total profits. See **22.7** for fuller details of these reliefs.

22.5 STEP 4: CALCULATE THE TAX

22.5.1 Basis of assessment (Finance Act 1988, s 117 and Sch 18)

The series of steps described so far will establish the company's taxable profit for the accounting period and the corporation tax will be calculated on that figure by applying the appropriate rate(s). Where the company's accounting period is a period different from the corporation tax financial year (1 April to 31 March (see **22.5.2**)) and the rates of tax have changed from one financial year to the next, it will be necessary to apply the different rates to the appropriate portions of the accounting period. If, for example, a company has an accounting period of 1 January to 31 December, one-quarter of the company's profit for 2025 (representing the first three months) will be taxed at the appropriate rate for Financial Year 2024 (ending 31 March 2025) and the remaining three-quarters of the profit will be taxed at the appropriate rate for Financial Year 2025.

22.5.2 Rates of corporation tax (CTA 2009, Part 2 and CTA 2010, Parts 2 and 3)

Corporation tax rates are fixed by reference to financial years, being the period from 1 April in one year to 31 March in the following year (this is different from the income tax year which runs from 6 April to 5 April in the following year). Financial years are described by reference to the period in which they commence, so the corporation tax year running from 1 April 2025 to 31 March 2026 is 'Financial Year 2025' (this is also different from the description of the income tax year, which is described by reference to the years in which it begins and ends).

For several years, up to and including Financial Year 2022, all companies were taxed at a flat rate of 19%. However, with effect from 1 April 2023, the rate of tax is determined by the level of the company's taxable profits in the accounting year:

- companies with taxable profits of up to £50,000 are subject to the standard small profits rate of 19%;
- companies with taxable profits of more than £250,000 are subject to the main rate of 25% (on the taxable profits in their entirety);
- companies with taxable profits above £50,000 but not exceeding £250,000 are subject to the marginal rate.

(The small profits and marginal rates do not apply to certain types of close companies.)

The marginal rate requires some explanation. Companies are given 'marginal relief' with the aim of smoothing the transition to the main rate. Under the legislation, the relief is achieved by charging the taxable profits at 25%, and then reducing the resulting sum by a fraction (set for each financial year). The result is that the rate is tapered so that a company is charged at an overall effective rate of tax somewhere between 19% and 25%; that effective rate gradually increasing the closer the profits are to the £250,000 threshold. The complexity of the statutory formula is beyond the scope of this book. For mainstream companies in receipt of straightforward trading profits, the amount of tax payable can be conveniently calculated by applying a rate of 19% to the first £50,000 of taxable profits and a rate of 26.5% to the balance (see example below).

As part of the Autumn 2024 Budget, the Government issued its 'roadmap' for corporate taxes in which it confirmed its intention to continue to cap corporation tax at 25% and retain the small profits and marginal rates regime.

22.6 ILLUSTRATION OF CORPORATION TAX CALCULATION

The accountant of D Co Ltd produces the following figures relevant to calculation of the company's income profits for its accounting period ending 31 March 2026:

(a) chargeable receipts are £95,000
(b) £18,000 is deductible in respect of salaries
(c) £10,000 is deductible in respect of capital allowances
(d) income from rents (after deductible expenditure) is £48,000.

In addition, the company has sold some land which was surplus to requirements and has made a chargeable gain of £50,000; it has no plans to buy replacement assets.

The company has paid in total £8,000 in dividends to its shareholders (these are not deductible – see **22.9**) and has made a qualifying donation to charity of £3,000.

The calculation of the company's corporation tax liability may be summarised as follows:

	£	£
Step 1 – Calculate income profits:		
• Trading Income:		
Chargeable receipts	95,000	
less		
Deductible expenditure (salaries)	18,000	
less		
Capital allowances	10,000	
Trading profit		67,000
• Property Income:		48,000
Total income profits		115,000
Step 2 – Calculate chargeable gains		50,000
Step 3 – Calculate total profits; apply reliefs available against total profits		
Income profits	115,000	
Chargeable gains	50,000	
Total profits		165,000
Apply relief against total profits (charity gift)		(3,000)
Taxable profits		162,000

Step 4 – Calculate the tax (on the taxable profits of £162,000)

£50,000 x 19% = £9,500

£112,000 x 26.5% = £29,680

The corporation tax due is £39,180

22.7 RELIEF FOR A TRADING LOSS

The illustration at **22.6** above shows a company that makes a trading profit. The calculation of trading income described at **22.2.1** may produce a trading loss rather than a profit. In that event, the company may be able to claim some tax relief for that loss.

There are various provisions in the CTA 2010 that allow a company in effect to deduct a trading loss from other profits in order to provide relief from corporation tax on those profits. Where the circumstances are such that relief could be claimed under more than one of the provisions described below, the company may choose which to claim. It may be that the company's trading loss for an accounting period is greater than can be relieved under just one of these provisions; if so, the company can claim as much relief as is available under one provision and then claim relief for the balance of its loss under any other available provision (although it cannot claim relief for the same loss twice over). Generally a company will want to claim relief under whichever provision is best for cash flow; two of the provisions described below may lead to a refund of tax previously paid, whilst the third acts to reduce the amount of corporation tax that will become payable in future.

22.7.1 In-year/carry-back relief for trading losses (CTA 2010, ss 37–38)

A company's trading loss for an accounting period can be set against total profits for the same accounting period. If these are insufficient to absorb (or fully absorb) the loss, the loss (or remaining loss) can then be carried back to be set against total profits from the accounting period(s) falling in the 12 months prior to the accounting period of the loss (provided that the company was then carrying on the same trade); in this way, the company may recover corporation tax previously paid.

EXAMPLE

A Co Ltd, a company with an accounting period that ends on 30 June each year, makes a trading loss in the accounting period ending 30 June 2025. The company can set the loss against any other profits it makes in the same accounting period (eg investment income and capital gains on the disposal of some premises). If any loss remains unused, it can be carried back and set against all profits in the accounting period ending 30 June 2024.

22.7.2 Terminal carry-back relief for trading losses (CTA 2010, s 39)

As an extension to the normal carry-back rules, when a company ceases to carry on a trade, a trading loss sustained in the final 12 months of the trade can be carried back and set against the company's total profits from any accounting period(s) falling in the three years previous to the start of that final 12 months, taking later periods first.

EXAMPLE

B Co Ltd, a company with an accounting period that ends on 31 December, makes a trading loss in 2025 and ceases trading on 31 December 2025. It could set the 2025 loss against any profits made in 2025, then (if necessary) 2024, 2023, and finally 2022.

Note:

(a) Where a company's accounting periods do not match exactly with the carry-back period, profits will be apportioned so that profits attributable to any part of an accounting period falling within the carry-back period will be eligible for reduction by available losses.

(b) A claim under s 37 or s 39 must usually be made within two years of the end of the accounting period in which the loss was incurred.

22.7.3 Carry-forward relief for trading losses (CTA 2010, ss 45–45B)

A company's trading loss for an accounting period can be carried forward to be set against subsequent profits. In the past, losses carried forward could only be set against profits of the same trade. However, trading losses arising in accounting periods beginning on or after 1 April 2017 can be set against the company's total profits in the next accounting period provided that certain conditions are met (eg the company continues to trade and is not concerned with certain types of trade such as farming, television and films). Any part of the loss which remains unrelieved can be carried forward again and set against total profits in subsequent years. The amount that can be relieved is restricted. Broadly, losses can only be set against 50% of profits exceeding an annual deductions allowance of £5,000,000.

A claim for losses to be set against total profits in a later period must usually be made within two years of the end of the later period.

If the company does not fulfil any of the conditions to set the loss against total profits, the loss can still be carried forward but it may only be set against profits of the same trade.

EXAMPLE

C Co Ltd, a company with an accounting period that ends on 31 March each year, makes a trading loss in the accounting period that ends 31 March 2023, but returns to profit in the following accounting period. The company can deduct the loss from the total profit made in the accounting period ending 31 March 2023. Any remaining loss can be carried forward to be used against trading profit made in the accounting period ending 31 March 2025, and so on until the loss is fully relieved.

Where trading losses arising on or after 1 April 2017 are carried forward to a period in which the trade ceases and the losses still remain unrelieved, a separate form of terminal loss relief enables the company to set the unrelieved losses against total profits (or trading profits if the company does not satisfy the conditions) in the preceding three years (CTA 2010, s 45F).

22.7.4 Summary

Section of CTA 2010	*When will the loss have occurred?*	*Against what will the loss be set?*	*Which accounting periods are relevant?*
s 37 (in-year/carry-back relief)	Any accounting period of trading	The company's total profits (at Step 3 of the tax calculation)	The accounting period of the loss and, thereafter, the accounting period(s) falling in the previous 12 months
s 39 (terminal carry-back relief)	The final 12 months of trading	The company's total profits (at Step 3 of the tax calculation)	The accounting period(s) of the loss and, thereafter, the accounting period(s) falling in the three years previous to the final 12 months of trading (taking later periods first)
s 45 (carry-forward relief)	Any accounting period of trading	The company's total profits (at Step 3 of the tax calculation). Subsequent profits of the same trade if the conditions are not met (at Step 1 of the tax calculation)	Subsequent accounting periods until the loss is absorbed

22.8 CORPORATION TAX ON GOODWILL AND INTELLECTUAL PROPERTY

The rules relating to the corporation tax treatment of goodwill and intellectual property (such as patents, trade marks, registered design, copyright and design rights) are in the CTA 2009, Part 8. Although such 'intangible fixed assets' are essentially capital in nature, they will generally be taxed as part of a company's income profit/loss calculation. The main features of the approach are as follows.

22.8.1 The general rule

Receipts from transactions in intangible fixed assets will generally be treated as income receipts, and expenditure on intangible fixed assets will generally be deductible in calculating a company's income profits (although not when the expenditure is part of the incorporation of a business).

22.8.2 Disposals of intangible fixed assets

Any profit on the disposal of intangible fixed assets may be rolled-over into the acquisition of replacement intangible fixed assets (provided the qualifying conditions are met) thus deferring any corporation tax charge arising from the disposal. Otherwise profits and losses on disposal will generally be accounted for in the income profit/loss calculation.

The treatment of intellectual property and goodwill for tax purposes will, in general, reflect Financial Reporting Standards and so reference will need to be made to a company's accounts to establish the exact effect of that treatment on a company's profit or loss for the accounting period in question.

22.9 DIVIDENDS

Dividends paid by a company are *not* deductible in calculating the company's taxable profit, but are treated as distributions of profit. Similarly, when a company buys back its own shares from shareholders, the payment is not deductible in calculating the company's taxable profit and that part of the price which is over and above the allotment price may be treated in the same way as a dividend (see **27.3**). Neither of these payments reduces the company's profits chargeable to corporation tax (CTA 2009, s 1305).

22.10 NOTIFICATION TO HMRC AND PAYMENT

22.10.1 Notification

Section 55 of the Finance Act 2004 requires a company to inform HMRC in writing of the beginning of its first accounting period (such notification to be within three months of the start of that period). Thereafter, a notice requiring delivery of a self-assessment corporation tax return will be issued.

22.10.2 Payment

For most companies, the corporation tax due under self-assessment is payable within nine months and one day from the end of the relevant accounting period (TMA 1970, s 59D). The company must make a payment to HMRC within this time limit in relation to its anticipated corporation tax liability for that period, even though the final assessment may not have been agreed with HMRC by that stage (the deadline for the self-assessment return itself is 12 months after the end of the relevant accounting period).

Large companies may, depending on the company's overall corporation tax liability, have to pay the tax in four instalments (TMA 1970, s 59E). A 'large' company for these purposes is one with annual taxable profits of £1,500,000 or over. The instalment due dates are calculated by HMRC as:

First	6 months and 13 days after the start of the accounting period
Second	3 months from the first instalment due date
Third	3 months from the second instalment due date
Fourth	3 months and 14 days after the end of the accounting period

EXAMPLE

Large Co plc has annual taxable profits of £3,000,000 and is required to pay corporation tax by instalments for its accounting period ending 31 December 2025. These instalments will be due on 14 July 2025, 14 October 2025, 14 January 2026 and 14 April 2026.

For accounting periods commencing on or after 1 April 2019, very large companies (ie those with annual taxable profits of over £20,000,000) must pay the tax in four instalments during the accounting period. The first instalment is due two months and 13 days after the start of the accounting period and the remaining instalments at three monthly intervals thereafter (Corporation Tax (Instalment Payments) (Amendment) Regulations 2017 (SI 2017/1072)).

22.11 COMPANIES AND VAT

A company that makes chargeable supplies in excess of £90,000 in any 12-month period will be required to register for value added tax (VAT). Details of the calculation and administration of VAT are contained in ***Legal Foundations***.

22.12 COMPANIES AND INHERITANCE TAX

A company cannot make a chargeable transfer for inheritance tax (IHT) purposes because a chargeable transfer is defined as being a transfer made by an individual. In certain circumstances, however, gifts made by companies do have IHT implications (see **23.2.4** for further details of the provisions applying to 'close companies').

22.13 COMPANY SHARES AND STAMP DUTY

When a person acquires company shares (or anything within the definition of 'stock' or 'marketable security' in the Stamp Act 1891), stamp duty (or stamp duty reserve tax in situations where the agreement to transfer the shares does not involve a transfer document) may be charged on the acquisition of those shares.

22.13.1 Basic rule

The duty is charged at 0.5% of the amount or value of the consideration for the shares (rounded up to the nearest multiple of £5).

EXAMPLE

John buys some shares in a company for £12,240. He must pay stamp duty of:

£12,240 x 0.5% = £61.20, rounded up to £65.

22.13.2 Exemptions and reliefs

There are various exemptions and reliefs from the charge, among the more important of which are set out below.

22.13.2.1 Consideration of £1,000 or less

No duty is charged where the consideration for the shares is £1,000 or less (therefore including gifts) provided the appropriate certificate is completed on the relevant instrument of transfer (usually on the back of the stock transfer form).

22.13.2.2 Transfers on a 'recognised growth market'

Shares traded on a 'recognised growth market' as defined are exempt from the duty. The main example of such a market is the Alternative Investment Market (AIM).

CHAPTER 23

Taxation of Companies II – Special Provisions Relating to Companies

LEARNING OUTCOMES

After reading this chapter you will be able to:

- understand the definition of 'close companies' and how they can affect a person's tax liability
- appreciate the general tax treatment of groups of companies.

23.1 INTRODUCTION

In addition to the general rules governing the taxation of companies, special provisions exist within the tax legislation with the aim of preventing the use of a company as a trading vehicle from being significantly more or less attractive (from a tax perspective) than trading as a sole trader or via a partnership.

The rules discussed in this chapter relate to companies controlled by a small number of persons ('close companies') and to groups of companies.

23.2 'CLOSE COMPANIES'

23.2.1 Definitions (CTA 2010, ss 439–454)

(a) A 'close company' is one which is controlled by five or fewer participators, or by participators (however many) who are directors (or shadow directors) (CTA 2010, s 439).

(b) A 'participator' is essentially a person owning, or having the right to acquire, shares in the company.

(c) Broadly, 'control' exists in the hands of those having, or having the right to acquire, more than half of the shares or more than half of the voting power. The test for 'control' does not depend on whether particular shareholders whose combined shareholdings represent a majority actually act together, but rather on whether, if they were to act together, the company would be under their control. In establishing who has control, any rights of a participator's 'associate' (defined so as to apply principally to a close relative or a business partner) are treated as rights of that participator.

(Note: although a subsidiary company is controlled by one participator (ie by its parent company), the subsidiary will not normally fall within the definition of close company unless the parent company is also a close company – CTA 2010, s 444.)

EXAMPLE 1

AB Company Ltd has nine shareholders. This must be a close company because, whatever the distribution of shareholdings, there must be at most five who, between them, own a majority – even if all nine shareholders have equal shareholdings, five of them must hold a majority compared with the other four.

EXAMPLE 2

CD Company Ltd has 100 shareholders of whom four own between them 51% of the shares. This is a close company.

EXAMPLE 3

EF Company Ltd has 18 shareholders, consisting of nine married couples. This is a close company because a married couple can be identified as a participator and an associate and therefore only counts as one person in assessing control. Effectively, therefore, there are nine participators for gauging control and five of them must hold a majority of the shares (as in Example 1).

EXAMPLE 4

GH Company Ltd has 25 equal shareholders, none of whom are 'associates' of one another. They are all directors. This is a close company under the second part of the s 439 definition because, although control is in the hands of 13 participators (being the bare majority), those participators are all directors.

23.2.2 The charge to tax imposed when a close company makes a loan to a participator

23.2.2.1 The company's position (CTA 2010, s 455)

Subject to exceptions (see **23.2.2.3**), when a close company makes a loan to a participator or to their associate, the company must pay to HMRC a sum equivalent to 33.75% of the loan. For example, it will cost a close company £133,750 to lend £100,000 to a participator or to their associate, because on top of the loan it must pay an additional £33,750 to HMRC.

The sum paid to HMRC is in the nature of a deposit since it will be refunded to the company if, and when, the recipient of the loan (the participator or their associate) repays the loan to the company or if the loan is written off.

23.2.2.2 The borrower's position (ITTOIA 2005, s 416)

From the borrower's point of view, the loan has the advantage that it is a receipt of money which is not taxable in their hands so long as it remains a loan; however, if the debt is written off by the company, it is charged under the income tax Savings and Investment Income provisions (ITTOIA 2005, Part 4, Ch 6) as if the borrower received a dividend (see **27.3.1**).

EXAMPLE

In June 2025 A Ltd, a close company, lends £100,000 to B, a participator (shareholder) in the company. In June 2026 the debt is written off by the company so B does not have to repay it.

(a) At the time of the loan A Ltd must pay £33,750 (33.75% of £100,000) to HMRC. There are no tax consequences for B at this stage.

> (b) When the debt is written off, HMRC will repay the £33,750 to A Ltd. B is treated as receiving a dividend payment of £100,000 which will form part of B's total income for 2026/27.

23.2.2.3 The exceptions (CTA 2010, s 456)

The charge to tax described does not apply:

(a) if the loan is made in the ordinary course of a money-lending business (eg a bank loan to someone who happens to hold shares in the company);

(b) if the loan (together with any outstanding loan to the same person) does not exceed £15,000 and the borrower works full-time for the company and owns no more than 5% of the company's ordinary shares.

23.2.2.4 The reason for the charge

These provisions play an important role in preventing tax avoidance. Without such provisions, a major tax saving could be achieved by the use of close companies, particularly for a participator who is a higher or additional rate income tax payer. Whereas any withdrawal of the company's profits in the form of salary (as employee/director) or dividend (as shareholder) will attract a charge to income tax in the hands of the recipient, money which is borrowed from the company is not income at all and therefore cannot in principle attract income tax.

A clear disadvantage to the borrower is that a loan must normally be repaid, perhaps with interest, but if the company is closely controlled the company may not enforce the obligation to repay for many years, if at all. Therefore, subject to that possible disadvantage, there would be a clear incentive to use the borrowing device to avoid the payment of income tax.

Section 455 of the CTA 2010 helps to close that loophole, although the use of loans may still help defer the payment of tax for the individual borrower which may have a cash flow advantage. A higher or additional rate taxpayer may also benefit by postponing the time when the payment is treated as chargeable in their hands to some future date when they may be a basic rate taxpayer (eg following retirement).

When loans are made to directors, consideration should also be given to the provisions of s 197 of the CA 2006.

23.2.3 Income tax relief on a shareholder's borrowings (Income Tax Act 2007, ss 383, 392–395)

Not all provisions relating to close companies are aimed at preventing tax avoidance. An individual shareholder who takes out a loan in order to purchase shares in a close company or to lend money to it may be able to claim income tax relief on the interest they pay on their borrowings.

23.2.3.1 The relief

Where a taxpayer pays interest on a loan taken for an eligible purpose, that interest qualifies for tax relief. The interest payments are deductible from the taxpayer's 'total income' at Step 2 of the income tax calculation.

23.2.3.2 Conditions

(a) To be eligible, a loan must be for the purchase of ordinary shares in a close company which carries on a trade, or for the borrower to lend money to such a company.

(b) It is a further condition that the borrower must either:
   - (i) control (by personal ownership or through another person) more than 5% of the company's ordinary share capital/assets; or
   - (ii) own ordinary shares in the company (with no 5% threshold) and work for the greater part of their time in the management or conduct of the company.

Any shares acquired as a result of the borrowing are counted in applying either limb of this condition if they are owned at the time the interest (for which relief is claimed) is paid.

The amount deductible from total income is capped at the greater of £50,000 or 25% of the taxpayer's total income in the relevant tax year (see **24.4.6** for further details).

> **EXAMPLE**
>
> Clare borrows £20,000 from Bigbank plc in order to buy 10% of the ordinary shares in E Co Ltd (which is a close company). In the tax year 2025/26 the interest payments that Bigbank plc charges Clare total £1,600. Clare can deduct £1,600 from her total income for 2025/26.

23.2.4 Inheritance tax and close companies (IHTA 1984, s 94)

A company cannot make a chargeable transfer for the purposes of IHT because the definition of a chargeable transfer in s 2 of the IHTA 1984 is limited to a transfer of value made by an individual. In order to prevent a company being used as a vehicle for making transfers which would otherwise escape IHT, special provisions apply to gifts made by close companies. These are complex but, broadly, a gift made by a close company is treated as a set of gifts by the participators in that company. This is achieved by apportioning the gift amongst the participators in accordance with their proportionate shareholdings in the company; each participator is then treated as having made a transfer of value of the appropriate fraction of the company's gift. Unless covered by an exemption and/or relief, this is a lifetime chargeable transfer rather than a potentially exempt transfer so that inheritance tax may become payable immediately. It is the company itself that is primarily liable for any tax arising.

The above provisions do not apply if the company's gift is charged to income tax in the hands of the recipient. The main examples of this would be:

(a) a dividend that is chargeable to income tax as Savings and Investment Income (ITTOIA 2005, Part 4);

(b) a benefit in kind provided for a director or employee that is chargeable to income tax under the ITEPA 2003.

23.3 GROUPS OF COMPANIES

23.3.1 Introduction

A group of companies may be a useful way of organising a business in terms of minimising risk, running a number of different trades, and streamlining the management structure of the business.

As regards taxation, each company in a group is treated as a separate entity for corporation tax purposes. The tax legislation contains provisions, however, with the aim of ensuring that trading via a group of companies is broadly 'tax neutral' – ie it does not lead to any major advantages or disadvantages when compared with trading via a single company.

The detail of the tax provisions relating to groups is beyond the scope of this book, but some of the more important rules relating to corporation tax are outlined below.

23.3.2 Group relief (CTA 2010, Part 5)

Group relief describes the process whereby certain losses and expenses incurred by a company can be transferred (or 'surrendered') to another company within the same qualifying group (to enable that company to use the loss/expense to reduce its own taxable profits). This relief is available only if both companies are within the definition of a group for these purposes (there are additional provisions applying to consortia).

23.3.2.1 Definition of a group for group relief (CTA 2010, ss 150–156)

For two companies to be within the same group, one must be the 75% subsidiary of the other, or both must be 75% subsidiaries of a third company. The test for a 75% subsidiary is complicated by anti-avoidance rules, but at its core is the requirement for the holding company to own (directly or indirectly) 75% or more of the subsidiary's ordinary share capital (widely defined in CTA 2010, s 1119).

EXAMPLE

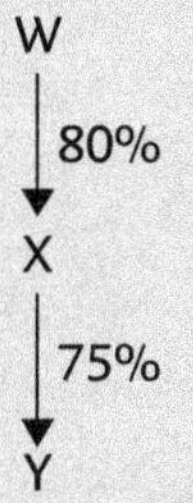

W and X are in a group together, as are X and Y, but W and Y are not part of the same group as W owns only an indirect shareholding of 60% in Y (80% x 75% = 60%).

23.3.2.2 The effect of group relief

If two companies are in the same group for group relief, certain items (most notably trading losses and management expenses) can be surrendered from the 'surrendering company' to the 'claimant company'. This is possible only to the extent that the loss/expense was incurred in the surrendering company's accounting period (or part period) that overlaps with the accounting period of the claimant company that generated the profit for which relief is sought.

EXAMPLE 1

Claimant Co and Surrender Co are in a group together for group relief purposes and both have accounting periods ending 31 March each year. In the year ending 31 March 2026, Surrender Co makes a trading loss of £400,000 and Claimant Co makes taxable profits of £1 million. Surrender Co may surrender its loss to Claimant Co which may use it to reduce its taxable profits to £600,000.

EXAMPLE 2

The facts are the same as in Example 1, except that Surrender Co made its trading loss of £400,000 in the year ending 31 March 2025. This loss can be carried forward to the year ending 31 March 2026 by Surrender Co (using CTA 2010, s 45), but cannot then be surrendered to Claimant Co in that year.

Group relief does not provide relief for capital losses, and there are further restrictions on the application of the relief where either the surrendering company has other profits and/or the claimant company has losses of its own.

23.3.3 A company's chargeable disposals (TCGA 1992, ss 170–181)

It may be possible for companies within a group to arrange for the disposal of a chargeable asset to be made by the company that will benefit most for tax purposes.

23.3.3.1 Definition of a group (TCGA 1992, s 170)

The definition of a group for chargeable gains purposes differs from that for group relief. Here a group will contain a company (a 'principal company'), its direct 75% subsidiaries and the direct 75% subsidiaries of those subsidiaries (and so on), provided that all of the subsidiaries are 'effective 51%' subsidiaries of the principal company (to pass the 'effective 51%' subsidiary test, the principal company must be beneficially entitled to more than 50% of the available profits and assets of the subsidiary as laid out in TCGA 1992, s 170(7)). A chargeable gains group may have only one principal company.

EXAMPLE 1

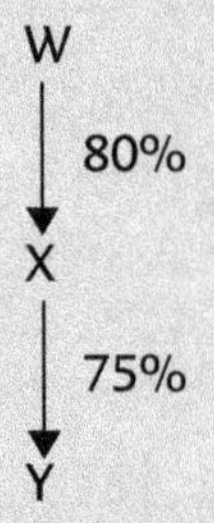

W (the principal company,) X and Y are in a group together for chargeable gains purposes as W owns at least 75% of X and X owns at least 75% of Y, plus W effectively 'owns' 60% of Y (80% x 75%) satisfying the 'effective 51%' test.

EXAMPLE 2

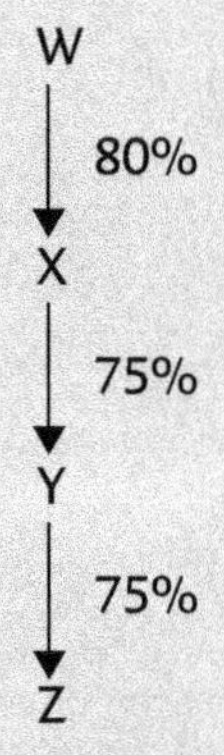

W, X and Y are in a group as before, but Z does not form part of the group as, although it satisfies the first part of the test (as Y's 75% subsidiary) it is not the effective 51% subsidiary of W as W effectively owns only 45% of Z (80% x 75% x 75%).

23.3.3.2 The available relief (TCGA 1992, ss 171–171A)

Where two companies are within a group for chargeable gains purposes, one can transfer a chargeable asset to the other on a tax neutral 'no gain, no loss' basis (so that the disposal is treated as being for such consideration as to give rise to neither a gain nor a loss by the transferor company). This is likely to be useful in two main situations:

EXAMPLE 1

Company A and Company B are in a group together. Company A owns a building with an unrealised gain of £300,000 which it wishes to sell to a third party. Company B has made a capital loss of £200,000 on the sale of some land and is not likely to make any chargeable gains in the near future. Company B may not set the capital loss against its trading profits, neither can it surrender the loss to Company A using group relief. What can happen, however, is that Company A transfers its property to Company B on a 'no gain, no loss' basis and then Company B sells it, realising the £300,000 gain against which it can set the £200,000 loss, so reducing the chargeable gain to £100,000.

> **EXAMPLE 2**
>
> Company C and Company D are in a group together. Company C owns some land with an unrealised loss of £400,000. Company D has just sold some premises, realising a £650,000 gain. If Company C transfers the land to Company D at no gain, no loss and Company D then sells it, Company D will make a £400,000 loss which it can set against its own gain of £650,000, so that its taxable chargeable gains for the year will be only £250,000.

In fact, if both companies elect under the TCGA 1992, s 171A, the same effect as described in the above examples can be achieved without any actual transfer within the group prior to the third party sale (thus saving, for example, the cost of conveyancing formalities). A similar form of relief is available for assets within the intangible assets regime (see **22.8**).

23.3.3.3 Roll-over relief (TCGA 1992, s 175)

When a company within a group for chargeable gains purposes disposes of a chargeable asset outside the group, it can roll-over its gain (if the usual roll-over relief criteria are satisfied – see **22.3.3.1**) into qualifying assets it acquires or, as an alternative, into qualifying assets acquired by another group company.

> **EXAMPLE**
>
> J Co sells a qualifying asset for £2 million in June 2025, realising a gain (after indexation) of £800,000. In October 2027, K Co (in the same group as J Co) acquires a qualifying asset for £3 million from a third party. If J Co's gain has not been relieved in some other way then it may be rolled over into K Co's acquisition so as to enable J Co to claim a reduction in its corporation tax liability.

Both group relief and the chargeable gains provisions are subject to numerous anti-avoidance provisions, which are beyond the scope of this book but which are designed, for example, to prevent the manipulation of the rules when companies join or leave a group.

23.3.4 VAT

A qualifying group of companies may be able to obtain a single registration for VAT purposes.

23.3.5 Stamp duty and stamp duty land tax

Provided certain conditions are met, stamp duty or stamp duty land tax will not be charged on transfers of assets between companies in a qualifying group.

CHAPTER 24

TAXATION OF SOLE TRADERS

LEARNING OUTCOMES

After reading this chapter you will be able to:

- explain how a sole trader's trading profit is taxed to income tax
- explain when payments of income tax are due from a sole trader
- understand when a sole trader can claim relief for a trading loss.

24.1 INTRODUCTION

In the course of running a sole trade, an individual must be aware of the impact of several different taxes.

24.1.1 Income profits and losses – income tax

The trading profits of a sole trader's business (calculated in accordance with the rules for trading income described in **Chapter 21**) form part of the sole trader's total income chargeable to income tax. (Other income related to the business, such as rents and loan interest will also form part of the individual's total income.) If the business makes a trading loss in an accounting period this may, in certain circumstances, be offset against the sole trader's other income and (more rarely) capital gains.

24.1.2 Capital profits and losses – capital gains tax

On the disposal of a chargeable asset used in their trade, a sole trader may realise a capital gain or loss. The treatment of capital gains realised by individuals is considered further in **Chapter 28**.

24.1.3 Gifts – inheritance tax

If a sole trader transfers a business asset (usually by gift) that results in a transfer of value for IHT purposes, an inheritance tax charge may arise. Details of this charge and available reliefs are described in **Chapter 28**.

24.1.4 VAT

A sole trader who makes chargeable supplies in excess of £90,000 in any 12-month period will be required to register for VAT. Details of the calculation and administration of VAT are contained in ***Legal Foundations***.

24.1.5 National Insurance contributions

As a self-employed person, a sole trader will pay Class 2 and Class 4 National Insurance contributions (although Class 2 contributions are no longer compulsory). If the sole trader employs any staff, they will pay Class 1 contributions in respect of their earnings (see **26.7**).

The remainder of this chapter concentrates on the treatment of the trading profit (or loss) of a sole trader's business.

Income tax, capital gains tax, inheritance tax (and, in due course, National Insurance contributions) are among the taxes subject to the 'general anti-abuse rule' ('GAAR'). The GAAR is an addition to the many existing specific anti-avoidance rules and is designed to allow HMRC to counteract 'abusive' tax avoidance schemes intended to exploit loopholes in the legislation governing the rules for calculating these taxes.

24.2 BASIS OF ASSESSMENT OF A TRADING PROFIT

Trading income is one of the components that comprise a person's total income at Step 1 of the income tax calculation (set out in the Income Tax Act (ITA) 2007, s 23). The detail of the steps is described in ***Legal Foundations***, but in outline they are:

Step 1: calculate 'total income'

Step 2: deduct allowable reliefs (to leave 'net income')

Step 3: deduct any personal allowance

Step 4: calculate tax at the applicable rate(s)

Step 5: add together the amounts of tax from Step 4 (to give the overall income tax liability)

(Steps 6 and 7 concern adjustments to the overall liability in defined circumstances and are beyond the scope of this book: see ITA 2007, ss 26 and 30 for further details.)

There is a trading allowance for income tax available to sole traders. In essence, the effect is that where gross trading income is less than £1,000, the allowance will reduce the amount of taxable income to nil. If the gross trading income exceeds £1,000, the sole trader can choose to claim the allowance as a deduction from chargeable receipts as an alternative to deducting expenditure. As the trading allowance will only be applicable to those receiving small amounts of trading income, it will not be considered further in this book.

As described in **Chapter 21**, taxable (trading) profits are calculated with reference to an accounting period (usually 12 months). This accounting period may not coincide with the tax year for income tax (running from 6 April to the following 5 April) in which case it will be necessary to apportion profits and losses between the different tax years. This will usually be done on the basis of the number of days of the accounting period falling in each tax year. However, another method of apportionment can be used if it is reasonable to do so (for example, where a business is highly seasonal, it may be reasonable to apportion the profits in order to spread them more evenly over the accounting period).

24.3 DATE FOR PAYMENT (TMA 1970, ss 59A and 59B)

A sole trader must register with HMRC within three months of starting the business (even if they already complete a self-assessment tax return).

Income tax assessed on a trading profit forms part of the income tax liability that is payable by two equal instalments, of which the first is due on 31 January in the tax year in question and the second is due on 31 July following the end of that tax year. Since the trader's taxable profit will not be known by the first of those dates, generally they will make their two payments based on the previous year's tax liability. On or before the 31 January following the end of the tax year, the taxpayer will make a tax return on which their actual liability to income tax will be self-assessed and an adjustment (by further payment or by repayment of tax) will be made. (Delaying submission of the tax return until the deadline of 31 January is not possible for taxpayers submitting paper returns. Here, an earlier deadline of the 31 October following the end of the tax year applies.)

No payments on account are required if the amount of tax due under these rules is less than £1,000 (or if more than 80% of the total tax bill has already been collected by deduction at source/ dividend tax credits).

> **EXAMPLE**
>
> A trader is taxed on profits in the tax year 2025/26. If their total tax due is £12,000 (estimated based on their tax liability on 2024/25 profits and assuming no deduction of tax at source), the first instalment of £6,000 will be due on 31 January 2026, the second (also of £6,000) will be due on 31 July 2026, with a balancing payment or rebate due on 31 January 2027 once the return for 2025/26 has been processed under the self-assessment system.

The current tax return system is being replaced by online digital tax accounts. The transition to digital accounts has been delayed several times and is now not expected to become compulsory until 2026 and, even then, only for sole traders with an annual gross income over £50,000.

24.4 RELIEF FOR A TRADING LOSS

The trading income calculations described in **Chapter 21** may produce a trading loss for which relief may be available.

There are various provisions in Part 4 of the ITA 2007 which allow the taxpayer, in effect, to deduct a trading loss from other income in order to provide relief from tax on that other income. Where the circumstances are such that relief could be claimed under more than one of the following provisions, the taxpayer may choose under which to claim. It may be that the taxpayer's loss is greater than can be relieved under just one of these provisions; if so, the taxpayer can claim as much relief as is available under one provision and then claim relief for the balance of their loss under any other available provision (although they cannot claim relief for the same loss twice over). Generally, the taxpayer will want to claim relief under whichever provision is best for cash-flow; some allow a repayment of tax previously paid, while others act to reduce the amount of tax that will become due in the future.

These losses are allowed for at Step 2 of the income tax calculation, and in some cases the loss is set against 'total income', whereas in others it is only set against a particular component of income.

Some of the reliefs are also subject to a cap on the amount of relief that can be claimed in any one tax year. The detail of that cap is set out at **24.4.6.**

24.4.1 Start-up loss relief (ITA 2007, ss 72–81)

Start-up loss relief (also known by HMRC as 'Early Trade Losses Relief') applies if the taxpayer suffers a loss which is assessed in any of the first four tax years of a new business. In that case, the loss can be carried back and set against the taxpayer's 'total income' in the three tax years prior to the tax year of the loss. This provision might be particularly useful to a person who starts a new business having previously had a steady income from a former business or employment. While the new business becomes established, it may make losses but the trader may be cushioned by claiming back from HMRC some income tax which they have paid in their previous business or employment in the earlier years. This would be especially beneficial if some or all of the income tax which the trader paid and is now able to claim back was at the higher or additional rate.

If the taxpayer elects to use this provision, the loss in question must be set against earlier years before later years – the taxpayer cannot pick and choose which year's income is reduced first.

A claim for relief must usually be made on or before the first anniversary of the 31 January following the tax year in which the loss is assessed (eg by 31 January 2028 for a loss assessed in 2025/26).

This relief is subject to the cap described at **24.4.6**.

EXAMPLE

Bruno commences a new business. In the first few months of trading, he incurs a lot of expense in setting up the business but has few customers. As a result, he makes a trading loss in the first tax year of assessment (2025/26) of £35,000.

Before starting his own business, Bruno had been an employee of a large company, and had the following income:

Tax year	2022/23	£30,000
	2023/24	£35,000
	2024/25	£48,000

If Bruno claims relief under s 72, his £35,000 trading loss will be relieved as follows:

£30,000 will be set against his income for 2022/23, reducing the revised income for 2022/23 to nil (so Bruno will get a tax rebate for that tax year).

The remaining £5,000 will be set against his income for 2023/24, reducing the revised income for 2023/24 to £30,000 (so Bruno will get a partial tax rebate for that tax year).

Note:

(a) The relief is given against total income at Step 2, ie before deduction of the personal allowance (at Step 3). For 2022/23, Bruno has, therefore, effectively wasted his personal allowance.

(b) The rule that a loss must be set against income from earlier years before later years means that Bruno has had his income reduced for years when he was a basic rate taxpayer, not when he became a higher rate taxpayer.

24.4.2 In-year/one year back relief for trading losses generally (ITA 2007, ss 64–71)

This relief (also known by HMRC as 'Trade Loss Relief against general income') comprises two aspects, the most important of which is the set off against the taxpayer's total income.

24.4.2.1 Set off against total income (ITA 2007, s 64)

A trading loss can be set against:

(a) the taxpayer's 'total income' in the tax year of the loss (defined as 'the loss-making year'); or

(b) the taxpayer's total income in the preceding tax year.

If the loss is big enough to reduce total income to nil using method (a) or (b), the taxpayer has the option to set the loss against:

(c) the taxpayer's total income in the loss-making year with the balance of any unused loss set against total income in the preceding tax year; or

(d) the taxpayer's total income in the preceding tax year, with the balance of any unused loss set against total income in the loss-making year.

As with start-up relief, if the taxpayer claims this relief, the loss must be set against total income which may result in them having no income left against which to set his personal allowance; this would mean that the personal allowance for that year is wasted since there is no provision for personal allowances to be carried forward to another year.

This relief is subject to the cap described at **24.4.6**.

In the example at **24.4.1**, Bruno may have preferred to claim relief for his trading loss under s 64 rather than s 72. This would have enabled him to set his loss of £35,000 against his total income of £48,000 in 2024/25 when he was a higher rate taxpayer.

24.4.2.2 Set off against capital gains (ITA 2007, s 71 and TCGA 1992, ss 261B and 261C)

If a claim is made under s 64 and the taxpayer's total income for the tax year in which the trading loss is used is effectively reduced to nil and some of the loss has still to be used then, if the taxpayer does not opt to relieve the excess loss in some other way (eg by using s 72 or s 83), it can be set against the taxpayer's chargeable gains (if any) for that tax year.

This is the only loss relief considered in this chapter which allows relief, in certain circumstances, against a taxpayer's chargeable capital gains as well as against income.

24.4.2.3 Claiming the relief

A claim for relief pursuant to s 64 must usually be made on or before the first anniversary of the 31 January following the tax year in which the loss is assessed (eg by 31 January 2027 for a loss assessed in 2025/26).

24.4.3 Carry-forward relief (ITA 2007, ss 83–85)

If a taxpayer suffers a trading loss in any year of a trade, the loss can be carried forward to be set against subsequent profits which the trade produces, taking earlier years first. This has two disadvantages for the taxpayer when compared with relief under s 64 (see **24.4.2**). First, the taxpayer must wait until future profits of the trade become taxable before they benefit from their loss relief. Secondly, s 83 is more restrictive than s 64 in that it only provides for the loss to be set against profits which the trade produces – it does not provide for relief against other sources of income or against capital gains.

However, the losses carried forward under s 83 can be carried forward indefinitely until a suitable profit from the trade arises to be relieved (although a claim confirming the intention to do this must be made no more than four years after the end of the tax year to which the loss relief claim relates). There is no cap on the amount of relief that can be claimed under this provision.

EXAMPLE

In 2023/24 Carl's business makes a trading loss of £40,000. In 2024/25 he makes a trading profit of £35,000 and in 2025/26 he makes a trading profit of £20,000. He has no other income. If Carl makes a claim under s 83, his income tax assessments will be based on:

Tax year	*Profit/(loss) £*
2023/24	(40,000)
2024/25	Nil – the £35,000 profit is fully covered by carried forward loss
2025/26	£15,000 – the £20,000 profit is reduced by remaining £5,000 loss.

24.4.4 Carry-back of terminal trading loss (ITA 2007, ss 89–94)

If a taxpayer suffers a trading loss in the final 12 months in which they carry on the trade, this loss can be carried across against trading profits made in the final tax year and then carried back to be set against their trading profit in the three tax years prior to their final tax year, taking later years before earlier years. The taxpayer may thus reclaim from HMRC tax which they have paid in earlier years. Note that s 89 does not allow relief against non-trading income or against capital gains. If any loss remains unrelieved, the other reliefs described in **24.4** are available if relevant in light of the taxpayer's situation.

A claim for relief must be made no more than four years after the end of the tax year to which the loss relief claim relates. There is no cap on the amount of relief that can be claimed under this provision.

> **EXAMPLE**
>
> After making a profit in its early years, Dee's organic aromatherapy business closes on 5 April 2026 making a loss in the final accounting period of £20,000. There is no profit in 2025/26 against which to set the loss, but it could be deducted from Dee's trading profit in the tax year 2024/25 with any remaining loss carried further back against trading profits assessed in 2023/24 and, finally, 2022/23.

24.4.5 Carry-forward relief on incorporation of business (ITA 2007, s 86)

If the taxpayer has suffered trading losses which have not been relieved and transfers the business to a company wholly or mainly in return for the issue to themselves of shares in the company, the losses can (unless otherwise relieved (eg by s 64 or s 89)) be carried forward and set against income which the taxpayer receives from the company, such as a salary as a director or dividends as a shareholder. In order to be 'wholly or mainly in return for the issue of shares', at least 80% of the consideration for the transfer must consist of shares in the company. Where the taxpayer receives more than one form of income from the company, the loss can be set off in the order most beneficial to the taxpayer. The loss can be carried forward indefinitely until fully used against income from the company (but a claim confirming the intention to do this must be made no more than four years after the end of the tax year to which the loss relief claim relates). There is no cap on the amount of relief that can be claimed under this provision.

> **EXAMPLE**
>
> On 30 November 2025, Ella transfers her business to a company wholly in return for shares in the company. Her trading loss from the business at that stage is £10,000. In the remainder of the 2025/26 tax year she receives a small salary from the company of £6,000. In the following tax year, 2026/27, she receives a salary from the company of £15,000 and her shareholding in the company produces dividends of £2,000. She has no other income. If Ella uses relief under s 86:
>
> (a) her income from the salary of £6,000 in 2025/26 is reduced to nil by the losses carried forward; and
>
> (b) the remaining loss of £4,000 can be set against her income of £17,000 in 2026/27 (reducing the salary by £4,000).

24.4.6 Restrictions on the use of certain loss reliefs

The Finance Act 2013 introduced restrictions on the amount of relief that can be claimed in any one tax year under some of the loss reliefs (and other reliefs mentioned below). The cap on relief is set at the greater of:

- £50,000; or
- 25% of the taxpayer's total income,

in the tax year where the relief is claimed. The cap only relates to income from sources other than the trade which produced the loss and so its impact in practice may be limited.

The reliefs covered in this book that are affected by the cap are:

- start-up relief (see **24.4.1**);
- carry-across/carry-back relief (see **24.4.2**);
- interest relief for loans to close companies (see **23.2.3**);

- interest relief for partnership investment (see **25.2.4**).

> **EXAMPLE**
>
> Frank makes a trading loss in 2026/27 of £200,000. In 2025/26 his profits from that trade were £70,000. He also has rental income in each tax year of £120,000.
>
> Frank's relief against the rental income is capped at £50,000 for both 2025/26 and 2026/27.
>
> Frank can therefore make a claim to carry across £50,000 of his trading loss to set against his 2026/27 rental income. He can then carry back £50,000 of his trading loss to set against his rental income in 2025/26. However, he can also carry back £70,000 of his trading loss to set against his 2025/26 profits from the same trade because that is not subject to the cap.
>
> At this stage, Frank has claimed relief for £170,000 of his original trading loss and he has exhausted the relief available to him under the carry-across/carry-back provisions. He still has £30,000 of his trading loss to use and he will be allowed to do that under one of the reliefs that is not subject to the cap, such as carry-forward relief.

In addition to the cap described above, a large number of specific anti-avoidance measures exist to prevent the manufacture of artificial losses, and HMRC will also be able to target such schemes using the GAAR.

24.4.7 Summary of reliefs for a trading loss

Section of ITA 2007	*When will the loss have occurred?*	*Against what will the loss be set?*	*Which periods are relevant?*
s 72 (start-up relief by carry-back)	The first four tax years of trading	Total income*	The three tax years preceding the tax year of the loss
s 64 (in-year/carry-back one year relief)	Any accounting year of trading	Total income* and (thereafter) chargeable gains	The tax year in which the accounting year of the loss ends and/or the preceding tax year
s 83 (carry-forward relief)	Any accounting year of trading	Subsequent profits of the same trade	Any subsequent tax year until the loss is absorbed
s 89 (terminal relief by carry-back)	The final 12 months of trading	Previous profits of the same trade	The final tax year and then the three tax years preceding the final tax year
s 86 (carry-forward relief on incorporation)	Up to incorporation	Subsequent income received from the company	Any subsequent tax year until the loss has been absorbed

* Subject to the cap described at **24.4.6**.

CHAPTER 25

TAXATION OF PARTNERSHIPS

LEARNING OUTCOMES

After reading this chapter you will be able to:

- explain how individual partners in a partnership are assessed to income tax, capital gains tax and inheritance tax
- explain how a corporate partner in a partnership is assessed to corporation tax
- appreciate the tax treatment of LLPs.

25.1 INTRODUCTION

For most tax purposes, a partnership falling within the definition contained in PA 1890 (see **Chapter 13**) is treated as 'transparent' so that any tax liability arising from the partnership's business is assessed not against the partnership as a whole, but against each of the members of the partnership. This chapter describes how each partner's share of income and capital profits is calculated and the subsequent tax liability that arises from that calculation. The rules governing the calculation differ depending on whether the partnership comprises only individuals or whether one or more of the partners is a company. The chapter concludes with a brief analysis of how a limited liability partnership (LLP) is taxed.

25.1.1 Partnerships comprising only individuals

An individual partner must consider their liability for income tax on trading profits and other income from the partnership, for capital gains tax on capital profits, and inheritance tax on transfers of value made by the partnership as a whole or by the individual partner.

25.1.2 Partnerships where one or more partner is a company

If a company is a partner additional provisions must be considered, given that a company pays corporation tax rather than income tax, capital gains tax or inheritance tax.

25.2 PARTNERSHIPS COMPRISING ONLY INDIVIDUALS – INCOME TAX

25.2.1 General principles

The principles described in **Chapter 24** for the income tax treatment of a sole trader apply, with modifications, to this type of partnership. These principles are:

(a) calculation of trading profits (see **Chapter 21**);

(b) the basis of assessing the taxable profit of a given tax year for each partner;

(c) income tax relief for trading losses.

25.2.2 Application of general principles to partnerships (ITTOIA 2005, Part 9)

As mentioned above, a partnership is not treated as an entity distinct from the partners themselves and so there is no assessment to income tax on the firm as a whole.

The assessment of income tax in the context of a partnership will therefore entail the following steps:

(a) The trading profit of the business will be calculated in the same way as if the business were run by a sole trader, applying the rules for trading income:

chargeable receipts
LESS
any deductible expenditure
LESS
any capital allowances
EQUALS
trading profit (or trading loss).

(b) The trading profit will be allocated between the partners according to the way in which income profits were shared under their agreement for that accounting period (eg 'salaries', interest on capital and then profit shares).

(c) Each partner's income from the partnership will then be included in their tax return and will be assessed in the ordinary way, taking account of whatever reliefs and allowances they are entitled to receive. Each partner is only liable to HMRC for income tax on their share of the profits – they cannot be required to pay income tax on the profits which are allocated to their partners.

EXAMPLE

W, X, Y and Z started a business on 6 April 2018. They share income profits as follows.

(a) W, X and Y each receive 'salaries' of £10,000 per annum to reflect the fact that they work full-time whereas Z only works part-time.

(b) All partners receive interest on capital at 10% per annum; their capital contributions were as follows:

W: £20,000
X: £20,000
Y: £10,000
Z: £50,000

(c) Profits remaining after 'salaries' and interest on capital are shared equally between the partners.

In 2025/26 the firm makes a taxable profit before allocation between the partners of £100,000. The partners' entitlement is:

	W	X	Y	Z	Totals
'Salary'	10,000	10,000	10,000	—	30,000
Interest	2,000	2,000	1,000	5,000	10,000
Profit	15,000	15,000	15,000	15,000	60,000
	£27,000	£27,000	£26,000	£20,000	£100,000

The figure produced at the foot of each partner's column (eg £27,000 for W) is the figure for inclusion in that individual's total income for the tax year 2025/26.

In the event of the business making a trading loss, that loss will be allocated between the partners for income tax purposes in accordance with the agreement for that accounting period and the partners then choose individually how they will claim the benefit of income tax relief for their share of the loss. See **24.4** for the possible alternatives for claiming relief for a trading loss and the restrictions that apply to using them.

25.2.3 Income tax relief on a partner's borrowings (ITA 2007, ss 383 and 398)

An individual who borrows money (eg from a bank) in order to buy a share in a partnership or to lend money to a partnership can deduct the interest they pay each year (on the money they have borrowed) from their total income. The relief is designed to encourage investment in business and a similar provision exists for investment in certain companies (see **23.2.3**).

This relief is subject to the cap described at **24.4.6**.

> **EXAMPLE**
>
> Brian borrows £20,000 from Bigbank plc in order to invest in a partnership. In the tax year 2025/26, the interest payments that Bigbank plc charges Brian total £1,600. Brian can deduct £1,600 from his total income for 2025/26.

25.3 PARTNERSHIPS COMPRISING ONLY INDIVIDUALS – CAPITAL GAINS TAX

25.3.1 General principles

Normal capital gains tax (CGT) principles apply to partnerships. Thus CGT may arise where there is a disposal of a chargeable asset resulting in a chargeable gain.

A partnership as a whole is unlikely to make gifts of the partnership assets and so the likely 'disposal' which is relevant is their sale. Bearing in mind that certain assets are not chargeable assets for CGT purposes, the partnership assets which are most likely to be subject to CGT are land and premises, goodwill and certain investments.

An individual partner may dispose (independently of the other partners) of their interest in an asset, or their interest in the partnership (see **Chapter 28**).

25.3.2 Disposal by the firm

Where the firm disposes of a chargeable asset, this is treated for capital gains tax purposes as being separate disposals by the partners of their individual interests in that asset. These interests are established by applying the terms of the partnership agreement relating to the sharing of capital profits (see **14.7**). The partners may have expressly agreed on the proportions (eg to share the capital profits in the same proportion as their capital contributions). If there is no express or implied agreement between the partners, capital profits are shared equally (PA 1890, s 24(1)).

> **EXAMPLE 1**
>
> If a firm consists of three partners who have equal shares in capital profits, then each partner is treated as owning one-third of each asset.

> **EXAMPLE 2**
>
> If the firm consists of three partners (A, B and C) who share capital profits in the ratio of A:2, B:1 and C:1, then A owns half of each asset, B one-quarter and C one-quarter.

25.3.3 Calculation of gain

When calculating the gain made by each partner arising from the firm's disposal of an asset, it is necessary to apportion the disposal proceeds and allowable expenditure (most importantly the acquisition cost) among the partners according to their fractional interest in the asset.

> **EXAMPLE**
>
> D, E, F and G have been partners for many years and share all profits equally. In 2006 they purchased shop premises, paying £120,000 as the purchase price. In July 2025, they sell the shop premises for £280,000. Each of the partners is taken to have disposed of one-quarter of the chargeable asset (the shop) at one-quarter of the sale price (ie £70,000). To each of them, there will be allocated one-quarter of the acquisition cost (£30,000) and of any other allowable expenditure.

25.3.4 Business reliefs

Once each partner has established whether the disposal of a partnership asset will give rise to a chargeable gain in their hands, they should consider whether that gain can be reduced, or the payment of tax on it postponed, by the use of one or more of the CGT reliefs currently available. In the context of the disposal of a business asset, the most common reliefs are:

(a) roll-over relief on the replacement of qualifying business assets;

(b) hold-over relief on gifts (and the gift element of sales at an undervalue) of business assets;

(c) roll-over relief on the incorporation of a business;

(d) business asset disposal relief.

The availability of each of the above reliefs (described in detail in **Chapter 28**) depends on the circumstances surrounding the disposal of the asset and the disponer's own circumstances. It may be, therefore, that one or more of the partners can claim relief(s) that are not available to other partners. If different reliefs are available to different partners, each individual may choose which relief (if any) they claim; there is no need for all the partners to treat their respective share of the gain on the disposal of a partnership asset in the same way.

> **EXAMPLE**
>
> If D disposes of his share in the shop premises for £70,000, having acquired his share for £30,000 (see previous example), his CGT calculation would be as follows:
>
> In order to show the calculation of D's gain (by way of illustration), the following assumptions will be made:
>
> (a) there was no allowable expenditure other than the purchase price;
>
> (b) no relief is available and D is a higher rate taxpayer for income tax.
>
> | | £ |
> |---|---|
> | Proceeds of disposal | 70,000 |
> | LESS | |
> | Acquisition cost | 30,000 |
> | Gain | 40,000 |
>
> D's gain will be aggregated with any other gains and losses he has made in the tax year 2025/26 and, following deduction of the annual exemption of £3,000, those gains will be taxed at 24%.

25.3.5 Payment of tax

Once each partner's chargeable gain and any resultant tax liability have been calculated, the tax is payable by that partner individually; as with income tax on the firm's income profits, CGT can only be assessed on each partner for their own share of the firm's gain.

25.3.6 Capital gains tax on disposals by partners individually

A partner may dispose of their fractional share in each of the partnership assets when the firm is not making a disposal.

25.3.6.1 Retirement

On retirement a partner may sell to their fellow partners (ie they are 'buying the retiring partner out') or the retiring partner may sell (or give away) their share to a third party. In these instances, the principles described in **25.3.2** and **25.3.3** will govern the identification of the retiring partner's fractional share, and the calculation of their gain. The reliefs listed in **25.3.4** may be available and any tax due as a result of the disposal will be payable in accordance with **25.3.5**.

25.3.6.2 A partner joins

When a new partner joins an existing partnership, they will usually buy into the partnership and so become entitled to a share in each of the partnership assets (at the value at the date of joining). The other partners are, therefore, each disposing of part of their existing share of the assets, leading to a possible CGT charge.

> **EXAMPLE**
>
> H and K own partnership assets equally. J joins the partnership in June 2025 and pays to acquire a one-third share in the partnership assets at their June 2025 values. As a result of this, H and K each make a disposal of one-sixth of the overall value of each asset so that H, K and J each end up owning two-sixths (ie one-third) of each asset. H and K have both made disposals on which the gain will need to be calculated (in the way described in **25.3.2** and **25.3.3**) even though the assets have not left the partnership as a whole.

(Note: the above example assumes that there has been a revaluation of the partnership assets when a new partner joins. For other possible accounting treatments in such a situation, and their possible tax consequences, see HMRC SPD/12.)

25.4 PARTNERSHIPS COMPRISING ONLY INDIVIDUALS – INHERITANCE TAX

As noted in **25.3.1**, it is unlikely that the partnership as a whole will make gifts of assets. If an individual partner disposes of their share of the partnership asset(s) at less than full value, IHT should be considered and the general inheritance tax rules apply to any transfer of value that a partner makes (eg on a gift of their share to a relative). Exemptions and reliefs which may be available are described in **Chapter 28**.

25.5 PARTNERSHIPS WHERE ONE OR MORE OF THE PARTNERS IS A COMPANY

Most partnerships are formed between individuals, but it is possible for a partnership's members to be companies or a mixture of companies and individuals. Special rules are needed for partnerships where one or more of the partners is a company, given that the income and capital profits of companies are assessed to corporation tax whereas, in the case of individuals, income tax and CGT are the relevant taxes. The detail of these special rules is beyond the scope of this book, but their general effect is described below.

25.5.1 Trading profits (CTA 2009, Part 17)

The trading profit (or loss) of a partnership for its accounting period will be split between the partners according to how the partners have agreed to share such profits (or losses).

The share of the partnership profit attributed to a partner who is an individual is taxed as part of their total income for the relevant tax year.

The position is more complex for a company. The share of the partnership profit attributed to a partner that is a company is taxed according to the company's own accounting period. This is relatively straightforward when the partnership's accounting period and that of the company synchronise (eg both have yearly accounting periods ending on 31 March). If, however, the accounting periods do not match (eg the partnership's accounting period ends on 31 December, and the company's accounting period ends on 30 June), then the company's share of the profit from the partnership must be apportioned between the company's two accounting periods that overlap with the partnership's accounting period.

EXAMPLE

X Ltd has an accounting period that ends on 30 June each year. It is a partner in a partnership with an accounting period that ends on 31 December each year. For the partnership accounting period ending 31 December 2025, X Ltd's share of the trading profit is £150,000. Half of that profit will be assessed in X Ltd's accounting period ending 30 June 2025, and the other half in the company's accounting period ending 30 June 2026.

25.5.2 Capital profits (TCGA 1992, s 59)

Where the partnership disposes of a chargeable asset, this is treated as being separate disposals by the partners of their interests in that asset (applying the terms of the partnership agreement as described in **25.3.2**).

The gain or loss arising from the disposal and attributable to a partner who is an individual is assessed in the tax year in which the disposal took place (using the rules for capital gains tax described in **25.3.3**).

The gain or loss arising from the disposal and attributable to a partner that is a company is assessed in the company's accounting period in which the disposal took place (using the rules and applying the reliefs for corporation tax described in **22.3**).

25.6 LIMITED LIABILITY PARTNERSHIPS

As described in **Chapter 18**, the Limited Liability Partnerships Act 2000 (LLPA 2000) was introduced to provide an element of protection from unlimited liability for the members of a partnership formed as an LLP, whilst allowing the LLP to be taxed in the same way as a partnership governed by the Partnership Act 1890 (despite the fact that an LLP is a body corporate). Accordingly, where an LLP is used to carry on a trade or a profession (but not if it is used to make investments), it will be treated for most UK tax purposes in the same way as an ordinary partnership. Particular points to note are mentioned below.

25.6.1 Trading profits

Trading profits will be calculated in the same way as for an ordinary partnership. If an ordinary partnership converts to an LLP, this will not trigger a balancing charge or allowance for the purposes of the capital allowances regime, and the partners will not be treated as ceasing one trade and starting another. An individual partner who borrows money to invest in an LLP or lend money to it will be able to claim interest relief on the loan in the same way as a partner in an ordinary partnership. There is, however, a difference in the availability of relief for a trading loss, with available loss relief being restricted in the case of a partner in an LLP in certain conditions (the detail of these provisions is beyond the scope of this book).

The Finance Act 2014 introduced measures to restrict the circumstances in which members of an LLP can benefit from the rules applicable to ordinary partnerships. If any member(s) of the LLP fall within the test for 'salaried member', such member(s) will be treated as employees of the LLP for income tax and national insurance purposes. The main consequences of this would be increased national insurance payments and the cash-flow disadvantage of having to account for income tax under the PAYE system rather than via partnership self-assessment rules.

25.6.2 Capital profits

Whilst the LLP is trading, capital gains will be assessed in the same way as for an ordinary partnership. If an ordinary partnership converts to an LLP, this will not trigger a disposal for capital gains purposes. A major change occurs, however, when an LLP ceases to trade and in certain situations it may stop being treated in the same way as an ordinary partnership and instead be treated as a body corporate. In advising on such cases, careful reference will need to be made to the provisions of s 59A of the TCGA 1992.

25.6.3 Inheritance tax

The usual inheritance tax rules apply to individual partners who make transfers of value. When an ordinary partnership converts to an LLP, this does not interrupt a partner's period of ownership for the purposes of claiming agricultural and/or business property relief.

25.7 VAT AND PARTNERSHIPS

A detailed discussion of VAT is beyond the scope of this book, but it should be noted that, unlike the position for the assessment and payment of income tax, capital gains tax, inheritance tax and corporation tax, VAT registration for a partnership can be in the name of the firm itself.

25.8 NATIONAL INSURANCE

Partners (other than 'sleeping' partners) will make National Insurance contributions on income earned as self-employed individuals. If the partnership employs staff, Class 1 contributions will be made in respect of those staff (see **26.7**).

CHAPTER 26

TAXATION OF EMPLOYEES AND DIRECTORS

LEARNING OUTCOMES

After reading this chapter you will be able to:

- explain how employees and directors are assessed to income tax
- appreciate the rules for payment of national insurance contributions from employers and employees.

26.1 INTRODUCTION

Income tax produces more revenue for HM Treasury than any other single tax, and the majority of that tax is collected from employees. Staff salaries will usually constitute one of the major expenses of any business and a substantial proportion (sometimes the whole) of the business's trading receipts may be absorbed by paying salaries or fees and other benefits to its employees (and, in the case of a company, also to its directors). As such payments are deductible expenditure in calculating trading profits, this means that a substantial proportion of the business's trading receipts may ultimately attract income tax as the income of its employees rather than being taxed as the employer business's taxable profit. The charge to income tax on employees (and company directors) is under the Income Tax (Earnings and Pensions) Act 2003 (ITEPA 2003).

In respect of the earnings of employees, both the employer and employee must also be aware of the impact of National Insurance contributions.

26.2 THE INCOME CHARGEABLE GENERALLY UNDER THE ITEPA 2003

Income tax is charged under the ITEPA 2003 on 'employment' income, 'pensions' income, and 'social security' income. This chapter concentrates on employment income. Employment income includes 'earnings'; that is all benefits received by the director or employee which derive from their office or employment as a reward for their services, whether they are paid by the employer or by a third party. Salaries, bonuses and tips are taxable; a gift on the other hand for purely personal reasons would not be taxable since it is not a reward for services. In relation to non-cash benefits such as company cars, there are particular provisions which require separate consideration.

26.3 CASH PAYMENTS

A cash salary usually forms the largest part of any remuneration package, but it is not the only cash payment that is taxable. A number of other receipts are chargeable under the ITEPA 2003, for example:

(a) a lump sum received at the beginning of the employment and referrable to future services (a 'golden hello');

(b) certain lump sums received at the end of the employment;

(c) a lump sum received in return for the employee entering into a covenant not to compete with the employer's trade (ITEPA 2003, s 225);

(d) other payments (ITEPA 2003, ss 401–416). A sum received on termination of office which is not otherwise chargeable to income tax is brought into charge by s 403 of the ITEPA 2003, even though it does not derive from the office or employment as a reward for services. Examples include compensation for unfair dismissal, damages for wrongful dismissal or even a gratuitous payment (a gift) on termination of the employment. However, the first £30,000 of any such sum is exempt.

26.4 NON-CASH BENEFITS

26.4.1 The general rules

Common examples of non-cash benefits provided or paid for by the employer are:

(a) the use of a 'company' car for private as well as business use;

(b) the provision of private medical insurance;

(c) an interest-free or low-interest loan;

(d) rent-free or low-rent living accommodation;

(e) an expenses allowance;

(f) vouchers exchangeable for goods or services (eg a season ticket for a football club).

Employees and company directors generally are liable to income tax under the ITEPA 2003 on all benefits which derive from the office or employment.

Generally, the taxable value of the benefit is taken as the amount of the cost incurred by the employer in providing that benefit (ITEPA 2003, s 204). For example, where the employer pays premiums for private medical insurance provided for the employee, pays rent for a house provided for the employee and pays for the employee's membership at their local gym, the employee will be assessed to income tax on the benefits valued on the amount of the premiums paid, the rent paid and the cost of the gym membership respectively. If the employee reimburses the employer to any extent (eg paying half of the rent), this reduces the cost incurred by the employer and hence reduces the taxable value of the benefit.

In some instances the taxable value of the benefit is calculated on a different basis; for example if the employer actually owns the asset, there may be no ongoing cost to the employer in providing that asset. In this case, the ITEPA 2003 sets prescribed methods for calculating the value of the benefit to the employee in each year. Particular examples are as follows:

(a) Private use of a 'company' car (ITEPA 2003, ss 114–172): the taxable value of the benefit to an employee from the private use of a car depends on the carbon dioxide emissions of the type of car in question. The charge is a fixed percentage of the list price of the car (and accessories), with a maximum charge being for cars with the greatest emissions (calculated in accordance with percentages prescribed in the Finance Act 2020).

(b) Private use of other company assets such as a house or a yacht (ITEPA 2003, s 205): the taxable value of the benefit is its annual value; for a house this will usually be its rateable value, whilst for other assets this will be 20% of the market value of the asset at the time it was first provided as a benefit.

(c) Loans at special rates by the employer (ITEPA 2003, ss 173–191): the taxable value of the benefit is the interest 'saved' by the director/employee as compared with the official interest rate as set from time to time. For 2025/26, the official rate is 3.75%. Thus if a director/employee pays no interest on a loan from their employer in 2025/26, the amount they have saved by not paying interest at 3.75% will be treated as part of their earnings. (However, see the exceptions mentioned in **26.4.2.**)

26.4.2 Exceptions

There are exceptions in certain cases, where the charge to tax described above will not apply. The following are common examples.

26.4.2.1 Certain accommodation (ITEPA 2003, s 315)

In certain instances, employees are not charged to tax (but generally directors are) on the benefit of rent-free or low-rent accommodation. Common examples are caretakers (exemption because occupation is necessary for the performance of the employee's duties) and police and fire officers (exemption because occupation is customary and for the better performance of the employee's duties).

26.4.2.2 Interest-free or low-interest loans (ITEPA 2003, s 180)

There is no charge to tax where the total outstanding on all special-rate loans from the employer does not exceed £10,000 at any time in the tax year.

26.4.2.3 Employer's pension contributions (ITEPA 2003, s 308)

The director/employee is not charged to tax on the benefit of contributions under HMRC-approved schemes.

26.4.3 Share schemes

The employer company may provide the employee or director with non-cash benefits which relate to shares in the company. These can take a variety of forms including a gift of the shares, a sale of the shares at a favourable price, a sale of the shares on terms where payment for them is postponed, an option to purchase shares in the future and various schemes involving the use of trusts. The tax treatment of such benefits requires more detailed explanation than is appropriate here, but it is worth noting that there are possible tax and other advantages to both the company employer and the employee or director in using these schemes. Part 7 of the ITEPA 2003 deals with the taxation of share-related income.

26.5 DEDUCTIBLE EXPENDITURE (ITEPA 2003, ss 327–385)

26.5.1 The general test (ITEPA 2003, s 336)

In calculating what is taxable within the ITEPA 2003, an employee or director is generally entitled only to deduct expenditure which is incurred 'wholly, exclusively and necessarily in the performance of their duties'. Travelling expenses and certain other items of expenditure are considered separately below. The 'wholly and exclusively' part of the test is the same as that considered in **21.3.2** in relation to trading income (ITTOIA 2005, Pt 2), where duality of purpose is generally fatal to a claim for deduction.

The ITEPA 2003 test is more severe in two respects:

(a) it contains the additional requirement of necessity, so that it must be shown that the employee's duties could not be performed without the expenditure in question;

(b) it contains the additional requirement that the expenditure was incurred in the performance of the duties so that, for example, expenditure incurred when preparing for the duties (eg in finding the job through an agency) is not deductible.

26.5.2 Particular kinds of expenses

The ITEPA 2003 test is so severe that there are few examples of expenditure that will satisfy the test. In a few instances the position is, therefore, modified.

26.5.2.1 Travelling expenses

Deductibility of travelling expenses depends on a slightly different test in that the expenditure must be necessarily incurred in the performance of the duties; it need not be wholly and exclusively incurred. It is clear that the employee/director who incurs expenditure when travelling from one place of work to another can treat that expenditure as deductible. However, this must be distinguished from travelling from home to the place of work; this travel cannot be in the performance of the duties, because the performance will only commence when the employee gets to work.

26.5.2.2 Pension contributions

An employee, or director, is entitled to deduct their contributions to an occupational pension scheme or to a personal pension scheme (although subject to restrictions). On the other hand, National Insurance contributions of the employee or director are not deductible.

26.6 COLLECTION OF TAX ON EMPLOYMENT INCOME (ITEPA 2003, Part 11)

Tax on most employment income is deducted at source by the employer under the PAYE (Pay As You Earn) system and paid to HMRC on the basis of earnings received in the tax year. This applies to most earnings, whether cash or non-cash (only the tax on non-cash benefits which are not readily convertible into cash is not collected via PAYE). Tax is collected at the appropriate rates (basic and higher). The system works by HMRC allocating to each taxpayer who is a director or an employee a code number based on information relating to their earnings and allowances. This code number is communicated to the employer, who is provided with Tables which enable the employer to calculate how much tax should be deducted before the director or employee's earnings are paid to them. The tax is then paid by the employer to HMRC. Employees/directors are, therefore, taxed on their income sooner under PAYE than a sole trader or partner who is assessed under the ITTOIA 2005, Part 2 (see **29.2.1**).

26.7 NATIONAL INSURANCE

After income tax, National Insurance contributions are the second largest source of receipts in the UK revenue system. Most of these contributions are made by employees and their employers in the form of 'Class 1' contributions on employees' earnings.

26.7.1 Employee (primary) contributions – 2025/26

An employee only has to make National Insurance contributions if their earnings exceed the earnings threshold (currently £242 per week). If that is the case, payment rates on earnings are:

First £242 per week	nil
Between £242 and £967 per week	8%
Above £967 per week	2%

26.7.2 Employer (secondary) contributions – 2025/26

An employer only has to make contributions in respect of an employee whose earnings exceed £5,000 per annum. The employer's rate of contribution for all earnings above that level is 15%. These contributions are in addition to those paid by the employee.

The employer may deduct its National Insurance contributions in calculating the taxable profit of the business for an accounting period, but an employee is not permitted to deduct their contributions when calculating their taxable income for a tax year. Contributions (like tax on employment income) are collected via the payroll.

CHAPTER 27

TAXATION OF SAVINGS AND INVESTMENT INCOME

LEARNING OUTCOMES

After reading this chapter you will be able to:

- understand the way in which interest payments are taxed when received by individuals and companies
- understand the taxation of dividends when received by a shareholder.

27.1 INTRODUCTION

This chapter describes the tax treatment of the income received by those who invest in business, either by way of making a loan to the business, or by buying shares in a company.

27.1.1 Interest received on loans/debentures

Both individuals and companies regularly make loans with a view to receiving interest on the loan. In the case of an individual, the interest forms income chargeable to income tax under Part 4, Ch 2 of the ITTOIA 2005. For a company, the interest is income chargeable to corporation tax, although the exact tax treatment of the interest depends on the reason for the loan (see **27.2.2**).

27.1.2 Income received by shareholders

A shareholder (whether an individual or a company) could receive payments from the company in which the shares are held (and relating to the shares) in a number of situations. The most common example of such payments are dividends, but other payments (see **27.3.1**) are also charged to tax and are collectively known as 'distributions'. The rules contained in Part 4, Ch 3 of the ITTOIA 2005 are relevant in order to determine the amount of income tax (in the case of an individual shareholder) due on a distribution. Again, the rules for companies differ from those for individuals.

27.2 TAXATION OF INTEREST

27.2.1 Income tax (ITTOIA 2005, Pt 4, Ch 2)

27.2.1.1 Interest received

For an individual who receives interest on a loan, Part 4, Ch 2 of the ITTOIA 2005 charges income tax on interest received in the current tax year. The lender must include the amount of interest in their total income for the tax year in question (see ***Legal Foundations*** for further details).

27.2.1.2 Deductible expenditure

There are no provisions in Part 4, Ch 2 of the ITTOIA 2005, for expenditure of any description to be deducted in calculating the amount of income that is taxable. For example, an individual lender cannot use their income from this source to obtain tax relief on any pension contributions they may be making (although certain sums may be deductible from the lender's total income when lending to a close company or a partnership – see **23.2.3** and **25.2.4** for details).

27.2.2 Corporation tax (CTA 2009, Parts 5 and 6)

The way in which a company is taxed on the interest it receives varies according to the company's purpose in making the loan, with different treatment for loans made in the course of a trade and loans made by way of investment. The rules are contained in the 'loan relationship' regime introduced by Finance Act 1996. The detail of the rules is beyond the scope of this book but, in general terms, interest paid or received as part of a company's trade is included in calculating the company's trading profit, whereas interest received on loans made by way of investment is assessed under CTA 2009, ss 299–301.

27.3 TAXATION OF SHAREHOLDERS

27.3.1 Income tax on distributions (ITTOIA 2005, Part 4, Ch 3)

27.3.1.1 Dividends

For an individual shareholder, Part 4, Ch 3 of the ITTOIA 2005 charges income tax on company dividends received in the current tax year. The shareholder must include the amount of the dividend in their total income for the tax year in question. (The taxation of dividends is described in ***Legal Foundations***.)

27.3.1.2 Written-off loan to a participator in a close company (ITTOIA 2005, s 416)

When a 'close company' makes a loan to a shareholder, there may ultimately be income tax consequences for the shareholder (see **23.2.2** for details).

27.3.1.3 'Profit' on sale of shares back to a company (CTA 2010, ss 1033–1048)

(a) Income tax treatment

A charge to income tax may be made when a shareholder sells their shares back to the company itself. The profit represented by the excess of the sale price over and above the issue price of the shares may be treated in the same way as a dividend (as described at **27.3.1.1**).

(b) Capital gains tax treatment

The income tax treatment of a sale of shares back to a company described above does not always apply and the shareholder's profit may attract CGT instead where certain conditions are satisfied. Broadly these conditions are:

(i) the buying company must be a trading company and its shares must not be listed on a recognised stock exchange (AIM is not included in the definition of stock exchange for these purposes); and

(ii) the purpose of the buy-back must not be to avoid tax; it must either be to raise cash to pay inheritance tax arising from a death or be for the benefit of the company's trade (this latter purpose might be achieved, for example, where the selling shareholder is at odds with the other shareholders so that the proper functioning of the company is best served by the dissenting shareholder selling their shares back to the company); and

(iii) the selling shareholder must have owned the shares being sold back for at least five years; and

(iv) the seller must either be selling all of their shares in the company or at least substantially reducing their percentage shareholding to no more than 30% of the issued share capital of the company. (A 'substantial' reduction in the shareholding is a reduction of at least 25%.)

(Note: It may be difficult to decide whether all of the above conditions are met (especially in cases where the buy-back must be shown to be for the benefit of the company's trade). In such situations it is possible to apply to HMRC for advance clearance of the proposed tax treatment of the buy-back.)

(c) The importance of the distinction between the income tax and capital gains tax treatment of a buy-back

The question of whether the income tax basis or CGT basis will apply to the sale of shares back to a company may be important to the selling shareholder in that a significant difference in their liability to tax may be involved.

If the CGT basis applies, the availability of reliefs and exemptions (such as business asset disposal relief and the annual exemption) may significantly reduce the shareholder's liability to that tax.

A basic rate taxpayer may prefer the income tax basis to apply, given that the ordinary income tax rate on dividends is 8.75% and a dividend allowance will be available. For a higher rate taxpayer, however, the rate at which the seller will pay income tax is 33.75% (the dividend upper rate). For an additional rate taxpayer, the income tax rate is 39.35%.

Which treatment is preferable will depend on the selling shareholder's own circumstances and it may be possible to structure the sale back to the company to ensure that the most favourable tax treatment is obtained. (The position is further complicated where the seller did not acquire the shares directly from the company but as a result of a subsequent share transfer. In such circumstances, both an income tax and a CGT calculation may be required on the disposal – the detail of the treatment of such a disposal is outside the scope of this book.)

(Note: As the company that buys back the shares must pay stamp duty on the purchase, a buy-back may have tax consequences for both parties and so requires careful consideration. Above the de minimis threshold of £1,000, stamp duty on shares is normally charged at 0.5% of the consideration (rounded up to the nearest multiple of £5).)

27.3.1.4 Tax treatment of 'treasury shares'

Certain companies can hold shares 'in treasury' rather than cancelling them following a sale back to the company by a shareholder. Section 195 of the Finance Act 2003 contains the tax treatment of such shares. In outline, shareholders are governed by the rules described at **27.3.1.3** when selling the shares to the company and the company must pay stamp duty on the purchase; whilst the shares are held in treasury, they are treated as if they do not exist for tax purposes; and a transfer by the company of shares previously held in treasury is treated as if it is an issue of new shares by the company.

27.3.2 Income tax relief for an individual shareholder

There are no provisions in Part 4, Ch 3 of the ITTOIA 2005, for expenditure of any description to be deducted in calculating the amount of income that is included in the individual shareholder's total income. To encourage individuals to invest in companies, however, the tax legislation does include two important income tax reliefs.

27.3.2.1 Income tax relief for a shareholder's borrowings (ITA 2007, ss 383, 392–395)

When an individual borrows in order to purchase ordinary shares in a close company that carries on a trade, or to lend to such a company, the relief described in **23.2.3** may be available (subject to the cap described at **24.4.6**).

27.3.2.2 Income tax relief under the Enterprise Investment Scheme (EIS)

When a qualifying individual invests money in a company whose shares qualify within the terms of the above scheme, a deduction from the individual's income tax liability is given in the tax year of the investment. The relief is described in ***Legal Foundations***.

27.3.3 Corporation tax on distributions

27.3.3.1 Dividends (CTA 2009, s 1285)

If a company receives dividends from shares it holds in another UK company, the general principle is that these dividends are taken into account when calculating its corporation tax liability. However, this is subject to a number of broad exceptions, the effect of which is to exempt most dividends from corporation tax. This prevents the double taxation that would otherwise arise on the distribution of profits that have already been assessed to tax on the paying company.

27.3.3.2 'Profit' on sale of shares back to a company (CTA 2010, ss 1033–1048)

When a company buys back shares from a shareholder that is another company, it is necessary to decide how any profit on the sale will be treated for the purposes of the selling company's corporation tax calculation. If the buy-back falls within the capital gains rules (using the test set out at **27.3.1.3**), the profit will be taxed as part of the selling company's chargeable gains (see **22.3**). If the capital gains treatment does not apply, the profit will be taxed as income (see **22.5.2**).

CHAPTER 28

BUSINESS RELIEFS FROM CGT AND IHT AVAILABLE TO INDIVIDUALS

LEARNING OUTCOMES

After reading this chapter you will be able to:

- explain the major business reliefs available to individuals liable to capital gains tax
- explain the reliefs from inheritance tax available in a business context.

28.1 INTRODUCTION

Any business, however structured, is ultimately run for the benefit of individuals (although, in the case of sophisticated corporate structures, there may be many layers of ownership including institutional investors such as pension funds between the business and those individuals who stand to benefit from its long-term success).

This chapter considers the tax implications for individuals, with direct involvement in a business venture, when they realise their investment in some way. The relevant taxes in this situation are CGT and IHT and, having identified the possible charge to tax, it is then necessary to identify what (if any) exemptions and/or reliefs may be available to reduce the amount of tax payable.

Capital gains tax and IHT are among the taxes subject to the 'general anti-abuse rule' ('GAAR'). The GAAR is an addition to the many existing specific anti-avoidance rules and is designed to allow HMRC to counteract 'abusive' tax avoidance schemes intended to exploit loopholes in the legislation governing the rules for calculating these taxes.

28.2 THE SUBJECT MATTER OF A CHARGE TO TAX

28.2.1 Sole trader

A sole trader may dispose of their business (or a part of it) which will comprise not only their tangible assets such as premises and fixtures but also their intangible asset of goodwill; disposal of these assets may have CGT implications. (The tangible assets will also include trading stock and perhaps machinery and plant, in relation to both of which a disposal may have income tax implications rather than CGT implications; the disposal of trading stock will be relevant to calculation of the final trading profit and the disposal of machinery and plant may result in a balancing charge or allowance for income tax purposes under the capital allowances system.) If the disposal is not a sale at full value, it may also have IHT implications.

28.2.2 Partner

An individual partner may dispose of their interest in the partnership business, comprising their fractional share in each of the assets of the business. This is equally the case if the firm is selling its business in that every partner is then disposing of their interest in the business. In addition, a partner may dispose of a particular asset (most notably the business premises) which is owned by them individually although used by the firm. (The sale of a particular asset by the firm is dealt with in detail at **25.3**.)

28.2.3 Shareholder

An individual shareholder in a company may dispose of their shares in the company and, perhaps, a particular asset owned by them individually although used by the company.

28.3 WHEN AND HOW CAPITAL TAXATION APPLIES: PRINCIPLES

Capital gains tax and inheritance tax are often referred to collectively as 'capital taxes', and this paragraph outlines the main occasions on which they will be chargeable in a business context.

28.3.1 Sale at full value

28.3.1.1 Capital gains tax

Where there is a disposal of assets (whether by a sole trader, an individual partner, partners acting together to sell a partnership asset, or a shareholder) and the disposal is a sale at full value, there may be a charge to CGT in so far as there is a disposal of chargeable assets which have increased in value during the period of ownership. For full details of the steps involved in calculating CGT, see **Legal Foundations**. In outline, the steps are as follows:

Step 1: *Identify a chargeable disposal*

In a business context, the most common examples of chargeable assets are likely to be land and buildings, goodwill, company shares or the individual's interest in such assets (although, if the disposal proceeds form part of the individual's income (eg regular sales of land as part of a property developer's trade), they will normally form part of the individual's total income rather than be taxed as chargeable gains). Plant and machinery will rarely produce a chargeable gain for the reasons detailed at **21.4.2**.

Step 2: *Calculate the gain (or loss)*

Proceeds of disposal
LESS
Costs of disposal
= Net proceeds of disposal
LESS
Other allowable expenditure
(eg acquisition cost, other incidental costs of acquisition, subsequent expenditure)
= GAIN or loss

Step 3: *Apply reliefs*

Step 4: *Aggregate gains and losses*

Deduct annual exemption

Step 5: *Apply the correct rate(s) of tax*

28.3.1.2 Inheritance tax

There is no liability to IHT on a sale at full value because there has been no 'transfer of value' under which the value of the disponer's estate is reduced.

28.3.2 Gift during lifetime

28.3.2.1 Capital gains tax

Where an individual makes a gift of a chargeable asset (or of their share in a chargeable asset in the case of a partner), this is a disposal which may give rise to a chargeable gain in the same way as a sale at full value except that in calculating the disponer's gain it is necessary to use the asset's market value at disposal (as opposed to sale price). The logic of this lies in the fact that the tax is imposed broadly on the increase in the asset's value during the period of ownership rather than on any gain in monetary terms that the disponer has actually realised.

28.3.2.2 Inheritance tax

Where an individual makes a gift of an asset, at the same time as being a disposal for CGT purposes this is a disposition which reduces the value of their estate and hence is a transfer of value for IHT purposes. For full details of the steps involved in calculating IHT, see **Legal Foundations.**

In outline, the steps are as follows:

Step 1: *Identify the transfer of value*

Step 2: *Find the value transferred*

Step 3: *Apply any relevant exemptions and reliefs:*

(a) spouse/civil partner or charity exemption
(b) agricultural property relief and/or business property relief
(c) lifetime only exemptions (eg annual exemption).

(Note: If the gift is to an individual (or some types of trusts) there will be no immediate charge to IHT if any value transferred remains after Step 3 because it will be a 'PET', a potentially exempt transfer, and a charge will arise only if the transferor dies within seven years of the gift. In the case of an 'LCT', a lifetime chargeable transfer (broadly, a gift to a company or most types of trusts), tax may become payable immediately and the charge may increase if the transferor dies within seven years of the gift.)

Step 4: *Calculate tax on a chargeable transfer at the appropriate rate (tapering relief may be available for transfers made more than three years before the transferor's death).*

28.3.3 Sale at an undervalue

Where a sale is at an undervalue, there may be liability to CGT as in **28.3.2.1** on the net increase in the asset's value during the period of ownership and possible liability to IHT on the loss to the disponer as a result of the gift element. The position is different if the disponer has sold at an undervalue merely as a result of making a bad bargain (eg through not recognising how much the asset is really worth). The implications of a sale at an undervalue with a gift element as distinguished from a bad bargain are considered separately below in relation to each of the possible charges to tax.

28.3.3.1 Capital gains tax

The significance of the distinction between a gift and a bad bargain is important to the calculation of the gain. If a sale is at an undervalue with a gift element, the gain, if any, will be calculated by reference to market value at disposal in the same way as with an outright gift; this prevents taxpayers avoiding CGT by fixing an artificially low sale price which would correspondingly produce an artificially low gain. If the sale is a bad bargain, the gain, if any, will be calculated by reference to the actual sale price. The problem of distinguishing between the two is often avoided by provisions in the Taxation of Chargeable Gains Act 1992 on 'connected persons' (TCGA 1992, s 286). A disposal to a connected person will be deemed to be made at market value rather than at the actual sale price; 'connected persons' include the spouse/civil partner of the disponer or other close relatives of the disponer or their spouse/civil partner (including parents, grandparents, children, grandchildren and siblings (and the spouses/civil partners of those people) but not, for example, aunts or uncles or nephews or nieces); business partners are also connected persons, but a disposal between such partners which is negotiated on a commercial basis will be taken to be at the actual sale price.

28.3.3.2 Inheritance tax

Section 10(1) of the IHTA 1984 provides that a disposition is not a transfer of value if the transferor had no intention to transfer a gratuitous benefit. Thus if the transferor can prove that they made a bad bargain, having no intention to confer a gratuitous benefit on another person, the loss to their estate resulting from that bad bargain will not have any IHT implications. As with the equivalent CGT point, there may be difficulty in establishing this distinction, although again the concept of a 'connected person' is used. For IHT purposes, the definition of connected person is wider than that for CGT as it is extended to include aunts or uncles or nephews or nieces (or their spouses/civil partners) (IHTA 1984, s 270). If the transaction is with a connected person, the burden on the transferor of proving that there was no 'transfer of value' is heavier because they must show that there was no intention to confer a gratuitous benefit and that the transaction was on the same terms as if it had been made with a person with whom they were not connected.

EXAMPLE 1

A, a sole trader, has decided to retire and to allow his son B to purchase the business from him. The net worth of the business is £100,000. B can afford to pay only £60,000 even by using all his savings and borrowing as much as he can. A sells to B at £60,000.

CGT: the fact that B is 'connected' to A is incidental on these facts because it is clearly a sale at an undervalue; A's gains must be calculated by reference to the market value of the chargeable assets of which he disposes.

IHT: again the fact that B is 'connected' to A is incidental because A is clearly going to be unable to prove that this was merely a bad bargain; A suffers a loss to his estate of £40,000 (the value of the business of £100,000 less the £60,000 paid for it) so that he has made a potentially exempt transfer which will become chargeable to IHT if A dies within seven years (subject to exemptions and reliefs).

EXAMPLE 2

C, a sole trader, receives an offer from DE Co Ltd (a company with which he has no connection) to purchase his business for £80,000. C accepts the offer and sells at this price without bothering to have the business professionally valued. In fact the business is worth at least £90,000.

CGT: the company is not 'connected' with C and therefore the transaction can be taken as being merely a bad bargain; the actual consideration will be used for calculation of C's gain.

IHT: since the company is not a connected person, C should have no difficulty in establishing that he had no intention to confer any gratuitous benefit on the company so that there are no IHT implications.

28.3.4 Death

28.3.4.1 Capital gains tax (TCGA 1992, s 62)

It is a fundamental principle of CGT that there can be no charge to the tax on death; technically, this position is achieved by providing that on death there is no disposal of assets. Also significant is the fact that any increase in the value of assets during the deceased's ownership will not attract any charge to CGT because the personal representatives (and eventually the person who inherits an asset) are deemed to acquire the deceased's assets at their market value at the date of death.

28.3.4.2 Inheritance tax

On death, there is a deemed transfer of value by the deceased of their entire estate immediately before death (IHTA 1984, s 4(1)); also, any potentially exempt transfers made by the deceased in the seven years preceding their death become chargeable transfers as a result of their death.

The charge to IHT is described in **Legal Foundations** but, in brief, is calculated as follows:

(a) IHT will be assessed on any potentially exempt transfers (and reassessed on any lifetime chargeable transfers) made in the seven years preceding death (see **28.3.2.2**);

(b) IHT will be assessed on the death estate using the following steps:

Step 1: *Identify the transfer of value (the deemed transfer on death)*

Step 2: *Find the value transferred*

Step 3: *Apply any relevant exemptions and reliefs:*

(a) *spouse/civil partner or charity exemption*

(b) *agricultural property relief and/or business property relief*

Step 4: *Calculate tax at the appropriate rates.*

28.4 CAPITAL GAINS TAX – BUSINESS RELIEFS

Having established the chargeable gain on the disposal of a chargeable asset, the available reliefs should be considered. The reliefs described below relate to business assets of various kinds, and have been introduced over the years to encourage investment in business. (Other reliefs of less general application are considered in other titles in this series.) The reliefs considered below are:

(a) roll-over relief on the replacement of qualifying business assets;

(b) hold-over relief on gifts of business assets;

(c) roll-over relief on the incorporation of a business;

(d) business asset disposal relief;

(e) other reliefs.

Several of the reliefs require that, in order to qualify for relief, assets being disposed of and/or acquired must be used in a 'trade' or, in the case of company shares, be shares in a 'trading company'. For the meaning of 'trade', see **21.2.1**.

Where it exists, the trading requirement is very important as it is designed to deny relief to disposals of assets held for non-trading purposes (typically where assets are held instead as investments).

(Where an asset is described below as being required to be used in a trade, that also includes, where appropriate, use in a vocation or profession.)

28.4.1 Roll-over relief on the replacement of qualifying business assets (TCGA 1992, ss 152–159)

This relief is designed to encourage businesses to expand and thrive by allowing the CGT due on the disposal of a 'qualifying asset' to be effectively postponed when the consideration obtained for the disposal is applied in acquiring another qualifying asset by way of replacement.

28.4.1.1 Conditions for the relief to apply

(a) Qualifying assets (TCGA 1992, s 155)

The principal qualifying assets for the purposes of the relief are land, buildings and goodwill.

The asset must be used in the trade of the business (as opposed to being held as an investment).

(Note:

(a) company shares are *not* qualifying assets;

(b) although 'fixed' plant and machinery is a qualifying asset, a sale of such an asset will rarely produce a gain (as most depreciate in value) and any roll-over relief when acquiring such assets will be restricted if they are wasting assets (TCGA 1992, s 154). What constitutes 'fixed' plant and machinery is, in itself, not straightforward. There is no statutory definition, so each case turns on its own facts, but claims are unlikely to succeed if the item in question is moveable and intended to be so to enable changes in the layout of the workplace.)

The relief can apply on the disposal of a qualifying asset owned by:

(i) a sole trader and used in their trade;

(ii) a partnership and used in the partnership trade;

(iii) an individual partner and used in the partnership trade;

(iv) an individual shareholder and used in the trade of the company in which they own shares. The company must be the shareholder's 'personal company' (ie the individual must own at least 5% of the voting shares in the company).

Provided both the asset disposed of, and the asset acquired fall within the definition of qualifying assets, they do not have to be the same type of asset. For example, it is possible to sell qualifying goodwill, and roll-over the gain into the purchase of qualifying buildings.

(b) Time limits

For the relief to apply, the disposal and acquisition must take place within certain time limits. The replacement asset must be acquired within one year before or three years after the disposal of the original asset, unless an extended period is allowed by HMRC.

> **EXAMPLE**
>
> If a sole trader disposes of a qualifying asset at the start of January 2025, a replacement qualifying asset would need to be acquired at some point in the period stretching from the start of January 2024 to the end of December 2027.

28.4.1.2 Application of the relief

If a qualifying asset is disposed of and, within the time limits, the proceeds of sale are used for the purchase of another qualifying asset to be used in a business, then any liability to CGT from the disposal can be postponed (at least until the disposal of the replacement asset) by rolling-over the gain on the disposal of the original asset into the acquisition cost of the replacement asset. This means that the gain is notionally deducted from the acquisition cost of the replacement asset to give a lower acquisition cost for use in subsequent CGT calculations. Thus a later disposal of the replacement asset may produce a gain that comprises both the rolled-over gain and any gain on the replacement asset itself (TCGA 1992, s 153 contains restrictions on the relief if part only of the value of the consideration on the disposal of the original asset is used to acquire the new asset).

Note that when an individual claims this relief the annual exemption cannot be set against the gain before it is rolled over.

Any claim for relief must be submitted no more than four years after the end of the tax year in which the replacement asset is acquired (or, if later, the original asset sold).

EXAMPLE

In September 2025, H, a sole trader, sells some premises that he has owned since 2005 for £70,000. He makes a gain of £30,000 (it is his only chargeable disposal in the 2025/26 tax year). Six months later, H buys some more premises for £80,000. If H claims roll-over relief on the replacement of qualifying assets:

(a) H will pay no CGT in 2025/26 as the gain on the disposal of the original premises is postponed;

(b) for the purposes of future CGT calculations the replacement premises will be treated as being acquired for £50,000 (£80,000 less £30,000);

(c) H will not be able to use his annual exemption for 2025/26.

Imagine that H then sells the new premises in 2028 for £125,000. The calculation of his gain will be:

Proceeds of disposal	125,000	
Less		
Adjusted acquisition cost	50,000	(without the effect of roll-over it would be 80,000)
Gain	75,000	(without the effect of roll-over it would be only 45,000)

Provided the qualifying conditions were met, the gain from the 2028 sale could itself be rolled over.

(Note:

(a) Although roll-over relief on the replacement of qualifying assets can apply in theory when a qualifying asset is given away, it would be unusual in practice for a donor to be so generous as to both make a gift and retain the CGT liability relating to that gift. The hold-over relief described at **28.4.2** is likely to be more relevant in these circumstances as liability for any future CGT on a disposal of the gifted asset passes to the donee under the terms of that relief.

(b) The roll-over relief contained in ss 152–159 of the TCGA 1992, is also available in a modified form to companies – see **22.4.3**.)

28.4.2 Hold-over relief on gifts (and the gift element in sales at an undervalue) of business assets (TCGA 1992, s 165 and Sch 7)

Hold-over relief on gifts is available to an individual who disposes of 'business assets' by way of gift or, to the extent of the gift element, by way of sale at an undervalue. Like roll-over relief, hold-over relief does not exempt any of the chargeable gain, but instead acts to postpone any tax liability. The relief is designed to allow business assets to be given away without a tax charge falling on the donor (who would not otherwise have any sale proceeds to fund the tax).

28.4.2.1 Conditions for the relief to apply

(a) Gift or gift element. The relief is available only on gifts, or on the gift element on a sale at an undervalue.

(b) Only the gain relating to chargeable business assets can be held over. 'Business assets' include the following:

  (i) assets which are used in the donor's trade or their interest in such assets. This applies to the assets of a sole trader or partnership;

  (ii) shares in a trading company which are not listed on a recognised stock exchange (AIM is not included in the definition of stock exchange for these purposes);

  (iii) shares in a *personal* trading company even if listed on a recognised stock exchange;

  (iv) assets owned by the shareholder and used by their *personal* trading company.

  (To be a 'personal company', the individual must own at least 5% of the company's voting shares.)

  Note: The relief does not apply to a gift of shares if the donee is a company.

(c) For the relief to apply, both donor and donee must so elect (as the donee is effectively taking on the liability for any CGT that eventually arises from the gift). The election must be made no more than four years after the end of the tax year of the disposal.

28.4.2.2 Application of the relief

To apply hold-over relief, the chargeable gain must be calculated in the usual way (taking market value as the consideration for the disposal), and then this gain will be deducted from the market value of the asset in order to establish an artificially low 'acquisition cost' for the donee.

When the donee eventually disposes of the asset, the artificially low acquisition cost (plus any qualifying expenditure – see **28.4.2.3**) is deducted from the sale price (on a sale at full value) or market value (on a gift) to find the gain of the donee. Thus the donee's gain will include the held-over gain plus any gain attributable to their own period of ownership. Having calculated the donee's chargeable gain, reliefs should be considered (including hold-over relief again if relevant). If the donee dies without having disposed of the asset, all gains then accumulated in respect of the asset will escape CGT altogether.

Note that the donor cannot set the annual exemption against the gain before it is held over.

EXAMPLE

J gives M, his son, the family business at a time when the business's chargeable assets are worth £100,000 and the total gains on those assets are £20,000. Eighteen months later M sells the business for £110,000 (he makes no other disposals in the same tax year).

(a) J pays no CGT on the disposal to M.

(b) J and M elect to hold over J's gain on the disposal to M, so that M's adjusted acquisition cost is £80,000 (£100,000 less £20,000). J's annual exemption for the year cannot be deducted from the held-over gain.

(c) on the sale of the business by M, his gain is:

	£
Sale price	110,000
Less: adjusted acquisition cost	80,000
Gain	30,000

M's annual exemption for the tax year of the sale can be used to reduce the gain.

28.4.2.3 Interaction with inheritance tax

In calculating the gain on any subsequent disposal by the donee as described in **28.4.2.2**, there is one item which may be deducted as an expense which would not usually occur. Given that this relief is relevant only to gifts or sales at an undervalue, the original disposal may lead to eventual charges to both IHT on the original disposal (eg if a potentially exempt transfer is followed by the death of the donor within seven years) and CGT (on the donee's eventual disposal) which will include the held-over gain from the original disposal. If a charge to IHT does occur, the IHT paid by the donee can be added to the acquisition cost of the asset, thus reducing the gain on the donee's eventual disposal. (The gain may be reduced to nil following this calculation, but it is not possible to use the IHT charge to produce a loss for CGT purposes.)

As most business assets qualify for 100% relief from IHT (see **28.5.2**), such an IHT charge will occur infrequently. An example of when it might occur is following a chargeable transfer of a minority holding of *quoted* shares (eg a gift followed by the donor's death within seven years). This transfer may qualify for hold-over relief for CGT purposes (as a shareholding of 5% or more of the company's shares) but not for IHT business property relief (as it is not a controlling shareholding).

EXAMPLE

M gives her 5% shareholding in B plc to her daughter D in September 2025 when the shares are valued at £100,000 (according to the price quoted on the Stock Exchange at the time). M acquired the shares several years previously – they were then valued at £30,000. There was no relevant expenditure to deduct in calculating M's gain. M and D claim hold-over relief on M's gain. M dies in January 2025 and D has to pay IHT of £40,000 in relation to the gift of shares from M (the PET becomes chargeable as a result of M's death within seven years and M's nil rate band had been exhausted by other gifts shortly before that to D).

In July 2026, D sells the shares for £110,000. She had no relevant expenditure to deduct in calculating her gain. Calculations for CGT purposes are as follows:

M's disposal (the gift to D)	£
Disposal value	100,000
LESS	
Acquisition value	30,000
M's gain held over	70,000
D's disposal (sale)	£
Disposal price	110,000
LESS	
Acquisition value as reduced by the gain held over on M's disposal (ie £100,000 less £70,000)	30,000
AND	
IHT paid by D as a result of M's PET becoming chargeable on the death of M	40,000
D's gain	40,000

D will be able to use her annual exemption for 2026/27 to reduce the gain further.

28.4.3 Roll-over relief on incorporation of a business (TCGA 1992, s 162)

Where a business is transferred by a sole trader or individual partners to a new or established company in return for shares in the company, a disposal occurs for CGT purposes. Roll-over relief on incorporation is given to allow any gain on the disposal to be deferred. The relief postpones the CGT payable on the disposal given that no cash has been realised with which to pay the tax arising.

28.4.3.1 Conditions for the relief to apply

(a) The business must be transferred as a going concern. This means that the business must essentially be carried on as the same business albeit with a change of owner; if, for example, the business premises are transferred but a different business is then carried on by the company, this is not a transfer as a going concern.

(b) The whole gain can be rolled over only if the consideration is all in shares issued by the company. If, for example, the company 'pays' for the business as to 50% by an issue of shares but as to the other 50% by an issue of debentures (ie this amount is treated as a loan to the company), then roll-over relief can apply to only 50% of the gain.

(c) The business must be transferred with all of its assets (although cash is ignored for this purpose). If, for example, a sole trader's business is transferred to a company as a going concern but ownership of the business premises is retained by the sole trader who will allow the company to use them, then roll-over relief will not apply.

28.4.3.2 Application of the relief

The gain on the disposal is rolled over by notionally deducting it from the acquisition cost of the shares.

Note that the annual exemption cannot be used to reduce the gain before it is rolled over.

EXAMPLE

X decides to sell his sole trade to Y Co Ltd. The business is valued at £100,000 and X receives £100,000 worth of shares in Y Co Ltd in exchange for the business. If X makes a chargeable gain of £25,000 on the disposal to Y Co Ltd and he rolls-over the gain on incorporation, he will not pay any CGT on the disposal but the acquisition cost of his shares in Y Co Ltd will, for tax purposes, be £75,000 (£100,000 less the gain of £25,000). When X eventually sells or gives away his shares, therefore, he will only be able to deduct an acquisition cost of £75,000 when calculating his gain on the disposal of the shares.

Note: Where the conditions for the relief are met, HMRC will apply it automatically unless the taxpayer elects not to use it. This election must be made no later than the second anniversary of the 31 January following the tax year of the incorporation (eg by 31 January 2028 for incorporations in 2024/25). If, however, the shares acquired as a result of the incorporation are sold before the end of the tax year that follows the tax year of incorporation, the election must be made no later than the first anniversary of the 31 January following the tax year of incorporation (eg by 31 January 2027 for incorporations in 2024/25).

28.4.4 Business asset disposal relief (TCGA 1992, ss 169H–169S)

This was previously called 'entrepreneurs' relief'. As the new name suggests, it applies on the disposal of certain business assets. However, not all business assets qualify for the relief.

28.4.4.1 Conditions for the relief to apply

For the relief to apply, there has to be a 'qualifying business disposal'. The conditions for this vary depending on the type of interest being disposed.

(a) Sole trade or partnership interests

(i) The disposal of the whole or part of a business (whether by a sole trader or an individual partner) may qualify. This includes situations where:

- (a) the business (or part of it) is disposed of as a going concern (not simply the disposal of individual asset(s) used in the business); or where
- (b) assets are disposed of following cessation of the business (provided the assets were used in the business at the time of cessation).

(ii) To be a qualifying disposal of part or the whole of a business, the interest in the business as a whole (as opposed to any one asset comprising it) must have been owned either:

(a) throughout the period of two years ending with the date of disposal; or

(b) throughout the period of two years ending with the cessation of the business (provided the disposal itself is within three years after that cessation).

(iii) Where there is a qualifying disposal of a sole trade or partnership interest, only assets used for the purposes of the business carried on by the individual or partnership are eligible for relief. Company shares and securities and any other assets held as investments are specifically excluded from this definition. Goodwill is also excluded from being a relevant business asset when the disposal is by an individual to a close company in which they or their associate(s) are participators (as defined in **23.2**).

> **EXAMPLE**
>
> Jagat has run a graphic design business for 10 years. He decides to retire, and cannot find a buyer for the business as a whole so stops trading. Two years later he sells the premises from which he traded, realising a chargeable gain. This is a qualifying business disposal for the purposes of business asset disposal relief.

(b) Company shares

(i) A disposal of company shares (including securities) may qualify for relief if:

(a) the company is a trading company and is the disponer's 'personal company' (so that they hold at least 5% of the ordinary share capital in the company and that holding gives at least 5% of the voting rights);

and either or both of the following conditions are met:

(i) by virtue of that holding, the disponer is beneficially entitled to at least 5% of the profits available for distribution to equity holders and, on a winding up, would be beneficially entitled to at least 5% of assets so available, or

(ii) in the event of a disposal of the whole of the ordinary share capital of the company, the disponer would be beneficially entitled to at least 5% of the proceeds; and

(b) the disponer is an employee or officer (such as a director) of the company.

(ii) For a qualifying disposal, the requirements detailed in (i) above must have been satisfied either:

(a) throughout the period of two years ending with the date of disposal; or

(b) throughout the period of two years ending with the date the company ceased to be a trading company (provided that the disposal itself is within three years of that cessation).

(iii) To be a 'trading company', the company must not have activities that include 'to a substantial extent activities other than trading activities'. This will restrict the extent to which the company can hold cash reserves or investments whilst still meeting the definition.

> **EXAMPLE**
>
> Kevin and Leanne each own 20% of the ordinary voting shares in KLR Optics Ltd, a company that makes precision lenses for scientific purposes. They formed the company together eight years ago and Kevin is the technical director, but Leanne resigned from her role in the company four years ago when she decided to take a career break to look after her children. They each sell their shareholding at a large profit when a competitor offers to buy the company. Kevin makes a qualifying business disposal but Leanne does not.

(c) Associated disposals

(i) Sometimes assets used by a business are not owned as part of the business but separately by an individual. Disposals of such assets owned by an individual outside of the business may qualify for relief if the asset was used for the purposes of the business run either by:

(a) a partnership in which the individual was a partner; or

(b) a company in which the individual's shares qualify under '(b) Company shares' above.

(ii) Disposals of such assets qualify only if the disposal of them is associated with a qualifying disposal of the individual's interest in the partnership or company shares as the case may be, and if the disposal is part of the withdrawal of the individual from the business carried on by the partnership or company. (Withdrawal means reducing the partnership share by at least 5% of the partnership assets or reducing the shareholding by at least 5% of the share capital.)

(iii) To be a qualifying disposal, the asset in question must have been owned by the individual for at least three years and used throughout the period of two years ending with the earlier of:

(a) the disposal of the interest or shares to which the disposal of the asset is associated; or

(b) the cessation of the business of the partnership or company which used the asset.

EXAMPLE

Milly sells her interest in a doctor's partnership to Neil after 20 years' involvement in the practice. Throughout that period, Milly had allowed the partnership to run its business from a surgery in some land she owns near her home. At the same time as selling her interest to Neil, Milly sells the surgery to the continuing partners. Both the sale of the partnership interest and the associated disposal of the surgery are qualifying business disposals.

(Note: further conditions apply if the shares being disposed of are in a company that is part of a group, or if the business or shares are owned as part of the assets of a trust).

28.4.4.2 Application of the relief

If the conditions for the relief are satisfied, the relief qualifies the gains concerned for a special tax rate of 14% for disposals after 6 April 2025 (18% for disposals after 6 April 2026).

There is, however, a restriction on the relief, in that an individual cannot claim the relief for more than £1 million of qualifying gains. This cap is a lifetime restriction, so that only £1 million of gains can qualify for the relief for each individual, whether those gains arise from just one business disposal or from a number of disposals spread over time. The lifetime cap has been set at various levels since the relief was first introduced.

(Note: there are further restrictions on the amount of gain on an associated disposal that can qualify for relief if the asset in question was not used for the purposes of the business throughout the disponer's period of ownership, if only part of the asset was used by the business, if the individual was involved in the business for only part of the time the asset was in use, or if rent was charged for the use of the asset.)

EXAMPLE 1

Otis is a sole trader who makes a gain on a qualifying business disposal of £450,000. He has never made any such disposals before. Otis can make a further £550,000 of gains in future that can qualify for the relief.

> **EXAMPLE 2**
>
> Petra makes a qualifying gain of £10 million when she sells her shares in a successful clothing company. She has not made any such disposals before. The first £1 million of the gain is eligible for the business asset disposal relief rate of tax. The remaining £9 million is not eligible and the relief has been exhausted and will not be available on any future disposals Petra makes.

Any claim for business asset disposal relief must be made on or before the first anniversary of the 31 January following the tax year in which the qualifying disposal was made (eg by 31 January 2028 for a disposal in 2025/26).

28.4.5 Other reliefs

In addition to the reliefs described above, there are many other CGT reliefs targeted at specific groups of investors. A selection of these are mentioned below.

28.4.5.1 Investors' relief (TCGA 1992, ss 169VA–169VR and Sch 7ZB)

Investors' relief applies to gains made on the disposal of qualifying shares in unlisted trading companies. In broad terms, in order to qualify, the shares must be fully paid ordinary shares which were issued to the investor in return for cash on or after 17 March 2016, and which the investor has held for at least three years from 6 April 2016. The relief operates in the same way as business asset disposal relief through the application of a special tax rate of 14% on the gain. The relief is subject to a lifetime cap of £1 million (separate from the lifetime cap on business asset disposal relief).

28.4.5.2 Deferral relief on reinvestment in EIS shares (TCGA 1992, s 150C and Sch 5B)

Unlimited deferral of capital gains arising on the disposal, by sale or gift, of any asset is available where an individual subscribes wholly for cash for shares in a company which qualifies under the Enterprise Investment Scheme (EIS). The Scheme is described in more detail in ***Legal Foundations***. (Note: as the shares must be acquired for cash, this relief will not usually be available to a partner or sole trader who transfers their business to a company, as the shares acquired following such a transfer are usually issued in return for the non-cash assets of the business.)

28.4.5.3 Other share based reliefs

To encourage share ownership, the Government sometimes introduces incentives by way of favourable CGT treatment for certain types of shareholding. The detail of these reliefs (which are often time limited) is beyond the scope of this book, but some of those currently available are the seed enterprise investment scheme ('SEIS'), enterprise management incentives ('EMI') and various other employee share schemes.

28.4.6 Annual exemption (TCGA 1992, s 3)

In each tax year, a prescribed amount (the first £3,000 for 2025/26) of an individual's gains is exempt from CGT. If the exemption is unused (in whole or in part) for any year, there is no provision for it to be carried forward and so any unused exemption is lost.

Where a person has gains that will be taxed at different rates (see below), the annual exemption can be allocated amongst those gains in the order that is most favourable to the taxpayer.

As mentioned above, the annual exemption cannot be used on a gain which is being rolled over or held over.

EXAMPLE 1

Rena makes two disposals in the 2025/26 tax year. Disposal 1 produces a gain of £30,000 that qualifies for business asset disposal relief. Disposal 2 produces a gain of £20,000 that does not qualify for any relief. Rena is a higher-rate taxpayer for income tax purposes. Rena can choose to set the annual exemption against the £20,000 gain that would otherwise all be taxed at 24%, rather than against the gain that qualifies for the business asset disposal relief rate of 14%:

Disposal 2:	£20,000	
	(£3,000)	annual exemption
	£17,000	taxable
Disposal 1:	£30,000	taxable

EXAMPLE 2

If, in Example 1, Rena had made a third disposal, creating a loss of £18,000, she could also have used that in the order most favourable to her. The loss would be set against the gain that did not qualify for business asset disposal relief, and the annual exemption against the balance of that gain before being set against the gain qualifying for business asset disposal relief:

Disposal 2:	£20,000	
	(£18,000)	loss from Disposal 3
	£2,000	
	(£2,000)	part of annual exemption
	0	taxable
Disposal 1:	£30,000	
	(£1,000)	remainder of annual exemption
	£29,000	taxable

28.4.7 Tax rates and payment

28.4.7.1 Tax rate(s)

There are three tax rates:

(a) *Business asset disposal relief rate* – for gains qualifying for business asset disposal relief, the tax rate is 14% (regardless of the taxpayer's income tax position).

(b) *Standard rate* – to the extent that the taxpayer's taxable income and any gains do not total more than the basic rate threshold for income tax (£37,700 in 2025/26) the tax rate is 18% on gains that do not qualify for business asset disposal relief.

(c) *Higher rate* – once the combination of taxable income and gains exceeds £37,700, any gains above that threshold that do not qualify for business asset disposal relief are subject to a tax rate of 24%.

In calculating how much (if any) of a taxpayer's gains are below the basic rate threshold, gains that qualify for business asset disposal relief are taxed before those that do not so qualify.

EXAMPLE 1

Sonia has taxable income in 2025/26 of £30,000. She has a taxable gain qualifying for business asset disposal relief of £40,000, and a gain that has no such relief of £20,000 (after deducting the annual exemption). The gain that qualifies for business asset disposal relief will be taxed at 14%. The other gain will all be taxed at 24% (because the combination of taxable income and the business asset disposal relief gain exceeds £37,700). Sonia's CGT liability will therefore be:

On gains qualifying for business asset disposal relief: £40,000 x 14%	£5,600
On gains not qualifying for business asset disposal relief: £20,000 x 24%	£4,800
Total CGT for the tax year	£10,400

EXAMPLE 2

Thor has taxable income in 2025/26 of £15,000 (£22,700 below the basic rate tax threshold). To supplement his income, he sells some shares that qualify for business asset disposal relief and some that do not. He has a taxable gain that qualifies for business asset disposal relief of £10,000, and other gains that have no such relief of £15,000 (after deducting the annual exemption). Thor's CGT liability will be:

On gains qualifying for business asset disposal relief: £10,000 x 14%	£1,400
On other gains under the basic rate threshold: £12,700 x 18%	£2,286
On other gains above the basic rate threshold: £2,300 x 24%	£552
Total CGT for the tax year	£4,238

28.4.7.2 Payment date

Any CGT due in respect of a tax year is normally payable on or before 31 January following the end of the tax year. The instalment option may be available in very limited circumstances (see below).

28.4.7.3 Instalment option (TCGA 1992, s 281)

In limited circumstances, payment may be made by 10 annual instalments, the first being on the usual date for payment of CGT (31 January following the tax year of the disposal), with interest being charged on the outstanding tax.

The conditions are:

(a) the disposal giving rise to the CGT must have been a gift; and

(b) hold-over relief must not be available (as opposed to merely not claimed); this means that the instalment option will rarely be relevant to disposal of business interests by sole traders, partners or shareholders in private companies except in relation to assets of the business which are investments; and

(c) the property disposed of must have been either land, a controlling shareholding in any company, or any shareholding (whether controlling or otherwise) in a company whose shares are unquoted.

EXAMPLE

Lionel gives away some land (held as an investment) in July 2025. He makes no other disposals during the 2025/26 tax year. His gain is £60,000 and he is a higher-rate taxpayer for income tax.

> Lionel can deduct his annual exemption of £3,000 from the gain of £60,000 to give a taxable amount of £57,000. Tax at 24% on this amount is £13,680 and the tax can be paid by 10 annual instalments, the first instalment being due on 31 January 2027.

28.4.8 Interrelation between reliefs and exemption

On any given disposal realising a gain it is possible that more than one relief could apply to it and that the disponer's annual exemption is available so that the taxpayer may have to choose which relief(s) to claim.

28.4.8.1 Roll-over relief on the replacement of qualifying assets

If a gain is to be rolled over, business asset disposal relief (if available) cannot apply to it, neither can the annual exemption be set against it. This roll-over relief cannot generally be used in conjunction with hold-over relief or roll-over relief on incorporation.

28.4.8.2 Hold-over relief on gifts of business assets

If a gain is to be held-over, business asset disposal relief (if available) cannot apply to it, neither can the donor's annual exemption be set against it. The relief cannot generally be used in conjunction with the roll-over reliefs.

28.4.8.3 Roll-over relief on the incorporation of a business

To the extent that a gain is to be rolled over when shares are received in consideration for the transfer of the business, business asset disposal relief (if available) cannot apply to it and neither can the annual exemption. The relief in these circumstances cannot be used at the same time as roll-over relief on replacement of qualifying assets (shares do not qualify) or hold-over relief (there is usually no gift).

If, however, part of the consideration is in cash and part in shares, it might, in certain circumstances, be possible to use the roll-over relief on incorporation for that proportion of the gain attributable to the part of the business exchanged for shares, leaving business asset disposal relief and the annual exemption to be used on the proportion of the gain attributable to the part of the business sold for cash.

28.4.8.4 Business asset disposal relief

From the above it can be seen that the business asset disposal relief rate cannot be claimed when using any of the hold-over or roll-over reliefs. The annual exemption, if available, can be used to reduce gains before the business asset disposal relief rate is applied.

28.4.8.5 The annual exemption

This is the final point to consider when looking at the various business reliefs and exemptions, and its interrelation with each of the other reliefs is set out above.

> **EXAMPLE**
>
> Malcolm has run a manufacturing business as a sole trader for 15 years (his only business venture). In July 2025, he gives the business to Patsy, his daughter. Malcolm's accountant advises him that the chargeable gain on the chargeable business assets is £135,000.
>
> *Option 1* – Malcolm and Patsy can claim hold-over relief for the £135,000 gain. This avoids Malcolm paying any CGT, but means HMRC will state that he cannot use business asset disposal relief or his annual exemption in respect of the gain. Patsy, therefore, effectively takes over liability for the whole £135,000 gain when she disposes of the business in future.

Option 2 – Malcolm could claim business asset disposal relief so that the £135,000 gain is reduced by Malcolm's annual exemption of £3,000, leaving a taxable amount of £132,000 to be taxed at 14%. The resulting bill of £18,480 would be Malcolm's liability to pay by 31 January 2027.

Assuming Malcolm is able to fund the tax bill arising from Option 2, he will have a choice of which option to take. The best option overall is likely to depend on whether Patsy will continue to run the business for long enough to qualify for business asset disposal relief in her own name. If she does then Option 1 may be most attractive – it will not matter that Malcolm did not claim any business asset disposal relief as Patsy will be able to do so instead (assuming that Patsy is at no risk of breaching her lifetime business asset disposal relief threshold).

28.5 INHERITANCE TAX – BUSINESS RELIEFS

As described in **28.3.2**, a relief may be available to reduce the value transferred by a transfer of value for IHT purposes. The reliefs should be considered after applying any spouse/civil partner or charity exemption (see ***Legal Foundations***). The reliefs are designed to try to ensure that businesses are not unnecessarily broken up by the burden of IHT following gifts made during the donor's life or on their death.

28.5.1 Business property relief (IHTA 1984, ss 103–114)

Business property relief ('BPR') operates to reduce the value transferred by a transfer of value of relevant business property by a certain percentage.

28.5.1.1 Conditions for the relief to apply

(a) **Relevant business property**

The amount of relief given depends on the type of property being transferred.

(i) A reduction of 100% of the value transferred is allowed for transfers of value where the value transferred is attributable to certain defined types of 'relevant business property' (meaning that there will be no charge to IHT in respect of those assets). These are:
  - (a) a business or an interest in a business (including a partnership share);
  - (b) company shares that are not listed on a recognised stock exchange (AIM is not included in the definition of stock exchange for these purposes). Only the value of the shares attributable to business/trading activities is eligible for the relief.

(ii) A reduction of 50% of the value transferred is allowed for transfers of value where the value transferred is attributable to any other relevant business property. They are:
  - (a) company shares that are listed on a recognised stock exchange if the transferor had voting control of the company immediately before the transfer;
  - (b) land, buildings, machinery or plant owned by the transferor personally but used for business purposes by a partnership of which the transferor is a member, or by a company (whether quoted or unquoted) of which the transferor has voting control.

Note: Voting control, for these purposes, means the ability to exercise over 50% of the votes on all resolutions. Such control may be denied by a provision in the company's articles of association that gives weighted voting rights on certain matters (eg a *Bushell v Faith* clause on a resolution to dismiss a director). The purpose and effect of such an article will be to prevent, for example, a majority shareholder from exercising their normal voting control on those matters and thus deprive them of control.

In assessing whether or not a person has voting control, separate shareholdings of spouses or civil partners can, in certain circumstances, be taken as one, so that if the combined percentage of the votes gives the couple voting control then the test will be satisfied (IHTA 1984, s 269).

(b) Time limits

(i) Transferor's ownership

To attract any relief at all, the asset or assets in question must have been owned by the transferor *for at least two years* at the time of the transfer or, broadly, must be a replacement for relevant business property where the combined period of ownership is two years (this would include the situation where a sole trader or individual partner incorporated their business; the shares in the company they received in return would be relevant business property). If property is inherited from a spouse or civil partner, the surviving spouse/civil partner is deemed to have owned the property from the date it was originally acquired by the deceased spouse/civil partner (but this rule does not apply to lifetime transfers between spouses/civil partners).

EXAMPLE

Claire has owned relevant business property (some unlisted trading company shares) for 18 months, having inherited them from her husband (who owned them for the previous five years). If Claire gives the shares to her daughter, Elizabeth, on 1 June 2025, they qualify for BPR at 100%.

(ii) Transferee's ownership

Where there is a lifetime transfer that is followed by the death of the transferor within seven years, the BPR given at the time of the lifetime transfer will be withdrawn unless the transferee still owns the business property (or qualifying substituted property) at the date of the transferor's death (or, if earlier, the transferee's own death).

EXAMPLE

Suppose that in the previous example, Elizabeth sells the company shares on 1 December 2025 and spends the proceeds on her house. Claire then dies on 1 March 2026. The BPR given at the time of the lifetime gift in June 2024 is withdrawn and the transfer is treated as if the BPR never applied. The transfer will therefore be taxed as a PET that has become chargeable due to the transferor's death within seven years after the transfer.

28.5.1.2 Application of the relief

A number of further points must be considered when applying BPR (at 100% or 50% as the case may be).

(a) The transfer need not be of the transferor's entire interest in the business or their entire shareholding.

(b) Where a person has entered into a contract for sale of their interest in a business (or their company shares), their interest is then taken to be in the proceeds of sale; since cash is not relevant business property, no relief will be available where there is a binding contract for sale. Examples of when such a situation may arise are:

   (i) partnership – under the terms of a partnership agreement which provides that on a partner's retirement or death, for example, the continuing partners *will* buy and the former partner (or their PRs) *will* sell the share of the former partner (as opposed to there merely being an option to sell/purchase);

(ii) company – under the terms of a shareholders' agreement which provides that on the occurrence of a given event, for example the shareholder's death, the shareholder's PRs *will* sell to the remaining shareholders who *will* buy those shares. (Again, the problem can be avoided by the use of an option to sell/ purchase.)

EXAMPLE 1

A is a 60% shareholder in XY plc (a quoted company) which he established many years ago. He gives half of his shares to his daughter on her 21st birthday. Three years later he gives the other half of his holding to his son on his 21st birthday. A dies in the following year.

Provided A's daughter still owns the shares on A's death (when the transfer becomes chargeable), the value transferred will be reduced by 50%. The gift to A's son will not qualify for any BPR because a 30% holding in a quoted company is not relevant business property.

EXAMPLE 2

For many years C and D have owned 55% and 25% respectively of the shares in a private company whose articles are in the form of Table A; they have also owned the business premises in equal shares as tenants in common. They are both killed in a road accident and their entire estates are inherited by C's son and D's daughter respectively.

C's shareholding and D's shareholding both qualify for 100% BPR. C's interest in the premises qualifies for relief at 50% because his shareholding gave 'control'; D's interest in the premises does not qualify for relief at all.

EXAMPLE 3

For many years E, F and G have been partners, sharing profits and losses equally; E and F have also owned the business premises in equal shares as tenants in common. There is no provision in their partnership agreement dealing with the purchase and sale of assets on the death or retirement of a partner. E and F are both killed in a road accident and their entire estates are inherited by E's son and F's daughter respectively.

The interest in the business of each partner qualifies for 100% BPR and also each partner's interest in the premises qualifies for BPR at 50%. (No relief at all would have been available if there was a partnership agreement under which there was a binding contract for the purchase and sale of the partners' interests.)

It can be seen that more favourable treatment is given to partners who own assets used by their business than to shareholders who own assets used by their company.

In the Autumn 2024 Budget, the Government announced significant changes to BPR to take effect from 6 April 2026. In essence, these changes will limit the availability of the 100% reduction to £1 million of the value of business property transferred, with the 50% reduction applying above this sum. In addition, the relief on unlisted shares will be reduced to 50%.

28.5.2 Agricultural property relief (IHTA 1984, ss 115–124)

28.5.2.1 Sole traders and partners

This relief operates to reduce the agricultural value of agricultural property (as defined) by a certain percentage. The 'agricultural value' is the value of the property if it were subject to a perpetual covenant prohibiting its use other than for agriculture. This will be significantly less than its market value if, for example, the land has development potential (eg for housing).

That part of the property's value which is over and above its 'agricultural value' will not qualify for any agricultural property relief, but may qualify for business property relief (see **28.5.1.3**). A reduction of 100% is allowed where either (broadly) the transferor had the right to vacant possession immediately before the transfer or where the property was subject to a letting commencing on or after 1 September 1995. A reduction of 50% is allowed in other cases. Further conditions which must also be satisfied for any relief are either that the property was occupied by the transferor for the purposes of agriculture for the two years prior to the transfer or that it was owned by them for the seven years prior to the transfer and was occupied by someone throughout that period for the purposes of agriculture.

Agricultural property relief will also be subject to the changes to take effect from 6 April 2026 referred to above. The £1 million limit will apply to agricultural property (the value of agricultural property is combined with that of business property for the purpose of the limit).

28.5.2.2 Shareholders

This relief is also available where the agricultural property is held by a company in which the transferor of shares had control. The value of the shares may be reduced by the appropriate percentage (100% or 50%) where the value of the shares is attributable to the agricultural value of the company's agricultural property. The company's occupancy or ownership of the land (for two years or for seven years (see **28.5.2.1**)) is treated as that of the transferor of shares and the transferor must also have held the shares for the qualifying two- or seven-year period (as the case may be).

28.5.2.3 Relationship with business property relief

Agricultural property relief is given in priority to business property relief (see **28.5.1**), but any of the value transferred not reduced by agricultural property relief may qualify for business property relief.

28.5.3 Instalment option (IHTA 1984, ss 227 and 228)

Provided the requirements described below are met, payment of IHT can be made by 10 annual instalments, the first being due when the tax would normally be due.

28.5.3.1 Qualifying assets

The instalment option is available in relation to tax on the following assets only:

(a) land;

(b) a business or an interest in a business;

(c) shares (whether quoted or unquoted) which gave the transferor control;

(d) in certain circumstances, non-controlling shares which are not listed on a recognised stock exchange, for example:

  (i) where the shares are worth over £20,000 and constitute at least 10% of the nominal value of the company's issued share capital; or

  (ii) where HMRC is satisfied that payment of tax in a lump sum would cause undue hardship; or

  (iii) where the IHT attributable to the shares and any other instalment option property in the estate amounts to at least 20% of the IHT payable on the estate following the deemed transfer of value made on death.

28.5.3.2 Application of the relief

The instalment option is available in certain circumstances only, primarily:

(a) where the recipient of a PET or LCT is paying the IHT. The instalment option applies where IHT is payable on the transfer, or where IHT (or additional IHT) becomes payable as a result of the transferor's death within seven years of the transfer and the transferee still owns the original asset (or a qualifying replacement) at the date of the death. If the asset is later sold, the outstanding tax must then be paid;

(b) where personal representatives are paying the tax. The instalment option applies where the transfer of value was the deemed transfer on death.

Interest is charged on the outstanding tax only if the asset in question is land which is not business or agricultural land, or is shares in an investment company, except that if an instalment is in arrears, interest then becomes chargeable on the overdue instalment.

28.6 SUMMARIES AND CHECKLISTS

(1) The occasions for a capital tax charge against an individual are:

CGT	IHT
Disposal by sale	Lifetime chargeable transfer (LCT)
Disposal by gift	PET where death occurs within seven years
[NOT death]	Death

(2) The possible business reliefs include:

CGT	IHT
Roll-over relief on replacement of qualifying assets	Agricultural property relief
Hold-over relief (gifts)	BPR
Roll-over relief on incorporation of a business	
Business asset disposal relief	

(3) When to consider the CGT reliefs:

Depending on the client's circumstances, one or more of the CGT reliefs listed at (2) above may be available on the disposal of a business interest, and a choice as to which relief to use may have to be made. Some examples of common scenarios are given below, along with the reliefs that may apply to the gain.

(a) Sale of sole trade or share in partnership:
  (i) business asset disposal relief (+ annual exemption); or
  (ii) roll-over relief on the replacement of qualifying assets

(b) Gift of sole trade or share in partnership:
  (i) business asset disposal relief (+ annual exemption); or
  (ii) hold-over relief.

(c) Sale of company shares:
  (i) business asset disposal relief (+ annual exemption).

(d) Gift of company shares:
  (i) business asset disposal relief (+ annual exemption); or
  (ii) hold-over relief.

(e) Transfer of sole trade or partnership to a company:
  (i) roll-over relief on incorporation; or
  (ii) business asset disposal relief (+ annual exemption).

Notes:

(1) In any of the above scenarios, consideration should also be given to the possibility of focussed CGT reliefs designed for particular situations (such as EIS relief).

(2) In scenarios (b) and (d), where gifts are being made, consideration should also be given to IHT and the availability of BPR.

CHAPTER 29

TAX CONSIDERATIONS IN CHOICE OF MEDIUM

LEARNING OUTCOMES

After reading this chapter you will be able to:

- appreciate how the choice of business organisation (sole trader, partnership or company) can affect the tax treatment of a business
- identify the reliefs available to different types of business medium.

29.1 INTRODUCTION

In order to compare the tax treatment of different forms of business organisations, it is necessary to consider not only the year-by-year treatment of the trading income generated by the business, but also the longer-term possibilities of capital taxation. Taxation of trading profits requires a comparison between taxation of the self-employed (ie sole trader or partners) and taxation of the incorporated business where profits may be taxed in the hands of the company, its directors and employees and/or its shareholders. Possible capital taxation involves a comparison between the reliefs available for sole traders or individual partners on the one hand and for a company and/or its shareholders on the other hand.

29.2 TRADING INCOME

Although the trading income of a company is calculated under broadly the same rules as that of a partnership or a sole trader (applying CTA 2009, Part 3 for a company and ITTOIA 2005, Part 2 for individuals carrying on a trade – see **Chapter 21**), significant differences arise from the fact that the company is a taxpayer in its own right, quite separate from its directors, employees and shareholders.

29.2.1 Comparing charging provisions and rates of tax

29.2.1.1 Profits withdrawn from the business

If *all* of the company's trading profit is withdrawn as directors' fees/employees' salaries, no corporation tax will be chargeable because the company is left with no taxable profit; the directors' fees/employees' salaries will suffer income tax under the employment income provisions in the ITEPA 2003. If the same business were run by a partnership or a sole trader, income tax would be charged on the income of the individual partners or the sole trader under the trading income provisions in Part 2 of the ITTOIA 2005. It follows, therefore, that a comparison of the tax treatment of the income of these businesses becomes a comparison between the application of tax on employment income in the context of the company's directors/employees and the application of trading income rules, in the context of the partnership or sole trader. Particular differences are:

(a) the rules on deductible expenditure are more generous under the trading income rules ('wholly and exclusively for the purposes of the trade') than under the ITEPA 2003 ('wholly, exclusively and necessarily in the performance of the employee's duties');

(b) there are rules under the ITEPA 2003 (but not under the trading income rules) for charging income tax on fringe benefits provided by the company, so that if a director/employee uses assets of the company (eg a dwelling) without payment to the company, there is a charge to income tax;

(c) the timing of payment of tax is more favourable under the trading income rules (tax in two instalments where calculation is based on profits of the accounting period which ends in the tax year) than under the ITEPA 2003 (tax on a current year basis collected at source under the PAYE system).

29.2.1.2 Profits retained in the business

If a business is run by a company and none (or only some) of the company's trading profit is withdrawn as salaries, the profits retained in the business attract corporation tax. If the same business were run by a partnership or a sole trader, income tax would be charged on the entire profits irrespective of whether or not they were withdrawn from the business as opposed to being 'ploughed back'. A comparison of the tax treatment of the income of these businesses is therefore between the payment of corporation tax and the payment of income tax. Differences arise as to rates of tax payable:

Company Profits		Income of Partners or Sole Trader	
Company's profit	Corporation tax rate	Individual's taxable income	Income tax rate
£	£	£	£
All profits	19%/25%	0–37,700	20%
		37,701–125,140	40%
		over 125,140	45%

For a company, the rate of corporation tax will never exceed 25%. Individual partners (or sole traders) will pay income tax on all of the trading profit, although they will also have their personal allowances to set against the income. This distinction is more likely to be significant when, in a profitable business, the profits are being ploughed back to finance growth: in a company, the retained profits will be taxed at 25% (or 19% if the standard small profits rate applies), while for an equivalent partnership or sole trader the higher rate of income tax (40%) or even the additional rate of 45% may be applicable.

29.2.2 Reliefs for a trading loss

Although most loss-relieving provisions applicable to companies have an equivalent provision applicable to individual partnerships and sole traders, there are three particular points worth noting.

29.2.2.1 Start-up relief (ITA 2007, s 72)

Start-up relief, which permits trading losses assessable in the first four tax years of a business to be carried back and set against the income of the taxpayer for the preceding three tax years, is only available to individual partners and sole traders (see **24.4.1**).

29.2.2.2 Carry-across reliefs – setting losses against other income or gains

A company's trading losses relieved under the CTA 2010, s 37 cannot be set against the income or gains of the persons running the company, whereas the trading losses of an individual partner or a sole trader can be set against that person's other income and, possibly, gains under s 64 of the ITA 2007 (see **22.7.1** and **24.4.2**).

29.2.2.3 Terminal loss relief by carry-back

When a company ceases to carry on a trade, a trading loss sustained in its final 12 months may be carried back and set against its profits of any description (income or capital) for the previous three years (CTA 2010, s 39). The position is more restrictive for sole traders or individual partners; for these taxpayers, a trading loss made in the final 12 months' trading has a three-tax-year carry back, but the loss can only be set against previous profits of the same trade (ITA 2007, s 89 (see **22.7.2** and **24.2.4**)).

29.2.3 Pension arrangements

The detail of the rules relating to pension payments is outside the scope of this book. However, the ability to make pension arrangements with the benefit of tax relief is greater for a company and its directors/employees through an occupational pension scheme or through the company contributing to the individual's personal pension scheme because two parties are contributing, both with the benefit of tax relief. Where a partner or sole trader is making pension arrangements, they are the only person contributing, albeit with tax relief.

29.2.4 National Insurance contributions

National Insurance contributions are subject to complex rules, and thresholds are adjusted each year. If a business is structured with employer and employees (almost inevitable in the case of a company whereas a partnership or sole trader may have the option of not employing staff), the Class 1 contributions may be greater than the Class 2 and 4 contributions made by the self-employed.

29.2.5 Relief for interest paid

An individual who pays interest on a loan to enable them to buy a share in a partnership or to lend to a partnership will obtain income tax relief for that interest (see **25.2.4**). An individual who pays interest on a loan to enable them to buy shares in a company or to lend to a company in which they are a shareholder will obtain income tax relief only if certain conditions are met; these conditions are that the company must be a close company and that the shareholder must either own more than 5% of the ordinary share capital or work for the greater part of their time in the management or conduct of the company (however few shares they hold – see **23.2.3**).

29.3 AVAILABLE RELIEFS FOR CAPITAL GAINS

29.3.1 Comparing companies with partners and sole traders

29.3.1.1 Indexation

Companies benefit from the indexation allowance throughout the period of ownership of a chargeable asset, whereas gains made by individuals do not. The lowest CGT rate of 10% tax for individuals is, however, almost half that of the corporation tax rate. Which regime is more favourable will depend on a number of factors, including the nature and amount of the gain, the rate of inflation and the length of ownership of the asset in question.

29.3.1.2 Roll-over relief on replacement of qualifying assets

The roll-over relief on replacement of qualifying assets is available on disposals by individuals and partners and, in a modified form, by companies.

29.3.1.3 Reliefs available only to companies

The main example to note in this category is the exemption for disposals of substantial shareholdings.

29.3.1.4 Key reliefs available only to individuals

(a) Hold-over relief on a gift of business assets.
(b) Roll-over relief on incorporation of an unincorporated business.
(c) Business asset disposal relief.

29.3.1.5 The annual exemption

The annual exemption is not available to companies.

29.3.2 Comparing individual shareholders with individual partners and sole traders

The details of the main available business reliefs were considered in **Chapter 28**. A general difference between the treatment of an individual shareholder on the one hand and individual partners or sole traders on the other lies in the fact that, for the shareholder to obtain relief, additional conditions must be satisfied which do not have to be satisfied by a partner or a sole trader.

29.3.2.1 Roll-over relief on the replacement of qualifying assets

A major difference is that shares do not count as qualifying assets for the purposes of roll-over relief on replacement, whereas a sole trader or partner will have an interest in qualifying assets (such as premises and goodwill). Where a shareholder disposes of a qualifying asset (such as premises) used by the company and acquires another qualifying asset, the company must be the personal trading company of that shareholder.

29.3.2.2 Hold-over relief

If the disposal is of company shares, the company need only be the shareholder's personal company if the shares are quoted (see **28.4.2**). Where a shareholder makes a disposal other than at arm's length of a business asset (eg premises) used by the company, the company must be the personal trading company of that shareholder.

29.3.2.3 Business asset disposal relief

Business asset disposal relief is available for shareholdings in both quoted and unquoted trading companies, but only if the shareholder is both an employee/officer and holds 5% or more of the company's voting shares. Assets held by the individual and used by the company will qualify for the relief only if the company is a qualifying company by reference to the individual owner.

29.4 POSSIBILITY OF DOUBLE TAXATION OF A COMPANY'S INCOME AND CAPITAL PROFITS

29.4.1 Distributions

Every pound of profit a company makes is charged to corporation tax at 25% (or 19% if the standard small profits rate applies) (see **22.5.2**). When that profit, net of tax, is distributed as a dividend to its individual shareholders, it is received as their Savings and Investment income (ITTOIA 2005, Part 4) (see **27.3.1**). The same profit is thus capable of attracting a double charge.

29.4.2 Capital gains tax

Because the company has a separate legal personality and therefore is a taxpayer separate from the shareholders who own it, there is a possibility that capital gains on the company's assets may give rise to charges to corporation tax against the company and CGT against the individuals concerned. Suppose, for example, that a company owns some land as an investment. The land has increased in value by £100,000 (after allowable expenditure and indexation) and correspondingly the shares in the company have increased in value by £81,000 (after allowing for a potential corporation tax charge of £19,000). If the company were to sell off the land and the shareholders were to sell some shares, the company would be liable to pay corporation tax on its gain and the individual shareholders would be liable to pay CGT on their gains. Even though the shareholders' gains are at least partly attributable to the gain on the premises which is charged to corporation tax, the shareholders are chargeable to CGT without credit for the corporation tax paid by the company. If, on the other hand, the land in the above situation was owned by a partnership, the individual partners might pay CGT on their disposal of the land, but there would be no equivalent of the second charge to tax which occurred in the company context.

29.4.3 Avoiding the double charge

To avoid the possibility of this double charge to taxation suffered by a company and its shareholders, it may be advisable for an appreciating asset, such as premises, to be owned by a shareholder or shareholders individually rather than by the company; the company may be allowed to use the premises under the terms of a lease or a licence. The advantage of individual ownership of assets used by the company is that, although the individual owner may suffer CGT on a disposal, there can be no second charge to tax as might occur if the company owned and disposed of the asset. There are, however, potential problems with such an arrangement from a tax perspective. For IHT business property relief, a maximum 50% relief will be available, and then only if the shareholder has voting control of the company (see **28.5.1**).

29.5 AVAILABLE RELIEFS FOR INHERITANCE TAX

The details of the available reliefs were considered in **Chapter 28**. As with CGT reliefs, there are additional conditions imposed on shareholders which may result in their receiving less favourable treatment than a sole trader or individual partner.

29.5.1 Agricultural property relief

For a shareholder to qualify in respect of their shareholding, they must have had control of the company at the time of the transfer; for a sole trader or partner, there is no equivalent of this condition.

29.5.2 Business property relief

For a shareholder, relief at 100% is available on the transfer of unquoted shares and at 50% on the transfer of quoted shares which give the shareholder a controlling interest. For a partner or sole trader transferring an interest in the business or the business, 100% relief is available.

Assets such as land, buildings, machinery or plant used by a partnership but owned by a partner will qualify for 50% BPR. This relief is available in the company context only if the owner is a shareholder whose holding yields control of the company.

29.5.3 Instalment option for payment of IHT

A business or an interest in a business held by a sole trader or individual partner always qualifies as property in relation to which the instalment option may be available, but a shareholding will qualify only if it is a controlling shareholding or, failing that, if further conditions are satisfied (see **28.5.3**).

29.6 CONCLUSION

Whether it is preferable to trade as a sole trader, in a partnership or via a company will depend, from a tax viewpoint, on the exact circumstances of the client's business and the tax regime in force at the time of consideration. It is not possible to say that one way of conducting business will always be more tax efficient than another.

Summary of Main Rates and Allowances

Value Added Tax

Rates:	Standard rate	20%
Registration threshold:		£90,000

Income Tax – 2025/26

(For 2025/26 the Welsh Parliament has set income tax rates in line with those for England.)

Rates:

Income (except savings and dividend income)		
	– basic rate (£1–37,700)	20%
	– higher rate (£37,701–125,140)	40%
	– additional rate (above £125,140)	45%
Savings income	– starting rate for savings (£1– £5,000) (only applicable to extent income (except savings and dividend income) is less than £5,000)	0%
	– basic rate	20%
	– higher rate	40%
	– additional rate	45%
Dividend income	– dividend ordinary rate (within basic rate band)	8.75%
	– dividend upper rate (within higher rate band)	33.75%
	– dividend additional rate	39.35%

Income Tax Allowances:

Personal Allowance £12,570
(restricted for those with net income above £100,000 and not available for those with net income of £125,140 or above)

Personal Saving Allowance	
Basic rate taxpayer	£1,000
Higher rate taxpayer	£500
Additional rate taxpayer	Nil
Dividend Allowance	£500

Capital Gains Tax – 2025/26

Rates:

Individuals	
Business asset disposal relief rate	– 14%
Standard rate	– 18%
Higher rate	– 24%
Annual exempt amount:	
Individuals	£3,000

Inheritance Tax – 2025/26

Rates:

£0 to £325,000	nil %*
over £325,000	40%**

* There is a separate Residence Nil Rate Band where the death estate includes a qualifying residential interest which is being closely inherited (see **Legal Foundations**).

** A lower rate of 36% applies where the charity gift conditions are met

Transfers on death

Full rates apply.

Lifetime transfers

(a) Potentially exempt transfers

Gifts to individuals, and gifts into certain trusts.

(i) On or within seven years of death

On death, the full rates apply with a tapered reduction in the tax payable on transfers as follows:

Years between gift and death	Percentage of full charge
0–3	100
3–4	80
4–5	60
5–6	40
6–7	20

Note: The scale in force at date of death applies

(ii) More than seven years before death – gift is exempt therefore NIL tax payable.

(b) Chargeable transfers

Gifts to most trusts and gifts involving companies.

At the time of gift, half the full rates apply. If the gift also falls within seven years of death, (a)(i) above applies but the lifetime tax will be credited against tax due on death.

Corporation Tax (effective rate) – Financial Year 2025/26

Profits up to £50,000 (all profits)	19%
Profits exceeding £250,000 (all profits)	25%

Marginal relief is available

Stamp Duty – main rates on sales – 2025/26

Shares and securities

£0–1,000	Nil
Over £1,000 (rounded up to nearest £5)	0.5%

Stamp Duty Land Tax (non-residential property)

Consideration:

£0–150,000	Nil
£150,001–£250,000	2%
Over £250,000	5%

PART V

SUMMARY – TAXATION

Topic	*Summary*	*References*
The lawyer's role	A lawyer advising a business on tax matters must, of course, understand the way in which relevant taxes are calculated. This is, however, only a means to an end. The lawyer's wider role is to help enable the business to structure its tax affairs in the most efficient manner possible within the legal framework provided by legislation, case law and professional practice. This summary highlights some of the important reliefs and exemptions that exist for each tax covered in Part V and which assist the lawyer in that role.	
Corporation tax – liability	Corporation tax should be considered in relation to the income and chargeable gains of companies.	
Corporation tax – income profits	In relation to its trading profits, a company will seek to maximise its available deductible (income) expenditure and capital allowances.	**21.3**
	The amount of any capital allowance will depend on the type of expenditure and date of the expenditure.	**21.4**
	It may be possible to set a company's trading losses against other profits of the company, depending on the circumstances surrounding the loss.	**22.3**
Corporation tax – chargeable gains	A company's chargeable gains may be relieved in a number of ways. Reliefs include roll-over relief (on replacement of qualifying assets) and the exemption for disposals of substantial shareholdings.	**22.4**
Corporation tax – special provisions	Companies defined as being 'close' or within a 'group' are subject to anti-avoidance measures but also provide planning opportunities to mitigate corporation tax for the company and/or income tax for shareholders in the company.	**Chapter 23**
Income tax – liability	Income tax should be considered in relation to the income of individuals, including sole traders, partners and shareholders.	

Topic	Summary	References
Income tax – trading income	For a business with trading income, relief may be provided by the capital allowances regime.	**21.4**
	It may be possible to set trading losses made by an individual against their other income (and possibly capital gains), depending on the circumstances surrounding the loss.	**24.4**
	The date of payment of tax can be adjusted depending on when a business's accounting period ends. For all individuals, use should be made of any allowable reliefs and the personal allowance for each tax year.	**24.2, 24.3** and **25.2**
Income tax – employment income	For employees, the ITEPA 2003 contains rules on what income is taxable and what deductions are allowable. Payment is largely governed by the PAYE system.	**Chapter 26**
Income tax – savings income	Interest and dividends have special rules.	**Chapter 27**
Capital gains tax (CGT) – liability	CGT should be considered in relation to chargeable disposals made by individuals, including sole traders, partners and shareholders.	
CGT – reliefs	A variety of reliefs exist which may be of assistance depending on the type of disposal in question. All are subject to conditions on availability and application. Key reliefs in a business context include roll-over relief (on the replacement of qualifying assets), hold-over relief (on gifts of business assets), roll-over relief on incorporation (of an unincorporated business) and business asset disposal relief. Where possible, use should also be made of an individual's annual exemption for each tax year.	**28.4**
Inheritance tax (IHT) – liability	IHT should be considered in relation to transfers of value by individuals, including sole traders, partners and shareholders.	
IHT – reliefs	The key relief in a business context is business property relief. Its availability depends on the length of ownership of the asset in question by the transferor, the type of asset and its use, and the retention of the asset by the transferee (following a lifetime transfer). Other reliefs which may be of use in transferring business assets include the spouse/civil partner exemption and the annual exemption.	**28.5**

PART VI

CONVERSION

CHAPTER 30

CONVERSION AND THE IMMEDIATE IMPLICATIONS

LEARNING OUTCOMES

After reading this chapter you will be able to:

- describe how certain businesses can convert from one format to another
- the tax implications of such a change.

30.1 INTRODUCTION

This chapter considers the steps and documentation which would be required to convert from sole trader to partnership, from unincorporated business to limited company and from private limited company to public limited company. The tax implications that might ensue as a direct result of the transactions are also considered. For the individuals involved, the possible implications of being a partner rather than a sole trader, or of being a director/shareholder rather than being a partner or sole trader may be appreciated from the topics covered earlier in this book.

30.2 CONVERTING FROM SOLE TRADER TO PARTNERSHIP

30.2.1 Formalities

In law, the creation of a partnership is simply a question of whether or not the statutory definition of partnership under s 1 of the PA 1890 is satisfied. It follows that there is no necessary formality to be observed in converting from sole trader to partnership. Nevertheless, certain questions should be considered.

30.2.1.1 To whom will the business assets belong?

It is inevitable that certain assets, particularly stock-in-trade and goodwill, will belong to the partners jointly. In relation to other assets, it will be necessary for the partners to reach agreement as to ownership of assets. Ownership of assets can simply be dealt with by means of a clause in the partnership agreement which declares which assets are partnership assets and which assets used by the partnership belong to a partner individually. In relation to premises, for example, this clause would operate as a declaration of trust, where legal title is to remain in the name of one partner alone but the beneficial ownership is to be shared by all the partners. The partners may prefer a formal transfer of title from the original owner to the partners jointly, in which case a conveyance or transfer of the title will be required.

30.2.1.2 Will there be a formal partnership agreement?

Partners should always have a formal partnership agreement prepared, not only to deal with the question of ownership of assets but also to deal with all other aspects of the relationship as described in **Chapter 14**.

30.2.1.3 Will the CA 2006, ss 1192–1208 apply?

If the name of the business is to differ from those of the partners, it will be necessary to set out the names of the partners, together with an address for each partner for service of documents, on all business stationery and on the business premises.

30.2.2 Income tax implications

The incoming person will be assessed to income tax under the rules described in **25.2.3**.

30.2.3 Capital gains tax implications

Where the sole trader agrees to share ownership of the business assets with their new partner, they will be disposing of a share in those assets. If the assets are chargeable assets for CGT purposes (such as premises and goodwill), there will be a possible charge to CGT on the disponer. Reliefs and exemptions that might be available include:

(a) hold-over relief if the disposal is by way of gift to the incoming partner;

(b) business asset disposal relief;

(c) the annual exemption.

30.2.4 Stamp Duty Land Tax

The FA 2004 introduced provisions to charge stamp duty land tax on certain transfers into and out of partnerships. For further detail on the structure of stamp duty land tax, see **30.3.4**.

30.2.5 Employees

Since the former sole trader continues as an employer, there are no necessary implications so far as the positions of employees are concerned.

30.3 CONVERTING FROM UNINCORPORATED BUSINESS TO LIMITED COMPANY

30.3.1 Formalities

Because the conversion from unincorporated business to limited company involves a sale of the business by the present owners (partners or sole trader) to a new owner (the company), there are many more formalities attached to this conversion than to that described in **30.2**.

(a) The present owners will need to form, or purchase off the shelf, a company of which they will be the sole directors and shareholders and to which they will sell the business. The consideration for the sale will normally consist exclusively of shares in the company but some of the consideration may be in the form of debentures (under which part of the agreed price is left outstanding as a loan to the company) or cash.

(b) Once the company is ready, it will buy the business from the present owners and it will be necessary for the company to observe the usual formalities on decision-making within the company, on filing returns with the Registrar of Companies and on maintaining the company's own records.

(c) The sale of the business will be effected under the terms of a contract (a sale agreement); typically this will:

  (i) describe the assets being sold to the company;

  (ii) describe the price and the way in which it will be paid by the company, normally wholly in shares;

(iii) apportion the price to show the value attributed to the various assets or groups of assets comprised in the business and being sold to the company;

(iv) contain covenants on the part of the company designed to indemnify the sellers in respect of any liability for the existing debts, liabilities and obligations connected with the business;

(v) contain the company's acceptance of the seller's title to the premises, for example, to ensure that no claim could be brought by the company against the sellers for a defective title (this might otherwise have been a possibility should the company eventually change hands, eg in liquidation); and

(vi) contain the company's acceptance of the equipment and stock in its current condition so that no claim can be brought by the company against the sellers on the basis of these items being defective or in poor condition.

The contract so far described is designed to ensure not only that ownership of the business and assets changes hands effectively, but also that the sellers (who will run the company but who will in future be protected by limited liability) obtain maximum protection from the company for any present or future liability. This differs significantly from a contract for the sale of a business to a person with whom the sellers are not connected. In such a situation (an arm's length sale), the buyer will be anxious to obtain maximum protection for its own position, including obtaining from the sellers warranties as to assets (eg that they are in a satisfactory state of repair and unencumbered state), employees (terms of their employment and the existence of any disputes), possible litigation (liabilities revealed to the buyer) and environmental matters (compliance with legislation on environmental matters).

In pursuance of the sale agreement, title to certain assets (notably the business premises) will, if appropriate, be transferred to the company by separate document, whilst the title to other assets may pass under the sale agreement (eg goodwill) or by physical delivery (eg stock).

If, as is common, the company takes over the previous name of the business and this is not the same as the company's name, it will be necessary for the company's stationery and a notice at the company's place of business to state the company's name and address (CA 2006, ss 1202, 1204).

30.3.2 Income tax implications

30.3.2.1 General

When the unincorporated business is sold to the company, this is a discontinuance of the business so far as the partnership (or sole trader) is concerned. The individual partners (or sole trader) will be assessed to income tax under the rules for the closing tax year of a business (see **24.2.4**) up to the date of the transfer of the business. The company must pay corporation tax on profits thereafter.

30.3.2.2 Capital allowances

In so far as the partnership (or sole trader) sells to the company assets on which capital allowances have been claimed (eg machinery and plant), there may be a balancing charge to income tax on any profit identified by comparing the sale proceeds with the assets' written-down value. Suppose, for example, that some machinery cost £50,000 when purchased three and a half years ago and capital allowances have been claimed totalling £22,432, so that the written-down value is £27,568. If the value attributed to this machinery on the sale was £30,000, there could be a balancing charge to income tax on the £2,432 'profit'. In other words, this 'profit' would be taxed as part of the trading income in the closing tax year. Conversely, if there is a loss calculated on the same basis, there will be a deduction from profits for the final year for income tax purposes, known as a balancing allowance. If the company is controlled by the sellers of the business, the company and the sellers can elect within two years that the company shall take over the position of the sellers so that no balancing charge occurs (CAA 2001, ss 266 and 267).

30.3.2.3 Trading losses

If the unincorporated business has made trading losses which have not been relieved when the business is transferred to the company, these losses can be carried forward and deducted from income which the former partners (or sole trader) receive from the company, such as a salary as director or dividends as shareholder. This relief is available only if the business is transferred to the company wholly or mainly in return for the issue of shares in the company (see **24.4.5**).

30.3.2.4 Interest on a qualifying loan – income tax relief for partners

Details of this relief are given at **25.2.4**. If a partnership is incorporated as a close company and the loan remains outstanding following incorporation, relief will continue to be given if the conditions for the relief that apply to close companies are met (see **23.2.3**).

30.3.3 Capital gains tax implications

When the business is transferred to the company there will be a disposal to the company by the individual partners (or sole trader) of any of the assets of the business which do not remain in their personal ownership. In so far as these assets are chargeable assets for CGT purposes, there may be a charge to CGT. Reliefs which may be available include the following.

30.3.3.1 Roll-over relief on incorporation of a business (TCGA 1992, s 162)

The details of this relief were considered at **28.4.3**. The conditions for the relief to apply include the condition that the business must be sold to the company as a going concern with all of its assets (although cash may be ignored for this purpose). Transferring all the assets may present certain disadvantages, including:

(a) possible SDLT on the transfer of land;

(b) various other expenses incurred in transferring assets, such as professional fees;

(c) possible double charge to taxation in relation to future gains on those assets transferred (see **30.4**);

(d) availability of those assets transferred for payment of the company creditors.

30.3.3.2 Other reliefs

The taxpayer may not wish to roll over their gain on incorporation of the business. This may be the case if the taxpayer wishes to use one or more of the following (if available – see **28.4**):

(a) EIS deferral relief;

(b) business asset disposal relief;

(c) the annual exemption.

30.3.4 Stamp duty land tax

Stamp duty land tax is chargeable on a 'land transaction' in accordance with Part 4 of the FA 2003, and this would include the acquisition by a company of land included as part of a business. The amount of the charge (if any) will depend on the value of the (usually non-residential) land.

30.3.5 VAT implications

If the company is not registered for VAT purposes before the sale to the company takes place, the sellers must charge VAT on the transaction. This is avoided by ensuring that the company is registered for VAT before the sale takes place (under the Transfer of Going Concern (TOGC) Rules).

30.3.6 Employees

As a result of the sale of the business, the owner of the business and therefore the employer will change. Under the Transfer of Undertakings (Protection of Employment) Regulations 2006 (SI 2006/246), the new employer (the company) is taken to stand in the shoes of the old employer and the rights of the employees are automatically transferred. If no change is made affecting the employees, then there will be no immediate implications of the change of employer.

30.4 CONVERTING FROM PRIVATE TO PUBLIC LIMITED COMPANY

30.4.1 Procedural requirements

For information on the re-registration of a private company as a public company, see **12.4.3** above.

30.4.2 Implications

Since the company remains the same person, there are no implications for the company in terms of taxation or in terms of the employees. The real implications for the company lie in the realm of the company's ability to raise finance by inviting the public to purchase its shares and by applying to have its shares dealt in on the London Stock Exchange.

For the shareholders in the company there may be implications as to the availability or otherwise of capital tax reliefs. For example, some IHT reliefs (such as BPR and the instalment option) operate less favourably for shareholdings in quoted companies than for shareholdings in unquoted companies. Some CGT reliefs (such as business asset disposal relief) are dependent on the company being a 'personal trading company', which is less likely to be established in a company whose shares are quoted on the London Stock Exchange.

PART VII

SOME ASPECTS OF TRADING

Part VII looks at some aspects of trading.

Chapter 31 concerns the basics of sale of goods.

Chapter 32 examines employment and other regulatory concerns in running a business.

Chapter 33 and **34** examine agency and distribution agreements, and **Chapter 35** considers the impact of competition law.

CHAPTER 31

SALE OF GOODS

LEARNING OUTCOMES

After reading this chapter you will be able to:

- describe the principal rights and obligations of the buyer and seller in a business to business sale of goods contract
- list some of the options available to a seller of goods to ensure that the buyer pays the price
- explain how exclusions of liability in a business to business sale of goods contract are regulated by the Unfair Contract Terms Act 1977 and the Consumer Rights Act 2015
- describe the principal characteristics of the reasonableness test in the Unfair Contract Terms Act 1977.

31.1 FORMATION OF THE CONTRACT

It is important not to lose sight of the basics of contract law. You need to differentiate between an invitation to treat on the one hand, and an offer on the other hand. In a well-publicised problem, Argos had an incorrect price on its Internet website. The price for one model of television was £3 when it should have been £300. A number of customers 'bought' televisions online at £3. However, Argos refused to supply them, stating that the advertisement on its website was only an invitation to treat. Any response from a customer was therefore an offer which Argos could reject. The aggrieved customers argued that the advertisement was an offer which they were accepting, and that Argos was therefore bound as a party to a contract for the sale of goods. What do you think?

Other aspects of contract law which should be kept in mind are:

(a) whose standard terms apply? – the 'battle of the forms' (eg *Rimeco Riggleson & Metal Co v Queenborough Rolling Mill Co Ltd* [1995] CLY 798, *Sauter Automation Ltd v Goodman (Mechanical Services) Ltd (in liquidation)* (1986) 34 Build LR 81);

(b) 'prevail' clauses (where one set of terms proclaim that they prevail over any other set of terms) are generally considered not to work;

(c) timing – were the terms brought to the other party's attention at the time the contract was made?
(d) signing a document is acceptance of its terms; and
(e) a collateral contract could be construed to exist between the parties, so include a 'whole agreement' clause in the terms to exclude this possibility.

31.2 RELEVANT LEGISLATION

The sale of goods between businesses is governed by the Sale of Goods Act 1979 (SGA 1979). Where between businesses goods are supplied along with services, the Supply of Goods and Services Act 1982 applies (SGSA 1982).

The Unfair Contract Terms Act 1977 (UCTA 1977) deals with exclusion clauses in sales between businesses, including exclusion of the implied terms under the SGA 1979.

The Consumer Rights Act 2015 (CRA 2015) governs many aspects of sales by businesses to consumers, including most of the matters that in sales between businesses are regulated by the SGA 1979, the SGSA 1982 and the UCTA 1977. The 2015 Act contains a comprehensive code governing the terms implied into contracts for the sale of goods, and also for the provision of services, by businesses (referred to as 'traders') to consumers, and also the exclusion of those terms. Some other aspects of contracts between traders and consumers – for example the rules on price, payment and delivery described below at **31.6** – are still regulated by the SGA 1979.

The CRA 2015 does not affect contracts between consumers. Certain aspects of contracts between consumers are governed by the SGA 1979 and the SGSA 1982.

This chapter is principally concerned with transactions between businesses. Except where the CRA 2015 is expressly mentioned, this chapter describes the rules governing transactions between businesses under the SGA 1979 (and, where relevant, the SGSA 1982) and the UCTA 1977.

There are various other pieces of legislation aimed at protecting consumers and which are not considered here, for example the Electronic Commerce (EC Directive) Regulations 2002 (SI 2002/2013) and the Consumer Contracts (Information, Cancellation and Additional Charges) Regulations 2013 (SI 2013/3134).

31.2.1 Excluding the provisions of the SGA 1979

Section 55 of the SGA 1979 provides that the terms implied into a contract for the sale of goods by the SGA 1979 may be excluded by the agreement of the parties, subject to the UCTA 1977 (see **31.10.1**). As noted above, neither the terms implied by the SGA 1979 nor the UCTA 1977 apply to contracts for the sale of goods by traders to consumers.

In many non-consumer contracts, therefore, the provisions implied into a sale of goods contract by the SGA 1979 are a fallback. They would often be unsuitable for a commercial contract, and it may be perfectly valid and proper to exclude them.

31.3 WHAT ARE 'GOODS'?

Usually it is perfectly obvious whether the subject matter of the contract is goods (eg buying a chocolate bar in a shop). Section 61 of the SGA 1979 defines goods as 'including all personal chattels other than things in action and money'.

One area where there has been uncertainty in sales between businesses is computer programs. Are they goods or services? The terms implied into the contract would be different for goods and for services. In *St Albans City and District Council v International Computers Ltd* [1996] 4 All ER 481, it was held obiter that programs were goods when they were supplied on a disk. In *Horace Holman Group Ltd v Sherwood International Group Ltd* [2002] EWCA Civ 170, there was a dispute as to whether software was goods, and *St Albans* was cited as the authority. This does not answer the question if the program is supplied over the Internet, and arrives in the computer via a telephone line.

In contracts governed by the CRA 2015, the supply of computer programs is regulated separately from that of goods and services, as the supply of 'digital content'. However, the case law remains relevant to contracts between businesses and contracts between consumers.

31.4 SALE OF GOODS

Section 2(1) of the SGA 1979 defines a contract of sale of goods as:

> A contract by which the seller transfers or agrees to transfer the property in goods to the buyer for a money consideration, called the price.

Section 2(4) defines a sale:

> Where under a contract of sale the property in the goods is transferred from the seller to the buyer the contract is called a sale.

These provisions indicate how a sale of goods differs, for example, from a contract for hire of goods because the property in the goods changes hands. It differs from a gift of the goods because the buyer pays the seller money for the goods.

31.4.1 Definition of 'price' in s 8 of the SGA 1979

Section 8 provides that:

> (1) The price in a contract of sale may be fixed by the contract, or may be left to be fixed in a manner agreed by the contract, or may be determined by the course of dealing between the parties.
>
> (2) Where the price is not determined as mentioned in subsection (1) above the buyer must pay a reasonable price.
>
> (3) What is a reasonable price is a question of fact dependent on the circumstances of each particular case.

The basic position is that the parties are free to fix their own price. The fallback position is that if they fail to do so, the price will be a reasonable one. One problem with s 8 is that it is debatable whether or not the parties have concluded a contract at all, if they have not agreed such a basic term of the contract as the price of the goods. If they have not agreed the price then the price has not been fixed by the contract. Alternatively, the parties may conclude the contract but agree that the price will be fixed at some point in the future. This is an 'agreement to agree', which is usually taken to be unenforceable in English law (see, eg, *Courtney & Fairbairn Ltd v Tolaini Bros (Hotels) Ltd* [1975] 1 WLR 297; cf the older case of *Foley v Classique Coaches Ltd* [1934] 2 KB 1, where there was an arbitration clause if the parties could not agree on the price and the contract was upheld).

In *Cable & Wireless plc v IBM United Kingdom Ltd* [2002] 2 All ER (Comm) 1041, it was held that although the law did not generally recognise agreements to agree, the situation here was different. The fact that the agreement prescribed the means by which dispute negotiation should take place, by the identification of a specific recognised procedure, meant that the requirement for contractual certainty was fulfilled and the agreement was thus enforceable.

31.4.2 Agreeing the price (SGA 1979, ss 8, 9)

In most circumstances, the parties will agree the price (or, if they do not, then s 8 applies). It could be by use of a price list, or it could be by quotation or by negotiation. The contract should provide that the price is fixed, or, if not, how price changes between signing and delivery are to be dealt with.

If the parties leave the price to be fixed by the valuation of a third party and the third party does not do so, the contract is void (s 9).

31.4.3 Value added tax

A price in a contract is taken as including value added tax (VAT) unless otherwise specified (Value Added Tax Act 1994, s 19(2)). If the prices are to be exclusive of VAT, that must be expressly stated. Failure to do this will result in the seller receiving 20% less for their goods than they wanted.

31.4.4 Contracts governed by the CRA 2015

Sections 2, 8 and 9 of the SGA 1979 apply to contracts that are governed by the CRA 2015.

31.5 DUTIES OF THE SELLER

The SGA 1979 implies various duties in to a contract for the sale of goods subject to agreement to the contrary. This section deals with the seller's duties.

31.5.1 Duty to pass a good title (SGA 1979, s 12)

Section 12(1) implies into the contract a term that the seller has the right to sell the goods, that is, the seller has good title to the goods.

Section 12(2) provides that there is an implied warranty:

(a) that the goods are free from any charge or encumbrance not already known to the buyer, and

(b) that the buyer will enjoy quiet possession of the goods.

For example, in *Rubicon Computer Systems Ltd v United Paints Ltd* [2000] 2 TCLR 453 it was held that the seller attaching a time lock to a computer system in order to deny access to the buyer was in breach of the 'quiet possession' term under s 12(2)(b).

Section 12 of the SGA 1979 applies to all contracts for the sale of goods, except for contracts for the supply of goods by traders to consumers. For these contracts, a similar term is implied by s 17 of the CRA 2015.

31.5.2 Duty to hand over the goods (SGA 1979, s 27–29)

Section 27 of the SGA 1979 provides that it is the duty of the seller to deliver the goods, and of the buyer to accept and pay for them, in accordance with the terms of the contract of sale. In this case 'deliver' means to pass the goods voluntarily to the buyer (SGA 1979, s 61). It does not mean 'deliver' in the sense that the seller is obliged to get on their bike and take the goods round to the buyer's premises (ie, transportation of goods).

Section 28 states that delivery of the goods and payment should happen at the same time. For example, this is the normal case when a customer buys goods in a shop – the customer pays the money to the shopkeeper and is handed the goods then and there.

Under s 29 there is no general duty to dispatch the goods to the buyer. The arrangements for that are a matter to be agreed between the parties.

Section 29 of the SGA 1979 applies to all contracts for the sale of goods, except for contracts for the supply of goods by traders to consumers. For these contracts, s 28 of the CRA 2015 places traders under a duty to deliver the goods to the consumer, subject to any agreement to the contrary.

31.5.3 Time of delivery (SGA 1979, s 10)

The basic position under the SGA 1979 is that time of payment is not of the essence in a sale of goods contract (s 10(1)). However, s 10(2) provides that the parties can agree whether or not time is of the essence with regard to any other term of the contract.

The courts have ruled on various aspects on time of delivery. In *Hartley v Hymans* [1920] 3 KB 475, it was held that in ordinary commercial contracts for the sale of goods, where a time for delivery has been agreed, the rule is that time is prima facie of the essence with respect to delivery.

If the buyer waives the delivery date before the goods are delivered, the buyer is entitled to give the seller reasonable notice that the buyer will not accept the goods after a certain date. See *Charles Rickards Ltd v Oppenheim* [1950] 1 KB 616, where the buyer waived the original delivery date but then gave the seller reasonable notice of a revised date. The seller failed to meet even the revised date, and the buyer was held to be entitled to refuse to accept the goods.

Section 28(3) of the CRA 2015 implies a default delivery period of 30 days from the date of the contract into contracts between traders and consumers, unless a different delivery period is agreed. The consumer is entitled to terminate the contract if the trader fails to deliver within a further period reasonably specified by the consumer.

31.5.4 Delivery of the right quantity (SGA 1979, ss 30–31)

The seller must deliver the correct quantity of goods. Section 30(1) of the SGA 1979 provides that the buyer may reject the goods if the quantity is less than the contract quantity. However, if the goods are accepted then the buyer has to pay for them at the contract rate. Section 31(1) provides that the buyer is not obliged to accept delivery in instalments.

31.5.5 Delivery of the right quality – sale by description (SGA 1979, s 13)

Section 13 of the SGA 1979 implies a term that the goods sold should comply with their description. This could apply to goods bought from a catalogue, for example. In *Beale v Taylor* [1967] 1 WLR 1193, the sale was held to be a sale by description even though the buyer inspected the car after having seen the advertisement for it in the local paper.

31.5.6 Delivery of the right quality – satisfactory quality (SGA 1979, s 14(2))

Section 14(2) of the SGA 1979 implies a term that, in a sale in the course of a business, the goods are to be of satisfactory quality. This includes fitness for the common purposes of the goods, appearance and finish, freedom from minor defects, safety and durability. It does not extend to matters specifically drawn to the buyer's attention before the contract is made.

31.5.7 Delivery of the right quality – fitness for purpose (SGA 1979, s 14(2) and (3))

As well as fitness for the common purposes of the goods under s 14(2), s 14(3) implies a term that the goods are fit for any particular purpose which the buyer makes known to the seller either expressly or by implication. (See *Micron Computer Systems Ltd v Wang (UK) Ltd*, QBD, 9 May 1990, where the buyer of a computer system failed to tell the seller of the particular purpose in question and was therefore unsuccessful in its claim.)

In *Jewson v Boyhan* [2003] EWCA Civ 1030, the seller was held by the Court of Appeal not to be liable for breach of the SGA 1979 in the supply of electrical heating equipment. The buyers alleged that the sale was in breach of s 14(2) and s 14(3), as the equipment had reduced the energy efficiency ratings of the flat conversions in question. The Court of Appeal held:

> Although there was considerable overlap between s 14(2) and s 14(3), the function of s 14(2) was to establish a general standard, and the function of s 14(3) was to impose a particular standard tailored to the individual circumstances of the case.

The equipment did work as heating equipment, so s 14(2) was held not to be applicable. As regards s 14(3), the buyer was held not to have relied on the sellers as regards the question of the 'particular' fitness for purpose of the effect of the heating equipment on the flats' energy efficiency ratings.

31.5.8 Delivery of the right quality – sale by sample (SGA 1979, s 15)

Section 15 of the SGA 1979 implies a term that, where the sale is by sample, the bulk of the goods will correspond with the sample in quality. The goods are also to be free of any defect not apparent on reasonable examination which would render the quality unsatisfactory.

31.5.9 Trade usage (SGA 1979, s 14(4))

Section 14(4) of the SGA 1979 states that an implied condition or warranty about quality or fitness for a particular purpose may be annexed to a contract of sale by usage in the course of a particular trade.

31.5.10 Description, quality, fitness for purpose and sale by sample: impact of the Consumer Rights Act 2015

Sections 13–15 of the SGA 1979 do not apply to contracts for the supply of goods by traders to consumers. Instead, similar terms are implied by ss 9–14 of the CRA 2015.

31.6 DUTIES OF THE BUYER

The SGA 1979 implies various duties into a contract for the sale of goods. This section deals with the buyer's duties. These apply to all contracts for the sale of goods.

31.6.1 Duty to pay the price (SGA 1979, ss 27–28)

It is the buyer's duty to pay the price (SGA 1979, s 27). The time for payment is prima facie when the goods are delivered, but the parties may agree otherwise (SGA 1979, s 28). The seller is not bound to accept anything but cash, subject to contrary agreement between the parties.

31.6.2 Duty to take delivery (SGA 1979, ss 27–28)

Under ss 27 and 28 of the SGA 1979 it is the duty of the buyer to accept and pay for the goods. The general rule is that delivery and payment takes place at the seller's premises. A buyer's failure to accept the goods does not by itself allow the seller to sell the goods to someone else but see s 48. Section 37 states that a buyer is liable for costs incurred by the seller due to the buyer's neglect or refusal to take delivery.

31.7 EFFECTS OF A SALE OF GOODS CONTRACT

31.7.1 Transfer of property (SGA 1979, ss 17–18)

The property in the goods, ie the title to the goods, passes when the parties intend it to pass (SGA 1979, s 17). Section 18 contains rules for ascertaining the intention of the parties, subject to their contrary intention.

Sections 17 and 18 apply to all contracts for the sale of goods.

31.7.2 Passing of risk (SGA 1979, s 20)

Section 20(1) of the SGA 1979 provides that the goods remain at the seller's risk until the property in them is transferred to the buyer whether or not delivery has been made, unless the parties agree otherwise.

This can be an important issue, for example, in the installation of a new computer system. The buyer will not want to pay the whole price until the system is running properly, yet the goods are on the buyer's premises and under their control while they are being installed. In such circumstances, the contract should provide that the risk in the goods passes to the buyer when the goods arrive at the buyer's premises. It is then up to the buyer to insure the goods, for example against theft or fire.

Section 20 of the SGA 1979 does not apply to contracts for the supply of goods by traders to consumers. Instead, s 29 of the CRA 2015 implies a term that risk passes when the goods come into the physical possession of the consumer.

31.7.3 Force majeure clause

A force majeure clause is included in a contract to deal with circumstances beyond the reasonable control of the parties and which would frustrate the contract. The terms of the clause are a matter of negotiation between the parties but would typically include the effects of government action, and extreme adverse weather.

31.8 RIGHTS OF THE SELLER

The provisions described below apply to all contracts for the sale of goods, although in practice they are unlikely to be of much relevance to sales to consumers.

31.8.1 Rights of an unpaid seller (SGA 1979, s 38)

The rights of the unpaid seller are:

(a) a lien on the goods;

(b) a right to stop the goods in transit;

(c) a right of resale;

(d) an action for the price of the goods; and

(e) a right to retain title to the goods until paid.

Section 38 of the SGA 1979 defines an unpaid seller. The rights in the SGA 1979 assume that the seller still has control over the goods. If this is not the case then the only possibility is a retention of title clause (see **31.8.7**).

31.8.2 Rights under s 39 of the SGA 1979

Section 39 provides that the unpaid seller has:

(a) a lien on the goods or right to retain them for the price;

(b) a right to stop the goods in transit if the buyer becomes insolvent; and

(c) a right of resale of the goods.

31.8.3 Seller's lien (SGA 1979, s 41)

Section 41 provides that an unpaid seller who is in possession of the goods is entitled to retain possession of them until paid, where any credit period has expired or the buyer has become insolvent.

The lien is lost when the goods are consigned to a carrier without the right to dispose of the goods, or the buyer has possession of the goods, or waiver by the seller.

31.8.4 Stoppage in transit (SGA 1979, ss 44–46)

Sections 44–46 provide that the seller may stop the goods in transit where the buyer has become insolvent, and retain them until paid.

31.8.5 Resale by seller (SGA 1979, s 48)

The unpaid seller who resells the goods to another buyer passes good title to the goods, even where the goods were subject to the unpaid seller's lien or were stopped in transit (s 48).

31.8.6 Action for the price, and damages (SGA 1979, ss 49 and 50)

Under s 49, the unpaid seller can sue the buyer for the price of the goods where the buyer has the property in the goods but has not paid for them.

Under s 50, where the buyer has refused to accept and pay for the goods the seller can sue the buyer for damages.

31.8.7 The seller who is not in possession of the goods (SGA 1979, ss 17 and 19)

The rights in **31.8.2–31.8.5** apply where the seller still has possession, or at least control, of the goods. A more difficult situation is where the goods are in the possession or control of the buyer but the seller has still not been paid. This is a major concern for the seller especially where the buyer is going insolvent. The danger is that the goods will be sold by a liquidator. The seller would be only an unsecured creditor and would be unlikely to be paid much, if anything, by the liquidator.

There is a right under ss 17 and 19 of the SGA 1979 to reserve title to the goods. This may be done in a contract of sale by inserting a retention of title clause (also called a *Romalpa* clause after *Aluminium Industrie Vaassen BV v Romalpa Aluminium* [1976] 1 WLR 676).

Typically, such a clause will reserve title to the seller until all monies owed to the seller by the buyer have been paid. It will also permit the seller to enter on to the buyer's premises to reclaim the goods, though one might query the efficacy of this if contested by a liquidator. There is also an exception. This is that, where the goods have been sold on to an innocent third party, s 25 of the SGA 1979 provides that the third party gets good title. There may be a provision seeking to trace the proceeds of onward sale of the goods through the buyer's bank account, but this is likely to be void against third parties for want of registration (see below).

There will be a requirement to keep the seller's goods identifiable, for example by separate storage.

A problem area is where the goods have been incorporated into other products. Generally, the original goods are considered to have been subsumed into the new products and the seller has no right to the new products. An attempt to 'reserve' title over the new products is likely to create a charge which will be void against third parties for want of registration (see below). However, where the goods are readily detachable, then it is appropriate to have a clause reserving the right of the seller to detach their goods and remove them. For example, in *Hendy Lennox Ltd v Graham Puttick Ltd* [1984] 1 WLR 485, it was held that the sellers were entitled to detach their diesel engines from electrical generating sets.

Retention of title clauses are generally not registrable as they are considered to operate by preventing the property in the goods from passing to the buyer in the first place (see *Clough Mill Ltd v Martin* [1985] 1 WLR 111). If the clause has the effect of the buyer creating an equitable charge over the goods or the proceeds of a sale of the goods, rather than being a retention of title, it is likely to be void against third parties for want of registration, as such charges are registrable under s 859A of the CA 2006.

31.9 RIGHTS OF THE BUYER

31.9.1 Right to reject the goods (SGA 1979, ss 15A, 35–36)

A buyer's primary right for breach of contract by the seller is to reject the goods and terminate the contract of sale. The seller's breach would have to go to the root of the contract to justify termination. The Sale and Supply of Goods Act 1994 made changes to this area of law, including by introducing s 15A into the SGA 1979.

Section 15A limits the right to reject the goods for breach of ss 13–15 of the SGA 1979. It provides that the right to reject is lost where the sale is not a consumer sale and the breach is so slight that it would be unreasonable for the buyer to reject the goods. Note that s 15A applies to breach of ss 13–15 only and not, for example, to breach of a stipulation concerning time of delivery.

Section 35 deals with the loss of the right to reject. So, for example, the buyer loses the right where they tell the seller that they have accepted the goods, or the buyer does something inconsistent with the seller's ownership after the goods have been delivered to the buyer. The buyer also loses the right to reject if the buyer retains the goods beyond a reasonable period of time (s 35(5)). In *Clegg v Olle Andersson (t/a Nordic Marine)* [2003] EWCA Civ 320, the Court of Appeal held that the Sale and Supply of Goods Act 1994 allowed the buyer to have time to ascertain the actions needed to modify or repair the goods. The case concerned an ocean-going yacht. The buyer took three weeks to assess the situation before rejecting the goods. This was in fact many months after delivery, as the seller was slow to respond to requests for information.

Section 36 of the SGA 1979 provides that, where the goods have been delivered to the buyer and the buyer rejects them, the buyer is not obliged to return them to the seller.

31.9.2 Action for damages (SGA 1979, s 53)

The buyer can sue for breach of a contract term, either express or implied (s 53). This is either where the term in question is classified as a warranty, or where it is a condition but the buyer has elected not to reject the goods.

Section 51 lays down the principles for calculating damages for non-delivery of the goods, and in particular s 51(3) provides:

> Where there is an available market for the goods in question the measure of damages is prima facie to be ascertained by the difference between the contract price and the market or current price of the goods at the time or times when they ought to have been delivered or (if no time was fixed) at the time of the refusal to deliver.

In other words, the buyer's loss is any increase in the price of equivalent goods obtained from another source.

A problem area is consequential loss. The governing principles are taken from the leading case of *Hadley v Baxendale* (1854) 9 Exch 341: the damages allowed are those that are considered either as arising naturally from the breach of the contract itself, or such as may reasonably be supposed to have been in the contemplation of the parties at the time they made the contract. The difficulty is that some losses – for example, loss of profit on resale of the goods – may be considered to be 'consequential loss' but are nonetheless 'direct loss' within the first limb of *Hadley v Baxendale*.

Limitation clauses in sale of goods contracts are often aimed at limiting or excluding consequential loss, subject to being disallowed under the UCTA 1977. The seller does not want to take on liabilities that might far exceed their profit on the sale. However, it can be difficult to know exactly what is intended by an exclusion of liability for 'consequential loss'.

31.9.3 Specific performance (SGA 1979, s 52)

The buyer's right to specific performance is regulated by s 52. The right applies only to contracts for specific or ascertained goods, that is goods identified and agreed upon at the time the contract is made. The right applies whether or not the property in the goods (title to the goods) has already passed to the buyer.

The right under s 52 does not extend to unascertained goods. These are goods which are not identified and agreed upon at the time a contract of sale is made. They may be divided into the following categories:

(a) a quantity of a type of goods in general, eg 5 kilos of potatoes;

(b) future goods – goods which are not yet in existence, eg next year's potatoes; or

(c) part of a larger quantity of ascertained goods, eg 5 kilos of potatoes out of the 2 tonnes in the Tesco shop in Chester.

In each case, the identity of the individual potatoes in question is not known.

However, there are some cases where an order for unascertained goods has been granted, albeit in exceptional circumstances. For example, in *Worldwide Dryers Ltd v Warner Howard Ltd and Others* (1982) *The Times*, 9 December, the buyer's business would have collapsed pending the full trial if the seller had cut off supplies of the goods which were imported from the United States. These would be 'future goods' under the classification above.

31.9.4 Rights of the buyer: impact of the Consumer Rights Act 2015

Sections 35, 52 and 53 of the SGA 1979 do not apply to contracts for the supply of goods by traders to consumers. Instead, provisions governing the rejection of goods by consumers and other consumer remedies are implied by ss 19–24 of the CRA 2015.

31.9.5 Rescission for misrepresentation

This is controlled by the Misrepresentation Act 1967. Section 1(a) of the Act provides that the fact that a pre-contractual representation has become a term of the contract does not necessarily stop the buyer from rescinding. Rescission is possible for innocent misrepresentation (s 1(b)).

Rescission for misrepresentation is barred by affirmation, lapse of time, inability to restore the parties to their original position, or the goods being acquired by an innocent third party.

Damages for misrepresentation are also a possibility but there can be no double recovery.

31.10 EXCLUSION OF SELLER'S LIABILITY

Exclusion clauses have to be incorporated into the contract in order to be relied upon by the seller. (See, for example, the difficulties with incorporation of a 'shrink-wrap' licence for computer software – *Beta Computers (Europe) Ltd v Adobe Systems (Europe) Ltd* [1996] FSR 367.) As a matter of construction, the exclusion clause must also apply to the facts of the particular matter in dispute. Any uncertainty will be construed against the person relying on the exclusion clause: the so-called '*contra proferentem*' rule.

Besides these issues of incorporation and construction, exclusion clauses are subject to extensive statutory regulation. The UCTA 1977 is the main legislation dealing with the exclusion of liability arising in contracts between businesses. It provides that certain exclusions of liability are void (see **31.10.1.1**), whilst others are effective only if they pass a 'reasonableness test'. See **31.10.1.2** for the exclusions of liability to which this test applies, and **31.10.3.1** for how the test works.

The CRA 2015 governs the exclusion of liability in contracts between businesses (referred to as 'traders') and consumers. It provides that certain types of liability cannot be excluded or restricted (see **31.10.2.2**), and that other terms in consumer contracts are not binding on the consumer if they are 'unfair' (see **31.10.2.3**). It also imposes a requirement that terms in consumer contracts must be 'transparent'.

There is no legislation affecting the exclusion of liability in contracts between consumers. (Section 1(3) of the UCTA 1977 makes it clear that its provisions apply only to business liability.)

Because the rules applicable to contracts between businesses are different from those applicable to contracts between businesses and consumers, solicitors drafting standard conditions of sale may wish to consider preparing different versions for use by their clients with business and consumer customers (see also **31.10.3.3**).

The following is a brief synopsis of the main points of the UCTA 1977 and, at **31.10.2**, the CRA 2015.

31.10.1 Business to business contracts: the effect of the UCTA 1977 on contractual terms

The provisions of the UCTA 1977 described here apply only to 'business liability'. By s 1(3), this is essentially liability for breach of obligations or duties arising in the course of a business or from the occupation of business premises. Each of the provisions described here expressly states that it does not apply to 'consumer contracts'. This is because exclusion clauses in those contracts are governed by the CRA 2015. 'Consumer contract' is defined in s 61 of the CRA 2015 as a contract between a trader and a consumer: see **31.10.2.1** for further details.

31.10.1.1 Void clauses under the UCTA

Section 2(1)

By s 2(1) of the UCTA 1977, a person cannot, either by reference to a contract term or a notice, exclude or restrict their liability for personal injury or death resulting from negligence.

Section 6(1)

By s 6(1) of the UCTA 1977, liability for breach of the implied condition of title under either s 12 of the SGA 1979 or s 8 of the Supply of Goods (Implied Terms) Act 1973 cannot be excluded or restricted by reference to any contract term.

Note that although the word 'void' is commonly used to describe the effect of ss 2(1) and 6(1) of the UCTA 1977, and is a convenient shorthand description, the Act does not actually use this word. Instead, it provides that the liability to which it refers cannot be excluded or restricted.

31.10.1.2 Clauses subject to the reasonableness test

The ways in which the contractual reasonableness test is most likely to apply are as follows.

Section 2(2)

By section 2(2) of the UCTA 1977, any attempt to exclude liability, by reference either to a contract term or to a notice, for damage caused by negligence other than death or personal injury is subject to the reasonableness test.

Section 3

Section 3 of the UCTA 1977 applies where one party deals on the other party's written standard terms of business. It imposes the reasonableness test on a wide variety of clauses, particularly any clause by which the party whose standard terms are used attempts to exclude any liability for breach of contract.

Section 6(1A)

By section 6(1A) of the UCTA 1977, any attempt to exclude liability for breach of the conditions implied by ss 13–15 of the SGA 1979 or ss 9–11 of the Supply of Goods (Implied Terms) Act 1973 is subject to the reasonableness test.

31.10.1.3 Other contracts under which goods pass

Section 7 of the UCTA 1977 applies to attempts to exclude liability in other contracts under which goods pass, including liability for breach of the statutory terms implied by the SGSA 1982. Its effect is similar to that of ss 6(1) and 6(1A), described in **31.10.1.1** and **31.10.1.2** above.

As well as s 7, s 3 of the UCTA 1977 applies the reasonableness test to clauses in such contracts where one party deals on the other party's written standard terms (see **31.10.1.2**).

31.10.2 Excluding liability in consumer contracts under the CRA 2015

The CRA 2015 is partly a consolidating statute, which brings disparate pieces of consumer law together in a single, easily accessed piece of legislation. It therefore makes relatively few changes to the pre-existing law. Many of the rules on exclusions of liability in consumer contracts, notably the rules on 'unfair' terms, are derived from the Unfair Terms in Consumer Contracts Regulations 1999. These Regulations have now been repealed, but it is likely that the courts will continue to refer to the pre-existing case law on their interpretation.

31.10.2.1 Scope and definitions

Critical definitions in the CRA 2015 include 'trader', 'consumer' and 'consumer contract'.

A 'trader' is defined in s 2(2) of the CRA 2015 as 'a person acting for purposes relating to that person's trade, business, craft or profession'. A 'consumer' is defined in s 2(3) as 'an individual acting for purposes that are wholly or mainly outside that individual's trade, business, craft or profession'. The effect of these definitions is that a *company* (or a government body) entering into a transaction which is not in the regular course of its business is not protected as a 'consumer'. The position of a partnership, or an individual running a business, entering into a transaction which is marginally incidental to its business, is perhaps less clear.

A 'consumer contract' is defined in s 61 of the CRA 2015 as 'a contract between a trader and a consumer'.

Chapter 2 of Pt 1 of the CRA 2015 applies to contracts for the supply of goods by a trader to a consumer (see s 3). (It therefore extends to the situation where goods are supplied along with services.) Sections 9–18 of Chapter 2 imply terms into contracts for the supply of goods which are in many cases similar to those implied by the SGA 1979 in non-consumer cases. (The CRA 2015 also contains equivalent provisions with regard to contracts for the provision of services, but they are beyond the scope of this chapter.)

The CRA 2015 contains two main groups of provisions relating to exclusions of liability in contracts for the supply of goods. First, certain types of liability cannot be excluded or restricted at all in a contract for the supply of goods (see **31.10.2.2**). Secondly, an exclusion or restriction of liability in *any* consumer contract will not be binding on the consumer if it is 'unfair' (see **31.10.2.3**). A solicitor drafting a contract that may be used with consumers will therefore need to have regard to both types of requirement. These two groups of provisions are described in more detail below.

Note that the concept of 'reasonableness', which is so important in the UCTA 1977, does not appear at all in the CRA 2015.

31.10.2.2 Liability that cannot be excluded or restricted

Section 31 of the CRA 2015 provides that terms of contracts to supply goods are not binding on consumers to the extent that they purport to exclude or restrict the trader's liability arising under certain specified provisions. These include the equivalents in the CRA 2015 to the terms implied under the SGA 1979 with regard to title, description and quality.

Section 65 of the CRA 2015 provides that a trader cannot, by a term of a consumer contract or by a notice given to a consumer, exclude or restrict liability for death or personal injury resulting from negligence. Note that s 65 extends to all consumer contracts, not just contracts for the supply of goods.

31.10.2.3 Unfair terms in consumer contracts

The rules on unfair terms in consumer contracts are contained in Part 2 of the CRA 2015. Note that they extend to all contracts between traders and consumers, not just contracts for the supply of goods, subject to certain exceptions referred to in s 64 of the CRA 2015. These rules implement Directive 93/13/EEC ([1993] OJ L095/29) on unfair terms in consumer contracts. The UK has now left the EU, but the UK courts may continue to have regard to EU rulings on this Directive unless UK law is amended.

Section 62(1) of the CRA 2015 provides that an unfair term of a consumer contract is not binding on the consumer. Section 62(4) then says that a term is unfair if, contrary to the requirement of good faith, it causes a significant imbalance in the parties' rights and obligations under the contract to the detriment of the consumer.

An 'indicative and non-exhaustive' list of terms which may be regarded as unfair is set out in Part 1 of Sch 2 to the CRA 2015.

31.10.2.4 The requirement for 'transparency'

By s 68 of the CRA 2015, a trader must ensure that a written term of a consumer contract is 'transparent'. To meet this requirement, it must be expressed in 'plain and intelligible language' and be legible. These concepts are not further defined. In a recent decision of the Court of Justice of the European Union, it was held that merely specifying an hourly rate is not sufficient to meet the requirement for transparency. The trader (in this case, a law firm) must at least give an indication of a minimum number of hours that the work is expected to entail, or agree to send regular bills or periodic reports of the number of hours worked.

Nor is it clear from the CRA 2015 what will happen if the requirement is not complied with. Perhaps the most appropriate conclusion is that it is one of the factors which may render a term unfair. Section 69 also provides that, if a term in a consumer contract could have different meanings, the meaning that is most favourable to the consumer is to prevail; compare the *contra proferentem* rule which applies in non-consumer cases (see **31.10**).

31.10.2.5 Enforcement

Section 70 of the CRA 2015 empowers the Competition and Markets Authority and various other regulators (including the Consumers' Association) to consider complaints about unfair contract terms and to seek a court order. In practice, day-to-day enforcement is likely to be left to local trading standards authorities.

31.10.3 Drafting for reasonableness: general principles

31.10.3.1 The contractual reasonableness test

In practice, when the UCTA 1977 applies to a commercial agreement, most (if not all) of the agreement's exclusion clauses will be subject to the reasonableness test, so it is usually against this test that the solicitor will need to assess a clause.

Section 11(1) of the UCTA 1977 provides:

> In relation to a contract term, the requirement of reasonableness ... is that the term shall have been a fair and reasonable one to be included having regard to the circumstances which were, or ought reasonably to have been, known to or in the contemplation of the parties when the contract was made.

It is, therefore, a test of reasonableness of incorporation, not reasonableness of reliance. If (in the light of the actual and constructive knowledge of the parties at the time) it is reasonable to include a particular clause when the contract is made, it should pass the reasonableness test: the court should not look at whether it was reasonable for the 'guilty' party to rely on the clause in the light of the events which actually happened (although it has to be said that it is not uncommon in practice for courts to do this). It is for the party claiming that a term satisfies the reasonableness test to show that it does (s 11(5)).

31.10.3.2 The Schedule 2 guidelines

The guidelines include: the relative bargaining power of the parties; whether the buyer was offered any inducement to accept the clause; whether any choice was available (could the buyer have acquired the goods elsewhere without the clause?); and the extent of the parties' knowledge of the existence and effect of the terms. The list is not intended to be exhaustive and, strictly speaking, applies only when the court is assessing reasonableness under ss 6(3) and 7(3) of the UCTA 1977. However, the courts often apply the guidelines when considering the reasonableness test in relation to other sections (notably s 3; see, for example, *Flamar Interocean Ltd v Denmac Ltd (formerly Denholm Maclay Co Ltd) (The 'Flamar Pride' and 'Flamar Progress')* [1990] 1 Lloyd's Rep 434). This approach was confirmed as appropriate by the Court of Appeal in *Overseas Medical Supplies Ltd v Orient Transport Services Ltd* [1999] 2 Lloyd's Rep 273. This case also contains a useful discussion and summary of the factors which are generally relevant to assessing the reasonableness of a clause.

31.10.3.3 Is the contract a consumer or a commercial contract?

In determining whether a clause will survive the application of the UCTA 1977 and the CRA 2015, the crucial factor is often whether the contract is a consumer or a commercial contract. For example, a clause that excludes liability for breach of s 14(2) or (3) of the SGA 1979 is only subject to the reasonableness test against a commercial buyer; it is void against a buyer who deals as consumer. If the client deals with both commercial and consumer buyers, it is important for the solicitor to recognise this when drafting. There may be several different ways of dealing with the problem, depending on how the client does business and the other relevant circumstances. For example, the solicitor may decide to draft two different forms of contracts, with the 'consumer' version either omitting certain exclusion clauses, or containing only modified versions. However, this may be risky; it would then be necessary to ensure that those operating the contract are able to distinguish between the two versions (perhaps print them on different coloured paper). A simpler solution (where possible) is to have one contract for all customers, but to draft any exclusion so that it will apply only to commercial customers.

31.10.3.4 No guarantee of success

Because of the way in which the contractual reasonableness test is worded, the factors that are relevant when drafting for reasonableness (see **31.10.3.1**) are often specific to the circumstances of each individual contract. The solicitor must therefore advise the client that even the best-drafted clause cannot be guaranteed to work in all circumstances. However, careful drafting can often significantly increase the likelihood of the clause passing the reasonableness test.

31.10.3.5 An example of reasonableness

In *SAM Business Systems Ltd v Hedley & Co* [2002] EWHC 2733, a computer supply company was held to have acted reasonably in excluding liability, not least as this was standard practice in the industry. The parties were of equal size and bargaining power. This also goes to indicate reasonableness. Computer supply companies will try to exclude most of their liability both for the implied terms under the SGA 1979 and the consequences of breach of contract, eg by capping their total liability to a specified amount. In this case, they succeeded. It is a typical UCTA type of dispute.

CHAPTER 32

Employment and Other Regulatory Concerns in Running a Business

LEARNING OUTCOMES

After reading this chapter you will be able to:

- identify statutory restrictions on an employer's general freedom to offer employment to whomever it wishes and on whatever terms it wishes
- explain the basis on which an employee might have a claim for wrongful dismissal, unfair dismissal or dismissal by reason of redundancy
- calculate the awards available to employees who bring successful claims of wrongful dismissal, unfair dismissal and/or dismissal by reason of redundancy.

32.1 INTRODUCTION

The new business will require personnel. The owner(s) of the business will need to be aware of statutory responsibilities and duties when recruiting employees, when acting as their employer and eventually, perhaps, when terminating their employment. Arrangements will have to be put in place for paying income tax (and corporation tax if the business is run by a company), for paying National Insurance contributions, and for collecting and paying VAT, if appropriate. Also, the product must be considered. Does the business need any licences, should the business carry insurances, or is there a need to protect the intellectual property rights of the business? There may be further matters to consider in relation to the business premises, such as planning consents, although these are not considered further in this book.

32.2 EMPLOYEES

32.2.1 Recruitment and dealings with employees

The general common law rule is that an employer is free to offer employment to whoever they choose (*Allen v Flood and Taylor* [1898] AC 1). This common law freedom has been restricted by statute. The employer may be in breach of statutory requirements if they discriminate against a person on the grounds of:

(a) sex;
(b) marriage and civil partnership;
(c) gender reassignment;
(d) race;
(e) religion or belief;
(f) sexual orientation;
(g) age;
(h) disability;
(i) pregnancy and maternity;
(j) trade union membership;
(k) part-time work;
(l) fixed (limited)-term work.

The Equality Act 2010 ('the Act') makes it unlawful to discriminate on recruitment, as to the employment terms offered, opportunities for promotion, transfers and training; on dismissal and on subjecting the employee to any other detriment (s 39). It also outlaws discrimination where a person is absent from work because of gender reassignment (s 16), and where absence is a result of pregnancy or related illness (s 18).

The Act identifies a list of 'Protected Characteristics' (s 4). They are those listed at (a)–(i) inclusive above. It then lists standard types of discrimination:

(a) direct discrimination (s 13);
(b) indirect discrimination (s 19);
(c) harassment (s 26); and
(d) victimisation (s 27);

in relation to each of the protected characteristics. (Pregnancy/maternity is excluded from indirect discrimination and harassment, whilst marriage/civil partnership is excluded from the harassment offence.)

There are three special types of discrimination:

(a) discrimination arising from disability (s 15);
(b) failure to make reasonable adjustments on disability (ss 20 and 21); and
(c) pregnancy and maternity discrimination (s 18).

In addition, the Act repeats the law previously contained in the Equal Pay Act 1970, designed to ensure that men and women within the same or equivalent employment receive equal pay.

The details of all these claims are beyond the scope of this book. The Government Equalities Office has a very useful web page providing links to all the relevant guidance, codes of practice and historical background to the Act.

32.2.2 Written statement of terms

By s 1 of the Employment Rights Act (ERA) 1996 (as amended by the Employment Act 2002), the employer must, within two months of employment commencing, give the employee a written statement of terms and conditions relating to the following particulars:

(a) identity of the parties;
(b) date employment began;
(c) date continuous employment began (taking into account any relevant employment with a previous employer);
(d) scale or rate of remuneration and intervals of pay;
(e) hours of work;

(f) any terms relating to:
   (i) holidays and holiday pay;
   (ii) sickness and sick pay;
   (iii) pensions and pension schemes;
(g) length of notice required to determine the contract;
(h) in the case of non-permanent employment, the period for which it is expected to continue or, if it is a fixed term, the date it is to end;
(i) job title or a brief description of work;
(j) place or places of work;
(k) particulars of any collective agreements which directly affect the terms and conditions of employment;
(l) where employees are required to work outside the UK for a period of more than one month, the period of such work, currency in which payment is made, benefits provided and terms relating to the return to the UK;
(m) details of the disciplinary and dismissal rules and grievance procedures;
(n) whether a contracting out certificate is in force (under the Pension Schemes Act 1993).

32.2.3 Dealings with employees

An employer should understand that they have certain statutory obligations towards their employee during the course of the employment in addition to those matters already described. These include:

(a) allowing employees time off work:
   (i) for ante-natal care;
   (ii) for trade union duties and activities;
   (iii) for public duties (eg those of magistrates);
   (iv) for maternity, paternity, adoption and parental leave; and
   (v) to care for dependants.
(b) allowing employees in certain situations to request flexible working;
(c) allowing an employee to return to work after maternity leave; and
(d) taking reasonable care for the employees' health and safety at work.

An employer should also understand the general rights and remedies of an employee whom the employer may wish to dismiss.

32.2.4 Informing and consulting employees

The Information and Consultation of Employees Regulations 2004 (SI 2004/3426) give employees in a relevant undertaking the right to be informed about the undertaking's economic situation, informed and consulted about employment prospects, and informed and consulted with a view to reaching agreement about decisions likely to lead to substantial changes in work organisation or contractual relations, including, but not limited to, collective redundancies and business transfers. The detail of the rights is beyond the scope of this chapter.

32.2.5 Dismissal of employees

An employer should understand the possible rights and remedies of an employee whom the employer wishes to dismiss. In addition to the discrimination claims mentioned at **32.2.1**, but which apply equally to dismissal (see **32.2.10**), there are three potential claims: the common law claim for wrongful dismissal and two statutory claims—the complaint of unfair dismissal and the claim for a statutory redundancy payment.

32.2.6 Wrongful dismissal

This is a common law claim which is based on the fact that the contract has been terminated by the employer in a manner which is a breach of the contract of employment. This is likely to be so if the employer terminates a contract for an indefinite term with no notice or with inadequate notice, or if a fixed-term contract is terminated before its expiry date.

Most employment contracts are for an indefinite term and terminable by either side giving the correct contractual notice. If the employer gives the proper period of notice, then no breach will have occurred and there will be no claim for wrongful dismissal whatever the reason for the termination. In a fixed-term contract, the contract is not usually terminable by notice. In the case of a fixed-term contract without a break clause, termination of the contract prior to its expiry date will be a breach of contract and the employee may claim wrongful dismissal.

The applicable notice period will usually be expressly agreed in the contract, and if the employer gives no notice or short notice the employer will be in breach. If an expressly agreed notice period is shorter than the statutory minimum period required by s 86 of the ERA 1996, then the longer statutory period of notice must be given. In the absence of an expressly agreed period of notice, there is an implied term that the employee is entitled to 'reasonable' notice. What will be a reasonable period will depend on the facts of the case. For more senior employees, a longer period will be implied. In any event, any such implied period is again subject to the statutory minimum period stipulated by s 86.

Where a contract of employment can be ended by notice, s 86 of the ERA 1996 provides for the following statutory minimum periods of notice (which prevail over any shorter contractual period, express or implied). The statutory minimum is:

(a) one week's notice after one month's continuous employment;
(b) two weeks' notice after two years' continuous employment;

and thereafter one additional week's notice for each year of continuous employment up to a maximum of 12 weeks' notice after 12 years' continuous employment.

It should be appreciated that the claim for wrongful dismissal requires a dismissal in breach of contract. Where an employee simply resigns, they will have no claim, since it is the employee who has then terminated the contract. The employee will be in breach of contract if they do not give the notice that they were required to give under the contract to end it, or, in the case of a fixed-term contract, they terminate it before the expiry date. (In indefinite contracts, the only statutory minimum notice required to be given by an employee is one week's notice after one month's continuous employment.) However, if the employer had committed a repudiatory breach of an express or implied term of the contract, the employee is entitled to treat the contract as discharged. In this case, the employee is entitled to leave, with or without notice and they can bring a claim of wrongful dismissal. Although they have not been actually dismissed by the employer they have been 'constructively dismissed' in breach of contract. However, in such a case, the employee must leave within a reasonable time of the employer's breach, otherwise they will be deemed to have affirmed the contract. Such a repudiatory breach may occur where the employer unilaterally alters the employee's contract or breaks the implied duty of good faith owed to employees (eg by humiliating the employee in front of colleagues or clients, imposing unreasonable work demands on them, etc).

It should be noted that even where there is a prima facie wrongful dismissal, the employer will have a defence if the employee had committed a repudiatory breach of an express or implied term of the contract, such as revealing confidential information or trade secrets, wilfully disobeying the employer's lawful orders or other serious misconduct. The employer can still use this defence even if the employer did not know of the employee's breach at the time the employer terminated the contract, but only discovered it afterwards.

Damages for wrongful dismissal are damages for breach of contract and the normal contractual rules apply. The aim is to put the employee in the position they would have been in, so far as money can do this, had the contract not been broken. Thus, in the case of an indefinite contract, the starting point for the calculation is the net salary or wages the employee would have earned during the proper notice period. In the case of a fixed-term contract, it is the net salary for the remainder of the fixed term. In addition, the employee may claim damages for loss of other benefits they would have been entitled to for the relevant period (eg lost commission or 'fringe' benefits such as pension rights or use of a company car). Damages can usually be claimed for pecuniary loss only, so they will not generally be awarded for loss of future prospects or for injured feelings.

The employee is under a duty to mitigate their loss. Once their employment has been terminated they will be expected to take reasonable steps to obtain suitable employment and they will not be awarded damages in respect of any loss which has been mitigated or would have been mitigated but for their breach of the duty to mitigate. Note that where an employer has made a payment in lieu of notice, this will be deducted from any damages.

The claim for wrongful dismissal can be brought in either the High Court or the county court, or in the employment tribunal. There is no limit to the amount of damages recoverable in a court action, although there is a restriction on tribunal awards. This is currently £25,000.

32.2.7 Unfair dismissal

Under s 94 of the ERA 1996 an employee has the right not to be unfairly dismissed. The claim is brought before the employment tribunal. The employee must prove that they are a 'qualifying employee'. For employees employed on or after 6 April 2012, they must have two years' continuous employment, starting when that employment began and ending with the dismissal.

The employee must prove that they have been dismissed. This includes actual dismissal and constructive dismissal. Actual dismissal is dismissal by the employer with or without notice. Constructive dismissal has been discussed at **32.2.6** in the context of wrongful dismissal. (There is another type of dismissal for the purposes of the statutory claim. This is where the contract was a fixed-term contract which was not renewed on its expiry.)

The burden of proof then moves to the employer. The employer must show the principal reason for the dismissal and that such reason is one of the five permitted reasons. If the employer can establish that, the employment tribunal must decide whether the employer acted reasonably in treating that reason as a sufficient reason for dismissing the employee. If either the employer cannot show one of the reasons or the tribunal considers that the employer acted unreasonably, the employee will win. The potentially fair reasons are:

(a) the *capability or qualifications* of the employee for doing work of the kind they were employed to do (this could include incompetence, or inability to do the job by reason of illness or injury);

(b) the *conduct* of the employee (this must generally relate to conduct within the employment – outside behaviour will be relevant only if it has a direct bearing on the employee's fitness to do the job);

(c) the employee was *redundant* (in this case the employee will be entitled to a redundancy payment (see below));

(d) the employee could not continue to work in the position held without *contravening some statutory enactment* (eg where a lorry driver loses their driving licence); and

(e) *some other substantial reason* justifying the dismissal of an employee holding the position which the employee held (it is not possible to give a comprehensive list of such reasons, but this category has been held to include dismissal where the employee refuses to accept a reorganisation affecting their working hours and a dismissal arising out of a personality clash between employees).

If the employer has demonstrated that the dismissal was for a fair reason, under s 98(4) of the ERA 1996 the tribunal must decide whether 'in the circumstances (including the size and administrative resources of the employer's undertaking) the employer acted reasonably or unreasonably in treating it as a sufficient reason for dismissing the employee [having regard] to equity and the substantial merits of the case.' The tribunal will see whether the employer had a genuine and reasonable belief in the facts based on a reasonable investigation and procedure leading to a reasonable decision. It will look at the size of the business – for instance, an employer with many employees may have found it easier to cope with an employee who has considerable sickness absence. In particular, the employer may be held to have dismissed unfairly if there are procedural defects.

Thus, in 'capability' cases, the employer should normally have warned the employee about their standard of work and given them the chance to improve, and perhaps offered additional training and supervision. Perhaps a reasonable employer would have moved the employee to a job within their competence rather than dismissing them. In dismissal for long-term sickness, the employer should consult with the employee as to the likely duration of the illness and its nature.

In 'conduct' cases, the employer should carry out a thorough investigation and allow the employee to state their case. The employer should not dismiss unless the misconduct is gross or persistent. Guidance on how to deal with misconduct is given by an ACAS Code of Practice, which in particular recommends a system of warnings for less serious misconduct. The Code does not have the force of law, but will be taken into account by the tribunal to see if the employer acted reasonably.

In cases of redundancy, the employer should warn and consult the affected employees or their representatives and adopt a fair basis of selection for redundancy. This usually involves employers drawing up a matrix of objective selection criteria and then fairly marking each employee against each criterion. A fair employer would also consider the possibility of redeployment of affected employees within the business.

The employer should generally give the employee the correct notice due under the contract (or payment in lieu of notice). Failure to do so (other than in cases of gross misconduct) may well lead to a finding of unfair dismissal (as well as exposing the employer to a claim for wrongful dismissal).

If the defence is based on the employee's misconduct, unlike wrongful dismissal, the employer cannot rely on misconduct which they only discovered after the dismissal (although, if such misconduct had occurred, the tribunal may reduce any compensation). The remedies for unfair dismissal are as follows.

32.2.7.1 Reinstatement (getting the old job back) or re-engagement (being given another comparable or suitable job with the same or an associated employer)

It is for the employee to ask for such remedies, and few such orders are made.

32.2.7.2 Compensation

This consists of two awards, considered below.

The basic award

This is calculated by reference to a statutory formula which reflects the employee's age, their pay and length of service. This formula remains untouched by age discrimination legislation. The statutory formula works by multiplying the employee's final gross week's pay (subject to a current maximum of £719; this is reviewed annually) by the following factors:

(a) their length of service (the maximum period taken into account is 20 years);

(b) a multiplier (as below) depending on the employee's age during those years' service (working backwards from the end of the employment):

for years worked when not below the age of 41 = 1½

for years worked when below 41 but not below 22 = 1

for years worked when below 22 = ½

EXAMPLE

Ernie starts work for A Co Ltd on his 30th birthday. His employment ends on his 57th birthday. His final gross week's pay is £750. On the basis of 20 years' service (the maximum), his basic award will be:

16 × 1½ × £719	17,256
4 × 1 × £719	2,876
	20,132

The compensatory award

In addition to the basic award, the tribunal will award such amount as it considers to be just and equitable having regard to the loss sustained by the employee in consequence of the dismissal in so far as that loss is attributable to the action taken by the employer. The award is subject to a maximum of £118,223 and is calculated under the following heads:

(a) immediate loss of net wages from the date of the dismissal to the date of the hearing, assuming the employee has not at that date got another job;

(b) future loss of net wages – based on an estimate as to how long it might take the employee to get another job (assuming they have not yet done so);

(c) loss of fringe benefits; and

(d) loss of statutory protection. In any new job, the employee will have to start building up as against a future employer their statutory rights to a redundancy payment and unfair dismissal protection, and a statutory minimum notice.

The tribunal will deduct from the compensatory award any payment in lieu of notice or ex gratia payment received from the employer. Both the basic award and the compensatory award can be reduced due to the employee's contributory fault.

In addition, if either party unreasonably failed to follow ACAS's recommended Code on discipline and grievance before the tribunal proceedings were started, the compensatory award may be adjusted. If the failure to comply is wholly or mainly the employee's, it may be reduced by up to 25%. If it is deemed to be wholly or mainly the employer's fault, it may be increased by up to 25%.

The unfair compensatory award is capped at the lower of 52 weeks' pay and the existing limit (£118,223). This maximum is applied after any deductions have been made and does not include fringe benefits.

32.2.8 Redundancy

The person primarily liable to pay a redundancy payment is the employer, and in most cases they pay it without dispute. Where they do not, or the employee disputes the calculation, the employee may refer the matter to an employment tribunal. There is a six-month time limit.

To claim a statutory redundancy payment, an employee must be 'qualified'. The factors are very similar to unfair dismissal.

As in unfair dismissal, the employee must prove that they have been dismissed (actually, constructively or by failure to renew a fixed-term contract on expiry) and that they have two years' continuous employment.

Once the above has been proved, a presumption arises that the employee has been dismissed for redundancy. The employer may be able to show a reason other than redundancy, but this may open the door to a claim for unfair dismissal. At this point, it is vital to consider whether or not the reason for the dismissal fits into the statutory definition of redundancy (contained in ERA 1996, s 139). The s 139 definition covers three situations:

(a) *complete closedown* (the fact that the employer has ceased or intends to cease to carry on the business for the purposes of which the employee was employed by the employer);

(b) *partial closedown* (the fact that the employer has ceased or intends to cease to carry on that business in the place where the employee was so employed); and

(c) *overmanning or a change in the type of work undertaken* (the fact that the requirements of the business for employees to carry out work of a particular kind, or for employees to carry out work of a particular kind in the place where the employee was employed by the employer, have ceased or diminished, or are expected to cease or diminish).

At this point, the employee may have a prima facie entitlement to a redundancy payment. However, it should be noted that an employee may lose their entitlement if they unreasonably refuse an offer of suitable alternative employment made by their employer.

The statutory redundancy payment is calculated in general in the same way as the basic award for unfair dismissal.

32.2.9 Overlapping claims

The employer should appreciate that a dismissed employee may have more than one potential claim against the employer. If the dismissal is unfair and without proper notice (or within a fixed term) the employee may claim both wrongful dismissal and unfair dismissal. Should the employee succeed in both claims, the basic principle is that compensation will not be awarded for the same loss twice. Immediate and future loss of wages form a substantial part of the compensatory award for unfair dismissal, and this would substantially reduce any damages awarded for wrongful dismissal.

An employee may have a claim for a redundancy and also for unfair dismissal. This could arise where an employee is unfairly selected for redundancy. The redundancy payment will be set against the unfair dismissal award and usually it simply offsets the basic award (since the two are calculated according to a similar formula). However, if the redundancy payment exceeds the basic award (as it might if the basic award were reduced because of the employee's own conduct) the balance will reduce the compensatory award.

32.2.10 Discriminatory dismissals, etc

If an employer discriminates on the unlawful grounds mentioned at **32.2.1** in dismissing an employee, the employee will be entitled to claim compensation from the employer. This also applies to subjecting the employee to any of the other detrimental treatments mentioned at **32.2.1** and **32.2.3**. This compensation is similar to the unfair dismissal compensation award. It is not subject to any maximum and can include compensation for injured feelings. Again if claimed in addition to other claims, compensation will not be awarded twice for the same loss.

32.2.11 Settlement agreements

Many complaints are agreed without a hearing before the employment tribunal, usually because the employer pays the employee a sum in settlement.

However, under s 203 of the ERA 1996, any provision in an agreement is void in so far as it purports to exclude or limit the operation of any of the provisions of the ERA 1996, or to stop someone bringing proceedings before an employment tribunal. The caveat is that this can be done if a conciliation officer has taken action under s 18 of the ERA 1996, or a settlement agreement has been entered into.

A settlement agreement is an agreement entered into by the parties. For it to be binding, it has to do the following:

(a) it must be in writing, identify the adviser, relate to the particular complaint and state that the relevant statutory conditions are satisfied;
(b) the employee or worker must have received advice from a relevant independent adviser as to the terms and effect of the proposed agreement and, in particular, its effect on their ability to pursue their rights before an employment tribunal; and
(c) there must be in force, when the adviser gives the advice, a contract of insurance, or an indemnity provided for members of a profession or professional body, covering the risk of a claim by the employer or worker in respect of loss arising in consequence of the advice.

The settlement agreement must relate only to the matter in dispute. It cannot purport to exclude all possible claims (see ERA 1996, s 203).

32.2.12 Directors and members

A director or a member (ie a shareholder) can also be an employee of the company – see *Secretary of State for Trade and Industry v Bottrill* [2000] 1 All ER 915. If a director is awarded a service contract for a fixed term that is guaranteed to exceed two years, the members must approve the term in advance by ordinary resolution. If they fail to pass an ordinary resolution, the contract will be valid, but the fixed term will be invalid and the contract will be terminable on 'reasonable notice' (see **32.2.6** above).

32.3 ACCOUNTING RECORDS FOR TAX PURPOSES

There is no statutory form of accounts which must be maintained, unless the business is run by a company, and only a company is required to have its accounts audited (see **8.1**). Nevertheless, it is necessary to maintain accounts which are sufficient to give a true and fair view of the affairs of a business so that the profits which are liable to tax can be ascertained.

32.4 NATIONAL INSURANCE

A sole trader or partner will pay Class 2 National Insurance contributions which are at a flat rate, and may also pay Class 4 National Insurance contributions which are calculated as a percentage of taxable profits. A limited company will pay the employer's National Insurance contributions in relation to each of its employees (including directors), and will collect and pay the employee's own Class 2 National Insurance contributions.

32.5 VALUE ADDED TAX

If the annual turnover of the business is expected to exceed £90,000 in the ensuing 30 days, the proprietor must register for VAT. This will mean that VAT must then be charged and accounted for on the output of goods or services by the business.

32.6 LICENCES

32.6.1 Consumer Credit Act 1974

If the business involves offering credit or hire facilities, the proprietor may require a licence under the Consumer Credit Act 1974, which may be obtained by application to the Office of Fair Trading.

32.6.2 Other licences

Particular types of businesses require a licence to operate obtained from the appropriate local administration office. Examples include licences for liquor sales (from the local authority), for food manufacture (from the environmental health department) and for children's nurseries (from the social services department).

32.7 INSURANCE

A range of possible insurances should be considered, two of which (employer's liability insurance and third party liability motor insurance) are compulsory. Examples of non-compulsory but advisable insurances include fire, theft, product liability, public liability and motor insurance (for more risks than the compulsory third party liability).

32.8 INTELLECTUAL PROPERTY

The business may be using brand names, inventions, designs or products which can be protected from copying by competitors by registration. A patent may be granted for an invention which is capable of industrial application following an application to the Patent Office. A design (ie the outward shape or decorative appearance of a product) may be registered at the Patent Office. A trade mark is a brand name or logo which distinguishes the product in the minds of the public (eg 'Coca-Cola' for soft drinks, or 'Honda' for motorcycles). It may be registered at the Trade Marks Registry, which is part of the Patent Office.

32.9 TERMS AND CONDITIONS OF TRADING

A business will want to set up the terms of the contracts it uses. These contracts could be for the provision of services or for the sale of goods, or a combination. Some aspects of trading are dealt with in **Chapters 31**, **33** and **34**.

CHAPTER 33

INTRODUCTION TO AGENCY AND DISTRIBUTION AGREEMENTS

LEARNING OUTCOMES

After reading this chapter you will be able to describe in outline the principles underlying:

- sales agency
- marketing agency
- distribution agreements
- franchising agreements.

33.1 INTRODUCTION

This chapter will look at differences between agency and distribution agreements, and will compare them with other types of commercial contracts, such as licensing and franchising agreements. **Chapter 34** will examine which factors are relevant in deciding whether to go for an agency or a distribution agreement.

33.2 AGENCY

Suppose Latham Ltd, a furniture manufacturer, decides to sell its furniture in France. However, what if Latham has little or no experience of the market conditions in France? It is likely that any marketing exercises it might undertake over there would be, at best, ill-informed. If Latham is still determined to sell in France, one solution is to find someone who does know the market in question, and to enter into an arrangement whereby that person markets the furniture on Latham's behalf.

One way of marketing the goods would be for Latham to appoint a French company as its agent for selling the furniture. The agency agreement is likely to be one of two main types.

33.2.1 'Sales' agency

Latham may authorise the agent (the French company) to enter into contracts with customers on its behalf; Latham will be 'the principal' under this arrangement. As a result, Latham will be in a direct contractual relationship with the French customers through the agent's actions. This is sometimes called a 'classical sales agency'.

33.2.2 'Marketing' agency

However, Latham may not be very happy with the idea of being bound into a contractual relationship with a customer whom it has never met. It may therefore prefer to give its agent a more limited type of agency authority, where Latham merely authorises the agent to find potential buyers, carry out preliminary discussions and put them directly in touch with Latham. This type of agency is sometimes known as a 'marketing', 'solicitation' or 'introducing' agency.

33.2.3 'Del credere' agency

This describes the situation where the agent agrees to guarantee the customer's performance of the contract in return for an additional commission. This is exceptional, since an agent is usually not liable at all on any contract which they negotiate on the principal's behalf.

33.3 DISTRIBUTION AGREEMENT

Another marketing possibility for Latham would be to sell the furniture to the French company, to enable that company to sell on to customers in France.

However, assume that, rather than simply selling the furniture to the French company and then leaving everything up to them, Latham wants to control the way in which the French company markets the furniture in France. For example, it wants to ensure that the French company exercises its best endeavours to sell as many of the products as possible, and that it uses advertising material which is appropriate to the products and accords with Latham's image. It also wants to ensure that the distributor will carry enough items of furniture to satisfy customer demand so that its goodwill in France will not be damaged by failure to make furniture available to customers. The French company agrees to all these conditions in return for the exclusive right to sell Latham's furniture in France. In other words, the parties enter into a distribution agreement, and both parties have accepted terms which limit their commercial freedom.

33.3.1 The nature of a distribution agreement

The basis of a distribution agreement is that one party (the distributor) buys goods from the other (the supplier) in order to resell them to the distributor's own customers. Thus, there is a contract between Latham and the distributor for the sale and purchase of the furniture, and a contract between the distributor and its customers (also for the sale and purchase of furniture), but no contract between Latham and the distributor's customer.

When goods are being marketed via a distribution agreement, there may be a number of levels of distribution between the producer of the goods and their ultimate consumer. For example, assume that a manufacturer of goods enters into a distribution agreement with a wholesaler. The wholesaler then enters into a distribution agreement of its own with one or more retailers. A supplier at any level of distribution may enter into a number of separate but identical agreements with different distributors, so that the goods can be marketed as widely as possible. The number of distributors appointed by each supplier is likely to increase as the goods move down the 'marketing chain'.

33.3.2 Distribution contrasted with agency and sale of goods

The relationship of supplier and distributor depends on the law of contract. A supplier and distributor will normally enter into a formal distribution agreement, which sets out the terms of their relationship. Central to this will be the terms on which the supplier sells the goods to the distributor (compare this with an agency agreement, where the principal is not selling the goods to the agent but there may be similar provisions relating to the terms upon which the agent contracts). These terms will cover matters such as the goods to be sold, price, payment, delivery and quality. Unlike an agent, a distributor will not receive commission in respect of goods sold. A distributor makes its profit from the margin between the price it pays for the goods and the price at which it sells them.

Although a distribution agreement is essentially a sale of goods contract, it is normally much more than that. In our example, of equal importance with the transfer of ownership in the furniture in return for payment (terms which characterise a sale of goods agreement) are the terms indicated at **33.3** under which the French company accepts certain obligations and restrictions in relation to its advertising and selling of the products and Latham agrees to give it exclusive rights to sell in the relevant territory.

33.3.3 Types of distribution agreements

The form and substance of distribution agreements can vary considerably, depending on the nature of the products being marketed and the level of distribution which has been reached.

Despite this variety, however, agreements tend to fall into a number of broad categories. For example, some are classified as 'selective distribution' agreements. In this case, the supplier attempts to control the sales which its distributor makes. A classic way in which this is done is by a manufacturer putting a term into its agreement with a wholesaler that the wholesaler can only sell the goods to persons who meet the manufacturer's suitability criteria. This may happen, for example, where the goods are luxury items and the manufacturer wants to ensure that any retail outlet to which the wholesaler sells has the appropriate ambience, or where the goods are highly technical and retailers need properly trained staff both to sell the goods and to provide effective after-sales service. In either case, the agreement must provide a set of clear and objective criteria for suitability, and even then, there may be problems with competition law (the impact of competition law on commercial agreements generally is considered in **Chapter 35**).

Another significant category of agreement is 'exclusive distribution'. Usually, this means that the supplier appoints a distributor as its only authorised representative in a certain area (in France, in our example), agreeing not to appoint any other distributors for that area and also not to supply customers in the area itself. This is probably what Latham and the French company have in mind when they agree that the French company is to have 'exclusive rights' to sell in France. It is also possible for the parties to enter into a 'sole distribution' agreement, where the supplier agrees not to appoint any other distributors for the area, but reserves the right to supply customers direct. It is a good idea, however, to avoid using these terms in the drafting of an agreement without further explanation, as businesses do in practice use the terms to mean different things. In our example, it would be important to check what the parties understood the expression 'exclusive rights' to mean.

33.3.4 Distribution agreements and competition law

Great care has to be taken in drafting distribution agreements as, without proper thought and advice, the parties may include terms which fall foul of competition law. This will be considered further in **Chapter 35**.

33.4 OTHER TYPES OF MARKETING AGREEMENTS

Agency and distribution agreements are not the only types of marketing agreements available. The remainder of this section will briefly consider three other possibilities:

(a) licensing agreements;

(b) franchising agreements; and

(c) joint ventures.

The various types of agreement are by no means mutually exclusive. For example, a distributor may also need some access to the intellectual property rights of the manufacturer to enable them to market the product to potential customers. The distribution agreement may therefore include a licence to the distributor of some of the manufacturer's rights (eg the right to use the manufacturer's trade mark).

33.4.1 Licensing

EXAMPLE

Lara, an inventor, has come up with a revolutionary new product with great sales potential. There may be various reasons why she does not want to manufacture and distribute that product herself:

(a) she may not have the facilities to manufacture or distribute the product. She may not be a manufacturer at all, or she may be a small manufacturer with insufficient resources to meet the costs involved in developing, advertising and supplying a sufficient quantity of the product in question;

(b) she may want to market the product in a particular territory and be compelled or encouraged by local laws in that territory to arrange for the product to be manufactured in the territory itself, rather than to manufacture it herself and sell it to a distributor in the usual way.

In such cases, Lara may consider granting a licence to a third party to manufacture and market the product on her behalf.

33.4.2 Franchising

The essence of a franchising agreement is that the franchisor establishes what is usually known as a 'uniform business format' and then authorises the franchisee (often known as the satellite business) to use it.

EXAMPLE

Felipe, a restaurateur, opens up an American-style restaurant in a large provincial town. The food is good, the atmosphere is agreeable and the decor distinctive. Before long, he is so busy he is turning customers away.

Felipe begins to have a vision of many other similar restaurants in other large provincial towns, all with the same name, the same decor, the same menu and the same ambience. However, he feels that he will not have the capacity to run these restaurants himself, and he does not want to employ managers to run them. He feels that someone with a financial stake in such a business is more likely to make a go of it.

The dilemma is one of control. Felipe does not want to be responsible for the satellite restaurants, but he does want to be able to control them, in the sense of ensuring that they retain the same format as the original restaurant. One solution to this problem would be to grant franchises to set up the new restaurants.

33.4.2.1 Advantages of a franchise

Felipe benefits since he can extend his business system without having to raise capital to do so. Also, since franchisees are independent owner-operators, Felipe:

(a) can usually count on a higher level of performance and profitability; and

(b) incurs less risk of legal liability to customers and staff.

Franchisees benefit because:

(a) they can use a business format or product already tested in the market which carries a name familiar to customers and suppliers;

(b) they can usually count on the franchisor's assistance and training during the risky start-up period (eg advice on the provision of equipment and stock); and

(c) they will often find it easier to raise the necessary bank and other finance to get the business off the ground.

33.4.2.2 Disadvantages of a franchise

Felipe may find it difficult in practice to maintain consistently high standards in the franchise and this may damage his reputation with third parties.

Franchisees may find the franchise frustrating because:

(a) the uniform business format leaves little room for individual initiative;

(b) the goodwill of the business remains in the franchisor (however hard the franchisee works to build up clientele); and

(c) the sale of the business therefore remains within the franchisor's control.

33.4.2.3 Conclusion

In practice, many shops, restaurants and other outlets are franchised, including many fast-food restaurants.

33.4.3 Joint ventures

The joint venture agreement commonly occurs where two or more businesses collaborate on a particular project or business enterprise. They may be similar businesses which are, in effect, pooling their resources. Alternatively, they may operate in different spheres and be collaborating on a project which involves the application of both of their areas of expertise.

Often, the parties involved will form a joint venture company and much thought will need to be given as to what powers each party has in respect of that company. However, there are other structures for joint ventures (see **Appendix 3**).

33.4.4 Impact of competition law

Licensing agreements, franchising agreements and joint venture agreements are normally all capable of being affected by both EU and UK competition law. The main provisions of EU competition law (and the main ways of avoiding its impact) are considered in outline in **Chapter 35**. For a summary of the potential impact of UK competition law, see ***Commercial and Intellectual Property Law and Practice***.

33.4.5 Other forms of agreement

There are many other forms of commercial agreements; however, further consideration of this area is outside the scope of this book.

CHAPTER 34

Choosing a Marketing Agreement

LEARNING OUTCOMES

After reading this chapter you will be able to explain some of the factors to be taken into account when choosing between agency and distribution, particularly:

- commercial considerations
- legal considerations.

34.1 INTRODUCTION

This chapter looks in outline at the various factors which might be relevant in choosing between an agency or a distribution agreement.

Before considering the choice between agency and distribution, note that a commercial client may not always require outside assistance in marketing its goods. For example, a large manufacturer intending to market a new line of goods may already be established (eg in the form of a subsidiary company) in its chosen market. It may then be appropriate to let the subsidiary handle the marketing (this can have competition law advantages: see **Chapter 35**).

However, where a client does need a 'trading partner' to help it find buyers and make sales, both agency and distribution agreements are potentially suitable. The client will naturally wish to market the goods as cheaply and efficiently as possible, as well as to promote demand for the goods in the chosen market. The best way of doing this will have to be assessed individually in each case, but the factors described in the following paragraphs should always be considered. Some of these factors may suggest whether an agency or distribution agreement is more suitable; others should always be borne in mind when considering marketing agreements generally.

34.2 COMMERCIAL FACTORS

Commercial factors play an important part in making the right choice of marketing agreement for a client. They may vary from case to case, but certain points are always worth considering.

34.2.1 Size and organisation of the client's business

A large business with considerable resources may be able to use existing subsidiaries, or set up new ones to handle marketing. In this way, it may be able to create an integrated marketing system which runs more efficiently than one in which goods are sold on down the marketing chain between different, independent businesses.

This may, however, not be possible for many clients; setting up a subsidiary (especially overseas) may be too expensive and time-consuming, in which case the client should consider appointing an independent agent or distributor. Bear in mind that a sales agency will need more supervision than a marketing agency or distribution agreement, because a sales agent binds its principal. A client which lacks the time or resources to keep a close check on its marketing operations should choose either a marketing agency or a distribution agreement.

34.2.2 Location and nature of proposed market

If the client is trying to penetrate an unfamiliar market (especially overseas), a distribution agreement is likely to be preferable to an agency agreement. Under a distribution agreement, the client does not have the risk of operating in the market itself (or direct responsibility to customers: see **34.2.4**), and can rely on the distributor's knowledge of local trading conditions and rules. This may be particularly helpful if there is a language barrier to be overcome. As an independent entrepreneur, a distributor may also have more incentive to exploit the market to the full; a distributor is acting for itself, and keeps the profit it earns.

34.2.3 Nature of goods to be marketed

If the client's goods are relatively straightforward to market (eg they are standard in specification, do not vary greatly according to customer requirements and do not require repackaging before they can be sold to customers) a distribution agreement is particularly suitable. If, however, it is essential for the client to be in touch with customers to give them the products they need (eg tailor-made goods, or goods requiring substantial modifications to suit individual customers), an agency agreement is more appropriate.

34.2.4 Client's responsibility to customers

In an agency agreement, the principal will have a contractual relationship with customers (ie the ultimate buyers of the goods); the agent will have either made the contract on the principal's behalf (sales agency) or found and introduced the customers to the principal (marketing agency). In a distribution agreement, the supplier is liable in contract only to the distributor, not to the ultimate customers. If the goods are defective, customers sue the distributor. The supplier's liability to the distributor will be subject to the terms of their agreement and the law governing that agreement, but it may be possible to define and control this liability more strictly than liability to customers. A supplier may, however, be liable to the distributor's customers in other ways (eg in certain circumstances under the Consumer Protection Act 1987 in the UK, or parallel provisions in EU Member States).

34.3 OVERSEAS OPERATIONS

If the parties to a marketing agreement are to be based in different countries (eg a UK supplier appoints a French distributor to market the supplier's goods in France), they should consider a number of points concerning the law which applies to the agreement.

34.3.1 Governing law

If the parties to an agency or distribution agreement are in different countries, they will have to decide what law they wish to govern the agreement. For example, the UK supplier and French distributor are likely to choose either English law or French law. If, however, they cannot agree on the law of one of the parties, they should find an acceptable compromise, such as the law of a neutral third country.

As far as the UK and most of the countries of Western Europe are concerned, contracts are governed by Regulation (EC) No 593/2008 ([2008] OJ L177/6) (referred to as 'Rome I'). Although Rome I is EU legislation, and the UK has now left the EU, Rome I continues to apply in the UK by virtue of the UK's Law Applicable to Contractual Obligations and Non-Contractual Obligations (Amendment etc) (EU Exit) Regulations 2019 (SI 2019/834). Under Rome I, the general principle is that the parties have complete freedom to decide which law governs their contract. However, this will not prevent certain mandatory rules applying to the contract.

For instance, where all the elements of the contract apply to one country only, the mandatory rules of that country cannot be excluded by merely choosing the law of a different country. For example, if both parties were resident in England and the contract were to be performed in England, the parties could not avoid the impact of English law on, for example, anti-competitive agreements, by opting for Swiss law. Even where some of the elements of the contract apply to a different country, certain mandatory rules protecting consumers and employees may be non-excludable.

The best advice must be to examine the terms of the Rome I Regulation before committing the client to a particular choice of law.

34.3.2 How will local law affect the agreement?

Local law (ie the law of the place where the agreement is performed) may be relevant even if the parties have chosen a different law to govern the agreement. Although detailed consideration of this aspect of the parties' relationship is beyond the scope of this chapter, the solicitor should be aware that, in some jurisdictions, provisions of local law may purport to exclude or override parts of the agreement.

34.3.3 Agency agreements

In drafting an agency agreement which is to operate within the EU, it is important to be aware of the impact of the Directive 86/653 on the Co-ordination of the Laws of Member States relating to Self-Employed Commercial Agents ([1986] OJ L382/17). The Directive attempts to harmonise national laws on commercial agency, and in particular provides for the way in which agents are to be remunerated and for the compulsory payment of sums of money by way of compensation or indemnity to an agent on termination of an agency agreement in certain circumstances. The UK implemented the Directive by the Commercial Agents (Council Directive) Regulations 1993 (SI 1993/3053). Detailed consideration of the Regulations is beyond the scope of this chapter, but it is important to note that their provisions on remuneration, termination and compensation considerably strengthen the agent's position under an agency agreement. Significantly, there is some evidence that, since the Regulations came into force, businesses which might in the past have appointed agents have tended to choose other forms of marketing arrangement, as they are concerned about the high level of protection which the Regulations give to agents. In this sense, the Regulations must now be counted as a factor in the choice between agency and distribution.

The Regulations are UK legislation, and so until they are repealed they will remain in force following the UK's withdrawal from the EU.

34.3.4 Specialist advice

If the client's agreement has an overseas element, it will usually be necessary to take the advice of a local lawyer. Local factors may affect the choice of agreement (eg in some countries, foreign businesses are not permitted to act as principals; they can trade only through a locally-run office). Specialist advice may also be needed on other matters, including the effect of local taxation. In addition, if the proposed agent is an individual, local employment or social security laws may apply to the agreement.

34.4 UK TAXATION

If both parties to an agency or distribution agreement are based in the UK, there are no particular tax advantages or disadvantages to either type of agreement. However, it may be important to advise a client on taxation when the principal or supplier is based overseas, with the agent or distributor in the UK, because the principal or supplier could in some circumstances be liable to pay UK corporation tax.

The detailed rules in this area are beyond the scope of this chapter; broadly speaking, however, if an overseas business trades in the UK through a branch or agency, it can be liable to UK corporation tax. For example, if a sales agent makes regular contracts on its principal's behalf here, the principal may become sufficiently established in the UK for tax purposes and the agent may have to account to HMRC for tax on the principal's profits on the principal's behalf. In a distribution agreement, the important factor in deciding whether a non-resident supplier may be liable for corporation tax is whether the supplier has established a sufficient business presence within the UK.

Other features of the agreement between the parties may also require special care from the tax point of view; in particular, whether there is any liability on either party to pay VAT. It may be necessary to take specialist advice on this matter.

34.5 COMPETITION LAW

The impact of EU competition law on both agency and distribution agreements is dealt with in **Chapter 35**.

For the purposes of this chapter, it is sufficient to note that genuine agency agreements are unaffected by EU competition law. This means that Article 101 TFEU cannot apply to the agreement (see further **35.8.2**).

Distribution agreements may run into difficulties with EU competition law. Many distribution agreements contain terms which could affect trade and competition (eg the supplier appoints the distributor to be its distributor for a defined territory, and then agrees to appoint no other distributors for that territory: see further **35.4.2**). It is often possible, however, to arrange matters so that the practical effect of competition law on the agreement is minimal. The EU competition law authorities are relatively sympathetic in their treatment of distribution agreements (especially those between smaller businesses), believing that such agreements may facilitate trade between Member States and help reinforce the single market.

As far as UK competition law is concerned, s 2 of the Competition Act 1998 contains a general prohibition on agreements and certain other business arrangements which may affect trade within the UK and have as their object or effect the prevention, restriction or distortion of competition within the UK. This is known as the 'Chapter I prohibition', and is almost identical in its wording to Article 101 TFEU. It is unlikely that this provision will apply to agency agreements, but it may affect some distribution agreements.

34.6 MAKING A CHOICE

The choice of marketing agreement must depend on the circumstances of each case. However, the following examples show how the choice might work in practice:

EXAMPLE 1: DISTRIBUTION AGREEMENT

Tea Time Ltd was set up five years ago. It is a small company which manufactures jams and pickles. The directors believe that the company's products will sell very well in France, but they are not confident about conducting business abroad and in a foreign language. They can spend some time on developing their overseas business, but feel that they need to concentrate on manufacturing. The jams and pickles can be easily exported in a form suitable for immediate resale.

These facts strongly suggest that a distribution agreement is the right choice. The company needs a trading partner, and wants to trade overseas in an unfamiliar market. The expertise of a local trading partner will help to overcome the language barrier, but the company will not be able to spare the time or resources to supervise that partner very closely. The goods can easily be marketed in the form in which they leave the company. One possible disadvantage of a distribution agreement when compared with an agency agreement is that EU competition law is more likely to apply, but if the trading partner is also a small business this is unlikely to be a major problem (see **35.8.3**).

EXAMPLE 2: AGENCY AGREEMENT

Wood Magic Ltd is a medium-sized company based in Chester. It has traded successfully for nearly 20 years, making luxury fitted furniture from woods such as yew and cherry. Its operations have so far been confined to northern England, but it now wishes to expand into the rest of the UK (and possibly into Continental Europe). The company has up to now handled its own marketing, because of the need to make each piece of furniture to each customer's exact requirements. However, its directors feel that they will require outside marketing assistance in making the planned expansion. They are happy to spend time working with and supervising their chosen trading partner; they feel that this will be necessary to maintain the excellent reputation of their products.

These facts suggest that an agency agreement is appropriate. The company is experienced in running its business, but needs a trading partner. Customer contact is absolutely vital. It may be a case where agency is appropriate for the projected overseas operations as well as those in the UK; the factor of customer contact may outweigh the drawbacks of operating an agency agreement abroad. Either sales or marketing agency may be suitable, although marketing agency does have the advantage of requiring less supervision. This may not, however, be crucial if Wood Magic Ltd is prepared to set aside plenty of time to keep a check on the agency.

CHAPTER 35

Competition Law

LEARNING OUTCOMES

After reading this chapter you will be able to:

- remember the key elements of Articles 101 and 102 TFEU
- explain some of the ways in which EU competition law may impact on commercial agreements, especially agency and distribution agreements
- identify the principal methods available to avoid the impact of Article 101 TFEU on vertical agreements
- describe the structure of the vertical agreements block exemption.

35.1 INTRODUCTION

This chapter builds on and develops the basic principles of EU competition law which were introduced in ***Legal Foundations***, placing particular emphasis on the application of EU competition law to individual commercial agreements. In order to prepare for this, a reminder of those basic principles is likely to be helpful.

The UK has now left the EU. However, EU competition law continues to be important for UK lawyers, as their clients will often be multinational and/or operate within Europe. In October 2024, the European Commission and the UK authorities announced that they had concluded technical negotiations on a new joint Competition Cooperation Agreement. The wording of this new agreement has yet to be finalised, and the detail of its content has not been made public, but it is thought to include cooperation and collaboration on the enforcement of competition law and the investigation of breaches. Moreover, the UK's domestic competition law (which is not described in detail in this chapter) is closely based on EU competition law. The principles underlying EU competition law are therefore important in domestic UK law. It is likely that they will remain important for many years to come after the UK leaves the EU, although it is possible that the two systems will develop in different directions over time.

35.2 PRINCIPLES AND SOURCES OF EU COMPETITION LAW

35.2.1 Direct effect

Articles 101 TFEU (formerly Article 81 EC) and 102 TFEU (formerly Article 82 EC) (see **35.5**) have direct effect and are directly applicable in all Member States. European Union law takes precedence over the law of Member States where there is a conflict between the two. Thus, if the law of a Member State permits a trading practice but EU competition law prohibits it, the practice is unlawful. EU competition law no longer has direct effect in the UK, but a claimant could use it to bring a claim against a UK company before the courts of an EU Member State.

35.2.2 Sources

There are four main sources of EU competition law:

(a) the relevant Articles of the EU Treaties (see **35.5**);

(b) secondary legislation issued under the authority of the Treaties by the Council of Ministers or European Commission (eg Regulation 2022/720 on the application of Article 101(3) of the Treaty on the Functioning of the European Union to categories of vertical agreements and concerted practices, commonly referred to as the 'Vertical Restraints Block Exemption': see **35.8.7**);

(c) case law (created by decisions of the Commission and judgments of the Court of First Instance (now the General Court) and the European Court of Justice (now the Court of Justice of the European Union));

(d) notices issued by the Commission indicating policy (eg the Notice on Agreements of Minor Importance: see **35.8.3**).

35.2.3 Operation of EU competition law: the institutions

35.2.3.1 The European Commission

The Council of Ministers has delegated power to the Commission to supervise the operation of EU competition law. The Commission, through its Competition Law Directorate-General, is therefore responsible for developing competition policy, investigating suspected infringements of competition law, issuing Decisions on most points of competition law and taking action against infringements if necessary. For more detail on the enforcement of EU competition law, see **35.6**.

35.2.3.2 The General Court and the Court of Justice of the European Union

Appeals against Decisions of the Commission are heard by the General Court. Appeal from the General Court is to the Court of Justice of the European Union ('the Court of Justice').

The Court of Justice also has jurisdiction under the general Article 267 TFEU reference procedure to give preliminary rulings on points of interpretation of EU competition law referred to it from national courts.

35.3 OTHER SYSTEMS OF COMPETITION LAW

35.3.1 Systems of Member States

It is important to note that most Member States have their own domestic systems of competition law and that, depending on the circumstances, it may be necessary to consider this domestic law in addition to EU law. Alternatively, domestic competition law may apply where EU law does not (eg where there is no effect on trade between Member States). Competition law in the UK is governed mainly by the Competition Act 1998. The system under this Act is based on Articles 101 and 102 TFEU. The emphasis of UK competition law is on prohibiting business arrangements which may affect trade within, and have the object or effect of preventing, restricting or distorting competition in, the UK and also on prohibiting abuse of a dominant position within the UK. Further, detailed consideration of UK competition law is outside the scope of this book, although the following sections will make some brief comparisons where appropriate.

35.3.2 US competition law

Probably the longest established system of competition law in the world is that of the USA. Like EU competition law, it shows the strong influence of political theory (although it lacks the EU dimension of being used as a means of creating a single internal market between different, independent countries) and has been even more heavily influenced by economic theory. The competition authorities of the USA and EU frequently liaise with each other, and so developments in US policy may influence EU thinking. Briefly, US competition law in its present form began with the Sherman Act 1890. This was designed to combat the anti-competitive practice by which trustees took control of independent companies, and then used that control to eliminate competition. US competition law is therefore known as 'anti-trust' law, although the term has come to refer to any action taken against anti-competitive practices. Its development has seen a number of different approaches to regulating the struggle between small and large businesses; each type of business has had periods of being in and out of favour with the law. By contrast, EU competition policy has always tended to favour smaller businesses.

35.4 EU COMPETITION LAW AND COMMERCIAL AGREEMENTS

35.4.1 Vertical and horizontal agreements

For competition law purposes, agreements are often classified as either 'vertical' or 'horizontal'. As a general principle, the EU competition authorities treat vertical agreements more leniently than horizontal agreements; broadly speaking, the same principle applies to English competition law.

35.4.1.1 Vertical agreements

Broadly speaking, a vertical agreement is an agreement between parties at different levels of the marketing 'chain', although EU law does have its own precise definition of 'vertical agreement' (see **35.8.7**). Examples include supply, distribution, agency and franchising agreements. The parties to a vertical agreement may wish to use terms in that agreement which potentially restrict competition. Assume, for example, that a manufacturer and a wholesaler entering into a distribution agreement agree that the wholesaler will buy all its goods for resale from the manufacturer, and that the manufacturer will sell to the wholesaler and no one else. This ties them to one another, and potentially reduces competition in the market in which the parties operate (eg other potential wholesalers may find it harder to break into the market because they cannot easily acquire suitable goods for resale). However, it is arguable that the potential restriction of competition may be beneficial to consumers of the goods in question, rather than harmful. The parties are secure in their relationship, which may allow them to invest more in the distribution of the goods and so encourage greater availability of the goods and more efficient supply.

As a result, EU competition law deals fairly leniently with most types of vertical agreements; see further **35.8.6**.

35.4.1.2 Horizontal agreements

A horizontal agreement is one between parties at the same level of supply; for example, where competing manufacturers agree to fix the prices at which they will sell their products, or to allocate product markets between themselves. This type of agreement (often referred to as a 'cartel') is likely to operate in a way which seriously reduces competition and harms consumers (eg prices are kept artificially high). European Union law rarely permits such restriction of competition.

35.4.2 Drafting vertical agreements: likely problem areas

Competition law may have a considerable effect on commercial agreements. It may, for example, influence the choice of agreement, as an agency agreement is less likely to infringe

Article 101(1) TFEU than a distribution agreement (see **35.8.2**). This chapter is, however, primarily concerned with the effect of competition law on the *drafting* of an agreement, once the type of agreement has been chosen. The following examples are based on the application of EU competition law; the position should be broadly the same in each case under the Competition Act where an agreement is capable of affecting trade and competition within the UK.

35.4.2.1 Grant of territory

Assume that a German company ('the supplier') is appointing a distributor to sell its goods in Italy. In order to get the distributorship firmly established, the supplier is prepared to offer the distributor some protection from competition. What the distributor wants in this respect is for the supplier not to appoint any other distributors to sell in Italy, and also for the supplier not to sell direct to Italian customers. Will it cause competition law problems if the supplier agrees to this? The term which the parties are contemplating (often referred to as the grant of 'exclusive territory') is a potential restriction on competition. It cuts down the sources from which consumers can buy the goods and, as a result, may keep the price artificially high. It may stop other sellers coming into the market. However, although this is a potential infringement of Article 101(1) TFEU, it should be permissible under the Vertical Restraints Block Exemption (see **35.8.7**).

35.4.2.2 Export ban

Assume that the grant of territory which has just been described is lawful. In return for making this concession, the supplier wants to ensure that the distributor concentrates on the Italian market by providing that the distributor will sell the goods only in Italy and not export them to Slovenia. Because one of the aims of EU competition law is to ensure that goods can circulate freely around the entire internal market, a term in the agreement which restricts or bans exports will cause problems. It will partition the internal market artificially along national lines. It may prevent consumers from being able to buy goods more cheaply from other Member States than they can at home, by impeding 'parallel imports'. Typically, these happen when a trader buys goods in a part of the EU where those goods are cheap, and resells in higher-priced areas, undercutting the higher prices and making them difficult to maintain. The Commission encourages parallel imports as a means of consolidating the single market; an outright export ban is therefore seen as a serious infringement of Article 101(1) TFEU and is unlikely to be permitted.

35.4.2.3 Unsolicited requests from outside the territory

Assume that the supplier wants to include a term in the agreement forbidding the distributor from selling the goods in response to sales requests from Greece. It may do this if it has granted exclusive distribution rights to its Greek distributor, in order to protect the Greek distributor from competition. The term is likely to impede the free flow of goods around the internal market, and potentially cuts off a source of goods for parallel imports. It is a potential restriction of competition and infringement of Article 101(1) TFEU. However, EU law will probably allow some compromise. The client may be able to stop the distributor actively seeking orders from outside Italy (making 'active' sales), but may not be able to stop it meeting unsolicited requests (making 'passive' sales). The point is considered further at **35.8.7**.

35.5 THE RELEVANT ARTICLES OF THE EU TREATIES

With the passing of the Treaty of Lisbon, the Treaty on European Union was split in two – the Treaty on European Union (TEU) and the Treaty on Functioning of the European Union (TFEU). Many of the operational treaty articles are thus now to be found in the TFEU. A consolidated version of the two treaties may be found at [2008] OJ C115/01.

35.5.1 Articles 3 and 4 TEU: general principles

Article 3 TEU sets out the EU's general aims of establishing an internal market and approximating the economic policies of Member States. The Commission and Courts often refer to Article 3 TEU in their decisions on Articles 101 and 102 TFEU, using the general principles as a starting point for the interpretation of the specific Articles.

35.5.2 Articles 34–36 TFEU: free movement of goods

Articles 34–36 TFEU deal with import and export restrictions on the free flow of goods around the internal market, and so are indirectly relevant to competition. Broadly, Article 34 TFEU prohibits measures enacted by Member States which impose total or partial restraints on imports (eg rules requiring import licences or inspection of imports). Article 35 TFEU does the same thing for export restraints (eg export licences). The emphasis is therefore on government restrictions on trade, rather than on arrangements between businesses. Article 36 TFEU, however, sets out circumstances in which such controls may be permitted. For a more detailed discussion of how Articles 34–36 TFEU operate, see ***Legal Foundations***.

35.5.3 Article 101 TFEU: principle, effect and exemption

Article 101(1) TFEU prohibits as incompatible with the internal market agreements between undertakings, decisions by associations of undertakings or concerted practices that may affect trade between Member States and which have as their object or effect the prevention, restriction or distortion of competition within the internal market. It also sets out a non-exhaustive list of business operations or practices which infringe this general principle (eg an agreement to share markets or to fix prices). By Article 101(2) TFEU, such agreements, decisions or practices are void. However, Article 101(3) TFEU allows exemption from the Article 101(1) prohibition in certain circumstances (see **35.8.9**). Article 101 TFEU is discussed in detail in ***Legal Foundations***.

35.5.4 Article 101 TFEU: a brief reminder of the key points

35.5.4.1 Agreements between undertakings

'Agreements' may be formal or informal, written or oral; for example, a formal written contract between two companies for one to distribute the other's products would be an 'agreement', but this would also be the case if nothing were put into writing. This chapter is largely concerned with the effect of Article 101 TFEU on agreements.

35.5.4.2 Decisions by associations of undertakings

A common example of this is where a trade association (ie an 'association of undertakings') makes a decision to fix the prices of products sold by its member businesses, instead of those businesses fixing their own prices in individual agreements with buyers. The price-fixing is likely to be well-organised and widespread, and so may be a potentially serious restriction of competition.

35.5.4.3 Concerted practices

'Concerted practices' can cover virtually any type of co-operation between undertakings (the basic test is whether the undertakings involved have knowingly substituted co-operation for competition). The concerted practice is most often found in relation to manufacturers, but possible examples in relation to vertical agreements include:

Informal co-operation

Two undertakings draft an agreement which does not infringe Article 101(1) TFEU, then abide by different, informally agreed, terms which do restrict competition (in practice, this sort of situation may constitute an informal agreement rather than a concerted practice; however, the precise classification is not usually significant for the purposes of Article 101(1) TFEU).

Networks

In a network of distribution agreements, one supplier enters into a number of agreements with different distributors. Even if none of these agreements contains any terms which directly restrict competition, the effect of the network of agreements may be to close off a market to new businesses trying to enter; it may mean that no new suppliers or distributors are required for that market.

35.5.4.4 Undertakings

The term 'undertakings' covers any entity which is engaged independently in economic activity, including (in the UK) sole traders, partnerships and companies.

35.5.4.5 May affect trade between Member States

The basic test is whether the relevant agreement, decision or practice alters or has the potential to alter the natural flow of trade between Member States. The effect on trade must be appreciable, but the agreement does not necessarily have to be between undertakings based in different Member States. An agreement between parties based in the same Member State and which appears at first sight only to concern that domestic market may have the potential to 'affect trade' in the way required by Article 101(1) TFEU. For example, two large businesses based in France which enter into a distribution agreement relating only to the French market may be able to close off that market so that competitors based elsewhere in the EU find it difficult to enter. It is also possible that an agreement where one party is based outside the EU (or EEA) and one within it may affect trade within the EU, especially where there is a strong trading relationship between the EU and the non-EU country involved.

The requirement for an effect on trade between Member States is what separates EU competition law from UK law. If an agreement, decision or concerted practice affects trade between Member States then it is governed by EU law; if it affects trade within the UK then it falls under UK law. However, the parties' behaviour may affect trade both between Member States and within the UK, and in such cases there is potential for both regimes to apply.

35.5.4.6 Object or effect

'Object' means that Article 101 TFEU applies to agreements containing terms such as price-fixing or export bans without any need for a market analysis; ie, by their very nature, they are assumed to fall within Article 101 TFEU. 'Effect' means that it also applies to agreements which, following analysis, have the effect of restricting competition. This gives the Commission an enormously wide discretion when applying Article 101 TFEU.

35.5.4.7 Prevention, restriction or distortion of competition within the internal market

The Commission gives these words their natural meaning. If an agreement has already been found to affect (or have the potential to affect) trade, it will normally be straightforward for the Commission to demonstrate the necessary effect on competition.

35.5.4.8 Article 101(2) TFEU

As far as individual commercial agreements are concerned, the effect of Article 101(2) TFEU may be to render the whole agreement void if it contains provisions which infringe Article 101(1) TFEU. However, it may be possible for a national court applying Article 101 TFEU to sever the offending provisions (in accordance with the severance rules of the national law governing the agreement) leaving the rest of the agreement valid. It can prove difficult for the court to do this in a distribution agreement, where the offending provisions (eg those relating to exclusive territory) are often part of the consideration offered to induce the potential distributor to accept the agreement (see **35.4.2**), and are therefore so central to the agreement that they cannot be severed.

35.5.4.9 Article 101(3) TFEU

Article 101(3) TFEU applies where an agreement, decision or practice infringes Article 101(1) TFEU but is worthy of exemption from the prohibition (so Article 101(2) TFEU does not apply). Exemption under Article 101(3) will be possible only if the agreement, etc is essentially pro-competitive (broadly, it must promote or improve trade, give consumers some benefit and not contain unnecessary restrictions of competition). For more detail of how this works in practice, see **35.8.9**.

35.5.5 Article 102 TFEU: the principle

Broadly, Article 102 TFEU prohibits as incompatible with the internal market the abuse by one or more undertakings of a dominant position within the internal market or a substantial part of it, in so far as that abuse may affect trade between Member States.

35.5.6 Article 102 TFEU: key points

35.5.6.1 One or more undertakings

The activities of one undertaking can infringe Article 102 TFEU. Unlike Article 101 TFEU, it is not necessary to have an agreement between undertakings (this might also be caught, although exactly when two or more unconnected undertakings can be 'collectively (ie jointly) dominant' in a market is still to some extent unclear; for guidance, see *Re Italian Flat Glass* [1990] 4 CMLR 535).

35.5.6.2 Dominant position

Broadly speaking, an undertaking enjoys a dominant position in a market when it is able to behave independently of its competitors and customers, to stop effective competition against itself and to maintain that state of affairs. There is no conclusive arithmetical test of 'dominance'; very broadly, the larger a business's market share, the more likely it is to be dominant, but the conditions of the relevant market must always be taken into account.

35.5.6.3 Market

The word 'market' includes both product and geographic markets. See ***Legal Foundations*** for a discussion of how to define and identify these markets.

35.5.6.4 Substantial part

Each Member State of the EU is likely to be a 'substantial part' of the internal market. Smaller divisions may be possible.

35.5.6.5 Abuse

Abuse is essentially behaviour by a dominant undertaking which is not normal commercial behaviour in the relevant markets and which is detrimental to competitors or consumers. Examples include:

(a) a dominant undertaking exploiting its customers by charging very high prices which bear no relation to the commercial value of goods, or charging very low prices in order to drive competitors out of the market ('predatory pricing');

(b) a dominant undertaking refusing to supply a customer for no commercially justifiable reason.

35.5.6.6 May affect trade

This is the same requirement as in Article 101 TFEU (see **35.5.4.5**).

35.5.7 Application of the Articles

Article 101 TFEU is more likely than Article 102 TFEU to be relevant to an individual commercial agreement (eg a distribution agreement). However, both Articles can apply to the same set of facts; equally, the fact that Article 101 TFEU does not apply will not rule out the application of Article 102 TFEU (and vice versa).

35.6 THE COMMISSION'S POWERS OF INVESTIGATION AND ENFORCEMENT

35.6.1 Attitude of the authorities

Both Articles 101 and 102 TFEU are expressed in wide terms, and the authorities are prepared to interpret them flexibly. It is unsafe to assume that they will be unable to discover an infringing agreement or practice; they take enforcement of the competition law rules very seriously and are endowed with considerable powers to track down infringements.

35.6.2 Regulation 1/2003

The way in which EU competition law is enforced is governed by Regulation 1/2003 ([2003] OJ L1/1). The Regulation places primary responsibility for the enforcement of EU competition law on national courts and national competition authorities. The Commission enjoys significant enforcement powers itself, but its role is more concerned with policing EU competition law than regulating this area.

The rules described below relate to enforcement by the Commission. Under Regulation 1/2003, national competition authorities also have power to enforce EU competition law. The detailed powers of enforcement are governed by national law, but in many Member States they are similar to the Commission's powers described below.

Since April 2014, competition enforcement in the UK has been carried out mainly by the Competition and Markets Authority. Now that the UK has left the EU and the implementation period has ended, Regulation 1/2003 no longer applies in the UK, and the Commission has no direct powers of investigation and enforcement here. Its ability to investigate possible breaches of EU competition law in the UK is limited to addressing written requests for information to the UK authorities.

35.6.3 Obtaining information

The Commission receives a considerable amount of unsolicited information about possible infringements. For example, information may come to the Commission from a party to an agreement which feels that it is being unfairly treated by the other party, or from a business claiming that a competitor is abusing a dominant position and driving it out of business. The Commission can also obtain information by request. Most requests are informal: the Commission can make a formal request, but this is uncommon. In both cases, the Commission can fine any undertaking which refuses to supply the information requested.

35.6.4 Investigations

When representatives of the Competition Law Directorate-General investigate an undertaking, they have power to inspect its premises, examine its books and records, and demand immediate explanations of 'suspicious' material or practices. Investigators can seek out information which they believe to be useful but which was not previously known to them (subject to the rules of privilege). The Competition Law Directorate-General may make both informal and formal investigations (the latter are usually known as a 'dawn raids'). An undertaking must submit to a dawn raid, which usually happens unannounced and at all the undertaking's premises; refusal to comply will usually result in a fine. Before the Commission makes a decision on the merits of a case, the undertakings concerned have the right to a hearing (the details of the procedure are outside the scope of this chapter).

35.6.5 Competition Cooperation Agreement

The new joint Competition Cooperation Agreement (see **35.1**) is thought to include provisions for cooperation on competition law investigations between the Commission and the UK Competition and Markets Authority. This is likely to be particularly relevant where the parties' behaviour could fall under both EU and UK competition law (see **35.4.5**) – the Commission would be able to investigate within the EU, and cooperate with the UK authority in its own investigations within the UK. Depending on the exact terms of the agreement, there may also be scope for the UK authorities to assist the Commission in obtaining evidence in relation to behaviour falling solely within EU competition law, and vice versa.

35.7 CONSEQUENCES OF INFRINGEMENT

35.7.1 Fines

The Commission can impose heavy fines in respect of infringements of both Articles 101 and 102 TFEU. By Article 23 of Regulation 1/2003, an undertaking which is found to have infringed either Article 101 or Article 102 can be fined a sum not exceeding 10% of its total turnover in the preceding business year. In deciding on the appropriate level of fines, Article 23 provides that the Commission will have regard to the gravity and duration of the infringement. In practice, the Commission will also look at matters such as the size of the undertakings involved, their market share, and (if relevant) how much the parties to the infringement have profited by keeping others out of their market. The Commission can and will fine in respect of unintentional infringements or behaviour which the Commission has not previously punished, although such fines are likely to be smaller than for deliberate infringements. Co-operation with the Commission during an investigation may be a mitigating factor.

35.7.2 Actions in national courts

It is possible for undertakings or consumers to bring actions in their national courts if they have suffered loss due to infringement of either Article 101 or Article 102 TFEU. Both Articles are directly effective. Directive 2020/1828 ([2020] OJ L409/1) requires EU Member States to make provision to enable representative actions to be brought on behalf of groups of affected consumers to obtain injunctions or seek compensation for breach of competition law. Member States had to implement the Directive by 25 June 2023. The intention is to make private enforcement by consumers easier and more cost-effective.

However, these remedies for breach of EU competition law are no longer available in the UK courts because Articles 101 and 102 no longer have direct effect in the UK. Conduct which breaches EU competition law may sometimes also breach UK competition law, and the UK courts can, of course, make orders and award damages for breaches of UK law.

The CRA 2015 (see **31.2** and **31.10**) has established the Competition Appeal Tribunal as a principal forum to hear claims arising from breaches of competition law. The UK also already has a regime for representative actions by consumers to seek remedies for breach of UK competition law, and this is generating substantial litigation.

35.7.3 UK law – the criminal cartel offence – the Enterprise Act 2002

Under the Enterprise Act 2002, criminal penalties may be imposed on an individual for serious cartels taking effect within the UK which breach Article 101. It is only the UK competition authorities that can apply for these sanctions – the Commission has no power to impose criminal sanctions on an individual. It is not necessary to prove that the defendant acted dishonestly. However, a defendant may have a defence if certain information about the cartel arrangement is disclosed to its customers.

35.7.4 Other consequences

Infringement can also have less tangible consequences. For example, a large manufacturer may impose on a small distributor an agreement which it knows to be suspect under Article 101 TFEU. If the distributor realises that the agreement may infringe Article 101 TFEU, it may be able to win concessions from the manufacturer by threatening to notify the authorities of the potential infringement. The manufacturer may then be forced to renegotiate the agreement from a position of weakness. Obviously, any undertaking which notified the Commission in these circumstances would itself be running risks, but it is possible that the distributor would be prepared to use the threat as a bargaining counter, significantly altering the normal balance of bargaining power.

35.8 AVOIDING INFRINGEMENT OF ARTICLE 101 TFEU

35.8.1 Difficulty of avoiding infringement

Subject to what is said at **35.8.8**, infringement of Article 101 TFEU cannot be avoided simply by using a particular form of agreement. The ways in which Article 101 TFEU may apply can sometimes be difficult to predict, and it may be impossible to advise a client with certainty on whether a particular agreement or practice is likely to amount to an infringement. However, depending on the nature of the agreement, it may be possible to take steps to minimise the risk.

35.8.2 Article 101(1) TFEU does not apply

It is sometimes possible to argue that an agreement containing potentially restrictive terms falls outside Article 101 TFEU altogether. This is particularly likely where the parties to an agreement cannot be described as two separate undertakings. Two important examples of this are: agreements between parent and subsidiary companies, and agency agreements.

35.8.2.1 Parent and subsidiary companies

An agreement between a parent and a subsidiary company is unlikely to infringe Article 101 TFEU; the Commission normally regards this sort of agreement as nothing more than allocation of business within a group of companies. The parties would never have been potential competitors, and so an agreement between them cannot have an effect on competition.

35.8.2.2 Agency agreements

Many agency agreements will fall outside the scope of Article 101 TFEU as a result of the Commission's Guidelines on Vertical Restraints ([2022] OJ C248/01), which set out guidance in relation to vertical restraints in general, and in particular on the application of the Vertical Restraints Block Exemption (see **35.8.6** for more explanation of how this block exemption works). Paragraphs 29–47 of the Guidelines deal specifically with agency agreements.

Paragraph 29 defines an agency agreement for this purpose. Broadly speaking, it is an agreement where one person (the agent) is 'entrusted with the power to negotiate and/or conclude contracts on behalf of another person (the principal)' for the sale or purchase of goods or services by the principal. Paragraph 30 indicates that the determining factor in assessing whether an agreement is treated as an agency agreement falling outside Article 101 TFEU is the 'financial or commercial risk' accepted by the agent.

Paragraph 41 says that, where an agency agreement falls outside Article 101 TFEU, the principal can impose limitations on the territory in which, or the customers to which, the agent may sell the contract goods or services, or the prices at which the agent must sell them. These restrictions are common in agency agreements, but they would be likely to breach Article 101 TFEU if it applied.

Paragraphs 31–40 discuss in more detail the types of financial or commercial risks which are material to assessing whether or not an agency agreement falls outside Article 101 TFEU. Article 101 TFEU will still apply if the agent accepts such risks, even to an insignificant degree. Paragraph 33 lists particular situations where an agent will *not* be accepting such risks. These include where the agent does not acquire property in the goods bought or sold under the agency agreement, or supply the services provided under it; where the agent does not contribute to the supply of goods or services; or where the agent is not required to invest in sales promotion, does not maintain at its own risk stocks of the contract goods, and does not offer after-sales services unless it is fully reimbursed by the principal.

However, online platforms – for example, platforms selling travel services, or insurance – will always be treated as distributors, even if they purport to be acting as agents (see para 46).

35.8.3 The Notice on Agreements of Minor Importance

Even if an agreement is made between two independent undertakings, and could affect trade between Member States, its effects may in practice be so small that the Commission will ignore the existence of the agreement. There are two main reasons for this. The Commission has the resources to investigate only the most seriously anti-competitive arrangements; in addition, it is prepared to encourage comparatively small undertakings by allowing them to make agreements which may in theory restrict competition, but which do not have an appreciable impact on market conditions. The Notice on Agreements of Minor Importance sets out guidelines as to when these 'small' agreements will not appreciably restrict competition. Broadly, the Notice can apply to all types of agreement, as long as the agreement satisfies an appropriate guideline (the 'thresholds').

The Notice ([2014] OJ C291/01) provides, in point 8, that the Commission 'holds the view' that agreements which affect trade between Member States do not in fact appreciably restrict competition within the meaning of Article 101(1) TFEU in two particular situations; each situation has a different market share threshold for the application of the Notice. These are:

(a) if the aggregate market share held by the parties to the agreement does not exceed 10% on any of the relevant markets affected by the agreement where the agreement is made between undertakings which are actual or potential competitors on any of these markets (agreements between competitors); or

(b) if the market share held by each of the parties to the agreement does not exceed 15% on any of the relevant markets affected by the agreement where the agreement is made by undertakings which are not actual or potential competitors on any of these markets (agreements between non-competitors).

Although the Notice does not say this as such, 'agreements between competitors' are likely to be horizontal agreements, and 'agreements between non-competitors' are likely to be vertical agreements.

The Notice imposes a further condition that must be fulfilled if the agreement is not going to fall within Article 101(1) TFEU. This condition is that the agreement must not have the prevention, restriction or distortion of competition as its *object*. Paragraph 13 provides that agreements which have the prevention, restriction or distortion of competition as their object include:

(a) agreements between competitors which have as their object the fixing of selling prices charged to third parties, the limitation of output or sales or the allocation of markets or customers;

(b) agreements which contain 'hardcore' restrictions listed in any current or future block exemption regulations (see **35.8.6–35.8.9**).

As vertical agreements are not usually concluded between competitors, it is likely that the Commission will look to the 'hardcore' restrictions in any relevant block exemption regulation to determine whether or not a restriction is an 'object' restriction. In other words, it is point (b) above that is likely to apply in relation to vertical agreements.

However, strictly speaking, the concept of 'object' restrictions is potentially broader, and may extend to other restrictions that are not listed in a block exemption regulation. At least in theory, it is possible that a restriction that is not listed could be an 'object' restriction and could prevent the Notice on Agreements of Minor Importance from applying.

If an agreement satisfies the appropriate market share threshold and does not contain any 'object' restrictions, Article 101 TFEU will not apply to the agreement: the Commission will, in effect, ignore it.

In cases where it is difficult to classify the agreement as being between competitors or non-competitors, the 10% threshold applies.

Point 10 of the Notice provides for what is called the 'cumulative foreclosure effect of parallel networks of agreements having similar effects on the market'. This is where competition in a relevant market is restricted by the cumulative effect of agreements for the sale of goods or services entered into by different suppliers or distributors: in this case, the market share thresholds under point 8 are reduced to 5% both for agreements between competitors and non-competitors. Such an effect is unlikely to exist if less than 30% of the relevant market is covered by parallel networks of agreements having similar effect.

Point 12 of the Notice provides some guidance on the potentially difficult question of how to determine the relevant market (so that in turn, market share can be calculated); in particular, it refers to the Commission's Notice on definition of the relevant market for the purposes of EU competition law. This Notice is also used, for example, to determine the relevant market for the purposes of Article 102 TFEU.

35.8.4 Effect of the Notice

Point 5 of the Notice provides that in cases covered by the Notice, the Commission will not institute proceedings (ie for infringement of Article 101 TFEU). It also provides that where undertakings assume 'in good faith' that an agreement is covered by the Notice but this turns out not to be the case, the Commission will not impose fines. Lastly, it notes that although the Notice is not binding on the courts and (competition) authorities of the Member States, it is intended to give guidance to them on the application of Article 101 TFEU.

The Court of Justice has confirmed (see Case C-226/11 *Expedia* [2012] ECR) that national competition authorities are not bound by the Notice when they are enforcing EU competition law. They are therefore free to apply Article 101(1) even if the parties' market shares are below the thresholds in the Notice, as long as the agreement restricts competition appreciably. In practice, however, they are likely to look to the Notice when deciding whether there is an appreciable restriction, unless they have a good reason not to do so.

Note also the existence of the Commission Notice ([2004] OJ C101/07) containing guidelines on the 'effect on trade' concept (which is common to both Articles 101 and 102 TFEU). This Notice is usually known as the 'NAAT' Notice, and works on similar principles to the Notice on Agreements of Minor Importance; there is deemed to be no appreciable effect on trade where the aggregate market share of the parties on any relevant market within the European Union does not exceed a certain level. There are, however, two substantial differences from the Notice on Agreements of Minor Importance: the NAAT Notice will apply only if the market share does not exceed 5%, and it can apply even if the agreement contains 'object' restrictions.

35.8.5 Agreements likely to infringe Article 101(1) TFEU

In the case of an agreement between substantial independent undertakings which is likely to have an appreciable effect on trade and competition within the internal market, there is a serious possibility that it will infringe Article 101(1) TFEU. This is particularly likely with distribution agreements, which often contain provisions (eg exclusive territory) considered by the parties to be essential to the workings of the agreement, but which have the potential to restrict competition. At this stage, the parties should consider whether the agreement could be redrafted to get the benefit of a block exemption.

35.8.6 Block exemptions

Block exemptions work by exempting defined categories of agreement from the prohibition in Article 101(1) TFEU. They are given in the form of Commission Regulations, and have been designed to ensure that the Commission does not have to investigate agreements which potentially infringe Article 101(1) TFEU, but do not in fact impose serious restrictions on competition, and which may actually benefit consumers. The exemption is granted under the provisions of Article 101(3) TFEU, which permits exemption for agreements which can be shown to have these characteristics (for more detail on Article 101(3), see **35.8.10**). There are block exemptions covering a variety of commercial agreements, including vertical agreements (see **35.8.7**) and agreements for the transfer of technology (eg the licensing of certain types of intellectual property, such as patents). Although there are some differences in format and presentation, block exemptions tend to follow a similar pattern; first, the Regulation states, in a preamble, the Commission's policy in allowing block exemption for the type of agreement concerned, and then outlines the conditions on which block exemption will be granted to that type of agreement.

35.8.7 An example of a block exemption in practice: Regulation 2022/720

The block exemption granted by Regulation 2022/720 ([2022] OJ L134/4) (commonly known as the 'Vertical Agreements' or 'Vertical Restraints' Block Exemption) has applied to vertical agreements (as defined in Article 1) since 1 June 2022. (It replaces the old Regulation 330/2010, which expired at the end of May 2022.) The Commission's Guidelines on Vertical Restraints ([2022] OJ C248/01) (see **35.8.2.2**) provide further guidance on its application. Regulation 2022/720 will expire on 31 May 2034

Broadly speaking, a 'vertical agreement' is defined in Regulation 2022/720 as an agreement for the supply of goods or services where the parties are at different levels of the supply chain (eg, a distribution agreement between a manufacturer and a wholesaler, or a franchise agreement).

The approach adopted in Regulation 2022/720 is similar to that taken in many block exemption regulations. It provides that Article 101 TFEU will not apply to a vertical agreement as long as:

(a) the parties' market shares do not exceed certain stated thresholds; and
(b) the agreement does not contain any prohibited terms.

These prohibited terms are listed in Articles 4 or 5 of Regulation 2022/720 (see below). Anything not listed in this way will normally be permissible, creating what is commonly referred to as a 'safe harbour' for agreements which do not contain prohibited terms.

The market share threshold is set out in Article 3: the block exemption applies to an agreement only if both the supplier and the distributor (referred to as the 'buyer') each have market shares of less than 30%. This has been seen as an attempt to bring some economic reality into the operation of the block exemption by restricting the benefit of exemption to small and medium-sized undertakings.

The main provisions of the Regulation are as follows:

Preamble explains the philosophy behind the grant of block exemption to vertical agreements, typically that small-scale agreements generally lead to an improvement in production or distribution and ultimately benefit consumers.

Article 1	defines various important phrases such as 'vertical agreement', 'non-compete obligation' and 'active sales' and 'passive sales' (see below).
Article 2	grants exemption to vertical agreements, subject to some limitations (see **35.8.7.1**).
Article 3	sets out the market share threshold above which the block exemption will not apply.
Article 4	lists a series of 'hard-core' restrictions, any one of which will prevent the block exemption from applying at all. Article 4 is explained in more detail at **35.8.7.2**.
Article 5	lists a series of 'excluded' restrictions which cannot benefit from the block exemption. They are explained in more detail at **35.8.7.3**. Such restrictions will be void under Article 101(2) TFEU. The rest of the agreement may still be valid if these restrictions can be severed from it (see **35.5.4.8**).

Note that, by Article 6, the block exemption may be withdrawn by the Commission.

35.8.7.1 Limitations of the block exemption

The application of the block exemption is restricted where the supplier and the distributor are competitors, for example where the supplier sells its goods or services online in parallel to the distributor ('dual distribution'). This is becoming increasingly common, particularly where suppliers who have appointed a distributor also sell their products from their own websites. To the extent that the supplier makes direct sales, it is competing with the distributor, operating at the same level of the supply chain. Article 2 contains detailed provisions setting out exactly when the block exemption can still apply if the supplier and the distributor are competing with one another.

The Commission is particularly concerned about competitors sharing information with one another, and so the block exemption does not apply to the exchange of information between the supplier and the distributor when they are competitors, unless it is directly related to the implementation of the agreement or is necessary to improve the production or distribution of the goods or services to which the agreement relates.

35.8.7.2 Article 4: hard-core restrictions

An agreement containing any of the restrictions listed in Article 4 cannot benefit from the block exemption. Article 4 deals separately with exclusive and non-exclusive distribution systems, and also selective distribution systems (see **33.3.3**). The rules which apply in each of these situations are similar, which means that there is quite a lot of duplication within Article 4. (The rules on selective distribution systems are beyond the scope of this book.)

The hard-core restrictions include:

(1) Fixing the prices at which the distributor can resell the goods or services (see Article 4(a)).

(2) Restricting the territories in which the distributor may resell the goods or services, or the customer groups to which it may resell them. However, the supplier can restrict the distributor from making 'active' sales into the exclusive territory allocated to a maximum of five other distributors (or into territory reserved exclusively to the supplier) – see Article 4(b)(i) and Article 4(d)(i). 'Active' sales are sales into territories where the distributor actively markets the goods or services (or to customer groups to which it actively markets them).

The supplier cannot restrict the distributor from making 'passive' sales. 'Passive' sales are sales into territories where the distributor does not market the goods or services (or to customer groups to which it does not market them).

(3) Preventing the distributor (or its customers) from using the internet to resell the supplier's goods or services. However, the Commission's Guidelines on Vertical

Restraints expressly state that a supplier can require a distributor to pay a different price for goods which are to be resold online (known as 'dual pricing').

35.8.7.3 Article 5: excluded restrictions

The excluded restrictions include:

(1) Preventing the distributor from competing with the supplier, if the obligation is indefinite or exceeds five years: Article 5(1)(a). This covers, for example, selling competing goods or services. The precise meaning of 'non-compete obligation' Is defined in Article 1.

(2) Post-termination non-compete obligations: Article 5(1)(b).

(3) Restrictions imposed by providers of online 'intermediation services' (such as booking platforms and price comparison websites) which prevent the businesses whose goods or services they sell (for example, hotels or insurance companies) from selling their goods or services on more favourable terms on other platforms (sometimes known as 'parity' obligations): Article 5(1)(d).

Thus a booking platform cannot prevent a hotel listed on the platform from selling its rooms more cheaply via another platform.

There are various detailed exceptions to the restrictions prohibited by Article 5.

35.8.8 Block exemptions in UK competition law

Following the expiry of the implementation period at the end of 2020, the EU's block exemptions remain in effect as 'retained exemptions' for the purposes of UK competition law, unless and until they are changed by the UK Government. The UK Government introduced its own version of the Vertical Restraints Block Exemption in June 2022, so EU Regulation 2022/720 does not apply in the UK. The UK's vertical restraints block exemption is contained in the Competition Act 1998 (Vertical Agreements Block Exemption) Order 2022 (SI 2022/516). It is commonly referred to as the VABEO (the 'Vertical Agreements Block Exemption Order').

Although the VABEO is structured rather differently from the EU's Vertical Restraints Block Exemption, its content is largely the same, differing only in points of detail.

For now, some other EU block exemptions remain in place in the UK as retained exemptions.

35.8.9 Advantages of block exemption

It is desirable to take advantage of a block exemption wherever possible, as it is likely to be cheaper, quicker and safer for the parties concerned. If an agreement is drafted in a way which closely follows any relevant block exemption, it is unlikely that the Commission will take an interest in the agreement unless circumstances change.

35.8.10 Article 101(3)

As noted at **35.5.4.9** above, Article 101(3) TFEU provides for the possibility that an agreement may be exempted from the prohibition in Article 101(1) TFEU if it satisfies the conditions in Article 101(3) TFEU. These are that the agreement:

(a) improves distribution or technical progress;

(b) allows consumers a fair share of the resulting benefits;

(c) does not impose restrictions that are not indispensable to achieving those benefits; and

(d) does not substantially eliminate competition.

As well as allowing for categories of agreements to be exempted from the prohibition (ie allowing block exemptions to be made by the Commission), Article 101(3) TFEU may also exempt individual agreements.

Under Regulation 1/2003:

(a) parties to an agreement are responsible for assessing whether or not their agreement satisfies the conditions laid down in Article 101(3) TFEU;

(b) in cases of dispute, national competition authorities or national courts have the power to decide whether or not an agreement does satisfy the conditions, and to grant exemption (see further **35.8.11**).

The Regulation 1/2003 system is often referred to as 'self-assessment'.

The Commission has the power under Regulation 1/2003 to pronounce informally on the status of agreements, although this is limited to difficult or novel cases, and there is little evidence of its use.

35.8.11 National courts and national competition authorities

Regulation 1/2003 devolves some of the power to enforce EU competition law to national courts and to national competition authorities (NCAs: essentially, these are the bodies in each Member State which enforce national competition law).

The Commission has provided guidance via a further regulation dealing with procedural issues and a series of Notices covering such matters as co-operation between NCAs, co-operation between the Commission and national courts, and Commission guidance for courts and NCAs on how to apply Article 101(3) TFEU.

It appears that, under English law, parties to an agreement would be able to apply to court for a declaration as to the status of an agreement. However, this would relate only to UK competition law, and in any case it is thought that courts will be reluctant to grant such declarations. In addition, the Competition and Markets Authority gives informal guidance on the status of agreements via guidelines on its website. Note that this is general guidance only rather than relating to specific agreements.

35.8.12 Practical impact of Regulation 1/2003

The following points may be made:

(a) parties may be well advised to rely on the block exemption or the Notice on Agreements of Minor Importance where appropriate;

(b) parties who want to rely on the self-assessment exemption under Article 101(3) need to assess their agreement carefully, and it may be advisable to take detailed legal advice on whether exemption will be possible;

(c) as noted at **35.8.11**, there are ways in which parties can obtain informal guidance from NCAs or a declaration from a court as to the status of their agreement under Article 101(3) TFEU. However, this is of limited availability and use, and the burden falls primarily on undertakings to assess their own agreements;

(d) if the parties have decided that Article 101(3) TFEU applies to their agreement, this conclusion may be challenged by a third party (possibly also by an NCA);

(e) if a challenge is made, the parties can apply to an NCA or court (as appropriate) to determine whether Article 101(3) TFEU applies or not.

35.9 APPLYING THE ARTICLES TO SPECIFIC COMMERCIAL AGREEMENTS

Although it is not always easy to predict the operation of Articles 101 and 102 TFEU in relation to a commercial agreement, it is worth considering certain points when drafting or reviewing an agreement from the point of view of EU law. In particular, the solicitor should try to establish two important points: are the Articles likely to apply, and how, if at all, can this be prevented? Bear in mind, however, that the answers may not be clear-cut, and that the following paragraphs provide guidance only on the points to consider.

35.9.1 Article 101 TFEU: agency agreements

When drafting or reviewing a client's agreement, consider the following points.

(a) Article 101(1) TFEU may not apply at all because one or more of the following statements is true.
   (i) The agreement is within the Commission's Guidelines on vertical restraints because the agreement is a 'genuine agency agreement': the agent is not acting independently in relation to the contract goods and, for example, accepts no financial risk under the agency agreement.
   (ii) The principal and agent are parent and subsidiary companies and therefore count as one undertaking.
   (iii) The agreement is otherwise incapable of affecting trade and competition within the internal market (eg it does not contain any restrictive terms).
(b) The agreement may fall within the Notice on Agreements of Minor Importance. If so, the Commission is unlikely to take an interest in the agreement.

If neither (a) nor (b) is relevant, the agency agreement will probably have to be treated in the same way as a distribution agreement (see below). Bear in mind, however, that there are no block exemptions which apply to agency agreements.

35.9.2 Article 101 TFEU: distribution agreements

When drafting or reviewing a client's distribution agreement, consider the following points:

(a) Article 101(1) TFEU may not apply because either of the following statements is (or both are) true:
   (i) The parties are parent and subsidiary companies and therefore count as one undertaking.
   (ii) The agreement is otherwise incapable of affecting trade and competition within the internal market (eg it does not contain any restrictive terms).
(b) Does the Notice on Agreements of Minor Importance or the NAAT Notice apply?
(c) If neither (a) nor (b) is relevant, consider the terms which the client wants to include in the agreement. If they are likely to restrict competition, it is probably best to assume that Article 101(1) TFEU applies, and then decide if it is possible to avoid infringement.
(d) (i) If drafting a new agreement, draft to get the benefit of the relevant block exemption (Regulation 2022/720) wherever possible.
   (ii) If reviewing an existing agreement, consider whether it could be redrafted to bring it within the block exemption.
(e) If none of the above is appropriate, consider whether Article 101(3) TFEU will apply to exempt the agreement.

35.9.3 Article 102 TFEU

Article 102 TFEU is far less likely to apply to individual commercial agreements than Article 101 TFEU. However, it must not be ignored, especially if one of the parties has a large market share (eg if a supplier with a large market share refused to supply a distributor and there was no good commercial reason for the refusal, it could in certain circumstances be abusing a dominant position). Bear in mind that there is no way of avoiding infringement if Article 102 TFEU does apply. Consider the following questions:

(a) Does the agreement involve one or more undertakings?
(b) Does the agreement involve an undertaking with a dominant position in the relevant markets?
(c) Is that dominant position within the internal market or a substantial part of it?
(d) Does the conduct of the dominant undertaking amount to abuse of a dominant position?

If the answer to all of these questions is 'Yes', Article 102 TFEU prohibits the abuse in so far as it may affect trade between Member States.

APPENDIX 1

Form IN01 – Application to Register a Company

Note. Pages 1, 2, 18, 19 and 25–34 are omitted. When the Economic Crime and Corporate Transparency Act 2023 comes fully into force, there will be further changes to this form. Always use the latest form available on the Companies House website, at <www.gov.uk/government/organisations/companies-house>.

In accordance with Section 9 of the Companies Act 2006.

DON'T STAPLE

IN01
Application to register a company

Companies House

A fee is payable with this form.
Please see 'How to pay' on the last page.

What this form is for
You may use this form to register a private or public company.

What this form is NOT for
You cannot use this form to register a limited liability partnership. To do this, please use form LL IN01. Do not use this form if any individual person with significant control is applying or has applied for protection from having their details disclosed on the public register. Contact secure@companieshouse.gov.uk to get a separate form.

For further information, please refer to our guidance at: gov.uk/companieshouse

Part 1 Company details

A1 Company name

Check if a company name is available by using our name availability search:

companieshouse.gov.uk/info

Please show the proposed company name below.

Proposed company name in full ❶

For official use

→ **Filling in this form**
Please complete in typescript or in bold black capitals.

All fields are mandatory unless specified or indicated by *

❶ **Duplicate names**
Duplicate names are not permitted. A list of registered names can be found on our website. There are various rules that may affect your choice of name. More information on this is available in our guidance at: gov.uk/companieshouse

A2 Company name restrictions ❷

Please tick the box only if the proposed company name contains sensitive or restricted words or expressions that require you to seek comments of a government department or other specified body.

☐ I confirm that the proposed company name contains sensitive or restricted words or expressions and that approval, where appropriate, has been sought of a government department or other specified body and I attach a copy of their response.

❷ **Company name restrictions**
A list of sensitive or restricted words or expressions that require consent can be found in our guidance at: gov.uk/companieshouse

A3 Exemption from name ending with 'Limited' or 'Cyfyngedig' ❸

Please tick the box if you wish to apply for exemption from the requirement to have the name ending with 'Limited', Cyfyngedig' or permitted alternative.

☐ I confirm that the above proposed company meets the conditions for exemption from the requirement to have a name ending with 'Limited', 'Cyfyngedig' or permitted alternative.

❸ **Name ending exemption**
Only private companies that are limited by guarantee and meet other specific requirements or private companies that are charities are eligible to apply for this. For more details, please go to our website: gov.uk/companieshouse

05/24 Version 10.0

IN01
Application to register a company

A4 Company type ❶

Please tick the box that describes the proposed company type and members' liability (only one box must be ticked):

☐ Public limited by shares
☐ Private limited by shares
☐ Private limited by guarantee
☐ Private unlimited with share capital
☐ Private unlimited without share capital

❶ **Company type**
If you are unsure of your company's type, please go to our website: gov.uk/companieshouse

A5 Principal business activity

Please show the trade classification code number(s) for the principal activity or activities. ❷

Classification code 1					
Classification code 2					
Classification code 3					
Classification code 4					

If you cannot determine a code, please give a brief description of the company's business activity below:

Principal activity description

❷ **Principal business activity**
You must provide a trade classification code (SIC code 2007) or a description of your company's main business in this section.

A full list of the trade classification codes is available on our website: gov.uk/companieshouse

A6 Situation of registered office ❸

Please tick the appropriate box below that describes the situation of the proposed registered office (only one box must be ticked):

☐ England and Wales
☐ Wales
☐ Scotland
☐ Northern Ireland

❸ **Registered office**
Every company must have a registered office and this is the address to which the Registrar will send correspondence.

For England and Wales companies, the address must be in England or Wales.

For Welsh, Scottish or Northern Ireland companies, the address must be in Wales, Scotland or Northern Ireland respectively.

IN01
Application to register a company

X

Registered email address

Do not cover this barcode

This page is not shown on the public record

A10 **Registered email address** ❶

Email address

❶ **You must give an appropriate email address.**
An email address is an "appropriate email address" if, in the ordinary course of events, emails sent to it by the registrar would be expected to come to the attention of a person acting on behalf of the company.
Only give one email address.

X

IN01
Application to register a company

X

Registered email address

Do not cover this barcode

This page is not shown on the public record

A10 **Registered email address** ❶

Email address

❶ **You must give an appropriate email address.**
An email address is an "appropriate email address" if, in the ordinary course of events, emails sent to it by the registrar would be expected to come to the attention of a person acting on behalf of the company.
Only give one email address.

X

IN01
Application to register a company

Part 2 Proposed officers

For private companies the appointment of a secretary is optional, however, if you do decide to appoint a company secretary you must provide the relevant details. Public companies are required to appoint at least one secretary.

Private companies must appoint at least one director who is an individual. Public companies must appoint at least two directors, one of which must be an individual.

For a secretary who is an individual, go to Section B1; For a corporate secretary, go to Section C1; For a director who is an individual, go to Section D1; For a corporate director, go to Section E1.

Secretary

B1 Secretary appointments ❶

Please use this section to list all the secretary appointments taken on formation. **For a corporate secretary, complete Sections C1-C4.**

Title*	
Full forename(s)	
Surname	
Former name(s) ❷	

❶ Corporate appointments
For corporate secretary appointments, please complete section C1-C4 instead of section B.

Additional appointments
If you wish to appoint more than one secretary, please use the 'Secretary appointments' continuation page.

❷ Former name(s)
Please provide any previous names (including maiden or married names) which have been used for business purposes in the last 20 years.

B2 Secretary's service address ❸

Building name/number	
Street	
Post town	
County/Region	
Postcode	
Country	

❸ Service address
This is the address that will appear on the public record. This does not have to be your usual residential address.

Please state 'The Company's Registered Office' if your service address will be recorded in the proposed company's register of secretaries as the company's registered office.

If you provide your residential address here it will appear on the public record.

05/24 Version 10.0

IN01
Application to register a company

Corporate secretary

C1 Corporate secretary appointments ❶

Please use this section to list all the corporate secretary appointments taken on formation.

Name of corporate body/firm

Building name/number

Street

Post town

County/Region

Postcode

Country

❶ Additional appointments
If you wish to appoint more than one corporate secretary, please use the 'Corporate secretary appointments' continuation page.

Registered or principal address
This is the address that will appear on the public record. This address must be a physical location for the delivery of documents. It cannot be a PO box number (unless contained within a full address), or DX number.

C2 Location of the registry of the corporate body or firm

Is the corporate secretary a limited company registered in the UK?

→ **Yes** Complete **Section C3 only**
→ **No** Complete **Section C4 only**

C3 UK-registered limited companies ❷

Please give the company registration number.

Registration number

❷ You can find the registration number on our website: companieshouse.gov.uk/info

C4 Other corporate bodies or firms

Please give details of the legal form of the corporate body or firm and the law by which it is governed. If applicable, please also give details of the register in which it is entered (including the state) and its registration number in that register.

Legal form of the corporate body or firm

Governing law

If applicable, where the company/firm is registered ❸

If applicable, the registration number

❸ Where you have provided details of the register (including state) where the company or firm is registered, you must also provide its number in that register.

IN01
Application to register a company

Director

D1 Director appointments ❶

Please use this section to list all the director appointments taken on formation.
For a corporate director, complete Sections E1-E4.

Title*	
Full forename(s)	
Surname	
Former name(s) ❷	
Country/State of residence ❸	
Nationality	
Month/year of birth ❹	X X m m y y y y
Business occupation (if any) ❺	

❶ Appointments
Private companies must appoint at least one director who is an individual. Public companies must appoint at least two directors, one of which must be an individual.

❷ Former name(s)
Please provide any previous names (including maiden or married names) which have been used for business purposes in the last 20 years.

❸ Country/State of residence
This is in respect of your usual residential address as stated in section D4.

❹ Month and year of birth
Please provide month and year only.

❺ Business occupation
If you have a business occupation, please enter here. If you do not, please leave blank.

Additional appointments
If you wish to appoint more than one director, please use the 'Director appointments' continuation page.

D2 Director's service address ❻

Please complete the service address below. You must also fill in the director's usual residential address in **Section D4.**

Building name/number	
Street	
Post town	
County/Region	
Postcode	
Country	

❻ Service address
This is the address that will appear on the public record. This does not have to be your usual residential address.

Please state 'The Company's Registered Office' if your service address will be recorded in the proposed company's register of directors as the company's registered office.

If you provide your residential address here it will appear on the public record.

05/24 Version 10.0

IN01
Application to register a company

X

This page is not shown on the public record

Do not cover this barcode

D3

New director's date of birth ❶

Please complete your full date of birth below.

Date of birth d d m m y y y y

❶ **Date of birth**
Please give the full date of birth. The day (dd) will not appear on the public record unless the subscribers have elected to hold LLP members information on the public register.

D4

Director's usual residential address ❷

Please complete your usual residential address below.

Building name/number

Street

Post town

County/Region

Postcode

Country

❷ **New director's usual residential address**
Please state 'Same as service address' in this section if your usual residential address is recorded in the company's proposed register of director's residential addresses as 'Same as service address'.

You cannot state 'Same as service address' if your service address has been stated in Section D2 as 'The Company's Registered Office'. You will need to complete the address in full.

This address cannot be a PO Box, or DX number.

Section 243 of Companies Act 2006

Section 243 exemption ❸

Only tick the box below if you are in the process of applying for, or have been granted, exemption by the Registrar from disclosing your usual residential address to credit reference agencies under section 243 of the Companies Act 2006.

☐

Different postal address:
If you are applying for, or have been granted, a section 243 exemption, please post this whole form to the different postal address below:
The Registrar of Companies, PO Box 4082, Cardiff, CF14 3WE.

Where you are applying for a section 243 exemption with this notice, the application and this form must be posted together.

❸ If you are currently in the process of applying for, or have been granted, a section 243 exemption, you may wish to check you have not entered your usual residential address in Section D2 as this will appear on the public record.

X

IN01
Application to register a company

Director

D1 Director appointments ❶

Please use this section to list all the director appointments taken on formation.
For a corporate director, complete Sections E1-E4.

Title*	
Full forename(s)	
Surname	
Former name(s) ❷	
Country/State of residence ❸	
Nationality	
Month/year of birth ❹	X X m m y y y y
Business occupation (if any) ❺	

❶ Appointments
Private companies must appoint at least one director who is an individual. Public companies must appoint at least two directors, one of which must be an individual.

❷ Former name(s)
Please provide any previous names (including maiden or married names) which have been used for business purposes in the last 20 years.

❸ Country/State of residence
This is in respect of your usual residential address as stated in section D4.

❹ Month and year of birth
Please provide month and year only.

❺ Business occupation
If you have a business occupation, please enter here. If you do not, please leave blank.

Additional appointments
If you wish to appoint more than one director, please use the 'Director appointments' continuation page.

D2 Director's service address ❻

Please complete the service address below. You must also fill in the director's usual residential address in **Section D4.**

Building name/number	
Street	
Post town	
County/Region	
Postcode	
Country	

❻ Service address
This is the address that will appear on the public record. This does not have to be your usual residential address.

Please state 'The Company's Registered Office' if your service address will be recorded in the proposed company's register of directors as the company's registered office.

If you provide your residential address here it will appear on the public record.

IN01
Application to register a company

X

This page is not shown on the public record

Do not cover this barcode

D3 New director's date of birth ❶

Please complete your full date of birth below.

Date of birth d d m m y y y y

❶ **Date of birth**
Please give the full date of birth. The day (dd) will not appear on the public record unless the subscribers have elected to hold LLP members information on the public register.

D4 Director's usual residential address ❷

Please complete your usual residential address below.

Building name/number

Street

Post town

County/Region

Postcode

Country

❷ **New director's usual residential address**
Please state 'Same as service address' in this section if your usual residential address is recorded in the company's proposed register of director's residential addresses as 'Same as service address'.

You cannot state 'Same as service address' if your service address has been stated in Section D2 as 'The Company's Registered Office'. You will need to complete the address in full.

This address cannot be a PO Box, or DX number.

Section 243 of Companies Act 2006

Section 243 exemption ❸

Only tick the box below if you are in the process of applying for, or have been granted, exemption by the Registrar from disclosing your usual residential address to credit reference agencies under section 243 of the Companies Act 2006.

☐

Different postal address:
If you are applying for, or have been granted, a section 243 exemption, please post this whole form to the different postal address below:
The Registrar of Companies, PO Box 4082, Cardiff, CF14 3WE.

Where you are applying for a section 243 exemption with this notice, the application and this form must be posted together.

❸ If you are currently in the process of applying for, or have been granted, a section 243 exemption, you may wish to check you have not entered your usual residential address in Section D2 as this will appear on the public record.

X

05/24 Version 10.0

IN01
Application to register a company

Corporate director

E1 Corporate director appointments ❶

Please use this section to list all the corporate directors taken on formation.

Name of corporate body or firm	
Building name/number	
Street	
Post town	
County/Region	
Postcode	
Country	

❶ **Additional appointments**
If you wish to appoint more than one corporate director, please use the 'Corporate director appointments' continuation page.

Registered or principal address
This is the address that will appear on the public record. This address must be a physical location for the delivery of documents. It cannot be a PO box number (unless contained within a full address), or DX number.

E2 Location of the registry of the corporate body or firm

Is the corporate director a limited company registered in the UK?

→ **Yes** Complete **Section E3 only**
→ **No** Complete **Section E4 only**

E3 UK-registered limited companies ❷

Please give the company registration number.

Registration number	

❷ You can find the registration number on our website: companieshouse.gov.uk/info

E4 Other corporate bodies or firms

Please give details of the legal form of the corporate body or firm and the law by which it is governed. If applicable, please also give details of the register in which it is entered (including the state) and its registration number in that register.

Legal form of the corporate body or firm	
Governing law	
If applicable, where the company/firm is registered ❸	
If applicable, the registration number	

❸ Where you have provided details of the register (including state) where the company or firm is registered, you must also provide its number in that register.

IN01
Application to register a company

Part 3 Statement of capital

Does your company have share capital?
→ **Yes** Complete the sections below.
→ **No** Go to **Part 4 (Statement of guarantee).**

F1 Statement of capital

Complete the table(s) below to show the share capital.

Complete a separate table for each currency (if appropriate). For example, add pound sterling in 'Currency table A' and Euros in 'Currency table B'. In each currency table show the total number of shares of each class issued in that currency.

Continuation pages
Please use a continuation page if necessary.

Currency Complete a separate table for each currency	**Class of shares** E.g. Ordinary/Preference etc.	**Number of shares**	**Aggregate nominal value** (£, €, $, etc) Number of shares issued multiplied by nominal value	**Total aggregate amount to be unpaid, if any** (£, €, $, etc) Including both the nominal value and any share premium
Currency table A				
	Totals (including any continuation pages)			
Currency table B				
	Totals (including any continuation pages)			
Currency table C				
	Totals (including any continuation pages)			

	Total number of shares	Total aggregate nominal value ❶	Total aggregate amount unpaid ❶
Totals (including continuation pages)			

❶ Please list total aggregate values in different currencies separately. For example: £100 + €100 + $10 etc.

IN01
Application to register a company

F2 **Statement of capital** (Prescribed particulars of rights attached to shares)

Please give the prescribed particulars of rights attached to shares for each class of share shown in the statement of capital share tables in **Section F1**.

Class of share	
Prescribed particulars ❶	

❶ Prescribed particulars of rights attached to shares

The particulars are:

a. particulars of any voting rights, including rights that arise only in certain circumstances;
b. particulars of any rights, as respects dividends, to participate in a distribution;
c. particulars of any rights, as respects capital, to participate in a distribution (including on winding up); and
d. whether the shares are to be redeemed or are liable to be redeemed at the option of the company or the shareholder.

A separate table must be used for each class of share.

Continuation pages
Please use the next page or a 'Statement of Capital (Prescribed particulars of rights attached to shares)' continuation page if necessary.

05/24 Version 10.0

IN01
Application to register a company

Class of share	
Prescribed particulars ❶	

❶ **Prescribed particulars of rights attached to shares**
The particulars are:
a. particulars of any voting rights, including rights that arise only in certain circumstances;
b. particulars of any rights, as respects dividends, to participate in a distribution;
c. particulars of any rights, as respects capital, to participate in a distribution (including on winding up); and
d. whether the shares are to be redeemed or are liable to be redeemed at the option of the company or the shareholder.

A separate table must be used for each class of share.

Continuation pages
Please use a 'Statement of capital (Prescribed particulars of rights attached to shares)' continuation page if necessary.

IN01
Application to register a company

F3 Initial shareholdings

This section should only be completed by companies incorporating with share capital.

Please complete the details below for each subscriber.

The addresses will appear on the public record. These do not need to be the subscribers' usual residential address.

Initial shareholdings
Please list the company's subscribers in alphabetical order.

Please use an 'Initial shareholdings' continuation page if necessary.

Subscriber's details	Class of share	Number of shares	Currency	Nominal value of each share	Amount (if any) to be unpaid on each share (including the nominal value and any share premium)	Amount to be paid on each share (including the nominal value and any share premium)
Name						
Address						
Name						
Address						
Name						
Address						
Name						
Address						

IN01
Application to register a company

Part 5 People with significant control (PSC)

Use this Part to tell us about people with significant control or registrable relevant legal entities in respect of the company. Do not use this Part to tell us about any individual people with significant control whose particulars must not be disclosed on the public record. You must use a separate form, which you can get by contacting us secure@companieshouse.gov.uk

If on incorporation there will be someone who will count as a person with significant control (either a registrable person or registrable relevant legal entity (RLE)) in relation to the company, tick the box in H1 and complete any relevant sections. If there will be no registrable person or RLE tick the box in H2 and go to **Part 6 Election to keep information on the public register**.

H1 Statement of initial significant control ❶

☐ On incorporation, there will be someone who will count as a person with significant control (either a registrable person or registrable RLE) in relation to the company.

❶ **Statement of initial significant control**
If there will be a registrable person (which includes 'other registrable persons') or RLE, please complete the appropriate details in sections I, J & K

Please use the PSC continuation pages if necessary

H2 Statement of no PSC

(Please tick the statement below if appropriate)

☐ The company knows or has reason to believe that there will be no person with significant control (either a registrable person or RLE) in relation to the company

IN01
Application to register a company

Individual PSC

I1 Individual's details

Use **sections I1-I7** as appropriate to tell us about individuals with significant control who are registrable persons and the nature of their control in relation to the company

Title*	
Full forename(s)	
Surname	
Country/State of residence ❶	
Nationality	
Month/year of birth ❷	X X m m y y y y

❶ **Country/State of residence**
This is in respect of the usual residential address as stated in section I4.

❷ **Month and year of birth**
Please provide month and year only.

I2 Individual's service address ❶

Please complete the individual's service address below. You must also complete the individual's usual residential address in **Section I4**.

Building name/number	
Street	
Post town	
County/Region	
Postcode	
Country	

❶ **Service address**
This is the address that will appear on the public record. This does not have to be the individual's usual residential address.

If you provide the individual's residential address here it will appear on the public record.

IN01

Application to register a company

X

This page is not shown on the public record

Do not cover this barcode

I3 Individual's date of birth ❶

Please complete the full date of birth below.

Date of birth	d d m m y y y y

❶ **Date of birth**
Please give the full date of birth. The day (dd) will not appear on the public record unless the subscribers have elected to hold PSC information on the public register

I4 Individual's usual residential address ❷

Please complete the individual's usual residential address below.

Building name/number	
Street	
Post town	
County/Region	
Postcode	
Country	

❷ **Individual's usual residential address**
You can state 'Same as service address' in this section if the usual residential address is same as the service address.

You cannot state 'Same as service address' if the service address has been stated in Section I2 as 'The Company's Registered Office'. You will need to complete the address in full.

This address cannot be a PO Box, or DX number.

Section 790ZF of Companies Act 2006

Section 790ZF exemption ❸

Only tick the box below if the individual is in the process of applying for, or has been granted, exemption by the Registrar from disclosing his or her usual residential address to credit reference agencies under section 790ZF of the Companies Act 2006.

☐

Different postal address:
If the individual is applying for, or has been granted, a section 790ZF exemption, please post this whole form to the different postal address below:
The Registrar of Companies, PO Box 4082, Cardiff, CF14 3WE.

Where the individual is applying for a section 790ZF exemption with this form, the application and this form must be posted together.

❸ If the individual is currently in the process of applying for, or has been granted, a section 790ZF exemption, you may wish to check you have not entered the individual's usual residential address in section I2 as this will appear on the public record.

X

IN01
Application to register a company

15 Nature of control for an individual

Please indicate how the individual is a person with significant control over the company

Ownership of shares

The individual holds, directly or indirectly, the following percentage of shares in the company (tick only one):

- ☐ more than 25% but not more than 50%
- ☐ more than 50% but less than 75%
- ☐ 75% or more

Ownership of voting rights

The individual holds, directly or indirectly, the following percentage of voting rights in the company (tick only one):

- ☐ more than 25% but not more than 50%
- ☐ more than 50% but less than 75%
- ☐ 75% or more

Ownership of right to appoint/remove directors

- ☐ The individual holds, directly or indirectly, the right to appoint or remove a majority of the board of directors of the company

Significant influence or control (Only tick if none of the above apply)

- ☐ The individual has the right to exercise, or actually exercises, significant influence or control over the company

Tick each that apply.

16 Nature of control by a firm over which the individual has significant control

The individual has the right to exercise or actually exercises significant influence or control over the activities of a firm that is not a legal person under its governing law, and:

the members of that firm (in their capacity as such) hold, directly or indirectly, the following percentage of shares in the company (tick only one):

- ☐ more than 25% but not more than 50%
- ☐ more than 50% but less than 75%
- ☐ 75% or more

the members of that firm (in their capacity as such) hold, directly or indirectly, the following percentage of voting rights in the company (tick only one):

- ☐ more than 25% but not more than 50%
- ☐ more than 50% but less than 75%
- ☐ 75% or more

- ☐ the members of that firm (in their capacity as such) hold the right, directly or indirectly, to appoint or remove a majority of the board of directors of the company

- ☐ the members of that firm (in their capacity as such) have the right to exercise, or actually exercise, significant influence or control over the company

Tick each that apply.

IN01
Application to register a company

17 Nature of control by a trust over which the individual has significant control ❶

The individual has the right to exercise or actually exercises significant influence or control over the activities of a trust and:

the trustees of that trust (in their capacity as such) hold, directly or indirectly, the following percentage of shares in the company (tick only one):

- ☐ more than 25% but not more than 50%
- ☐ more than 50% but less than 75%
- ☐ 75% or more

the trustees of that trust (in their capacity as such) hold, directly or indirectly, the following percentage of voting rights in the company (tick only one):

- ☐ more than 25% but not more than 50%
- ☐ more than 50% but less than 75%
- ☐ 75% or more

- ☐ the trustees of that trust (in their capacity as such) hold the right, directly or indirectly, to appoint or remove a majority of the board of directors of the company

- ☐ the trustees of that trust (in their capacity as such) have the right to exercise, or actually exercise, significant influence or control over the company

❶ **Tick each that apply.**

IN01
Application to register a company

Part 6 Election to keep information on the public register (if applicable)

The subscribers of a private company can agree to elect to keep certain information on the public register at Companies House, rather than keeping their own registers. Tick the appropriate box to show which information the subscribers are electing to keep on the public register. If the subscribers have not agreed to keep any of this information on the public register, go to Part 7 Consent to Act

L1 Election to keep secretaries' register information on the public register ❶

☐ All subscribers elect to keep secretaries' register information on the public register

❶ only applies if the proposed company will have a secretary.

L2 Election to keep directors' register information on the public register

IMPORTANT:
If the subscribers elect to keep this information on the public register, everyone who is an individual director while the election is in force will have their full date of birth available on the public record❷

☐ All subscribers elect to keep directors' register information on the public register

❷ If the subscribers don't make this election, only the month and year of birth will be available on the public record.

L3 Election to keep directors' usual residential address (URA) register information on the public register

If the subscribers elect to keep this information on the public register, the URA will **not** be publicly available

☐ All subscribers elect to keep directors' URA register information on the public register.

L4 Election to keep members' register information on the public register

IMPORTANT:
If the subscribers elect to keep this information on the public register, everyone who is a member while the election is in place will have their name and address available on the public record

☐ All subscribers elect to keep members' register information on the public register

☐ All company will be a single member company (Tick if applicable).

L5 Election to keep PSC register information on the public register

IMPORTANT:
If the subscribers elect to keep this information on the public register, everyone who is an individual PSC while the election is in force will have their full date of birth available on the public record❸

☐ All subscribers elect to keep PSC register information on the public register

☐ No objection was received by the subscribers from any eligible person ❹ within the notice period before making the election.

❸ If the subscribers don't make this election, only the month and year of birth will be available on the public record.

❹ **Eligible person**
An eligible person is a person whose details would have to be entered in the company's PSC register

05/24 Version 10.0

IN01
Application to register a company

Part 7 Consent to act

M1 **Consent statement**

☐ The subscribers confirm that each of the persons named as a director or secretary has consented to act in that capacity.

Part 8 Statement about individual PSC particulars

N1 **Particulars of an individual PSC** ❶

Please tick the box to confirm.

☐ The subscribers confirm that each person named in this application as an individual PSC knows that their particulars are being supplied as part of this application.

❶ Only tick this if you have completed details of one or more individual PSCs in sections I1-I7

Part 9 Lawful purpose statement

O1 **Lawful purpose**

Please tick the box to confirm.

☐ The subscribers wish to form the company for lawful purposes.

IN01
Application to register a company

Part 10 Statement of compliance ❶

This section must be completed by all companies.

Is the application by an agent on behalf of all the subscribers?

→ **No** Go to **Section P1** (Statement of compliance delivered by the subscribers).
→ **Yes** Go to **Section P2** (Statement of compliance delivered by an agent).

❶ **Authentication**
What ever you give here will appear on the public record.

P1 Statement of compliance delivered by the subscribers ❷

Please complete this section if the application is not delivered by an agent for the subscribers of the memorandum of association.
I confirm that the requirements of the Companies Act 2006 as to registration have been complied with.

Subscriber's name — **Enter your printed name.** You do not need to include a signature.

Subscriber's name — **Enter your printed name.** You do not need to include a signature.

Subscriber's name — **Enter your printed name.** You do not need to include a signature.

Subscriber's name — **Enter your printed name.** You do not need to include a signature.

❷ **Statement of compliance delivered by the subscribers**
Every subscriber to the memorandum of association must authenticate the statement of compliance.

Continuation pages
Please use a 'Statement of compliance delivered by the subscribers' continuation page if more subscribers need to authenticate.

P2 Statement of compliance delivered by an agent

Please complete this section if this application is delivered by an agent for the subscribers to the memorandum of association.

Agent's name	
Building name/number	
Street	
Post town	
County/Region	
Postcode	
Country	

I confirm that the requirements of the Companies Act 2006 as to registration have been complied with.

Agent's name — **Enter your printed name.** You do not need to include a signature.

IN01

Application to register a company

Presenter information

You do not have to give any contact information, but if you do it will help Companies House if there is a query on the form. The contact information you give will be visible to searchers of the public record.

Contact name

Company name

Address

Post town

County/Region

Postcode

Country

DX

Telephone

Certificate

We will send your certificate to the presenters address (shown above) or if indicated to another address shown below:

☐ At the registered office address (Given in Section A7).
☐ At the agents address (Given in Section N2).

Checklist

We may return forms completed incorrectly or with information missing.

Please make sure you have remembered the following:

☐ You have checked that the proposed company name is available as well as the various rules that may affect your choice of name. More information can be found in guidance on our website.
☐ If the name of the company is the same as one already on the register as permitted by The Company LLP and Business (Names and Trading Disclosures) Regulations 2015, please attach consent.
☐ All addresses given must be physical addresses.
☐ You have given a registered email address.
☐ You have used the correct appointment sections.
☐ The document has been authenticated, where indicated.
☐ All relevant attachments have been included.
☐ You have enclosed the Memorandum of Association.
☐ You have enclosed the correct fee.

Important information

Please note that all information on this form will appear on the public record, apart from information relating to usual residential addresses and registered email address. Day of birth will only be shown on the public record if the subscribers have elected to keep PSC and/or directors' information on the public register.

How to pay

A fee of £71 is payable on this form.
Make cheques or postal orders payable to 'Companies House'. For information on fees, go to: gov.uk/companieshouse

How to send your form

You can upload certain forms to Companies House instead of sending them by post.

If you need to post your form, you must send it to the correct address.

For more information on where to send the form visit:

gov.uk/companies-house/offices

Section 243 or 790ZF exemption
If you are applying for, or have been granted a section 243 or 790ZF exemption, please post this whole form to the different postal address below:
The Registrar of Companies, PO Box 4082, Cardiff, CF14 3WE.

Further information

For further information, please see the guidance notes on the website at gov.uk/companieshouse or email enquiries@companieshouse.gov.uk

This form is available in an alternative format. Please visit the forms page on our website: **gov.uk/companieshouse**

APPENDIX 2

Company Documents

(A) MEMORANDUM OF ASSOCIATION (CA 2006)

COMPANY HAVING A SHARE CAPITAL

Memorandum of association of ABCD1234 Limited

Each subscriber to this memorandum of association wishes to form a company under the Companies Act 2006 and agrees to become a member of the company and to take at least one share.

Name of each subscriber	***Authentication***
Jane Smith Dated: [ ]/[ ]/20[ ]	Authenticated Electronically*

* This memorandum is for an electronic registration. If it were a paper registration the document would be identical save that this phrase would be replaced by Jane Smith's actual signature.

(B) CERTIFICATE OF INCORPORATION OF A PRIVATE LIMITED COMPANY

CERTIFICATE OF INCORPORATION

OF A PRIVATE LIMITED COMPANY

Company No. 000000001

The Registrar of Companies for England and Wales hereby certifies that

ABCD1234 LIMITED

is this day incorporated under the Companies Act 2006 as a private company limited by shares.

Given at Companies House, Cardiff, the [ ] 20[ ].

Authorised signature

For the Registrar of Companies.

Companies House

for the record

(C) MEMORANDUM OF ASSOCIATION (CA 1985)

THE COMPANIES ACTS 1985 TO 1989

PRIVATE COMPANY LIMITED BY SHARES

MEMORANDUM OF ASSOCIATION OF

[ ] LIMITED

1. The Company's name is "[ ] Limited".
2. The registered office is to be situated in England and Wales.
3. The object of the Company is to carry on business as a general commercial company.
4. The liability of the members is limited.
5. The Company's share capital is £100 divided into 100 shares of £1 each.

WE, the subscribers to this Memorandum of Association, wish to be formed into a Company pursuant to this Memorandum; and we agree to take the number of shares shown opposite our respective names.

Signatures, names and addresses subscribers	Number of shares taken by each subscriber
1. ***[signature]***	
[name]	One
[address]	
2. ***[signature]***	
[name]	One
[address]	

Dated [ ]

Witness to the above signatures:

[name]

[address]

APPENDIX 3

JOINT VENTURES

1 REASONS FOR JOINT VENTURES

Reasons for setting up a joint venture (JV) of whatever structure include the following.

(a) **Cost savings**: the costs of research and development, or capital investment programmes can be shared, especially in industries when there are high investment costs such as electronics or pharmaceuticals.

(b) **Risk sharing**: a similar rationale is the objective of sharing the significant financial risks in a speculative or capital intensive project (eg the PFI and PPP projects in the public sector to build, and often to operate, major infrastructure projects such as a new power station, roads, prisons, hospitals).

(c) **Access to technology**: a JV may provide a way to gain access to the other parties' technology skills.

(d) **Extension of the customer base**: international JVs can provide an effective route for one party to utilise the other party's strength in different geographic markets and/or use the other party's distribution or a sales network in another territory.

(e) **Entry into new geographical markets**: a JV with a local entity may provide the only realistic route for entering emerging markets such as eastern Europe or Asia.

(f) **Entry into new technical markets**: the rapid pace of technological change produces new markets, and the best way of 'hitting the ground running' is to collaborate with another entity which has a technical start in that field.

(g) **Pressures of global competition**: the merger of similar business between two or more entities may establish economies of scale, wider access to customers throughout the world, better purchasing power or a pooling of capital investment resources needed to meet international competition (eg the proposed alliance between American Airlines and British Airways, but which is now defunct due to competition law issues).

2 TYPES OF JOINT VENTURES

Joint ventures come in all shapes and sizes and can include those below.

(a) **Short-term collaborations**, for example to undertake a particular project.

(b) **'Limited function' joint ventures**, for example to build a new production facility for the supply of components to the joint venture parties.

(c) **'Full function'** start-up business ventures based on new technology.

(d) **Full-scale worldwide mergers** of existing businesses (eg Shell and Texaco have merged their industrial lubricants businesses in the US to produce 'Equilon' to deal with these types of products).

3 PROBLEMS WITH JOINT VENTURES

(a) **Sharing management:** a JV needs to have management input from each of the JV parties. However, one party may dominate the management structure causing tensions within the JV.

(b) **Differences in culture:** JVs require the various parties to work together. There can be a consequent difference in approach within the JV management, which can affect the harmony and speed of operations.

(c) **The 'Trojan horse' problem:** the fear is that the other party in a JV may use the JV to 'steal' the technology or market knowledge of the other party, and then compete independently.

(d) **Different commercial objectives:** the parties may have different objectives for the same JV.

(e) **Who is in charge?** Is it the management of the companies which are the parties to the JV, or is it the management team of the JV itself?

(f) **Disagreements:** these will need to be resolved by the senior management.

(g) **Extra management time:** the management of the parties will need to devote time and energy to managing the JV.

(h) **Long and costly negotiations:** these add to the costs of setting up the JV.

(i) **Competition law problems:** it may be anti-competitive and may be struck down by the Monopolies and Mergers Commission or the EU Commission.

(j) **Exit:** all JVs come to an end some day, so each party needs to have an eye on the exit route.

4 STRUCTURES FOR JOINT VENTURES

Possible structures are:

(a) contractual JV;

(b) collaboration agreements;

(c) corporate JV;

(d) partnership (general or limited liability) which can be:
   - (i) for a fixed term;
   - (ii) 'at will' (continues until dissolved); or
   - (iii) for a specific project;

(e) European Economic Interest Grouping 'EEIG'. This is a creation of the EU. It is not suitable for ordinary profit-making businesses. It has been used for cross-border alliances of, for example, accountants and for research collaboration between existing companies in different jurisdictions. It has a separate legal identity, rather like a company.

5 ADVANTAGES/DISADVANTAGES OF A PARTNERSHIP STRUCTURE FOR A JOINT VENTURE

5.1 Advantages

(a) **Flexibility and simplicity:** there are no formalities for formation of a partnership; the governing rules will be contained in a partnership agreement agreed by the parties themselves (ie there is no equivalent of the model articles for private companies or Table A articles).

(b) **Tax transparency:** tax relief can be readily obtained for capital expenditure or losses incurred in the early stages of trading.

(c) **No public filings:** the lack of any need to incur the publicity or expense of making submissions to any regulator, eg Companies House, can be a major advantage. There is also no need for public audited accounts.

5.2 Disadvantages

(a) **Liability:** there is joint and several liability of partners for liabilities incurred by a partnership, or by any of the partners acting within the express or implied authority of a partnership.

(b) **Absence of a corporate identity:** contrast this with a corporate structure which would own the assets, and contain the liabilities, independently of shareholders.

(c) **External finance:** there are fewer places to obtain the external finance. A company can borrow money on the security of a floating charge, or could sell its shares to an investor. This cannot be the case with a partnership. A partnership cannot create a floating charge, nor can it issue shares.

(d) **The Partnership Act 1890:** this implies certain terms into a partnership which the partners would often wish to exclude by including contrary terms in the partnership agreement.

(e) **Imprecise structure:** there does not have to be any written partnership agreement.

6 PARTICULAR ISSUES WITH PARTNERSHIP: THE PARTNERSHIP ACT 1890

(a) **Starting date:** remember that the partnership comes into being when the s 1(1) criteria are met, which is not necessarily when the parties would like it to (eg as stated in the partnership agreement).

(b) **Liability:** each partner is an agent of the partnership and can bind the partnership in the usual course of business. Each partner has unlimited liability for the debts and obligations of the partnership (ss 9, 10).

(c) **Management:** the management structure will depend on contractual agreement between the parties.

(d) **Variation by agreement:** s 19 provides that the partners can vary their rights and duties, including those under the PA 1890, by consent of all the partners. Such consent may be express or inferred from a course of dealing. (Note that the articles of a company cannot be altered in a manner inconsistent with the CA 2006.)

(e) **Profits and losses:** the agreement should provide rules for calculating division of profit and any losses, otherwise each will be allocated equally to the partners (s 24(1)).

(f) **General implied terms:**

  (i) loans from the partners to the partnership bear interest at 5% per annum (s 24(3));

  (ii) a partner is not entitled to interest on capital payments made to the firm (s 24(4));

  (iii) every partner is entitled to take part in the management of the partnership (s 24(5));

  (iv) no new partner can be introduced without the consent of all existing partners (s 24(7)); and

  (v) a change in the nature of the business requires consent of all the partners (s 24(8)).

(g) **Termination:** if the partnership has no fixed term, a partner may terminate it by notice (s 26).

(h) **Fiduciary duties:** partnership is a fiduciary relationship. Every partner is bound to render accounts and information to any other partner (s 28), including profits from a competing business of the same nature as the firm, unless the firm has consented to them running that business (ss 29, 30).

7 EXIT ROUTES

7.1 Dissolution under the PA 1890

(a) Section 32 provides that a partnership dissolves (subject to contrary agreement between the parties):
  (i) if a partnership for a fixed term, by expiry of that term
  (ii) if for a single venture, then when that venture is terminated or
  (iii) if for an unlimited time, then when a partner gives notice to the others of his intent to dissolve the partnership.

(b) Section 35 – dissolution by the court, especially (c) breach of the agreement, and (f) just and equitable grounds.

  See also ss 33, 34 on other grounds for dissolution under the PA 1890, which are very unlikely to apply to JVs.

7.2 Dissolution under the partnership agreement

There will usually be a JV agreement between the parties which will provide for dissolution of the partnership, and an exit route before that. Just how those rights are formulated will depend on the agreement itself. The general rule would be that a party's interest cannot be transferred without the consent of the other party or parties to the JV.

Sometimes, there is a need for a detailed procedure rather like the transfer of shares in a private company. This is often dictated in a partnership JV by the regulatory regime in which the JV operates, eg the licences from the UK government for North Sea oil exploration.

7.3 General exit clauses

Two general examples of exit clause that can be used in JVs are known as 'Russian roulette' and a 'Texas shoot-out' clauses.

7.3.1 'Russian roulette' clause

(a) Party A wants to terminate the JV.

(b) Party A serves a notice on Party B offering to sell its shares (or share in the partnership) for a price set out in the notice.

(c) Party B is obliged either to:
  (i) accept the offer; or
  (ii) reject it, whereupon Party B becomes obliged to sell its shares (or partnership share) to Party A for the price specified on the original notice.

7.3.1.1 'Texas shoot-out' clause

(a) Party A wishes to terminate the JV as above.

(b) Party A serves a 'buy notice' on Party B offering to buy Party B's share for a specified price.

(c) Party B then serves a counter notice that either:
  (i) it is prepared to sell its interest to Party A; or
  (ii) it wishes to buy Party A's interest at a higher price than that in Party A's notice.

(d) A sealed bid system is used if both parties want to buy the other's interest.

7.3.1.2 Miscellaneous exit events

There can also be compulsory termination events in the JV agreement, eg for material default by one party, or insolvency.

8 ROLE OF THE LAWYER IN THE JOINT VENTURE

Various areas which are relevant in JVs include corporate, regulatory, tax, pensions, employment and IP. The role of the lawyer will normally be to:

(a) help structure the JV in line with the client's business objectives;

(b) alert the client to important legal issues and the solutions available;

(c) carry out legal due diligence;

(d) obtain any regulatory clearance or consents;

(e) draft the JV documentation so that it accurately encapsulates the commercial instructions; and

(f) manage the legal and other steps necessary to establish the joint venture.

APPENDIX 4

COMPANY ACCOUNTS

1 THE FORM OF COMPANY ACCOUNTS

1.1 The profit and loss and appropriation account

The profit and loss account of a company, like that of a partnership, contains an appropriation section which shows the purposes for which the profit will be used.

A company's legal nature differs from that of an unincorporated business and this is reflected in the way in which items are divided between the profit and loss section and the appropriation section of the account.

Note particularly:

(a) **Directors' salaries**

A director may, in fact, be a shareholder in the company but a director is regarded as an employee. Hence directors' remuneration (unlike a 'salary' for a partner) appears as an expense on the profit and loss account.

(b) **Debenture interest**

Such interest is always shown as an expense on the profit and loss account even if it is payable to a shareholder.

EXAMPLE

PROFIT AND LOSS A/C FOR YEAR —

	£m	£m
Turnover		3,000
Less		
Cost of Sales		(2,700)
Gross Profit		300
Less		
Expenses (inc directors' fees)	(100)	
Debenture interest	(50)	
		(150)
		250
Profit Before Tax		150
Appropriations		
Less Tax on Profit		(40)(1)
Profit After Tax		110
Less Dividend		(30)(2)
Profit Retained (Reserves)		80(3)
Add Profit brought forward from previous years		2,420(4)
		2,500(5)

Notes

(1) Tax is not yet payable. It will be paid nine months after the end of the accounting period. The provision on the appropriation account merely makes it clear that this amount is not available for distribution to shareholders.

(2) The dividend has not yet been paid. It must be authorised by the shareholders at the annual general meeting.

(3) The remaining profit is retained by the company.

(4) This represents profit retained in previous years.

(5) The total is the amount by which the company's successful trading has increased its assets.

1.2 The balance sheet

The Capital Employed section will show amounts owed to shareholders ('shareholders' funds') separately from amounts owed to outsiders.

As is usual on any balance sheet liabilities repayable within 12 months will be shown as current liabilities. Other liabilities will be shown as long-term liabilities.

EXAMPLE

BALANCE SHEET AS AT—

		£m	£m
ASSETS EMPLOYED			
Fixed Assets			2,600
Current Assets			
	Stock	200	
	Debtors	600	
	Cash	100	
		900	
Less	**Current Liabilities**		
	Creditors	(130)	
	Tax	(40) (1)	
	Dividends	(30) (1)	
		(200)	
Net Current Assets			700
			3,300
Debenture			(200)
			3,100
CAPITAL EMPLOYED			
Share Capital			200
Share Premium			400 (3)
Profit and Loss Reserve			2,500 (2)
			3,100

Notes

(1) These items have not been paid at the end of the accounting period, but will be paid within the next 12 months. Hence they are current liabilities.

(2) The item 'Profit and Loss Reserve' is an amount owed to shareholders in undistributed profits.

(3) This is also an amount 'owed' to shareholders. If a share is issued for more than its original value the excess over nominal value must be recorded separately. The combined consideration is 'owed' to shareholders and is regarded as capital not normally distributable to shareholders during the lifetime of the company.

2 THE LIMITATIONS OF ACCOUNTS

You must be able to understand what is in the accounts, but looking at accounts alone may provide a misleading picture of the state of a business. Accounts are produced only *after* events have occurred.

Furthermore, accounts can produce information of only a financial nature. Thus, a Balance Sheet will only list assets and liabilities of the business. It will not indicate the health or otherwise of labour relations, despite the fact that many people would regard good staff relations as a very important asset. A poor trade reputation would be regarded by many people as a liability, but it has no place on a financial statement.

There may also be matters entirely beyond the control of management, such as a declining market for the firm's products. In other words, the accounts provide only part of the information needed in the analysis of the position of a business.

3 WHAT INFORMATION DO YOU NEED?

It is important to have a general picture of the firm that you are investigating:

(a) It is large or small?
(b) Is it growing or contracting?
(c) What is the nature of its business?
(d) Does it operate in an expanding or declining market?
(e) Does it depend heavily on a particular product or products?

The questions which you should ask depend on the circumstances and are largely a matter of common sense.

3.1 Public companies

A public company must prepare an annual report. The report has two main purposes:

(a) It complies with the requirements of the Companies Act 2006 to produce certain information and accounts.
(b) It gives the company an opportunity to promote itself, to its shareholders, to prospective investors and to analysts.

As you read any company's report, be very aware of the need to question and check everything:

(a) Are any of the figures in the accounts not clear? Is there an explanation in the Chairperson's Statement or the Directors' Report? Do the notes help?
(b) Is the chairperson expressing over-optimistic hopes in his statement? Do they look as though they can be supported by the company's current financial position? Do they look sensible in the light of the economy here and abroad?

It is unlikely, although not impossible, that you would find a direct lie in a company's report, but you should always look at the information critically to see whether a particular proposal or intention looks as if it can be justified.

Some of the items in a report are included because they must be, while some are included because the company wants to include them. The following must be included in any public company's report:

(a) Directors' Report.
(b) Auditors' Report.
(c) Balance Sheet – company and group.
(d) Profit and Loss Account – company or, if there is a group, then group only.
(e) Cash Flow Statement – company or, if there is a group, then group only.
(f) Notes giving the required information.
(g) Details of directors' interests.

Other items are optional, but you would generally be surprised if the following were not there in some form:

(a) Chairperson's Statement. What is there to hide?
(b) Ten-year record missing? Has the company not been performing consistently in the long term?

In a sense, reading a company report is something that lawyers are well trained to do – you check and question everything before accepting it as true.

Remember, when you are reading the report, that there are other sources of information as well. Keep an eye on newspaper reports, television news, etc.

3.2 Partnerships and sole practitioners

There will be no published accounts for partnerships and sole practitioners, though there will be for LLPs. Even so, you should get copies of the accounts they produce and study them.

Be aware that the requirements as to the format and content of reports which apply to companies do not apply to unincorporated bodies to anywhere near the same extent.

In these circumstances, you must get as much information about the business as you can. Find out the following:

(a) Are its premises in a suitable area?

(b) Does it seem to be busy?

(c) Is it dealing in something which is going to provide an income in the long term?

(d) What sort of reputation does it have locally?

(e) What can you find out about the proprietors?

You can then look at the accounts in the light of that information. When your analysis raises further questions, you can get down to detailed discussions of the problems with the proprietors or their advisers.

Obviously, the amount of information you can get will depend on what your relationship is, or is to be, with the business.

4 PRELIMINARY STEPS

As well as obtaining as much general information about the business as you can, there are a number of preliminary steps you should take before launching into a detailed analysis of the accounts. These involve, in part, checking the accuracy and reliability of the figures presented and, in part, building up a general picture of the business and the market in which it operates, so that the information extracted can be considered in a proper context. What might be normal for a small business might be very unusual for a large one. A particular level of profitability may be commendable in a time of recession but disappointing in a period when business generally is 'booming'.

Common preliminary steps are as follows.

(1) *Obtain the accounts for several years.* If you are going to make a realistic assessment of a business, it is important that you obtain its accounts for several years rather than for the previous year alone. One year's accounts will reveal important information – the extent of borrowings, the value of fixed assets, the amount of unpaid bills, the value of stock in hand – but it is difficult to reach reliable conclusions without making comparisons with earlier years.

(2) *Check the date of the Balance Sheet.* A business can choose a Balance Sheet date to suit itself. If the business is seasonal, then a Balance Sheet drawn up at one date could include figures which would show the business in a much more favourable light than a Balance Sheet drawn up at another date.

EXAMPLE

A business manufactures Christmas decorations. It sells the decorations to department stores in September. A Balance Sheet drawn up in September would show a healthy cash balance and probably substantial debtors. By contrast, a Balance Sheet drawn up in July would show substantial stock, a high creditors figure and, probably, a large overdraft.

Always consider whether you have to take the date of the Balance Sheet into account when you are analysing the figures.

(a) Check the method of valuing fixed assets.

(b) When were the assets last valued? Freehold premises purchased 20 years earlier for £5,000 may still be shown in the Balance Sheet at that value. Their current value will probably be quite different.

(c) Has provision been made for depreciation? If so, what method has been used?

In the case of a company, you will be looking for the answers to these and other questions in the notes and the statement of accounting policies included in the company's published accounts. If you are dealing with a partnership or sole trader, you should ask for that information from the partners or proprietor.

(3) *Check how the closing stock is valued.* The normal method is to value stock at the lower of cost or current market value. If you want to do the job thoroughly, you should inspect the stock. It may be that it includes items which are no longer readily saleable. For example, in the fashion trade, a business may have purchased items some months ago, which are now out of fashion. They could still be appearing in the accounts under 'Stock' at cost price, when in fact their current market value is little or nothing.

(4) *Analyse the figure given for debtors.* Will all the debts really be paid? Has a provision been made for bad debts? It is quite possible for a business not to write off bad debts so that the debtors figure appears larger than the amount of cash which the business can readily expect to receive.

(5) *Look for unusual or exceptional items or major changes.* The picture given by the Profit and Loss Account and Balance Sheet for a particular year can sometimes be distorted because of some exceptional event or major change either in circumstances or in accounting policy.

EXAMPLE

A business may have borrowed a substantial amount to invest in new plant or machinery. In the short term, profit may be reduced because there has been no time to use the new machinery to increase profits, yet interest charges will already have been incurred. However, in the long term, there may be prospects of rapid growth in future years.

Fixed assets such as land and buildings may have been revalued for the first time in many years. This will make the Balance Sheet look quite different, but in reality nothing has changed.

You will have to take all these matters into account, particularly if you are going to make comparisons with previous years.

5 SOME GENERAL CONSIDERATIONS

5.1 Profitability, solvency and liquidity

The two main questions which people ask when reading the accounts of a business are:

(a) Is the business profitable?

(b) Is the business solvent?

Profitability is not the same as solvency. The Profit and Loss Account shows whether the business has made a profit. The Balance Sheet shows whether it is solvent (ie, whether its assets exceed its liabilities).

The fact that the accounts reveal that a profit has been made does not necessarily mean that the money is in the bank.

The Trading and Profit and Loss Accounts of a business will record sales or levels of professional charges which in turn will determine the amount of profit, but, although the goods may have been sold or bills issued, payment may not yet have been received. Thus, although the Profit and Loss Account may show a large profit, the Balance Sheet may record a high figure under debtors and there may be no cash in the bank.

Alternatively, the business may have sold goods or delivered bills and been paid; however, it may have purchased expensive new premises paying cash. The result is that while the Profit and Loss Account will show a profit, there is no money in the bank.

In either example, if the proprietors relied on the Profit and Loss Account to try to withdraw large amounts of cash, they would find they could not because there was no money in the bank.

It is therefore a misconception to think that if a business is profitable it must be solvent (ie, able to pay its debts). This is not so. Obviously, a business which is unprofitable is not likely to be solvent for long, but just because a business is profitable does not necessarily mean that it is able to pay its debts at once. A profitable business may be driven into liquidation if it is unable to pay its debts as they fall due.

Liquidity is an even more important issue for a business. A business can only use current assets to meet its liabilities if it is to continue in business. If it has to sell fixed assets to meet liabilities, it will eventually be unable to continue trading. It is, therefore, important that the business does not run short of current assets. Cash is the most liquid of current assets. Debtors are also liquid as, even if they are not yet due for payment, the business can always turn them into cash quickly by selling them on to someone else to collect. Stock is less liquid as it may be difficult to sell quickly. Some items can only be sold at certain times of year.

5.2 Treatment of bank overdrafts

It is necessary to decide how to deal with a bank overdraft, particularly if this is substantial. It will normally appear in the Balance Sheet as a current liability because, in theory at least, it is repayable on demand. The reality may be quite different. The business may maintain a high overdraft indefinitely and finance its activities from it. Unless the business runs into difficulties, the bank will not take steps to call in the money owing.

As a current liability, the bank overdraft will not appear as part of the capital employed in the business. Instead, it will be deducted from the current assets. If, however, it is a source of long-term finance, it should be treated as such in calculating the return on capital which the business is achieving. Again, in calculating whether a business can pay its debts by examining the ratio of current or liquid assets to current liabilities, a totally misleading picture may emerge if no distinction is made between the bank overdraft and ordinary trade creditors.

5.3 The impact of inflation

It is necessary to make allowance for the impact of inflation. If profits are increasing at the rate of 2% pa when inflation is running at 4% pa, then in real terms profits are falling.

6 RATIO ANALYSIS

6.1 Why use ratio analysis?

Ratio analysis relates two figures together. The result can be expressed as a percentage or as a ratio. Once you have a percentage or ratio, it is easy to compare the results of different years or of different businesses. You can use ratio analysis to check the profitability and efficiency of a business and also the liquidity.

6.2 Profitability and efficiency

6.2.1 Return on capital

When looking at a set of accounts, the first thing you are likely to want to know is whether or not the business is making a profit. However, you will then want answers to some further questions:

(a) Is the amount of profit made satisfactory when compared with the amount of capital invested in the business?

(b) Is it more or less than the amount of profit similar businesses make from their capital?

To answer these questions, you need to relate the amount of profit produced to the amount of capital used to produce it. This is referred to as the 'return on capital'. It is normally expressed as a percentage:

$$\frac{\text{Net Profit}}{\text{Capital}} \times 100 = \%$$

You can calculate the return on the amount of capital the proprietor has invested or the amount of capital provided from all sources (for example, from bank loans). A proprietor will consider whether the return on capital is satisfactory by reference to the return that could be obtained on other investments.

When calculating the return, you may choose to take the capital figure at the start of the year, the end of the year or an average figure. It is normally easiest to take the figure at the end of the year, although arguably it is more accurate to take the figure at the start of the year as that was the amount invested during the relevant trading period.

EXAMPLE

The balance on the proprietor's capital account at the end of the accounting period is £200,000; net profit for the accounting period was £40,000. The return on capital is:

$$\frac{£40{,}000}{£200{,}000} \times 100 = 20\%$$

This compares very favourably with putting the money in a bank or building society account. How does it compare with other similar businesses?

6.2.2 Net profit percentage

If the return on capital is unsatisfactory, a proprietor may want to increase net profit. There are only two ways to make more profit. You can increase income or reduce expenses. To increase income you can either sell more items or make more profit on each item sold. The 'net profit percentage' shows the amount of profit made on each item sold.

$$\frac{\text{Net Profit}}{\text{Sales}} \times 100 = \%$$

A business can improve profit by putting up prices. However, a business will usually try to avoid putting up prices as this may drive away customers. It will prefer to reduce expenses or sell more items.

EXAMPLE

A business has sales of £400,000 and a net profit of £40,000. The net profit percentage is:

$$\frac{£40{,}000}{£400{,}000} \times 100 = 10\%$$

This means that out of every £1 of sales, 90p goes in expenses and 10p is profit. We would need figures from comparable businesses to decide whether or not the business was performing satisfactorily.

6.3 Liquidity tests

6.3.1 Current ratio

The current ratio compares current assets with current liabilities. The result is normally expressed as a ratio.

$$\frac{\text{Current assets}}{\text{Current liabilities}} = ?:1$$

A cautious business will want a current ratio of at least 1.5:1. However, many retail businesses manage with current ratios which are much lower. This is because they buy goods on credit but sell mainly for cash. Each day, they know that large amounts of cash will be injected. In general, therefore, they can meet liabilities due on a particular day from cash received on that day and need only a small amount of additional liquid funds in reserve.

6.3.2 Acid test

As we saw earlier, stock may not be quickly saleable. Also, there may be doubts as to whether it is saleable at all. Changes in fashion and technology may make stock obsolete. Many prepayments, treated as current assets, cannot be turned into ready cash, for example prepaid rent. The acid test is the ratio between current liabilities and current assets excluding stock and prepayments. (In a non-trading business, we would exclude work in progress as it is uncertain how quickly it can be turned into cash.) These assets are referred to as 'liquid assets':

$$\frac{\text{Liquid assets}}{\text{Current liabilities}} = ?:1$$

An acid test of 1:1 means that the business has £1 of liquid assets for every £1 of current liabilities. The lower the ratio, the greater the risk of the business being unable to meet its debts as they fall due.

EXAMPLE

The following is an extract from a Balance Sheet:

Current Assets		
Stock	65,000	
Debtors	50,000	
Cash	4,000	
Prepayments	1,000	
		120,000
Current Liabilities		
Creditors	(40,000)	
Accruals	(10,000)	
		(50,000)
Net Current Assets		70,000

The current ratio is:

$$\frac{£120{,}000}{£50{,}000} = 2.4:1$$

The acid test is

$$\frac{£54{,}000}{£50{,}000} = 1.08:1$$

There are an enormous number of other ratios which can be applied to a set of accounts. However, these are sufficient to show the way in which ratio analysis can give insight into the true position of a business.

Index